Edgardo M. Velasco
Cathay Pacific Steel Corp.
Cainta Rizal

655 1143

AutoCAD®:
The Professional Reference
Second Edition

Kurt Hampe

Glenn Hilley

Valda Hilley

William Valaski

NRP
NEW RIDERS
PUBLISHING

New Riders Publishing, Carmel, Indiana

AutoCAD: The Professional Reference, Second Edition

By Kurt Hampe, Glenn Hilley, Valda Hilley, and William Valaski

Published by:
New Riders Publishing
11711 N. College Ave., Suite 140
Carmel, IN 46032 USA

Printed in the United States of America 1 2 3 4 5 6 7 8 9 0

Library of Congress Cataloging-in-Publication Data

```
AutoCAD--the professional reference / Kurt Hampe… [et al.]. --2nd ed.
     p. cm.
     Includes index.
   ISBN 1-56205-059-1 : $39.95
1. Computer graphics.  2. AutoCAD (Computer file)
I. Hampe, Kurt, 1969- .
T385.A886    1993
620'.0042'02855369--dc20        93-20218
        CIP
```

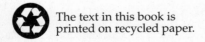

The text in this book is printed on recycled paper.

Publisher

David P. Ewing

Associate Publisher

Tim Huddleston

Acquisitions Editor

John Pont

Managing Editor

Cheri Robinson

Product Director

Kurt Hampe

Production Editor

Nancy E. Sixsmith

Editors

Geneil Breeze
Patrice Hartmann
Tim Huddleston
Richard Limacher
Rob Tidrow
Lisa Wilson

Technical Editors

David Dye
Kurt Hampe
Kevin McWhirter

Editorial Secretary

Karen Opal

Book Design and Production

Amy Peppler-Adams
Christine Cook
Aaron Davis
Jerry Ellis
Tim Groeling
Dennis Clay Hager
Michelle Self
Dennis Sheehan
Greg Simsic
Susan VandeWalle

Proofreaders

Carla Hall-Batton
Howard Jones
John Kane
R. Sean Medlock

Indexed by

Jeanne Clark
Joy Dean Lee
Tina Trettin

About the Authors

Kurt Hampe

Kurt Hampe is a freelance computer-applications consultant and instructor in Louisville, Kentucky. He is an author, editor, and illustrator of several books, including *Inside AutoCAD, AutoCAD for Beginners, Inside AutoLISP,* and *New Riders' Reference Guide to AutoCAD.* When not engaged in literary tasks, Mr. Hampe is a programmer, draftsperson, and instructor. He attended Kentucky Polytechnic Institute, from which he graduated with honors in 1988.

Glenn Hilley

Glenn Hilley is president and owner of The Graphx Lab, a computer graphics firm in Cincinnati, Ohio. The firm specializes in providing PC graphics applications and systems consulting in the areas of CAD, 3D photorealism, digital imaging, graphic design, presentation graphics, and desktop publishing for DOS and Windows. For fifteen years, Mr. Hilley has worked as a design engineer for the aerospace, military, and commercial industries. His computer expertise covers mainframe systems (CADAM, CATIA, Prime Medusa) and PC CAD systems (AutoCAD, Microstation, Cadkey). He is a member of the Cincinnati PCUG, and participates as a production volunteer for WCTV cable access. He can be reached on Compuserve: 72147,3322.

Valda Hilley

Valda Hilley is an engineer and systems designer with more than twelve years of experience in providing technical expertise for commercial, military, and aerospace industries. Ms. Hilley has worked on mainframe CAD systems and PC CAD systems (including AutoCAD and Cadkey). She has expertise in a wide variety of PC software, including word processing, desktop publishing, and graphics.

Ms. Hilley founded SCIFAX Technical Resources, which is a technical consulting firm in Cincinnati that specializes in applying PC-based computing to business and engineering problem solving. She is the author of *Design Smart!,* which contains integrated solutions for design and engineering, and features Windows-specific technical and business applications. Ms. Hilley serves as contributing editor to the *Windows Journal* and is a member of the National Society of Professional Engineers.

Bill Valaski

Bill Valaski graduated from the University of Cincinnati with a degree in Architectural Engineering. He works for CDS Associates, Inc., an A/E firm in Cincinnati, Ohio, at which he manages computer operations and is training to become a registered architect. Mr. Valaski is also a partner in CPU (Computer Projects Unlimited), a computer consulting firm, with Bob Knight, another noted AutoCAD author. Together, they have authored several books, including *AutoCAD: The Professional Reference, Using AutoCAD, Second Edition, The AutoCAD Quick Reference,* and *New Riders' Reference Guide to AutoCAD Release 12.*

Acknowledgments

Kurt Hampe gratefully acknowledges The MACHINE.

New Riders Publishing expresses sincere thanks to the following individuals for their contributions:

Kurt Hampe, for developing and nurturing the project, excellent authoring skills, and morale-boosting when the going got tough.

David Dye and Kevin McWhirter, for ensuring the book's technical accuracy.

Tim Huddleston, for helping to make order out of chaos.

Cheri Robinson, for her management (and crisis management) expertise.

John Pont, for collecting the authoring team and riding herd when necessary.

Nancy Sixsmith, for managing the project through its many stages and steering the book through the production process.

The editors—Geneil Breeze, Patrice Hartmann, Tim Huddleston, Rich Limacher, Rob Tidrow, and Lisa Wilson—for their cheerful demeanors, tireless efforts, and attention to detail.

Karen Opal, for acquisitions and editorial assistance wherever needed.

Jerry Ellis, as always, for "going the extra yard" to ensure quality figures.

The members of Prentice Hall Computer Publishing's production and manufacturing staff, for their extraordinary efforts.

Kurt Hampe gratefully acknowledges The MACHINE.

Trademark Acknowledgments

New Riders Publishing has made every attempt to supply trademark information about company names, products, and services mentioned in this book. Trademarks indicated below were derived from various sources. New Riders Publishing cannot attest to the accuracy of this information.

3Com is a registered trademark of the 3Com Corporation.

ACAD, Advanced Modeling Extension, Autodesk 3D Studio, AutoFlix, and Animator Pro are trademarks; and ADI, AutoCAD, AutoCAD for Windows, Autodesk, Autodesk Animator, AutoLISP, and AutoShade are registered trademarks of Autodesk, Inc.

CompuServe is a registered trademark of CompuServe, Inc.

HP and Hewlett-Packard are registered trademarks of Hewlett-Packard Co.

IBM, IBM PC, and PC DOS are trademarks of International Business Machines Corporation.

Informix is a registered trademark of Informix Software, Inc.

Lotus and 1-2-3 are registered trademarks of Lotus Development Corporation.

Manifest is a trademark of Quarterdeck Office Systems.

Microsoft, MS-DOS, Windows, Word, and Word for Windows are registered trademarks of Microsoft Corporation.

Norton Utilities and Unerase are trademarks of Symantec Corporation.

Oracle is a registered trademark of Oracle Corporation.

Paradox is a registered trademark of Borland/Ansa Software.

Phar Lap is a registered trademark of Phar Lap Software, Inc.

Sun and Sun Microsystems are registered trademarks of Sun Microsystems, Inc.

UNIX is a trademark of American Telephone and Telegraph Corp.

WordPerfect is a registered trademark of WordPerfect Corporation.

Trademarks of other products mentioned in this book are held by the companies producing them.

Warning and Disclaimer

This book is designed to provide information about the AutoCAD Release 12 computer program. Every effort has been made to make this book as complete and as accurate as possible, but no warranty or fitness is implied.

The information is provided on an "as is" basis. The author and New Riders Publishing shall have neither liability nor responsibility to any person or entity with respect to any loss or damages arising from the information contained in this book or from the use of the disks or programs that may accompany it.

Table of Contents

Part One: Installation and Configuration of AutoCAD

1

2

3

Part Two: Selected Topics and Techniques

4

5

Blocks, Attributes, and External References 141

xiii

8

The Solid Modeling Extension 237

9

Part Three: Customization

10

11

Importing and Exporting Files 387

Part Four: Troubleshooting AutoCAD

12

13

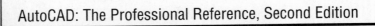
Part Five

Part Six

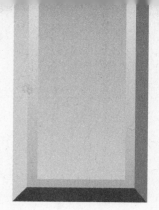

Introduction

AutoCAD is the premier computer-aided drafting and design software package. Autodesk has registered more than 800,000 AutoCAD users, and this number is growing every day. With the introduction of Release 12, AutoCAD has presented the most complete, powerful, and easy-to-use version of AutoCAD to date. In fact, Release 12 has been hailed as "the wish list release" and "the user's release" by AutoCAD users and developers alike.

AutoCAD: The Professional Reference, Second Edition is both a guide and a reference to installing and using the many features of AutoCAD. Thousands of AutoCAD users have used the first edition of *AutoCAD: The Professional Reference*.

This book provides useful information to Release 11 and Release 12 users. *AutoCAD: The Professional Reference, Second Edition* helps you upgrade, install, troubleshoot, and customize AutoCAD. The newest, most powerful features of AutoCAD are explained to enable new users to get up and running, and to enable experienced users to work faster and more productively.

Whenever possible, the differences between different AutoCAD platforms are addressed to provide a more complete discussion of

1

AutoCAD. The actual AutoCAD program does not vary much from platform to platform; often, the platform itself introduces new features.

AutoCAD Release 12 for Windows offers several new features that are exclusive to the Windows release and operating environment. These features are discussed in detail in *AutoCAD: The Professional Reference, Second Edition*.

How this Book is Different from Most AutoCAD Books

AutoCAD: The Professional Reference, Second Edition is designed to accommodate the way you work. The authors and editors at New Riders Publishing know that you probably do not have a great deal of time to explore the many features of AutoCAD, and that you are anxious to increase your AutoCAD knowledge to be more productive in your daily work.

This book presents clear, concise examples and explanations for installing AutoCAD and using its features. Each chapter introduces you to an important facet of AutoCAD, and quickly shows you how these aspects of AutoCAD relate to other AutoCAD features, commands, and your system. The chapters also lead you through the steps necessary to employ the concepts discussed in the chapter.

Who Should Read this Book?

AutoCAD: The Professional Reference, Second Edition is intended primarily for users who are already familiar with basic AutoCAD drafting techniques. If you are a new user, you will still find plenty of useful and understandable information.

Benefits of this Book for New AutoCAD Users

If you are a new AutoCAD user, you need to learn basic AutoCAD drafting techniques. Because Release 12 offers many new basic drafting features, new and experienced users alike need to learn from scratch. This book discusses the new features of Release 12 in detail, including basic examples and reference material. Part 5, the AutoCAD Command Reference, explains every AutoCAD command and provides a brief example of the way each command is used.

To learn more about the basic drafting features of AutoCAD, see *Inside AutoCAD Release 12 for Beginners* or *Inside AutoCAD Release 12*, available from New Riders Publishing.

Benefits of this Book for Intermediate and Advanced Users

AutoCAD: The Professional Reference, Second Edition, is an in-depth reference of AutoCAD commands, system variables, and techniques. This book explains the features of AutoCAD and how to access them. The command and system variable references offer the most complete listings and explanations that are in print.

As an intermediate or advanced user, you are interested in learning about the more advanced AutoCAD features and customizations. To this end, each chapter introduces material, and then explains it in a straightforward fashion. Although the steps for accessing an AutoCAD feature are explained, tutorials for the features are not provided.

Users Upgrading to Release 12

If you are presently using an earlier version of AutoCAD and are considering upgrading to Release 12, or if you have just upgraded to Release 12, you will find many helpful features in this book. Of particular interest to upgraders are the installation, configuration, and troubleshooting chapters; and the chapters that discuss the new features of Release 12. Because of the examples and directions, you will be able to acclimate to Release 12 quickly.

How this Book is Organized

AutoCAD: The Professional Reference, Second Edition, is designed as a reference to the major features of AutoCAD. The book is divided into six parts that discuss the complete range of AutoCAD use. Each section is intended primarily as a reference; examples and steps to follow are provided to increase your efficiency.

Part One: Installation and Configuration of AutoCAD

Part One introduces the various platform versions of AutoCAD, the requirements of each platform, and installation and configuration information.

Chapter One, "Getting Started in AutoCAD Release 12," discusses each of the platform-specific versions of AutoCAD, its special features, and the hardware required to run each version.

Chapter Two, "Installing and Configuring AutoCAD," discusses the process of installing AutoCAD on your platform and configuring AutoCAD to work with your peripherals. You also learn the specifics of configuring your operating system to run AutoCAD.

Chapter Three, "Memory Management and Performance," studies the memory considerations of the operating-system environments under which AutoCAD can run. You also learn ways to configure and use AutoCAD to work better within the restrictions of your operating system and hardware.

Part Two: Selected Topics and Techniques

Part Two discusses selected features of the AutoCAD program. The features discussed are new or changed for Release 12, or the features involve multiple commands, making them difficult to explain adequately in the Command Reference alone.

Chapter Four, "Grip Mode Editing," offers a look at the new noun/verb object selection features of Release 12 and tells you how to control them.

Chapter Five, "Blocks, Attributes, and External References," examines AutoCAD's capabilities to group entities together and to provide information about those entities. These features are discussed because they offer new commands and options for Release 12, and because the features require multiple commands.

Chapter Six, "Dimensioning," examines AutoCAD's dimensioning capabilities. The chapter focuses on dimension types and techniques, and the new dimensioning dialog boxes for Release 12. The chapter also lists the dimensioning variables and explains each one.

Chapter Seven, "Paper Space and Plotting," examines two of AutoCAD's most important presentation features. The discussion on paper space provides an understanding of paper space and how to use it to your best advantage. The discussion of plotting discusses model- and paper-space plots, as well as the new plot dialog box for Release 12.

Chapter Eight, "The Solid Modeling Extension," examines the most innovative 3D features of AutoCAD. You learn about the techniques and pitfalls of 3D design, drafting, and rendering. The chapter also includes a complete listing of the solid modeling system variables.

Chapter Nine, "The Structured Query Language," examines the single most important feature for data exchange in AutoCAD. You are presented with the SQL commands, the SQL language, and some of the techniques for employing SQL in AutoLISP programs.

Part Three: Customization

Part Three offers a look at the many opportunities for customization and optimization that AutoCAD provides.

Chapter Ten, "Customizing AutoCAD," looks at the many modifications and additions you can use with AutoCAD to make it work for you. Although the chapter does not attempt to teach you the precise "how-to" steps of customizing AutoCAD, you learn about the available customizations, and you see examples of many customization techniques and their results.

Chapter Eleven, "Importing and Exporting Files," discusses the many file formats that can be used with AutoCAD. This information benefits you, both for customizing AutoCAD and for developing the necessary data exchange between other users and you.

Part Four: Troubleshooting AutoCAD

Part Four offers help for troubleshooting AutoCAD and your platform. You learn about the most commonly occurring problems and error messages and what to do about them. You also learn ways to detect and prevent error-causing hardware and software.

Chapter Twelve, "Troubleshooting AutoCAD," addresses the most common problems that occur while using AutoCAD. Drawing-file recovery techniques and system problems are also discussed.

Chapter Thirteen, "AutoCAD Error Messages," lists the error messages that occur most often, discusses why they happen, and tells you what to do about them. The chapter also discusses the ERRNO system variable and how it is used and accessed by AutoLISP and ADS programs.

Part Five: AutoCAD Command Reference

Part Five is a complete Command Reference. For each command, the reference lists the following:

- The command and a category for the command
- Ways to access the command through the menus
- A description of the command's purpose
- A list of the command's prompts
- An example of the command at work
- Related commands
- Related system variables

Part Six: AutoCAD System Variable Reference

Part Six is a complete system variable reference. For each system variable, the reference lists the following:

- The system variable name
- The system variable type
- Any commands that can set the system variable
- The default value of the system variable
- The location at which the system variable is saved

The system variables are then listed by category, described, and the valid values are listed or defined.

Conventions Used in this Book

To help you find your way through this book, you should familiarize yourself with the different conventions used in the text. You will find special notes, tips, and warnings throughout the text, as well as special typesetting conventions that will help you distinguish AutoCAD's prompts and messages, and information that you need to enter.

When you are instructed to enter information at a program prompt, the information you type is printed in **bold typeface.**

Variable elements appear in *italic typeface*.

Prompts or messages that a program displays on-screen appear in this `special typeface`.

Notes, Tips, and Warnings

Notes, tips, and warnings appear with special margin icons. These special bits of text contain "extra" information that can help you boost your system's productivity or provide additional details about AutoCAD commands and features.

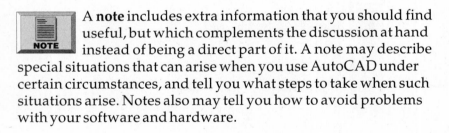

A **note** includes extra information that you should find useful, but which complements the discussion at hand instead of being a direct part of it. A note may describe special situations that can arise when you use AutoCAD under certain circumstances, and tell you what steps to take when such situations arise. Notes also may tell you how to avoid problems with your software and hardware.

A **tip** provides you with quick instructions for getting the most from AutoCAD as you follow the steps outlined in the general discussion. A tip might show you how to speed up a procedure or how to perform one of many time-saving techniques, for example.

A **warning** tells you when a procedure may be dangerous—when you run the risk of losing data, locking up your system, or even damaging your hardware. Warnings tell you how to avoid such losses or describe the steps you can take to remedy them.

Example Formats

The examples used in this book show you the steps to complete a given procedure. Due to the reference nature of the book, more emphasis is placed on the command in question and less emphasis is placed on exercise setup or step explanations. A sample exercise is shown here:

Example

In this example, you create a single solid-box primitive using the SOLBOX command. The entity that you create is shown in figure SOLBOX.1.

```
Command: SOLBOX ↵
Baseplane/Center/<Corner of box> <0,0,0>: ↵
Cube/Length/<Other corner>: ①
Height: 5
```

File Listings and AutoCAD Text

Throughout this book, there are file listings, AutoCAD prompts, and AutoCAD-generated text. All of this text is presented in a special font. The following example shows a configuration command prompt, as seen on the text screen:.

```
Select rendering hard copy device:

   1. None (Null rendering device)
   2. P386 Autodesk Device Interface rendering driver
   3. Rendering file (256 color map)
   4. Rendering file (continuous color)

Rendering hard copy selection: <1>
```

9

Table I.1
Icons Used in this Book

Icon	Description
R12	This icon indicates a command new to Release 12, or an existing command that has a new feature or option in Release 12.
	These commands create or edit two-dimensional objects, although the objects may be located anywhere in 3D space.
	These commands create or edit three-dimensional objects.
	These commands affect how AutoCAD is displayed on the screen, as well as how the drawing is shown on-screen.
	This icon indicates any type of command that creates an AutoCAD entity, such as a line or circle.
	These commands enable you to modify AutoCAD entities.
?	The Inquiry commands display information about the drawing, entities, or the operating system that you are using.
	These commands enable you to organize your drawing information into a more manageable drawing file.
	These commands affect the actions of other AutoCAD commands.
	These commands relate to the new Release 12 Region Modeler.
,	This group of commands can be executed from within other commands, without first having to cancel the active command.
	The Utility commands perform functions that are not necessarily related to the basic act of creating your drawing.

Icon	Description
SQL	This icon means that ASE must be loaded to use this command.
AME	This icon indicates that AME 2.1 must be loaded to use this command.

Other AutoCAD Titles from New Riders Publishing

New Riders Publishing offers a wide selection of books on AutoCAD. The following are examples of books that are currently available from New Riders:

Inside AutoCAD Release 12 is written for beginning-to-intermediate AutoCAD users. This book covers all of the material that most users ever need to use the basic AutoCAD package.

Inside AutoCAD Release 12 for Beginners is written for beginning AutoCAD users. It covers the 80 percent of AutoCAD tasks that most users use in everyday work, packaged into an easy-to-use text.

For comprehensive coverage of the several Autodesk products that can be used to create 3D designs and presentations, see *AutoCAD 3D Design and Presentation*. The book includes coverage of AutoCAD 3D, AME solid modeling, AutoShade, RenderMan, Autodesk Animator Pro, 3D Studio, and AutoFlix.

If you want to turn your AutoCAD drawings into animated presentations, see *Inside Autodesk Animator*.

If you want a quick, comprehensive reference, see *New Riders' Reference Guide to AutoCAD Release 12*.

If you want a tutorial, or if you need to pass the Certified AutoCAD Operator's Exam, refer to *The AutoCAD Tutor*. This book was written specifically to help new AutoCAD users prepare for this exam.

If you manage other AutoCAD users, with or without a network, read *Managing and Networking AutoCAD*. This book provides a comprehensive discussion of the issues facing an AutoCAD manager or network administrator.

If you do technical drafting in 2D or 3D, see *AutoCAD Drafting and 3D Design*, which was written around ANSI Y14.5M standards.

For a complete discussion of AutoCAD Release 12 for Windows, see *Inside AutoCAD Release 12 for Windows*.

New Riders Publishing

The staff of New Riders Publishing is committed to bringing you the very best in computer reference material. Each New Riders book is the result of months of work by authors and staff, who research and refine the information contained within its covers.

As part of this commitment to you, the NRP reader, New Riders invites your input. Please let us know if you enjoy this book, if you have trouble with the information and examples presented, or if you have a suggestion for the next edition.

Please note, however, that the New Riders staff cannot serve as a technical resource for AutoCAD or AutoCAD application-related questions, including hardware or software problems. Refer to your documentation, your AutoCAD dealer, or AutoCAD technical support for information.

If you have a question or comment about any New Riders book, please write to NRP at the following address. We will respond to as many readers as we can. Your name, address, or phone number will never become part of a mailing list or be used for any other purpose other that to help us continue to bring you the best books possible.

New Riders Publishing
Prentice Hall Computer Publishing
Attn: Associate Producer
11711 N. College Avenue
Carmel, IN 46032

If you prefer, you can send a FAX to New Riders Publishing at the following number:

(317) 571-3484

Thank you for selecting *AutoCAD: The Professional Reference, Second Edition*!

Part One: Installation and Configuration of AutoCAD

Getting Started in AutoCAD Release 12
Installing and Configuring AutoCAD
Memory Management and Performance

Getting Started in AutoCAD Release 12

Before you begin creating complex and accurate 2D and 3D drawings with AutoCAD, you need to understand the ways in which AutoCAD works with your computer—and with you. AutoCAD runs on a wide variety of computer/operating system combinations, or *platforms*. The program looks and acts very much the same on all the platforms it supports, but each platform has idiosyncrasies and features that make it slightly different from other systems.

Several different versions of AutoCAD Release 12 exist, and each one is designed for use on a specific platform. This chapter describes the different versions of AutoCAD Release 12 and the hardware and operating system that each version needs in order to operate. This chapter also discusses the subtle—and sometimes not so subtle— differences that make each version of AutoCAD unique. If you do not already have AutoCAD Release 12, this chapter may help you decide which version and platform best meet your particular drafting and computing needs.

This chapter also shows you the different ways in which you, the computer user, can communicate with AutoCAD. Like most other computer programs, AutoCAD uses commands to perform its work. When you give AutoCAD a command to tell it which task to perform, AutoCAD does it. The program, however, does not lock you into one method of command entry—you can enter commands in several ways. This chapter describes all of the standard methods of command entry in AutoCAD, which you can use in any version of the program.

This chapter ends by showing you how to get help directly from AutoCAD itself when using the program. AutoCAD features a powerful built-in help system that can assist you in entering commands or drawing objects. By mastering the help system, you avoid hours spent thumbing through documentation for help with difficult commands or drafting concepts.

Understanding Release 12 Versions and Their Requirements

AutoCAD Release 12 is available for three operating systems: DOS, UNIX, and Windows. (For more information on AutoCAD Release 12 for Windows, see *Inside AutoCAD Release 12 for Windows*, by New Riders Publishing.) If a computer system is widely used by design and engineering professionals, that system is supported by a platform-specific version of AutoCAD, which has been optimized for use with that system. Whenever a computing platform or operating system becomes popular, Autodesk evaluates it to determine the feasibility of creating a new version of AutoCAD for that environment. Consequently, platform-specific versions of AutoCAD come and go, as customers demand them and as business economics permit their development.

Each version of AutoCAD is designed to run on a particular combination of computer hardware and an operating system or operating environment. An *operating environment* is a program that offers a set of operating-system features and makes certain capabilities available to programs such as AutoCAD. Because these capabilities can vary from one operating environment to another, one version of AutoCAD may have capabilities that another does not have. To take advantage of these capabilities, the computer may need different system resources, such as different microprocessor chips, different amounts of random-access memory (RAM) or hard disk space, or different peripheral devices.

The following sections discuss the different platform versions and features of AutoCAD that were available at the time this book was written. Each section describes the system requirements for a particular version of AutoCAD. The requirements listed here are the generally accepted minimum requirements for each type of system. In most cases, you can improve your system's performance any time you exceed these minimum requirements.

By adding more RAM or hard disk space, or by installing a superior video display adapter and monitor, for example, you can improve performance in almost every case. Of course, these systems vary widely in cost—a factor you must weigh against the benefits any system offers when used with AutoCAD.

Special Features

AutoCAD Release 12 contains more than 170 different improvements and enhancements, including the following:

- Release 12 enables you to input, display, and print PostScript text fonts and images to produce extremely high-quality output.
- AutoCAD supports multiple-output devices by handling configurations for up to 29 separate devices and enabling you to select the output device at the time of printing.
- You can now render and display shaded images from within AutoCAD.
- The new Region Modeler feature enables you to create and develop two-dimensional shapes.

- The AutoCAD SQL Extension provides a set of commands that enable you to create interactive links between nongraphic data stored in external database and all graphic entities within an AutoCAD drawing.

Another feature common to all Release 12 platforms is the AutoCAD Development System (ADS). ADS is a powerful programming interface for C and other high-level languages. Using ADS, third-party developers can write AutoCAD applications in a manner similar to AutoLISP, yet in the more powerful C language. This implementation of the AutoCAD Development System features real-mode ADS, enabling ADS to compile and execute in real-mode on MS-DOS platforms.

Each AutoCAD Release 12 package comes with ADS programming library files, header files, and sample files. A programmer can use these files and a supported compiler to create executable files that can run on any AutoCAD Release 12 system.

A good example of an ADS program is the Advanced Modeling Extension (AME). AME 2.1 is available only with AutoCAD Release 12. AME enables you to do sophisticated solid modeling within AutoCAD Release 12. *Solid modeling*, a method of designing 3D objects, takes into account not only the surfaces that make up an object but also its mass properties.

 For more information on AME and solid modeling in AutoCAD, see Chapter 8.

AutoCAD 386 Release 12 for DOS

AutoCAD Release 12 for DOS is a high-performance version of Auto-CAD that is designed to take advantage of the speed and power of the 386/486 platform. Release 12 is the most powerful and fastest version of AutoCAD to date. This release incorporates more improvements and enhancements than any previous release of AutoCAD.

System Requirements

AutoCAD 386 Release 12 is specifically designed for IBM-compatible 80386- or 80486-class machines, and it requires the following special hardware:

- A 387 math coprocessor is required. On the 486DX, the 487 coprocessor is an integral part of the 486DX chip. On the 486SX, you need to add a 487 coprocessor.

- At least 8M of RAM is recommended; memory above 1M must be extended—not expanded—memory. You can improve performance with additional memory.

- A hard disk with approximately 26M of available space is required to install AutoCAD's full complement, including the optional Advanced Modeling Extension (AME). The minimum installation of executable and support files requires 11M of free hard disk space. Bonus and sample files require another 2.6M. The AutoCAD virtual-memory system needs additional free disk space, especially when editing large drawings.

- A 1.2M, 5.25-inch floppy disk drive; or a 1.44M, 3.5-inch floppy disk drive.

- MS-DOS or PC DOS Version 3.3 or higher (Autodesk recommends DOS 5.0 or higher).

- Microsoft Windows version 3.1 or higher (optional). You need this to run AutoCAD as a full-screen DOS application under Windows.

- An AutoCAD-supported video display.

- An AutoCAD-supported digitizer or mouse (optional).

- A plotter or printer-plotter (optional).

The AutoCAD Release 12 Interface

Release 12 features an intuitive graphical interface that enables you to execute commands using pull-down menus, icon menus, dialog boxes, the command line, or a digitizer template.

AutoCAD Versions for UNIX

Two different versions of the UNIX operating system are now available for engineering workstations. AutoCAD is available for use under both Sun OS and Sun Solaris. The primary difference between AutoCAD when it runs on UNIX and when it runs on DOS is that UNIX versions of AutoCAD feature multiuser, multitasking, and virtual-memory capabilities.

UNIX enables multiple users to share the same computer. This multi-user capability creates an economical network or a secure way of enabling several people to share one computer (on different shifts, for example). UNIX security also works for the general benefit of single users by protecting against accidental file erasures and other data accidents.

UNIX multitasking capabilities enhance the productivity of AutoCAD users. UNIX can support the simultaneous operation of multiple programs by multiple users. One application runs in the foreground and interacts with the user; one or more other programs run unattended in the background. The user can switch from one program to another at will.

The following sections briefly describe the way AutoCAD runs on the UNIX variants supported at the time of this writing: Sun OS and Sun Solaris.

AutoCAD Release 12 for SPARCstation

AutoCAD for the Sun Microsystems Sun-4 and SPARCstation runs under Sun OS 4.1.1 or higher. Release 12 on this platform is an X Window System implementation with an OpenLook interface. The following is a list of hardware and software requirements:

- Sun-4 or SPARCstation
- SunOS operating system version 4.1.1 or higher; or Solaris 2.1 or higher, consisting of Sun OS 5.1 and OpenWindows 3.1.

- OpenWindows version 3.0
- At least 32M of RAM
- At least 30M of free hard disk space
- A swap partition that is twice as large as the amount of RAM on your machine
- 2M of hard disk space (in the directory defined by the `sharedretainpath` option in your OpenWindows startup script) for each session of AutoCAD running if you are using the XGL video driver
- Optional digitizer, plotter, or printer

When you launch AutoCAD on a SPARCstation, AutoCAD opens two windows—one window for graphics and one for text. Text can be copied and pasted into the AutoCAD text window as it can with other programs. Using a digitizing device, you can reduce a window to an icon, open a window from an icon, or move a window or icon. You can also use it to resize a window, place a window in front or behind all other windows, repaint the window, or quit the program in the window. You can quit an AutoCAD window only from within AutoCAD itself, however.

AutoCAD runs very quickly under Sun OS. Like AutoCAD Release 12 for DOS, Sun OS is a 32-bit operating system, and AutoCAD takes full advantage of the 32-bit power. Multitasking multiple sessions of AutoCAD under Sun OS is as simple as starting AutoCAD in another window. Only the first session has control over the digitizer; other sessions must be used for plotting or other less input-intensive operations.

Another nice feature of Sun OS is its capability to associate data files with their applications. You can double-click on an AutoCAD drawing file from within the Sun OS file, for instance, and the Organizer (directory manager) automatically begins AutoCAD with the selected file. The Sun platform also enjoys popular support from other major DOS application developers. Almost all of your favorite DOS programs have a Sun version, and the Sun is the most popular platform for AutoCAD third-party applications.

AutoCAD can use either a plotter configured directly with AutoCAD or spool plot files in the background. To spool plots, you can set a UNIX command or script-file name in the AutoCAD environment variable ACADPLCMD or ACADPPCMD. Then, when you create an AutoCAD plot file with the name AUTOSPOOL from within AutoCAD, it goes to a spool directory and the real file name is supplied to the UNIX command or script.

Other than these small differences, AutoCAD looks and behaves under Sun OS in much the same way that it looks and behaves under DOS.

The Open Look Interface

The SPARCstation version of AutoCAD runs on the Sun Open Look interface, which is a graphical user interface designed to run on top of the Sun Operating System (Sun OS). That process is similar to the way Microsoft Windows runs on top of MS-DOS.

Using AutoCAD's Interfaces

You can interact with the AutoCAD program in a number of ways. AutoCAD provides several different interfaces that display information on-screen and accept input from you. Any combination of these interfaces can be used as you work with AutoCAD. You may prefer to use only certain interfaces, each of which has advantages for specific operations, while disabling other ones.

> **NOTE** The following sections give you a brief tour of AutoCAD's different interfaces by using the most popular platform, DOS, as the sample platform. If you use AutoCAD on a different platform, you may need to refer to the previous discussions to relate these interfaces to your platform.

The Drawing Editor

Upon opening AutoCAD Release 12, you are taken directly to the AutoCAD's graphic workspace—the *drawing editor*. Once in the drawing editor workspace, you may be prompted by a dialog box to provide a login name so you can log in to AutoCAD. AutoCAD uses this information to monitor the number of users that are executing AutoCAD. You can make AutoCAD save the login name in your configuration file. In subsequent sessions, you will not be prompted for a login name.

 See Chapter 2 for more information on AutoCAD configuration.

When you successfully log in, your drawing appears in the center of the graphics screen with the crosshairs, pick box, and aperture cursors. (You learn about these different cursors later in the book.) In this graphics area, you use AutoCAD's commands to create your drawing's geometry. The graphics area is surrounded by three text areas, one for status display and two for command entry, as illustrated in figure 1.1. The text areas are detailed in the following sections.

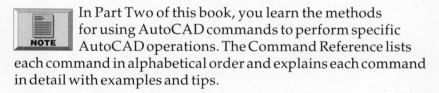 In Part Two of this book, you learn the methods for using AutoCAD commands to perform specific AutoCAD operations. The Command Reference lists each command in alphabetical order and explains each command in detail with examples and tips.

When you first face the AutoCAD drawing editor, your drawing tasks may seem daunting. AutoCAD Release 12 includes over 250 standard commands, the Advanced Modeling Extension adds even more commands, and you can enter commands as well as their associated options and parameters in six different ways.

The following sections discuss the AutoCAD status-line area, menu areas, and the `Command:` prompt, which are the means by which AutoCAD enables you to enter commands, select options, and see current parameters. Depending on your hardware, you may not have access to all of the menu facilities described here. (See the earlier discussion of hardware requirements.)

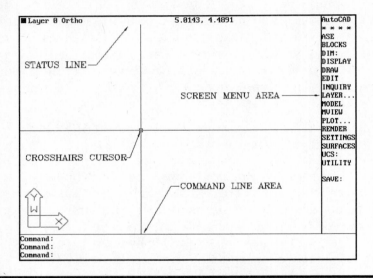

Figure 1.1:
The AutoCAD drawing editor's screen elements.

> **NOTE** You may be interested in the customization possibilities available in AutoCAD, which enable you to customize all of AutoCAD's built-in menus. Menu customization is discussed in Chapter 10.

The Status Line

Depending on your hardware's capabilities, a status-line area may appear at the top of the graphics screen. This line of text displays your current drawing layer, the state of certain drawing aids (such as Grid, Ortho, and Snap), and your current drawing coordinates.

The Command Line

The most direct way to enter AutoCAD commands is by typing them from your keyboard at the command line, which appears at the bottom of the AutoCAD graphics screen. The Command: prompt displays whenever AutoCAD is waiting for you to enter a command.

After a command is entered, additional prompts and pieces of information appear in the command-line area. By using video drivers that are supplied with AutoCAD, you can configure this portion of the screen to hold up to three lines of text. Some ADI drivers enable you to configure additional lines of text. As commands are completed and text output is displayed, the command-line area scrolls to display new Command: prompts or informational items.

As you type in a command, you can use the keyboard's Backspace key to move back through the command name to edit characters. You must press Enter to input commands that have text with spaces. (In such cases, pressing the space bar does not submit the command.)

If you enter a command name incorrectly, AutoCAD responds with the message Unknown command. Type ? for list of commands. If this message occurs, retype the command with the name spelled correctly. If you want to view a list of AutoCAD commands, enter ? at the Command: prompt. This invokes AutoCAD's Help command, which is discussed later.

You can press Ctrl-X to delete a complete line of command input, or Ctrl-C to cancel a command, at any time during command entry or execution. Table 1.1 lists the Ctrl-key combinations you can use in AutoCAD, and their functions.

Table 1.1
AutoCAD's Ctrl-Key Functions

Ctrl-Key Combination	Function
Ctrl-C	Cancels a command
Ctrl-B	Turns Snap mode on or off
Ctrl-O	Turns Ortho mode on or off
Ctrl-G	Turns Grid mode on or off
Ctrl-D	Turns Coordinate Display on or off
Ctrl-E	Toggles Isoplane mode to left, top, or right plane
Ctrl-T	Turns Tablet mode on or off

Text Screens

Sometimes AutoCAD displays more than three lines of text information in response to a command. When this happens, the text can scroll through the three-line command area and you may miss some information. To avoid this problem, press the F1 function key (another key may be required on non-DOS systems) to turn off the graphics screen and display the drawing editor's text screen. On AutoCAD systems running in windows-based systems, the Flip Screen key (F1 or another key) brings the AutoCAD text window to the foreground if it is obscured by another window. Figure 1.2 shows the text screen.

All AutoCAD text output is continuously scrolled up the text screen during operation. You can flip to the text screen at any time to see additional or past text output. When you want to return to the graphics screen, press the Flip Screen key again.

```
0 entities in UNNAMED
Model space limits are X:      0.0000  Y:      0.0000  (Off)
                       X:     12.0000  Y:      9.0000
Model space uses       *Nothing*
Display shows          X:      0.0000  Y:      0.0000
                       X:     12.4867  Y:      9.0000
Insertion base is      X:      0.0000  Y:      0.0000  Z:      0.0000
Snap resolution is     X:      1.0000  Y:      1.0000
Grid spacing is        X:      0.0000  Y:      0.0000

Current space:         Model space
Current layer:         0
Current color:         BYLAYER -- 7 (white)
Current linetype:      BYLAYER -- CONTINUOUS
Current elevation:     0.0000  thickness:      0.0000
Fill on  Grid off  Ortho off  Qtext off  Snap off  Tablet off
Object snap modes:     None
Free disk: 15474688 bytes
Virtual memory allocated to program: 3452 KB
Amount of program in physical memory/Total (virtual) program size: 57%
Total conventional memory: 432 KB      Total extended memory: 7104 KB
-- Press RETURN for more --
Swap file size: 388 KB
Command:
```

Figure 1.2:
The drawing editor's text screen.

> **TIP** Some computer systems can be configured with two display adapter cards and monitors at the same time. On these systems, AutoCAD can often be configured so that it sends text output to one display and graphics to the other. In these situations, you should configure AutoCAD without a command-line area on the graphics screen to make more room for drawing geometry. When so configured, all AutoCAD prompts and responses appear on the text display for easy viewing. For more information on setting up a dual-monitor system, consult your AutoCAD dealer.

Screen Menus

The AutoCAD *screen menu* is located along the right edge of the drawing editor's graphics screen. The screen menu presents a vertical list of submenu and command names, which can be highlighted and executed. When you first enter the drawing editor, AutoCAD presents the screen menu's *root menu*, which is the first menu set in the screen-menu system. Because it has hundreds of command and option selections, the standard AutoCAD screen menu is divided into many submenus—called *pages*—which are arranged in hierarchical order. When you pick a submenu name from the root menu, AutoCAD replaces the root menu with another menu of related command names or command option selections (see fig. 1.3).

Each menu page provides a selection that enables you to move to a different menu without executing a specific command or option. To return to the previous screen menu page, you can select the LAST option. To move to the next page, select the next option. You can also skip from any menu page to the DRAW or EDIT screen menus by selecting the DRAW or EDIT options (see fig. 1.3). If you pick the AutoCAD option, which appears at the top of each menu page, you return to the root menu. The * * * * selection, which also is constantly visible, displays object snap overrides and other commands.

Each menu selection in uppercase signifies that a submenu is displayed by that selection. Selections ending with a colon (:) cancel any current command, execute the command named by the selection, and display command options for that command. Mixed-case or lowercase menu selections simply enter their characters when picked as a response to a prompt.

To pick from the screen menu, you can use your pointing device to move the cursor over the desired menu selection and then press the device's pick button. You can also use the keyboard to make menu selections. To do that, press the Menu Cursor key (the Ins key on DOS systems) and highlight any item on a screen menu. You then can use the arrow keys to move up and down the screen menu to highlight your choice. Press the Menu Cursor key again to execute the selection.

You also can make selections by typing the desired menu selection after first pressing the Menu Cursor key. AutoCAD attempts to match each character you type with a menu-selection name. When AutoCAD correctly matches your typed characters with a menu selection, press the Menu Cursor key again to execute it. As you execute a command or make a command- option selection, the command's prompts and its responses appear in the command-line area.

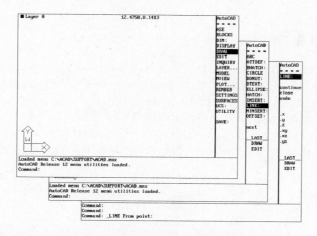

Figure 1.3:
Hierarchical screen menu pages.

If you become accustomed to another menu interface and seldom use the screen-menu area, you can configure AutoCAD to disable the screen-menu display, making more screen area usable for drawing. To disable the screen-menu area, reconfigure your video display (by selecting Configure from the File menu, then following the subsequent instructions), and enter your preference when prompted during the configuration dialogue.

You do not have to accept the standard AutoCAD screen menu. The screen menu, and other menus, are completely customizable and replaceable. Third-party application developers supply discipline-specific menu systems that make drawing with AutoCAD much easier and productive.

31

You can also easily create your own menu selections and command macros, as described in Chapter 10.

Pull-Down Menus

If your system is configured with a display driver that supports the Advanced User Interface (AUI), and you move your cursor above the graphics-display area, the pull-down menu bar appears and replaces the status line, as shown in figure 1.4. The AUI includes AutoCAD's pull-down menus and dialog boxes (which are discussed later). Pull-down menus are available only if you enable the status line during display configuration.

Figure 1.4:
The pull-down menu bar with one menu displayed.

The standard AutoCAD pull-down menu provides nine selections. If you click your pointing device's pick button on one of the names, its associated pull-down menu appears below the menu bar and temporarily overlays the graphics screen. Figure 1.4, for example, shows that picking Draw from the menu bar causes the Draw pull-down menu to appear.

Each pull-down menu contains a number of AutoCAD commands or submenu names for selection. Submenu names typically end with an angle bracket (>), as shown in figure 1.5. Selections ending with an ellipsis (...) present an icon menu or dialog box when selected, as illustrated in figure 1.6. Icon menus are described in the next section.

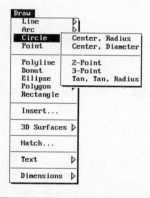

Figure 1.5:
A submenu, displayed by picking a pull-down menu selection.

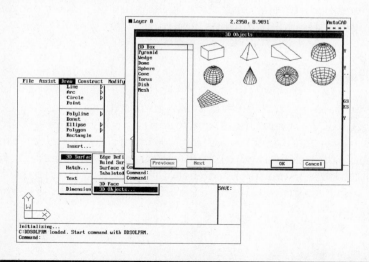

Figure 1.6:
An icon menu, displayed by picking a pull-down menu selection.

To execute a command from a pull-down menu, pick the command's name from the menu. For example, you can start the LINE command by picking Line from the Draw pull-down menu. When you pick a submenu name, the submenu replaces the pull-down menu with another list of options.

The pull-down menu disappears when you select a command name. If you want to remove the menu from the screen without selecting a command, however, you can move the cursor into any blank area of the drawing screen and press the pointing device's pick button. You can also remove a menu from the screen by typing a character at the keyboard. You must backspace over the character before typing anything else at the Command: prompt.

 Pull-down menus cannot be activated from the keyboard. AutoCAD disables the pull-down menu system while certain commands are being executed.

You can customize AutoCAD's pull-down menus by replacing a standard pull-down menu with one of your own making. Third-party developers also offer customization options for pull-down menus. (See Chapter 10 for more information.)

Icon Menus

When a pull-down menu selection that ends with an ellipsis (...) is chosen, AutoCAD presents an icon menu or dialog box of additional options. *Icon menus* display selections for command options that are more easily represented with graphics than with text, such as fonts and symbols. Each icon menu can consist of four, nine, or 16 separate icons, each of which features its own pick button. Figure 1.7 shows a typical icon menu.

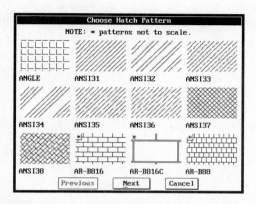

Figure 1.7:
An icon menu of hatch patterns.

When an icon menu is displayed, the crosshair cursor becomes an arrow cursor, which you use to select an icon. As you move the cursor over the menu, a box appears around the nearest icon. If the menu is in a series of icon menus, it usually has a selection for moving back to the previous icon menu or ahead to the next menu. A selection is also often available for exiting from the menu without making a selection. Still another selection may be available to cancel the current command.

AutoCAD uses simple slide files to display icon menus, which makes it easy to create your own icon menus. See Chapter 10 for details.

Dialog Boxes

Several AutoCAD commands display graphical *dialog boxes* for inputting various command options and parameters. Dialog boxes are also part of the Advanced User Interface, and can display only when the proper driver is installed. A dialog box enables you to quickly set and review many command parameters before the command acts on all your choices at once. Some commands even display multiple dialog boxes, one on top of the other.

When a dialog box is visible, the crosshair cursor once again becomes an arrow cursor for operating available buttons, for using slider bars, or for editing text boxes (see fig. 1.8). Any default values for command parameters are displayed within text boxes; you can edit the values by clicking on the box at the characters to be edited.

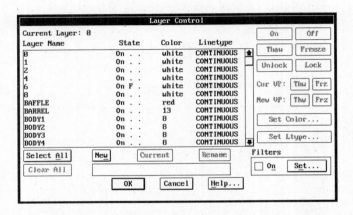

Figure 1.8:
Typical dialog-box components.

You can edit the text by pressing the arrow-movement keys, Del, or Backspace. Press Ctrl-X to highlight all text characters in the text box.

Some dialog box selections are *toggles*, and are indicated by a check mark in a box near a label. You can click on the box to turn the check mark on or off, depending on its current status. Some dialog boxes, such as those that display lists of files or layers, may contain too many items to be displayed at once. Such long lists have *slider bars* at the side with which you can scroll. You can drag the slider box up and down the slider bar to see corresponding sections of the list.

Clicking above or below the slider box scrolls the list in single-page increments in either direction. Clicking on the arrows at either end of the scroll bars scrolls the list up or down, one item at a time. When you finish setting all the values you have chosen, you must click on the OK button or press Enter for the changes to take effect. Click on the Cancel button in the dialog box, press Ctrl-C, or press Esc to abort the command without changes.

NOTE The commands that use dialog boxes all begin with the letters DD (which stands for Dynamic Dialog box). If FILEDIA is set to 0, file dialog boxes are disabled. To access a file dialog box when FILEDIA is set to 0, type a tilde (~) at the file-name prompt and press Enter. Figure 1.9 shows the Open Drawing dialog box.

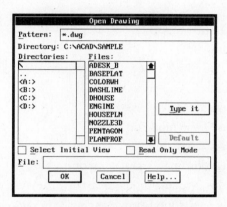

Figure 1.9:
The Open Drawing dialog box.

Button Menus

You can easily select commands from menus by using your input device. If your input device has many buttons, you have a quick alternative to using the keyboard or menus for certain types of input. With today's sophisticated input devices, you can pick commands simply by pressing a single button. Many digitizers and mice are equipped with 16 or more buttons to help you input commands.

In addition to the pick button on your mouse or digitizer puck, the other buttons on your pointing device perform various functions. Each of the extra buttons on your pointing device can execute a frequently used command. Table 1.2 lists the functions assigned to pointing-device buttons by the standard AutoCAD menu file (ACAD.MNU). The device's first button is always reserved as the pick button.

Table 1.2
Pointing-Device Button Assignments

Button	Function
1	Pick button
2	Enter
3	Activates the Assist pull-down menu
4	Cancels a command
5	Turns Snap mode on or off
6	Turns Ortho mode on or off
7	Turns Grid display on or off
8	Turns coordinate display on or off
9	Toggles Isoplane mode to left, top, or right plane
10	Turns Tablet mode on or off

A button performs the assigned action at any time while within the drawing editor. You can also replace the default function by assigning commands of your own to any of the buttons, up to the maximum number supported by your pointing device.

Tablet Menus

One of the fastest ways to draw with AutoCAD without going through pages of screen menus is to enter AutoCAD commands from a *digitizer-tablet menu*. Tablet menus are also one of the most productive interfaces for third-party applications. If you have a digitizer-tablet menu, you can configure AutoCAD to use a portion of the tablet's surface for entering commands. Another portion of the surface, usually in the center of the command-entry area, is used for the screen-pointing area in which you enter points in your drawing. Some or all of your digitizer-tablet area can be used to input paper drawings into an AutoCAD drawing.

You enter commands from a tablet menu by picking a point on the tablet surface within a smaller rectangular area, called a *cell*. A paper or plastic sheet with arrays of cells, called a *template*, must be attached to the tablet's surface and calibrated electronically with AutoCAD to record its position on the tablet. The TABLET>DWG drawing in your sample directory contains the default tablet menu.

Each cell can have a command name or icon printed in it, which identifies the command or action to be performed when you use the pointing device to pick the cell. Tablet picks are often coordinated with screen menus or pull-down menus to display options for further selection. You can also customize or replace the tablet menu, just as you can customize or replace the other menu interfaces described so far. The blank area at the top of the AutoCAD tablet menu template is available for adding your own commands.

Your movements do not display on the AutoCAD graphics screen when you move your pointing device over the command-cell area of the template. When you move the device into the screen-display area, your pointing device then controls the crosshair cursor.

Getting Help

If you invoke a command, and you need help providing information for it, AutoCAD has a built-in system that helps you complete the command. You can use the HELP command at any `Command:` prompt to get pointers on any single command or to see a list of all available commands and system variables (including those used by the Advanced Modeling Extension). Help selections are also available on the screen, pull-down, and tablet menus. You can get help, even in the middle of most commands, by invoking the HELP command transparently. To do this, enter an apostrophe before the word:'**HELP**. The HELP command then gives you information about the current command prompt, if available.

For more information on the HELP command, see the Command Reference.

Summary

In this chapter, you were introduced to the different versions of AutoCAD Release 12 and their platforms. You learned the hardware requirements for each version and some of the special features of each version. You also learned your way around the graphic interface.

Installing and Configuring AutoCAD

This chapter shows you ways to install AutoCAD Release 12 on MS-DOS and SPARCstation platforms for a single user on a stand-alone machine or on a network. This chapter also describes program configuration to help you set up the program so that it runs efficiently on your computer platform.

You do not need to install, configure, or optimize AutoCAD. An established AutoCAD dealer channel exists to perform these tasks for you. If you purchase a complete system, including computer and software, from an authorized AutoCAD dealer, Autodesk requires the dealer to perform the following services:

- Install hardware required by AutoCAD, such as a hard drive and math coprocessor

- Prepare the system for operation by formatting the hard drive, loading and configuring the operating system, and loading and configuring AutoCAD for your system
- Provide eight hours of AutoCAD training
- Provide telephone and on-site support (the dealer may charge for these services)

Autodesk recommends that you buy AutoCAD through an authorized dealer. AutoCAD is a very complex program, and you need many hours to master it. You also need in-depth knowledge of your computer's hardware and operating system to make AutoCAD perform at its optimum level. The aid of a qualified and knowledgeable dealer can prove invaluable in helping you gain the expertise you need to get the most out of AutoCAD.

Installing AutoCAD

The basic installation process is similar for each platform. AutoCAD is available to do the following:

- Run the Install program
- Select the AutoCAD components for installation
- Personalize the executable file
- Complete the installation

You must use the installation program included with AutoCAD to install AutoCAD. The AutoCAD release disks contain compressed files that must be expanded by the installation program. Before installing AutoCAD, make sure that you have enough free hard disk space to install AutoCAD successfully. The full complement of AutoCAD occupies from 26M to 30M of disk space, depending on the platform on which it is installed.

Each version of AutoCAD provides an easy-to-use, menu-based installation program for transferring files from the release disks into the appropriate subdirectories of your hard disk.

Upgrading from a Previous Release

If you are upgrading from Release 11 or an earlier version of AutoCAD, follow these guidelines:

- Leave the earlier version installed on your computer until you are confident that Release 12 has been installed and runs correctly. Install Release 12 in a different directory or on a different drive from the older version (permanently, or at least until Release 12 is up and running). This takes up a large part of your hard disk drive, so confirm that you have enough space to accommodate both. To conserve disk space, you can choose to install only that part of Release 12 that is necessary to run the program.

- Make backup copies on floppy disks of any customized files you have created or installed. These may include AutoLISP programs (LSP), prototype drawings (DWG), shape and text font files (SHP and SHX), customized help files (HLP and HDX), menu files (MNU and MNX), custom linetype files (LIN), and hatch-pattern files (PAT).

- After Release 12 is running, update your AUTOEXEC.BAT and CONFIG.SYS files.

Hardware Locking

When you purchase or upgrade an international version of AutoCAD on certain platforms, a small device called a *hardware lock* is enclosed with your AutoCAD product. If it is included with your package, AutoCAD will not operate without the hardware lock properly installed on your computer.

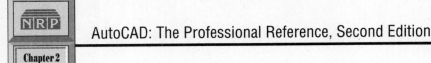

 The hardware lock is used only with the international version of AutoCAD.

The hardware lock is an integral part of AutoCAD's software, so if the lock is lost, stolen, or destroyed, you must buy another complete copy of AutoCAD to replace it. If your hardware lock is damaged or faulty, contact your dealer (in Europe, contact your Autodesk country office). Autodesk will replace the defective device upon return of the original lock.

The AutoCAD license agreement enables you to install a single copy of AutoCAD on as many computers as you want, provided you use it on only one computer at a time. Installing AutoCAD on more than one computer means that you must move the lock to the computer on which you plan to use AutoCAD.

How the Hardware Lock Works

The hardware lock is designed to affect AutoCAD only; it should not affect peripheral devices connected to the same parallel-interface port. It is not necessary to remove the hardware lock to run other programs. The hardware lock does not prevent you from making backup copies of the software disks or from loading AutoCAD on your hard disk. Also, you do not need a key disk to run AutoCAD.

 Other programs using a different hardware-lock device might not run properly with the AutoCAD lock installed. AutoCAD should work fine with hardware locks for other programs attached, provided that the AutoCAD hardware lock is also installed.

Installing the Hardware Lock

To install the hardware lock, follow these steps:

1. Shut down the computer and all peripheral devices.
2. Attach the male connector (the end labeled "computer") of the hardware lock to your computer's parallel-port connector. AutoCAD is now able to run.

 If all of your parallel ports are occupied, disconnect one of the peripheral devices, and then connect the hardware lock to the open parallel port. Next, reconnect the peripheral device you disconnected to the female end (labeled "peripheral") of the hardware lock.

 Some caution must be taken when using the lock. Never connect or disconnect a peripheral device when the computer is turned on. Low voltages and signals passing through the parallel interface could damage your computer, peripheral devices, hardware lock, or data. Also, you should always turn off the computer before installing or removing the hardware lock.

Finally, turning a peripheral device off or on that is connected to the hardware lock while you are using AutoCAD causes the hardware lock to fail. Make sure that each peripheral you intend to use is turned on before you start AutoCAD, and leave those peripherals turned on while AutoCAD is running.

Testing the Hardware Lock

To test the hardware lock, simply start AutoCAD. If AutoCAD runs, you have installed the lock properly. If the lock is not installed properly, dislodged, or not connected, AutoCAD displays the following message:

```
Hardware Lock error
Retry, Fail?
```

After this message, AutoCAD enables you to recheck the connection or correct any problem. After you correct the problem, press **R** for retry; AutoCAD should run normally. If the message is repeated, it is a good indication that there may be a problem with the lock. Contact your dealer (in Europe, contact your Autodesk country office).

Using the AutoCAD Install Program

To install AutoCAD, you must use the installation program that comes with AutoCAD. Before beginning the installation process, make backup copies of your AutoCAD disks (the AutoCAD License Agreement permits you to make one copy). The DOS DISKCOPY command works best for this purpose. (For instructions on the use of DISKCOPY, see your DOS reference manual.)

If you see `Error reading drive A` messages while attempting to use the DISKCOPY command, contact your AutoCAD dealer before continuing. Your disks may be defective; if they are, your dealer can return them to Autodesk for a new copy.

If you install AutoCAD from your backup copy and see the error message `Program too big to fit in memory`, the installation program may be infected with a virus, or an interruption to the DISKCOPY command during the copying procedure may have corrupted the backup. You need to scan the disk from which you are installing to discover the virus or repeat the DISKCOPY backup procedure. Your AutoCAD dealer can provide you with valuable help in these situations. Do not hesitate to call on your AutoCAD dealer whenever you encounter difficulties.

To begin the installation program, place disk 1, titled Executables 1, in drive A and make it the current drive by entering **A:** at the DOS prompt. When you see the DOS prompt reappear, type **INSTALL**.

If your AutoCAD release disks are 1.44M, 3 1/2-inch media, substitute drive **B** wherever you see drive A in the installation instructions.

A message appears on-screen to tell you that you must personalize AutoCAD before you can complete the installation, and to warn you that the disk in drive A cannot be write-protected (the personalization procedure writes information back to the floppy disk). Press any key to continue.

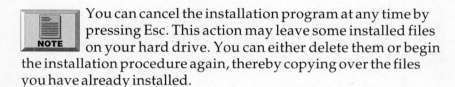 You can cancel the installation program at any time by pressing Esc. This action may leave some installed files on your hard drive. You can either delete them or begin the installation procedure again, thereby copying over the files you have already installed.

Personalizing AutoCAD

Figure 2.1 shows the AutoCAD program personalization screen. On this screen, you enter information to personalize your copy of AutoCAD. The Install program permanently imprints the software with your name, the name of the company you work for, and the dealer's name and telephone number. Whenever you run AutoCAD, this information is displayed in the banner at the top of the main menu.

The Install program's personalization screen contains four fields in which you place data. Type the data and use the Tab key or the up- and down-arrow keys to move between the fields. The Backspace key deletes characters; typing characters overwrites any existing characters. The left- and right-arrow keys move the cursor within a field. Each field must contain at least four characters. If you do not know your dealer's name and telephone number, enter at least four random characters in the two dealer-information fields.

47

After you have entered all of the required information, press Enter. The Install program then asks you (twice) to verify the information you have entered, and writes the data to the floppy disk and displays the information.

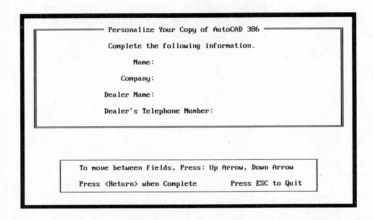

```
┌─────────── Personalize Your Copy of AutoCAD 386 ───────────┐
│                                                            │
│          Complete the following information.               │
│                                                            │
│               Name:                                        │
│                                                            │
│            Company:                                        │
│                                                            │
│        Dealer Name:                                        │
│                                                            │
│        Dealer's Telephone Number:                          │
│                                                            │
└────────────────────────────────────────────────────────────┘


        ┌──────────────────────────────────────────────────┐
        │ To move between fields, Press: Up Arrow, Down Arrow │
        │                                                  │
        │ Press <Return> when Complete      Press ESC to Quit │
        └──────────────────────────────────────────────────┘
```

Figure 2.1:
AutoCAD personalization screen.

Selecting the Files To Install

After personalizing the software, the Install program asks which files you want to install (see fig. 2.2). The Install program enables you to install as much or as little of AutoCAD as you need by letting you choose file groups.

Depending on the platform, your interests, and how you plan to use AutoCAD, you also can install any or all of the following portions of the program:

Files	Function
Bonus/Sample files	Sample AutoCAD drawings and AutoLISP routines
Source files	Standard menu file and source font files
IGES font files	IGES text fonts and text source files; AutoCAD drawings of IGES symbols
ADS files	AutoCAD Development System files
AME files	Advanced Modeling Extension files
API files	Application Programming Interface files

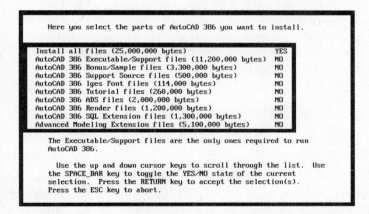

Figure 2.2:
The Select Files to Install screen.

To run AutoCAD, all you need are the executable and support files, but you may want some of the other groups installed as well. Scroll through the list, using the up- and down-arrow keys; press the spacebar to select each group you want to install. After you have made your selections, press Enter. At this point, AutoCAD gives you the option of quitting or continuing.

If you choose to install all the files or AME only, the program asks whether you purchased the Advanced Modeling Extension. You can choose to install the AME files, but unless you purchased the AME option and received the authorization code that activates the AME program, you will not be able to use the program.

Choosing Files To Install

After selecting file groups for installation, the Install program determines whether your hard drive has enough free space to accommodate the files you have chosen to install. If there is not enough available, the Install program tells you how much space you need to free up. If you are sure that you have enough space, you can respond **Yes** at the prompt to continue installation. Otherwise, respond **No** and exit to DOS. If you respond **Yes**, the program begins to install AutoCAD, prompting you each time it needs a new release disk.

Selecting a Hard Drive and Directories

After you finish the personalization routine, a new screen appears, displaying information about the installation program. Press any key to display a list of hard drives available on your system for the AutoCAD installation (see fig. 2.3). If you do not see the drive you want, use the down-arrow key to scroll to other drive names. When the name of the desired hard drive is highlighted, press Enter.

Specifying the AutoCAD Subdirectory

Next, enter the name of the directory in which you want AutoCAD installed. As you can see in figure 2.4, the program provides the default directory \ACAD. Press Enter to accept it, or type the name of another directory you want to use. If you are upgrading a previous version that you want to leave on your hard drive, make sure that you specify a different directory name if the earlier version is installed in a directory named ACAD.

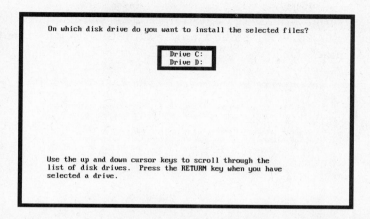

On which disk drive do you want to install the selected files?

```
Drive C:
Drive D:
```

Use the up and down cursor keys to scroll through the
list of disk drives. Press the RETURN key when you have
selected a drive.

Figure 2.3:
Selecting a drive to store AutoCAD.

After you specify a subdirectory for the program, another screen
appears and prompts you for the name of the directory in which
AutoCAD's support files are to be transferred. You can use the directory name you selected in the previous screen, or enter a new directory
name. Many users create a subdirectory called SUPPORT under
the AutoCAD directory, as shown in figure 2.5. To do so, type
\ACAD\SUPPORT (assuming that you called your AutoCAD directory ACAD) and press Enter. If the directory already exists, the program warns you of this and asks if you want to overwrite the existing
files in that directory.

Installing AME

You can install AME at the same time you install AutoCAD, or you can
install it separately. To install AutoCAD 12 and AME 2.1 at the same
time, follow the instructions outlined in the previous section or use the
following procedure:

1. Insert the disk labeled "AME 1Disk" into drive A:.
2. Run the Install program by entering **a:install**.

51

The Install program assumes that AutoCAD Release 12 is already installed. AME must be installed into the same directory in which you installed AutoCAD.

```
Here you specify the name of the directory where the selected files
will be installed.  By default, the name of this directory is:
   \ACAD.
The program locates it below the root directory of the disk
drive you selected.  If you have no preference, choose the
default by pressing the RETURN key.

To change the directory name, backspace over the directory name
and type a new name.  Press the RETURN key when you have finished
typing the name.




                         ===== Which subdirectory ? =====
 \ACAD
```

Figure 2.4:
The installation screen, showing the directory for AutoCAD.

```
Here you specify the name of the directory where AutoCAD 386
support files will be installed.  By default, the name of this
directory is:
   \ACAD12\SUPPORT

The program locates it below the root directory of the disk
drive you selected.  If you have no preference, choose the
default by pressing the RETURN key.

To change the directory name, backspace over the directory name
and type a new name.  Press the RETURN key when you have finished
typing the name.



                    ===== Support files subdirectory ? =====
 \ACAD12\SUPPORT
```

Figure 2.5:
Selecting a subdirectory to store AutoCAD.

Installing AutoCAD on a Network

AutoCAD provides explicit network support in Release 12 through file-locking and server authorization. With file-locking enabled, no single file can be used simultaneously by more than one person. AutoCAD locks drawing files, menu files, and font files, among others.

Server authorization enables more than one person to use a single copy of AutoCAD at the same time. In networked environments, AutoCAD often is installed on a central computer, called a *file server*, to which all other computers on the network are linked. You can authorize one copy of AutoCAD on the server to allow a specific number of users to use the program simultaneously. When that number of users is running AutoCAD, additional users cannot gain access to the program. You can increase the number of authorized users at any time; contact your AutoCAD dealer for more information.

Preparing To Install AutoCAD on a Network

Before you actually install AutoCAD on your network, you must decide whether you want AutoCAD to place its temporary files on the local workstations or on the central server. If you decide to use the workstations, you must create the directories in which the files will be stored before you install AutoCAD.

Some networks (most notably 3Com) require that you store shared files in a read-write directory. If you decide to use the server for temporary file storage, check the documentation for your network software to determine the network's requirements. If your network requires that shared directories be read-write, you must configure AutoCAD to place its temporary files in a read-write directory, and set the necessary read-write permissions for the directory you choose.

Next, log in to your network from a workstation as the supervisor or system administrator. Link or map a drive letter to the directory in which you store your applications. You need to have write permission to this directory.

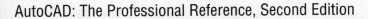
Begin the AutoCAD installation program and personalize the software. When you are prompted for the drive in which to install AutoCAD, use the letter you designated by mapping or linking to a directory on the server in the previous step.

The next two steps in the installation program prompt for a directory in which to install AutoCAD's program files and a directory for AutoCAD's support files. Name a subdirectory under your application directory for the program files and a subdirectory under that one for the support files. Select the portions of AutoCAD you want to install, and then complete the installation process.

After installing AutoCAD, run it to begin the configuration process. During configuration, you tell AutoCAD how many users are authorized to use the program simultaneously, enter passwords that help guard against unauthorized changes to the server authorization, and supply the server-authorization code for your copy of AutoCAD. After configuration, run AutoCAD to make sure that it functions properly.

As a normal user, log on to each workstation and configure it to run AutoCAD. You may want to write a batch file to start AutoCAD from each station, and to set the DOS environment variables (such as ACAD and ACADCFG) that AutoCAD uses to customize its environment on a particular workstation. If you prefer, you can set these variables in the system or in user login scripts rather than with a batch file.

You also need to run AutoCAD and configure it for the peripherals (graphics card, digitizer, plotter, printer) that each workstation uses. You must select a unique, three-character, network-node name for each workstation. AutoCAD uses the network-node name as an extension to the names of each workstation's temporary files so that they are not overwritten by another user's files. After configuration, run AutoCAD at each workstation to make sure that it runs properly.

When the program finishes installation, it checks your CONFIG.SYS file for the statement Files=40. If the file does not contain this statement, or if the installation program finds that Files have been set to a value less than 40, the program offers to edit your CONFIG.SYS file.

If you answer **No**, the program asks if you want it to write a CONFIG.CAD file containing the correct files statement to drive C.

If you do not allow the program to edit your CONFIG.SYS file, do not forget to edit the file yourself.

Finally, the program offers to write an ACADR12.BAT file that you can use to start AutoCAD. There is no harm in answering **Yes** to this question. In fact, the batch file provides information that can be quite useful as a guide to editing your AUTOEXEC.BAT file to set appropriate environment variables.

If you allowed the Install program to edit your CONFIG.SYS file, the program tells you to reboot your computer so that the changes take effect. The Install program exits to DOS in the directory in which it installed AutoCAD. Now you are ready to configure AutoCAD for the specific devices with which you intend to use it.

Running AutoCAD 386 under Windows

If you run Microsoft Windows on at least a 386-class machine, you can run AutoCAD as a full-screen DOS application under Windows, which enables you to run AutoCAD without exiting from the Windows environment. The following sections describe this process.

Setting Up AutoCAD under Windows 3.1

Setup consists of the following five steps:

- Installing the PHARLAP.386 device driver
- Creating a PIF file
- Setting environment variables in your AUTOEXEC.BAT file
- Setting up a Windows icon for AutoCAD (these instructions assume that AutoCAD is installed and configured properly on your system)
- Installing the PHARLAP.386 device driver

To run AutoCAD as a DOS application under Windows 3.1, the Windows device driver PHARLAP.386 must be installed in the Windows SYSTEM.INI file by adding the following line to the 386Enh section of the file:

```
[386Enh]
...
device=pharlap.386
```

Copy PHARLAP.386 from your AutoCAD directory \ACAD into your Windows directory d:\windows:

```
copy c:\acad\pharlap.386 d:\windows.
```

Creating a PIF File

To optimize performance of AutoCAD under Windows, first create a PIF file. PIF stands for *program information file,* and it is the Windows convention for specifying the amount of memory required for DOS-based applications.

Without a PIF file, AutoCAD Release 12 does not run well under Windows. AutoCAD requires access to several megabytes of extended memory. The PIF file specifies the memory needed for AutoCAD. For your convenience, Autodesk supplies a sample PIF file called ACAD.PIF in the Autocad \ACAD executable directory. Copy this file into your Windows 3.1 directory. If Windows 3.1 is installed in D:\WINDOWS, for example, and AutoCAD is installed in C:\ACAD, use the following command:

```
copy c:\acad\acad.pif d:\windows
```

Figure 2.6 shows a sample PIF Editor dialog box for ACAD.PIF.

To display this dialog box, run the PIF editor from the main window in the Program Manager. Select **F**ile, **O**pen from the top line menu of the main window, and open ACAD.PIF in the \WINDOWS EXECUTABLES directory.

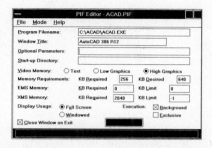

Figure 2.6:
A sample PIF Editor dialog box for AutoCAD.

The settings are as follows:

- Memory Requirements. AutoCAD requires at least 256K of conventional memory to start.
- XMS Memory. AutoCAD requires at least 3M of extended memory. The -1 setting in the KB Limit edit box tells Windows to give AutoCAD all the available extended memory it needs.
- Display usage. AutoCAD should be run only as a full-screen application.

Creating an AutoCAD Icon

The easiest way to launch a program in Windows is to associate an icon with it. From the Program Manager, select New from the File menu. Choose Program Item to create an icon for AutoCAD Release 12.

Restart Windows after completing these steps to initialize your SYSTEM.INI file and enable AutoCAD to run when you re-enter Windows.

Environment Files

Proper system setup is essential for AutoCAD to operate efficiently on your computer system. If you are running AutoCAD under DOS, you can use DOS to improve AutoCAD's performance. Like many programs, AutoCAD uses factors called *environment variables* to set program parameters, such as what directories to look in for support files or how much memory to devote to specific program functions. In DOS, the SET command establishes an environment variable's conditions. The SET command takes the following syntax:

```
SET environment variable=value
```

AutoCAD uses an environment variable called ACAD to determine the location of support files (such as menu files, AutoLISP routines, and text-font files). The following statement establishes that location:

```
SET ACAD=directoryname
```

Like the PATH command, environment-variable values established by the SET command vanish when the computer reboots; thus, most people set commonly used variables in their AUTOEXEC.BAT file. You can remove an environment variable by issuing the following command:

```
SET variable name=
```

You can view all currently set variables by typing **SET** at the DOS prompt.

Other settings, such as files and buffers, also affect the way AutoCAD works with your DOS-compatible hardware. This section discusses the following:

- Uses and settings for the AUTOEXEC.BAT and CONFIG.SYS files
- Startup batch files
- AutoCAD environment variables

AUTOEXEC.BAT

Batch files (executable files that have the BAT extension) consist of a series of DOS commands that DOS performs sequentially when you execute the file. When your computer starts up, it looks for the batch file named AUTOEXEC.BAT; if DOS finds this file, the operating system carries out the commands contained in the file. You can place any commands you regularly run upon starting your computer in your AUTOEXEC.BAT file. Practical uses for an AUTOEXEC.BAT file include setting a DOS path, setting environment variables with SET, and loading memory-resident programs, such as TSRs or ADI real-mode drivers.

AutoCAD uses the AUTOEXEC.BAT file to do the following:

- Specify the AutoCAD directory in the PATH statement that tells DOS where to find all the programs and executable files not in the current directory.
- Issue set commands for environment variables, such as ACAD, ACADDRV, and ACADCFG, which are discussed later in this chapter.

CONFIG.SYS

At startup, and before running the AUTOEXEC.BAT file, DOS also looks for a file called CONFIG.SYS. This file loads device drivers into memory, such as network drivers and expanded-memory managers. It also sets such DOS-configuration parameters as the number of files that can be open at any one time and the amount of memory to set aside for storage of environment-variable settings.

Files Statement

AutoCAD often needs to access several of its program files simultaneously (such as AutoLISP functions and text fonts). DOS, however, places limitations on the number of files that a program can have open at one time. AutoCAD is a large collection of program files and support files, and it can sometimes exceed DOS' default limit (eight) of open files. The number of files AutoCAD can open at one time is determined by the `Files` statement in the CONFIG.SYS file.

When AutoCAD's Install program finishes installation, it checks your CONFIG.SYS file for the statement `Files=40`. If the file does not contain this statement, or if the installation program finds that files have been set to a value less than 40, the program offers to edit your CONFIG.SYS file. If you answer **No**, the program asks if you want it to write a CONFIG.CAD file containing the correct `Files` statement to drive C. If you do not allow the program to edit your CONFIG.SYS file, do not forget to edit the file yourself.

 With `Files` set at 40, AutoLISP can open a maximum of about 20 files at the same time.

Buffers

DOS reserves a small amount of memory to use as input/output *buffers* for temporary data storage. Buffers have little effect on AutoCAD's performance because of the large amount of memory available and the way the DOS extender manages that memory. (The DOS extender is discussed in Chapter 3.)

Startup Batch Files

Although AutoCAD can use the AUTOEXEC.BAT file, running several programs that require special settings can make your AUTOEXEC.BAT file cumbersome to manage. You can create a long PATH statement or set up a conflict between programs, for example. One solution is to use a startup batch file, such as ACADR12.BAT, which was created by the Install program. An example of the ACAD12.BAT file is shown here:

```
set  acad=c:\acad\support;c:\acad\fonts;\c:\acad\ads
set  acadcfg=c:\acad
```

```
set acaddrv=c:\acad\drv
C:\ACAD\ACAD %1 %2
```

In the example, the environment variable ACAD is set to search multiple directories for support files. In the last statement, %1 and %2 allow parameters for drawing and script files. For instance, if you want to start AutoCAD with the drawing SAM.DWG and run a script called STARTUP.SCR to set AutoCAD system variables, enter the following:

```
C:>acadr12 sam startup
```

If you do not add parameters, AutoCAD starts in the normal manner.

Add the following statements to your AUTOEXEC.BAT file so that AutoCAD can run properly under Windows. The AutoCAD startup batch file, ACAD12.BAT, does not affect Windows, so these statements must reside in the AUTOEXEC.BAT file.

```
Set  acad=c:\acad\support;c:\acad\fonts;\c:\acad\ads
set  acadcfg=c:\acad
set  acaddrv=c:\acad\drv
```

If your AutoCAD directory is not \ACAD on the C drive, substitute the correct drive and path when you set the variables.

Configuring AutoCAD

Configuration gives AutoCAD the information it needs to handle the graphics and printing devices connected to your computer, such as the video display, digitizer, and plotter. AutoCAD cannot be used until it is configured.

AutoCAD is a single product that can be configured for any authorized number of users. The same configuration procedure is used for stand-alone and networked machines. When you configure AutoCAD, the configuration information (authorization code if required, device selections, operating parameters, and so on) is stored in a special configuration file called ACAD.CFG.

Initial Configuration

When you run AutoCAD for the first time after installing it, the program displays the following message:

```
AutoCAD is not yet configured.
```

You must specify the devices to which AutoCAD will interface. AutoCAD then walks you through the configuration procedure, in which you specify which graphics card, input device, and plotter you will use.

Configuring AutoCAD for Your Display Adapter

The first step in the configuration process is to select and configure your video card. After AutoCAD displays the `AutoCAD is not yet configured.` message, AutoCAD searches along the ACADDRV path for ADI drivers. It then displays a list of available video displays. Select a video display driver from the displayed list.

AutoCAD asks you a series of questions about the video monitor you have connected to your system. Check the manufacturer's documentation if you are not sure how to answer any of the questions.

After selecting an appropriate video display, AutoCAD presents the following configuration options for the selected display driver:

- **Aspect ratio.** AutoCAD gives you the opportunity to adjust the size of the square on your graphics screen. Each display driver supported by AutoCAD has a default aspect ratio, but if your monitor deviates from the default, you can adjust the aspect ratio by entering a value at this time.

- **Status line.** You can enable or disable the status line. The default for most monitors is to have a status line.

- **Menu and Prompt Areas.** You can disable the screen menu on some displays to make more room for graphics. The command-prompt area also can be disabled to enlarge the drawing area.

Digitizer Drivers

After setting the video-display configuration, AutoCAD searches for *digitizer drivers*. It then displays a list of available digitizers. Some differences exist between a digitizer and a mouse. A mouse interacts only with the screen, so you can point to, and select on-screen, menu functions and work in the screen-graphics area. You also can use the pull-down menus at the top of the screen in the drawing editor.

A digitizer has all the capabilities of a mouse and also enables you to use tablet menus. After you have surveyed the digitizer listing, enter the number corresponding to the digitizing device connected to your system, and press Enter to continue.

Depending on the type of pointing device you select, you may be asked to provide information about the adapter port to which the device connects. Standard ports are COM1 and COM2. If this information is requested, type the name of the communications port used by your digitizer.

Depending on the type of digitizer you select, you may need to configure the digitizer. AutoCAD prompts you for information about the size of your digitizing area.

Plotter Configuration

Next, AutoCAD searches for plotter drivers and displays a list of available plotters when found. If you have one of the listed plotters, press the appropriate number. Like the digitizer configuration, you need to indicate to which communications port the printer or plotter is connected. AutoCAD next offers you a chance to calibrate your plotter.

You are prompted with a series of questions related to your plotter settings. The exact questions vary from plotter to plotter. Check your plotter's documentation for information on your plotter settings.

Login Name

Next, AutoCAD prompts you for a login name. If you press Enter, AutoCAD uses the name under which you personalized the program when you installed it. If that name happens to be your company name or another name that is inappropriate, you can enter your own name here. If you enter a single period (.), AutoCAD prompts you for a login name whenever you run the program.

The login name appears on the AutoCAD banner at the top of the main menu when you enter AutoCAD. AutoCAD uses the login name to identify the owners of locked files. If you run AutoCAD on a network, you should choose a unique login name to avoid confusion. If you are running AutoCAD on a single workstation, but intend that it be used by more than one person, use the single-period option so that AutoCAD prompts for a login name each time the program is used. Figure 2.7 shows the login name screen.

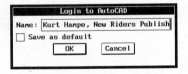

Figure 2.7:
AutoCAD login name screen.

Server Authorization

If you are running AutoCAD on a network, you must specify the number of people using your copy of AutoCAD. If you are running AutoCAD on a stand-alone machine with only one user at a time, accept the default (1). AutoCAD enables you to enter any number at this point. If the number does not equal that for which AutoCAD has been authorized, however, AutoCAD generates an error message whenever you try to enter the drawing editor.

AutoCAD then asks for the server-authorization code, which is an eight-digit hexadecimal number supplied to you by your AutoCAD dealer. Enter the number and, before accepting it, double-check to make sure that you have entered it correctly.

The next prompt asks if you want to run AutoCAD from a read-only directory. Some network environments (such as 3Com) require that you do this. If you answer **Yes** to this question, AutoCAD prompts for the directory's name. Then AutoCAD asks for a password to be used to guard against unauthorized changes to the server authorization. Autodesk recommends using a password; to omit one, type a period (.) at the prompt.

File-Locking

Next, AutoCAD asks if you want to enable file-locking (see fig. 2.8), which is a feature that enables you to run AutoCAD on a network and prevent more than one person from using a file simultaneously. If you are running the program on a stand-alone workstation, answer **No**. If you answer **Yes** and AutoCAD crashes, you have to unlock the menu and drawing files before you can edit the drawing again.

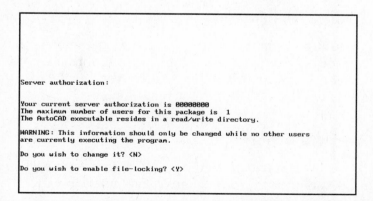

```
Server authorization:

Your current server authorization is 00000000
The maximum number of users for this package is  1
The AutoCAD executable resides in a read/write directory.

WARNING: This information should only be changed while no other users
are currently executing the program.

Do you wish to change it? <N>

Do you wish to enable file-locking? <Y>
```

Figure 2.8:
The AutoCAD network-configuration screen.

The Configuration Menu

At the end of the initial configuration process, AutoCAD displays the current configuration; simply press Enter until the configuration menu appears.

The main configuration menu includes eight options, each of which is described briefly in the following sections:

Exit to Drawing Editor

This option enables you to save the changes you have made during your configuration session and returns you to the drawing editor.

Show Current Configuration

This option displays the current configuration settings used by AutoCAD on-screen. It displays settings for the video display, digitizer, plotter or printer, and then prompts you to press Enter to return to the main configuration menu.

Allow Detailed Configuration

Options 3 through 7 enable you to tweak device parameters and operating modes. Some devices prompt you for information that is suppressed during normal configuration. Option 2 enables you to fine-tune these devices beyond the normal requirements.

Configure Video Display

This option enables you to configure your computer's video display adapter. Use this option if you change your adapter card after the initial configuration.

Configure Digitizer

Use this option to configure your computer's digitizer. Use this option if you change your adapter card after the initial configuration.

Configure Plotter

This option enables you to configure your computer's plotter. Use this option if you change your plotter after the initial configuration.

Configure System Console

This option does not apply to IBM-PCs and compatibles. Sun Microsystems computers, however, have configurable system-console parameters.

Configure Operating System

This option takes you to a secondary configuration menu.

Exit to Configuration Menu

This option takes you back to the main configuration menu.

Alarm on Error

Activating this option causes AutoCAD to beep whenever you make an input error.

Initial Drawing Setup

Use this option to identify a drawing that you use as a prototype.

Default Plot File Name

Use this option to specify a standard output file name for all the files you generate using the plot menu's plot-to-file feature.

Plot Spooler Directory

This option enables you to specify the directory for the plot spooler.

Placement of Temporary Files

AutoCAD uses disk space to swap drawings and temporary files in and out of memory. This option enables you to specify a directory in which AutoCAD places temporary files.

Network Node Name

With this option, each user in a network can configure AutoCAD to use a different network-node name.

Automatic-Save

AutoCAD can perform a timed save of your current drawing. You can select an interval from one to 600 minutes. Select 0 to disable timed saves.

Full-Time CRC Validation

CRC (cyclic redundancy check) is an error-checking mechanism. Use this option if you suspect that your drawing files are being corrupted. Full-time validation means that the check is done each time an entity is read into the drawing.

Automatic Audit after IGESIN, DXFIN, DXBIN

AutoCAD issues the Audit command whenever a drawing is opened with one of these drawing-interchange commands.

Select Release 11 Hidden Line Removal Algorithm

Use this option to select the AutoCAD Release 11 algorithm. The AutoCAD Release 11 hidden-line removal algorithm takes up less memory than does Release 12's. Release 11's algorithm, however, is slower.

Log In Name

This option enables you to change the login name.

Server Authorization and File Locking

Use this option to change the server of authorization code.

Saving the Configuration

AutoCAD now shows you a screen that displays the choices you made during configuration. If you press Enter while this screen is active, AutoCAD displays the Configuration menu. If you accept the default of 0, AutoCAD displays a message telling you that typing **N** at this point discards all configuration changes and asks if you want to keep them. Answer **Y** to exit from the Configuration menu to AutoCAD's drawing editor.

Maintaining Multiple Configurations

Whenever you configure AutoCAD, the program writes the information you supplied in the configuration process to a file called ACAD.CFG.

AutoCAD recognizes an environment variable, called ACADCFG, that points to the directory in which the ACAD.CFG file resides. If you use more than one set of peripheral devices and do not want to reconfigure AutoCAD each time you use a different set, you can create separate ACAD.CFG files for each set of peripherals, and then place the files in separate subdirectories. You can then write several startup batch files that initialize the different configuration directories.

To create this structure, follow these steps:

1. Create the subdirectories in which you plan to store the individual ACAD.CFG files.

2. Set the ACADCFG variable to one of these subdirectories, using the following syntax at the DOS prompt:

   ```
   SET ACADCFG=subdirectory name
   ```

   If, for example, you want a separate ACAD.CFG file for your CalComp plotter to be stored in a subdirectory called CALCOMP under the ACAD directory on the C drive, use the following version of the SET command:

   ```
   SET ACADCFG=C:\ACAD\CALCOMP
   ```

3. Change to the directory from which you load AutoCAD, and delete any ACAD.CFG file there. (Back it up to a floppy disk if you want to save it.)

4. Run AutoCAD. AutoCAD tells you that it is not yet configured, and walks you through the configuration process. When you have finished, AutoCAD writes the ACAD.CFG file in the directory to which ACADCFG pointed.

5. Exit from AutoCAD and repeat steps 2 through 4 for the next subdirectory in which you want to store a separate ACAD.CFG file. Continue until you have created all the ACAD.CFG files you need.

Whenever you want to switch peripherals, reset the directory to which ACADCFG points. AutoCAD reads the ACAD.CFG information from that directory and works correctly for the devices you are using.

Using Autodesk Device Interface Drivers

The Autodesk Device Interface (ADI) is a set of standards that peripheral hardware and software developers use to write drivers that interface peripherals with AutoCAD. The ADI drivers designed to work with AutoCAD Release 12 conform to ADI Version 4.2.

Because ADI standards enable developers to write their own device drivers, developers can issue new or improved drivers quickly, and Autodesk does not have to write a driver for every possible display, digitizer, or plotter that works with AutoCAD. The standard also helps prevent conflicts between different ADI drivers and the system on which AutoCAD is running. A final benefit is that the installation and configuration of ADI drivers is not very complex.

ADI drivers come in two types: protected-mode and real-mode. Each driver type is described in the following sections, along with the configuration information necessary to run the drivers. A final section discusses the limitations and needs of pre-4.2 drivers of both types.

Protected-Mode Drivers

Protected-mode drivers are started and run by AutoCAD when AutoCAD loads the ACAD.CFG configuration file. Protected-mode drivers are designated with a P386 ADI label and have EXP extensions. Protected-mode ADI drivers are run in 32-bit mode and are loaded into 32-bit extended memory. Because protected-mode drivers are run by AutoCAD and are placed in extended memory, they tend to be less troublesome than real-mode drivers. Their ease of use, combined with the speed of full 32-bit extended-memory processing, makes protected-mode drivers preferable to real-mode drivers.

Environment Variables

Environment variables tell AutoCAD where to look for protected-mode drivers. AutoCAD uses this information to list the protected-mode drivers during configuration. After AutoCAD is configured, the desired protected-mode drivers are loaded into memory and run each time the ACAD.CFG file is loaded.

ACADDRV

The ACADDRV environment variable tells AutoCAD exactly where to search for protected-mode drivers. Typically, the search path is directed to the DRV subdirectory of your AutoCAD directory, as shown in the following:

```
C:\>SET ACADDRV=C:\ACAD\DRV
```

If ACADDRV is not set, AutoCAD uses a much wider search path, which can lead to trouble if you have multiple versions and copies of AutoCAD within the search path. ACADDRV must be set before you start AutoCAD. If you intend to use the ADI drivers regularly, you should place the ACADDRV SET statement in your AUTOEXEC.BAT file or AutoCAD startup batch file.

If you are using a third-party protected-mode ADI driver, consult the manufacturer's documentation to ensure that all environment variables are set.

If you are using AutoCAD Render with separate display and rendering protected-mode drivers, set a search path for the display and hardcopy rendering drivers. Your hardcopy driver may require file-format information as well.

RDPADI

Set RDPADI to designate the path to the render display driver.

RHPADI

Set RHPADI to designate the path to the render hardcopy driver.

AVERDFILE

Set AVERDFILE to control the limits set on hardcopy RND files

Configuration

Protected-mode ADI drivers must be installed on your system before you can configure AutoCAD to use the drivers. The drivers supplied by AutoCAD are automatically loaded into the DRV subdirectory of the AutoCAD directory when AutoCAD is installed. Any third-party drivers must be installed according to the manufacturers' specifications. After the drivers are installed, make sure that all of the necessary environment variables are set.

For pre-Release 12 versions of AutoCAD, select Configuration from the main menu; for Release 12, run the CONFIG command from the drawing editor. Select the device you want to configure.

AutoCAD searches for the protected-mode drivers according to the search path designated by the ACADDRV environment variable. Select the desired driver from the list of drivers presented, then answer any questions you are prompted. Consult the documentation supplied by the driver's manufacturer if you have any trouble answering the questions. If the driver is supplied by AutoCAD, consult the *AutoCAD Interface, Installation, and Performance Guide*. When you are finished making selections, save and exit the Configuration menu.

Pre-4.2 Protected-Mode Drivers and Release 12

Pre-4.2 protected-mode drivers often can be used with Release 12 of AutoCAD. You may, however, experience some loss of Release 12 capabilities and you may have to take special steps to configure your drivers and AutoCAD.

Priveleged/Unprivileged Mode

AutoCAD Release 12 is an unprivileged application. An *unprivileged application* can run concurrently with other unprivileged applications without memory conflicts. Being unprivileged enables AutoCAD Release 12 to run under Windows.

Previous releases of AutoCAD are *privileged applications*, meaning that they cannot be run concurrent with unprivileged applications without risking memory conflicts. Protected-mode drivers written to comply with pre-4.2 standards, such as 4.0 and 4.1, expect AutoCAD to be privileged. If you attempt to run pre-4.2 protected-mode drivers with Release 12, you may experience difficulties, particularly with display drivers. Digitizer and plotter drivers usually are not concerned about the privileged or unprivileged state of AutoCAD.

To make AutoCAD privileged, run CFIG386.EXE with the -PRIV switch, as follows:

```
C:\ACAD>CFIG ACAD -PRIV
```

CFIG386 controls AutoCAD's virtual-memory management settings. To make AutoCAD Release 12 unprivileged again, use the -UNPRIV switch, as follows:

```
C:\ACAD>CFIG ACAD -UNPRIV
```

 If AutoCAD is set to privileged mode, it does not run as an application under Windows.

 Do not alter AutoCAD's DOS extender settings unless you have a specific reason and fully understand the consequences of any change you make. Changing the DOS extender settings can change the ACAD.EXE program.

Special Prefixes

AutoCAD Release 12 uses special file-name prefixes and the EXP extension to identify protected-mode drivers along the ACADDRV driver search path. If you want to use a pre-4.2 protected-mode driver, rename the driver to include the appropriate prefix. The prefixes are listed in table 2.1.

Table 2.1
Special Prefixes

Driver	Prefix
Display Driver	DS
Combined Display and Rendering Driver	RC
Plotter	PL
Digitizer	DG

A display protected-mode driver called DISP.EXP should be renamed to DSDISP.EXP.

Rendering Drivers

Release 12 of AutoCAD comes with Autodesk's Render. To properly use this feature, you must have drivers loaded and configured for rendering and hard-copy output. Your display driver may already support rendering. Before you can load and configure your rendering protected-mode drivers, you should have the RDPADI and RHPADI environment variables set. Your drivers must be copied onto the hard drive in the path designated by the ACADDRV environment variable.

WARNING The rendering display and rendering hardcopy drivers are loaded into memory when AutoCAD loads the Render program. The memory used by these drivers is not available while Render is loaded. This can have a profound effect on your system's speed if you are low on memory.

To select the drivers for rendering, choose Render, then Preferences. AutoCAD displays the Rendering Preferences dialog box.

Click on Reconfigure. AutoCAD now prompts you in text mode for rendering and hardcopy driver information.

If you configured your video display with the AutoCAD-supplied P386 4.2 combined display/rendering driver, select option 1. You are then prompted to select the mode to run combined display/rendering driver.

If your display can render to a viewport, select option 1 to render to a viewport. If your display cannot render to a viewport, you must select option 2 to render to a rendering screen.

The location of the rendering screen depends on your environment. A single screen in a non-windowing environment uses the entire screen as the rendering screen. A single screen in a windowing environment can use a separate window for the rendering screen. A dual-screen system uses the second screen as the rendering screen.

You may be prompted for additional information, depending on the combined display rendering driver you have installed.

If you have installed a protected-mode rendering driver, select option 2. Select the desired rendering driver. You may be prompted for additional information, depending on the rendering driver you have selected.

You must set the RDPADI environment variable before running AutoCAD. RDPADI tells AutoCAD where to find the rendering driver.

If you are not rendering to the display device, you do not have to load or configure a rendering display driver. Select option 3 if you do not need a rendering display driver.

After the rendering display driver has been set, you are prompted for information on the rendering hardcopy driver. The hardcopy driver sets the peripheral device or file format.

If you do not need to produce hard-copy output of your rendering, select option 1.

If you have installed an Autodesk-supplied protected-mode rendering driver, select option 2.

 You must set the RHPADI environment variable before running AutoCAD. RHPADI tells AutoCAD where to find the hardcopy driver.

To create a rendering file for a device that uses a 256-color map file, select option 3. Before you start AutoCAD, you must set the AVERDFILE environment variable according to the following format:

```
AVERDFILE=MAX_X,MAX_Y,PIXEL_WIDTH,PIXEL_HEIGHT,#_COLORS,#_SHADES
```

Consult your hardware documentation; the *AutoCAD Interface, Installation, and Performance Guide*; and the *AutoCAD Render Reference Manual* for the correct values for your device.

To create a rendering file for a device that uses a continuous color file, select option 4. Before you start AutoCAD, you must set the AVERDFILE environment variable according to the following format:

```
AVERDFILE=MAX_X,MAX_Y,PIXEL_WIDTH,PIXEL_HEIGHT
```

Consult your hardware documentation; the *AutoCAD Interface, Installation, and Performance Guide*; and the *AutoCAD Render Reference Manual* for the correct values for your device.

Real-Mode Drivers

Real-mode drivers are separate programs that are run before AutoCAD is started. Real-mode drivers run in 16-bit low memory as terminate-and-stay resident (TSR) programs. Real-mode drivers conform to ADI

Version 4.1 and earlier, making them an outmoded way of communicating with peripherals in AutoCAD Release 12. Real-mode drivers often work with Release 12, but you may lose some Release 12 features.

 Because real-mode drivers do not conform to the ADI 4.2 standards, you may not be able to use all of the features available in Release 12.

Conflicts

Because real-mode drivers are separate programs from AutoCAD, there is a risk of memory, processor, or interrupt conflict when using real-mode drivers. When using any real-mode driver, make sure that each of your peripheral drivers uses a different interrupt. Consult your hardware and driver documentation to determine which interrupts the peripherals and drivers use.

Configuration

Configuring real-mode drivers requires the driver to be installed and run before AutoCAD is started. You can select pre-4.2 real-mode drivers as an option from the configuration menus. You must then supply AutoCAD with the interrupt code in hexadecimal.

Display Drivers

At the configuration menu, select option 3 to configure the video display. You can select one of two options for real-mode drivers. ADI display 4.0 tells AutoCAD that you are using an ADI 4.0 or earlier display driver; ADI display 4.1 tells AutoCAD that you are using an ADI 4.1 display driver. You are prompted with the following:

```
Hexadecimal interrupt code (INT 0XXh) <7A>:
```

Enter the hexadecimal value of the interrupt your peripheral uses, which should be listed in the hardware documentation. Do not set up your hardware to use the same interrupt at the same time with two different peripherals.

Digitizer Drivers

At the configuration menu, select option 4 to configure the digitizer. Select ADI Digitizer (Real Mode). You are prompted with the following:

```
Hexadecimal interrupt code (INT 0XXh) <7A>:
```

Enter the hexadecimal value of the interrupt your peripheral uses, which should be listed in the hardware documentation. Do not set up your hardware to use the same interrupt at the same time with two different peripherals.

Plotter Drivers

At the Configuration menu, select option 5 to configure the plotter. Select ADI plotter or printer (installed pre-4.1) by Autodesk. You are prompted with the following:

```
1 Plotter (vector output)
2 Printer-plotter (raster output)
Enter selection, 1 or 2 <1>:
```

Select the appropriate device for your plotter or printer. If you have a vector plotter, select 1. If you have a raster plotter, select 2. After selecting the plotter type, you are prompted with the following:

```
Hexadecimal interrupt code (INT 0XXh) <78h>:
```

Enter the hexadecimal value of the interrupt your peripheral uses, which should be listed in the hardware documentation. Do not set up your hardware to use the same interrupt at the same time with two different peripherals.

Raster-Plotter Drivers

Raster-plotter drivers are configured exactly like plotter drivers, with the addition of two more prompts for the maximum horizontal plot size and the horizontal dots-per-inch that your plotter plots. AutoCAD prompts for this information to prevent memory-overflow problems.

When plotting to a raster plotter, AutoCAD transfers each row of pixel information into real memory for the raster-plotter driver. AutoCAD has 2,048 bytes set aside to hold the pixel information as it is sent to the raster plotter. The amount of information taken from AutoCAD limits the plot's horizontal size. A color display can send up to 4,096 pixels in a horizontal line. A monochrome display can send up to 32,768 pixels in a horizontal line.

To determine the number of dots-per-inch, consult your plotter's documentation. To determine the plot size, divide the number of pixels your display can send (4,096 or 38,768) by the plotter's resolution (dots-per-inch).

Reserving Memory

DOS operating systems allocate memory when the system is turned on. AutoCAD takes all available memory when it is loaded and reserves this memory for AutoCAD's use. Some ADI drivers may require memory to be set aside for their use. To prevent out-of-memory problems when the ADI driver attempts to allocate its memory, you must configure AutoCAD to use only some of the available memory. This is done with the DOS-extender switches and the CFIG386.EXE utility.

Simulated Expanded Memory

If you are using a VCPI-compatible 386-memory manager to convert your extended memory into simulated expanded memory, and you need to limit the amount of the expanded memory AutoCAD allocates, use the -MAXVCPI switch. The -MAXVGCPI switch limits the amount of VCPI-style expanded memory that AutoCAD allocates. The following line shows the DOS command line that limits AutoCAD to the first 6M available after the 1M that DOS allocates.

```
C:\ACAD>CFIG386 ACAD.EXE -MAXVCPI 6252000
```

The 6252000 is calculated by multiplying the number of megabytes AutoCAD is limited to (6) by 1M (1024000). All memory left after the 1M allocated by DOS and the 6M allocated by AutoCAD is available.

Extended Memory

Some real-mode ADI display list drivers use extended memory to store the display list. By default, AutoCAD 386 allocates all extended memory, after 1M up to 4G. To reserve extended memory for use by a program other than AutoCAD, you need to configure AutoCAD with the -EXTLOW and -EXTHIGH switches. AutoCAD allocates the available memory between the addresses set by these switches.

-EXTLOW

The -EXTLOW switch sets the hexadecimal address of the lowest extended-memory address available to AutoCAD. If any program has allocated memory above this address, AutoCAD starts allocating memory above the occupying program.

-EXTHIGH

The -EXTHIGH switch sets the hexadecimal address of the highest memory address available to AutoCAD. If another program has allocated memory below this address, AutoCAD allocates up to the memory occupied by the other program.

The following example shows setting the lowest and highest memory addressed available to AutoCAD:

```
C:\ACAD>CFIG ACAD.EXE -EXTLOW 2048000 -EXTHIGH 5120000
```

Pre-4.2 ADI Drivers

Pre-4.2 ADI drivers, both protected-mode and real-mode, have some limitations. You may have to set special environment variables to use the drivers, and you may experience a loss on some Release 12 features.

IGNORE_BIG_SCREEN

IGNORE_BIG_SCREEN sets display-list drivers to be nondisplay list drivers in Release 12. Setting IGNORE_BIG_SCREEN to any non-null value enables AutoCAD to use the entire Release 12 regeneration space size. This reduces the number of regenerations performed by AutoCAD, but you cannot use the display-list drivers' features for faster ZOOMS and PANS.

Not setting IGNORE_BIG_SCREEN enables AutoCAD to use the display features of your display-list driver, which may enable faster zooms and pans. If you are using a pre-4.2 display-list driver, you are limited to the Release 11 regeneration space size, which is smaller than Release 12's, and causes more regenerations.

If you have a 4.2 ADI display-list driver, you should be able to use the complete Release 12 regeneration space size and the special features of the display-list driver. If you have Release 12 and a 4.2 ADI display list driver, you should not have to set IGNORE_BIG_SCREEN.

 IGNORE_BIG_SCREEN sets any version of an ADI display-list driver used with AutoCAD Release 12 to a nondisplay list driver.

Limitations

The precise limitations imposed by a pre-4.2 ADI driver depend on the peripheral and the driver used. Display drivers are limited in their capability to use the complete Release 12 regeneration space size and provide fast zooms and pans. They cannot render in a viewport or work with Windows.

Real-mode display drivers do not support Render, and many cannot display dialog boxes correctly. Digitizer drivers cannot provide extended-digitizer space, even if the digitizer has the space available. Plotter drivers do not support 256 colors or smart fills, even if the plotter supports these features. Real-mode plotter drivers do not support AUTOSPOOL.

All pre-4.2 drivers appear with an asterisk on the Release 12 Configuration menu to indicate that they are older drivers.

Summary

In this chapter, you learned how to install AutoCAD on a network or stand-alone PC. You also learned how to configure AutoCAD to run with your peripherals and how to create multiple configurations. Finally, you received the details of ADI drivers and learned to configure them to work with AutoCAD.

Memory Management and Performance

Chapter 1 defined the minimum system requirements for AutoCAD Release 12's various platforms. Across these platforms is one common resource that affects the operation and performance of AutoCAD. That resource is memory. This chapter describes memory-management techniques to help you maximize the speed and efficiency of AutoCAD.

Understanding Physical Memory

A personal computer system generally can have three different kinds of physical memory: conventional, extended, and expanded.

- **Conventional memory** consists of the first 640K of memory available on your machine. When you power up your computer, DOS runs the utilities and applications listed in the CONFIG.SYS and AUTOEXEC.BAT files. These files often use conventional memory to function. The remaining memory is available for running other applications such as AutoCAD.

- **Extended memory** is an extension of the original one-megabyte address space available in the memory of 80386 and 80486 machines. Extended memory always starts where the upper-memory area ends. The first 64K of extended memory is referred to as the high-memory area (HMA).

- **Expanded memory** on an 80386 or 80486 machine can be emulated by an expanded-memory manager (EMM). The EMM software maps pages of expanded memory onto the system's upper-memory area (from 640K to 1024K). Applications must be designed to interact with EMM software to take advantage of expanded memory.

Understanding Virtual Memory

Virtual memory has been used for years with mainframes, but it first came to PCs with the introduction of the IBM/Microsoft OS/2 operating system. AutoCAD uses a virtual-memory system, called the AutoCAD pager, for drawings. The *AutoCAD pager* causes pages of your current drawing to automatically be written out to your hard disk when not enough physical memory (RAM) is available to accommodate them. This enables your AutoCAD drawings to grow beyond your system's available physical memory.

These pages are moved back into physical memory as needed, and other pages, usually ones not used recently, are written out to disk. This is generally known as *swapping*. The pages are stored on disk in one large swap file, controlled by AutoCAD's pager.

Virtual memory is like an overflow container whose capacity is determined by the combination of available physical RAM and the free disk space on the partition containing the swap file. The total amount of virtual memory required by AutoCAD depends on the following:

- The size and type (complexity) of the drawing being edited.
- The size of the additional application programs (such as ADS and AutoLISP programs) that are loaded and executed.

Virtual-memory requirements are dynamic. The amount of virtual memory needed can increase with each subsequent editing operation. As drawings become more complex, more virtual memory can be required. Hidden-line removal operations also can increase virtual memory requirements.

Using Disk-Cache Programs

The keys to optimal performance with a virtual-memory manager are RAM and free hard disk space.

Autodesk recommends that you have at least three times the drawing size available on disk at startup. AutoCAD cannot load with less than one-half megabyte of free disk space.

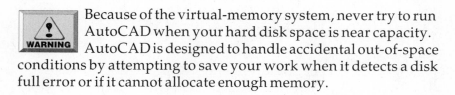

Because of the virtual-memory system, never try to run AutoCAD when your hard disk space is near capacity. AutoCAD is designed to handle accidental out-of-space conditions by attempting to save your work when it detects a disk full error or if it cannot allocate enough memory.

Disk-cache programs have become common in today's computing arena. Most computer manufacturers bundle disk-cache programs with their machines. A *disk-cache program* keeps recently referenced disk sectors in memory, so that the system does not need to get them from disk the next time you reference them. The disk-cache program intercepts function calls to your hard disk and controls read-write access to the disk. Caching improves the system's overall performance. Applications are much faster because the cache reduces the time needed to save and retrieve data or swap out parts of the application from the hard disk.

Using RAM Disks with AutoCAD

Extended memory also can be used for a RAM disk. *RAM disks* simulate the actions of a disk drive in memory. Because accessing RAM is much faster than accessing a disk, RAM disks can significantly speed up a program's performance.

AutoCAD does not recognize all RAM disk drivers. To verify that AutoCAD recognizes the one you intend to use, bring up AutoCAD without the RAM disk enabled, and note the amount of extended I/O page space that AutoCAD's STATUS command reports.

Run AutoCAD with the RAM disk enabled, and again check the amount of extended I/O page space available. The I/O page-space figure should drop by the size of the RAM disk you configured. If I/O page space does not drop, AutoCAD does not recognize the RAM disk and may try to use memory also used by the RAM disk. Any information stored in the RAM disk is destroyed when AutoCAD writes to the RAM disk area. You can exclude AutoCAD from these memory areas by setting a starting address with ACADXMEM.

 Remember that any data stored in a RAM disk is lost when you turn off the computer or otherwise interrupt its power supply. Always make sure to save backup copies of any files you copy to the RAM disk.

Using AutoCAD 386 Release 12

In Release 12, AutoCAD makes a more aggressive use of memory than ever before. Various commands, such as HIDE, REGEN, and RENDER, use memory intensively, and in most cases run faster or offer extended capabilities. Because of these changes, optimizing memory use and the location of temporary and paging files are increasingly important.

Managing DOS for AutoCAD

The changes in DOS 5.0 make it a more robust platform for AutoCAD, enhancing its capability to make the best use of your system's memory. Upgrading to DOS 5.0 is one of the best things you can do to increase AutoCAD's performance. On 80386 and 80486 PCs, with DOS 5.0 you can load memory-resident programs such as device drivers, TSRs, and network software into the upper-memory area to free conventional memory.

The DOS Memory Map

With the release of DOS 5.0 and its Extended Memory Specification (XMS), DOS now differentiates between five kinds of random access memory (RAM), as follows:

- Base RAM
- Upper-memory blocks (UMB)
- High-memory area (HMA)
- Extended memory
- Expanded memory

The first 640K of your computer's memory is *base RAM. Upper-memory blocks* lie between the 640K and 1M addresses. Although DOS usually reserves the UMB area for video and system ROM, programs such as expanded-memory managers and AutoCAD can use the UMB under certain circumstances. DOS versions prior to 4.0 did not recognize memory above 640K. Special programs, such as RAM-driven drivers, expanded-memory managers, or expanded-memory boards were required to access it.

The XMS specification defines *HMA* as the first 64K of memory above 1M (fewer than 16 bytes). *Extended memory* begins at the 1M address, unless the HMA has been defined, in which case it begins above the HMA. *Expanded memory* consists of a 64K "window" of memory, called a *page frame*, that lies within the UMB, and a memory-expansion card from which the computer grabs 64K-chunks of memory that it swaps into the page frame for processing.

Expanded-memory managers, such as QEMM and 386Max, now allow expanded-memory simulation in extended memory, thus fooling programs that require expanded memory into "thinking" that they are running in expanded memory when they actually are in an extended-memory area.

> **NOTE** Throughout the first years of DOS' existence, application programs and the data files they created quickly grew too large to easily fit into 640K of RAM, which is the maximum amount addressable by DOS. The expanded-memory specification was implemented to help break the 640K barrier.

To implement expanded memory, an expanded-memory board is installed in the computer to increase the amount of RAM installed beyond 640K. An expanded-memory manager program creates a page frame, which is a reserved 64K-memory area that usually lies between the 640K and 1M memory addresses. The page frame is divided into four 16K-segments called *pages*. A program that can use expanded memory stores data in the expanded-memory board's memory in 16K-pages. When the program requires some of that data, the expanded memory moves the page that contains the data into one of the pages in the page frame for the program to access and use. This process is called *swapping*.

AutoCAD uses all of these types of memory except HMA, although the way the memory is used and how much memory is used depends on the version of AutoCAD. The way you configure AutoCAD to use your computer's memory significantly affects AutoCAD's performance. You should configure AutoCAD to postpone the necessity of its using your hard drive for any purpose. AutoCAD can keep in RAM only part of itself and the data on which it operates. When it needs data or code not currently in RAM, AutoCAD swaps part of itself or some data to disk in exchange for the information it needs. Because swapping slows AutoCAD considerably, the more AutoCAD you can keep in RAM at any one time, the better.

AUTOEXEC.BAT and CONFIG.SYS Files

As mentioned earlier, DOS recognizes three kinds of executable files. An *executable file* is one that causes the computer to do something when you type the file's name at the DOS prompt. Executable files have the extensions EXE, COM, and BAT.

Batch files (executable files that have the BAT extension) consist of a series of DOS commands that DOS performs sequentially when you execute the file; they are similar to AutoCAD scripts. When your computer starts up, it looks for the batch file named AUTOEXEC.BAT; if DOS finds this file, the operating system carries out the commands contained in the file. You can place in your AUTOEXEC.BAT file any commands you regularly run upon starting your computer. Practical uses for an AUTOEXEC.BAT file include setting a DOS path, setting environment variables with SET, and loading memory-resident programs such as TSRs or real-mode ADI drivers.

Upon startup and before running the AUTOEXEC.BAT file, DOS also looks for a file called CONFIG.SYS. This file loads device drivers into memory, such as network drivers and expanded-memory managers. It also sets DOS-configuration parameters, such as the number of files that can be open at any one time and the amount of memory to set aside for storage of environment-variable settings.

AutoCAD 386 and the Phar Lap DOS Extender

Limitations in DOS prevent programs from directly using more than
640K of RAM. Standard DOS versions of AutoCAD can use up to 4M of
extended or expanded RAM for extended I/O *paging space*, which is
memory used by AutoCAD for paging data into and out of its work
space. You also can configure a part of extended RAM as a RAM disk,
to which frequently accessed files can be copied. These operations
require some complex configuration maneuvers, however, if AutoCAD
is to perform at its peak level.

The Phar Lap DOS Extender technology used in AutoCAD 386 eliminates the need for such maneuvers by giving AutoCAD direct access to
any extended RAM that is not currently being used by another program. AutoCAD 386 also uses an extension to the Extender, called the
virtual-memory manager (VMM), which allows AutoCAD to see any
unused hard drive space as an extension to RAM. With the DOS
Extender and VMM, AutoCAD 386 can directly access four gigabytes
of memory in any combination of RAM and disk space. The DOS
Extender loads and runs automatically when you start AutoCAD.

CFIGPHAR and CFIG386—Configuring the DOS Extender

The DOS Extender and VMM contain many software-configuration
switches that you can set to influence their behavior. Most AutoCAD
386 users never need to set these switches or reset them from their
default values. Nevertheless, this section describes how to use two
programs included with AutoCAD (CFIG386 and CFIGPHAR) to
change switch settings. See the following section about DOS Extender
switches for an explanation of some of the switches and their functions.

You can set or change a switch's value by using either the CFIG386
program at the DOS command line or CFIGPHAR, a menu-based
program. CFIGPHAR writes a batch file called CONF386.BAT, which
runs CFIG386 and actually sets the switches. Autodesk includes both
CFIG386 and CFIGPHAR with AutoCAD 386.

Running CFIG386

To use CFIG386, issue the following command at the DOS prompt:

```
CFIG386 ACAD.EXE -switch name parameter
```

If you set switches and then want to return them to their default values, use the following command to clear the previously-set switches:

```
CFIG386 ACAD -CLEAR
```

Then issue the following command and switch settings:

```
CFIG386 ACAD -minswfsize 400000 -swapdefdisk -swapchk off -
intmap 8 -vscan 20000
```

For an explanation of the preceding switches, see the section on DOS Extender switches.

Running CFIGPHAR

To run CFIGPHAR, type its name at the DOS prompt. You should find it wherever your ACAD.EXE file was installed when you loaded Auto-CAD on your hard drive. After you start the program, you are asked whether you have a monochrome or color monitor, as shown in figure 3.1.

Figure 3.1:
The CFIGPHAR opening screen.

After you press the appropriate key, the program's main menu is displayed. To choose from this menu, move to one of its options by pressing the left- or right-arrow key, and then pressing Enter. Use the up- and down-arrow keys to move to the item you want, and then press Enter to choose it.

If you press Enter at the main menu's Configure Switches item, a pull-down menu lists the switch categories shown in figure 3.2.

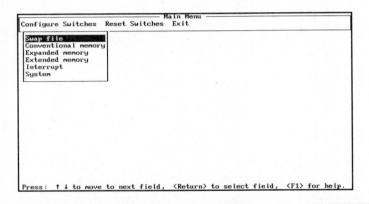

Figure 3.2:
The Configure Switches pull-down menu.

Choosing one of these items displays a list of switches, whose values you can then change. When you choose some of them, additional menus pop up, listing various options for the specific switch. After you make a change to any switch, press F2 to save it. To change another switch, choose Configure Switches again from the main menu.

After you have made and saved all the necessary changes, select Exit and then choose End from the main menu (see fig. 3.3). At this point, if you choose **No** when prompted to save the current settings, the program cancels all the changes you made and returns you to DOS. If you choose **Yes**, CFIGPHAR writes the CONF386.BAT file. If one already exists, CFIGPHAR asks if you want to create a new batch file. If you answer **Yes**, CFIGPHAR displays all the current switch settings. Press any key to write the new batch file and return to DOS. Now you need to run the CONF386.BAT file in the directory in which your ACAD.EXE file resides.

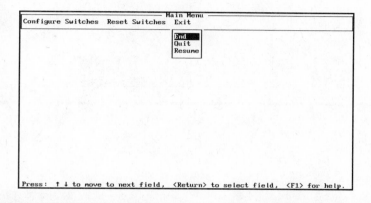

Figure 3.3:
The CFIGPHAR Exit pull-down menu.

To change switch settings back to their default values with CFIGPHAR, choose Reset Switches from the main menu. You have only one choice at this point: make a batch file with default settings (see fig. 3.4). If CONF386.BAT does not exist, CFIGPHAR writes one. If the file already exists, the program asks if you want to replace it. Choose **Yes** and press any key to write the new batch file and return to the main menu. Then choose Exit to return to DOS.

DOS Extender Switches

This section describes the functions of the Phar Lap DOS Extender switches that most affect AutoCAD's performance.

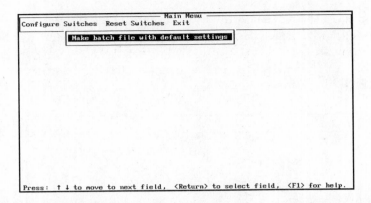

Figure 3.4:
The Reset switches pull-down menu.

-vdisk

Some programs do not adhere to the VDISK driver protocol for allocating extended memory. If the DOS Extender cannot run because it does not recognize a configured VDISK, you can set the -vdisk switch to enable the Extender to use the larger of the two extended-memory allocations that have been configured.

Before setting -vdisk, check the size allocations printed in the error message that Phar Lap generates when it tries to run AutoCAD. If the larger number seems wrong, programs other than the VDISK may be using extended memory. You need to calculate the amount of RAM that those other programs use, and then use the -extlow switch (described next) to prevent the DOS Extender from using that amount. Use CFIG386 to set the -vdisk switch by issuing the following command at the DOS prompt:

```
CFIG386 ACAD -vdisk
```

-extlow/-exthigh

Use the -extlow and -exthigh switches to restrict the amount of extended memory that the DOS Extender allocates for AutoCAD's use. Do not change the default settings for these switches unless you are running programs that use extended memory that do not adhere to one of the following standards:

- The VDISK or RAMDRIVE standards for allocating memory above 1M
- The INT 15h function 88h BIOS call for allocating extended memory from the top down

Refer to your DOS manual or encyclopedia for more information about these standards.

The DOS Extender uses only memory above the address specified by -extlow and below the address specified by -exthigh, unless other programs already use that memory area. In that case, the DOS Extender uses only memory above or below that used by the other programs. Such programs include RAM drives, disk-caching software, and expanded-memory managers such as QEMM.

The -extlow switch defaults to the 1M memory address (100000h); -exthigh defaults to 4G (FFFFFFFFh). If you want to use CFIG386 to reset these switches, you must supply a physical memory address for each. The following example sets -extlow to the 1.8M address and -exthigh to 4M:

```
CFIG386 ACAD -extlow 180000h -exthigh 400000h
```

-maxvcpi

The -maxvcpi switch restricts the amount of memory that the DOS Extender can use. The memory must be configured by an expanded-memory manager (EMM) such as QEMM, which uses the Virtual Control Program Interface (VCPI) protocol. When this switch is not set, the DOS Extender uses all available EMM-configured memory. By setting the switch, you free EMM-configured memory for use by another program. You can use CFIG386 to set this switch by using the following syntax:

```
CFIG386 ACAD -maxvcpi number of bytes
```

-b0

AutoCAD 386 runs only on 80386 systems with a step b0 (or later) CPU. Unless you set this switch, however, the DOS Extender verifies only whether a step b1 or later chip is installed. If your computer has a step b0 chip installed, you must set this switch for AutoCAD to run (the b0 chip was produced earlier than the step b1 chip). You can use CFIG386 to set the switch by issuing the following command:

```
CFIG386 ACAD -b0
```

-hwivec/-privec

The -hwivec and -privec switches specify the interrupt vectors for hardware interrupts. The hardware interrupts IRQ0 through IRQ7, and the one for the BIOS print-screen function call must be relocated because the DOS Extender uses them for processor exceptions.

The -hwivec switch relocates the IRQ interrupts by specifying the interrupt-vector number for IRQ0; the other seven interrupts follow in consecutive sequence. The -privec switch relocates the BIOS print-screen function call. The default values for these switches work on most computers; do not change them unless you have a specific reason, such as a hardware conflict of some kind. You can use CFIG386 to change the settings of these switches, as follows:

```
CFIG386 ACAD -hwivec interrupt -privec interrupt
```

-intmap/-primap

As with -hwivec and -privec, these switches apply to hardware interrupts IRQ0-IRQ7 and the BIOS print-screen function call, respectively.
By setting these switches, you enable protected-mode, memory-
resident programs to be installed and ensure compatibility with other
programs that relocate interrupts. These switches disable the DOS
Extender's hardware-interrupt remapping and specify the interrupts to
which they already are mapped. The -intmap switch is set to a default
of 8; you should not have to reset it. You can use CFIG386 to reset these
switches, as follows:

```
CFIG386 ACAD -intmap 8 -primap 5
```

-a20

The -a20 switch specifies the manner in which address line 20 is enabled
and disabled. In its default mode, the DOS Extender enables a20 when
entering AutoCAD and disables it when exiting. If the switch is set, a20
is enabled each time the 80386 chip enters real mode from protected
mode; it is disabled when the chip exits from real mode to protected
mode. This mode can be required if you are running programs that rely
on 1M addressing wraparound (although few programs do).

By setting this switch, however, you exact a performance penalty when
you run AutoCAD because each switch to and from the a20 state
requires several microseconds to several milliseconds, depending on
your computer's architecture. You can use CFIG386 to set this switch, as
follows:

```
CFIG386 ACAD -a20
```

The Virtual-Memory Manager (VMM)

As mentioned earlier, AutoCAD 386 uses an extension to the Phar Lap
DOS Extender called the *virtual-memory manager* (VMM). The VMM
enables AutoCAD to view free hard-drive space as an extension to

RAM, providing a seamless interface between RAM and the disk for paging operations. VMM enables AutoCAD, while running, to grow larger than physical memory (RAM) actually can hold.

Virtual-memory management works like this: the computer's RAM, called *physical memory*, is divided into 4K-chunks called *physical pages*. AutoCAD is divided into 4K-chunks called *virtual pages*.

VMM overlays AutoCAD's virtual pages onto the computer's physical pages until the VMM fills the computer's physical memory. When AutoCAD requires data from a virtual page not in a physical page, the 80386 chip issues a page-fault exception, and VMM swaps out one of the virtual pages in memory and swaps in the virtual page that contains the required information. VMM maintains a table, called a *page table*, which lists which virtual pages are in physical memory and which are on disk.

Because swapping slows AutoCAD, the VMM uses an algorithm to determine which page, when swapped, causes the least delay. The worst candidate is a page that must be swapped back into physical memory immediately after it has been swapped out to disk. VMM, therefore, tries to swap either the least frequently used page currently in physical memory or one that is not used recently. A VMM switch enables you to specify which algorithm it uses.

VMM stores the virtual pages on disk in a swap file it creates when AutoCAD starts. VMM deletes the swap file when AutoCAD ends. Should AutoCAD end abnormally, the swap file remains on your disk. You can delete it.

VMM Switches

You can set the following VMM switches by using the CFIG386 or CFIGPHAR programs described earlier in this chapter.

-swapchk

VMM uses -swpchk to determine when the swap file should increase in size. Larger swap files are needed when VMM needs to increase virtual address space or when page faults occur. The -swapchk switch has four options: Off, On, Max, and Force. AutoCAD 386 uses Off as a default, so that the swap file grows as page faults occur. With -swapchk set to Off, VMM does not verify that enough disk space is available to enlarge the swap file before making the attempt; if not enough disk space is available to increase the swap file by the required amount, AutoCAD cannot continue, and exits to DOS.

When -swapchk is set to On, the swap file grows only when page faults occur (as it does when the switch is set to Off). When set to On, -swapchk also checks for available disk space any other time VMM allocates additional virtual memory. This check ensures that the page-fault handler always has enough swap space.

If you set -swapchk to Force, the swap file grows whenever additional memory space is allocated, but only by an amount equal to the program's virtual space minus the amount of physical memory available.

When -swapchk is set to Max, VMM makes the swap file as large as the virtual address space the program uses. This most conservative option ensures that the program does not run out of swap space, but can create large swap files.

You can use CFIG386 to set -swapchk. To set the switch to On, for example, use the following syntax:

```
CFIG386 ACAD -swapchk on
```

-nopgexp

As a rule, VMM does not place actual AutoCAD code pages into the swap file; rather, it reads them from AutoCAD's executable file on disk. This procedure can lead to unacceptably slow performance in network environments, in which a single executable file is stored on a central server. The -nopgexp switch forces VMM to place all of the code pages into the swap file, which usually exists on a local workstation where the file can be retrieved much more rapidly. To use CFIG386 to set -nopgexp, use the following syntax:

```
CFIG386 ACAD -nopgexp
```

By default, this switch is not set, enabling VMM to read code pages from AutoCAD's executable file.

-codesize

Even though VMM obtains code pages from AutoCAD's executable file on disk, some part of the code must always remain in physical memory to maintain acceptable performance (if not, VMM would constantly be swapping code pages in and out of memory). Clearly, because physical memory used by code cannot be used for data, more data must be stored on disk in the swap file. In terms of performance, a trade-off exists between the amount of physical memory allocated to code and the amount allocated to data.

The -codesize switch enables you to manipulate that trade-off by specifying the amount of physical memory, in bytes, to be used for code. A larger number means that less code is placed in memory, leaving more on disk. Too large a value leads to disk-drive thrashing as VMM spends more and more time swapping code pages in and out of memory. The -codesize switch equals the size of the executable file, minus the amount that should stay in memory. To set this switch with CFIG386, use the following syntax:

```
CFIG386 ACAD -codesize number in bytes
```

If you have large amounts of RAM, or you generate small drawing files in relation to your RAM size, you may want to experiment with setting codesize to a higher value, leaving more code in RAM so that less paging is required.

-swfgrow1st/-noswfgrow1st

When a page must be swapped and the swap file has no more free pages, the page-fault handler can either increase the size of the swap file by one page, or it can take a swap page away from a virtual page currently in physical memory (this process is called *reclaiming*).

These two switches determine the order in which the page-fault handler tries those options. If -swfgrow1st is set, the page-fault handler first tries to enlarge the swap file, reclaiming a swap page only if not enough disk space is available for the swap file to grow. With -noswfgrow1st set, the page-fault handler tries to reclaim a page before it tries to enlarge the swap file.

Swap files continue to grow as long as you remain in AutoCAD. Simply ending a drawing does not decrease the swap file's size. If you have limited disk space, and you intend to spend long hours working with AutoCAD, set the -noswfgrow1st switch. Although this may cause AutoCAD to run more slowly, you are less likely to run out of disk space. To set one of these switches with CFIG386, use the following syntax:

```
CFIG386 ACAD -swfgrow1st
```

You can improve performance by exiting to DOS occasionally. This action deletes the swap, freeing up disk space and enabling the swap to begin growing again.

-swapdefdisk/-swapdir

You can use the -swapdefdisk and -swapdir switches to instruct VMM where to create a swap file. By default, swap files are created in the root directory of the drive from which AutoCAD was loaded.

The -swapdefdisk switch forces VMM to create the swap file in the root directory of the current drive. When you are running AutoCAD on a network, it may run unacceptably slowly because the swap file is located on a remote server. You may need to use this switch.

With -swapdir, you can specify any drive and directory in which to place the swap file. This switch's setting takes precedence over any -swapdefdisk setting. This switch is useful if you intend to configure a large partition on your hard drive specifically for a swap file, where it can grow as much as it needs. You also can use -swapdir to relocate the swap file to a local disk drive when running AutoCAD on a network. To set one of these switches, use the following syntax:

```
CFIG386 ACAD -swapdefdisk drive name
```

or

```
CFIG386 ACAD -swapdir drive:\directory
```

Do not end the directory path in the -swapdir setting with a backslash (\) because VMM automatically attaches a backslash to the beginning of the swap file's name.

-minswfsize/-maxswfsize

These switches set minimum and maximum swap-file sizes. AutoCAD uses 40,000 as the -minswfsize default. If -maxswfsize is not set, the swap file grows continually until the disk is full, or until you exit from AutoCAD. To set -minswfsize and -maxswfsize, use the following syntax:

```
CFIG386 ACAD -minswfsize number of bytes
```

and

```
CFIG386 ACAD -maxswfsize number of bytes
```

-nur

The -nur switch tells VMM to use the not-used-recently algorithm rather than the default least-frequently-used (LFU) algorithm when determining the most suitable virtual page to be swapped to disk. To set this switch, use the following syntax:

```
CFIG386 ACAD -nur
```

-vscan

Set -vscan equal to a number that tells VMM how often, in milliseconds, to scan the page tables to update their age information. The page-replacement algorithm uses the age information to determine which pages should be swapped. AutoCAD uses a default of 20,000 milliseconds.

If you use a *polled-mode driver* for your digitizer, notice that the crosshairs hesitate occasionally in the AutoCAD drawing editor. (A polled-mode driver periodically checks to see if any instructions have been received from the digitizer, and, if so, implements them.) This hesitation is caused by the scanning of the page tables. Although you cannot eliminate the hesitation, you can increase the amount of time between pauses by increasing the -vscan setting. Use the following syntax to set -vscan:

```
CFIG386 ACAD -vscan number greater than 999
```

-novm

This switch tells the DOS Extender not to load the VMM driver. Because this switch causes AutoCAD to run painfully slowly, its use is not recommended unless AutoCAD will not run if -novm is not set. To set -novm, use the following syntax:

```
CFIG386 ACAD -novm
```

Running AutoCAD 386 Release 12 as an Application under Windows

When AutoCAD or an ADS application is running under Windows 3.1, 386 virtual memory manager settings have no effect. The Windows DOS Protected Mode Interface (DPMI) server allocates all extended memory; memory management is handled by Windows and not the 386 VMM. Because Windows is a multitasking system, it might not be as efficient as the Phar Lap virtual memory manager.

> **NOTE** The DOS Protected Mode Interface (DPMI) was developed by a group of industry leaders. Several members of the DPMI committee also helped create the Virtual Control Program Interface (VCPI). DPMI is primarily a creation of Microsoft, and VCPI was formulated primarily by Phar Lap Systems. DPMI and VCPI solve two different problems.

Applications that use DOS Extenders can execute code in the protected mode of the 80286 or 80386 processor. DPMI provides a standard method for such applications to switch the 80286 processor to protected mode and to allocate extended memory. Hundreds of applications use various types of DOS Extenders, and those that do not already support DPMI require minor modifications to do so.

VCPI provides an interface that enables applications that use DOS Extenders on 80386 machines to run simultaneously with 386 expanded-memory managers. For example, QEMM.EXE, 386MAX.EXE, and CEMM.EXE support the VCPI specification. Windows 3.1 supports VCPI in both standard mode and 386-enhanced mode. Windows 3.0 does not support VCPI.

Windows 386-enhanced mode provides access to extended memory for non-Windows applications by creating virtual machines up to 640K in size, or the size defined by the `CommandEnvSize=` entry in the `[NonWindowsApp]` section of SYSTEM.INI.

Each virtual machine inherits the environment that was present before you started Windows. This means that every driver and terminate-and-stay-resident (TSR) program loaded before running Windows consumes memory in every subsequent virtual machine. The memory available within each virtual machine under 386-enhanced mode is slightly less than the free memory available at the command prompt before you start Windows, depending on your system configuration.

Using AutoCAD for Windows

When running AutoCAD for Windows, AutoCAD relies upon the AutoCAD pager and virtual memory services built into Windows for memory management. Windows virtual-memory management systems work like AutoCAD's VMM, described earlier in this chapter. Windows can simulate additional memory, as needed, by swapping information out to the hard disk to make room in memory for other programs and data. Through swapping, Windows can provide more memory than your system physically has.

AutoCAD uses the AutoCAD pager to handle drawing that is generated during a drawing session. Normally, the AutoCAD pager uses all available RAM to store its data. This works fine for a small drawing. As the drawing grows in size and complexity, the AutoCAD pager creates a temporary file on disk to hold various bits of information about the drawing. AutoCAD then pages out parts of the drawing to the temporary file to make room in RAM for other parts. The pager now operates as a virtual-memory system, reading files from disk and back into memory as needed.

For program memory, AutoCAD relinquishes control to Windows' virtual-memory management system. Much like the pager, Windows VMM writes pages of the program to a swap file on your hard disk when not enough RAM is available to hold them. These pages are swapped back into memory as needed, and other pages are swapped out.

When virtual memory is used with Windows 386-enhanced mode, some of the program code and data is kept in physical memory, while the rest is swapped to the hard disk in a swap file. Whenever a reference is made to a memory address, it can be used without interruption if the information is currently in physical memory. If the information is not in physical memory, a page fault occurs and the Windows virtual memory manager (VMM) takes control, pulling the required information back into physical memory and, if necessary, swapping other information to the disk. All this activity is invisible to the user, who only sees some hard disk activity.

Windows applications can use virtual memory without being specially written to take advantage of it. Windows handles the memory management, allocating however much memory the application requests. With Windows managing virtual memory, you see much more memory available than is actually installed in your machine when you choose About Program Manager or About File Manager from the Help menu.

A major benefit of using virtual memory is that you can run more programs simultaneously than your system's physical memory would usually allow. The drawbacks are the disk space required for the virtual memory swap file and the decreased execution speed when page swapping is required. It usually is better to run a program slowly in virtual memory than to not be able to run it at all.

Creating Swap Files for Virtual Memory

You can create either a temporary or a permanent swap file. A permanent swap file improves the speed of the Windows virtual-memory system because the file is contiguous. Thus, accessing it requires less overhead than the normal DOS file created for a temporary swap file.

A temporary swap file named WIN386.SWP is created on the hard disk while Windows is running, then deleted automatically when you exit Windows. This swap file is not a hidden or system file, and it can shrink or grow in size as necessary. You need about 1.5M of free hard disk space on the paging drive for a temporary swap file.

A permanent swap file is a hidden file named 386PART.PAR, which has a system attribute and is always created in the root directory of the specified drive. Windows also creates a read-only SPART.PAR file in the WINDOWS directory that tells Windows where and how large the permanent swap file is. Because a permanent swap file must be contiguous, you cannot create a permanent swap file bigger than the largest contiguous free segment of your hard disk. You should compact your hard disk with a disk-compacting utility. If an error message reports that your swap file is corrupted, delete the current swap file and create a new one.

You can optimize Windows' virtual-memory performance by creating a permanent swap file on your hard disk. Autodesk recommends creating a swap file at least four times the amount of physical memory. For example, if your machine has 8M of physical memory, create a swap file of 32M. Do not attempt to create a swap file on a RAM disk. Creating a swap file on a RAM disk is self-defeating because you sacrifice physical memory to create virtual memory.

Using a Plot Spooler

A *plot spooler* is a DOS-executable program that enables you to send a plot file to a device for printing in the background while you continue working in AutoCAD. The following section explains how to use the plot-spooling feature.

To use the plot-spooler feature, you must set the AutoCAD environment variable ACADPLCMD before you start AutoCAD. This variable, when set, creates an interface between AutoCAD and the plot spooler.

After this variable has been set, you plot from AutoCAD to a file named AUTOSPOOL. If you configure AutoCAD to plot to a file, you must specify a file name for the plot file. If you accept the default file name AUTOSPOOL, AutoCAD queues plots to a user-specified background spooling program. AutoCAD generates a unique file name in the spooler directory, specified by using option 4 of the Operating Parameters menu. Refer to Chapter 2 for a description of the Operating Parameters menu.

Setting Up for Plot Spooling

Make a directory on your hard disk for plot spooling. AutoCAD and the spooler program read and write to this directory.

NOTE The default spooler directory is \SPFILES\, but you can configure AutoCAD for the directory of your choice.

Enter the following command to set the ACADPLCMD environment variable before starting AutoCAD.

```
C> set ACADPLCMD=spoolpl %s
```

The preceding example assumes that the plot-spooler program is SPOOLPL.EXE, and is able to accept a plot file name as a parameter.

WARNING If the plot-spooler program operates as a TSR (terminate-and-stay resident) program, be sure to install it before starting AutoCAD. Loading the TSR with ACADPLCMD at plot time or using the SHELL command may be fatal to both the TSR and AutoCAD.

Start AutoCAD and configure for a plotter. Refer to Chapter 2 or your AutoCAD installation and configuration manual for detailed configuration instructions.

Plotting after Spooling Setup

First, enter the PLOT command. Verify all plotting parameters, then enter the plot-file name. The default file name AUTOSPOOL is listed if you configured for this, or the drawing name appears. Accept the AUTOSPOOL default or enter **AUTOSPOOL** as the file name.

AutoCAD now begins plotting to file. It substitutes a unique name for the %s parameter in the ACADPLCMD variable, and then sends the command to DOS. AutoCAD then returns to the Command: prompt so that you can continue working.

Summary

In this chapter, you learned about the different types of memory on DOS-based systems. You also learned which forms of memory AutoCAD uses. The CFIGPHAR and CFIG386 programs were explained, as well as the Extended switches used to configure the AutoCAD DOS Extender. AutoCAD for Windows memory management was explained and print spooling was discussed. With this information, you can configure your system to operate as quickly and correctly as possible.

Part Two:
Selected Topics
and Techniques

Grip Mode Editing

Entity grips are one of the most exciting new features of AutoCAD Release 12. First pioneered in AutoCAD Release 11 for the Macintosh, and more at home in the Macintosh environment than on DOS systems, entity handles—or *grips*, as they are now called by Autodesk—are selection points on entities. Each type of AutoCAD entity has its own unique set of selection points. You can use these selection points to perform editing operations on the chosen entities.

Before the addition of grips to AutoCAD, you could edit entities only by first issuing a command, such as MOVE, and then choosing the entities you wanted to modify. Grips enable you to pre-select the entities you will edit before you issue the editing command. In some cases, entity grips let you stretch or mirror an entity much more quickly than you can by using the STRETCH or MIRROR command.

With grips, you can perform the following types of editing: moving, copying, stretching, scaling, mirroring, and rotating. These operations are discussed later in this chapter.

Using Grips

The following sections show you how to use entity grips within a typical editing session. Although the use of grips requires you to change your thinking about editing, AutoCAD's editing capabilities do not change when you use grips.

Selecting Grips

By default, AutoCAD leaves entity grips turned on. To turn on an entity's grips, simply place the crosshairs over the desired entity and pick it. The selected entity is highlighted on-screen when you pick it, just as any normal selection set is highlighted. If grips are active, how-ever, the entity's grip points also appear as boxes. Figure 4.1 shows a simple example of this. In the figure, a line has been selected at one of its endpoints. The line is highlighted and its three grips—one at the midpoint and one at each endpoint—appear as boxes.

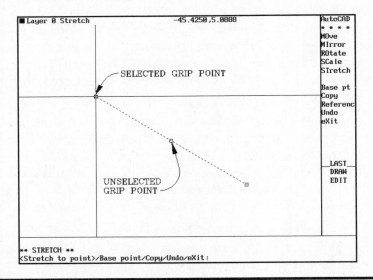

Figure 4.1:
The grip points on a line entity.

116

Grips reside at certain points on an entity. When you place the crosshairs close to a grip, they automatically snap to the grip—as they do when you use an object snap. If you pick the grip where the crosshairs are currently located, the box changes from empty to filled, and the grip-editing options become active. These options enable you to move, copy, stretch, and perform other editing options on the selected entities. These options are discussed in more detail in the next few sections.

Table 4.1 describes the locations of grip points on each different type of AutoCAD entity. Figures 4.2 and 4.3 show the grip points for the majority of the listed entities.

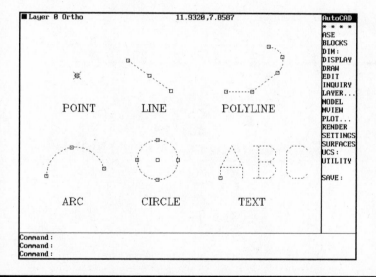

Figure 4.2:
Entity grip points.

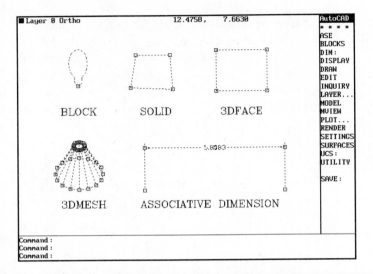

Figure 4.3:
Entity grip points.

Table 4.1
Grip Locations on AutoCAD Entities

Entity	Grip Locations
Point	At the point itself.
Line	At the line's endpoints and midpoint.
Polyline	At each vertex.
Arc	At the arc's endpoints and midpoint.
Circle	At each quadrant and the center of the circle.
Shape	At the insertion point of the shape entity.
Trace	At the four corners of the trace entity.
Text	At the insertion point of the text entity.
Blocks/Xrefs	At the block/external reference insertion point, or at the normal grip points of the block entities if the GRIPBLOCK variable is set to 1.

Entity	Grip Locations
Attribute Definition.	At the insertion point of the attribute-definition entity.
Attribute	At the insertion point of the attribute entity.
Solid	At each corner of the solid entity.
3DFace	At each vertex of the entity.
3DMesh	At all vertices of the mesh entity.
Pface	At each vertex of the Pface entity.
Viewport	At each corner of the viewport entity.
Associative Dimension	For normal, rotated, and aligned dimensions, the grip points lie at the extension points, the endpoints of the dimension line, and the center of the dimension text. Grips for angular dimensions lie at the dimension endpoints, the center of the text, and the location you chose for placing the arc. Radius and diameter dimensions display grip blocks at the center of the dimension text and the endpoints of the dimension. Ordinate dimensions display grip blocks at the dimensioned point, the point chosen by the user to locate the leader, and the center of the dimension text.

Clearing Grips

An entity's grip points remain constant through all commands. If you use the ERASE command to delete an entity, that entity's grips are erased along with the entity. When you execute any other command (such as a display command), however, the selected entities and their grips remain highlighted.

To clear the grips from an entity, press Ctrl-C twice. If you press Ctrl-C only once, you clear the entities from the current selection set, but the grip boxes continue to appear on the entity grip points.

Controlling Grips

Remember that entity grips are a luxury, not a feature that you are forced to use. If you elect to use grips, you can take advantage of several new command and system variables, which help you control the way grips are used. The following sections show you how to use these new features to make grips easier to work with.

The Grips Dialog Box

General control of the grip feature in Release 12 is handled by the Grips dialog box. This dialog box, shown in figure 4.4, controls all of the grip settings. To display this dialog box, enter **DDGRIP** at the Command: prompt, or choose Settings Grips from the pull-down menu. The dialog box presents the following options:

Figure 4.4:
The DDGRIP dialog box.

- **Enable Grips**. This check box turns the grip editing feature on and off. When grip editing is turned on, a small square appears at the crosshairs' intersection between commands.

- **Enable Grips Within Blocks.** When this check box is not checked, the grip point for a block is its insertion point. When checked, the entities that make up the block have their grips shown instead.

 Be careful about using grips within block entities, especially external references. If you accidentally pick a large external reference, the sheer number of entities that make up the entity may hold your computer in limbo for several hours while the individual grip points are being rendered.

- **Unselected**. When a grip is not selected, it appears as an empty box. You can choose this box's color by clicking on this button and selecting the desired color from the Standard Color dialog box.

- **Selected**. When a grip is selected, it appears as a filled box. You can choose the fill color by clicking on this button and selecting the desired color from the Standard Color dialog box.

- **Grip Size**. This slider bar enables you to adjust the size of the grip boxes when they appear on an entity. By clicking on one of the arrows or sliding the button, you can see a graphic representation of the grip-block size in the image area to the right of the slider bar.

DDSELECT

You can use the DDSELECT command to implement noun-verb editing and to determine how entities can be selected. When you issue the DDSELECT command or choose Settings Selections Settings from the pull-down menu, the Entity Selection Settings dialog box appears, as shown in figure 4.5. The following two options affect the implementation of entity grips:

121

- **Noun/Verb Selection.** When this radio button is checked, AutoCAD Release 12 lets you pre-select entities to be modified by AutoCAD editing commands. Before Release 12, AutoCAD always used a verb/noun-based selection; that is, you had to first activate the editing command and then choose entities to edit. Now you can choose the entities by activating their grips, and then run a command such as CHANGE. Because AutoCAD recognizes that you have already chosen the entities, the program skips the `Select objects:` prompt and goes directly to the first prompt of the editing command. In Release 12, the following commands enable you to pre-select entities for editing:

  ARRAY
  BLOCK
  CHANGE
  CHPROP
  COPY
  DDCHPROP
  DVIEW
  ERASE
  EXPLODE
  HATCH
  LIST
  MIRROR
  MOVE
  ROTATE
  SCALE
  STRETCH
  WBLOCK

All other AutoCAD commands that require the selection of entities, such as EXTEND or TRIM, still require you to choose the entities to manipulate after you enter the command.

- **Use Shift to Add.** This radio button determines the way in which you can add extra items to a current selection set. Although this affects normal selection sets chosen at the `Select objects:` prompt, this is the most intuitive manner of adding entities to a pre-selected set. Normally, when you are picking entities to display the entity handles, you can choose only one entity at a time. By holding down the Shift key as you pick additional entities, you add those new entities to the current selection group.

 For information on the other options in the Entity Selection Settings dialog box, see the DDSELECT command's entry in this book's Command Reference.

Figure 4.5:
The Entity Selection Settings dialog box.

Grip System Variables

The following AutoCAD variables control the way entity grips are used and displayed within the drawing editor (they can be set at the `Command:` prompt):

- **GRIPS**. If you set the GRIPS system variable to a value of 1, grip editing is allowed in the current editing session.
- **GRIPBLOCK**. If GRIPBLOCK is set to 0, the insertion point of a block or external reference also serves as the grip point. If you set this variable to 1, all entities within the block or external reference display their unique grip points.
- **GRIPCOLOR**. This variable contains the color number for all unselected grips.
- **GRIPHOT**. This variable contains the color number for all selected grips.
- **GRIPSIZE**. This variable specifies the size, in pixels, of the grip boxes.
- **PICKADD**. If PICKADD is set to 1, AutoCAD enables you to add or remove an entity from the current selection set by holding down the Shift key and selecting the entity.
- **PICKFIRST**. If this variable is set to 1, AutoCAD enables you to select entities before issuing an editing command.

Using Grips as Editing Tools

Grips have been implemented in AutoCAD Release 12 for two reasons. First, grips enable you to edit your drawings much more quickly than is possible with AutoCAD's traditional editing tools. Second, grips ease the transition for users of Macintosh and Windows drawing programs who want to switch to AutoCAD. With the first reason firmly in mind, the following sections explain how to use grips to your advantage, to edit your drawings in less time, and to make the use of AutoCAD a more intuitive process.

The following sections discuss the grip-editing modes. These modes enable you to do basic editing functions: stretching, moving, copying, rotating, mirroring, and scaling. You can initiate these features when you select a "hot spot" on a currently selected entity. Press the space bar after the hot spot is selected, or enter the editing mode mnemonic, which is explained in the following sections.

Grips are also tied into *autoedit mode*, which enables you to take any entities that are currently preselected (showing their grip points), and use them as the selection set for editing commands such as ARRAY, ERASE, and SCALE.

Stretch

Stretch editing with grips is very similar to stretching an entity with the normal STRETCH command. The biggest difference is that, instead of using a crossing selection to choose the points to stretch, you select the grips that you can relocate to stretch the object. This method of performing a stretch edit is best used when you need to only modify a single entity at a time.

When you choose one or more grips on the desired entity, AutoCAD automatically displays the Stretch edit prompt, which shows what actions you may take by using the Stretch option:

```
<Stretch to point>/Base point/Copy/Undo/eXit:
```

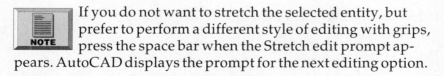

If you do not want to stretch the selected entity, but prefer to perform a different style of editing with grips, press the space bar when the Stretch edit prompt appears. AutoCAD displays the prompt for the next editing option.

By default, the point you have chosen as the selected grip becomes the base point for stretching the entity. If you choose multiple hot spots on

125

the entity, each relocates by the same value as the selected base point. You can start editing by taking one of the following actions:

1. Locate the point to which the entity will be stretched.
2. Select one of the options shown in the Stretch prompt, by pressing the option's capital letter.
3. Press the space bar to get to the next grip-editing option.

Options for Stretching

When you use grips to stretch an entity, AutoCAD offers five editing options:

- **Stretch to point.** This default option enables you to select a new point to which the selected grip(s) will be stretched.
- **Base point.** The Base point option enables you to select a base point that is different than the selected grip point.
- **Copy.** The Copy option creates a copy of the selected entity at the new stretch point location. This copy is the modified version, having been stretched as part of the editing operation. The original entity is unchanged.
- **Undo.** The Undo option reverses the effects of the editing you have performed, one step at a time.
- **eXit.** The eXit option exits completely from grip editing and returns you to the Command: prompt. The selected entities still show their grip points, and they are still highlighted, indicating that they are part of a selection set.

Using Grips To Stretch Paper Space Viewports

Viewports are special entities that show various areas of your drawing. In paper space, viewports are similar to regular entities that can be scaled or stretched. Editing a viewport is different than editing other entities because viewports cannot have angled edges. Because a viewport's sides always remain at 90-degree angles, stretching them with grips is a simple operation.

When you stretch a viewport by the grips, the sides anchored by the grip are moved perpendicular to their original orientation. Figure 4.6 shows a highlighted viewport.

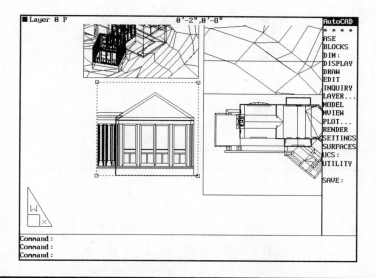

Figure 4.6
A viewport with grips activated.

In figure 4.7, the grip in the lower left corner of the viewport has been selected, and serves as the hot spot for the original stretch operation. As the viewport edges are stretched, the sides remain at 90-degree angles to each other.

Figure 4.8 shows Stretch to Point, which finishes the viewport resizing and shows the enlarged model-space display.

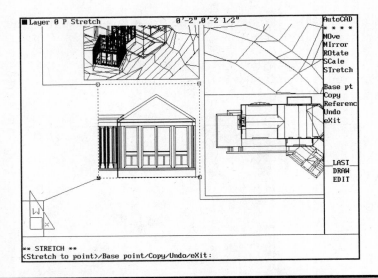

Figure 4.7:
Stretching a viewport with grip mode editing.

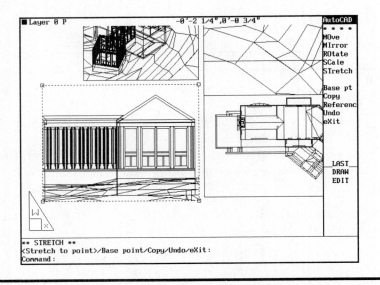

Figure 4.8:
A viewport stretched with grip mode editing.

Using Grips To Modify Associative Dimensions

Associative dimensions are tricky entities to edit—the text may overlap or the dimension line needs to be moved. Using grips, however, makes this type of editing simple.

When an associative dimension is picked, the grips appear at the extension endpoints, the dimension-line endpoints, and the center of the text (see fig. 4.9).

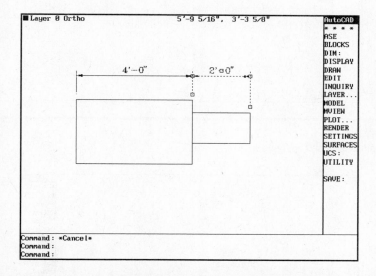

Figure 4.9:
A dimension with grips activated.

You can pick the text grip point and, with the Stretch mode active, move the dimension text to a new location, as shown in figures 4.10 and 4.11.

129

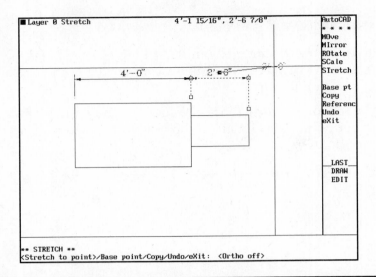

Figure 4.10:
Moving dimension text with grips.

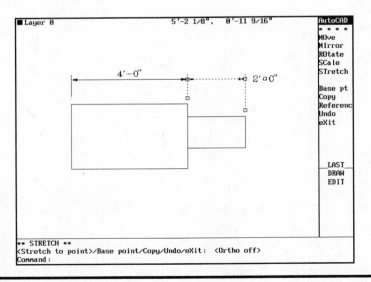

Figure 4.11:
Dimensions after moving text with grip mode editing.

If you choose one of the dimension endpoints (see fig. 4.12), the dimension line moves to a new location when you pick a Stretch to point (see fig. 4.13).

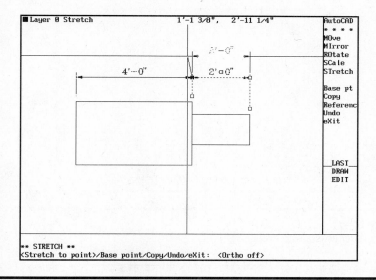

Figure 4.12:
Dimension with an endpoint grip selected.

If you choose one of the extension-line endpoints (see fig. 4.14), its new location updates the dimension text value as it relocates (see fig. 4.15).

 If you create any 3D entities by using the REVSURF, RULESURF, BOX, CONE, or the other 3DMesh commands, remember that these entities are easily disrupted by the Stretch editing option. When you select one of the grips to stretch, each of the vertices that are anchored to the selected grip remain stationary. This may cause some unrealistic faces to be shown within the selected entity.

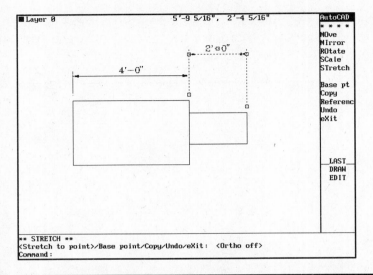

Figure 4.13:
Dimension after editing with endpoint grip.

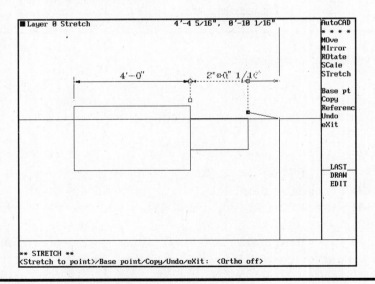

Figure 4.14:
Stretching an associative dimension with grip mode editing.

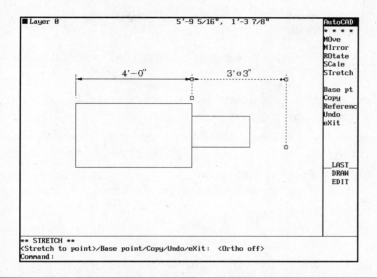

Figure 4.15:
An associative dimension after stretching.

Move

You can use grips to move an entity in much the same way that you use the normal MOVE command. Pick the entities you want to edit, select the base grip point, and then press the space bar until the Move prompt appears, as follows:

```
<Move to point>/Base point/Copy/Undo/eXit:
```

You also can type **M** or **MOVE**, and the Move prompt appears.

By default, the point you have chosen as the selected grip becomes the base point for moving the entity. You can begin editing the entity by taking one of the following actions:

1. Locate a new point where the entity will be relocated.
2. Select the capital letter of one of the other Move options.
3. Press the space bar to switch to the next editing option.

133

Options for Moving

When you use grips to move an entity, AutoCAD offers five editing options:

- **Move to point.** This default option enables you to move the selected entities to a new point.
- **Base point.** The Base point option enables you to select a base point that is different from the selected grip point.
- **Copy.** The Copy option creates a copy of the selected entity at the new move point location. The original entity is left in its current position.
- **Undo.** The Undo option reverses the effects of the editing you have performed, one step at a time.
- **eXit.** The eXit option exits completely from grip editing and returns you to the `Command:` prompt. The selected entities still maintain their grip points.

Rotate

You can use grips to rotate an entity in much the same way that you use the normal ROTATE command, except that AutoCAD does not prompt you to select any entities. To access the rotate options, enter **ROTATE** or **RO** after selecting the grip base point. The Rotate prompt appears as follows:

```
<Rotation angle>/Base point/Copy/Undo/Reference/eXit:
```

By default, the selected grip becomes the base point for rotating the entity. You can begin editing the selected entity by taking one of the following actions:

1. Enter the desired rotation angle.
2. Select the capital letter of one of the other Rotate options.
3. Press the space bar to switch to the next set of editing options.

Options for Rotating

When you use grips to rotate an entity, AutoCAD offers six editing options:

- **Rotation angle.** This default option enables you to define the rotation value to apply to the selected entities.
- **Base point.** The Base point option enables you to select a base point that is different from the selected grip point.
- **Copy.** The Copy option creates a copy of the selected entity using the new rotation value. The original entity is left in its initial position.
- **Undo.** The Undo option reverses the effects of the editing you have performed, one step at a time.
- **Reference.** The Reference option provides a reference angle for the rotation value. With this option, you define the angle you are starting at, and then the new angle to which to rotate the entities.
- **eXit.** The eXit option exits completely from grip-editing mode and returns you to the `Command:` prompt. The selected entities still show their grip points.

Scale

You can use grips to scale an entity in much the same way that you use the normal SCALE command. To access the scale options, enter **SCALE** or **SC** after you select the grip base point. The Scale prompt appears as follows:

```
<Scale factor>/Base point/Copy/Undo/Reference/eXit:
```

By default, the selected grip becomes the base point for scaling the entity. You can begin editing by taking one of the following actions:

1. Enter the desired scaling factor.
2. Select the capital letter of one of the other Scale options.
3. Press the space bar to switch to the next set of editing options.

Options for Scaling

When you use grips to scale an entity, AutoCAD offers six editing options:

- **Scale factor.** This default option automatically scales the selected entities by the value you enter.
- **Base point.** The Base point option enables you to select a base point that is different from the selected grip point.
- **Copy.** The Copy option creates a copy of the scaled entity, leaving the original entity untouched.
- **Undo.** The Undo option reverses the effects of the editing you have performed, one step at a time.
- **Reference.** The Reference option is used to provide a reference scale factor. With this option, you define the starting scale factor and a final scale factor. AutoCAD determines how much scaling to apply to the entity.
- **eXit.** The eXit option exits completely from grip-editing mode and returns you to the Command: prompt. The selected entities still show their grip points.

Mirror

The final grip-editing option, Mirror, enables you to create a mirror copy of the selected entity, much like the normal MIRROR command. To address the mirror options, enter **MIRROR** or **MI** after you select the grip base point. The Mirror prompt appears as follows:

```
<Second point>/Base point/Copy/Undo/eXit:
```

By default, the point you have chosen as the selected grip becomes the base point for mirroring the entity. You can begin editing by taking one of the following actions:

1. Pick a second point to form the mirror line.
2. Select the capital letter of one of the other Mirror options.
3. Press the space bar to switch to the next set of editing options.

Options for Mirroring

When you use grips to mirror an entity, AutoCAD offers five editing options:

- **Second point.** This default option enables you to define the second point on the mirror line. The entity hot spot is the first point on the mirror line.
- **Base point.** The Base point option enables you to select a base point that is different from the selected grip point.
- **Copy.** The Copy option creates a copy of the entity to be mirrored, leaving the original entity untouched.
- **Undo.** The Undo option reverses the effects of the editing you have performed, one step at a time.
- **eXit.** The eXit option exits completely from grip-editing mode and returns you to the `Command:` prompt. The selected entities still show their grip points, and they are still highlighted, indicating that they are part of a selection set.

Grip Editing Extras

In addition to all the editing you can do with grips, each editing mode can be enhanced with the addition of the Shift key. After you choose the base point for the selected entity (see fig. 4.16), you can hold down the Shift key as you select the second point for the editing option. When you use the Shift key, AutoCAD automatically switches to copy mode. When you choose the next point, AutoCAD places a copy of the selected entities at that point (see fig. 4.17).

If you continue to hold down the Shift key while you select new locations, AutoCAD switches to offset-copy mode. Any new entity copies that are created maintain the same distance and angle as between the original entity and the first copy (see fig. 4.18). This provides an easy method for performing entity offsets without leaving grip-editing mode.

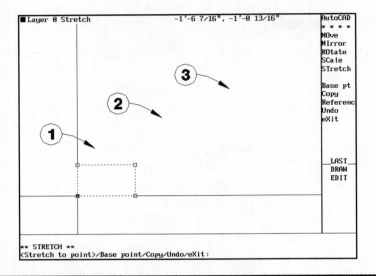

Figure 4.16:
Selecting a base point.

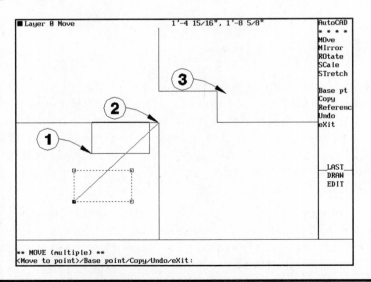

Figure 4.17:
Copying with grips.

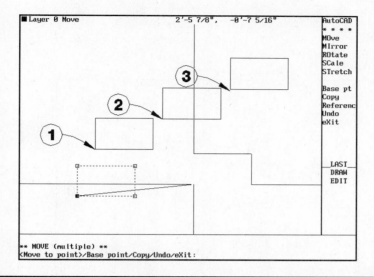

Figure 4.18:
Offset copies using grips.

Example

This example demonstrates grip editing mode with a five-sided polygon. Figure 4.19 shows both the initial entity and the modified version as you perform the following steps:

Command: *Select the polygon*

Command: *Select the grip at* ①

```
** STRETCH **
<Stretch to point>/Base
point/Copy/Undo/eXit:
```
Stretch the selected vertex to ②

Command: *Select the grip now located at* ②
and hold down the Shift key

```
** STRETCH (multiple) **
<Stretch to point>/Base
point/Copy/Undo/eXit:
```
Stretch/copy the selected vertex to ③

139

```
** STRETCH (multiple) **
<Stretch to point>/Base
point/Copy/Undo/eXit: X
```

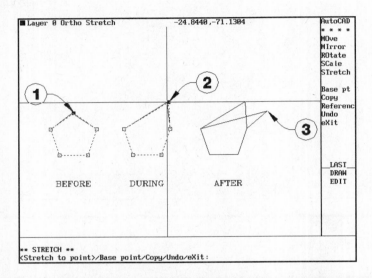

Figure 4.19:
Modifying an entity by using grip-editing mode.

Summary

Entity grips further increase AutoCAD's already wide range of editing tools and make the editing process not only faster, but easier, as well. The use of grips to pre-select your selection sets—as well as the built-in editing commands for grip-editing mode—enables you not only to continue to work with the methods you have always used, but also makes you more productive than ever before.

Blocks, Attributes, and External References

Organization is the key to running a successful drafting department. A continuity from drawing to drawing must be maintained, and AutoCAD has been instrumental in keeping this consistency. One powerful advantage of AutoCAD is its capability to group drawing entities into one single entity, then to reuse these entities in the same or other drawings. This transference of drawing information can simplify the enormous task of creating a complex set of drawings.

Three powerful features for manipulating drawing information are blocks, attributes, and external references.

Using Blocks

A *block* is an entity or group of entities that is saved under a special name for repetitive use in CAD drawings. Once the block is inserted into a drawing, you can manipulate it as one group. A group of blocks can be grouped into a single block—these blocks are called *nested blocks*.

Blocks can be pieced together in nested blocks or exploded apart into different levels of object entities (a single block or a drawing entity, such as a line or circle).

Advantages of Blocks

Blocks can be defined from any set of objects on any drawing, so a drafter (or a drafting department) should only have to draw it one time. Once an object, or a part, is created, it can be used over and over. Repeated parts can become standardized parts and maintained in a parts library or a symbol library. Blocks can be redefined and reinserted in single or multiple drawing files, even if the part changes through revisions or design changes. Any reference to that block is automatically updated.

Every entity added to a drawing increases its file size. The AutoCAD database records every point, line, or circle of each entity represented on the drawing. By creating blocks out of similar or multiple entities, AutoCAD only has to record one definition for each entity, regardless of how many smaller entities it takes to construct the larger one. Thus, blocks save valuable disk space when you produce large, complex drawings

Blocks also allow for a great deal of flexibility. Each time a block is inserted into a drawing, it can be rotated or rescaled (with different X and Y values).

A block is much like a complex entity because it can be exploded into individual entities. Once you explode a block, which enables you to edit the entities, the object no longer is part of the original block.

Symbol Libraries

As your stock of symbols increases, it becomes difficult to find a symbol quickly. A good tactic is to gather your symbols into a *library* (a special drawing that contains nothing but related blocks). A library drawing can be inserted as a block into your current drawing.

The library collection is a nested collection of blocks, and it can be inserted beside the drawing being created. Once the library drawing has been inserted, EXPLODE it once to separate the individual blocks into their own entities. Blocks can now be moved or copied into place on the new drawing. When the drawing is completed, the library drawing can be deleted to save disk space.

If space is a concern when constructing your drawing, library blocks associated with library drawings can be inserted without inserting the drawing. Insert the library-drawing name at the prompt, as you would any other block. When you are prompted for the insertion point, press Ctrl-C. All of the blocks from the library drawing are loaded. They can then be inserted when needed by their names (to request all of the block names, enter **?** at the prompt).

When a drawing is finished and ready to be archived, you can delete all of your used blocks, as well as linetypes, text styles, layers, and dimension styles by issuing a PURGE command. Drawing objects can be selectively deleted any time after entering the drawing until you add or delete to or from the drawing database.

Each PURGE command deletes one level of reference for used blocks. To PURGE every unused object in the database, save the drawing by issuing the END command, and then repeat the process two or three more times or until all objects are deleted.

You also can use the XREF/XBIND commands (discussed at the end of this chapter) to load the blocks you want.

Library parts and symbols should all be drawn at a 1:1 scale. Parts then can be inserted at whatever scale the drawing is generated to.

Creating Blocks

The BLOCK command enables you to create blocks. Once you have drawn your part or entity to be grouped as a block, select the BLOCK command. You are prompted for a block name, then an insertion point or base reference point by which the block is inserted. This point is also used as the pivot point on which the block can be scaled from or rotated around.

Once you have chosen the block's name and reference point, select the drawing entities that you want to include in the block. Any AutoCAD method of selection (single, window, crossing) is acceptable. After the entities have been selected and entered, the entities are erased. If you do not want these entities to be erased, use the OOPS command immediately after the entities are erased to restore these entities.

The BLOCK command is covered in depth in the Command Reference.

Redefining Blocks

Blocks can be redefined, both from within the current drawing and from an external file. When you start the BLOCK command and answer the "BLOCK NAME?" prompt with the name of a block already defined in the drawing, it asks you if you want to redefine it. Do so, and all existing instances of the block insertion are redefined. This is a handy option when you want to change your insertion point, or if an error occurred previously in defining the block.

Inserting Blocks

The INSERT command puts a previously defined block or drawing into the current drawing. It first prompts you for the block name. If the block cannot be found in the drawing database, AutoCAD searches the current default directory on the disk for a drawing of that name to insert. If AutoCAD cannot find the block name or drawing, you are prompted for the path and name. After a name is selected, an insertion point must be specified, as well as options for rotating and scaling the block. The block is then inserted into the drawing (see fig. 5.1).

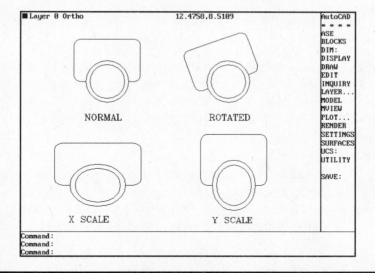

Figure 5.1:
Insert Options, either rotated or scaled.

INSERT can be initiated from the command line, side bar, or the pull-down menu that involves the DDINSERT command. This command

145

opens up the Insert dialog box. You can specify all of the block's parameters inside this dialog box (see fig. 5.2).

Insert
Select Block Name

Figure 5.2:
Insert dialog box.

MINSERT is another insert command that creates multiple instances of the block in an array. You are prompted with the same questions as the INSERT command. MINSERT prompts for the number of rows, the number of columns, and the distance between the columns to be used for the array.

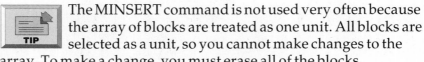

The MINSERT command is not used very often because the array of blocks are treated as one unit. All blocks are selected as a unit, so you cannot make changes to the array. To make a change, you must erase all of the blocks.

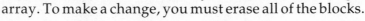

The INSERT command is covered in depth in the Command Reference later in the book.

WBlocks

The WBLOCK (Write Block) command saves a block to a disk file as a drawing file. This is an excellent way to create a standardized library of symbols and parts.

Users can write blocks out to external files by using the WBLOCK command. You are prompted with the same information as with the BLOCK command. See the Command Reference for more information.

Using Attributes

This section highlights a way of making blocks even more useful by storing nongraphical data as attributes. *Smart blocks* can be created with tags such as names, part numbers, and prices. The nongraphical data you attach to a block are called *attributes*. Attributes can be displayed as part of the drawing or they can be hidden, but the information that they contain always is available (see fig. 5.3).

The uses for attributes are limited only by imagination. For example, an architect can use attributed blocks for door and window symbols, a facilities planner can use them to keep track of equipment and personnel, and a mechanical designer can use them to keep track of the materials used for unique parts.

Any type of information used in a dedicated database-management program can be attached to a block as an attribute.

Creating Attributed Blocks

Attributes are essentially a part of blocks. You may first want to create the drawing entities, and then define the attribute, or define the attribute first—the choice is arbitrary. Once they are defined, the attributes and the drawing entities are saved as a block.

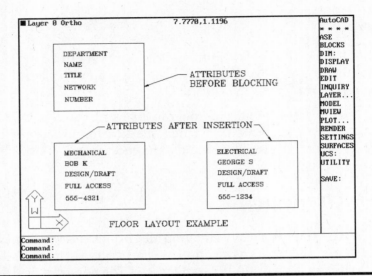

Figure 5.3:
Attribute appearances, before and after insertion.

Attributes are initially defined with either the DDATTDEF dialog box (see figure 5.4), or the ATTDEF command. Both commands can create attributes with the same modes: (I) invisible, (C) constant or fixed variable, (V) verify attribute at insertion, and (P) preset or default value. These modes are all optional and can be turned off or on.

Attributes consist of a tag name, a prompt name, and values. The *tag* identifies the name of the attribute. You can use any characters except blank spaces. All lowercase letters are translated to uppercase. The tag must not be null—you must enter some type of reference name.

When the block is inserted onto the drawing, you are then prompted for a name or character string to be associated with the block. This is the *prompt*. If you enter a null response (by pressing Enter), the attribute tag is used instead.

Finally, you are requested for a default value. You may enter a value or a null response if a value is not needed. If the Constant mode is turned on, AutoCAD prompts you for a permanent value instead of the default value. This value is used each time the block is inserted into the drawing.

```
┌─────────────────────────────────────────────────────────┐
│                   Attribute Definition                   │
│ Mode                  Attribute                          │
│  ☐ Invisible          Tag:    DEPARTMENT                 │
│  ☐ Constant           Prompt: DEPARTMENT TYPE?           │
│  ☐ Verify             Value:  MECHANICAL                 │
│  ☐ Preset                                                │
│ Insertion Point       Text Options                       │
│  ┌───────────────┐    Justification: Left          ▼    │
│  │ Pick Point <  │                                       │
│  └───────────────┘    Text Style:    ROMANC        ▼    │
│  X:  1.8164                                               │
│  Y:  7.7500           ┌ Height <  ┐   0.2000             │
│  Z:  0.0000           ┌ Rotation < ┐  0                  │
│  ☐ Align below previous attribute                        │
│           ┌─ OK ─┐  ┌ Cancel ┐  ┌ Help... ┐             │
└─────────────────────────────────────────────────────────┘
```

Figure 5.4:
The Attribute Definition dialog box.

When the block is inserted, you are prompted to enter values for each defined tag. Depending on how the system variable ATTDIA is set, the prompting occurs at the bottom of the screen in the command-prompt area or through the Edit Attribute dialog box.

Editing Attributes

AutoCAD offers a number of ways to edit attributes after they are placed on the drawing. ATTEDIT enables you to edit attribute values independently of the blocks. Editing can be done individually (changing any attribute property) or globally (only the attribute-string values can be edited). An easier method of editing attributes is by using the DDATTE command (see fig. 5.4). In this manner, editing attributes is like editing database records.

You may want to see all the values on the drawing, even if you defined the attributes so that some should be invisible. The ATTDISP (Attribute

149

Display) command enables you to choose between displaying all attribute values on the drawing, making them all invisible, or displaying them the way you defined them.

```
                    Edit Attributes
Block name: DESK

number               555-4321

ACCESS LEVEL         FULL ACCESS

TITLE                DESIGN/DRAFT

NAME                 BOB K

DEPARTMENT TYPE?     MECHANICAL




        OK    Cancel   Previous   Next   Help...
```

Figure 5.5:
The Edit Attributes dialog box.

Attribute Extraction

The additional information you store in your drawing files is even more useful if you can do more with it than display it in a dialog box. The attribute command, ATTEXT (Attribute Extraction), enables you to do many more things with your information.

Attribute extraction is a two-step process. First, you create an ASCII-template file that the command uses to "shape" the data from the attributed blocks into tabular form. Each line in the template file represents one field, consisting of the tag name, a designation as a numeric (N) or character (C) value, field width (www), and number of decimal places (ddd) for numeric values (see table 5.1).

Table 5.1
Template Fields

Field Name	Format	Return Value
BL:LEVEL	Nwww000	Block nesting level
BL:NAME	Cwww000	Block name
BL:X	Nwwwddd	X coordinate of block insertion point
BL:Y	Nwwwddd	Y coordinate
BL:Z	Nwwwddd	Z coordinate
BL:NUMBER	Nwww000	Block counter; same for all members of a MINSERT
BL:HANDLE	Cwww000	Block's handle; same for all members of a MINSERT
BL:LAYER	Cwww000	Block insertion-layer name
BL:ORIENT	Nwwwddd	Block-rotation angle
BL:XSCALE	Nwwwddd	X-scale factor of Block
BL:YSCALE	Nwwwddd	Y-scale factor
BL:ZSCALE	Nwwwddd	Z-scale factor
BL:XEXTRUDE	Nwwwddd	X component of block's extrusion direction
BL:YEXTRUDE	Nwwwddd	Y component
BL:ZEXTRUDE	Nwwwddd	Z component
OTHER	Cwwwddd	Attribute tag, character
OTHER	Nwwwddd	Attribute tag, numeric

A template file for the block shown in figure 5.3 is written as follows:

```
Department      C020000
Name            C015000
Type            C020000
Network         C020000
Phone           N010000
```

The preceding file can be created by using any text editor that saves files as ASCII text files (giving it a TXT extension).

AutoCAD can output to three different file formats, each one used for different applications. The DXF format is AutoCAD's own Data eXchange File and does not require a template file to be used. The Comma Delimited Format (CDF) is a universal data file, in which each attribute is separated by a comma, and each entry line represents one record or block. An example of the CDF format is:

```
'MECHANICAL'  'BOB K'  'DESIGN/DRAFT''FULL'  '555-4321'
```

The Space Delimited Format (SDF) file, which is the standard for many database software packages, is slightly different. Each attribute is separated by a space, and each entry line represents one record or block.

```
MECHANICAL  BOB K  DESIGN/DRAFT  FULL  555-4321
```

The Entities option under the ATTEXT command enables you to select blocks instead of using the entire drawing.

The data file that ATTEXT creates can be exported to external programs, such as dBASE IV or Lotus 1-2-3 for manipulation.

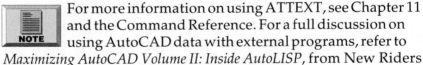 For more information on using ATTEXT, see Chapter 11 and the Command Reference. For a full discussion on using AutoCAD data with external programs, refer to *Maximizing AutoCAD Volume II: Inside AutoLISP*, from New Riders Publishing.

Using External-Reference Files

AutoCAD users often have to refer to other drawing files. For example, you may need to verify that a layout you create is not going to interfere with something else that is already placed in a master drawing. Or you may want to use a symbol from another drawing that is not in your block library. One solution is to insert the desired reference or source drawing into the current drawing as a block.

You now know how much work you can save by creating and inserting blocks. Inserting a whole drawing, however, has limited value for the following reasons:

- Inserting an entire drawing as a block substantially increases the size of the drawing file.

- Any changes you make to the source drawing after it is inserted are missed.

- Any items you want to "capture" from the source drawing must be blocks, or the source drawing must be exploded.

External-Reference Files

An alternative to inserting entire drawings as blocks is to attach them as *external references* with the XREF command. This command is similar to the INSERT command, in that it enables you to bring another drawing into your current one. There are, however, important differences in the way each command works.

The INSERT command inserts a drawing into the current drawing as a block. The inserted drawing's geometry becomes part of the current drawing and increases the size of the drawing. The inserted drawing never changes unless it is exploded and edited in the current drawing.

Attaching External References

The XREF command *attaches* a drawing to the current drawing. The attached drawing's geometry remains outside the current drawing database and does not increase its size. When one drawing is attached to a second drawing, the latest version of the first drawing is attached to it each time the second drawing is loaded.

Externally-referenced drawings always are current because, as the name indicates, the original drawing itself is referenced from the hard drive. When you attach a drawing as an external reference, only the information required to display it is included in the current drawing.

Although external references can be more useful than blocks, blocks are more convenient for individual symbols. Any layers in the referenced drawing are added to the layer list of the current drawing. For example, suppose you have a drawing named WIDGET.DWG, with layers called red, blue, and green. When the reference is attached to your drawing, AutoCAD adds these layers to your layer list:

```
widget|red
widget|blue
widget|green
```

Binding External References

Many options are available to make external references more useful. The Command Reference covers them all in detail, but one noteworthy one is Xref BIND, which makes an external reference a permanent part of the current drawing.

Similar to the XREF command is XBIND, which enables you to "capture" a named item (referred to as a *dependent symbol*) from an external reference and make it part of your current drawing. You can use XBIND on blocks, dimstyles, layers, linetypes, and text styles. Dependent symbols added with XBIND are represented in your drawing with three new characters. For instance, if you bind a dependent layer named XYZ | WIDGET, it is renamed XYZ0WIDGET.

Although Xref BIND makes the entire reference drawing a permanent part of the current drawing, XBIND makes permanent only the items that you select. Named items go through another change when they are "Xbound". This helps keep the size of the drawing file smaller, and limits the information in the drawing database only to what is really needed.

Each time you invoke the XREF command, AutoCAD records your actions in an ASCII-format log file that has the same name as the current drawing with an XLG extension. This file is only created if the XRECTL system variable is set to 1. The information in this file is written to an ASCII file, and it may or may not be useful. The more you use the command, however, the larger the file becomes. It is perfectly safe to delete it at any time. Of course, if you do not need or want this file, set the XRECTL variable to 0.

Summary

In this chapter, you learned about AutoCAD's powerful features for manipulating drawing information: blocks, attributes, and external references.

6

Dimensioning

This book has shown you new and exciting methods of creating objects with AutoCAD and viewing them on-screen. Most companies, however, still want the finished product—the working drawing—to look just like the ones drawn by hand. Widely recognized standards exist, such as ANSIY14.5M, that provide basic guidelines for placement of views, dimensioning standards, and tolerancing. In addition, some industry groups or large companies develop their own drawing standards that CAD software vendors have been encouraged to conform to; and now, with AutoCAD in its tenth year, many companies have established their own internal dimensioning standards that they expect employees to adhere to.

This chapter concentrates on ways to take advantage of the advance capabilities of AutoCAD's dimensioning commands. This chapter covers ways to dimension entities within the drawing editor, how to modify the dimensions you place, and how to set up dimensioning styles that enable you to maintain consistent dimensioning across drawings. It also discusses the dimensioning variables that ultimately control the way these entities appear in your drawing.

Dimensioning in AutoCAD

AutoCAD users often say that dimensioning is one of the more challenging tasks facing new CAD users. This is true for two reasons. First, skill is needed to determine the type of dimensions to use and where to place the dimensions in relationship to other drawing entities. Second, AutoCAD offers many options to suit a wide range of users and applications, and these options can seem overwhelming.

Release 12 has eased this burden with the new DDIM command. This command uses interactive dialog boxes to detail the changes you can make to the dimensioning variables, which then affect the way dimensions are shown in your drawing. Couple this with AutoCAD's dimension styles, and you have a simple method for maintaining consistency between drawings.

Automatic Dimensioning

A *dimension* is a type of drawing annotation that displays, in the clearest possible form, the distance between two points. The term *automatic dimensioning* is much like the term *three-dimensional* when used to describe the capability of CAD software—it says little but implies great capabilities. Figure 6.1 shows the components of a typical dimension.

① **Dimension value.** This text string indicates the distance between the points chosen by the user.

② **Dimension line.** This line usually is parallel to the object being dimensioned and stretches between the two extension lines.

③ **Pointers.** These entities (commonly arrowheads) serve as a punctuation mark on each end of the dimension line; they make it clear where the dimension begins and ends.

④ **Extension (witness) lines.** These lines guide the viewer from the object being dimensioned to the dimension itself.

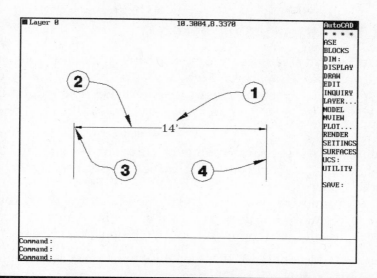

Figure 6.1:
The basic dimension and its component parts.

Fortunately, these components do not have to be drawn individually in AutoCAD. A typical dimensioning command in AutoCAD asks which object to dimension and where to place the dimension components. AutoCAD then automatically places the dimensions in the drawing.

NOTE The automatic dimensioning commands are very helpful for verifying the accuracy of the drawing, assuming that everything was drawn precisely to scale. If entities are improperly sized or located, the dimensioning commands point this out and enable you to correct the problem by changing the value of the dimension text or by correcting the appearance of the dimensioned entity.

AutoCAD: The Professional Reference, Second Edition

AutoCAD's Dimensioning Mode

AutoCAD actually features two dimensioning commands: DIM and DIM1. If you enter **Dim**, AutoCAD's Command: prompt is replaced with a special Dim: prompt. This prompt indicates that AutoCAD has switched to *dimensioning mode* and will accept only dimensioning-specific commands.

None of AutoCAD's regular commands are available from the Dim: prompt except those commands that can be called transparently. When you finish dimensioning, type **Exit** at the Dim: prompt; AutoCAD then returns to normal drawing mode and the familiar Command: prompt reappears. If you want to use several dimensioning commands at the same time, use the DIM command to enter dimensioning mode.

The second DIM command, DIM1, enables you to execute a single dimensioning command and then return to the Command: prompt when the dimensioning command is complete. When you issue the DIM1 command, the Dim: prompt appears. If you want to put a reference dimension on the drawing (when you forget one dimension), or if you want to modify a dimension with a single command, use the DIM1 command.

AutoCAD provides the following four locations from which to execute the dimensioning commands. The way the commands are executed depends largely on your understanding of the commands and your preference of input.

- **Keyboard.** All of the dimensioning commands and options can be entered at the keyboard.
- **Screen menu.** The AutoCAD screen menu contains all the dimensioning commands under the DIM: menu.
- **Tablet menu.** If you use a tablet menu, you can find many of the common dimensioning commands there.

- **Pull-down menu.** Release 12 offers the DIM command from the Draw pull-down menu. In Release 11, this menu was more helpful to the new user because it used icon selections to help determine the intended results of the command. In Release 12, however, the pull-down menu only allows for the selection of the type of dimensioning to be done. You will use examples of both the pull-down menus and figures to show the types of dimensioning each option creates.

In this chapter, many of the dimensioning commands' names appear with the first two or three letters capitalized. This is done to show you the abbreviation that you can type at the `Dim:` prompt to issue these commands.

Associative Dimensions

AutoCAD uses a single complex entity or a series of primitive entities to place dimensions on a drawing. When AutoCAD treats a dimension's components as a single entity, that dimension is called an *associative dimension*. If you select any part of an associative dimension for editing, the entire dimension is highlighted.

A dimension that consists of a number of separate entities is a *nonassociative dimension*. AutoCAD makes dimensions associative or nonassociative, according to the setting of the DIMASO dimensioning variable (dimensioning variables are discussed later in this chapter).

Whenever you modify an object that has an associative dimension, the dimension automatically updates to reflect the change in the object. Figure 6.2, for example, shows the effect of extending a part that has an associative dimension. As the line is extended, the dimension "stretches," dynamically updating as the line changes in length. When the line is extended to the desired length, the associative dimension shows the new length.

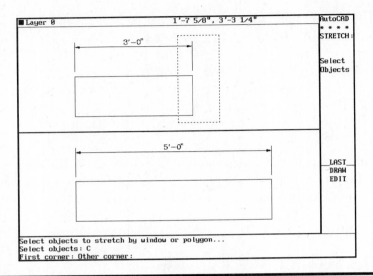

Figure 6.2:
Stretching a part with an associative dimension.

You can modify the associative dimensions themselves—individually or globally—by using the UPdate dimensioning command. The drawing's associative dimensions' appearance and values can change after the dimensioning variables are modified with the DDIM command. Also, if you are using dimension style, updating the variables that make up the dimension style automatically updates any dimensions based on the style.

When dimensions are set to be nonassociative, their parts are placed in the drawing as separate entities. If no other variables are changed, a single dimension consists of three lines (two extension lines and the dimension line), two points at the first and second points of the dimension, two triangular solids (the arrows), and a text string. None of AutoCAD's dimension-editing utilities work on nonassociative dimensions, but you can use AutoCAD's regular editing commands to modify nonassociative dimensions.

AutoCAD creates associative dimensions by default, but you can set the program so that dimensions always are nonassociative (although it is strongly recommended that you do not).

You can make an associative dimension nonassociative by using the EXPLODE command to break it into its separate entities. You cannot, however, make a nonassociative dimension associative. When you explode a dimension, its lines, solids, and text go to Layer 0, and the color of all the entities is set to 7. If you want the dimensions to be on your normal dimension layer, you must transfer them manually and set their color to BYLAYER.

When you are using associative dimensions, AutoCAD creates two point entities at the defining points of the dimension. *Point entities* are the first and second points you pick, or the endpoints of the entity you select. These points are placed on a special layer, which is named DEFPOINTS.

Point entities make the dimensions associative, and they must be included in a Stretch Window option if they are to be used to update the dimension.

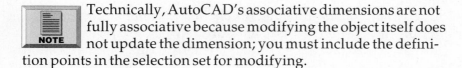

Technically, AutoCAD's associative dimensions are not fully associative because modifying the object itself does not update the dimension; you must include the definition points in the selection set for modifying.

AutoCAD's Dimensioning Commands

When you select the Dimensions option from the Draw pull-down menu, AutoCAD presents the dimension-creation commands that enable you to create new dimensions. In the following sections, the dimension-creation commands are discussed first, followed by the commands that can be used to modify the created entities.

AutoCAD's dimension-creation commands are broken down into the following groups:

- **Linear dimensions.** Show the straight-line distance from one point to another.
- **Radial (circular) dimensions.** Label an arc or circle with its radius or diameter.
- **Ordinate (datum) dimensions.** Measure a number of points from a common origin.
- **Angular dimensions.** Label an angle (internal or external) in whichever form of degrees has been preset in the UNITS command.
- **Leader dimensions.** Not "true" dimensions; they are labels with leaders that point to a feature in your drawing.

Each category of dimensions differ in the information they show. Each of these categories are explained in the following sections.

Linear Dimensions

The linear-dimensioning commands display the distance between two specified points on the drawing. In general, the command begins by prompting for the two points to measure between. (To pick the points accurately, use object snaps.) AutoCAD then prompts for the location of the dimension on the drawing. An additional prompt shows the default value of dimension to enable you to make changes or additions if necessary.

The dimension pull-down menu, shown in figure 6.3, shows the six types of linear dimensions: horizontal, vertical, aligned, rotated, continuous, and baseline. These dimension types are discussed in the next section; the dimension information that each one creates is shown in figure 6.4.

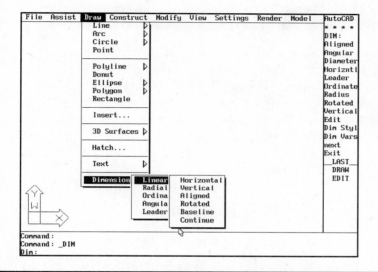

Figure 6.3:
The linear dimensions pull-down menu.

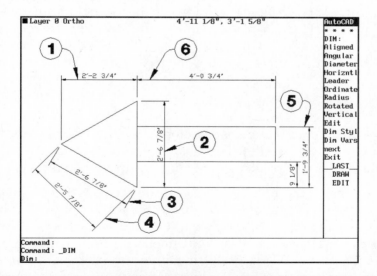

Figure 6.4:
Dimensions created by using the linear options.

The HOrizontal and VErtical Commands

Horizontal dimensions and *vertical dimensions* are the most commonly used types of dimensions created in AutoCAD. As their names imply, horizontal and vertical dimensions always are parallel and perpendicular to the current X and Y axes. (In fig. 6.4, the horizontal dimension is shown at ①, and the vertical dimension is shown at ②.) The two selected points do not have to be aligned in the X and Y direction because AutoCAD automatically determines the horizontal and vertical distance between the two points.

The ALigned and ROtated Commands

When linear dimensions do not lie parallel to the X and Y axes, you must use the ALigned and ROtated commands. The ALigned command, which was used to create the dimension shown at ③, aligns the dimension between the two selected points and displays the absolute distance between the points. Rotated dimensions are used when the dimensions are not to be aligned between the two points but placed at specific angles. The dimension pointed to by ④ was given a rotation angle of -45 degrees. The distance measured by this dimension is taken across the supplied angle—not between the dimension points.

The COntinue and BASeline Commands

You often need several dimensions along the horizontal or vertical edges of a view to show the placement of various features. AutoCAD provides two shortcuts for placing multiple dimensions on a view.

The BASeline command creates multiple dimensions that originate from the same baseline, as shown by the dimensions pointed to by ⑤. The BASeline command also kicks in automatically if AutoCAD does not have enough room to place two dimensions in a limited space. In such a case, AutoCAD places the first dimension with its text outside the extension lines (rather than between them), and it then offsets the second dimension from the first. The distance between baseline dimensions is set by the dimension variable DIMDLI, or in the Dimension Line dialog box of the DDIM command.

The COntinue command is used immediately after a horizontal or vertical dimension. Because the new dimension's first point is the second point of the last dimension, and the placement is in line with the previous dimension, only one point—the next point to be dimensioned—must be selected for the COntinue command. The dimension pointed to by ⑥ shows a continued dimension, based off of a single horizontal dimension.

 Both the Baseline and Continue dimensions use the value of the DIMDLI variable to control the way they are placed in relation to the originating dimension. For *baseline dimensions*, provide a gap between the dimension lines (but do not for continuous dimensions). *Continuous dimensions* are typically shown with the dimension line continuous across the group of dimensions. Set the value of DIMDLI to 0 to make sure that your continuous dimensions are created in this manner.

Radial Dimensions

Radial dimensions are selected by using the Radial option of the Draw Dimension pull-down menu (see fig. 6.5.) You can dimension the diameter of a circle and the radius of an arc or a circle by using the RADius and DIAmeter dimensioning commands. You also can use these commands to place center marks on circles and arcs, or place a center mark for these entities, without also creating an associated dimension. When you select an arc or circle, AutoCAD automatically generates the size of the entity from the database. The types of dimensions created by using these commands are shown in figure 6.6.

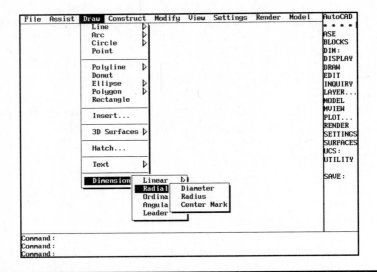

Figure 6.5:
The Radial dimensions pull-down menu.

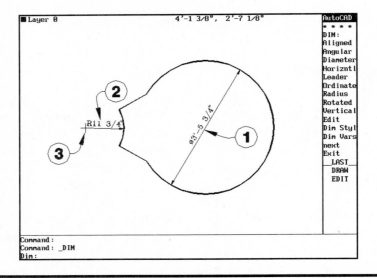

Figure 6.6:
Dimensions created by using the radial options.

The DIAmeter and RADius Commands

The DIAmeter and RADius commands are very similar. The RADius command displays an R and the radius value (see the dimension pointed to by ②). DIAmeter displays the diameter symbol and the diameter value (see the dimension pointed to by ①). The text and dimension line can be inside or outside the arc, depending on the size of the arc and certain dimensioning variables (discussed later in this chapter).

The DIAmeter and RADius commands start by prompting you to select an arc or circle. The point at which you select the entity is very important because it determines the dimension line's location.

The CENter Command

The CENter dimensioning command enables you to place center marks and lines on arcs and circles. CENter responds according to the current setting of the DIMCEN dimensioning variable, which can be modified through the DDIM command's Extension Lines dialog box.

See the examples of the DIMCEN settings in the DIM: Radius and DIM: Diameter discussion in the Command Reference.

A negative DIMCEN value extends the centers past the outside of an arc or circle by that amount. Also, the RADius and DIAmeter commands place centers according to the DIMCEN variable's setting if there are no dimension lines created through the arc center.

Ordinate (Datum) Dimensions

Ordinate dimensions are used by mechanical engineers because they enable entities to be dimensioned from a single starting (or *datum*) point. These types of dimensions only give a value within a certain axis, either the X- or Y-axis dimension, which enables the drawing to be kept fairly clutter-free. Ordinate dimensions are called from the Ordinate option of the Draw Dimensions pull-down menu, shown in figure 6.7. The X and Y datum dimensions are shown in figure 6.8.

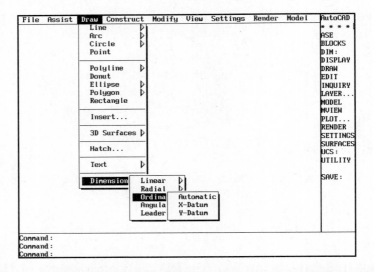

Figure 6.7:
The Ordinate dimensions pull-down menu.

 Ordinate dimension values are calculated from the origin point of the User Coordinate System. This point may be relocated by using the UCS Origin option.

Angular Dimensions

The ANgular dimensioning command is very flexible for showing the angle between two lines. The command asks for the two lines of the angle that needs to be dimensioned, and it then asks for a point where the dimension arc is to be placed. The dimension text is centered on the dimension arc unless you select an optional fourth point showing the text placement. Angular dimensions are called from the Angular option of the Draw Dimensions pull-down menu, shown in figure 6.9. Figure 6.10 shows an angular dimension pointed to by ①.

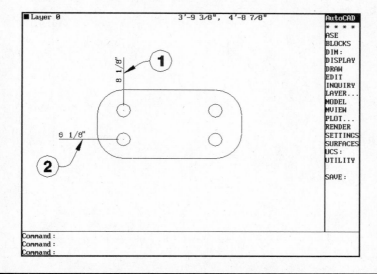

Figure 6.8:
X datum ① and Y datum ② dimensions, created by using the ordinate options.

 An extension line for another dimension cannot be used as the selected line unless the dimension is exploded. If necessary, you should draw a short construction line from which to dimension.

Leaders

Leaders often are used to show a size or specification when no other dimensioning command seems appropriate. *Leaders* are lines and

171

arrows (see ② of fig. 6.10) that point from one or several lines of dimension text toward the object that has been dimensioned. Although leaders are not really dimensions, AutoCAD creates them by using dimension variables.

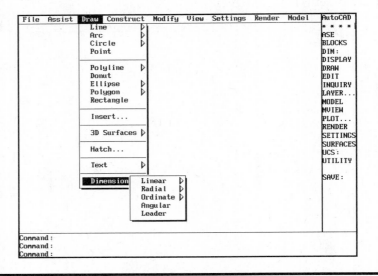

Figure 6.9:
The Angular option in the Dimensions pull-down menu.

Because you use the LEAder dimensioning command to create leaders, you can draw leaders only from the `Dim:` prompt. Unlike other types of dimensions, leaders are individual entities that are composed of lines, solids, and text. Leader dimensions are called from the Leader option of the Draw Dimensions pull-down menu (shown in fig. 6.9).

AutoCAD's LEAder command has one drawback: the command enables you to enter only one line of text (most annotations have more than one line of text). If you want multiline leaders, you must enter the DIM command, create the leader and first line of text, exit from dimensioning mode, and start the TEXT or DTEXT command to add the remaining lines.

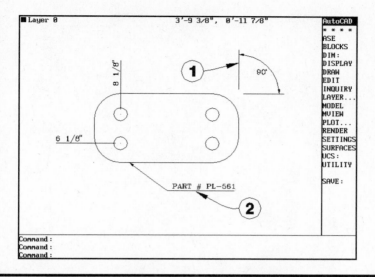

Figure 6.10:
Angular ① and Leader ② dimensions shown for an entity.

Dimension-Editing Routines

If your dimensions are associative, you can edit them as if they are
single entities. One of the more typical types of editing is to move the
dimension line or dimension text. Although this can be accomplished
using the STRETCH command, it is simpler to use entity grips.

Grips, which are discussed in Chapter 4, enable you to perform selected
editing operations on an entity without having to call the required
editing command. Look at figure 6.11, for example. The dimension in
the upper half of the screen has been picked with the cursor, and its
entity grips are shown. If you want to move the text to a new position,
place the cursor over the text hot spot and pick the grip. Immediately
you are placed in Stretch edit mode, which enables you to relocate the
text to a new position (see the bottom half of the screen). This type of
editing can be done with any of the dimension entity-grip points.

173

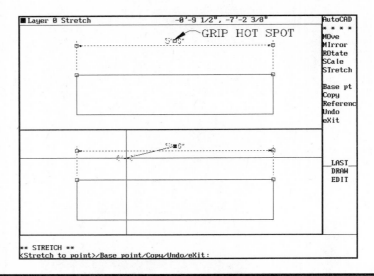

Figure 6.11:
Using grip-mode editing to modify an associative dimension.

Like the dimension-creating commands, the dimension-editing commands are available from the Modify Dimensions pull-down menu, shown in figure 6.12. In Release 11, AutoCAD used icon menus to show how these commands modified associative dimensions, but that has been discontinued in Release 12. This chapter describes the effects of each of these commands—see the Command Reference for examples of these commands at work.

Moving the Dimension Text's Location

The options to modify an associative dimension's text string are available from the Dimension Text options of the Modify Edit Dims pull-down menu, shown in figure 6.13. You can use AutoCAD's Gripmode Stretch option or the TEdit dimensioning command (Move Text on the pull-down menu) to move the text of a dimension and leave the rest of it where it is. You should do this, for example, if the default position of the text is on top of another entity.

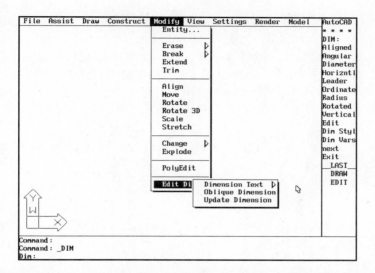

Figure 6.12:
The Modify Edit Dims pull-down menu.

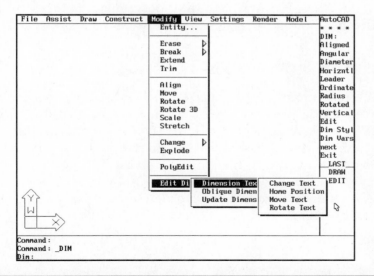

Figure 6.13:
The Dimension Text options menu.

The TEdit command, like Gripmode Stretch, makes the task of moving dimension text easier by prompting you to select the dimension you want to adjust. TEdit's only purpose (and the only purpose of TRotate) is to adjust the text's location or angle in associative dimensions. Note that TRotate (Rotate Text on the pull-down menu) changes only the text's angle; it does not turn a horizontal dimension into a rotated one.

The DIM: TEdit command explanation in the Command Reference provides a good example of moving dimension text.

Because AutoCAD centers text in a dimension, the text may interfere with existing entities. Use TEdit to move the text to a better location if necessary.

The HOMetext command enables you to change your mind and undo any changes you make to the text's location or angle of rotation. HOMetext (Home Position on the pull-down menu) returns the text to its default position.

Changing the Dimension Text

The NEWtext command (Change Text in the pull-down menu) enables you to replace the default dimension value with a new value. You may want to change a dimension's value to a text string plus the dimensions value, for instance. An easy way to note a rough opening in a wall is to dimension the opening normally, and then use NEWtext to change the dimension value to ROUGH OPENING - <>. The two arrow brackets tell the NEWtext command where to place the entered text in the current dimension value.

Another common method of changing text in a dimension is to interfere with the default text in the dimension command. After appropriate points are selected, the Dimension text <xyz>: prompt appears (*xyz* represents the default text). You can press Enter to accept the default dimension, or press the spacebar and Enter to enter no dimension text. You also can enter substitute dimensioning text. In addition, you can add a prefix or suffix by typing it with empty default brackets (<>) to show where the default text should appear.

The UPDate Command

The UPDate dimensioning command enables you to apply modified dimension-variable settings to existing dimensions. You can update dimensions individually or by windowing all the dimensions on a drawing. The UPDate command appears in the Modify Edit Dims pull-down menu, shown in figure 6.12.

Suppose, for example, that you receive a drawing from a colleague that contains associative dimensions. The only problem is that the dimensions in his drawing do not match your office standards. You can use the DDIM command to change the dimension variables to the proper values, and then use the UPDate command to change the appearance of the existing dimensions.

The OBLique Command

The OBLique command angles the dimension-leader lines to shift the dimension away from entities it may be obstructing.

For an example of using the OBLique command, see the Command Reference section under DIM: OBLIQUE.

Dimension Utilities

Actually placing dimensions on an AutoCAD drawing is not difficult. The challenging part is getting AutoCAD to display the dimensions in a format that conforms to company standards while producing a professional-looking document. The next sections on dimension styles and dimension variables discuss how to take the unwieldy process of setting up dimensions and bring it under control.

Setting Dimension Styles

One of the greatest features of AutoCAD Release 11 was the addition of dimension styles. These settings enable you to maintain uniformity across a wide group of files because they can be placed in your ACAD.DWG file, and they are automatically included with any new file you create.

Dimension styles take the values of each of the dimensioning variables and store them under a name you supply. These settings can be retrieved at any time. In Release 12, Autodesk has created a new command, DDIM, that simplifies the use and setting of the dimension variables, which in turn simplifies the creation of dimension styles.

The DDIM command uses a dialog box (see fig. 6.14) that breaks down into seven dialog boxes that control all aspects of dimension creation. In the main dialog box, any current dimension styles are shown, as well as the style *UNNAMED, which indicates no active style. To define a dimension style, type the name of the style you want to create at the Dimension Style: edit box. The current settings for all dimension variables are saved with that name. If you want to edit the setting of a particular style, highlight its name in the list box, and then select the button for the settings you want to revise. Any changes you make to the dimension style's settings are automatically saved when you exit from the main dialog box.

The next sections discuss how the dialog boxes of the DDIM command affect the creation and placement of dimension elements.

Figure 6.14:
The Dimension Styles and Variables dialog box.

Modifying Dimension Lines

The first dialog box of the DDIM command enables you to change the settings that affect the creation of dimension lines (see fig. 6.15). These settings affect only the dimension-line entity (see fig. 6.2 to view this element). You could use the dimension variables to change these settings, but the DDIM command lays everything out for you in fairly plain language.

Figure 6.15:
The Dimension Line settings dialog box.

The first three elements of every dialog box are the following: the name of the current dimensions style, an element called **F**eature Scaling, and a check box labeled Use **P**aper Space Scaling.

Feature Scaling relates to the scaling factor that is applied to the variables that are set using DDIM, and directly relates to the scale at which a drawing is plotted. Typically, this value is the same as the value you enter at the PLOT command. If you plot a drawing with 1/8" = 1'-0", for example, your feature scale is 96.

The check box for paper-space scaling sets the scaling value based upon the scaling factor in the current paper-space viewport. This enables you to let the viewport control the scale that is used for creating dimension entities.

The next option, Dimension Line Color, enables you to set the color used for the dimension line. The edit box enables you to enter a color number (the color is shown in the graphic to the right of this edit box).

The last four options control the dimension line. The first, Force **I**nterior Lines, ensures that a dimension line is placed between the extension lines, even if the text is placed outside of the extension lines. The Basic **D**imension checkbox creates a box around the dimension text, which draws attention to a certain dimension.

The Text **G**ap edit box enables you to define the amount of space between the dimension text and the broken dimension line. This is exclusively used for dimension strings in which the text is centered within the dimension line, not above it.

The **B**aseline Increment edit box determines where continuous dimensions are placed in relation to the starting dimension. When using the Baseline dimensioning command, for example, you want a gap between each successive dimension string, so you should enter a positive value. For continuous dimensions created with the CONTINUE command, each dimension should line up with the previous one. Enter a value of **0** in this edit box.

The settings that you edit using this dialog box affect the following dimension variables:

DIMSCALE	DIMTOFL
DIMCLRD	DIMGAP
DIMOXD	DIMDLI

Modifying Extension Lines

The next dialog box of the DDIM command enables you to change the settings that affect the creation of extension lines (see fig. 6.16). These affect only the extension-line entity (see figure 6.2 to view this element).

Figure 6.16:
The Extension Line settings dialog box.

The last group of options control the creation of the extension lines. The first option is Extension Above Line, which defines how far above the dimension line the extension lines end.

Next is an edit box, labeled Feature **O**ffset, which sets the distance from the extension-line location pick point to the beginning of the extension line. The Visibilit**y** drop-down list box enables you to define whether both extension lines are drawn, if none are drawn, or if only one is drawn.

The **C**enter Mark Size edit box sets the size of any center marks placed at the center of arcs or circles that are dimensioned with the CENTER, RADIUS, or DIAMETER commands. The **M**ark with Center Lines checkbox creates actual center lines for a circular object that is dimensioned with the CENTER, RADIUS, or DIAMETER commands.

The settings that you edit using this dialog box affect the following dimension variables:

DIMSCALE	DIMTSE1
DIMCLRE	DIMSE2
DIMEXE	DIMCEN
DIMEXO	

Modifying Dimension Arrows

The Arrows dialog box enables you to change the settings that affect the creation of arrows (see fig. 6.17). Using this dialog box, you control not only the types of arrows that are drawn, but also their placement and scale. These settings affect only the arrows that are drawn at the ends of each dimension line (see fig. 6.2 to view this element).

The Dimension **L**ine Color option enables you to set the color used for both the arrows and the dimension lines. Technically speaking, AutoCAD considers arrows to be part of the dimension line, which is why this value controls both. The edit box enables you to enter a color number, the color of which is shown in the graphic to the right of this edit box.

Figure 6.17:
The Arrows settings dialog box.

The next options control the creation of the arrows. They are a series of radio buttons that control which type of arrows are shown on the dimension line. You can choose from a "true" arrow-type entity, a tick mark, a dot, or a user-supplied block that will be used as the arrow. No matter which type you choose, its size is determined by the value entered in the Arrow Size edit box. This value, like any dimension-size value, is scaled by the Feature Scaling value.

The next options appear grayed-out unless you use a user-defined arrow block. The User Arrow edit box holds the name of a user-defined arrow block. The Separate Arrows check box enables you to define a different block for the first and second arrows by typing the appropriate block name for each arrow. The Tick Extension value is used when you pick the Tick radio button. This value determines how far past the extension lines the dimension line extends.

The settings that you edit using this dialog box affect the following dimension variables:

DIMSCALE	DIMBLK1
DIMCLRD	DIMBLK2
DIMASZ	DIMSAH
DIMTSZ	DIMDLE
DIMBLK	

Modifying Dimension-Text Location

The Text Location dialog box enables you to change the settings that affect where text is placed in relation to the dimension line (see fig. 6.18). This dialog box controls text height, text color, and the position—both horizontally and vertically—of dimension-text elements. These settings affect only the text drawn with the dimensioning commands (see fig. 6.2 to view this element).

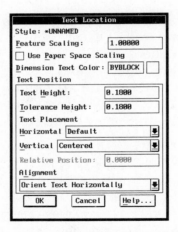

Figure 6.18:
The Text Location dialog box.

The **D**imension Text Color option enables you to set the color used for the dimension text color. You can enter a color number, the color of which is shown in the graphic to the right of this edit box.

The text position options ultimately control the creation of the dimension-text element. The first option sets the text height. Enter a value that will be scaled by the **F**eature Scaling value. When sizing text, keep in mind the size of the final plotted entity. If the text needs to be 3/32 inches tall on the plotted drawing, type **3/32**.

The **T**olerance Height value sets the size of tolerance text. These elements are used often in mechanical design, in which a machined dimension must be created within a certain tolerance from the main dimensions. These tolerances then are placed next to the dimensions text.

Two drop-down list boxes enable you to determine where text is placed in relation to the dimension line. The options for horizontal placement are the following: Default, which places the text between the extension lines (if it fits); Force Text Inside, which ensures that, even if the arrow does not fit, the text is placed between extension lines; and Text, Arrows Inside, which places everything between the dimension lines.

The second drop-down list box controls vertical text placement. Its options are the following: Centered, which places the text within the area where the dimension line is drawn; Above, which places the dimension text above the dimension line; and Relative, which uses the value of the Relative Position edit box to locate the text. A positive value places the text above the dimension line; a negative value places the text below the dimension line.

The A**l**ignment drop-down list box controls general placement of the text with relation to the dimension line. Its options are the following: Orient Text Horizontally, which forces the text to remain horizontal—even in vertical dimensions; Align with Dimension Line, which draws the dimension text at the same angle as the dimension line; Aligned when Inside Only, which only aligns dimension text if it fits between the dimension lines; and Aligned when Outside Only, which aligns the text if it is forced outside of the extension lines.

The settings that you edit using this dialog box affect the following dimension variables:

DIMSCALE	DIMSOXD
DIMCLRT	DIMTAD
DIMTXT	DIMTVP
DIMTFAC	DIMTIH
DIMTIX	DIMTOH

Controlling Dimension-Text Format

The Text Format dialog box enables you to set the elements that affect the way text is formatted when placed in the dimension line (see fig. 6.19). This dialog box controls tolerance values, displays zeros in feet and inches, and displays alternate units.

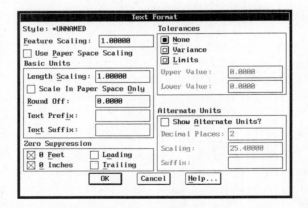

Figure 6.19:
The Text Format dialog box.

The following options control the basic units with which text is displayed. Length Scaling is a value used to multiply by the dimension value before placing it in the dimension string. This value only affects the contents of the dimension text, not the dimension or the entities being dimensioned. The check box that follows uses the Length Scaling value only when creating dimensions in paper space. The Round Off value is used to round off all dimension values based on a certain factor. If you wanted all dimensions rounded to the nearest 1/2-inch, for example, you enter a value of **.5** here.

The Text Pre**f**ix and Te**x**t Suffix edit boxes enable you to assign a text value placed before or after the dimension text, such as **"5'-0" R.O."** or **"Approx. 5'-0"**.

The Zero Suppression check boxes determine where zeros are placed in dimension text. Checking any of these boxes disables the use of zeros in the locations specified. If you dimension an entity that is 10 inches long, and the 0 **F**eet check box is not set, for example, the dimension string placed is 0'-10".

Leading and trailing only affect decimal dimensions. A dimension of 1/2-inch, for example, is displayed as 0.5000 if neither box is checked, or .5 if both are checked.

Tolerances control the placement and value of any tolerances placed with the dimension text. The **N**one radio button disables the placement of any tolerance values. The **V**ariance button uses the values stored in the U**p**per Value and Lo**w**er Value edit boxes to control what sort of tolerance is placed. (See fig. 6.20 to view the different options controlled by this radio button and these values.)

The **L**imits radio button takes the values in the U**p**per Value and Lo**w**er Value check boxes and presents both the addition and subtraction value of the dimension text.

Alternate Units enables you to display the dimensions, not only in units of feet and inches, but in any units of measurement. If you want to show all dimensions in centimeters, for example, click on the Show Alternate Units? check box to enable this feature. Type **2.54** in the S**c**aling edit box and **cm** in the S**u**ffix edit box. Finally, use the Decimal Places edit box to show the number of decimal places for the value in centimeters.

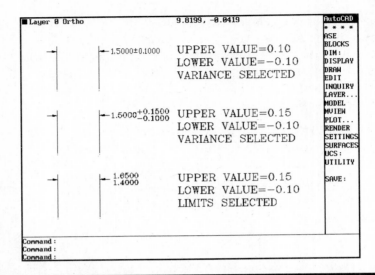

Figure 6.20:
The effect of tolerance settings from within DDIM.

The settings that you edit using this dialog box affect the following dimension variables:

DIMSCALE	DIMLIM
DIMLFAC	DIMTM
DIMRND	DIMTP
DIMPOST	DIMALT
DIMZIN	DIMALTF
DIMTOL	ALTD
DIMAPOST	

Reviewing Dimension-Style Features

This dialog box of the DDIM command combines all the features of the four previous dialog boxes to enable you to quickly peruse all of the settings for a particular dimension style (see fig. 6.21). To find the meaning of each of these options, review the previous sections.

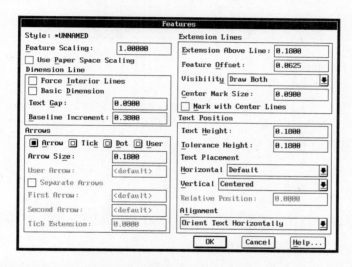

Figure 6.21:
The Features dialog box.

Controlling Dimension Colors

The Colors dialog box of the DDIM command sets the colors of the various dimension-entity elements (see fig. 6.22). Using this dialog box, you can set the color of the Dimension line and arrows, the extension lines, and the dimension text.

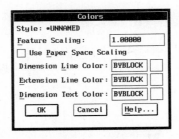

Figure 6.22:
The Colors dialog box.

The settings that you edit using this dialog box affect the following dimension variables:

DIMSCALE	DIMCLRD
DIMLCLRE	DIMCLRT

Using Dimensioning Variables To Modify Dimensions

AutoCAD has 216 settings that determine the way that commands function. These settings are called *system variables* and are discussed in detail in Part 6.

The following sections examine a subset of system variables, called *dimensioning variables*, which control the creation and appearance of dimensions. When they have been set, dimensioning variables usually are left alone to maintain a consistent appearance for all drawing output. You can use these variables to modify the appearance of AutoCAD's dimensions so that the dimensions you create suit any standards.

You can set the dimensioning variables at the `Command:` prompt the same way that you set other AutoCAD variables.

It is easier to set these values using the new DDIM dialog box group than it is to remember the value of all of these variables.

- **DIMALT.** If set to 1, enables alternate units dimensioning (see fig. 6.23).
- **DIMALTD.** If DIMALT is set to 1, this variable sets the number of decimal places used to edit the alternate measurement.
- **DIMALTF.** If DIMALT is set to 1, all linear dimensions are multiplied by this factor to produce a value in an alternate system of measurement.
- **DIMAPOST.** Places the defined text string after any alternate dimensions. To disable a set text string, enter a period (see fig. 6.23).

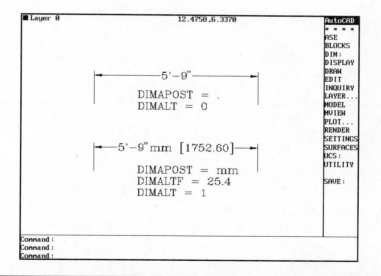

Figure 6.23:
Dimensions, with and without alternate values.

- **DIMASO.** If set to 1, only associative dimensions are created.
- **DIMASZ.** Determines the size of arrows or arrow blocks at the ends of the dimension line. If DIMTSZ is not equal to 0, this setting is ignored (see fig. 6.24).

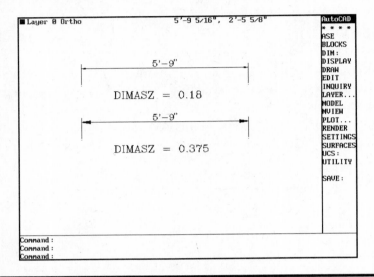

Figure 6.24:
Dimensions with small and large arrows.

- **DIMBLK.** This variable contains the name of a block to be used for the dimension arrows.
- **DIMBLK1** and **DIMBLK2.** If DIMSAH is set to 1, these two variables contain the names of blocks to be used for the first and second arrows.
- **DIMCEN.** If set to 0, no center lines or marks are created for circular entities. If the value is greater than 0, a center mark of the set size is created. If it is less than zero, center marks are placed in the entity (see fig. 6.25).

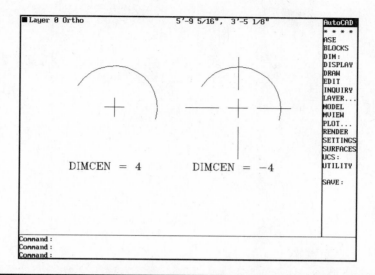

Figure 6.25:
The effects of DIMCEN.

- **DIMCLRD.** Sets the color of the dimension lines, arrowheads, and dimension-line leaders.

- **DIMCLRE.** Sets the color of the dimension extension lines. It can take on any valid color number or the special logicals Byblock and Bylayer.

- **DIMCLRT.** Sets the color of the dimension text.

- **DIMDLE.** When ticks are used for arrows (DIMTSZ is greater than 0), this value extends the dimension line past the extension lines (see fig. 6.26).

- **DIMDLI.** Sets the dimension-line increment for continuous linear dimensioning with the BASELINE and CONTINUE dimensioning subcommands (see fig. 6.27).

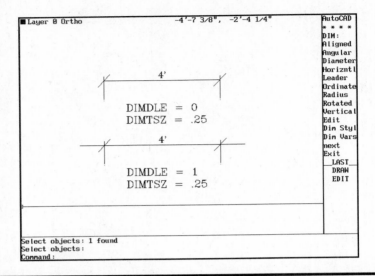

Figure 6.26:
Dimensions, with and without extended dimension lines.

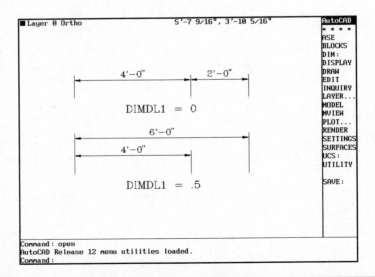

Figure 6.27:
Dimensions, with and without dimension-line increments.

- **DIMEXE.** Sets the distance specifying how far extension lines extend beyond the dimension line (see fig. 6.28).
- **DIMEXO.** Sets the distance specifying how far extension lines are offset from the origin points chosen by the user (see fig. 6.28).

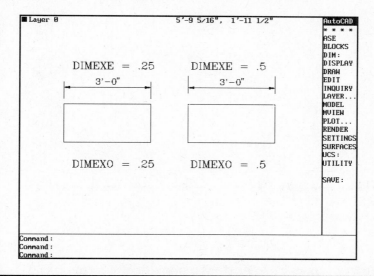

Figure 6.28:
Dimensions with varying extension line offset and height.

- **DIMGAP.** If greater than 0, determines how far from the dimensions text the dimension line stops. If less than 0, draws a box around the dimension text (see fig. 6.29).
- **DIMLFAC.** Used as a scaling factor for all dimension-text values when used in model space. In paper space, if value is less than 0, dimensions are scaled by the absolute value of this variable. If the viewport option is enabled, a scaling factor based on the selected viewport is used.
- **DIMLIM.** If set to 1, generates dimension limits by default.

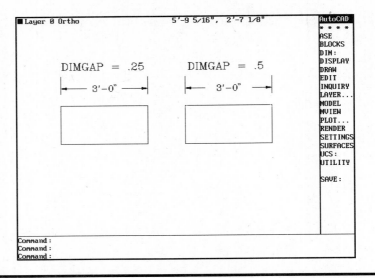

Figure 6.29:
Dimensions with varying dimension-line gaps.

 Turning on DIMLIM automatically turns off DIMTOL, and vice versa.

- **DIMPOST.** Used to set dimension-text prefixes or suffixes. Use with the angle brackets to place the defined dimension within the text string (see fig. 6.30).
- **DIMRND.** Rounds all dimensions to this value (see fig. 6.31).

 The number of decimal places shown in dimension text is controlled by the UNITS commands or the LUPREC system variable.

- **DIMSAH.** If DIMSAH is set to 1, the alternate dimension blocks DIMBLK1 and DIMBLK2 are used at each end of the dimension line.

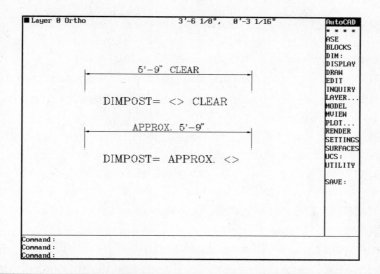

Figure 6.30:
Dimensions with prefixes and suffixes.

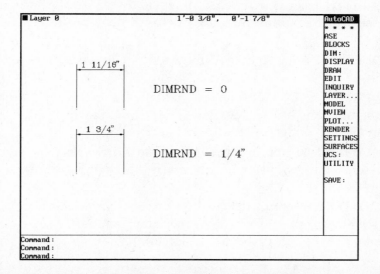

Figure 6.31:
The effects of DIMRND.

- **DIMSCALE.** The scale factor applied to all general dimension values. Does not affect tolerances or actual measured distances. If set to 0, uses the current viewport's scaling factor.
- **DIMSE1.** If set to 1, suppresses creation of the first extension line.
- **DIMSE2.** If set to 1, suppresses creation of the second extension line.
- **DIMSHO.** If set to 1, associative dimension values are recomputed as the dimension is dragged.
- **DIMSOXD.** If set to 1, prevents the dimension line from being drawn, as long as DIMTIX also is set to 1.
- **DIMSTYLE.** Sets the name of the current dimension style.
- **DIMTAD.** If set to 1, dimension text is placed above the dimension line. If set to 0, text placement is controlled by DIMTVP.
- **DIMTFAC.** Sets the scale factor for the text height of tolerance values, which is relative to the normal dimension-text height set by DIMTXT.
- **DIMTIH.** If set to 1, dimensions text is always drawn horizontally. If set to 0, text follows the angle of the dimension line (see fig. 6.32).
- **DIMTIX.** If set to 1, forces dimension text between the extension lines.
- **DIMTM and DIMTP.** These variables contain the dimension tolerance and limit values. DIMTP specifies the upper tolerance and DIMTM specifies the lower tolerance.
- **DIMTOFL.** If set to 1, a dimension line is drawn between the extension lines, even when the text is placed outside the extension lines (see fig. 6.33).
- **DIMTOH.** If set to 1, dimensions text always is drawn horizontally for text placed outside of the extension lines. If set to 0, text follows the angle of the dimension line.

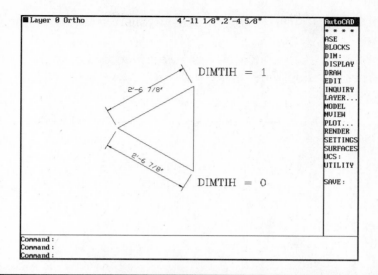

Figure 6.32:
Dimensions, with and without forced horizontal text.

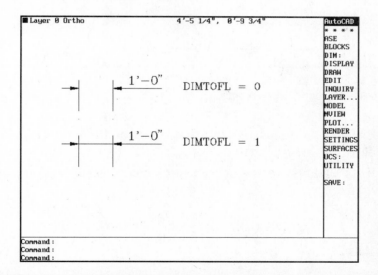

Figure 6.33:
Dimensions, with and without a forced dimension line.

- **DIMTOL.** If set to 1, adds dimension tolerances to the dimension text.
- **DIMTSZ.** Used to size the tick marks placed at the ends of the dimension line. If this is used, arrows and arrow blocks are turned off (see fig. 6.34).

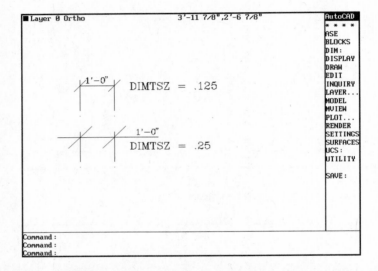

Figure 6.34:
Dimensions with different tick-mark sizes.

- **DIMTVP.** Controls the vertical position of dimension text above or below the dimension line.
- **DIMTXT.** Sets the height of the dimension text unless preassigned when using a fixed height text style.

 A text style with a fixed height overrides the DIMTXT setting.

- **DIMZIN.** Enables you to suppress the inches portion of a feet-and-inches dimension when the distance is an integral number of feet, or the feet portion when the distance is less than one foot.

Dimensioning in Paper Space

The last chapter looked at the differences between AutoCAD's two working environments, model space and paper space. You know that the primary purpose of paper space is to simplify the construction of multiscale and multiview hard-copy drawings. It is thus logical to use model space to create models and paper space to document them.

In many cases, you can work this way by using the two environments. You can create a full-size model in model space, use paper space to set up a drawing sheet with a title block, and then create untiled viewports to look at the model. You also can place general notes and annotations in paper space.

You can even dimension in paper space. Because the dimensions always relate to objects in model space, however, it is better to also keep your dimensions in model space. Paper-space dimensioning can be done, though, and two of the dimension settings discussed with the DDIM command are specific to paper space.

DIMSCALE=0

The normal purpose of DIMSCALE (**F**eature Scaling in DDIM) is to set the size and distances of all visible dimension entities. In model space, DIMSCALE should normally be the reciprocal of the plot scale. On a drawing that is plotted at 1/8"=1'-0" (or 1/96th full size), for example, DIMSCALE should be 96; on a drawing that is plotted at full scale, DIMSCALE should be 1.

When DIMSCALE is set to 0, the DIMSCALE value takes on a real value: the reciprocal of the Zoom XP factor previously applied to the viewport entity. If you set up an untiled viewport, zoom 1/48XP, and insert a house plan in it, you can set DIMSCALE to 0 in that viewport, and DIMSCALE assumes a value of 48. You can simply begin dimensioning and all dimension entities are then created at the right size.

DIMLFAC=V

The second paper space-specific setting of a dimension variable is DIMLFAC=V (use **P**aper Space Scaling checkbox in DDIM). DIMLFAC stands for DIMension Linear FACtor, which is a multiplier that the DIM command applies to all distances before it places the dimension text.

DIMLFAC's V argument stands for viewport. When DIMLFAC is set to V, AutoCAD looks at the viewport's scale factor, sets the multiplication factor to its reciprocal, and uses that as the multiplier for the dimension entity. This only affects dimension entities created in paper space.

Remember that both of these settings are necessary to dimension model-space entities correctly in paper space. Both settings examine the scale factor of the untiled viewport and apply the reciprocal of that scale factor—one to the size of the dimension entities and the other to the dimension value.

> **TIP**
>
> Dimensioning in the paper-space environment is not practical for several reasons. First, there is no virtual screen in paper space, which means that every pan and zoom requires a regeneration. If 30 to 40 percent of the time is spent annotating and dimensioning, the process takes much longer in paper space. Second, because the dimensions are in paper space, they do not update when you change your model.

Keep your dimensions in model space with the rest of your model. The advantages, which include tying the dimensions to the object and transparent display commands, outweigh the disadvantages of having to remember model space DIMSCALE factors and keeping documentation entities in the model environment.

Summary

In this chapter, you learned about the different types of dimensions and how to control their appearance. The chapter discussed ways to access each dimension, how to format the dimension, and how to edit each one. You also learned how to exploit paper space to ease dimension scaling. The chapter ended with a list of the names of the dimension variables and their effects.

Paper Space and Plotting

At first, paper space and plotting seem to have nothing in common.
They both, however, are concerned with the look of the drawing.
Paper space is a feature used by the operator to arrange the contents of
the drawing; *plotting* is used to take the actual drawing and place it on
paper by using pens of varying widths or colors. Paper space works
with plotting because it enables you to arrange your drawing using
normal measurements. You are not forced to scale text and other elements so that a correct plot is produced.

This chapter explores the capabilities of paper space and the revised
PLOT command to make your job of producing documents as easy as
possible. When you have worked and become familiar with these two
fundamental elements of AutoCAD, you will be on the road to creating
concise drawings with a minimum of effort.

Working in Paper Space

The paper-space feature, which debuted in AutoCAD Release 11, arranges multiple-scaled views of your drawing file, and provides advanced features to keep the number of entities within the drawing file to a minimum. Paper space is still one of the more difficult AutoCAD concepts to grasp and work with intelligently. This chapter describes paper space and provides tips on its use.

Suppose that you have a street map of your city, and you place a piece of glass on top of the map. In the simplest terms, the map represents model space; the glass is paper space. The glass does not interfere with your use of the map. Any text or graphics drawn on the glass is visible but kept separate from the map. If you change the view or scale of the map, the text and graphics on the sheet of glass remain unchanged. Because paper space is a work surface independent of model space size and scale, it is useful for adding borders, title blocks, and notations that are not part of the model.

When you draw in paper space, everything is kept on the glass, which enables you to annotate the map, but not have the annotations get in the way of the map elements. By the same token, you can modify the elements in your map, such as rotating the map, without affecting the entities you created in paper space.

Starting a Drawing in Paper Space

Working in paper space is controlled with the TILEMODE system variable and the PSPACE command (discussed later in this chapter). Under AutoCAD R11, the TILEMODE variable was a crutch used to ensure compatibility for routines designed to work in Release 10. But now, its use has opened up a whole new world for creating and composing AutoCAD drawings.

To use paper space, the TILEMODE variable must first be set to 0. The screen regenerates, and, if you have not previously created any paper space elements, AutoCAD displays a blank screen (see fig. 7.1).

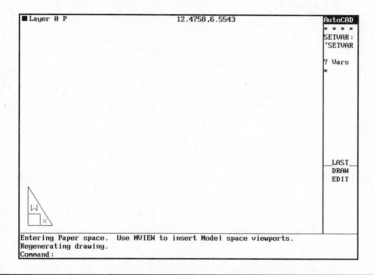

Figure 7.1:
The initial paper-space screen.

Notice that the coordinate-system icon is different. When you are drawing in paper space, this icon always appears as the triangle shown in figure 7.1. A P appears on the status bar when you are in paper space.

All the things you can do in model space (with few exceptions), you can also do in paper space. You can create entities, define views, zoom, pan, and otherwise interact in the same ways. The one thing you cannot do in model space is to create and compose many different views of your drawing on a sheet. This feature, which makes paper space unique, is described in the next section.

207

Creating Multiple Viewports

In paper space, *viewports* are the windows into your drawing. These windows are actually entities created using the MVIEW command. Similar to the VPORTS command for dividing the screen into viewports in model-space, MVIEW enables you to create each rectangular area to view the model-space entities within. You are not limited to creating the viewports based on the screen size—each viewport can be a different size, and you can create as many viewports as you like. The only restriction is that you can only have 16 viewports active at any one time on DOS systems.

The drawing shown in figure 7.2 shows a viewport created in paper space using the MVIEW command. The viewport was created by choosing two points that defined the size of the entity. When the viewport is created, a regeneration occurs as the model-space drawing extents are displayed within the viewport. You can scale the drawing within the viewport using the ZOOM command (discussed in the next section).

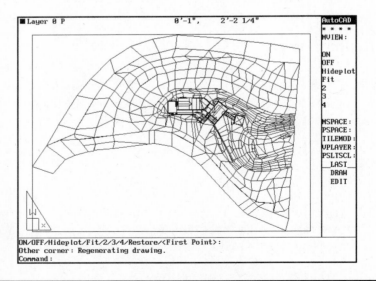

Figure 7.2:
A single paper-space viewport.

You can create as many viewports as you need. For example, look at the drawing shown in figure 7.3. In this drawing, multiple viewports are used to display different views of a house and the land it sits on. The author of this drawing created the full 3D site and house in model space, and then used the advanced features of paper space to show various views of his creation in the drawing sheet.

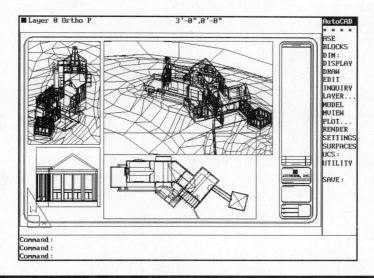

Figure 7.3:
A typical use for paper-space viewports.

Viewports are exactly like other AutoCAD entities. This means that viewport entities can be copied, scaled, stretched, or deleted. This is also the key to making the viewport entities invisible. Once you open the viewport and are displaying the entities you want to see, you do not really want to see the viewport edges. You can place the viewport entity on a layer that is turned off, which gives the effect of hiding the viewport edges while still displaying the entities within the viewport.

Once you have created the viewports, you can use them right away with the MSPACE and PSPACE commands. These two commands can only be used when the TILEMODE variable is set to 0. They enable you to draw in one of the viewports (in model space) or on top of the viewports (in paper space). If you use the MSPACE command, the crosshairs are restricted to the limits of the current viewport entity. This is a good reminder of the space in which you are creating entities. To go back to paper space, enter **PSPACE**. Your crosshairs now extend the length of the drawing screen, and any entities you now create are placed in paper space.

The MSPACE and PSPACE commands can be abbreviated as MS and PS.

You cannot select paper-space entities while in a model space viewport, nor can you choose model-space entities while in paper space.

Scaling Viewports

Now that you have created your viewports, how do you actually use them? The first thing to do is set up a viewport-scale factor. Do not confuse viewport scaling with using the SCALE command on a viewport entity. *Scaling viewports* refers to applying a scaling factor to the entities shown within the viewport using the ZOOM command.

One of the ZOOM command's options is ZOOM XP, which sets the scaling factor between paper space and the viewport. Typically, you enter this value as a fraction, the same value you use if you are plotting the entities normally. For example, to plot the entities at a scale factor of 1/8" = 1'-0", you first position yourself within the viewport with the MSPACE command, and then enter **ZOOM 1/96XP**. The drawing shown in figure 7.4 has two viewports: one in which no scaling factor has been applied, and one with a scaling factor of 1/96XP.

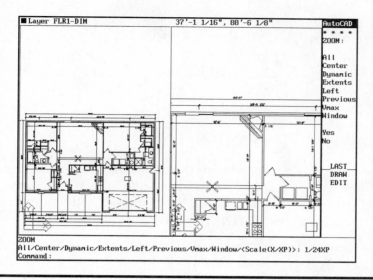

Figure 7.4:
Scaled and non-scaled viewports.

When you plot the drawing containing the viewport at a scale of 1=1, the entities shown in the viewport plot at 1/8-inch scale. This may seem confusing, because you typically think of applying the scale factor at plot time, but paper space frees you of this restriction. This procedure also enables you to mix multiscale viewports with relative ease.

Before, when you wanted to show two elements of a drawing at different scales, one had to be physically scaled with a SCALE command. Now you can continue to draw at natural, 1=1 scale, and use viewport scaling to display the elements at the correct size.

Once you have set up the proper scale within a viewport, be careful when you use the ZOOM command. Zooming in or out disrupts the scale factor you have set, and unless you go back to the original view with a ZOOM Previous, the scale will be incorrect when the viewport is plotted.

Use the PAN command instead because it does not disrupt the current scale factor. If you need to zoom in on the model space information in order to work with it effectively, you may be better off setting the TILEMODE variable to 1, which turns off paper space and enables you to work only in model space. Once you have finished modifying your model-space drawing, set TILEMODE back to 0, and your paper space information will reappear.

Annotating in Paper Space

Because drawing in paper space is the same as in model space, there is no problem with annotating paper-space elements. When you draw text, text entities are created. The LINE command still creates lines. Keep the following in mind when annotating your drawings:

- **Scale.** When you wanted to plot a drawing sheet at 1/8-inch scale (prior to paper space), you had to draw a border that was 96 times its natural, plotted size. At plot time, you entered a scale factor, which then created the drawing at the correct size. Now, you can draw and annotate the border sheet in paper space at normal, 1=1 scale.

- **Dimensions.** You should keep all dimensions in model space. Although you can use paper-space scaling to dimension model-space entities from within paper space, resist the temptation! When you stretch the model-space entities, the dimension does not update to the new length. If you have to move the entities in model space, you then have to go back to paper space to move the dimensions.

- **Linetypes.** AutoCAD Release 11's greatest failure when dealing with paper space is its lack of proper linetype handling. If you used viewports with different scale factors, the linetypes displayed differently in each viewport. In Release 12, the problem has been addressed by the PSLTSCALE variable. If PSLTSCALE is set to 1, all lines, whether created in model space or paper space, use the same scaling factor. Linetype scale factor is set with LTSCALE. Typically, you set LTSCALE to a value of 1, which, when you plot your drawing at a scale of 1=1, correctly draws the lines.

- **Text.** There is no rule about whether text relating to a drawing should be placed in paper space or model space. The advantage to using paper space for text is that you do not need to scale the entity so that it plots at the proper size. If you know text should be 1/8-inch high, simply draw it that way in paper space. Also, if you create a drawing with viewports at various scales, it may be easier to do all your annotation in paper space. On the other hand, if you have text that must be duplicated among a group of viewports, it is easier to create the text only once in model space, and then to make sure the layer containing the text is active in all selected viewports.

- **Moving entities between spaces.** There are occasions in which you have entities in model space that you may decide would be better in paper space. AutoCAD has no direct command to move entities from one space to another, but you can use the WBLOCK command instead. This command removes the selected entities to a new drawing file, which you can then insert into paper space. Do not forget to scale down the entities so they fit properly on your sheet when you use the INSERT command.

- **WBlocks.** Entities in paper space are not inserted into a drawing by using the INSERT command. If a drawing contains paper-space entities, and you insert that drawing as a WBLOCK using the INSERT command, the paper-space entities are not inserted. You first need to transfer any paper-space entities into model space before they can be inserted into another drawing.

- **Entities.** Always be aware of the space you are in when drawing. One of the easiest mistakes to make is to draw an entity in paper space that should be in model space. In paper space, you can select model space entity snap points with object snap overrides. This makes it easy to appear to draw entities that are part of your model but are actually in paper space. This leads to confusion when you are in paper space, trying to select an entity that looks like it is part of your model but it is not. When you are in paper space, a P appears in the status bar, and you see the paper-space icon in the lower-left corner of the screen. When you are in model space, the screen icon displays the UCS or WCS.

Although you can draw 3D objects in paper space, you cannot change the viewport in paper space. Any entities you draw as part of the model should be in model space.

Composing a Plot in Paper Space

Similar to annotating a drawing in paper space, composing a plot is very simple. Remember that you are plotting your paper-space drawing at a scale of 1=1. Text heights and entity sizes that you normally expect to set do not need to be scaled up or down to plot at the proper size.

Become familiar with the VPLAYER and MVSETUP commands. VPLAYER is used to control visibility of a layer within individual viewports. This feature is extremely useful because it enables you to keep the number of duplicate entities within your drawing to a minimum. For example, suppose you want to show both a floor plan and ceiling plan in the same sheet. You open up two paper-space viewports, showing the wall lines in both, and then freeze out the layers that do not pertain to each viewport by using the VPLAYER command. The drawing in figure 7.5 shows this feature.

The VPLAYER command is command-line driven—you have to type in the names of all layers that you wish to freeze out, and then select the viewports in which this will take effect. You can also use the DDLMODES command to freeze or thaw layers within the current viewport.

MVSETUP is a generalized viewport creation and configuration program. It enables you to rotate the image seen within a viewport and line up the contents of viewports. The rotation capability is handy for drawings that must maintain proper coordinate locations (such as a surveying drawing) but are aligned incorrectly within AutoCAD to produce a plot. For example, look at the two viewports in figure 7.6. The left viewport shows the entities as they actually appear in model space; the right viewport has had the display rotated so it can be plotted length-wise.

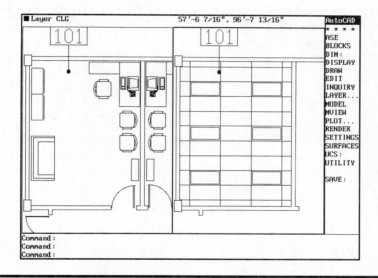

Figure 7.5:
Restricting layer display within viewports.

MVSETUP is also a very handy routine for performing all of your paper space setup routines. With it, you can insert custom borders, create and size multiple viewports, and alter the display of model space within each viewport. See the *Command Reference* for a full description of the capabilities of this command.

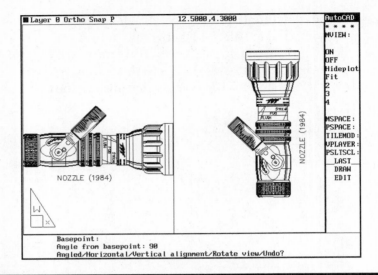

Figure 7.6:
A normal and rotated viewport display.

Plotting the Drawing

The final step in any project is to plot the drawing. You can then check on drawing content, line weights, and the general correctness of your drawing. Although you can review a drawing directly on the computer, not everyone is computer literate yet, and reviewing a computer drawing is more fatiguing than doing it on paper.

This section discusses ways to take advantage of AutoCAD's newly revised PLOT command, the benefits offered by such facilities as plot preview and multiple-device selection, the types of plotters currently in use in most offices today, and some options for increasing the speed of plotting, which is still the largest bottleneck in any CADD implementation.

Types of Plotters

Five years ago, the plotter market was pretty simple—there were pen plotters or print plotters. Since then, new technologies have come of age and plot solutions that once cost over $30,000 have been reduced to an economical $8,000.

The quality of a plotter is a direct reflection of the quality of your work. This section discusses the types of plotting devices available, so you can decide which one best suits your needs.

There are two broad categories of plotters: vector and raster. *Vector plotters* are pen-based. They are slow because vector plotters take the AutoCAD vector information and redraw each entity from start to finish.

Raster plotters translate the AutoCAD vector information into a series of dots, which form drawing images when output on the plotter. Although this process involves a second step before the plot is actually created, it is still much faster than the vector-plotter process.

The other feature that differentiates these plotters is the output resolution. Most raster plotters have a resolution of 300 dots-per-inch (dpi), with some achieving up to 600 dpi. Vector plotters have a typical resolution of more than 2000 steps-per-inch.

Pen Plotters

Pen-plotter technology has been around for a generation. The computer sends instructions to the plotter; the plotter mechanism then rolls the paper back and forth, and moves the pen holder from side to side at the same time. Quality pen plotters create beautiful output because of their high resolution, but they can be slow—a complex E-size drawing, for example, can take an hour or more to plot.

You can choose from several types of plotting media as well as a wide range of sizes—each depends on the type of plotting you must do. Translucent bond usually is specified for check plots; plotter vellum or mylar is specified for final plots. Many users find that translucent bond is perfectly adequate for final plots as well.

 Make sure your pen speed and pen weight are set correctly (usually on the plotter) for the type of media you are using.

Pen plotters are designed to accept the standard range of precut sheets. These include A-size through E-size, in both architectural and engineering standards (engineering sheets are slightly smaller than architectural sheets), as well as metric sheet sizes A0 through A4. Most offices use architectural D-size (24"×36") or E-size (36"×48") plotters for final output. Many large-size plotters also have a roll-feed option, which allows for plots of any length or continuous plotting.

You can choose from a variety of pen types. Because mylar film wears down ordinary steel tips very quickly, tungsten-tipped pens are available for use with film. You also can choose disposable or refillable liquid-ink pens. Refillable pens are slightly cheaper than disposables, but some users find that the chore of cleaning pens is not worth the savings. You can use ball-point and felt-tip plotter pens on bond and vellum rather than liquid-ink plotter pens in high-speed pen plotters. Felt-tip pens offer the further advantage of a range of color.

Pen plotters typically have resolutions between 1500 and 2000 steps-per-inch. Pen plotters usually are used to create working (final) drawings due to this increased crispness of the final image. To produce lines of varying widths on a pen plotter you have two options: using different width pens or plotting wide polylines. Similar to technical drafting pens, disposable plotter pens come in standard widths of 0.25, 0.35, 0.50, and 0.70 millimeters.

If you also use refillable pens you can get finer and broader lines. For any line in your drawing that exceeds the width of the pen you are using, you can create a polyline with the required width. The pen plotter then takes the pen and draws the line to the width you specified within AutoCAD.

Electrostatic, Laser, and Thermal Plotters

Electrostatic, laser, and thermal plotters are the new cutting edge for plotters within most medium-sized firms. The proliferation of the technology and software to use these devices has drastically reduced their price to being within the budget of many firms. Each of these plotters uses an AutoCAD driver that converts the vector information into dots (*raster data*), which is then output from the plotter.

Electrostatic and laser plotters are fairly similar. Both rely on a toner cartridge to supply the ink that is fused to the paper. *Electrostatic plotters,* because of the technology on which they are based, typically require a well-regulated environment in order to operate properly. Laser plotters, like laser printers, use laser ionization to place the toner and electric heat to fuse the toner ink into the paper. They are much less sensitive to the surrounding environment and are often less of a burden to maintain.

Thermal plotters use heat to induce a reaction from the media on which they plot. When heat is applied, the media changes color, which produces the image. Black-and-white, two-color, and full-color thermal plotters are available. Thermal plotters are by far the easiest to maintain because there is no ink to refill or cartridges to replace, but the media may need to be cared for in special ways. Because it is heat-sensitive, the media may darken when taken to a professional blueprinting office. If you use thermal plotters, warn your blueprinter to slow down the speed of the blueprint machines and not damage the plotted original.

All of these devices are set up to use roll-fed paper. This is a great convenience, especially when running large plot jobs. Multiple plots can be sent to the plotter, and the plot operator only needs to worry about the paper running out or the wrong media being in the plotter. These plotters also have a fairly good plot resolution: usually in the range of 300-400 dpi.

By far, these types of plotters have the best support for both variable line weights and line patterns. Most raster plotters have widths from 0.005-inch up to 1.25-inch, in increments of 0.005-inch, which give quite a broad range.

Setting up pen widths on a raster plotter involves setting up default weight tables that are stored by the plotter. If you do not accept the manufacturer's defaults, you need to specify what width should be used for which pens that AutoCAD specifies. This is a fairly detailed operation—it may take hours before line weights are acceptable by you and your co-workers. Once it is done, though, you will never need to change widths again. This also helps eliminate the need for wide polylines in your drawing because you can simply choose a wide plotter line when plotting a certain color.

Inkjet Plotters

This new breed of raster plotter has been spurred on by the strong sales of inkjet printers during the early 1990s. These types of plotters are very much the same as their desktop brethren—both use the same technology to create the image. *Inkjet plotters* apply an electrical charge to the print head, which causes a bead of ink to form. As the charge is increased, the bubble is ejected from the print head onto the media. Although may seem like a messy way to plot, the current group of inkjet plotters have resolutions up to 600 dpi.

Inkjet plotters also appear to be more versatile than most of the other plotters on the market. They accept both single-sheet and roll-fed media in many lengths. The average width for these types of plotters is 24 inches or 36 inches. In comparison to the electrostatic and thermal plotters, the inkjet printer is slower, but not by much. This is due to the fact that the inkjet head is similar to a normal printer head that must pass back and forth over the media before the media advance. The other plotters have a print "head" that extends the width of the media, so the image is being created on all parts of the paper at a single point.

In addition to normal blackline inkjet plotters, color inkjets are beginning to emerge on the market. These plotters are priced in the same range as other inkjet plotters, but their resolution tends to not be as fine. Inkjet plotters, like other raster plotters, can be specified when plotting your drawings. You may need to modify some of the plotter internal values in order to get all the line widths in the plotter to be addressed by AutoCAD's 255 colors, but once it is done, you probably do not have to change it again.

Printer Plotters

Printer plotters are standard office printers that can produce graphics. *Dot-matrix printers* come in standard or wide-carriage models and can create printer plots at different resolutions; some are also capable of color output. Printer plotters usually are used for check plots because of their low resolution and general availability. Although each station may have its own printer, it is not likely that each CADD station would have its own laser or pen plotter. Printers are an inexpensive alternative.

The quality of printer plots can vary widely. Resolution is poor on nine-pin dot-matrix printers (around 180 dpi); it is adequate to good on 24-pin printers (up to 360 dpi). Many printers also create color plots. This is usually done by using a color ribbon and specifying the proper pens from within AutoCAD.

Because of their simple nature, most printer plotters do not give much control over pen weights. Still, many users are happy with their results from printer plotting and do not need to use a large pen or electrostatic plotter.

The Plot Dialog Box

When Autodesk updated the user interface for Release 12 with dialog boxes, the PLOT command changed and the PRPLOT command was dropped. For many years, the PLOT command was one of the least intuitive, most difficult commands to use effectively. In essence, it was too easy to screw up! The new PLOT dialog box, shown in figure 7.7, makes the whole process a lot more accurate.

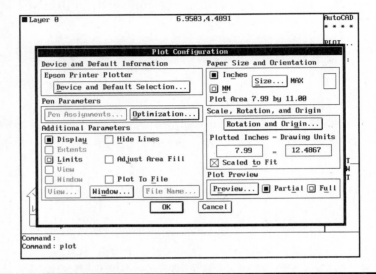

Figure 7.7:
The new PLOT command dialog box.

The next sections discuss the new format of the PLOT command and how it can be used to benefit you most.

Plot Device Selection

In previous releases of AutoCAD, you only had two choices for output devices: a printer plotter or a normal plotter. To use anything else, you had to reconfigure AutoCAD for a different device. In AutoCAD Release 12, you have the option of creating 29 possible plot devices, and you can access any at the time you issue the PLOT command. The configuration of these devices is handled through the CONFIG command. For an in-depth discussion of setting up multiple configurations, see Chapter 2.

When issuing the PLOT command, the currently selected plot device is shown in the upper left corner of the dialog box under Device and Default Information. No matter how many plot devices you have, you can select among them by picking the **D**evice and Default Selection button. This button brings up a dialog box, shown in figure 7.8, which displays all the currently configured plotters. This list may contain a mixture of printers, pen, inkjet, and raster plotters, but only the descriptions of these devices tell you what they are. (These descriptions are supplied by the person who set up your copy of AutoCAD.)

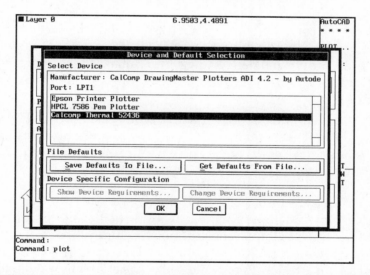

Figure 7.8:
Multiple plot device selection.

To select the device you want to plot to, highlight its name in the list, and press the OK button. This is a great improvement over the old method of choosing plotters, and by using this type of interface, Autodesk has eliminated the PRPLOT command, which was used to send a plot to the printer.

In addition to choosing which plotter device you want to plot to, you can set and retrieve plot-configuration parameter defaults, and show and modify plotter-device requirements. A Plot Configuration Parameters (PCP) file is used to store pen settings in an ASCII format. AutoCAD enables you to map all 256 colors to create a PCP file and save these settings, rather than manually setting the pen assignments with each different plot you produce. When you want to use a particular pen setup, retrieve the PCP file that contains the settings you wish to use.

 Most raster plotters, such as thermal and electrostatic plotters, enable you to map all 256 AutoCAD colors to individual pen settings. You can use the PCP file to provide the direct relationship between colors and pens to use on a daily basis.

First, save your current setting with the **S**ave Defaults To File button. When you want to alter the pen mappings, do it through the Pen Assignments dialog box. To use the default, restore the mappings with the **G**et Defaults From File button.

The Show Device Requirements and Change Device Requirements buttons display and modify any hardware-specific options that may be available with your plotter. These options include plot density, copies, rotation, or mirroring. Check the *AutoCAD Interface, Installation, and Performance Guide* to see if your selected plot device allows you to modify any of these parameters.

Most raster plotters allow a variety of pen weights, giving you the ability to do grayscale plots in one step.

Pen Parameters

When AutoCAD plots a drawing, it sends entities of a certain color to a specified pen on the plotter. This method enables you to control the way the elements of the drawing are shown in the hard copy that you produce. When you click on the Pen Assignments button in the PLOT dialog box, you see the Pen Assignments dialog box, shown in figure 7.9.

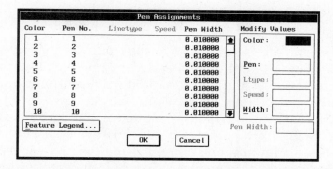

Figure 7.9:
The Pen Assignments dialog box.

This dialog box is similar in behavior to the DDLMODES dialog box: when you select a color number, you can modify the pen it is mapping to, the hardware linetype, the pen speed, and the width value. If you select multiple colors, your settings in the edit boxes are applied to all the selected colors.

The ways that you can modify these elements depend on the capabilities of the plot device. If you are working with an eight-pen plotter, you cannot assign a color to pen 9. Unless there is a specific reason for using hardware linetypes, you should map all colors to the plotter's continuous linetype, and let AutoCAD control the look of the lines. This simplifies the exchange of the drawing file with another person.

Pen-speed control adjusts the speed at which the plotter moves a pen, which is necessary if a pen skips because it is moving too fast. This control may also be necessary when plotting to mylar, because it allows the ink more time to flow onto the media to produce consistent lines.

The Pen Width setting informs AutoCAD about the size of any physical pens when using a pen plotter. This enables AutoCAD to determine how many times it must travel over a line to fill it with ink when solids and wide polylines are used in a drawing. If your plotter supports any features such as hardware linetypes, speed settings, or widths, you can view them by clicking on the Feature Legend button.

The final element of pen parameters is the **O**ptimization button in the PLOT dialog box. This button is intended for true pen plotters because it allows for the fastest transmission of data by performing optimizations based on pen motion. The pen information can be sorted so that all entities that use a certain pen are plotted at once, or all the vector information with a certain area to be sent in order to keep the plotter's movements to a minimum and more. You may want to experiment with these settings to determine which one produces the fastest, most accurate plot.

Plot-Area Selection

The Additional Parameters settings in the PLOT dialog box describe to AutoCAD the area of the drawing you want to plot. Similar to the ZOOM command's options, you select the area—for example, the current display or drawing extents—to be output to the plotter. Simply check the radio button that conforms to the area of the drawing that you want to plot.

If you plot a drawing view, first click on the View button and select the name of a currently defined view. This is the most trouble-free method of defining a plot area because a view describes an area of the drawing editor, regardless of any other elements. Settings, such as extents and limits, are easily changed when drawing elements exceed the areas in which you think the current extents or limits lie.

NOTE The views must be defined before the View buttons are available for use.

You can also select to plot a drawing window by clicking on the Window button. The dialog box disappears, and enables you to select two points that define the plot window. Once a window is defined, the Window radio button is available. You can then select the defined window by clicking on the button.

Three additional settings that control the creation of your plot display in the Additional Parameters area. These are check boxes for Hide Lines, Adjust Area Fill, and Plot to File. To make hidden-line plots of three-dimensional elements, you must click on the Hide Lines box.

You cannot create a hidden-line plot by executing the HIDE command and then plotting normally. In fact, you do not need to run the HIDE command before you do a hidden-line plot; simply check this box prior to creating the plot. Hidden lines are removed from the output. If you use paper space, you can put hidden-line plots in individual viewports by turning on the MVIEW command's Hideplot option. When AutoCAD plots each viewport, it removes any hidden lines before sending the information to the plotter.

The Adjust Area Fill setting is used to make detailed line-fill plots. By checking this box, AutoCAD offsets the pen by half of its width into the filled area. This ensures that the edge of the fill is exactly where the drawing element indicates it should be.

The Plot to File check box creates a plot file instead of the normal hard-copy output from the PLOT command. You can use this file in several ways. If you are on a network, you can place the plot file in a queue at the network plotter. You can dedicate a computer as a plotter server, and transfer the plot-file from your AutoCAD station to this machine for plotting. The plot-file name is set by clicking on the File Name button and entering a file name.

If you only have a single computer, you can use plot-spooling software to send your plot file to the plotter in the background while you continue to use AutoCAD. In an office in which you are not networked (but you have several CADD stations that need to send files to the plotter), creating plot files is a timesaving method for creating output.

When you configure AutoCAD to plot to file, it writes all the drawing information and instructions on sheet size and pen numbers to a file that has the same name as the drawing, with the extension PLT. You can use the DOS PRINT or COPY commands to send a plot file to the plotter. By using plot files, you do not force the single CADD station that may be hooked up to your plotter to process all of the files for plotting. The plot file contains all the instructions that the plotter needs to create its plot, which ultimately speeds up transmission and creation of each plot.

Plotting to file is more than a technique to speed up your work; you also can use plot files to send graphics to other programs. For instance, if your current plot device is configured as a Hewlett-Packard plotter, you can import plot files directly into other programs that accept HPGL files, such as Microsoft Word for Windows or WordPerfect.

Paper Parameters

The Paper Size and Orientation portion of the PLOT dialog box describes the size of paper to which your drawing will be plotted. The Plot Preview feature determines whether the plot fits on the selected piece of paper. The first two radio buttons are used by AutoCAD to define the way it displays the paper sizes and current plot. Your choices are Inches or Millimeters (MM). This area also contains a button to select from other paper sizes and a graphic that displays the way your plotter is currently orienting the paper—in either landscape or portrait mode. Paper orientation is discussed in the next section.

When you click on the Size button, you see the dialog box shown in figure 7.10. This dialog box presents you with a list of default paper sizes in ANSI format, as well as the dimensions for each default size. The list can also contain a value titled MAX, which is the maximum size that may be plotted on your current device. You can select the paper size that matches what you are plotting on by clicking on the appropriate letter and pressing the OK button, or, if you need to create a special paper size, enter its dimensions in the User sections. Once you have defined this specialized size, it appears in the list box along with the default paper sizes.

Size	Width	Height		Size	Width	Height
A	10.50	8.00		USER:		
B	16.00	10.00				
C	21.00	16.00		USER1:		
D	33.00	21.00				
E	43.00	33.00		USER2:		
F	40.00	28.00				
G	90.00	11.00		USER3:		
H	143.00	28.00				
A4	11.20	7.80		USER4:		
A3	15.60	10.70				
A2	22.40	15.60				
A1	32.20	22.40		Orientation is landscape		
A0	45.90	32.20				

OK   Cancel

Figure 7.10:
The Paper Size dialog box.

The paper size that you select works with the Plot Preview feature to determine whether the area of the drawing you have selected fits on the paper. If your plot exceeds the paper, you may have to select a larger sheet, plot a different area, or change the scale you have selected for plotting.

Scale and Rotation Parameters

The Scale, Rotation, and Origin area of the PLOT dialog box determines to what size the drawing must be scaled in order to fit on the paper. The Rotation and Origin button in this area displays the dialog box shown in figure 7.11.

This dialog box enables you to rotate the plot as it is drawn on the paper, or provide an offset from the starting corner to give the plot a small buffer from the paper edge. Plot rotation is used as a paper saver, especially in plotters that have a full 36-inch width. By rotating the plot 90 degrees, you do not waste as much paper. The Origin settings are useful for printer plotters in which the plot may start over the paper perforation. By supplying an offset, you can place the plot within the main body of the paper.

Figure 7.11:
The Plot Rotation and Origin dialog box.

To actually define the scale used to put the drawing entities on your paper correctly, enter the appropriate values in the Plotted Inches=Drawing Units edit boxes. For plotting model-space areas, use a value based on typical scales for your profession. For example, architects typically plot floor or ceiling plans at scales of 1/8" = 1'-0" or 1/4" = 1'-0"; engineers plot a site plan at a scale of 1 = 20. When plotting paper-space areas, you use a value of 1=1 because you use paper-space viewports to perform the scaling for all of your model-space elements. If you want the defined plot area placed on the selected piece of paper, check the Scaled to Fit check box, which determines the appropriate scale automatically.

Plot Preview

Among all of the new features of Release 12, Plot Preview will make the greatest impact on the casual user. There are two preview options: Partial or Full. Partial Preview displays only outlines of the current plot area and the selected sheet size, as well as any rotations or origin offsets applied to the plot. Figure 7.12 shows an example of a partial plot preview. You can make a quick determination as to whether the plot will fit on the sheet. On color screens, the current sheet size is displayed in blue; the plot area is displayed in red. The small triangular icon in the corner of the plot indicates the lower left corner of the plot area. If you have selected a plot rotation, this icon displays in different locations in the plot area.

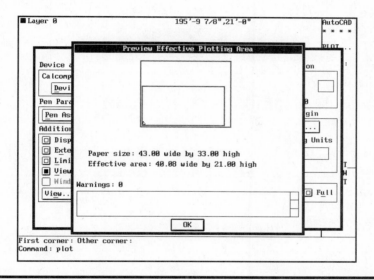

Figure 7.12:
The Partial plot preview display.

In a Full preview, AutoCAD renders the plot area in the exact way it will send it to the plotter. This means that you see the full drawing as it would appear on the paper, including any origin offsets and rotations. Figure 7.13 shows the display of a full plot preview. The dialog box at the center of the display enables you to perform limited zooms and pans within the drawing. This is similar to the ZOOM Dynamic option, which enables you to define the area of the plot preview you want to enlarge. Another useful capability of full plot previews is that of checking the drawing for hidden-line removal.

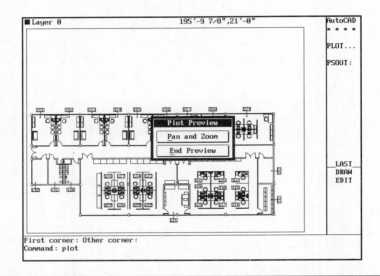

Figure 7.13:
The Fu̲ll plot preview display.

Plot-Only AutoCAD

For many years, Autodesk has been asked to produce a low-priced version of AutoCAD to be used only for producing plots. At $3000 per licensee, many firms found it hard to justify the purchase of a copy of AutoCAD strictly for plotting. Now, in Release 12, Autodesk has introduced *freeplotting*, which is a plot-only version of AutoCAD that is integrated with the normal version of the program.

The freeplotting feature is accessed by typing **ACAD -P** at the DOS command line. This runs the plot-only version of AutoCAD, in which the only commands you can execute are the PLOT command and the commands to exit AutoCAD. When you run the PLOT command, you first see the dialog box for selecting a file to plot. Once you have chosen the file, you see the normal PLOT dialog box, which enables you to set the plot parameters and send the selected file to the plotter.

Plotting Tips

Before you issue the PLOT command, remember that plotting is a time-consuming process. The following tips ensure that your drawing is set up so that it plots correctly the first time:

- Freeze any unnecessary layers—do not waste time processing layers that will not be plotted.
- Make sure that what you tell AutoCAD to plot is what you really want. If you use the PLOT command's Extents option, issue ZOOM Extents first to make sure that nothing exists "out in space" that may cause errors in the plot.
- Try and plot views instead of drawing extents or limits. It is too easy to modify the extents or limits of a drawing—views are easier to set up and maintain.
- Use the QTEXT command to accelerate check plots as it accelerates regenerations on-screen.
- Define a working text style with the TXT font, while you work on your drawing, and for check plots. (The TXT font uses the fewest entities of any AutoCAD font.) Before you create the final plot, redefine the style with a more attractive font.

 One cautionary note: AutoCAD's different fonts have letters of differing widths; a block of text with a redefined font may thus use a different amount of space.

- Use block redefinition as well as text redefinition. A dual-library system of blocks enables you to keep a simple plotted version in your drawing until the final plot. You can then substitute it for the finished, more complex version.

233

- To do check plots, turn FILLMODE off so that you do not waste time and ink if your drawing contains solids, traces, wide polylines, and so forth.

- AutoCAD does not always give you the correct plotting area for your plotter; you may have to experiment to find the correct areas. To ensure that AutoCAD has the correct information for your plotter, draw a simple rectangle (the size of the largest plot that your documentation says your plotter will do) in a new drawing, use ZOOM Extents, and then use PLOT Extents. Select MAX as the plot size, and then tell AutoCAD to plot the drawing to fit the page. Your plotter should draw all four sides of the rectangle.

- If AutoCAD does not draw the right side or top, you need to find the correct maximum size. Do this by shortening the distance to the edge that did not plot. When you find the greatest distance that plots, you can save it as a new size, called USER, in AutoCAD's plotter-configuration menu.

Plot Buffers and Spooling

The plotting process usually is the "bottleneck" of drawing production. Even raster plotters halt everything after you issue the PLOT command. This problem is solved when the plotter includes a *plotter buffer*, which is dedicated memory within the plotter itself that can store large parts of the drawing and feed the information to the plotter as quickly as the plotter accepts it. Plotter buffers can also be purchased as separate hardware components. A software-based solution is the inclusion of a *plot spooler*, which uses the computer's memory to store plot information and feed it to the plotter. Spoolers offer the further advantage of handling plot files.

Note, however, that your plotter still will not work any more quickly if you use a spooler. A drawing that is on the plotter for 20 minutes is still on the plotter for 20 minutes, whether you use a spooler or not. The spooler returns control of the computer, however, as soon as the plot file is created, which reduces the time the computer is tied up by as much as 75 percent.

A plot spooler does this and much more; it can manage a plotter that serves several AutoCAD stations, and it can *queue* (line up) plot files for unattended plotting. This is typically how plotting is handled within network environments.

Summary

In this chapter, you learned how to enter paper space and set up viewports to model space. The chapter discussed ways to take your drawing, either as paper space or model space, and plot it. This information will help you set up complex plots with ease, and to choose the plotter and plot methods to best suit your situation.

The Solid Modeling Extension

The Advanced Modeling Extension (AME) is a separate executable program that operates within AutoCAD. This option creates solid, three-dimensional geometry that can analyze technical integrity, as well as verify manufacturing processes. Solid modeling provides a desktop prototyping environment by simulating shop processes such as milling or drilling operations. This enables early detection of design error, which minimizes drawing revisions while improving quality and lowering cost.

Through Release 10, AutoCAD's three-dimensional modeling capabilities were limited to wireframes and surface models. Release 11 included new facilities for 3D solid modeling, in the form of AMElite, as well as the extra-cost option, AME Release 1. With Release 12 of AutoCAD, the internal features of AMElite have been discontinued, making solid modeling an option only. However, AME Release 2.1 and AutoCAD Release 12 provide an improved operating environment and many new features over the original release. These include:

- Revamped pull-down menus and dialog boxes
- A geometry calculator that evaluates numeric or point input
- IGES support through AMELINK, which outputs solids to other solid modeling and analysis programs
- Rendering support from AutoCAD Render
- The Region Modeler for creating and analyzing 2D regions
- New options for constructing solids: BASEPLAN defines a temporary UCS on which a *primitive* is created, CONSTRUCTION PLANE (CP) defines a temporary USC on which *points* can be created, SOLCUT enables you to divide a solid with a plane into separate solids, and SOLINTERF locates interferences between solids (handy in checking for tolerance buildup)
- Additional options for primitives creation, reduced file size, improved performance, double-precision accuracy of mathematical computations, and external application support.

Characterizing Solid versus Surface Modeling

A *surface model* is intended to model an object's visual appearance. A *solid model* not only models an object's visual appearance, it also models the aspects of an object's characteristics. A solid model stores more information about a physical object than does a surface model, and it can be used for more types of analyses. The following sections offer a comparison of AutoCAD's three types of 3D models.

Wireframes

The most elementary type of 3D model is a *wireframe* model. It is constructed of linear entities such as lines, circles, arcs, and polylines, as shown in figure 8.1. Each linear entity represents an edge of a surface.

You need at least three entities in order to represent a surface, and they must connect end-to-end to form a closed shape.

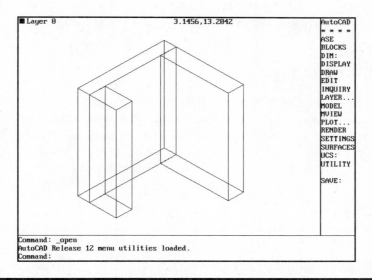

Figure 8.1:
A wireframe model.

The surfaces represented by a wireframe's edges must enclose some volume of space to accurately represent a 3D object. Each edge actually represents the intersection of two surfaces. However, AutoCAD can create wireframes that are not representative of real-world objects (edges that are not connected, for example), because AutoCAD does not store information about the relationships between entities that represent edges.

Wireframes are only skeletal models; they do not supply surface information about the arrangement of edges in the model. Because they are transparent by definition, wireframes cannot be shaded or processed for hidden-line removal.

AutoCAD has no provision for the construction of wireframe models (that is, the program has no composite objects corresponding to wireframes), although you can use blocks to group the edges of a wireframe and maintain their geometric relationships. Similarly, you can use attributes to store descriptions of surfaces or their properties.

Surface Models

A *surface* model stores not only edge information (essentially the same information as stored in a wireframe), but also information about the surfaces bounded by the edges (as shown in fig. 8.2). Depending on the system's capabilities, the model can store information about contours, surface texture, reflectivity, and other properties. Because surface entities store information about the surface, AutoCAD can process a shaded display and remove hidden lines from the view.

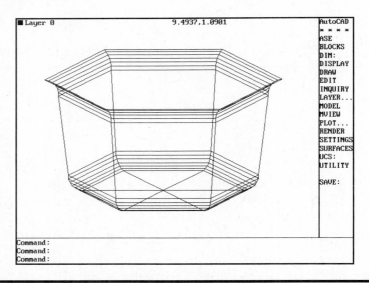

Figure 8.2:
A surface model.

You construct surface models from either *surface entities* or 3D polygon meshes by using commands such as EDGESURF or REVSURF. AutoCAD's surface-modeling facilities are based on a plane surface patch, or polygon. By placing several polygons so they share edges, you can approximate complex surfaces. However, a surface model does not store information about the nature of the space it encloses. It cannot distinguish between tangible matter and empty space.

Surface models are useful for modeling and displaying the surface geometry and appearance of real objects. By using external commands or AutoLISP programs, you can analyze surface models that are supplemented with attributes regarding various material properties and their associated behaviors.

Solid Models

A solid model not only contains information about the edges and surfaces, but it also contains the nature of the space enclosed by those surfaces (for example, whether it represents tangible matter, as well as the nature of such matter). Figure 8.3 illustrates a solid model in AutoCAD. Solids give you the most realistic representations of computer models. You can also shade or render solids, because they are opaque.

Solid models are constructed of solid primitives or entities. A *solid primitive* is a three-dimensional entity that has height, width, depth, and a closed surface. Again, only one general solid primitive is necessary for the construction of approximate models, but the modeling process is more efficient if an assortment of less general primitives is available. AutoCAD incorporates an assortment of solid primitives.

Because a solid model contains information about the nature of the space it encloses, you can use a solid model to represent more than just the appearance of a real object. A solid model can, for example, represent the static and kinematic behaviors of an object under the influence of external forces.

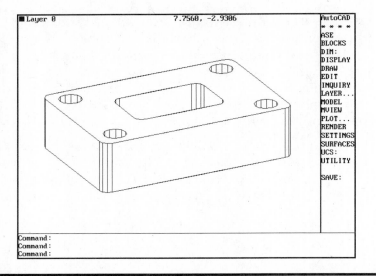

Figure 8.3:
A solid model.

NOTE Solid modeling offers many advantages to the designer. One outstanding benefit is the ability to check dimensional interferences. The SOLINTERF command finds interferences between two or more solids. Designers must account for real-world manufacturing processes by including tolerances in their design. *Tolerances* enable interchangeability between mating parts and assemblies. Designers can include tolerances in their solids to study form, fit, and function, and to eliminate ambiguity in interpreting designs.

Displaying Solid Models

Just as an AME solid object only *represents* a real object, the lines and arcs on-screen at the workstation only represent the solid object, as defined in the AutoCAD database. In fact, AME uses wireframes and surface models for the display of its solid objects.

When AME defines a solid object, the program also creates a wireframe representation of the object and displays its wireframe on-screen. In fact, AutoCAD's solid primitives are not visible because the visible wireframe contains only the edges of the surfaces that bind the solid object. In order to see these surfaces or to remove hidden lines and surfaces, you need to mesh the wireframe.

Just as AutoCAD can create a wireframe from the information that defines a solid object, it also can create and display a surface model from that information. You then can process the surface model to create a display that is shaded or whose hidden lines have been removed. The surface model derived from a solid model is subject to the same limitations as other AutoCAD surface models (for example, whether their surfaces are faceted).

Representing Solids in the Database

The database representation of solid objects differs from that of linear entities and surface entities. A solid object appears in the conventional database (whether wireframe or mesh) as a block insert on the current layer with color set to BYLAYER. The solid information, however, appears in the *Extended Entity Data (Xdata)* section of the database. Xdata contains the handles to secondary entities that consist of components (the child nodes) of the composite model, the block name of the wireframe or mesh, and the B-rep information.

Composite model data are represented in a CSG tree and denoted by an object handle. AME keeps track of these objects by their handles on a special layer called AME_FRZ.

 By destroying the handles of your objects, solid information is corrupted and/or lost forever. Never edit the contents of this layer. Leave the data intact and the layer frozen.

You can list solid information on primitives and composites by using the SOLLIST command. Refer to the Command Reference for more information on SOLLIST.

Working with Solid Entities

Just as a 2D drawing consists of 2D entities and a 3D model consists of 3D entities, a solid model consists of solid entities. Solid entities are the solid modeler's building blocks.

Solid Primitives

Solid primitives are basic solid shapes that cannot be broken down into more elementary solid shapes. In a sense, solid primitives are composite objects because they are a combination of several 2D and 3D entities. As noted in the preceding section, a solid object appears in the database as a block reference with solid-specific information stored in the Xdata section. The block reference contains lines, polylines, circles, and arcs. You can explode a solid primitive into those more elementary entities. When the solid primitive's block reference is exploded, however, the solid information is lost.

Solid primitives have regular shapes: slabs, cones, cylinders, spheres, tori, wedges, extrusions, and revolutions. Figure 8.4 shows examples of AutoCAD's solid primitives. A solid model of a real object typically consists of many solid primitives assembled like building blocks. The number of primitives you need to construct a model often depends on the kinds of primitives you choose.

AutoCAD's AME does not prevent the definition of overlapping solid primitives. Theoretically, you can model any solid by using a collection of nonoverlapping solid primitives, although it is often expedient to create the model from overlapping solids. Overlapping solids usually create a correct appearance, but they do not model material properties accurately.

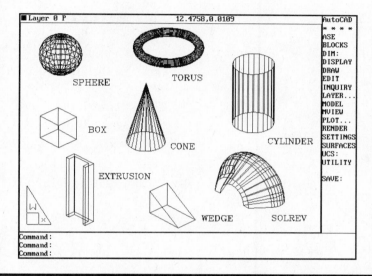

Figure 8.4:
Examples of AutoCAD's solid primitives.

Solid Commands

The AME command structure is divided into seven distinct groups: solid primitives, composite solids and regions, editing commands, inquiry commands, solid representation, drafting aids, and utility commands. Users can select commands from the pull-down menu, the tablet, or the keyboard.

Table 8.1 briefly describes the AME commands. For more detailed discussions of these commands, see the Command Reference.

Table 8.1
AME Release 2.1 Commands

Command	Type	Description
SOLAREA	Inquiry	Analyzes surface and regional areas
SOLBOX	Primitive	Creates a solid box
SOLCHAM	Editing	Creates a chamfer or beveled edge
SOLCHP	Editing	Changes properties of a solid
SOLCONE	Primitive	Creates a solid cone
SOLCUT	Editing	Divides solids across a plane
SOLCYL	Primitive	Creates a solid cylinder
SOLEXT	Primitive	Extrudes 2D objects into 3D solids
SOLFEAT	Drafting Aid	Creates a 2D feature from a 3D face
SOLFILL	Editing	Creates a fillet or rounded edge
SOLIDIFY	Primitive	Creates solids from 2D and 3D objects
SOLIN	Utility	Imports AutoSolid files
SOLINT	Composite	Creates solids from intersecting solids
SOLINTERF	Inquiry	Calculates interference between solids
SOLLIST	Inquiry	Displays solid data information
DDSOLMASSP/ SOLMASSP	Inquiry	Calculates mass properties
DDSOLMAT/ SOLMAT	Utility	Defines solid material type
SOLMESH	Representation	Displays a meshed solid or region

Command	Type	Description
SOLMOVE	Editing	Moves or rotates a solid or region
SOLOUT	Utility	Exports solids into AutoSolid
SOLPROF	Drafting Aid	Creates 2D profile view of a solid
SOLPURGE	Utility	Removes entities from solid files
SOLREV	Primitive	Creates a revolving solid
SOLSECT	Drafting Aid	Creates a cross-section of a solid
SOLSEP	Composite	Separates composite solids into component primitives
SOLSPHERE	Primitive	Creates a solid sphere
SOLSUB	Composite	Creates solids by subtracting solids
SOLTORUS	Primitive	Creates a solid torus (donut)
SOLUCS	Utility	Aligns UCS to a solid face or edge
SOLUNION	Composite	Creates solids from a union of solids
SOLVAR	Utility	Defines AME system-variable values
SOLWEDGE	Primitive	Creates a solid wedge
SOLWIRE	Representation	Displays a wireframe solid or region

Understanding the Structure of Solid Objects

Solid modelers use two general techniques of solid modeling: Constructive Solid Geometry (CSG) and Boundary Representation (B-rep). AutoCAD AME is based on a combination of these two techniques and the Parts and Assembly Description Language (PADL), which was developed at the University of Rochester, New York. The following sections briefly describe these modeling techniques.

Constructive Solid Geometry (CSG)

Constructive Solid Geometry (CSG) refers to the technique of assembling complex solid objects from simpler ones, which may be primitives or other complex solids. In AutoCAD terminology, you refer to any solid other than a solid primitive as a *composite solid*, which comprises member solids that may be primitives or other composites. In AutoCAD's implementation, CSG can describe the structure of a solid object, but not its visual appearance. Figure 8.5 illustrates the concept of CSG information.

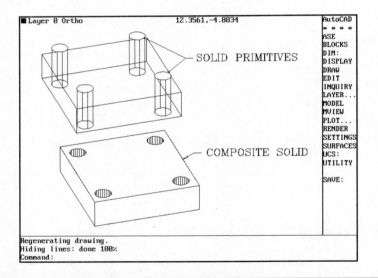

Figure 8.5:
Solid primitives and a composite solid.

Using CSG, you can describe a composite-solid object by listing its member solids and the relationships between those solids. To automate the tasks of forming and manipulating solid objects, you can use mathematical descriptions of the objects and their relationships.

A composite solid is described through a data structure called the *CSG tree*, an example of which is shown in figure 8.6. The CSG tree is a form of the binary tree used in many database management systems to index data. The tree begins with a single node—the root—which represents the top-level composite solid. That node is linked to two other nodes, which represent the two solids that make up the top-level solid. Each node, in turn, is linked to two lower-level nodes or solids. At the bottom of the tree are the leaves, which represent solid primitives. The relationships between the member solids are binary in nature: two member solids combine to form the next higher-level solid.

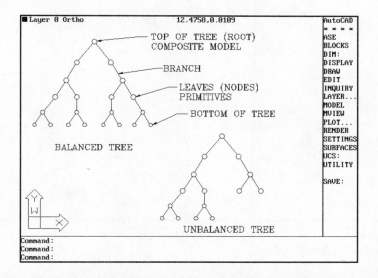

Figure 8.6:
The CSG tree data structure.

The CSG tree of a given solid object essentially describes the volume of space-containing material that belongs to the solid. From this description of the solid object, AutoCAD and AME can determine how to display, analyze, and manipulate the solid.

Boundary Representation (B-rep)

AutoCAD uses a second solid-modeling technique, Boundary Representation (B-rep) to represent the appearance of solid objects. When a solid (whether a primitive or a composite) is defined, and AME calculates its boundaries (the surfaces that separate its "matter" from AutoCAD's "ether") by displaying the message, boundary evaluation begins. AME uses the B-rep information to construct the screen display. Figure 8.7 illustrates the concept of B-rep information.

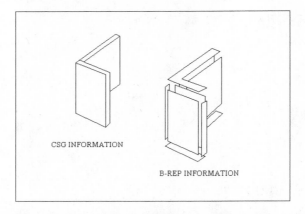

CSG INFORMATION

B-REP INFORMATION

Figure 8.7:
B-rep information describing surfaces.

Every time you create a solid, additional B-rep information is added to the drawing. If you combine two slabs to form an angle iron, for example, AutoCAD generates B-rep information for each slab and for the combination of the two. Because B-rep information is attached to every solid, AME can display the composite solid or its member solids at any time.

Composite Solids

As mentioned earlier, composite solids are solids composed of solid primitives or other composite solids. Figure 8.8 illustrates the various methods of creating composite solids. The lower-level solids that make up a composite solid are called *member solids* or *component solids*. Only the top-level component solid usually is visible on-screen.

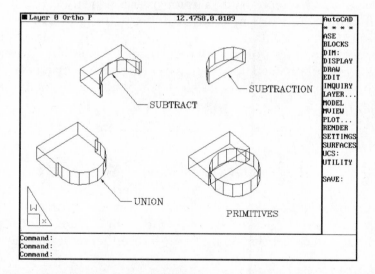

Figure 8.8:
Composite solids constructed with Boolean operations.

A composite solid appears in the drawing database as a block reference and is treated as a single object. The structure of a composite solid is described in a CSG tree that is part of the block reference.

Boolean Operations

AutoCAD uses Boolean operations to combine solid objects into more complex solid objects. AutoCAD's Boolean operations are essentially the same as the Boolean operations of logic and sets. AutoCAD uses three basic Boolean operations: union, subtraction, and intersection. The following sections describe these operations.

Union

The *union* of two solids is the volume of space that belongs to one member or the other. A union is similar to the logical OR. If the two members of a solid created with a union overlap, the union encloses a smaller volume than the sum of the volumes of the two-member solids. If the two-member solids do not overlap, the union encloses a volume equal to the sum of the volumes of the two-member solids. The member solids of a union need not overlap or be immediately adjacent. A union, however, is treated as a single object, whether or not the member solids overlap.

Subtraction

The *subtraction* of two solids encloses the space of the first solid but not the space of the second solid. The two-member solids of a subtraction must overlap. A solid cannot be subtracted from a solid that it does not overlap; otherwise, the result is a null solid, which AutoCAD does not allow. If two solids overlap, you can subtract either one from the other.

Intersection

The *intersection* of two solids encloses the space that is common to both solids. An intersection is similar to a logical AND. The two-member solids of an intersection must overlap. An intersection of two non-overlapping solids is a null solid, which AutoCAD does not allow.

The SOLSEP command separates a composite solid into its individual components. For more information about the SOLSEP command, see the Command Reference.

Building Models with Solids

Constructing solid models is a complex, changing process. The following section is a synopsis (not a tutorial) of AME.

Setting Up Models

Sometimes producing solid models can be as simple as loading the program and creating the objects. However, depending upon your application, you may want to change the values of the AME system variables from their default settings. You can make changes either from the command line or through the AME System Variables dialog box. Table 8.2 summarizes the AME system variables.

Table 8.2
AME System Variables

Variable Name	Type	Initial Value	Possible Value	Description
SOLAMECOMP	String	AME2	AME1,AME2	Tells AME to prompt with AME R1 or AME R2 syntax.
SOLAMEVER	String	R2.1	(Read-Only)	Lists the AME release number; unlike SOLAMECOMP, this cannot be changed.

continues

253

Table 8.2
Continued

Variable Name	Type	Initial Value	Possible Value	Description
SOLAREAU	String	sq cm	Area units	Determines the units used to calculate a solid area. See ACAD.UNT file for a list of all units.
SOLAXCOL	Integer	3	1 through 255	Sets the Motion Coordinate System icon's color. Valid values are display-dependent.
SOLDECOMP	String	X	X,Y,Z	The direction of ray projection used in mass property calculations.
SOLDELENT	Integer	3	1,2,3	Determines whether selected 2D entities are retained after they are solidified, extruded, or revolved.
SOLDISPLAY	String	WIRE	WIRE,MESH	Sets the default display for new solids.

Variable Name	Type	Initial Value	Possible Value	Description
SOLHANGLE	Real	45.00	A real number	Sets the hatch-pattern angle for new region and solid section representation.
SOLHPAT	String	U	Hatch patterns	Sets the hatch pattern for new region and solid representations. See ACAD.PAT for a list of valid patterns.
SOLHSIZE	Real	1.00	A (+) real no.	Sets the hatch-pattern scale for new region and solid section representations.
SOLLENGTH	String	cm	Length units	Sets the unit of measure used in solid length calculations.
SOLMASS	String	gm	Mass units	Sets the unit of measure used in solid mass property calculations.
SOLMATCURR	String	MILD_STEEL	(Read-Only)	Lists the current solid mass material.

continues

Table 8.2
Continued

Variable Name	Type	Initial Value	Possible Value	Description
SOLPAGELEN	Integer	25	0 through 1000	Sets the length of the text screen page used by SOLLIST, SOLMASSP, and SOLMAT commands.
SOLRENDER	String	CSG	CSG,UNIFORM	Sets the render-color method for new solids.
SOLSECTYPE	Integer	1	1,2,3	Determines whether SOLSECT creates a wireframe, polyline, or region.
SOLSERVMSG	Integer	3	0,1,2,3	Sets the level of command-line reporting in solid computations.
SOLSOLIDIFY	Integer	3	1,2,3	Sets the level of prompting for automatic solid conver-sion with the SOLIDIFY command.

Variable Name	Type	Initial Value	Possible Value	Description
SOLSUBDIV	Integer	3	1 through 8	Sets the accuracy level of SOLMASSP mass-property calculations.
SOLUPGRADE	Integer	0	0,1	Determines whether or not single precision AME R1 solids should be converted to double precision AME R2 solids.
SOLVOLUME	String	cu cm	Volume units	Sets the volumn unit of measure for mass property calculations. See ACAD.UNT for valid values.
SOLWDENS	Integer	1	1 through 12	Sets the wire density of new wireframe representations of solids and regions.

Selecting the Coordinate System

AutoCAD creates drawing entities—2D, 3D, and solid—in the X,Y construction plane of the current coordinate system (either the World Coordinate System or User Coordinate System). You can create solids in a single coordinate system and rotate them to the desired orientation, or you can create solids in a UCS so that reorientation is not required. AutoCAD drawing entities, solids included, are not linked to the coordinate system in which they were created. Whether a solid is created in one coordinate system and rotated, or created in a coordinate system that does not require reorientation, the coordinate system has no effect on the structure of the model.

> **TIP** An easy method of determining positive axis coordination (either WCS or UCS) is by using the right-hand rule. As represented in figure 8.9, the thumb points in the positive X-axis direction, the index finger points in the positive Y-axis direction, and the middle finger points in the positive Z-axis direction. The last two fingers are curled; they represent positive axis rotation or angle rotation.

AutoCAD creates solids with a characteristic profile in the X,Y plane—elevation equaling zero. You can take various approaches to position a solid at the correct elevation. A UCS can be defined so that the solid is located with the characteristic profile at elevation zero, or a UCS can be defined so that its origin coincides with the WCS or some other coordinate system, and its elevation is set with the ELEV command. Otherwise, you can create the solid at one elevation and move it to the desired elevation.

Creating Solid Primitives

The solid-modeling process begins with the creation of solid primitives, assuming that a suitable coordinate system has been defined. You can create solid primitives any time, so you do not need to begin the modeling process by immediately creating all of the solid primitives required for the model.

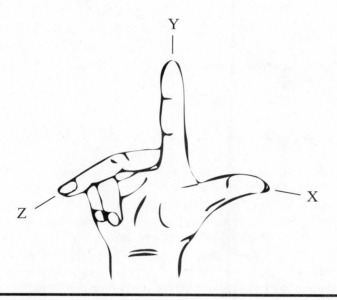

Figure 8.9
The right-hand rule.

You can save time by creating all of the solid primitives required for a given composite solid before you actually create the composite. A composite solid can be visualized if all its primitives are displayed on-screen, even though the composite has not actually been formed.

Forming Composite Solids

As described earlier, you can form composite solids from solid primitives and other composite solids by using the Boolean commands

SOLINT, SOLSUB, and SOLUNION, and the solid-modification commands SOLFILL and SOLCHAM. Most composite solids can be formed in various sequences. You can apply the Boolean operation commands to successive pairs of objects or to entire groups of objects.

If Boolean operation commands are applied to successive pairs of solid objects, the sequence in which they are applied determines the structure of the CSG tree. If you apply a Boolean command to a group of objects, AME applies the Boolean operation repeatedly to pairs of solid objects—and so determines the structure of the CSG tree.

NOTE A CSG tree can be balanced or unbalanced (see fig. 8.6). In a *balanced tree*, all paths from the root to a leaf are the same distance. In an *unbalanced tree*, some paths are longer than others; that is, the depth of the tree is greater in some branches. An unbalanced tree is a less efficient data structure than a balanced one. If AME selects the sequence in which it combines the solids selected for a Boolean operation command, it attempts to create a balanced tree. The user can apply the same strategy by combining primitives into pairs, then the pairs into pairs of pairs, and so on, rather than repeatedly adding single primitives to a composite object.

Although most composite solids can be formed in several different ways, the sequence in which Boolean operations are applied to a given set of primitives affects the final appearance of the composite solid. The key to forming composite solids quickly and efficiently is to mentally break down the desired shape into the primitives available under AME. When the desired shape is visualized as a collection of primitive shapes, it is a straightforward task to build the shape on-screen.

Most shapes can be created from a large number of simple primitives and a large number of Boolean operations, or from a smaller number of more complex primitives (extrusions) and a smaller number of Boolean operations. There are advantages to both approaches. A model built from a few extrusions may be more compact, but the model built from many simple primitives is easier to edit. You often may find it appropriate to develop the model with the simpler primitives and then to convert the final model to objects built primarily from extrusions, by using AME's SOLSECT command to generate the characteristic profile.

Manipulating Solids

You can manipulate solids—that is, translate, rotate, scale, mirror, array, and copy them—by using the normal AutoCAD commands MOVE, ROTATE, SCALE, MIRROR, ARRAY, and COPY. These commands, however, generally manipulate objects in the X,Y plane of the current UCS. In some cases, you can specify 3D displacements with precision input (keyboard input of coordinates), but if you want to input the displacements graphically, you first must define and select an appropriate UCS.

On the other hand, you can use the AME SOLMOVE command to manipulate solids three-dimensionally. This command accepts three-dimensional motion description codes in relation to a temporary coordinate system, called the Motion Coordinate System (MCS). AME displays a 3D icon to show the orientation of the MCS. You can orient and position the MCS by using the SOLMOVE command's options. Figure 8.10 shows the screen as it appears during the SOLMOVE command.

Editing Primitives

You can use normal AutoCAD commands to perform a limited amount of editing on primitives, such as erasing, scaling, and mirroring. These commands, however, generally operate in the X,Y orientation of the current UCS. The SCALE command, for example, applies the same scale factor in the Z direction as in the X and Y directions. You can also use the CHPROP command to change a solid primitive's color or layer, but not its linetype.

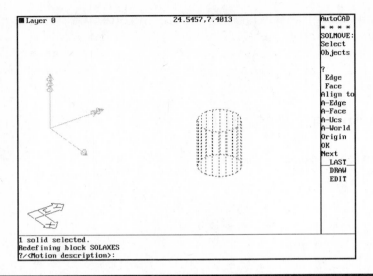

Figure 8.10:
The SOLMOVE command displays the Motion Control System icon.

Solid properties can be changed with the AME SOLCHP command. This command can change the color, size, move the solid, delete it, make an instance (copy), and replace it. For more information on SOLCHP, see the Command Reference.

Editing Composite Solids

Composite solids can be erased, moved, copied, mirrored, scaled, and rotated with normal AutoCAD commands. You cannot use normal AutoCAD commands, however, to edit the member solids of a composite solid unless the solid is decomposed into primitives and then reconstructed after the member solids are edited. The limitations regarding the editing of primitive solids with normal AutoCAD commands apply also to composite solids.

You can use the SOLCHP command to edit the member solids of a composite solid without decomposing it into primitives. SOLCHP makes all primitives temporarily visible for editing. Primitives can be moved, copied, deleted, replaced, scaled independently in all three axes, and assigned a new color. SOLCHP does not display the structure of the CSG tree or limit access to the primitives based on the structure of the CSG tree. Figure 8.11 illustrates the appearance of a composite solid when the SOLCHP command is active.

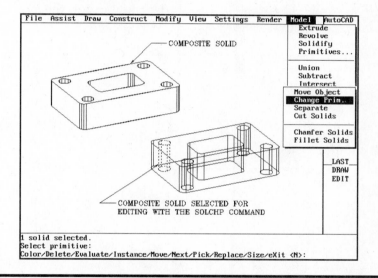

Figure 8.11:
A composite solid with SOLCHP inactive versus active.

Viewing Solid Models

All of AutoCAD's normal viewing commands apply to solid models, as well as to 3D surface models and 2D drawings. Solids are normally created with a wireframe representation and thus cannot be shaded or processed to remove hidden lines. You must use the SOLMESH command to mesh a solid before you can process the object to produce an opaque display. Meshing creates a surface representation of the solid, which can be processed by the HIDE and SHADE commands.

You can view solids in tiled viewports or MVIEW (paper space) viewports, as shown in figure 8.12. In either case, if you rotate the viewing direction, you do not change the model's orientation with respect to the WCS. By viewing a solid in multiple viewports, you can more easily visualize the desired model and monitor the modeling process.

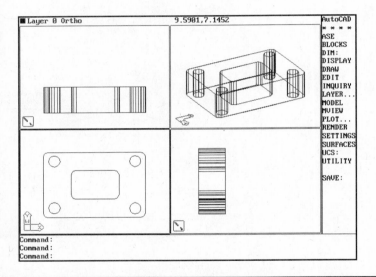

Figure 8.12:
A solid model from different viewpoints.

Creating Features, Sections, and Profiles

AME provides the designer with drafting utilities to transfer solids information to production drawings. Three such utilities are features, sections, and profiles.

AME includes commands that can generate cross-sections and profile views of solid objects, as well as commands that can copy the edges and faces of solid objects. You can use these capabilities to generate 2D drawings and 3D wireframe and surface models from solid models.

Sections, profiles, edges, and faces made from solids are not linked to the solids from which they are generated. If the original solid is edited after a section is taken, for example, the section is not updated to reflect the changes in the solid. The blocks generated with these commands can be moved away from the original solid and used to develop 2D drawings, or left in place and viewed in paper-space viewports with the aid of the VPLAYER command.

2D features, sections, and profiles created by AME are not always complete 2D entities as created by AutoCAD (LINES, ARCS, CIRCLES, and so on.). Points generated from these entities are sometimes not parallel to the same UCS, and the AutoLisp program PROJECT does not help much in alleviating this problem. Dimensioning these entities is a drafting nightmare. Therefore, drawings produced by using these entities do not always produce the best geometry to use as a production drawing. However, these entities are useful for visualizing and defining views that need to be drafted.

By leaving the blocks in place and controlling visibility with layers, you provide yourself with a reminder to generate new sections, profiles, and auxiliary views when the original solid is changed.

The following sections describe the AME commands that enable you to create cross-sections and profile views of solids. For more information on these commands, see the Command Reference.

SOLSECT

The SOLSECT command generates a cross-section from the intersection of the selected solids with the X,Y plane of the current UCS (or WCS). You must define and select the UCS before you issue the SOLSECT command. AME generates the cross-section as a block and leaves it in position, highlighted. After the screen is refreshed, however, the section is not highlighted and it is generally not apparent. You can use the Last option to select the section and move it into a location suitable for use as a detail. You also can select the section with the Window or Crossing options. SOLSECT works in model space and creates the section in model space. Figure 8.13 shows a section created with SOLSECT.

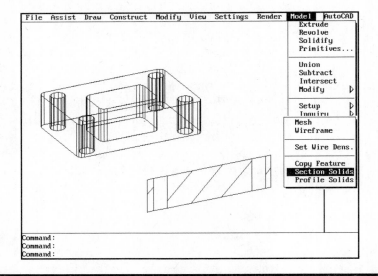

Figure 8.13:
SOLSECT generates a solid's cross-section.

SOLPROF

SOLPROF generates a profile of a solid from the current viewing direction. This profile is a 3D shape, consisting of linear entities that define the edges of the selected solids and silhouettes of curved surfaces. AME separates hidden lines as an option, but hidden-line views are correct only for the viewing direction that was current when the profile was generated. The profile is generated as a block and can be moved away from the original solid.

Alternatively, you can turn off the layer containing the original solid, to display the profile by itself. Figure 8.14 shows a profile created with SOLPROF.

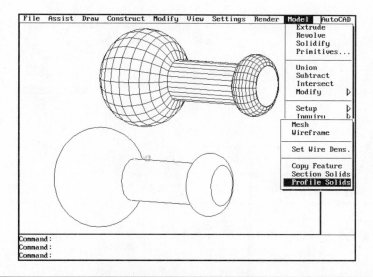

Figure 8.14:
A profile created by SOLPROF.

SOLFEAT

SOLFEAT copies an edge or a face of a solid as a block consisting of lines, circles, arcs, and polylines, as required. The block remains in place, highlighted until the screen is refreshed. Copies of edges and faces created in this way can be used as the basis of 2D auxiliary views of the solid object. Figure 8.15 illustrates the use of SOLFEAT to copy a face of a solid.

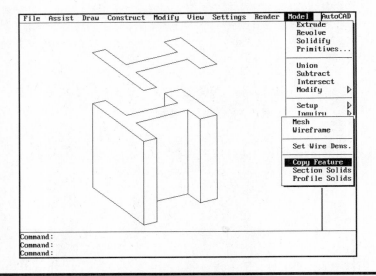

Figure 8.15:
SOLFEAT copies edges and faces of solid objects.

Presenting Solid Models in Multiple Views

For presentation purposes, a solid model can usually be effectively displayed from a single viewing direction. If you are using the model as the basis of a set of drawings, you generally should display it in several different orientations (as shown in fig. 8.12). To arrange the orientations, leave the model itself in a single position in the WCS, and then define the viewports required to display the model as a series of conventional drawing views.

For editing purposes, you can define multiple views by setting TILEMODE 1 or 0, as desired. For plots, define the multiple views in paper space (with TILEMODE set to 0) to plot several views in a single drawing. Use the V PLAYER command to control the layer visibility of paper-space viewports independently.

Adding Drawing References

When you use solid models for design documentation rather than presentations, you must supplement the models with drawing reference symbols, such as titles, title blocks, notes, dimensions, feature-control symbols, section marks, and hatch patterns. The solid objects of a solid model can be viewed from any viewing direction because they are three-dimensional. Drawing reference symbols, however, are inherently two-dimensional and are appropriate only in a single view.

AutoCAD does not distinguish between entities used for drawing reference symboling and entities used for model construction. Thus, a line of text or a dimension is visible in all views, oriented as it was created. If such entities are added directly to the solid model in various views, but on a single layer, the symbols tend to obscure each other. They also tend to obscure the model for editing.

If reference symbols must be attached directly to the model, you can place them on layers that can be controlled with the VPLAYER command, enabling them to be visible only in the appropriate view.

Notes, borders, title blocks, and titles are best created in paper space, as a 2D overlay, after the model is essentially complete, as shown in figure 8.16. You then can turn off the reference symboling by re-entering model space for subsequent editing of the model.

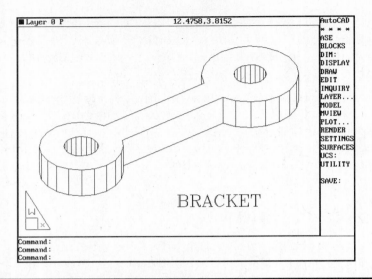

Figure 8.16:
Reference symboling in paper space.

You also can add reference symboling to the model by using external references. The actual drawing file that is finally plotted contains only reference symboling, and the model is attached as an external reference. This method ensures that changes made to the model are reflected (but not updated) in the drawing files where the model is visible.

Building Complex Solid Models with Blocks and Xrefs

Solid-model drawing files tend to become very large as the model becomes more complex. You can use blocks and xrefs to control the size of individual drawing files. In addition, many components tend to occur in multiples and patterns. To minimize the size of the drawing's database, you should model such components with block references rather than with copies of the first item. By using block references for solid models of components, you also ensure that changes to a component are propagated throughout the drawing.

You can construct a complex solid model with xrefs. By modeling each component of an assembly in a separate file, you can minimize the file's size and the system's response time during the modeling process. When the individual components are modeled, you can attach them to a subassembly drawing file as xrefs. The subassembly drawing files can in turn be attached to assembly files, and the assembly files can in turn be attached to a final assembly file, as shown in figure 8.17. A map of the nested external references is a graphical description of the bill of materials—the product structure. The individual component model files should be constructed so that the origin of the file corresponds to a natural "handle" for the component in the other files.

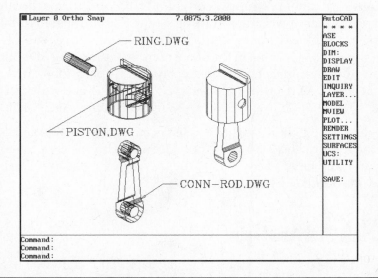

Figure 8.17:
Complex solid models constructed in assembly files.

Use insertion point 0,0,0 for each component when attaching xrefs. This is a common point of reference for all files comprised in a large, complex assembly file. New drawing files can be easily be created by overlaying xrefs for fit references, and later be detached to archive as a single file. You can keep one single file for a master assembly, and build detail models off of this master file.

Region Modeler

The Region Modeler command set, a subset of AME, enables you to create closed 2D areas by combining several entities into a single entity. This powerful new feature can analyze regions such as its area, centroid, moments of inertia, products of inertia, and radii of gyration.

Although AME does not supply commands that specifically create region primitives, it solidifies existing AutoCAD entities such as 2D polylines and circles by using the SOLIDIFY command. Creating composite regions is done in the same manner as creating 3D solids by using the union, subtract, and intersect Boolean operations. After you create a region, AME cross-hatches it with the settings defined in the SOLHPAT, SOLHSIZE, and SOLHANGLE variables (see fig. 8.18).

Regions are closed 2D areas that consist of *outer loops* (the outer boundary of the region) and *inner loops* (holes). These entities are planar (lie on one plane), and have a zero Z-axis thickness. However, they can be located or oriented anywhere in the WCS.

Materials and Analysis

Solid Modeling provides the engineer a particular insight into the problems of design. AME's strength lies in its powerful analyzing tools to provide an understanding of material relationships and characteristics.

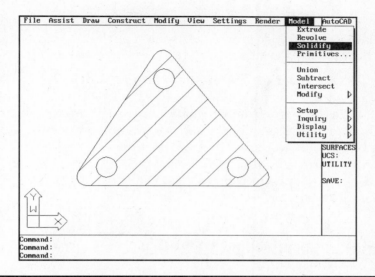

Figure 8.18:
A composite region.

Properties of Real Materials

Mass properties are characteristics of real matter such as density, thermal conductivity, elasticity, and electrical conductivity. These properties determine the behavior of real materials in response to external influences such as heat, physical force, and electrical potential. AutoCAD's solid objects, on the other hand, are mathematical constructs with no actual physical properties, and they exhibit no behavior in response to the external influences that affect real objects.

As an analyst, you usually want to predict a real object's behavior in response to external influences. This objective can be accomplished mathematically, with the use of scale models and real prototypes. One reason for working with solid models is that they are generally easier and more economical to construct than real models. In order to model the behavior of real objects, however, solid models must incorporate the properties of real materials.

Properties such as density and elasticity are unit properties. For example, a sheet of a given steel alloy has the same density and modulus of elasticity as the ingot from which it was rolled. Properties such as mass and weight are functions of volume and unit properties. Real objects also exhibit properties that are functions of unit properties, volume, and form (a hollow tube, for instance, is stiffer than a solid rod of the same weight per unit length). AME solid objects can store this type of information.

Material Properties in AME Solids

AME stores material properties in solid objects by using an indexing system. Each object incorporates a data field that stores the name of a material, which is described in detail in a material file. When AME creates a solid object, it assigns the default material to the object in the same way that it assigns a default layer assignment or color. Analysis commands that require material properties use the material name to look up the properties. AutoCAD includes a standard material file, ACAD.MAT, to describe a number of commonly used materials.

The following properties are included for each material listed in the material file:

- Density
- Young's modulus
- Poisson's ratio
- Yield strength
- Ultimate tensile strength
- Thermal conductivity
- Coefficient of linear expansion
- Specific heat

All property values are defined at a temperature of 25 degrees Centigrade. Properties are defined with a single set of values but can be used in SI, English, or CGS units.

> **NOTE** Notice that the material file lists only selected properties. Materials whose properties vary with direction, such as composites, cannot be modeled accurately. Concrete, for example, is a common material that cannot be described accurately in this format because concrete's tensile strength differs substantially from its compressive strength.

Material Definitions

You can define new materials by adding entries in the ACAD.MAT file, or by creating and loading another material file. The easiest method of defining new materials is by the Material Properties dialog box (see fig. 8.19). New materials can be defined or edited by name, description, properties, and values.

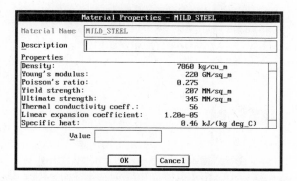

Figure 8.19:
Material Properties dialog box.

Material files are managed with the SOLMAT command, which enables you to change a material assignment, edit a material's definition, list a material's property values, load a material file, remove a material, and set the default material.

Analysis of Solid Mass Properties

The principal analysis command in AME is the SOLMASSP command. This command calculates and lists mass properties of one or more solid objects in reference to the current UCS. SOLMASSP calculates the following properties:

- Total mass
- Volume
- Bounding box
- Centroid
- Moments of inertia
- Products of inertia
- Radii of gyration
- Principal moments

You also can use the SOLMASSP command to write the calculated properties to an external data file.

The Ray-Firing Technique

AME uses a *ray-firing* technique to calculate mass properties in reference to an arbitrary coordinate system. To implement this technique, AME divides a box enclosing the selected solid or set of solids into a preset number of subdivisions. For each subdivision, AME "fires" a ray or vector along a preset direction, and determines whether the ray intersects the solid. With this technique, AME can determine the extent of the solid in relation to an arbitrary coordinate system, which is the current UCS. The method is statistical in nature, and admittedly does not provide exact results.

You can use AME system variables to control the accuracy of the ray-firing algorithm. A larger number of subdivisions increases the accuracy of the calculations, at the expense of time. Shapes with small details and curved surfaces should be analyzed with a large number of subdivisions to ensure that the details are detected and accounted for in the calculations. The direction in which rays are fired—the *decomposition direction*—also can affect the accuracy of the calculations and can be controlled with a system variable setting. Both direction and divisions can be set in the Mass Properties dialog box (see fig. 8.20). The decomposition direction should be perpendicular to the smallest cross-section of the object.

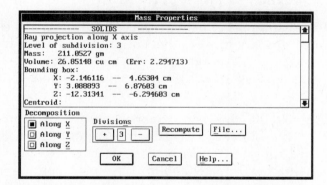

Figure 8.20:
Mass Properties dialog box.

Error Estimates

Because of the statistical nature of AME's ray-firing technique, errors are inherent in the mass-property calculations. The SOLMASSP command lists an error estimate for the volume, centroid location, moments of inertia, and products of inertia calculations. Although error estimates are not exact, high error estimates indicate that the calculations should be repeated with higher subdivision levels or a different decomposition direction.

Rendering Solid Models

Shading and rendering solid models can communicate design processes by enhancing visualization. The following section explains the options AME offers.

Wireframe versus Mesh Representation

AutoCAD can display solids in two forms: wireframe and mesh. *Wireframes* are transparent; they cannot be processed to produce opaque displays of the model. *Meshes* are surfaces, and can be processed to produce an opaque display, either shaded or with hidden lines removed.

Although AutoCAD's wireframes cannot be processed to remove hidden lines or to produce a shaded display, AutoCAD enhances wireframes to display the shapes of the surfaces represented by the edges. When AutoCAD creates a solid, it calculates contour lines for each surface at intervals that are determined by system variable settings. These contour lines are called *tessellation lines*, which are not part of the solid object or of its surface. Tessellation lines are used as devices to indicate the shape of the surface and to reflect the true shape of the surface where they are drawn. That is, the tessellation lines on the surface of a sphere are arcs.

The mesh representation of a solid is a polyface mesh that approximates the shape of the solid's surface. It is characteristic of AutoCAD's polyface mesh that all edges consist of straight-line segments and that all surfaces are faceted. Thus, each individual face in the mesh is a plane surface. The advantage of displaying the mesh representation is that it can be processed to produce an opaque display. After the mesh representation is created, the display of a solid object can be switched between the wireframe and mesh modes without additional calculations.

Meshed Solids

The SOLMESH command generates a polyface-mesh representation of a selected object. It hides the wireframe representation and displays the solid as polyface entities. The SOLWDENS variable controls the density of the displayed mesh. If you use a Boolean operation to combine two meshed solids to form a composite solid, the resulting solid is displayed in wireframe form—a mesh representation is not created automatically. You must use SOLMESH to mesh the composite solid.

Hidden-Line Removal

The HIDE command produces an opaque display of the drawing or model. It removes entities and parts of entities that are not visible from the current viewpoint. AutoCAD considers surface entities—variants of polyfaces and polyface meshes—as opaque surfaces. HIDE also processes some closed 2D entities and 2D entities with nonzero thickness as surfaces. HIDE does not consider areas enclosed by lines and arcs to be opaque surfaces. This limitation applies to the lines and arcs that make up the tessellation lines of wireframe representations of solid objects. Thus, solids displayed in wireframe form remain transparent when processed with HIDE.

If a display's hidden lines have been removed, that display is temporary. Any command that causes regeneration of the drawing restores it to a transparent display. When you remove the display's hidden lines, the transparent wireframe seems less ambiguous.

Shaded Displays

The SHADE command produces a simple shaded rendering of a 3D drawing. It basically produces an image that removes hidden lines and displays the faces in their original color with a single direct light source (no shadows). This shading method is similar to the QUICKSHADE command in AutoShade 2.0.

Four different kinds of shading are available with the SHADE command. They are determined by the SHADEDGE system variables, as described in table 8.3.

Table 8.3
SHADEDGE Settings

SHADEDGE Setting	Type of Shaded Rendering
0	Shaded faces, no edge highlighting. Used with 256-color displays.
1	Shaded faces, edges highlighted in the background color. Used with 256-color displays.
2	Simulated hidden-line rendering. Works with any display.
3	Faces are not shaded, but are drawn in their original color. AutoCAD hides hidden faces and traces their visible edges in the background color. Works on any display.

The quality of the shaded image depends on the number of colors available. Graphics boards that can display 256 or more colors produce simulated lighting effects; less than 256 colors produce color-filled renderings without lighting effects.

The SHADE command considers surfaces and 2D entities with nonzero thickness to be opaque. Solids displayed in wireframe form are not considered opaque and remain transparent after processing. Solids displayed in mesh form are considered opaque and are shaded.

The shaded image is only temporary, and it is replaced with the original drawing at regeneration. However, you can make a slide view with the MSLIDE command. This is a handy means of compiling a progression of images for checking the progress of a model.

The Render Module

A new feature with Release 12 is a built-in, three-dimensional rendering module called Render. With this rendering utility, you can control the appearance of your models with lighting, surface color, and features such as *reflection*. *Rendering* helps you to visualize designs more accurately by seeing actual surfaces instead of line entities. Also, it can verify surface parameters and eliminate ambiguities in communicating design specifications.

Features of AutoCAD Render include adding variable light sources to the drawing, such as ambient, distant, and point lighting; defining and saving views and scenes; and altering surface finishes and colors. You can change the reflective quality of your surfaces, making them either dull or shiny. In fact, you can give your surfaces a wide range of finishes, from smooth metallic to rough stone.

After modeling your entities, you begin the rendering process by defining your view with the DVIEW command. (See the Command Reference.) Select and save the view or views you want to render, and add lights to your view. Proper lighting determines the realistic quality of your objects and surfaces by giving them a three-dimensional appearance. You add lights through the pull-down menu's dialog box.

By adjusting the type, location, and intensity, you can define your *scene*, which is a combination of views, lights, and surface-finish definitions that you can save as one entity. To finalize the scene, you define the characteristics of your object surfaces in the Finishes dialog box. You can define or refine the color from the RGB or HLS slider bars, and adjust the settings that control ambient, diffuse, specular, and roughness.

When your scene is complete, you are ready to render. For a fast preview of your scene, select the QUICK RENDER option from the Rendering Preferences dialog box and then choose RENDER from the pulldown menu. If you are satisfied with your scene or would like to see more detail, generate a full rendering by changing the option in the dialog box to FULL RENDER.

Rendering is a process of adjustment. However, many options of this process and in using AutoCAD Render go beyond the scope of this book. For more information on these options, see the *AutoCAD Render Reference Manual*.

Plotting Solid Models

Isolated orthographic views of solid models can be confusing. If you want to plot a solid model in a single view, it should be off-axis, such as a true isometric or axonometric view. However, you should not rotate the model itself to achieve an off-axis view. Instead, define a UCS so a plan view in that UCS produces the desired apparent orientation of the model. There is no rule for selecting the "best" viewing direction.

An effective technique for determining the best view of a solid object is to use the DVIEW command to rotate the viewpoint, and then define and save a UCS that is aligned with that view.

Plotting solid models can enhance the understanding associated with constructing the model. Plots can be used for design reviews or for presentations. The following sections discuss the options and problems of plotting solid models.

Wireframe Plots

Wireframe plots are transparent; that is, all of the solid object's edges are visible. Wireframe plots tend to be ambiguous, but they illustrate surface contours accurately with tessellation lines. By default, AutoCAD plots drawings without removing hidden lines. Also, AutoCAD plots unmeshed solid objects in wireframe form.

Plots with Hidden Lines Removed

You can instruct AutoCAD to remove hidden lines during plotting. Note that surfaces and entities with nonzero thicknesses are plotted as opaque surfaces, and hidden lines are removed. You must mesh solids before plotting, however, in order to produce such a plot. This type of plot generally is less ambiguous than a wireframe plot.

Traditional engineering drawings generally show hidden lines in orthographic views, but not in isometric or pictorial views. In orthographic views, hidden lines appear as dashed lines. AutoCAD has no provision for displaying hidden lines in a hidden linetype. You can use the SOLPROF command, however, to construct profiles of solid objects with visible lines on one layer and hidden lines on another.

You can set the layer that contains the hidden lines to display hidden lines in the Hidden linetype. If the SOLPROF command is applied in several principal views, the VPLAYER command can display the profiles without solid models in several viewports, with hidden lines correctly shown in the Hidden linetype. Leaving the profiles in place and controlling visibility with VPLAYER serves as a reminder to generate new profiles when the solid model is revised.

Multiple-View Plots

The most effective way to present a solid model is to plot it in multiple views: two or more orthographic views and one or more axonometric or perspective views for design documentation. You can plot multiple views of the model in a single plot by using MVIEW's paper-space viewports. You can plot several views of the same model on the same sheet of paper by running multiple plots with different origins, but you cannot view all of the drawings on-screen as they are to be plotted.

It is important to plan when you plot multiple views of a model. Drawing entities that should appear in only one view must be placed on separate layers so they can be made visible in the correct viewport. You also should define a User Coordinate System for each viewing direction, and name the UCS so that its relation to a viewport is apparent.

Multiple-view drawings must be plotted with TILEMODE set to 0, in order to enable the display of paper-space viewports.

Improving Performance Considerations

AutoCAD is a large, complex program that requires a high-performance hardware platform for responsive operation. AME increases the size and complexity of the program, and thus increases the need for a high-performance platform. Even on the fastest microcomputers, AME is considerably less responsive than AutoCAD because AME must perform complex and time-consuming calculations that are not required in conventional 2D or 3D drafting tasks. Although you cannot make AME as responsive as the basic AutoCAD package, you can minimize its effect on your productivity.

Hardware Considerations

AutoCAD has always been an application that places demands on hardware, and AME is even more demanding. Both programs can operate using several different options and hardware platforms. The most optimum setup used does not always need to be state-of-the-art, but it should provide a fast, stable operating environment. For instance, on PC DOS platforms you can choose ISA, EISA, or VESA local bus architecture. Of course, "faster is better" for operating AME to its full potential; however, for medium-size to complex solid models, it is best to have at least the following minimum configuration:

- 486DX-33 MHz CPU with 256K cache
- 8M RAM
- 200M hard drive with fast access time
- VGA graphics card with 1M VRAM
- Large SuperVGA noninterlaced monitor, 1028x768 resolution
- 1.2M 5.25" & 1.44M 3.5" drives
- Mouse or tablet input

The AME platform should feature a high-speed, high-capacity disk drive. Solid models tend to be large and AutoCAD creates many temporary files in any case. A solid-modeling session should not be started without several megabytes of free disk space available both on the disk that holds AutoCAD and on the disk that holds the drawing files. A "disk full" error in a solid-modeling session can result in the loss of a significant amount of time-consuming work.

The AME graphics display device should be high-resolution, high-performance, and capable of displaying at least 256 colors. The SHADE command does not produce lighting effects with graphic boards that display fewer than 256 colors.

AME makes no special demands on hard copy output devices used for wireframe or hidden-line removed plots. AutoCAD does not plot a shaded image, although slides can be made of shaded images. If a third-party, screen-capture program is installed, you can capture and print shaded images. Printing shaded images generally requires a raster-type hard copy device, rather than the traditional pen plotter.

Boolean Operations and Storage Considerations

Solid models require more storage space than normal AutoCAD entities, because more information is required to describe a solid object than a linear object. Boolean operations also require storage space. A Boolean operation forms a new solid, but the member solids also remain in the drawing database.

Meshing a solid increases the size of the drawing database. When a new solid is formed with a Boolean operation, the new solid does not inherit the mesh representations of the component solids. If the new solid is meshed, the size of the drawing database increases again.

Optimizing the Modeling Process

Successful solid modeling relies on visualizing the prototype in terms of primitives and composite Boolean operations. Creating a solid model is like constructing a puzzle or carving a sculpture. Each piece must be carefully conceived and meticulously put together. As a designer, you first conceptualize what the whole piece is supposed to look like in its final state. Then, you must fabricate each piece to fit into or join together with other pieces in order to complete the picture. Designers have always faced this challenge in orthographic projection by visualizing each view separately. However, modeling enhances this process by providing a new set of tools and a new way to design.

During the development of a design, you may find it advantageous to construct composite solids from a relatively large number of simple primitives, such as boxes and cylinders. Composite solids constructed in this manner can be edited easily with the SOLCHP command.

If analysis is not immediately required, you can construct a useful solid model with a minimum number of Boolean operations. Placing solid primitives in position—but not combining them with Boolean operations—often yields a reasonable approximation of the final composite solid. For ease of manipulation, you can combine such groups of primitives with the BLOCK command and then insert them as block references. When Boolean operations are required, you can explode the block references.

As the solid model develops, you can create a given solid in an alternative form. A solid consisting of a large number of primitives and Boolean operations can often be replaced with a few extrusions and a smaller number of Boolean operations. Composite solids based on extrusions are more difficult to edit than those built from simpler solids, but they are often more compact and require less storage space.

You may find it useful to construct a solid model in the same way the real prototype is to be made, without regard to compactness of storage space or ease of editing. By simulating fabrication methods, as well as the form and properties of the prototype, you increase the amount of information that the model contains. For example, if two slabs are combined and then filleted with the SOLFILL command, the fillet primitive that AME creates is a close approximation of the amount of weld material required to join two steel plates in the prototype. Similarly, the cylinders that represent drilled holes in a piece of stock accurately represent the amount of material that must be removed by machining.

Reducing the Size of the Database

AME solid models of complex prototypes tend to be very large. Some of the information that is added to the drawing file during the modeling process need not be stored permanently because it can be reconstructed at any time from the basic descriptions of solid. One way of reducing the size of the drawing database is to build models in the most compact form to avoid unnecessary operations.

The SOLPURGE command can be used to reduce the size of the drawing database prior to storage, or at the conclusion of a session with a particular solid. SOLPURGE can be used to release memory that AME allocated to a particular solid when it was selected for an AME command. If you select that solid for a subsequent operation, AME again allocates memory for it.

You can use SOLPURGE to remove boundary representation (Bfile) and mesh information from the drawing file. AME can reconstruct this information at any time from the basic definitions of solids in the drawing file. Reducing the drawing file's size before ending a drawing session reduces the amount of disk space required for permanent storage. Reducing the drawing file's size during an editing session also reduces the amount of time required to regenerate the drawing.

Summary

In this chapter, you learned about AutoCAD's Advanced Modeling Extension (AME), which creates three-dimensional geometry that can analyze technical integrity and verify manufacturing processes. The chapter discussed how to work with solid entities, build models with solids, manipulate solids, and build models with blocks and xrefs.

The Structured Query Language

AutoCAD Release 12 comes with the AutoCAD SQL Extension (ASE), a Structured Query Language (SQL) interface. The SQL feature is invaluable because it allows two-way data flow between AutoCAD drawings and databases. This chapter looks at the SQL feature from several perspectives. First, you learn what SQL is and what the benefits of using SQL with AutoCAD are. From there you look at AutoCAD's ASE commands and features. The chapter also discusses the specifics of supported ASE drivers. The chapter ends with a discussion of using ASE with AutoLISP and SQL.

 For a detailed explanation of the commands mentioned in this chapter, see the Command Reference.

Using the Structured Query Language

To understand the benefits of the SQL feature, you need to start by looking at some concepts independent of AutoCAD. To begin with, SQL allows for two-way data flow between an AutoCAD drawing and a database. *Two-way flow* means that changes can be brought about in the drawing or the database by changing the data in either one of them. Changes to the database affect the drawing, and changes to the drawing affect the database.

The database is external to AutoCAD and therefore available for use even if AutoCAD is not running. This enables you to use all the data-query and report-writing features of the database package on the stored drawing data. Before going any further, you need to have two terms defined, database and SQL.

Database Concepts

A *database* is a software package used to store and manipulate data. Databases are defined best by describing their components. The smallest element in a database is a *field*. A field can hold a single piece of information, such as a person's name, age, or social security number. A group of related fields make a *record*. One person's name, age, and social security number can be a record; the next person's name, age, and social security number can be the next record.

All of the records together make up a *file*. Because you often must keep track of several different groups of data, you may have several files. Databases provide a feature called an *index* to speed access to the data in a file. An index works like a card catalog to identify a specific record or records, based on the value of a field. The field used to organize an index is called an *indexed field*. All of your files and indexes make up a database.

The data in a database is useless if you cannot get to it and modify it. The software for managing databases is called a *database management system* (DBMS). The particular DBMS you have may use different names for the parts of a database, but they all perform the same basic functions. Table 9.1 shows the terms used by SQL, their meanings, and the equivalent term from the description.

Table 9.1
SQL Terminology

SQL Term	Meaning	Database Term
Database	A collection of tables and their supporting files	Database
Table	A collection of related rows	File
Row	A collection of related columns	Record
Column	A single piece of information	Field
Key	A reference field	Indexed field

SQL

SQL (Structured Query Language) is a language used to query databases. Because of its narrow focus, SQL is somewhat limited in its capabilities. SQL cannot be used to create fancy data-entry forms or to write complex reports, for example. These needs are left to the DBMS's own language. SQL is useful, however, because it uses relatively few commands in a flexible way to retrieve data from a database.

The main attraction of SQL is that the user does not need to know how the database is put together to get data back. The user asks for the desired data, and SQL figures out how to get the data. Because microcomputer database packages are starting to support SQL, a common interface to several database packages is now available. AutoCAD uses this common interface to "talk" to the different supported database packages. Table 9.2 lists the database packages currently available to AutoCAD through the SQL interface.

Table 9.2
Supported DBMSs

Database Management Systems

dBASE III PLUS for DOS and Sun SPARC stations

dBASE IV for DOS

INFORMIX 4.1 for Sun SPARC stations

ORACLE 6.0 for Sun SPACE stations

Paradox 3.5 for DOS

 dBASE III, dBASE IV, and Paradox do not have to be installed in order for the SQL feature to work with databases created in those packages. ORACLE and INFORMIX must be installed in order for the SQL feature to work with their databases.

Because many people are not familiar with SQL, most software packages that use SQL also have interfaces to access data. AutoCAD provides several easy-to-use dialog boxes for this purpose. Although you can use the SQL interface without learning much of the SQL language, you must know the SQL language for some programming applications.

Configuring ASE

Before you can use the SQL interface, you must load the SQL files and configure your system to run SQL. The SQL files do not have to be installed to run AutoCAD, so make sure that they are installed before you try to use the SQL interface. You also must load the SQL interface into memory and assign the appropriate DBMS information.

Configuring SQL

Each database supported by AutoCAD places certain restrictions, limitations, and requirements on the system. The points mentioned here are general and apply to AutoCAD. For specific limitations and needs of your database package, refer to your database's documentation, the *AutoCAD Interface, Installation, and Performance Guide,* and the *AutoCAD SQL Extension Reference Manual.*

General Environment Variables

You should have the ACAD environment variable set to include the search path for the support directory.

For package-specific environment variables, check the information listed with your database in the next section.

Database-Specific Settings

Each of the databases supported by AutoCAD has specific system settings that must be made before the database can be used with AutoCAD.

For more information on each database, see "Choosing a DBMS Driver," later in this chapter.

dBASE III

dBASE III itself does not have to be installed to use or create dBASE III data files. AutoCAD needs a user-named environment variable that tells AutoCAD the search path to the directory with the dBASE III data files. Use the DOS SET command to set the system variable. AutoCAD prompts for the name of this variable in the Set DBMS Driver dialog box, displayed by the ASESETDBMS command.

dBASE IV

dBASE IV SQL needs to be installed in order to use the dBASE IV DBMS driver. AutoCAD needs a dBASE IV system table that lists each of the databases used. AutoCAD also needs an environment variable, called SQLHOME, which tells AutoCAD the search path to the dBASE IV system tables. Use the DOS SET command to set the system variable.

Paradox

Paradox does not have to be installed in order to use or create Paradox data files. AutoCAD needs a user-named environment variable that tells AutoCAD the search path to the directory with the Paradox data files. Use the DOS SET command to set the system variable. AutoCAD prompts for the name of this variable in the Set DBMS Driver dialog box, displayed by the ASESETDBMS command.

ORACLE

ORACLE must be installed to use the SQL interface. The CONFIG.ORA file must include a DYN=*xxxx* line, in which *xxxx* is the amount of memory your ORACLE server requires. Enter **CFIG 386 ACAD.EXE -EXTLOW 200000H** at the OS prompt to configure AutoCAD and ORACLE to properly run together. You can start ORACLE, and then start AutoCAD.

INFORMIX

INFORMIX must be installed in order to use the SQL interface. Although the database name is the directory in which the INFORMIX data files can be found, AutoCAD does not require an environment variable to be set. The directory name is entered in the Set DBMS Driver dialog box. Your system requires the QEMM386.SYS device to be loaded in the CONFIG.SYS file. Start INFORMIX, and then start AutoCAD.

If you change the CONFIG.SYS file, you need to reset your system in order for the change to take effect.

Required Files

AutoCAD comes with all the files needed to run the AutoCAD side of the SQL interface. The exact files needed vary slightly from platform to platform. The following list describes each of the files AutoCAD uses with SQL:

- **ASE.DCL**. This dialog box file contains the dialog boxes used with the AutoCAD SQL interface.

- **ACAD.ASE**. This file lists the aliases used to select a driver from within AutoCAD, then the platform (real or protected mode), and finally the location and name of the driver file needed to use the database. The default ACAD.ASE file for DOS systems is as follows:

```
;  ACAD.ASE file for DOS Protected Mode:
;  ASE drivers for dBASE database

dBASE3  ,PHARLAP386,asidb3ph.exp
dBASE4  ,PHARLAP386,asidb4ph.exp

;  ASE drivers for PARADOX 3.5 database
PARADOX ,PHARLAP86 ,asipdxpm.exe
;  End driver list
```

- **ASE.EXP**. ASE.EXP is the ADS application that provides the ASE commands. The file is automatically loaded when you select ASE from the AutoCAD menus.

- **ASEMMNG.EXP** (DOS platforms only). ASEMMNG.EXP is the ASE memory manager. It is installed in the ACAD directory. When ASE is loaded, ASEMMNG.EXP is loaded automatically.

- **ACAD.ADS**. ACAD.ADS lists the names of ADS applications to be loaded when AutoCAD starts. You can add ASE to the file to load ASE.EXP when AutoCAD starts.

- **ACAD.MNL**. ACAD.MNL contains the AutoLISP functions used by the ASE menus. It is loaded automatically, provided that you leave it in the same directory as ACAD.MNU.
- **ASE.LSP**. This file contains the ASE commands that can be implemented as AutoLISP routines. The file is loaded automatically through ACAD.MNU.

Loading SQL

After AutoCAD is started, you must load ASE. To load ASE, use the Initialize option in the ASE cascading menu of the Files pull-down menu; or select the ASE screen menu, and then choose InitASE. You also can use XLOAD to load ASE.EXP, use LOAD to load ASE.LSP, and then run ASEINIT to initialize ASE. The initialization process loads ASE, and creates a layer called ACADASE in your drawing. Do not alter the layer or its contents in any way because AutoCAD uses this layer, called the *control database*, to store database information.

The control database is AutoCAD's way of keeping track of the links created between AutoCAD entities and the records in your external database.

DBMS Assignments

After ASE is initialized, tell AutoCAD which DBMS driver you are using and where the databases can be found. This is a two-step process.

First, call ASESETDBMS and enter the desired DBMS driver. The available DBMS drivers are listed in your ACAD.ASE file. Although more than one DMBS can be attached to a drawing, only one DBMS can be used at a time. If you have already attached DBMS drivers to a drawing, the attached drivers are listed in the Set DBMS dialog box, enabling you to select the desired driver. The next step is to set the database.

Set the database with the ASESETDB command. The exact entry depends on the DBMS driver you are using. For dBASE III and Paradox, enter the name of the environment variable set to the data directory. For dBASE IV, the database name is the system table that lists the data files. For ORACLE, the database name is the actual name of the database you want to access. For INFORMIX, the database is the name of the directory with the data files.

After entering the database, you are prompted for a user name and password. Enter the appropriate values or press Enter if your database and operating system do not require a user name and password.

After the DBMS and database are assigned, list the specific tables you want to access and the key (reference) field in the table. The *key field* must have a unique entry in each record to ensure that AutoCAD accesses the proper row during data searches.

To list the tables you want to access, use ASESETTABLE. You are not provided with a list of available tables—you must already know the names of the tables you want. If you already have attached tables, these attached tables are listed in the dialog box. After you specify a table, you have to pick a key column. Because the key column should be unique to each record, you may have to pick more than one column to get a unique combination.

 The value stored in the fields marked as the key column must be unique to each record. If a key column value is duplicated, all records with the duplicate value are edited or deleted when any one record is accessed. Any attempt to access the records returns the first record with the key column value.

The *current table* is the one that you have access to at the moment. You can use ASESETTABLE to make the desired table current.

Using SQL

The SQL interface provides you with several tools. This section covers ways to access external data while you are in AutoCAD, linking the external data to entities, using links, exporting data, and error-checking and prevention.

Modifying External Data from within AutoCAD

The data that are stored in external databases can be accessed by key values, search queries, or graphical selections. The graphical selections require links to have been made from graphic entities to the database rows. Because links are discussed next, this section discusses ways to access external data by using key column or search queries.

Setting the Current Row

Before external data can be modified, the row of data to modify must be set current. To set the current row, use ASESETROW. ASESETROW has three options for setting the current row: you can specify a key value, specify a search criterion, or select an entity linked to the desired row. The syntax of the search statements is the where clause portion of an SQL statement. If you click on Search without specifying a criterion, you can step through all the rows in the table. Figure 9.1 shows the Set Row dialog box.

Figure 9.2 shows the Set Current Row By Search Criteria dialog box.

 The Set Current Row by Search Criteria dialog box translates your entry in the Criteria box to a full SQL statement and displays it above the row information.

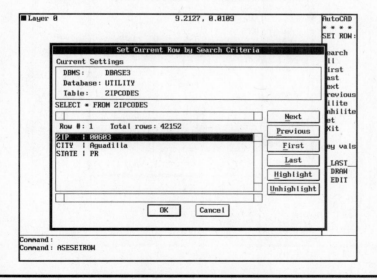

Figure 9.1:
The Set Row dialog box.

Figure 9.2:
The Set Current Row by Search Criteria dialog box.

Viewing Data

To view a row, make it current with ASESETROW, and then issue the ASEVIEWROW command. ASEVIEWROW displays the current row in a list box. If you have a link between a graphic entity and the row you want to display, use the ASEQVIEW command to set the current row and view it in one step.

Adding Data

Data is added to the current table with ASEADDROW. Remember, you can set the current table with ASESETTABLE. When you add a new row to a table (see fig. 9.3), the values of the current row are displayed as default values. You can use these values as starting points when entering the new row's data. The current row's values do not change in any way. When you are finished, the new row is the current one.

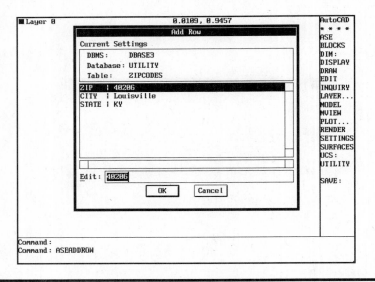

Figure 9.3:
The Add Row dialog box.

Editing Data

You can edit data from within AutoCAD by using ASEEDITROW (see fig. 9.4). ASEEDITROW edits the current row. If any rows have duplicate key-column values, all of the duplicate rows will reflect the editing change. If you select Cancel while working in the dialog box, however, your changes are disregarded. Use the ASEQEDIT command to set the current row and edit it in one step.

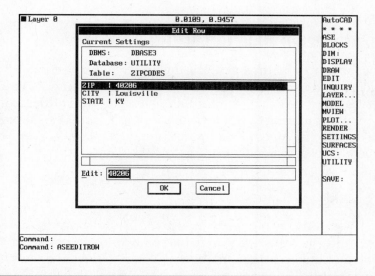

Figure 9.4:
The Edit Row dialog box.

Deleting Data

To delete data from an external table, use the ASEDELROW command. The effect that this command has on the table varies with the DBMS. Check your DBMS documentation to see if you must pack the database after records have been deleted (*packing* a database completely removes deleted records). The ASEDELROW command deletes the current row from the current table. You should not have duplications of your key value. If there are multiple rows with the same key value as the current row, they also are deleted.

 ASEDELROW automatically removes any links between the drawing and the database before deleting the row.

Linking External Data to Entities

The most powerful feature of SQL is the link that can be created between a graphic entity and a row in a table. This link enables you to create two-way data flow—manipulating the graphic entities from the table and manipulating the table from the graphic entities. Before you explore the specific types of manipulations available, however, you must make links between the entities and the tables.

Adding Links

A *link* associates a graphic entity in AutoCAD with a row in a table. You can have multiple entities linked to the same row, and you can have multiple rows linked to the same entity. You also can have rows from multiple tables linked to one entity. The only restriction is that each row must have a unique key value.

Links are made in two ways. You can set the current row and then use ASEMAKELINK; or you can use ASEQLINK, which combines setting the row with ASESETROW and making the link with ASEMAKELINK. Use the ASEQLINK command to set the current row and link it to a graphic entity in one step.

Editing Links

As your drawing changes, you may have to alter the links between graphic entities and tables. To reset existing links, issue the ASEEDITLINK command.

Deleting Links

As drawings are changed, you may need to delete a link. Always delete a link if you are going to erase linked data from a table or a linked graphic entity from a drawing. To delete a link, issue the ASEDELLINK command. ASEDELLINK does not affect the entity or the data being linked—only the link itself is removed. You can limit the scope of the links being deleted from an entity to a row, table, database, or DBMS.

 ASEDELROW automatically removes links before deleting any data.

Using Links

Now that you know how to manipulate data and links, you are ready to put SQL to work for you. By using a link set in a drawing, you can display table information in the drawing, display data with graphic selections, and select entities based on a table query.

Displayable Attributes

Displayable attributes enable you to display select values from the current row in the drawing. Use the ASEQMAKEDA command to set the current row and make a link at the same time. The exact column or columns displayed is up to the user.

Although you can display data from rows that are not linked to an entity, you often have a link between a nearby entity and the row whose values you are displaying. After a displayable attribute is in place, it is automatically linked to the row and columns that the attribute displays (see fig. 9.5).

As your data changes, your displayable attributes may become out-of-date. You can reload all or selected displayable attributes by using the ASERELOAD command.

 ASERELOADDA causes a complete drawing regeneration. If you have a large drawing, this can be a time-consuming task.

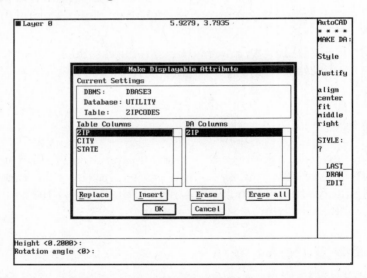

Figure 9.5:
The Make Displayable Attribute dialog box.

Displaying Tables with Graphic Selection

After you have linked an entity to a row in a table, you can display that row by selecting the entity. You can do this in two ways. You can use ASESETROW with the Graphical option and then use ASEVIEWROW; or you can use ASEQVIEW, which combines these two commands.

Selecting Entities with a Query

Another advantage of the SQL interface is its capability to select graphic entities based on a table query. You can use ASESETROW and the Highlight option to draw attention to entities based on a query. You also can use ASESELECT to create a select set that is a union, subtraction, or intersection of graphic entities selected with the cursor and graphic entities selected by a query.

Exporting Data

Exporting data refers to creating lists of data in external files, or running reports written in the database's programming language. This section deals with exporting data by using the ASEEXPORT and ASESELECT commands. The ASEMAKEREP command is also used to run programs written in the database's programming language or in any other language that can access the database tables.

The specifics of running external reports vary, depending on the DBMS you are using. Consult your DBMS documentation for details on how to run those reports.

As the name Structured Query Language suggests, the focus of SQL is not on report generation. The two commands that create an external file are ASEEXPORT and ASESELECT. The files that these two commands create are not lists of the data in the desired table or row. What you get is a file that lists the key-field value in a row and the handle of the entity to which it is linked. This is useful for determining how many graphic entities are linked to a given row, or how many rows are linked to a given graphic entity.

Both commands enable you to choose from Comma-delimited (CDF), Space-delimited (SDF), and Native file formats. *Native file format* creates files using the format of the DBMS you are using, and adds the name of the key column to the key attributes and entity handles exported.

You must have database-creation privileges in your DBMS before you can create exported data files in Native file format.

Error-Checking

Errors can occur in your drawing when linked entities and data are modified. If you delete a linked row with the external DBMS, you leave an entity with a link to nothing. Conversely, if you use ERASE to delete an entity without first deleting the link, you have data linked to nothing. Although both cases can cause problems when it is time to use the links, these errors can be reported and fixed by using the ASEPORT command.

If you delete the link between a displayable attribute and the row to which it is linked, the displayable attribute disappears.

If you have performed any ASE commands, you should save your drawing when you quit to prevent errors in your control database.

Editing the Control Database

The *control database* is a list of attached DBMS drivers, databases, tables, and data links. The control database data is kept on the ACADASE layer. You should leave this layer unchanged. You can use ASE commands to selectively delete information from the control database.

 You should use the control database commands with extreme caution. These commands are irreversible, even with the UNDO command.

 Displayable attributes that are linked to the deleted database or DBMS reference will be erased.

Deleting Items from the Control Database

By selectively deleting tables, databases, or DBMS drivers from the control database, you can clear all references to the deleted item in the drawing. To delete all references to a database, issue the ASEERASEDB command. ASEERASEDB deletes the database name from the list of attached databases, deletes all tables in the database from the list of attached tables, and removes all links to rows in the erased database. To delete all references to a DBMS driver, issue the ASEERASEDBMS command. ASEERASEDBMS deletes the DBMS driver's name from the list of attached drivers, deletes all references to the databases using the driver, and deletes all links to the data in the databases being removed.

Deleting the Control Database

The entire control database can be deleted with the ASEERASEALL command. ASEERASEALL erases all references to any DBMS, database, table, or link in the drawing. Run this command only if you no longer need the control database in your drawing and want to reduce the drawing size.

307

Closing Databases and Exiting ASE

The last action you take with the SQL interface is to close all open databases and unload ASE. By closing a database, you prevent any data from being lost or garbled. To close a database, issue the ASECLOSEDB command.

To close a DBMS driver and free the memory it uses, issue the ASETERMDBMS command.

 By closing any DBMS drivers that you are not currently using, you can free system memory and improve performance.

Unloading ASE frees system memory for other tasks. This can enhance your system's performance significantly if you are low on memory. To unload ASE, issue the ASETERM command. ASETERM closes any open database files and unloads the SQL interface. If you want to access the data again, you must reinitialize ASE.

Using the ASE Command Reference

This section gives a brief list of all ASE commands. Because so many ASE commands use dialog boxes, the setting of the CDMDIA system variable is important. If CMDDIA is set to 1, dialog boxes appear. If CMDDIA is set to 0, you are prompted from the command-line area. When ASE commands are used in AutoLISP, they respond according to the CMDDIA setting. (For a more complete explanation of each command and its options, see the Command Reference.)

ASE Commands and Syntax

The ASE commands can be divided into four categories, according to purpose. *Administrative commands* are used to initialize ASE, open and close DBMSs, and set the component parts of a DBMS. *Manipulative commands* enable you to add, edit, delete, or view rows. *Link commands* enable you to add, edit, delete, or view links. *Utility commands* execute SQL commands, run reports, and perform maintenance on the links. The ASE commands are listed and described as follows:

Administrative Commands

Several Administrative commands affect the control database. The control database is created by AutoCAD to store ASE information. When a command's primary purpose is to delete information from the control database, your data in the linked databases is not deleted. Use these commands with extreme caution, however, because you can lose references to your data or databases.

ASECLOSEDB

ASECLOSEDB closes an open database. Closing an open database does not remove any references in the control database or delete data. Typically, this command is used when your DBMS driver does not enable you to open multiple databases at the same time, or when you finish using SQL.

ASEERASEALL

ASEERASEALL deletes the control database, which removes all links between your drawing and any external data. All databases are closed and their references are removed, all drivers are unloaded and their references are removed, and all displayable attributes are erased from the drawing. ASE remains initialized, so ASE commands are still available. If you use an ASE command after running ASEERASEALL, you are prompted for DBMS and database information. UNDO does not reverse this command.

ASEERASEDB

ASEERASEDB removes the selected database from the control database. The selected database is closed, and all links and displayable attributes associated with the database are deleted. You do not lose any data in the database, but all references to the database are removed from the drawing. UNDO does not reverse this command.

ASEERASEDBMS

ASEERASEDBMS removes all references to the DBMS from the control database. All databases in the DBMS are closed, and the DBMS driver is unloaded. The reference to the DBMS is removed from the control database. All links and displayable attributes associated with the DBMS are deleted. UNDO does not reverse this command.

ASEERASETABLE

ASEERASETABLE removes all references to the specified table from the control database. All links and displayable attributes associated with the table are deleted. This command cannot be reversed with UNDO.

ASEINIT

ASEINIT is used to initialize ASE and to create the control database. Before you can run ASEINIT, xload ASE.EXP and load ASE.LSP. The results of issuing ASEINIT depend on whether ASE has been intialized previously in the drawing. If you open a drawing that had ASE initialized when you ended the drawing session, ASEINIT reloads the DBMS and database automatically. When you run ASEINIT for the first time in a drawing, you must use ASESETDBMS and ASESETDB to set the DBMS and database.

ASESETDB

ASESETDB sets the current database. If the DBMS has not been set, the ASESETDBMS command is automatically run first.

ASESETDBMS

ASESETDBMS sets the current DBMS. Your options are determined by the drivers listed in the ACAD.ASE file.

ASESETROW

ASESETROW sets the current row in the current table. The current row can be selected by specifying a key value, specifying a search criteria, or selecting an entity linked to the desired row.

ASESETTABLE

ASESETTABLE sets the current table. If you have not initialized the DBMS or database, the ASESETDBMS and ASESETDB commands are run automatically. AutoCAD does not list any tables in the current database until the tables have been attached to the drawing. Thus, you cannot get a list of all tables in the current database that can be attached—you must know the name of the table before you can attach it.

If you are setting the table for the first time, you must specify a *key column*, which can be a single column or several columns. The value of the key column should not be duplicated in another row in the same table. If your DBMS cannot prevent duplications, you should use the CREATE UNIQUE INDEX command to create an index of the key column that does not allow duplications.

ASETERM

ASETERM closes all databases and deactivates all drivers, which does not cause a loss of data or links. The SQL interface is simply deactivated, and the memory it was using is freed. ASE is terminated automatically when you END a drawing session.

ASETERMDBMS

ASETERMDBMS deactivates a DBMS and frees the memory it occupies. No data is lost in the control database or in the DBMS. ASETERMDBMS usually is used to deactivate a DBMS that is not being used, however, you can deactivate the current DBMS.

Manipulative Commands

Manipulative commands work on one row in a table. You can use them to add, edit, delete, and view rows in a table.

ASEADDROW

ASEADDROW adds a new row to the current table. Entries must conform to all DBMS restrictions, and no duplicate values should be used in the key column. After you have added a row, it becomes the current row.

ASEDELROW

ASEDELROW deletes the current row from the current table. If you delete a row with ASEDELROW, all links with that row are automatically deleted.

ASEEDITROW

ASEEDITROW edits the contents of the current row in the current table. Any rows with the same key value are also updated with the new values.

ASEQEDIT

ASEQEDIT makes a row current and edits its contents. The command is a combination of the ASESETROW command, the Graphic option, and the ASEEDITROW command. Before a dialog box appears or you are prompted for further information, you are asked to select the entity that is linked to the row you want to edit. If the entity is not linked to a row, the message No links found displays.

ASEQVIEW

ASEQVIEW makes a row current and views its contents. The command is a combination of the ASESETROW command, the Graphic option, and the ASEVIEWROW command. Before a dialog box displays or you are prompted for further information, you are asked to select the entity linked to the row you want to view. If the entity is not linked to a row, the message No links found displays.

ASEVIEWROW

ASEVIEWROW views the current row in the current table. If no row has been set current, an alert box displays the message No Current Row.

Link Commands

Link commands attach entities in a drawing with rows in a table.

ASEDELLINK

ASEDELLINK deletes the links between an entity and the DBMS. The links that are removed depend on the scope specified at the prompt.

ASEEDITLINK

ASEEDITLINK deletes links between the selected object and the DBMS. The links that are edited depend on the scope specified at the prompt.

ASEMAKEDA

ASEMAKEDA makes displayable attributes. A *displayable attribute* is a text string in the drawing with a value corresponding to a column in a linked row. If an error prevents the attribute from being displayed, an asterisk (*) displays.

ASEMAKELINK

ASEMAKELINK links the selected objects with the current row. Use ASESETROW to make the correct row current before running ASEMAKELINK.

ASERELOADDA

ASERELOADDA redisplays the selected displayable attributes with the current column values. When you edit a row with displayable attributes, you must run ASERELOADDA to get the new values to replace the old ones in the drawing. If an error occurs, an asterisk (*) displays.

ASEQLINK

ASEQLINK sets the current row and links the selected entities with it. This works like a combination of the ASESETROW command without the Graphic option and the ASEMAKELINK command.

ASEQMAKEDA

ASEQMAKEDA sets the current row and creates a displayable attribute from it. This works like a combination of the ASESETROW command (without the Graphic option) and the ASEMAKEDQ command.

ASEVIEWLINK

ASEVIEWLINK displays all links for the selected object. The View Link dialog box is displayed. Use the Next, Previous, First, and Last buttons to view the links attached to the entity.

Utility Commands

Utility commands export data, run reports, create select sets, run SQL commands, and error-check the SQL interface.

ASEEXPORT

ASEEXPORT creates a file that contains the key-column value of a row and the entity handle with which the row is linked. Native format files also contain the name of the key column. If a row is linked to more than one entity, a line appears in the report for each entity with which the row is linked.

ASEMAKEREP

ASEMAKEREP runs a report written with the DBMS's programming language or a compatible report generator. The exact format of the command issued varies, depending on the DBMS and the report generator. Consult your DBMS documentation for the specifics of your DBMS.

ASEPOST

ASEPOST checks the ASE interface between the drawing and the control database (this is called *synchronizing* the drawing with the database). You can use ASEPOST to report on any errors or to fix errors. Errors are likely when a linked entity or a linked row was deleted using the ASESQLED command.

ASESELECT

ASESELECT reports or creates a select set of entities by comparing a graphic selection with an SQL where clause. You can perform a Boolean intersect, subtract, or union the graphic and text selection.

ASESQLED

ASESQLED executes an SQL command from within AutoCAD. You must follow proper DBMS procedure when using ASESQLED. If you delete a row that is linked, you are not warned that the link exists, and the link is not removed.

Learning the SQL Language

SQL was developed in the 1970s as a language for manipulating relational databases. At that time, databases were stored and manipulated on mainframes, and SQL became a common query language used by mainframe operators. With the introduction of powerful personal computers in the late 1980s, large-scale databases became available on PCs. If you are one of the many PC users who has never used a mainframe, you may not be familiar with the SQL language. This section introduces you to the SQL commands supported by AutoCAD and shows examples of the syntax.

Although a recognized standard for SQL commands and syntax exists, most software developers create their own dialect of SQL to mesh with their software needs. AutoCAD provides some nonstandard command syntax, and the particular database you are linked with may not support all the SQL commands. Consult your AutoCAD *SQL Extension Reference Manual* and your database software documentation to learn the limits of your particular database management system.

SQL Syntax

SQL is intended to be written like English. Because everybody approaches language a little bit differently, and computers need a given amount of information, the syntax is a compromise.

ASESQLED

The ASESQLED command enters SQL commands through a dialog box or the command prompt. When you use ASESETROW and ASEVIEWROW, you enter the where-clause portion of an SQL Select statement only, so you may find them less cumbersome to use for straight queries. The ASESQLED command, however, gives you access to all SQL commands supported by your DBMS. For this reason, you should become familiar with the basics of SQL. You also may find this information useful when programming SQL commands.

Reference and Syntax of Basic SQL Statements

The intent of an SQL statement is that you can read and write it in an English-like syntax. SQL statements begin with an SQL command that is a verb. You use SELECT for queries and CREATE to make a table, for example. After the verb, you supply a subject—what you want to SELECT or CREATE, for example. The remainder of the SQL statement depends on the command you are using. In each case, however, the flow is like English. The following examples show you the commands available to all the DBMSs.

In these examples, options are listed in square brackets and repeatable phrases are followed by an ellipsis. There are two rules to follow: SQL is case-sensitive when searching for column values, and text-column values should be enclosed in single quotes.

The examples of command syntax in the SQL reference use two databases (ZONE and STATION). The database definitions are as follows:

- **ZONE.DBF:**

  ZONE_NAME. A text column, 15 characters wide, which keeps track of the exchange-zone name.

  ZONE_NO. A numeric column, two digits wide, which identifies each exchange zone.

  MARKET. A number column, five digits wide with two decimal places, which tracks the market share in the exchange zone.

  NO_UNITS. A numeric column, two digits wide, which keeps track of the number of switching stations in the exchange zone.

- **STATION.DBF:**

  STATION_ID. A numeric column, two digits wide, which identifies the switching station.

  ST_NAME. A text column, 15 characters wide, which stores the switching station's name.

  ZONE_NO. A numeric column, two characters wide, which identifies within which exchange zone the switching station is located.

  TECHNOLOGY. A numeric column, two digits wide, which stores a numeric code for the type of technology used by the switching station. The options are 01 (Digital) or 02 (Analog).

  ST_TYPE. A text column, four characters wide, which identifies the type of switching station. The options are MAIN and SUB.

SELECT

Because SQL is a query language, the first command you examine is SELECT. SELECT is used to return all the rows in a table that meet a given condition. You even can control the order of the returned information. The SELECT command uses the following format:

```
SELECT [data]
FROM [table name...] [WHERE search condition ]
[GROUP BY [column name...] [HAVING search condition]]
[ORDER BY sort specifications... ]
```

The format for each of the options is as follows:

- *data*. List each column, separated by a comma. An asterisk (*) references all columns. You can specify an aggregate function of SUM, MIN, MAX, AVG, or COUNT.

- *table name*. List the tables you want to have searched, separated by a comma.

- *search condition*. Specify expectable values in certain columns. The logical operators, often called *predicates,* that are available for search conditions are listed in table 9.3. The compound logical operators are listed in table 9.4.

Table 9.3
SQL Logical Operators

Logical Operator	Meaning
=	Equal.
<>	Not equal.
>	Greater than.
<	Less than.
>=	Greater than or equal to.
<=	Less than or equal to.
[NOT] BETWEEN *value_1* AND *value_2*	Lists all rows in which a column's value is >= value 1 and <= value 2.
[NOT] IN *value_list or subquery*	Lists all rows in which a column's value is in the value list or return of a subquery.

continues

319

Table 9.3
Continued

Logical Operator	Meaning
[NOT] LIKE *pattern*	Lists all rows in which a column's value matches the pattern. The pattern can be any letters, numbers, symbols, or % and _. % is equal to any character and any number of characters. _ is equal to any character, but to only one.
IS [NOT] NULL	Lists all rows in which a column's value equals null.
comparison All *subquery*	Lists all rows in which a column's value =,<,>,<=,>=,or <> all of the values returned from a subquery.
comparison ANY *subquery*	Lists all rows in which a column's value =,<,>,<=,>=,or <> any of the values returned from a subquery.
EXIST *subquery*	Returns a true if there is a return from the subquery and a false if the return is null.

Table 9.4
SQL Compound Logical Operators

Compound Operator	Meaning
column AND column	Lists all rows when both column values are met
column OR column	Lists all rows when either column value is met
column NOT column	Reverses a logical relation

- *column name*. List the columns by which you want to group. This column must use all columns entered after SELECT except those with aggregate operators.
- *sort specification*. List the columns by which you want to sort.

The following examples show you how to use the SELECT command with the zone and station tables.

To list all columns and all rows in the zone table, issue the following command:

```
SELECT * FROM zone
```

To list all columns in the rows from zone number 4 in the ZONE table, issue this command:

```
SELECT * FROM zone WHERE zone_no = 4
```

To list the zone name and number columns in the rows from the zone named CENTRAL, enter this command:

```
SELECT zone_name, zone_no FROM zone WHERE zone_name = 'CENTRAL'
```

To list all columns in the rows between zone number 4 and 6, inclusive, in the zone table, issue the following command:

```
SELECT * FROM zone WHERE zone_no BETWEEN 4 AND 6
```

To list the stations grouped by zone number, enter this command:

```
SELECT st_name FROM station GROUP BY st_name
```

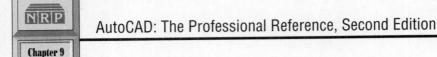

To list the information in the last query, plus the average of the technology type, issue the following command:

```
SELECT st_name, AVG(technology) FROM station group by st_name
```

INSERT INTO

The INSERT INTO command enters data into a table. The INSERT INTO command uses the following syntax:

```
[INSERT INTO table [column name...]
VALUES new_value and/or query_result...
```

- *table name*. List the table into which you want to enter data.
- *column name*. List the columns into which you want to enter data.
- *new_value*. List the values to place in the corresponding columns.
- *query_result*. Use a SELECT statement to generate the new value.

The following examples show you ways to use the INSERT INTO command with the zone and station tables.

To insert a new row into the zone table, with values for the zone-name and zone-number columns, use this command:

```
INSERT INTO zone (zone_name, zone_no) VALUE ('Western', 8)
```

To insert the values of the zone name and zone number from every row in the station table, in which the zone name is 8 and the station type is MAIN, into new rows in the zone table, issue this command:

```
INSERT INTO zone (zone_name, zone_no) SELECT st_name, zone_no
FROM station WHERE zone_no = 8 and st_type = 'MAIN'
```

DELETE FROM

The DELETE FROM command deletes rows from a table.

 If you delete a linked row with the ASESQLED command, the link is not deleted, and you have to run ASEPOST to fix the error.

The DELETE FROM command uses the following syntax:

```
DELETE FROM table name
WHERE search condition
```

- *table name*. List the table from which you want to delete data.
- *search condition*. Specify rows to delete with a where clause, such as the SELECT command.

The following example shows ways to delete rows from the zone and station tables.

To delete all rows from the station table with a zone number of 3, issue the following command:

```
DELETE FROM station WHERE zone_no = 3
```

UPDATE

The UPDATE command changes the values in an existing row or rows. The UPDATE command uses the following syntax:

```
UPDATE table name
SET column name = value...
WHERE search condition
```

- *table name*. List the table you want to have updated.
- *set*. List the columns to update and the values with which to update.
- *search condition*. Specify rows to update. The search condition works like the SELECT command where clause.

The following examples show ways to use the UPDATE command with the zone and station tables:

To change all the stations with zone number = 5 to zone number = 6, use this command:

```
UPDATE station SET zone_no = 9 WHERE zone_no = 5
```

To update all stations to technology type 2, issue the following command:

```
UPDATE station SET technology = 2
```

CREATE TABLE

The CREATE TABLE command creates a new table in the database. The CREATE TABLE command uses the following syntax:

```
CREATE TABLE table name (table element...)
```

- *table name.* List the table you want to create.
- *table element.* List the column name, data type, and length (where necessary). Valid data types are shown in table 9.5.

Table 9.5
Data Types

Date Type	Description
CHARACTER	Any text, numbers, or symbols. Include the value of a character in single quotes. You must specify a length.
NUMERIC	Numbers and a decimal point. You must specify a length, and you can specify a number of decimal places.
DECIMAL	Numbers and a decimal point. You must specify a length, and you can specify a number of decimal places.
INTEGER	Numbers.
SMALLINT	Integers with a maximum of ten significant digits.
FLOAT	Numbers and a decimal point. You must specify a length. The number of decimal places varies.
REAL	Numbers and a decimal point.
DOUBLE PRECISION	Numbers and a decimal point. The Double precision type holds more significant digits than the Real type.

The following example shows ways to use the CREATE TABLE command.

To create a table called phone with a last name and telephone number field, issue this command:

```
CREATE TABLE phone (lastname character(15), telephone character
(8))
```

DROP TABLE

The DROP TABLE command deletes a table from the DBMS. Be careful with this command—when a table is deleted, you cannot get it back without an undelete utility. The DROP TABLE command uses the following syntax:

```
DROP TABLE table name
```

- *table name*. List the table you want to delete.

The following example shows you how to delete a table.

To delete the zone table, issue the following command:

```
DROP TABLE zone
```

CREATE INDEX

The CREATE INDEX command creates an index to speed the searching and sorting of data in a table. The CREATE INDEX command uses the following format:

```
CREATE [unique] INDEX index name
ON table name (column name[order]...)
```

- *unique*. Add this option to prevent duplications in the index.
- *index name*. List the name of the index you want to create.
- *table name*. List the table in which you want to create an index.
- *column name*. List the columns to include in the index, separated by a comma.
- *order*. Select ASC for ascending or DESC for descending order.

325

The following examples show ways to use the CREATE INDEX command with the station table.

To create an index called st_id on the station-number field with no duplications in the station table, enter the following command:

```
CREATE unique INDEX st_id ON station (station_id)
```

To create an index called id_type on the station number and type in the station table, issue this command:

```
CREATE INDEX id_type ON station (station_id, st_type)
```

DROP INDEX

The DROP INDEX command deletes an index from the DBMS. If you delete an index and then decide you want it back, use CREATE INDEX. The DROP TABLE command uses the following format:

```
DROP INDEX index name
```

- *index name.* List the name of the index you want to delete.

The following example shows you how to delete an index.

To delete the id_type index, enter this command:

```
DROP INDEX id_type
```

Using ASE Commands in AutoLISP

Programming with ASE commands adds an extra degree of flexibility to ASE use. With ASE programming, you can write your own programs that execute ASE commands only when the user should execute the commands, and only in the order that the commands should be executed. This kind of coding enables you to create a user-friendly and data-safe environment.

For the most part, the existing ASE commands enable you to do anything you want to do in SQL. The major reason for writing AutoLISP programs is that they relieve the burden of tedious tasks. A dialog box, for example, can be written to load ASE, a specific DBMS, and a database; and then supplies a predetermined list of tables.

This dialog box can be displayed with a simple command name such as SQL. Type **SQL**, and then pick the desired table. You can even write commands that load a specific table. Your goal in programming with ASE commands should not be to reinvent ASE—the general ASE functions have been written. You should use these commands to automate your work. The examples provided here use the ZONE and EXCHANGE databases, described in the SQL Command Reference.

 Some of the ASE commands do not execute properly if called while a dialog box is displayed. If you want to call ASE commands from a dialog box, hide the dialog box first.

Before you can run ASE commands, you must xload ASE.EXP, load ASE.LSP, and run ASEINIT. You can test whether ASE has been loaded by running ASEINIT. If the return value is nil, ASE is not yet loaded.

The format for executing an ASE command in AutoLISP is as follows:

```
(C:ASEcommand [arg1] [arg1] ...)
```

The ASE command can be any of the ASE commands listed under the ASE Command Reference. For example, you can run ASESETROW like this:

```
(C:ASESETROW)
```

The arguments are optional and depend on the command. A few rules that apply to the arguments of an ASE command are as follows:

- You cannot automatically insert a value into the Username: and Password: prompts of the ASESETDB command and ASEINIT commands.

- All option names and text values should be included in quotes.

- A `Select objects:` prompt cannot be given an entity name; you must pass a select set.
- A `Select object:` prompt can be given an entity name because the prompt wants only one entity.
- Coordinate values must be entered as a point list: for example, '(1 1 0).
- To enter a NULL value, enter "" as the pass parameter, which is the equivalent of pressing Enter on a blank prompt.

To continue with the preceding example, you can use ASESETROW with arguments to set a specific row current, as shown in the following:

```
(C:ASESETROW "S" "zone_no = 5")
```

The preceding example uses the Search criteria option with a search criteria of "zone_no = 5" to set the row.

The following example of an ASE command uses the ASEADDROW command to add a row to the table:

```
(setq zone (gettext "Enter the zone name: "))

(setq number (getint "Enter the zone number: "))

(setq share (getreal "Enter the market share: "))

(setq units (getint "Enter the number of stations: "))

(C:ASEADDROW zone number share units)
```

You can provide default values and perform error-checking on entries before using the ASE commands. This reduces the time spent setting and resetting tables and rows, and increases accuracy.

Error-checking can be done on the ASE commands with the ASE_ERRNO variable. ASE_ERRNO is set when an ASE command reports an error. Check the value of ASE_ERRNO in your programs immediately after an ASE command is executed if you need to confirm that the command worked. An ASE_ERRNO of zero indicates that there were no errors. A complete list of all 53 error codes can be found in Appendix C of the *AutoCAD SQL Extension Reference Manual*.

The following example makes use of a dialog box to offer a set of options to the user (see fig. 9.6). Because you can select the desired commands by clicking on buttons, your speed and accuracy are improved significantly.

The SQL.DCL file used in this example is as follows:

```
sqltool : dialog
{
   label = "ASE Commands";
   : boxed_row
   {
        label = "AutoCAD SQL Extension";
        : button
        {
             label = "Start";
             key = "start";
        }
        : button
        {
             label = "Stop";
             key = "stop";
        }
   }
   :boxed_row
   {
        : column
        {
             : button
```

```
                                {
                                        label = "Use Zone";
                                        key = "set_zone";
                                }
                        : button
                        {
                                label = "Use Station";
                                key = "set_st";
                        }
                        : button
                        {
                                label = "Set Row";
                                key = "set_row";
                        }
                }
                :column
                {
                        : button
                        {
                                label = "Add Row";
                                key = "add_row";
                        }
                        : button
                        {
                                label = "Delete Row";
                                key = "del_row";
                        }
```

```
            : button
            {
                    label = "View Row";
                    key = "view_row";
            }
        }
    }
    ok_cancel;
}
```

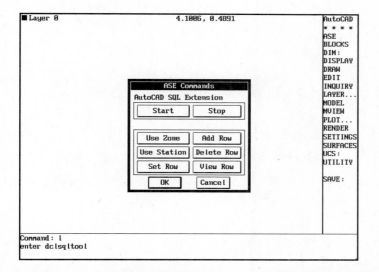

Figure 9.6
The ASE Commands dialog box.

As you can see, the DCL file is not complex. The file simply creates buttons and assigns a label and key to each button.

The SQL.LSP AutoLISP driver for the dialog box is as follows:

```
;* SQL displays the SQL dialog box. Each of the options hide the
;* dialog box and then run an ASE command.
;;; init_ase initializes SQL and loads the DBMS, database, and
;;; tables. The key columns for the tables are set.

(defun init_ase()
  (if (= nil c:aseinit) ;tests for return of aseinit. If nil
                        ;ase is not loaded
    (progn
      (xload "ase")       ;loads ASE.EXP
      (load "ase")        ;loads ASE.LSP
      (c:aseinit)         ;initialized ASE
      (c:asesetdbms "DBASE3") ;sets the DBMS to dBASE3
      (c:asesetdb "EXCHANGE" " " " ") ;set database to Exchange
      (c:asesettable "zone" "zone_no" "") ;set zone table
      (c:asesettable "station" "station_id" "") ;station table
    ) ;end progn
    (alert "ASE is already loaded. Please proceed")
  ) ;end if aseinit = nil
) ;end defun


;;; stop_ase closes the database, unloads the DBMS driver, and
;;; disconnects the ASE interface.
(defun stop_ase()
  (if (/= nil c:aseinit) ;confirms ase is loaded
    (progn
      (c:aseterm) ;terminates ASE
    ) ;end progn
```

```lisp
      (alert "ASE is already unloaded")
   ) ;end if aseinit /= nil
) ;end defun


;;; set_zone makes the zone table current
(defun set_zone()
   (if (/= nil c:aseinit) ;confirms ase is loaded
     (progn
       (c:asesettable "zone") ;sets zone current
     ) ;end progn
     (alert "ASE is not loaded")
   ) ;end if aseinit /= nil
) ;end defun


;;; set_st makes the station table current
(defun set_st()
   (if (/= nil c:aseinit) ;confirms ase is loaded
     (progn
       (c:asesettable "station") ;sets station current
     ) ;end progn
     (alert "ASE is not loaded")
   ) ;end if aseinit /= nil
) ;end defun


;;; set_row runs ASESETROW
(defun set_row()
   (if (/= nil c:aseinit) ;confirms ase is loaded
     (progn
       (c:asesetrow) ;runs ASESETROW
```

```
    ) ;end progn
    (alert "ASE is not loaded")
  ) ;end if aseinit /= nil
) ;end defun


;;; add_row runs ASEADDROW
(defun add_row()
  (if (/= nil c:aseinit) ;confirms ase is loaded
    (progn
      (c:aseaddrow) ;runs ASEADDROW
    ) ;end progn
    (alert "ASE is not loaded")
  ) ;end if aseinit /= nil
) ;end defun


;;; del_row run ASEDELROW
(defun del_row()
  (if (/= nil c:aseinit) ;confirms ase is loaded
    (progn
      (c:asedelrow) ;runs ASEDELROW
    ) ;end progn
    (alert "ASE is not loaded")
  ) ;end if aseinit /= nil
) ;end defun


;;; view_row runs ASEVIEWROW
(defun view_row()
  (if (/= nil c:aseinit) ; confirms ase is loaded
    (progn
```

```
        (c:aseviewrow) ;runs ASEVIEWROW
    ) ;end progn
    (alert "ASE is not loaded")
  ) ;end if aseinit /= nil
) ;end defun


;;; C:SQL - the main function that displays the dialog box and
;;; drives the selections
(defun C:SQL (/ index do_what)
  (if (> (setq index (load_dialog "SQL")) 0) ;load SQL.DCL
    (progn
      (setq do_what 11)
        (while (< 2 do_what) ;while done_dialog is user defined
          (setvar "cmdecho" 0)
          (if (new_dialog "sqltool" index) ;displays dialog box
            (progn
                ;;the action declarations initialize the dialog
                ;;box call backs.
                (action_tile "start" "(done_dialog 3)")
                (action_tile "stop" "(done_dialog 4)")
                (action_tile "set_zone" "(done_dialog 5)")
                (action_tile "set_st" "(done_dialog 6)")
                (action_tile "set_row" "(done_dialog 7)")
                (action_tile "add_row" "(done_dialog 8)")
                (action_tile "del_row" "(done_dialog 9)")
                (action_tile "view_row" "(done_dialog 10)")
                (setq do_what (start_dialog)) ;starts dialog box
                (cond
                  ;; the reason for done_dialog is tested and
                  ;; the appropriate function is called
```

335

```
                          ((= do_what 3)  (init_ase))
                          ((= do_what 4)  (stop_ase))
                          ((= do_what 5)  (set_zone))
                          ((= do_what 6)  (set_st))
                          ((= do_what 7)  (set_row))
                          ((= do_what 8)  (add_row))
                          ((= do_what 9)  (del_row))
                          ((= do_what 10) (view_row))
                     ) ;end cond
                  ) ;end progn
                  (progn
                    (prompt "Unable to display dialog box")
                      (setq do_what 0)
                  ) ;end progn
                ) ;end if new_dialog
              ) ;end while
          (unload_dialog index)
          (setvar "cmdecho" 1)
        ) ;end progn
        (prompt "Unable to load dialog box")
      ) ;end load dialog
    (princ); clear buffer
  ) ;end defun SQL
```

ASE commands have one major limitation: they do not provide a return value that can be assigned to an AutoLISP variable. You can use variables as arguments, but you cannot assign a value to a variable as a result of an ASE command. This means that you cannot extract column values from a row into an AutoLISP variable with the ASE commands. Fortunately, some ASI commands are supported by AutoLISP that can provide column values. The next section covers the AutoLISP-supported ASI commands.

Accessing External Files in AutoLISP and API Programs

The SQL interface provides new and better methods to access information stored outside of AutoCAD. You can use this capability to link data and entities, or you can use only one direction of the data flow to import or export data.

AutoLISP

As mentioned before, one limitation of using the ASE commands in AutoLISP is that you cannot extract a value from a column. The capability to pull data from a table and analyze it in a drawing is important. If you want to create your own application-specific dialog boxes that display information from a table, you must be able to read the table values. If you want to write functions that read a row and draw a specific entity based on the column values, you must be able to read the table values. The AutoCAD Programming Interface (API) provides commands for accessing a column's values.

The API commands you can use in AutoLISP are provided on the CD-ROM that comes with Release 12. Unfortunately, these commands have some errors in them. AutoCAD has provided a fix in the form of the LISPSQL.ZIP file, which is available on CompuServe or from AutoCAD's own BBS. LISPSQL.ZIP includes LISPSQL.EXP, LISPSQL.C, and LISPSQL.DOC. Before you can run the commands in LISPSQL.EXP, you must xload the file with the following:

```
(XLOAD "LISPSQL")
```

API

The AutoCAD Programming Interface provides a wide variety of commands for accessing external data through the SQL interface. To use the API interface. you must be familiar with C. If you are willing to make the effort that C programming for AutoCAD requires, you will be rewarded with speed and flexibility beyond AutoLISP's capabilities.

Accessing External Data

Whether you use the AutoLISP-supported API commands or API itself, you must follow the same basic steps when programming. These steps are as follows:

1. Initialize the DBMS driver
2. Log on to the database
3. Open a communications handle with the database
4. Create an SQL statement to execute
5. Execute the SQL statement
6. Examine the resulting data
7. Close the communications handle with the database
8. Log off the database
9. Unload the DBMS driver

The first three steps are performed once to initialize the SQL interface. Steps four, five, and six are repeated for as many actions as you need to take with the database. The final three steps are taken to unload the SQL interface.

Summary

In this chapter, you learned about the AutoCAD SQL Extension (ASE), which is an SQL (Structured Query Language) interface. The chapter discussed SQL and its advantages. You learned about AutoCAD's ASE commands and features, and the specifics of supported ASE drivers. The chapter ended with a discussion of using ASE with AutoLISP and SQL.

Part Three: Customization

Customizing AutoCAD
Importing and Exporting Files

Customizing AutoCAD

One of the biggest selling points of AutoCAD is the capability to customize it to your needs. Customization can take many forms from, the simplest prototype file to the most complex programming applications. Each way of customizing provides different and potentially beneficial changes to AutoCAD.

The main reason AutoCAD is customized is user speed. The more you can modify the AutoCAD environment based on the task you need to perform, the faster you can perform the task. This chapter dicusses many of the types of customization available with AutoCAD, and what you need to know and do to perform them. The chapter does not explain the details of how to perform the customization. For more information on the details of how to customize AutoCAD, see *Maximizing AutoCAD Release 12* and *Maximizing AutoLISP*, by New Riders Publishing.

NOTE Before you begin any major customization project, consult *The AutoCAD Resource Guide*, which comes with AutoCAD. *The Resource Guide* lists platforms that support AutoCAD, existing applications and developers, peripheral suppliers, learning resource material, and a summary of Autodesk products.

Customizing the Basic AutoCAD Environment

Making changes to the basic AutoCAD environment is the easiest way to make large-scale changes to AutoCAD. Many of the changes discussed here take effect automatically when you load AutoCAD. Many of the types of customization discussed later in this chapter can be included with changes to the AutoCAD environment to automatically load your custom menus, macros, programs, and more. The first type of customization concern changes made to an AutoCAD support file before AutoCAD is ever started.

ACAD.PGP

The ACAD.PGP file, or ProGram Parameter file, is an AutoCAD support file defining external programs that can be run from within AutoCAD, and command aliases used in AutoCAD. The external programs usually are operating-system commands, but they can be any program that will run concurrent with AutoCAD. *Command aliases* are abbreviations of the names of existing AutoCAD commands.

TIP If you make changes to the ACAD.PGP file while you are running AutoCAD, you can reload ACAD.PGP with the REINIT command or RE-INIT system variable.

External Commands

The following is the external command section of the DOS platform
ACAD.PGP file. Notice that the OS command request in the SH and
SHELL commands is left blank, enabling you to specify any command
to be run at the OS prompt. The memory-reserve parameter of all of the
external commands is set to 0. This parameter is always 0, and it is
included to maintain compatibility with older versions of AutoCAD.

```
; External Command format:

;   <Command name>,[<DOS request>],<Memory
reserve>,[*]<Prompt>,<Return code>

; Examples of External Commands for DOS

CATALOG,DIR /W,0,File specification: ,0
DEL,DEL,    0,File to delete: ,4
DIR,DIR,    0,File specification: ,0
EDIT,EDIT,   0,File to edit: ,4
SH,,       0,*OS Command: ,4
SHELL,,    0,*OS Command: ,4
TYPE,TYPE,  0,File to list: ,0
```

An example of a quick change to the ACAD.PGP file is to change
EDLIN to EDIT for users of DOS 5.0 and up. This enables you to use the
EDIT text-file editor instead of the EDLIN line editor while inside
AutoCAD.

```
EDIT,EDIT0,File to edit: ,4
```

Users of multitasking environments, such as UNIX, usually do not need
to define external commands in the ACAD.PGP file unless they are
adapting third-party software written for the DOS environment. Another advantage of UNIX is that it can suspend one program while
another is running, enabling programs to run concurrently with
AutoCAD. You do not need to integrate an access to the program into
AutoCAD.

Command Aliases

The other purpose of the ACAD.PGP file is to define command aliases. The following is a portion of the command alias section of ACAD.PGP.:

```
;  Command_alias format:
;   <Alias>,*<Full command name>
;  Sample aliases for AutoCAD Commands
;  These examples reflect the most frequently used commands.
;  Each alias uses a small amount of memory, so don't go
;  overboard on systems with tight memory.

A,    *ARC
C,    *CIRCLE
CP,   *COPY
DV,   *DVIEW
E,    *ERASE
L,    *LINE
LA,   *LAYER
M,    *MOVE
MS,   *MSPACE
P,    *PAN
PS,   *PSPACE
PL,   *PLINE
R,    *REDRAW
Z,    *ZOOM
```

Command aliases are limited to one word that precludes the addition of any command options. Transparent aliases also can be defined for transparent commands.

Memory Considerations

If you are running into memory problems with external commands, you may need to increase the amount of available memory. This is done with the SHROOM program in the sample subdirectory of your AutoCAD directory. Each command alias takes up a small amount of memory, so you should avoid defining command aliases unnecessarily. If you are very tight on memory, you may want to delete the command aliases you do not use. Many aisles for AME commands exist; if you did not buy or install AME you may want to consider deleting these command aliases.

Prototype Drawings

A *prototype drawing* is loaded with each new drawing. The prototype defines many of the basic default parameters of an AutoCAD drawing. When you start a new drawing, you can name a specific file to use as a prototype drawing, or you can accept AutoCAD's default settings. You also can tell AutoCAD to retain your prototype as the default to use each time a new drawing is begun. Changes made to the drawing have no effect on the prototype drawing.

Prototypes

Layers, blocks, menus, linetypes, text styles, limits, views, and external references can be defined in a prototype. These features are available at startup, when the prototype is used. If you want to create a prototype that is automatically loaded, call it ACAD.DWG. To add a menu to a prototype, load the menu with the MENU command, and save the prototype. AutoCAD remembers the last menu file loaded and reloads that menu when the drawing is opened or used as a prototype.

Inserts

In addition to defining a prototype drawing in the standard way, you can insert any drawing into another and add many of the inserted drawings features. A common use for this technique is a *block library file*, in which several blocks are defined in one drawing, and then the drawing is saved. The block library file can then be inserted into other drawings, making all of the blocks available for use. Any layers, linetypes, or text styles that are defined in a drawing that is inserted also are available for use. Using this technique, you can insert any number of drawings to add specific sets of features to your drawings.

System Variables

System variable settings can be changed to modify your drawing environment. You probably already do this with the basic setup commands each time you start a new drawing. An example of this is the UNITS command, which can set six system variables. For a complete discussion of the system variables, see the "AutoCAD System Variable Reference."

 System variables saved in the ACAD.CFG configuration file will be stored and used for every drawing.

 System variables saved in the current drawing file will be stored and used every time the drawing is edited.

Grips

The grip edit mode, noun/verb object selection, and octal tree entity search method are three major improvements to Release 12 of AutoCAD. These features can be customized to your preferences using the DDGRIPS and DDSELECT commands.

 For more information on grips, see Chapter 4.

DDGRIPS

DDGRIPS changes the appearance of the grips used in grip-mode editing. The following system variables are affected:

GRIPBLOCK	GRIPHOT
GRIPCOLOR	GRIPSIZE

DDSELECT

DDSELECT controls the use of grips, noun/verb selection, and the entity-sort order. The following system variables are affected:

GRIPS	PICKDRAG
PICKADD	PICKFIRST
PICKAUTO	SORTENTS

Automatic Save

The automatic save feature of AutoCAD enables you to specify an automatic save file name and a time duration between automatic file saves. The default setting is to save to AUTO.SV$ every 120 minutes. You can change these settings by setting the SAVENAME and SAVETIME system variables.

Units

The drawing units and precision are controlled with the DDUNITS command. Figure 10.1 shows the Units Control dialog box. You can specify the desired unit of measure and precision for both linear and angular measurements. The following system variables are affected:

ANGBASE	AUPREC
ANGDIR	LUNITS
AUNITS	LUPREC

Miscellaneous System Variables

Over 180 system variables control AutoCAD's behavior. Some are read-only and cannot be changed, others can only be changed with an AutoCAD command. Many of them pass unnoticed the entire time you use AutoCAD. The following list of system variables control some of the basic drawing features and menu responses:

Drawing Features

CECOLOR	ELEVATION	PDSIZE	SPLINETYPE
CELTYPE	FILLETRAD	PFACEVMAX	SURFTAB1
CHAMFERA	LIMCHECK	PLINEGEN	SURFTAB2
CHAMFERB	LIMMAX	PLINEWID	SURFTYPE
CIRCLERAD	LIMMIN	POLYSIDES	SURFU
CLAYER	LTSCALE	PSLTSCALE	SURFV
DONUTID	OFFSETDIST	SPLFRAME	THICKNESS
DONUTOD	PDMODE	SPLINESEGS	TRACEWID

Menu Responses

CMDDIA	MENUECHO
FILEDIA	SCREENBOXES
MAXSORT	SCREENMODE
MENUCTL	TABMODE

Figure 10.1:
The Units Control dialog box.

Start-Up LISP Files

AutoCAD functions can be written in AutoLISP and loaded into
the drawing editor for your use. Three AutoLISP files can be loaded

into the drawing editor automatically at start-up: ACADR12.LSP, ACAD.LSP, and MENUNAME.MNL. For more information on AutoLISP, see *Maximizing AutoLISP*, published by New Riders Publishing.

 Before you modify any AutoCAD or third-party supplied AutoLISP files, make a backup of the files.

ACADR12.LSP

ACADR12.LSP is the AutoLISP file that contains many of AutoCAD's external functions. ACADR12.LSP can be found in the Support subdirectory of your AutoCAD directory. If you know AutoLISP, you can modify the commands in ACADR12.LSP, or you can add your own new commands.

ACAD.LSP

ACAD.LSP previously was used when ACADR12.LSP is used in Release 12. The file name has been retained as one that is searched for and loaded whenever a drawing is loaded. This enables you to create a library of AutoLISP routines that is automatically loaded without having to modify ACADR12.LSP.

MENUNAME.MNL

MNL files are AutoLISP files that support menus. When a menu is loaded, AutoCAD searches for a file with the same name and an MNL extension. If the MENUNAME.MNL file is found, it is loaded with the menu. In this way, you can write AutoLISP drivers for menus without having to worry about how to get them loaded. The practical upshot of this is that you can add any functions to the MENUNAME.MNL file that is loaded with your drawing. ACAD.MNL is the AutoLISP file that supports ACAD.MNU, and it is automatically loaded unless you have specified a different menu in your drawing or prototype drawing. ACAD.MNL can be found in the Support directory of your AutoCAD directory.

Creating Text and Dimension Styles

AutoCAD provides a wide variety of settings for text and dimension styles. Several styles can be defined in a drawing and made current when needed. The styles are saved with the drawing.

Text

Text styles are created using the STYLE command or selecting Text Style from the Entity Creation Modes dialog box. You can specify the style's name, font, height, width factor, oblique angle, backwards, upside-down, and vertical settings. The fonts are shape files and PostScript font files. For more information on PostScript, see Chapter 11. You can create your own font files externally by creating a shape file. Figure 10.2 shows the Select Text Style dialog box.

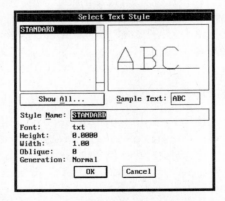

Figure 10.2:
The Select Text Style dialog box.

Dimension

Dimension styles are created using the Dim:SAVE and the DDIM commands. Many of the dimension variables can be set with DDIM and saved with Dim:SAVE. A Dim:STYLE command is available that sets the current text style. For more information on dimensions and dimension styles, see Chapter 6. Figure 10.3 shows the Dimension Styles and Variables dialog box.

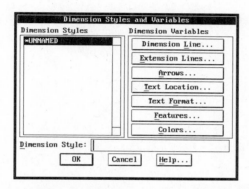

Figure 10.3:
The Dimension Styles and Variables dialog box.

Shapes and Fonts

Shapes are externally defined entities similar to blocks. The shape's definition is stored in an external file even after the shape has been added to a drawing. You can have several definitions in one shape file. Unlike blocks, this can significantly decrease the potential size of a drawing file. Because shapes are external files, whole libraries of related shapes can be purchased from third-party developers, and added to your drawings very easily. Font files are shape files that contain several shape definitions that look like letters. Shapes have two disadvantages, shapes can be constructed from only a few simple entities and defining a shape is a tedious, exacting process.

Shapes

Shapes are entities made of lines, arcs, and circles only. These lines, arcs, and circles are defined in an external file containing programming codes and vectors. The following shape definition is for the resistor shown in figure 10.4.

Figure 10.4:
Shape 129a resistor.

*129,12,RES

3,20,020,023,04D,043,04D,043,04D,023,020,0

After the shape file has been defined, it must be compiled with the COMPILE command and loaded with the LOAD command before the shape can be inserted with the SHAPE command. Obviously, more effort is involved with shapes than with blocks or external references. In some cases, having several shapes defined in one file without adding much to the drawing database can make up for the effort of preparing a shape.

Fonts

Fonts are an ideal use of shapes. A single shape file can have 255 separate definitions. This enables a single font file to have a shape for nearly every letter or symbol you might need in a given font style. Each font file that comes with AutoCAD defines the basic letters and symbols needed for text with a different font style. All of the font files provide a large library of fonts available for use. Figure 10.5 shows the Select Text Font dialog box.

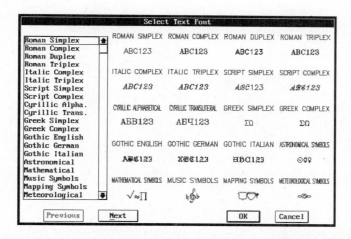

Figure 10.5:
The Select Text Font dialog box.

Bigfonts

Bigfonts are complex shape codes that enable the definition of large shapes that represent fonts. The symbols of the Japanese and Chinese language are examples of the need for bigfont files.

Using Blocks, Wblocks, and Xrefs

Blocks, wblocks, external references (xrefs), and shapes are three ways you can store entities for insertion into drawings. Blocks, wblocks, and xrefs are discussed in the following section.

For more information on blocks and xrefs, see Chapter 5.

Blocks

A *block* is a group of entities that have been joined together and treated as one complex entity. The block's definition is stored in the Insert Table of the drawing database. After a block is defined with the BLOCK command, it can be placed in the drawing over and over, using the INSERT command. Each time the block is inserted, the Insert Table is referenced. The individual entities of the block do not have to be entered into the drawing database each time a block is inserted, saving large amounts of disk space. Blocks are limited to the drawing in which they are defined.

The Inserts section of the Prototype Drawing portion of this chapter mentions block libraries. A *block library* takes advantage of the fact that multiple blocks can be defined and saved in one drawing. This drawing then can be inserted into other drawings using the INSERT command, making all of the original blocks available for use. All of the blocks in a block library are stored in the new drawing's database block table. You may not need all of the blocks that come in the library.

Use the PURGE command to remove unwanted block definitions from a drawing file. This keeps your drawing size down and speeds up your database search.

Another advantage to blocks is the use of attributes. *Attributes* enable you to define parametric text strings in the block. Each time you insert the block, you are prompted for the strings' value. The value is then stored along with the block. Attributes can be displayed or made invisible; they can have constant values, default values, or any value you want, depending on the attribute definition. Attributes are defined with the DDATTDEF and ATTDEF commands.

Attribute values can be edited with the DDATTE and ATTEDIT commands. One of the most important and valuable aspects of attributes is the capability to extract the text string from the drawing and insert it into a text file. This enables you to insert your blocks at random and then extract all of the necessary information on your blocks and their attributes when you are finished. This technique is useful any time you need to keep track of specific drawing contents. In the following example, a block of a desk with phone attributes has been inserted several times. Figure 10.6 shows a series of blocks with attributes.

```
■ Layer 0              12.2148,8.9891         AutoCAD
                                              * * * *
                                              ASE
                                              BLOCKS
      MAGGIE           JAMES                  DIM:
      OSTER    📞       WINGER   📞             DISPLAY
      234              567                     DRAW
                                              EDIT
                                              INQUIRY
                                              LAYER...
                                              MODEL
      TIM              KURT                    MVIEW
      SMITH    📞       HAMPE    📞             PLOT...
      345              678                     RENDER
                                              SETTINGS
                                              SURFACES
                                              UCS:
      JAMES            DAVID                   UTILITY
      KAISER   📞       KING     📞
      456              789                     SAVE:


Command :
Command :
Command :
```

Figure 10.6:
Blocks with attributes.

The following is some of the data that can be extracted from the attributes.

'PHONE', 2, 8, 'MAGGIE', 'OSTER', '234'
'PHONE', 2, 6, 'TIM', 'SMITH', '345'
'PHONE', 2, 3, 'JAMES', 'KAISER', '456'
'PHONE', 7, 8, 'JAMES', 'WINGER', '567'
'PHONE', 7, 6, 'KURT', 'HAMPE', '678'
'PHONE', 7, 3, 'DAVID', 'KING', '789'

 You can use the SQL extension of AutoCAD in place of attributes and have a two-way communication between your drawing and a database.

Wblocks

Wblocks are blocks with definitions that are stored in separate disk files before the blocks are inserted. Wblocks are created with the WBLOCK command. The steps for defining a WBLOCK are the same as the BLOCK command, with the additional step of entering the file name in which the WBLOCK will be stored. Wblock files can be accessed and edited just as any other drawing file. In fact, any drawing file can be inserted into another drawing file as if it were a wblock. Unlike block files, wblock files can be inserted into any drawing.

 Wblocks can have attributes just like blocks. You can insert these attributes into any drawing.

Xrefs

Xrefs (external references) are drawing files that are attached to other drawing files. An xref drawing can be any drawing file, and you do not need any special definition. Xrefs are attached to drawings with the

XREF command. The difference between an xref and a wblock is that the xref's definition is never imported into the host drawing. Each time the drawing is loaded, xrefs are reloaded from their file.

Xrefs have two major advantages. The first advantage is drawing-file size. When an xref is attached to another drawing, the host drawing's database does not have to absorb the xref's entities in the database or Insert Table. The second advantage is in updates. Because the xref is reloaded each time the host drawing is reloaded, the xref updates according to its drawing file. Xrefs enable you to divide a project among several drafters without worrying about everyone having the most up-to-date blocks.

A potential advantage or disadvantage to xrefs involves editing referenced files. An xref's drawing file cannot be edited from within the host drawing. One definite disadvantage of an xref is that you must give both the host drawing file and the xref drawing file to anyone who needs the complete drawing.

Creating Linetypes, Hatches, and PostScript Fills

AutoCAD enables you to use and define custom linetype and fill patterns in your drawings. Linetypes and file patterns are defined in external files and loaded as needed.

Linetypes

Linetype patterns, such as hidden or phantom, are defined with the LINETYPE command or externally with a text editor. Linetypes are stored in LIN files and loaded and set current with LINETYPE when they are needed. LIN files can contain several linetypes but only the ones loaded from the file will be available. ACAD.LIN is the default linetype.

Linetype definitions consist of positive numbers representing the lengths of dashes, negative numbers representing the lengths of blanks, and zeros representing dots. All linetypes are scaled the same, according to the linetype scale set with LTSCALE. Figure 10.7 shows a phantom linetype.

PHANTOM

Figure 10.7:
The phantom linetype.

The linetype definition for the phantom line is shown here.

```
*PHANTOM,_____  __  __  _____  __  __  _____  __  __  _____  __  __
A,1.25,-.25,.25,-.25,.25,-.25
```

Linetypes are limited in the following ways:

- The entire line must be on one layer.
- The segments of a line cannot be scaled differently from one another.
- All of the lines in a drawing are governed by the scale factor.
- A linetype cannot be exploded into its individual segments.

Hatches

Hatch patterns define a fill pattern that is inserted in a block. Simple hatch patterns can be defined using the BHATCH or HATCH commands. More complex hatches are defined externally with a text editor. Hatch patterns are stored in PAT files, which are loaded with the BHATCH or HATCH commands.

Hatch patterns consist of a pattern name and a series of descriptors that include the X origin, Y origin, delta X, and delta Y coordinates of the pattern. Additional numbers, representing dashed lines, also can be added. All hatches are scaled according to the current LTSCALE setting. Figure 10.8 shows the Escher hatch pattern.

Figure 10.8:
The Escher hatch pattern.

The following is the hatch definition for the Escher hatch. This is a complex hatch pattern—most are easier to define.

```
*ESCHER, Escher pattern
60, 0,0, -.6,1.039230484, 1.1,-.1
180, 0,0, -.6,1.039230484, 1.1,-.1
300, 0,0, .6,1.039230484, 1.1,-.1
60, .1,0, -.6,1.039230484, .2,-1
```

```
300, .1,0, .6,1.039230484, .2,-1
60, -.05,.08660254, -.6,1.039230484, .2,-1
180, -.05,.08660254, -.6,1.039230484, .2,-1
300, -.05,-.08660254, .6,1.039230484, .2,-1
180, -.05,-.08660254, -.6,1.039230484, .2,-1
60, -.4,0, -.6,1.039230484, .2,-1
300, -.4,0, .6,1.039230484, .2,-1
60, .2,-.346410161, -.6,1.039230484, .2,-1
180, .2,-.346410161, -.6,1.039230484, .2,-1
300, .2,.346410161, .6,1.039230484, .2,-1
180, .2,.346410161, -.6,1.039230484, .2,-1
0, .2,.173205081, -.6,1.039230484, .7,-.5
0, .2,-.173205081, -.6,1.039230484, .7,-.5
120, .05,.259807621, .6,1.039230484, .7,-.5
120, -.25,.08660254, .6,1.039230484, .7,-.5
240, -.25,-.08660254, .6,1.039230484, .7,-.5
240, .05,-.259807621, .6,1.039230484, .7,-.5
```

 You cannot edit a hatch pattern without first exploding it.

 If you explode a hatch pattern, all of its individual segments are entered into the drawing database, increasing the size of your drawing significantly.

PostScript Fills

A *PostScript fill* is a graphic fill pattern that is applied to a closed polyline area by the PSFILL command. Fill patterns are defined with a text editor using the PostScript language and stored in external .PSF files. The default PostScript fill pattern file is ACAD.PSF. The following is the code for the brick fill pattern:

```
%@Fill
/Brick %Brick,5, Scale=1.0, LineWidth=1,
BrickGray1=100, BrickGray2=50, BackGroundGray=0
  {
  /Bgray exch 0 100 Rangefilter def
  /Fgray2 exch 0 100 Rangefilter def
  /Fgray1 exch 0 100 Rangefilter def
  /LineWidth exch 0 100 Rangefilter def
  /Scale exch 1 10000 Rangefilter def
  /newfont 10 dict def
  newfont begin
  /FontMatrix [1 0 0 1 0 0] def
  /FontType 3 def
  /FontBBox [0 0 1 1] def
  /Encoding 256 array def
  0 1 255 {Encoding exch /.notdef put} for
  Encoding 97 /Fill1 put
  Encoding 98 /Fill2 put
  Encoding 99 /Lines put
  /CharProcs 4 dict def
  CharProcs begin
  /.notdef {} def
  /Fill1
   {
   .025 .975 moveto
   .025 .525 lineto
   .975 .525 lineto
   .975 .975 lineto
   .025 .975 lineto
   closepath
   fill
   } def
  /Fill2
   {
   .000 .475 moveto
   .000 .025 lineto
   .475 .025 lineto
   .475 .475 lineto
```

```
.000 .475 lineto
1.000 .475 moveto
1.000 .025 lineto
.525 .025 lineto
.525 .475 lineto
1.000 .475 lineto
closepath
fill
} def
/Lines
{
newpath
1.000 .025 moveto
.525 .025 lineto
.525 .475 lineto
1.000 .475 lineto
.000 .025 moveto
.475 .025 lineto
.475 .475 lineto
.000 .475 lineto
.025 .975 moveto
.025 .525 lineto
.975 .525 lineto
.975 .975 lineto
.025 .975 lineto
LineWidth 100 div setlinewidth
stroke
} def
end

/BuildChar
{ 1 0
  0 0 1 1
  setcachedevice
  exch begin
  Encoding exch get
  CharProcs exch get
  end
  exec
} def
end
```

```
/pntsize 1000 Scale mul def
/FillFont newfont definefont pop
/FillFont findfont pntsize scalefont setfont
eoclip
Bgray 100 div 1 exch sub setgray fill
Fgray1 100 div 1 exch sub setgray
Bblly pntsize Bbury
 { Bbllx pntsize Bburx
   { 1 index moveto
   (a) show
   } for
 pop
 } for
Fgray2 100 div 1 exch sub setgray
Bblly pntsize Bbury
 { Bbllx pntsize Bburx
   { 1 index moveto
   (b) show
   } for
 pop
 } for
0 setgray
Bblly pntsize Bbury
   { Bbllx pntsize Bburx
   { 1 index moveto
   (c)show
   } for
 pop
 } for
} bind def
```

Using Scripts and Slides

Script and slide files are two separate features of AutoCAD that often are used together. A *script* is a text file containing AutoCAD commands. A *slide* is a captured screen image of an AutoCAD drawing. Using the two together enables you to create automated slide shows on your video display.

363

Scripts

Scripts are text files containing AutoCAD commands. All script files have the extension SCR. Script files can be invoked inside a drawing or when a drawing file is loaded. To run a script from within AutoCAD, use the SCRIPT command. To invoke a script file when loading a drawing, type the script file name after the name of the drawing you want to load.

```
OS PROMPT>ACAD DRAWING_NAME SCRIPT_NAME
```

 To preserve compatibility with older versions of AutoCAD, the PICKADD system variable is assumed to be 1 and the PICKAUTO system variable is assumed to be 0 whenever a script is run.

The following commands have been added to AutoCAD to make the process of running a script easier:

DELAY	RESUME
GRAPHSCR	TEXTSCR
RCRIPT	

The following is a sample script file. This script file sets the snap on, loads the custom1 linetype from the CUSTOM.LIN linetype file, and makes a new layer called TEST with the custom1 linetype.

```
SNAP ON
LINETYPE LOAD CUSTOM1 CUSTOM

LAYER MAKE TEST LT CUSTOM1 TEST
```

Unlike many types of external files, script files do not ignore blank lines. Blank lines are interpreted as a Return. The preceding file listing has a block line after the linetype and layer commands to end each command.

Slides

Slides are drawing images shown on your computer screen. The image in a slide does not have any vector or entity information. You cannot edit a slide or select it. Slides are made with the MSLIDE command and displayed with the VSLIDE command.

Slides are stored in external files in one of two ways. The first is an *.SLD file. This file contains a single slide image. You can also store slides in a slide library file.

Slide library files contain many slide definitions and have the extension *.SLB. The default AutoCAD slide file is ACAD.SLB. Slide libraries are created by following these steps:

1. Create the individual slide files with MSLIDE.
2. Exit AutoCAD and create a text file containing the names of the slide files to put in the library file.
3. Use the SLIDELIB.EXE program to create a slide library file of the slides listed in the text file created in step 2.

The icons used in the standard AutoCAD icon menus, such as Text, Viewpoint, and Hatch Pattern menus, are all slides. These slides are stored in the ACAD.SLB slide library file and accessed by the menu code when needed. Slides also can be used on the Image tiles and Image Buttons of a dialog box. The slides used in a dialog box can be individual slides or slides from a slide library.

Do not try to edit displayed slides. You may inadvertently edit the drawing entities that the slide is covering.

If you are in paper space, MSLIDE captures the entire display screen, including all viewports on the screen. If you are in model space, MSLIDE captures the current viewport only. VSLIDE scales slides to fit the current viewport in paper space or model space.

Chapter 10

Customizing Menus and Macros

Menus and macros are used to ease access to AutoCAD commands and to automate AutoCAD commands. This is accomplished by defining a menus appearance and then assigning an activity to each menu option in the form of a macro. Menu definitions and actions are stored in external *.MNU text files. Menus are loaded with the MENU commands. When a menu is loaded, it is automatically compiled and stored as an *.MNX file. The default AutoCAD menu file is ACAD.MNU, which is compiled to ACAD.MNX. After a menu is compiled, the compiled menu is loaded instead of the MNU file. If an MNU file is changed, AutoCAD automatically recompiles it when the menu is loaded.

Macros

Macros are used to drive the options of AutoCAD menus. Macros are little more than AutoCAD commands, their options, and some special codes strung together. Macros can call AutoCAD commands, set the command options, pause for input, and automatically repeat. An example of a macro that lists the available views, and then sets a user selected view current, is shown here. The backslash (\) enables the macro to pause for input; semicolons (;) are used for Returns.

```
[Set View]view;?;;;r;\
```

NOTE Macros interpret spaces as a space, which usually is equivalent to a carriage return (when you press Enter). Macros assume a return at the end of each line. Use the plus (+) key to string lines together without issuing a return.

Macros can call dialog boxes, but macros cannot provide input to dialog boxes. If you have a macro call a dialog box, you must provide all of the input manually. You cannot automate the dialog-box settings.

DIESEL

The DIESEL language (Direct Interpretively Evaluated String Expression Language) is an AutoCAD programming language. Many of the functions of the DIESEL language are similar to AutoLISP functions in name and in purpose. DIESEL expressions can be imbedded in macros to run special functions. When a DIESEL expression is encountered, AutoCAD evaluates the expression and returns a string value in the DIESEL strings place.

The major advantage to including DIESEL expressions is that they are interpreted every time AutoCAD runs into them. This enables you to create menus that can respond interactively with the AutoCAD environment. In addition to its interactive nature, DIESEL gives you three other benefits. DIESEL expressions are an efficient way of making and reading changes to the AutoCAD environment, they do not suffer from re-entry errors the way AutoLISP does when it is used interactively, and they enable you to create parametric custom status lines when used with the MODEMACRO system variable. An example of a DIESEL expression that returns a 1 or 0, based on the value of the UCSFOLLOW system variable, is shown here. The $M= code indicates that the DIESEL expression is in a menu macro.

```
$M=$(if,$(getvar,pickadd),0,1)
```

 The DIESEL language is not fully functional for all AutoCAD platforms. Check your README.DOC file or your *AutoCAD Interface, Installation, and Performance Guide* for compatibility details.

AutoLISP

AutoLISP can be used with the DIESEL language in menu macros. Some limitations exist, however, when using AutoLISP this way. Any AutoLISP code over 255 characters must be broken up with a semicolon (;). Using AutoLISP interactively can produce re-entry errors, which prevent AutoLISP from continuing.

The best way to use AutoLISP in menu files is to have your macros call AutoLISP functions that are defined in a separate file. If you name your AutoLISP file with the same name as the menu file and an extension of MNL, the AutoLISP file loads automatically at the same time as the menu.

Screen Menus

A *screen menu* is the AutoCAD menu that runs down the right side of your graphics screen. A screen menu lists a single page of options that can call macros or other pages of the screen menu. These menus also are driven by keyboard selection if the MENUCTL system variable is set to 1. Figure 10.9 shows the first page of the default screen menu for AutoCAD.

The following is the code for the first page of the screen menu:

```
***SCREEN
**S
[AutoCAD]^C^C^P(ai_rootmenus)  ^P
[* * * *]$S=OSNAPB
[ASE]^C^C^P(ai_aseinit_chk)  ^P
[BLOCKS]$S=X  $S=BL
[DIM:]^C^C_DIM
[DISPLAY]$S=X  $S=DS
[DRAW]$S=X  $S=DR
[EDIT]$S=X  $S=ED
[INQUIRY]$S=X  $S=INQ
[LAYER...]$S=LAYER  '_DDLMODES
[MODEL]$S=X  $S=SOLIDS
```

```
[MVIEW]$S=MVIEW
[PLOT...]^C^C_PLOT
[RENDER]$S=X  $S=RENDER
[SETTINGS]$S=X  $S=SET
[SURFACES]$S=X  $S=3D
[UCS:]^C^C_UCS
[UTILITY]$S=X  $S=UT

[SAVE:]^C^C_QSAVE
```

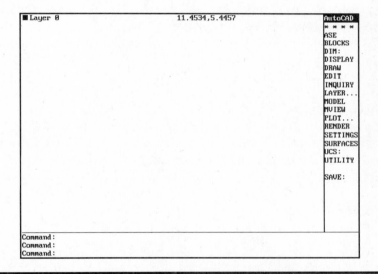

Figure 10.9:
The default screen menu's first page.

Button and Auxiliary Menus

Button and auxiliary menus define the actions taken with digitizer buttons. *Button menus* are used if a system does not have a system mouse and *auxiliary menus* are used if a system has a system mouse.

NOTE SPARCstations and Macintoshes have a system mouse and use the auxiliary menus.

A maximum of four button and auxiliary menus can be used. By default, your system uses the Buttons1 or Aux1 menu. If you press the Shift key when you use the digitizer buttons, the Buttons2 or Aux2 menu is used. If you press the Ctrl key when you use the digitizer buttons, the Buttons3 or Aux3 menu is used. If you press the Ctrl-Shift keys at the same time when you use the digitizer buttons, the Buttons4 or Aux4 menu is used. Having access to four different sets of button menus enables you to define four completely different sets of tasks for the same buttons. Each line of a button or auxiliary menu lists the action that a button should take. The first line lists the action for the second digitizer button, and each line after that is for the next digitizer button. You can have as many lines as you want in the menu because your digitizer will be able to access as many lines as the digitizer has definable buttons. The first digitizer button is the pick button, which cannot be redefined. The default Buttons1 and Aux1 menus follow:

```
***BUTTONS1
;
$p0=*
^C^C
^B
^O
^G
^D
^E
^T

***AUX1
;
$p0=*
^C^C
^B
^O
^G
^D
^E
^T
```

Tablet Menus

Tablets control the actions taken by menu selections on a digitizing tablet. You can define four menu areas on your tablet, each one with a maximum of 32766 menu items. Each table item is identified by a row letter and column number. The top of the Tablet1 menu that comes in ACAD.MNU has several blank definitions that are available for your use. Some of the lines have been defined for use by the AME and RENDER commands. AutoDESK recommends against redefining any of the lines following box [I-25] on the tablet menu.

Pull-Down Menus

Pull-down menus are vertical lists of menu options accessed from the status line. You can define a maximum of 17 pull-down menus. Each menu is identified as ***POPn, in which n is the number of the menu. ***POP1 through ***POP16 define the menus accessed by the status line. Each menu can have as many as 999 menu items. By default, AutoCAD uses ***POP1 through ***POP9 to define the standard pull-down menus.

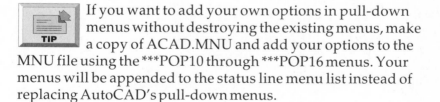

If you want to add your own options in pull-down menus without destroying the existing menus, make a copy of ACAD.MNU and add your options to the MNU file using the ***POP10 through ***POP16 menus. Your menus will be appended to the status line menu list instead of replacing AutoCAD's pull-down menus.

Each pull-down menu can access a cascading menu. A *cascading menu*, like a pull-down menu, is a vertical listing of menu options. This enables you to have your menus show AutoCAD commands and display a cascading menu of the command options. Figure 10.10 shows the ***POP2 pull-down menu and the Inquiry cascading menu.

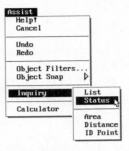

Figure 10.10:
The Assist pull-down menu and Inquiry cascading menu.

The following is the code for the ***POP2 pull-down menu and the associated cursor menus:

```
***POP2
[Assist]
[Help!]'?
[Cancel]^C^C^C
[--]
[Undo]_U
[Redo]^C^C_redo
[--]
[Object Filters...]'filter
[->Object Snap]
 [Center]_center
 [Endpoint]_endp
 [Insert]_ins
 [Intersection]_int
 [Midpoint]_mid
 [Nearest]_nea
 [Node]_nod
 [Perpendicular]_per
 [Quadrant]_qua
 [Tangent]_tan
 [<-None]_non
[--]
```

```
[->Inquiry]
 [List]^C^C_list
 [Status]'_status
 [--]
 [Area]^C^C_area
 [Distance]^C^C'_dist
 [<-ID Point]'_id
[--]
[Calculator]'cal
```

Cursor Menus

The *cursor menu* is a pull-down menu that appears at the cursor location when the third digitizer button is pressed. If you have a two-button mouse, press the Shift key and the second digitizer button to get the cursor menu. The cursor-menu options are defined in the ***POP0 pull-down menu. Aside from its location, the cursor menu is defined exactly like a regular pull-down menu. The cursor menu can have 499 menu options and cascading menus. Figure 10.11 shows the default cursor menu.

Figure 10.11:
The default cursor menu.

The following is the code for the default cursor menu:

```
***POP0
[Osnap]
[Center]_center
[Endpoint]_endp
[Insert]_ins
[Intersection]_int
[Midpoint]_mid
[Nearest]_nea
[Node]_nod
[Perpendicular]_per
[Quadrant]_qua
[Tangent]_tan
[None]_non
[->Filters]
 [.X].X
 [.Y].Y
 [.Z].Z
 [.XY].XY
 [.XZ].XZ
 [<-.YZ].YZ
[Calculator]'cal
```

Icon Menu

Icon menus display a list of graphic options in a dialog box. An icon menu uses slide files or slides from a slide library file to show the available options. Only one ***Icon menu is available in a menu file but it can have several subsections, each section defining a different icon menu.

The default ***Icon menu includes definitions for the Set Spline Fit Variables, 3D Object, Text Font, and Tiled Viewport Layout icon menus. Figure 10.12 shows the 3D Objects icon menu.

The following is the code for part of the ***ICON menu, including the 3D Objects icon menu:

```
**3DObjects
[3D Objects]
```

```
[acad(box3d,3D Box)]^C^Cai_box
[acad(Pyramid)]^C^Cai_pyramid
[acad(Wedge)]^C^Cai_wedge
[acad(Dome)]^C^Cai_dome
[acad(Sphere)]^C^Cai_sphere
[acad(Cone)]^C^Cai_cone
[acad(Torus)]^C^Cai_torus
[acad(Dish)]^C^Cai_dish
[acad(Mesh)]^C^Cai_mesh
```

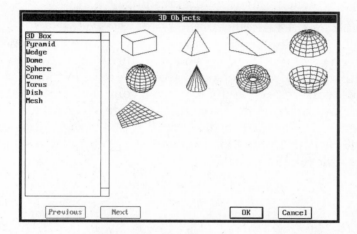

Figure 10.12:
The 3D Objects icon menu.

Developing Functions with AutoLISP and ADS

The two main programming languages for AutoCAD are AutoLISP and the AutoCAD Development System (ADS). Both languages can be used to develop applications for AutoCAD, and each has its own advantages and disadvantages. Whether you use AutoLISP or ADS, you must have a basic understanding of programming techniques.

375

AutoLISP

AutoLISP is a LISP-based interpreted language. AutoLISP code can be entered directly at the Command: prompt to develop temporary functions, or saved in a text file to create permanent functions. AutoLISP is forgiving and requires little structure to function properly. AutoLISP pays for these nice features, however, with a speed penalty. Being interpreted, AutoLISP also is relatively easy to debug because it runs until an error is encountered before crashing.

You should consider that the original AutoLISP code listing must be maintained because it is interpreted each time the function is needed. Anyone can access your code. If you are a third-party developer in a competitive market segment, open access to your product may be a problem. If you are developing AutoCAD commands for your own use, you may find AutoLISP to be the language of choice because it is easy to use in development. The following code listing is an example of the AutoLISP code needed to display a dialog box called test1 in a dialog-box file called TEST.DCL.

```
(defun display_dialog (/ dialog_index)
 (if (> (setq dialog_index (load_dialog "TEST")) 0)
  (progn
   (if (new_dialog "test1" index_dialog)
    (progn
      ;dialog box driver code
    )
    (alert "Unable to display dialog box")
   )
  )
  (alert "Unable to open dialog box")
 )
)
```

AutoLISP also enables you to undefine and redefine existing AutoCAD commands using the UNDEFINE and REDEFINE commands. This enables you to remove existing AutoCAD commands or assign a new meaning to an existing command name.

A command that is undefined can still be accessed if you precede the command name with a period (.).

ADS

ADS is a C-based compiled language. ADS functions cannot be entered at the Command: prompt. ADS functions must be entered into a text file and compiled with a supported C compiler. AutoCAD provides header files to include in your code to support the functions necessary to work in AutoCAD. The C compilers supported depend on your platform; consult your *Interface, Installation, and Performance Guide.* Your C compiler must support the math coprocessor and should compile 32-bit code.

ADS offers three main advantages over AutoLISP. The first is flexibility. You can do more with the ADS language than you can with AutoLISP. ADS has more functions. The second advantage is speed. ADS creates an executable file that can be run much faster than AutoLISP can be interpreted. The final reason for using ADS is security. Because ADS compiles your code to an executable file, your code is protected from prying eyes. Although executable code can be unassembled into assembler code, anyone who can do this and understand the results can probably write their own functions from scratch just as easily.

ADS also has some drawbacks. First, C is a very structured language that requires a lot of attention to detail and setup. Second, most functions are more complex because C requires the use of memory buffers for most operations. Third, the code must be completely correct before it can be compiled and run, and because the code cannot be run until it is correct, debugging can be more difficult.

If your primary concerns are speed or security, or you need a function that AutoLISP does not provide, use ADS. Many of the newer features of AutoCAD, such as SQL and AME, are supported better by ADS than

AutoLISP. The following code listing is an example of the ADS code needed to display a dialog box called test1 in a dialog box file called TEST.DCL.

```
int display_dialog()
{
 int dialog_index, dialog_status;
 ads_hdlg dialog_handle;
 if (ads_load_dialog("test", &dialog_index) == RTNORM)
   {
     if (ads_new_dialog("test", dialog_index, NULLCB,
     &dialog_handle) == RTNORM)
       {
        /* dialog box driver code
        {
      else
        {
         ads_alert("Unable to load dialog box");
        }
     }
   else
     {
      ads_alert("Unable to load dialog box");
     }
}
```

Customizing Dialog Boxes

Dialog boxes are interactive menus that present the user with a list of options in a natural, easily accessible, self-explanatory manner. Dialog boxes offer several advantages over most conventional menus. Dialog boxes are used interactively, enabling the dialog box to make subtle changes in response to a user's actions. Dialog boxes present you with all of the options of a command in a simple, easy-to-interpret manner. Dialog boxes are driven by digitizer cursor and shortcut key selections, enabling fast access to the options presented. Dialog boxes automatically conform to the graphic user interface (GUI) of the host system so that you do not have to alter your programming to maintain conformity with each platform GUI. Finally, dialog boxes provide many ways of presenting the necessary information and options to the user.

  Shortcut keys are not supported on all platforms.

Disadvantages of dialog boxes also exist. You must create the dialog box in the Dialog Control Language (DCL), which means that you must use another language. The DCL language is very easy to learn, however.

Dialog boxes require complex drivers to operate properly. The two previous code listings in the AutoLISP and ADS sections are the code necessary to start a dialog box. Dialog boxes require a lot of planning in the design phase to get a useful result that is easily supported. After you are familiar with dialog-box programming, however, you will be able to create very complex user interfaces without too much effort.

Figure 10.13 shows a simple dialog box with a text tile and a pop-up list. The dialog box's actions in response to user selections and the names in the pop-up list are supplied by a separate driver program.

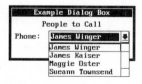

Figure 10.13:
The Test dialog box.

The following is the DCL code for the dialog box in figure 10.13:

```
test : dialog
{
  label = "Example Dialog Box";
```

```
: text
{
 alignment = centered;
 label = "People to Call";
}
: popup_list
{
 key = "phone_list";
 label = "Phone: ";
 edit_width = 16;
}
ok_only;
}
```

The driver for the dialog box can be written in AutoLISP or ADS. The following is an example AutoLISP driver for the dialog box in figure 10.13:

```
(defun build_list ()
 (start_list "phone_list")
 (add_list "James Winger")
 (add_list "James Kaiser")
 (add_list "Maggie Oster")
 (add_list "Sueann Townsend")
 (end_list)
)

(defun c:dd (/ dialog_index)
 (if (> (setq dialog_index (load_dialog "test")) 0)
  (progn
   (if (new_dialog "test" dialog_index)
    (progn
     (build_list)
     (start_dialog)
    )
    (alert "Unable to display dialog box")
   )
   (unload_dialog dialog_index)
  )
  (alert "Unable to open dialog box")
 )
)
```

Customizing AutoCAD for Windows

AutoCAD for Windows enables some customizations that are not available on other platforms. This is due in part to the differences between the Windows-based GUI and the standard AutoCAD GUI.

ACAD.INI

The ACAD.INI file is the initialization file for AutoCAD for Windows. This file contains many of the settings that define the default appearance and behavior of AutoCAD for Windows. You can edit the file manually or allow AutoCAD to edit the file for you by using the built-in customization feature. The following is a listing of the AutoCAD General part of the ACAD.INI file:

```
[AutoCAD General]
ToolBarSize=16
ToolBar1=(if (null tbox)(xload "atoolbox"))(tboxdlg)
^TOOLBOX1^
ToolBar2=\3\3OPEN ^OPEN^
ToolBar3=\3\3QSAVE ^SAVE^
ToolBar4=\3\3PLOT ^PLOT^
ToolBar5=ZOOM WINDOW ^ZOOM^
ToolBar6=
ToolBar7=
ToolBar8=
ToolBar9=
ToolBar10=
ToolBar11=
ToolBar12=
ToolBar13=
ToolBar14=
MonoVectors=0
ToolBar15=
ToolBar16=
ToolBar17=
ToolBar18=
ToolBar19=
```

```
ToolBar20=
ToolBar21=
ToolBar22=
ToolBar23=
ToolBar24=
ToolBar25=
ToolBar26=
UseControlPanelPrinter=1
ACAD=C:\ACADWIN\SUPPORT;C:\ACADWIN\FONTS
Drawing1=C:\NRP\JOB1.DWG
Drawing2=C:\NRP\JOB2
```

You can make changes to the ACAD.INI file automatically with the AutoCAD Environment Settings dialog box or by using the customization features of the toolbar.

Toolbar

The *toolbar* is the row of buttons directly below the status line. You can modify the toolbar by editing the ACAD.INI file or by selecting the button to change with the right mouse button. This displays the AutoCAD Toolbar Button dialog box which enables you to assign a new task and letter or icon to a button.

Toolbox

The *toolbox* is a movable menu covered with buttons that perform either AutoCAD or user-defined tasks. The size of the toolbar menu and the function of the buttons on it is controlled by clicking on the desired toolbox button with the right mouse button. This action displays the Toolbox Customization dialog box.

Menu Bit Maps

AutoCAD for Windows enables you to make several modifications based on bit maps. You can tell AutoCAD to display bit maps in place of text in the Draw, Construct, and Modify menus by selecting the Menu Bitmaps option of the Settings menu. You also can create your own bit maps in a bit-map resource editor and import them into AutoCAD for use with other menus. Menus that use bit maps have an additional file with the same name and a DLL extension. DLL files store the bit maps used in the menus. You can add icons to a DLL file with a Windows resource editor.

The code listing for the Construct bit map pull-down menu is shown here. The bit-map names are the names preceded and followed by a control character (^) in the square brackets([]) that hold the menu label.

```
**p6bitmaps
[/CConstruct]
[->^X21^/AArray]
 [/2Array 2D]^C^C_array
 [<-/3Array 3D]^C^C3darray
[^X20^/ CCopy]$M=$(if,$(eq,$(substr,$(getvar,cmdnames),
1,4),GRIP),_copy,^C^C_copy)
[->^X25^/MMirror]
 [/2Mirror
2D]$M=$(if,$(eq,$(substr,$(getvar,cmdnames),1,4),GRIP)
,_mirror,^C^C_mirror)
 [<-/3Mirror 3D]^C^Cmirror3d
[^X19^/hChamfer]^C^C_chamfer
[^X32^/FFillet]^C^C_fillet
[^X23^/DDivide]^C^C_divide
[^X33^/eMeasure]^C^C_measure
[^X22^/OOffset]^C^C_offset
[^X31^/BBlock]^C^C_block
```

Customizing Help Files

Help files are external text files that provide information for AutoCAD's help dialog box. Help files have an HLP extension. The default help file is ACAD.HLP. AutoCAD also creates a help index file automatically when you open the help file for the first time. Help index files have an HDX extension.

If you modify a help file, AutoCAD usually, but not always, re-creates the index file. To ensure that the index file is up to date, delete the existing *.HDX file before opening the help file again.

You can modify or append information to AutoCAD's help file or create your own help files as needed. Help files are divided into several sections to identity commands and their options in the help file. Because the HELP command can be used transparently to display context sensitive help, you should completely describe all of your command options in a custom help file.

 You can display the Help dialog box from any AutoLISP or ADS program by using the ACAD_HELPDLG function.

The following is the listing for the LINE command in the ACAD.HLP file:

```
\LINE
The LINE command allows you to draw straight Lines. You can
specify the desired endpoints using either 2D or 3D coordinates,
or
a combination. If you enter 2D coordinates, AutoCAD uses the
current elevation as the Z component of the point.

Format: LINE
    From point: (point)
    To point: (point)
    To point: (point)
    To point: ...RETURN to end line sequence

To erase the latest line segment without exiting the LINE command,
enter "u" when prompted for a "To" point.

You can continue the previous Line or Arc by responding to the
"From point:" prompt with a space or RETURN. If you are drawing
a sequence of Lines that will become a closed polygon, you can
reply to the "To point" prompt with "c" to draw the last segment
(close the polygon).
```

Lines can be constrained to horizontal or vertical by the ORTHO command.
\LINE,From
The LINE command is asking you to pick a point (or enter a coordinate) for the starting point of the Line.

You can continue the previous Line or Arc by responding to this prompt with a space or RETURN.
\LINE,To
The LINE command is asking you to pick a point (or enter a coordinate) to complete the line segment.

If you have drawn more than one segment, you can reply to the "To point" prompt with "c" to draw the last segment (close the polygon).

To erase the latest line segment without exiting the LINE command, enter "u" at this prompt.

Relative, cylindrical, and spherical coordinate point entry is allowed. Also, Object Snap can be used to specify particular points (endpoints of Lines, centers of Circles, etc.) of previously drawn entities.

For more information about customizing, AutoCAD consult *The AutoCAD Resource Guide*, *The AutoCAD Customization Manual*, *Maximizing AutoCAD Release 12* (New Riders Publishing), and *Maximizing AutoLISP* (New Riders Publishing).

Summary

In this chapter, you learned about customizing AutoCAD, from simple prototype files to complex programming applications. The chapter discussed customizing the basic AutoCAD environment: using shapes and fonts; and creating linetypes, hatches, and fills. Also discussed were scripts and slides, customizing menus and macros, customizing dialog boxes, and customizing AutoCAD for Windows.

Importing and Exporting Files

AutoCAD imports and exports a variety of file formats, in addition to drawing files. These file formats are useful if you work with your drawings in other programs or bring files from other programs into AutoCAD. This chapter discusses the exchange of drawing files among different versions of AutoCAD, describes the file formats that AutoCAD supports, and shows you ways to import raster files into the drawing editor.

Interversion Drawing—File Compatibility

You can import drawing files created in earlier versions of AutoCAD into later versions without any kind of conversion process. This feature is known as *upward compatibility*. You can simply call an AutoCAD Release 10 drawing into AutoCAD Release 12, for example, just as you would a Release 12 drawing.

Since Release 9, AutoCAD users have been able to pass drawings directly between the different platform versions of AutoCAD.

Assuming that you can transfer the file through a network, a modem, or a compatible disk format; a drawing created in AutoCAD on a Macintosh can be imported directly into AutoCAD on a Sun SPARCstation, or into AutoCAD 386, or AutoCAD on a DEC VAX computer. This platform compatibility also applies to most of the other files AutoCAD creates, such as AutoLISP files, menu files, and font files.

AutoCAD Release 12 drawings can be used on AutoCAD Release 11. Only a few minor limitations exist—locked layers and linetypes. *Locked layers* (a new feature of Release 12) cannot be unlocked or made current on Release 11. You can modify entities on locked layers, however. Polyline linetypes are elaborated only from vertex to vertex, and linetype-pattern scaling is varied with the viewport's zoom factor. Both occur, regardless of the PLINEGEN variable setting in Release 12.

For a complete list of the differences between Release 11 and Release 12, see Appendix B of the *AutoCAD Reference Manual, Release 12*.

Every new release of AutoCAD contains entity and structure definitions that are not found in earlier versions, making backward compatibility a problematic proposition. Recent third-party programs, however, provide this capability by using filters to remove any features from a drawing file that are not supported in earlier incarnations of the program, and writing a DXF or DWG file that is compatible with the earlier version. Of course, your drawing then may have gaps in it where those entities existed in the later version.

Autodesk also provides such a utility. This program, called DXFIX, enables you to convert a Release 12 drawing file into earlier releases of AutoCAD. DXFIX is included with shipping copies of Release 12, or it can be obtained through an authorized AutoCAD dealer or from the Autodesk AutoCAD Forum on CompuServe.

AutoCAD's Native File Types

AutoCAD creates several drawing-based file types that can be useful in transferring drawing information to other programs. These include ASCII and binary DXF, DXB, IGES, SLD, FLM, and several plotter/printer language files. All file types except DXB and the plotter/printer language files can be written directly from the drawing editor with native AutoCAD commands.

ASCII and Binary Drawing Interchange (DXF) Files

Autodesk invented the DXF file format. The programmers at Autodesk knew that AutoCAD drawing files would be useful for other purposes. They did not want to document the drawing file format, however, because that format changes with every new release of AutoCAD. Whenever a new version of AutoCAD was released, developers had to change their programs that depended on the drawing format. DXF was intended to be an easily understood format to facilitate the exchange of drawing file information with other applications. The DXF format has become a de facto standard for file exchanges among CAD programs.

A DXF file contains a full description of every entity in a drawing and the drawing's environment. The default file format is a straight ASCII text file that you can read with any text editor or word processor. AutoCAD Release 10 introduced a more compact binary form of DXF (typically, about 25 percent smaller than the ASCII form) that contains a full depiction of the drawing file. AutoCAD can read and write this form five times faster than the older one.

AutoCAD automatically writes the binary files at the full accuracy of the drawing file; the ASCII form can preserve full accuracy, but more accurate depictions lead to correspondingly larger drawing files. You can choose the level of accuracy in decimal places (.000000 = 6) in your ASCII DXF file while you write it.

You create a DXF file from the AutoCAD drawing editor by using the DXFOUT command. When you enter **DXFOUT** at the Command: prompt, AutoCAD prompts you to provide a name for the DXF file. AutoCAD uses the current drawing file's name as the default name for the DXF file, or you can specify a new name.

If you select the Entities option, AutoCAD writes a partial DXF file, composed of the entities you choose. You can select the desired entities by using AutoCAD's standard object-selection methods. After you choose the entities you want to include in the DXF file, AutoCAD again prompts for the level of accuracy you want.

If you choose to write an entities-only DXF file, only the definitions of the entities are included in the file; no information about the drawing file's environment is written.

 For a list of the ASCII DXF file codes, see the appendixes of the *AutoCAD Reference Manual*; they include full documentation of both the ASCII and binary DXF file format.

As noted earlier, DXF is a de facto standard for drawing-file exchange among different PC-based CAD programs and even among some minicomputer- and mainframe-based programs. If someone wants to use your drawing file's data in a CAD package other than AutoCAD, chances are good that the DXF format will fit the bill. Other kinds of programs also are beginning to accept DXF files, including paint and page-layout programs and even some word processing programs (WordPerfect, for example). DXF also is used to translate drawing data into engineering applications, such as FEA, CAM, and stereo lithography. Of course, many Autodesk products, including Autodesk 3D Studio, AutoSketch, and Generic CADD, read and write DXF files.

 For more information on the DXFOUT and DXFIN commands, see the Command Reference.

Drawing Interchange Binary (DXB) Files

The DXB file format (not to be confused with binary DXF) provides an extremely compact, but limited, description of the drawing file. The DXB format supports only the most basic AutoCAD entities (lines, arcs, circles, traces, solids, polylines, and 3D faces), and does not convey much drawing-environment information (such as layer names, block base, polyline vertices, arc bulge and width, and entity color). DXB files can be valuable, however, for conveying necessary information in a small package.

You cannot create a DXB file directly (in other words, there is no DXBOUT command). To write one of these files, you must first configure AutoCAD to use an ADI plotter or printer. AutoCAD prompts you to choose one of four output formats: ASCII file, binary file, AutoCAD DXB file, or installed INT driver. Choose the AutoCAD DXB file format and complete the configuration procedure. Then plot the drawing from which you want to create the DXB file. Accept the default values in the plot routine. AutoCAD plots the drawing to a file on your hard drive rather than to a plotter. That file will be your DXB file.

Initial Graphics Exchange Specification (IGES) Files

A consortium of industry and government agencies created the IGES standard to provide a universal CAD-file translation format. AutoCAD reads and writes IGES files. IGES contains hundreds of defined entities, of which AutoCAD supports a subset. IGESIN and IGESOUT commands enable a two-way translation of drawings between AutoCAD and other systems by means of files that conform to the Initial Graphics Exchange Specification (IGES) version 4.0, as described in National Bureau of Standards document NBSIR 86-3359.

Because AutoCAD supports a subset of IGES entities, importing an IGES file written by AutoCAD into another CAD system may not yield an exact, one-to-one representation of the AutoCAD drawing. In fact, an IGES file created from an AutoCAD drawing may look different when it is imported back into AutoCAD. As is the case in many translations, certain concepts that can be expressed succinctly in one "language" may require many more "words" when translated to another language. Conveying the original meaning exactly in the translated version is often impossible. For instance, AutoCAD approximates space curves in an incoming IGES file by means of 3D polylines, which consist entirely of line segments. Similarly, IGES has no way of expressing certain AutoCAD constructs, such as attribute definitions.

AutoCAD's IGESIN and IGESOUT commands are used to import and export IGES files. See the Command Reference for more information on the IGESOUT command.

Slide (SLD) Files

AutoCAD can create screen shots of a particular drawing view and save them in a slide file with the extension SLD. AutoCAD's MSLIDE (Make Slide) command creates slide files, and the VSLIDE (view slide) command views slide files. You also can use an AutoCAD script to replay a series of slides for demonstrations and presentations. AutoCAD's DELAY command is provided especially for such uses; it enables you to specify the amount of time a certain image should remain on-screen before AutoCAD shows the next one.

 Autodesk's animation programs (AutoFlix, Autodesk Animator, and Autodesk Animator Pro) can animate a series of slide files for specific instructions (see the documentation for these programs). If you want to write your own slide-file applications, the slide format is completely documented in the *AutoCAD Reference Manual* appendixes.

For more information on the VSLIDE and MSLIDE commands, see the Command Reference.

Filmroll (FLM) Files

Autodesk's rendering program, AutoShade, uses filmroll files to create its rendered images. Autodesk 3D Studio also can import filmroll files, which are documented in the *AutoShade Reference Manual* appendixes. The *AutoShade Reference Manual* contains complete instructions for creating filmroll files.

Plot (PLT) Files

AutoCAD creates plot and printer-plot files (Release 11 only) by sending data to a file, rather than directly to your output device. AutoCAD offers this choice during the plotting-command sequences or at initial configuration setup. With Release 12, you can install multiple plotter or printer devices and configurations. Plotting devices can be selected from the Plot Configuration dialog box (see fig. 11.1) and directed to plot to a file by checking the Plot to File checkbox.

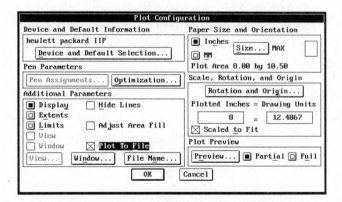

Figure 11.1:
Plot Configuration dialog box.

Having multiple-plotter configuration to either plotters or printers in Release 12 eliminated the PRPLOT command. Release 11 can be configured for a single plotter/printer combination that can be reconfigured from the main menu. File output is directed through the PLOT or PRPLOT commands.

In general, plot and printer-plot files are useful for plot spoolers and other batch-plotting devices on which you can queue up a number of files for unattended plotting.

PostScript Files

AutoCAD drawings are a visual means of communication, and can be used in other media besides production drawings for manufacturing. Release 12 now incorporates PostScript capability into its file repertoire. PostScript is the standard page description language for publishing and graphics. It provides designers with a flexible means of incorporating drawings into technical illustrations used in desktop publishing projects, 35MM slides, or overheads for presentations.

PostScript Fonts

AutoCAD reads Adobe Type 1 (PostScript) fonts that can be loaded into compiled Shape/Font (SHX) files or compiled into conventional Shape/Font files. Both deal with PostScript fonts in the same manner as AutoCAD-compiled Shape/Fonts.

Select PostScript fonts from the STYLE command and specify a file name with the file type PFB. If the fonts already are compiled, use the file extension SHX instead. After loading the font definition, any text that is typed appears in the PostScript typeface in the outline form. When you export the drawing to a PostScript device with the PSOUT command, the font will be filled (if designed to be filled). See the Command Reference for more information on the PSOUT command.

Encapsulated PostScript (EPS) Files

Encapsulated PostScript (EPS) is a popular graphic-image format used in desktop publishing. It supports drawing entities (lines and curves) in much the same way as vector-based CAD programs, such as AutoCAD, support drawing entities.

Exporting AutoCAD drawings to an EPS file is accomplished with the PSOUT command. AutoCAD then displays a dialog box for creating PostScript files. The procedure used to create these files is similar to that used to create a plot file with the PLOT command.

After you select the drawing entities to be exported, you are asked if you want a screen-preview image included with the file. It is sometimes necessary to include an image preview for layout in desktop publishing. You will be asked to chose a NONE, EPSI, or TIFF file format, and the pixel resolution to use: 128×128, 256×256, or 512×512. The larger the resolution, the larger your file grows. Because the preview image is only used for sizing an area for layout, high resolutions, such as 512×512, are not necessary unless detail is needed to distinguish the file. After entering the resolution or entering **NONE** for no preview, AutoCAD generates the file by displaying the effective plotting area, much like the PLOT command.

Screen previews generally are intended for desktop publishing or graphic programs. To preview the image, you need a program that reads one of these graphics formats.

AutoCAD Render also can produce EPS files by printing the file to a PostScript device. This can be done by configuring AutoCAD to set the Hardcopy rendering device to PostScript output and setting the rendering destination output in the Rendering Preferences dialog box to Hardcopy.

EPS files also can be imported with the PSIN command. PostScript files are loaded into a drawing as an anonymous block that is representative of the image. EPS files are imported in the same manner as other files using the Import/Export option on the File pull-down menu.

The PSDRAG command controls the visual appearance of the imported EPS image while the image is being dragged into place by the PSIN command. You have two choices at the prompt: 0 (the default) displays the image as a bounding box; 1 displays the image as a rendered PostScript image in a resolution dictated by the PSQUALITY system variable in pixel units.

PostScript Fill Patterns

PostScript provides greater flexibility in creating technical illustrations, especially in the area of shades and fills. You can specify gray scale, gradients, zigzag, and other effective patterns to emphasize or control the appearance of an illustration, for example. You can even add new patterns to the ACAD.PSF by redefining or adding to it.

Using the PSFILL command enables you to fill 2D-polyline outlines with any PostScript fill patterns defined in the ACAD.PSF support file.

 Although AutoCAD does not output these fills to the screen, it does recognize them.

To fill a 2D polyline outline, enter **PSFILL**. Select the polyline and enter the name of the pattern, or list pattern names with a question mark at the prompt. Type the name of the pattern. If you select Grayscale, Lineargray, or Radialgray, you are prompted for the density of the pattern: 0 is white and 100 is black. If you select Lineargray and Radialgray, you must further specify both foreground gray and background gray. Technical illustrators use these types of fills to indicate highlights and to shape 2D objects into 3D abstract drawings.

 For more information on the PSFILL command, see the Command Reference.

Attribute ATTEXT Files

Drawing documentation is more than just producing drawings. AutoCAD's attributes are an excellent way to assign text to blocks. This text also can be exported to another program, such as a database, to aid in generating a bill of materials.

The DDATTEXT and ATTEXT commands extract attribute entities to a disk file. The DDATTEXT command displays the Attribute Extraction dialog box, and the ATTEXT commands extracts attributes at the command line.

If you invoke either command, you must choose a file format to export to: a Comma Delimited File (CDF), a Space Delimited File (SDF), or a Drawing Interchange File (DXF). The CDF and the SDF format extraction processes are similar.

In the CDF format, the fields of each attribute record are separated by a comma, with character fields enclosed in quotes. In the SDF format, the fields are separated by a space. The fields of each record have a fixed width, with no separators or character-string delimiters used. Most PC database programs can read this format, including dBASE III. You also can export to a DXF file, which is an ASCII file that has other information included besides attribute information.

 See Chapter 5 and the Command Reference for more information on these commands.

Importing Raster Files

Two general forms of graphics files exist: *vector-based*, such as those created by AutoCAD, and *raster-based*, such as those created by a scanning device. Entities are described in raster files as a series of dots. A vector-based program that wants to incorporate a raster-file must use a translation mechanism to convert the dots into a single-line vector.

Raster files can now be imported into AutoCAD Release 12 via an ADS application called Rasterin. This new feature enables users to import 256-color images in three types of raster-file formats: GIF, PCX, and TIFF. Rasterin controls the image display through the following variable settings:

- RIASPECTL: image-aspect ratio
- RIAACKG: background color
- RIEDGE: edge detection
- RIGAMUT: number (gamut) of colors
- RIGREY: gray-scale compression
- RITHRESH: brightness threshold

You can access Rasterin to import raster files by using three new commands: GIFIN, which imports GIF files; PCXIN, which imports PCX files; and TIFFIN, which imports TIFF files. To import one of the file formats, type the command name followed by the file name. For example:

```
Command: PCXIN filename
```

Each command takes the file and converts the raster images into a block of solids. Using Rasterin, you can trace over converted raster images with AutoCAD geometry. Although this process may be a crude file conversion for processing raster files to vector files, it is useful when only a few relatively simple files need to be converted. Converted raster files can be manipulated with the MOVE, SCALE, MIRROR, and ROTATE commands, and then deleted when finished. Another way you can translate a file is by taping a printout of the raster image onto your digitizer and tracing over it.

For more intensive situations, in which large numbers of files must be converted (a large engineering firm wants to scan and convert all of its hand-drafted work to CAD, for example), translation software provides a more cost-effective solution.

Several third-party developers have produced translation software. Two approaches have been tried. One is a stand-alone program that converts scanner files (usually in the TIFF format) into DXF format. You then use AutoCAD's DXFIN command to bring the file into the drawing editor. This method works fine, but it can be slow and can create large DXF files. In addition, you must clean up the drawing after it has been imported to AutoCAD by erasing unwanted vectors and redrawing incorrect or incomplete vectors. The amount of work required depends on the quality of the original scanned sheets.

> **NOTE** The AutoCAD CompuServe forum provides user feedback and support through messages and shareware. Many outstanding third-party programs are available that can enhance AutoCAD's capability to support graphics. BMP2DXF and PCXDXB are utility programs that convert bit-map or raster images to AutoCAD's DXF or DXB file formats, PLTGIF converts GIF files into Hewlett-Packard Graphics Language (HPGL), and Plotmanager converts HPGL files into DXF format.

Interchanging Files with AutoCAD for Windows

The Windows operating environment provides a flexible means of exchanging data. Windows has a built-in file-management system that supports drag-and-drop file exchange, a Clipboard interface for cutting and pasting data, and other sophisticated options for sharing data.

File importing and exporting is handled under the File menu. It can handle the same data-exchange formats as the DOS version of AutoCAD, with a few exceptions. You can import and export Windows Metafiles format (WMF), which is Windows' file format for handling both bit-map and vector graphics.

Dynamic Data Exchange (DDE)

AutoCAD for Windows also supports Dynamic Data Exchange (DDE). This feature enables you to integrate information across other Windows applications. You can create a link between AutoCAD and a spreadsheet, for example, that automatically updates and modifies a drawing file. Because AutoCAD can act as the client or server, the exchange of information can flow in either direction.

The Clipboard

One simplified solution for sharing data information is through the Clipboard. The Windows Clipboard is a temporary storage for holding graphics or text you want to transfer. Information is cut or copied from your file and stored in the Clipboard, where it remains until it is pasted or placed into a file, or until other data or graphics replace it. Text and graphics can originate from any Windows application, such as word processors, graphics programs, spreadsheets, or databases.

 The Clipboard Viewer lets you view, save, retrieve, and delete the contents of the Clipboard. Files that are saved with the Clipboard use the CLP extension.

There are three commands under the Edit menu that transfer information with the Clipboard.

COPY IMAGE copies either a selected vector or bit-map image to the Clipboard in Windows Metafile format (WMF). The method for copying an image into the Clipboard is as follows:

1. Choose the COPY IMAGE command from the Edit menu.
2. Use the mouse to diagonally choose the area you want to copy.
3. Click the mouse button, and the image is sent to the Clipboard.

COPY VECTORS copies selected entities of both AutoCAD and Windows Metafile format (WMF). The method for copying vectors into the Clipboard is as follows:

1. Select the entities to be copied into the Clipboard.
2. Choose the COPY VECTORS from the Edit menu, and the entities are copied.

COPY OBJECT copies objects for object linking and embedding (OLE) applications.

Object Linking and Embedding

Object Linking and Embedding (OLE) enables Windows programs to transfer and share information. This facility enables you to use several applications to generate one single document. That document directly starts all applications involved in producing it, and reflects the most recent updated versions between the saved files.

An AutoCAD drawing, for instance, can be linked into a proposal created in another Windows program, such as Microsoft Word. Each time the proposal document is opened, the most recent revision of your AutoCAD drawing is linked and pasted into the Word document. *Linking* is a process of dynamically updating the information in the source file to be received in the destination file.

On the other hand, *embedding* is the process of packaging a set of information into another document. This is similar to copying from the Clipboard. To make changes to an embedded object, such as an AutoCAD drawing embedded into a Word document, however, click on the object and AutoCAD opens with the object ready to be edited. Embedded information is an image of your source document and is not automatically updated as with linking.

To preview the image, you need a program that can read the graphics format.

AutoCAD Render also can produce EPS files by printing the file to PostScript.

Summary

In this chapter, you learned how to exchange drawing files from different versions of AutoCAD. The chapter discussed the file formats AutoCAD enables you to use for exporting information into other programs, and for importing data from other programs into AutoCAD. You also learned about raster files and how they are used in AutoCAD.

Part Four: Troubleshooting AutoCAD

Troubleshooting AutoCAD
AutoCAD Error Messages

Troubleshooting AutoCAD

While using AutoCAD, you may see a cryptic Fatal Error message (usually as you are being dumped from the drawing editor). Frustrated, you read and reread the error message, trying to figure out where the problem lies. The message seldom gives you a clue. You reach for your *AutoCAD Reference Manual* to find an explanation, but to no avail. Crossing your fingers, you re-enter the drawing editor, hoping that you never come across the problem again.

This chapter looks beyond those cryptic error messages to try to give you a starting place for solving the problem. This chapter suggests some strategies you can use to discover the cause of an error message so that you can recover from the error and avoid it in the future.

Error Troubleshooting or Corruption Deduction

Corruption is the common culprit in many of the explanations of AutoCAD and Phar Lap error messages. These errors almost always occur as a result of one of the following:

- The drawing file AutoCAD is reading
- The temporary files AutoCAD has generated
- AutoCAD's working environment

Temporary-file and working-environment corruption usually stem from software conflicts or hardware malfunction.

Drawing-File Corruption

Because drawing files are quite complex, yet fragile, the data is easily corrupted. Data corruption can occur due to bad storage media; bent or dirty floppy disks; disk drives that need cleaning and aligning; or a highly fragmented, overheated, or almost full hard disk. All these conditions may cause data to be stored in bad sectors.

If your computer suffers a voltage spike while reading or writing to disk, data can be corrupted. Other misfortunes, too numerous to list here, can ruin your drawing files.

Preventive Medicine

Your best course of action is to never allow conditions to exist under which file corruption can occur. Keep your computer well-maintained and place it in a healthy environment. In particular, keep the room in which the computer operates as pollution-free as possible; do not allow smoke or dust near the computer. Buy brand-name floppy disks and maintain current backup copies of all your drawing files.

A backup routine cannot be overemphasized. You should institute standard backup procedures that become part of your daily routine. Backups are as critical as getting the job out the door—make time to do them. For a thorough discussion of data backups and AutoCAD systems, see *Managing and Networking AutoCAD*, by New Riders Publishing.

Drawing Diagnostics

It is a good idea to check your drawing status when you have a sluggish drawing. Two commands that help you streamline drawing maintenance are STATUS and AUDIT.

The STATUS command displays drawing statistics and memory usage. It reports the current values of AutoCAD's drawing parameters without searching through the file settings in the drawing editor. More importantly, the STATUS command shows the amount of memory and free disk space left to allocate the current drawing. If AutoCAD runs out of disk space, it tries to save the current completed work, and terminates the program.

The AUDIT command examines the integrity of the current drawing and fixes errors associated with it. You can either fix any errors found by entering **Y**, or be given a report of any errors found by entering **N**, at the Command: prompt. If the drawing contains errors that AUDIT cannot fix, you can use the RECOVER command to recover the damaged drawing.

Recovery Procedures

Even if you maintain your equipment and backups religiously, you may be forced at some point to try to recover corrupted drawing files. AutoCAD features a few diagnostic and drawing-recovery tools to fill the bill.

AutoCAD maintains a built-in error-checking mechanism that checks each byte in your drawing file for verification. This is called a *cyclic redundancy check* (CRC). This procedure is performed each time the drawing is loaded for editing, or plotted. Option 8 on the Operating Parameters menu from the Configuration menu enables this option. If an error is found, AutoCAD will not load the drawing—the file must be recovered with the RECOVER command. The RECOVER command recovers the file and loads it into the AutoCAD drawing editor when the recovery is finished.

The RECOVER command can be issued in two ways. The OPEN command automatically performs a recovery if it detects a damaged drawing. Similarly, you can enter **RECOVER** at the command line, and the standard drawing file dialog box opens for a file name. Either way, the RECOVER command obtains a drawing header, copies each section of the database, validates the database with CRC, and performs an AUDIT to correct the more complex problems. RECOVER extracts only the necessary data needed to rebuild the file, so you may still lose some of your drawing file.

If the RECOVER command procedure does not recover as much of the drawing as you need, you must go back to a previous version or the backup (BAK) file. The BAK file contains the drawing as it existed before you last issued the END or SAVE command. If you use the BAK file to replace the drawing file, you may have to redo several hours of work, but the process may be faster than reproducing the entire drawing from scratch. AutoCAD cannot read a BAK file directly; you must rename it as a DWG file or copy it to a DWG file.

If you cannot locate the BAK file, or if it proves unacceptable, try the following procedure to recover a drawing:

1. Start loading the drawing into the drawing editor.
2. Press Ctrl-C before AutoCAD encounters the error and dumps you out of the drawing editor.

3. If the Command: prompt appears before AutoCAD encounters the corrupted area of the drawing file, use the DXFOUT command to write a DXF file.

4. Load the ASCII DXF file into your favorite text editor or word processor, and examine it for any data that seems wrong or does not make sense. If you find such faulty data, remove the data.

5. Begin a new drawing in AutoCAD.

6. Use the DXFIN command to import the edited DXF file.

The data you removed when you edited the DXF file probably defined some entities in the original drawing file. If so, those entities will be missing from this version; you must redraw that section of the drawing.

If the BAK file does not work for you, and the Ctrl-C/DXF editing procedure fails, you can turn to one of the commercially available drawing-recovery programs. Such a program can analyze drawing files for corrupted data, and either change the data to a value that makes sense or remove it from the drawing file. The recovery program then writes a clean drawing or DXF file.

Unerased Files

Sometimes you encounter inadvertently-erased drawing files that have been reconstructed by one of the popular file-recovery programs, such as Norton Utilities Unerase or the DOS UNDELETE command. Drawing files created with AutoCAD versions earlier than Release 2.62 were simple enough to be recovered successfully by an unerase program. Drawings created with AutoCAD Release 12, however, are too complex for these programs; when they are unerased, they almost always contain corrupted entities. In this situation, try the DXFOUT strategy discussed in the preceding section, or use a drawing-recovery program to resurrect the unerased drawing files.

Identifying Temporary-File Corruption

Temporary files can be corrupted at runtime for the same reasons that drawing files are corrupted, as well as by improper configuration. Your machine, for example, can contain extended memory, part of which has been set aside for RAM or an expanded-memory manager. If AutoCAD fails to recognize RAM or expanded memory, the memory allocated to them may be absorbed by AutoCAD for its own use as extended I/O page space. The next time AutoCAD or some other program writes to RAM or an expanded memory partition, the I/O page data stored in the same area is overwritten.

In DOS, AutoCAD establishes and maintains a tight working environment that uses memory blocks, data resources, and software interrupts. If an ill-behaved TSR program or device driver alters this carefully maintained state without AutoCAD's knowledge, any data AutoCAD is operating on risks being corrupted.

Whenever these error messages appear, AutoCAD is almost certainly reporting a genuine case of data or environment corruption. On rare occasions, these errors may point to a software bug within AutoCAD. Such cases are almost always repeatable, and they occur because of a specific sequence of events. If you encounter an error whenever you draw a circle and trim it to 1/4-inch of its radius, for example, you may have discovered a software bug.

Identifying Software Conflicts

Problems inherent in one single drawing file may or may not indicate software problems in the AutoCAD program. Using a systematic approach to troubleshooting, however, eliminates a lot of the time wasted by haphazardly trying to solve the problem.

Make sure AutoCAD is properly configured to at least the minimum recommended requirements from Autodesk. AutoCAD recommends at least 8M of RAM, for instance. The program runs with 4M of RAM, but large drawing files may not run. Be sure the system is configured with the proper settings: CONFIG.SYS, AUTOEXEC.BAT, and your ACADR12.BAT file (or whatever name you assign to it).

For more information on configuring AutoCAD, see Chapter 2 of this book or the *AutoCAD Interface, Installation, and Performance Guide.*

You can attempt to eliminate the obvious problems by trying the simplest solutions. Open an older drawing or an AutoCAD sample drawing to see whether the same problem or a recurring problem exists. If a problem does exist, quite often it may be a memory conflict. You can clear the memory by restarting or rebooting your computer. If this does not solve the problem, reboot your computer with a basic system setup. The easiest way to do this is with a dedicated system disk for troubleshooting.

Setting Up a Dedicated System Disk

Format a floppy disk in the A: drive with the /S option to make it a bootable system disk. Make a new stripped down version of your CONFIG.SYS file with `FILES=40` and `BUFFERS=15` (the default value). Do not install any device drivers, terminate-and-stay resident programs (TSRs), or memory managers. Make a stripped-down version of your AUTOEXEC.BAT file. Keep your path statement (be sure to include your AutoCAD directory, AutoCAD support directory, and AutoCAD driver directory in the statement).

Configuring AutoCAD for Troubleshooting

Move your current ACAD.CFG file into a temporary directory, and configure AutoCAD with a simple setup by using a VGA display and a mouse-pointing device. You can keep a copy of this file on your troubleshooting disk and copy it into the ACAD directory when needed.

After either copying the ACAD.CFG to the ACAD directory or reconfiguring AutoCAD to the simple setup, reboot your computer with the floppy system disk. Start AutoCAD from the ACAD directory by using the ACAD.EXE file. This runs a basic AutoCAD program that should operate on any system. Test a couple of drawing files to ensure that the AutoCAD program runs properly. If the program checks out, you next should rebuild your system setup by adding your device drivers and DOS statements back into your CONFIG.SYS and AUTOEXEC.BAT files. Be sure to add just one statement at a time until the problem recurs and you can pinpoint the problem.

 To discover any software or ADI conflicts, it helps to clean your computer of all ADI drivers and software statements that might conflict with each other.

This process eliminates every possible source of conflict from the environment. Then, by adding lines back to the CONFIG.SYS and AUTOEXEC.BAT files, one at a time, until AutoCAD fails, you may discover the source of the problem.

 Keep backups of your current CONFIG.SYS and AUTOEXEC.BAT files. This eliminates the hassle of reinstalling some of your other computer application parameters, such as Windows.

If you are running AutoCAD on a network, and have just eliminated your network drivers, you must install a copy of AutoCAD locally on the machine you are testing.

If you get your AUTOEXEC.BAT and CONFIG.SYS files back to their original states without any problems, then reconfigure AutoCAD to use your ADI drivers if you need any (again, one at a time). (See Chapter 2 for more information on ADI drivers.) This procedure can result in one of the following situations:

1. AutoCAD still refuses to run after you strip your system.

2. You discover a specific item that, when added back into the configuration, causes AutoCAD to crash.

3. You return your system to its normal state.

> **NOTE** Be sure to use the latest ADI drivers for your graphics card or other peripheral hardware. Manufacturers try to keep abreast of the problems that their hardware might be having with AutoCAD; most manufacturers will send you an update for their driver by mail or through their bulletin board. A good source for ADI drivers is the AutoCAD forum on CompuServe.

If you strip your system and AutoCAD still refuses to run, your computer may either be damaged, or it may not be completely compatible for Release 11 or 12 of AutoCAD. If you can run AutoCAD successfully on a different 80386 or 80486 computer of the same brand, for example, you may have an older BIOS version of your 386 or 486 processor. You can upgrade your BIOS by replacing it yourself or having your computer serviced by a reliable repair service.

If you find a specific program that consistently causes AutoCAD to fail, check the program's documentation to see whether it can be installed differently—in a way that does not conflict with AutoCAD. Many memory-resident programs use system resources called *interrupts* to gain the computer's attention when they are called on to do something.

Any attempt by AutoCAD and another program to use the same interrupt simultaneously is a common cause of AutoCAD malfunctions. Most programs can be configured to use different interrupts; by doing this, you may be able to eliminate conflicts and still use all your favorite programs.

Many helpful diagnostic programs are available to help you set up your system or list your system parameters. Checkit PC Diagnostic Software from Touchstone Software Corporation can identify system interrupts, COM ports, peripheral settings, and much more. Memory-management programs, such as Manifest from Quarterdeck, also can tell which interrupts are being used. These commercial programs and many shareware programs can be a great help in tracking down system conflicts.

If an interrupt conflict is not the reason another program causes AutoCAD to fail, the two programs may be incompatible. Contact the program's manufacturers to find out if they know about the problem and whether a workaround or update is available to solve the problem.

ADI-Driver Problems

The Autodesk Device Interface (ADI) is the standard specification that manufacturers use to write device drivers for their peripheral hardware. AutoCAD can use either protected-mode drivers (EXP files) or real-mode drivers (EXE files). Release 12 uses ADI versions 4.2, 4.1, and 4.0 for protected-mode drivers; and ADI versions 4.1, 4.0, and some earlier versions for real-mode drivers (see Chapter 2).

Some Release 12 features are not supported by the older drivers.

If you use an ADI driver, check its documentation to see whether it came with a stand-alone configuration program. These programs often allow detailed customization, enabling you to change the screen colors and the size of text in the menu bar and status line. If your ADI driver has a separate configuration program, you may be able to use it to recover your display's original state.

In Release 11, protected-mode ADI drivers must be identified by setting an environment variable (DSPADI in your ACAD.BAT. file) that points to the directory containing the driver. For example, note the following line, in which *drvname* is the name of your ADI driver:

```
SET DSPADI = drvname.exp
```

If AutoCAD tells you that an inconsistency exists in the protected-mode ADI driver, and it does not allow you to enter the drawing editor, make sure that you have set DSPADI, and that it points to the correct directory.

If you use a real-mode ADI driver, and AutoCAD tells you that no driver is installed at address 7Ah or 78h when you try to enter the drawing editor, make sure that you loaded the driver before entering AutoCAD. Real-mode ADI drivers are executable TSR programs that you must run before entering AutoCAD. Read your graphics card's ADI-driver documentation for information about installing the driver.

Using AutoCAD 386 as a Full-Screen Application in Windows

AutoCAD 386 can run as a full-screen DOS application under Windows 3.1. Although you must set up several Windows parameters, you create a smoothly running Windows application and eliminate future problems.

Be sure to copy the pharlap.386 file from your AutoCAD directory into your Windows directory, and have the following line in the SYSTEM.INI file:

```
[386Enh]
device=pharlap.386
```

Also, be sure to create a Program Information File (PIF) for Windows to allocate the proper memory settings. Check the following settings for proper configuration:

Memory Requirements	256K Required (Minimum)
XMS Memory	2048K Required (K Limit -1)
Display Usage	Full-Screen

The proper environmental variables should be set in your AutoCAD Startup batch file. This is not different from running a DOS application; it just ensures that AutoCAD will find the correct support files and drivers.

Solving Problems with Peripheral Hardware

If a piece of peripheral hardware is causing problems, you should be able to spot the trouble fairly easily. The screen fills with gibberish (indicating a graphics-card problem), the crosshairs refuse to move (digitizer problem), the plotter draws weird lines (plotter problem), or nonsense appears on your printer plots (printer-plotter problem).

If the device itself is broken, you can do little to fix it, which means that you must call the repairman for service, or the dealer or manufacturer for a replacement. Although you can control certain system parameters, there can be problems if they are set incorrectly. The following sections discuss these specific problems.

Graphics-Card Problems

If your screen looks odd, first check the monitor's controls. Most modern computer monitors have controls with which you can adjust vertical and horizontal size, and position and vertical hold (to control rolling, as on a television). You can even program some of the more advanced monitors to remember desired configurations for specific software applications or graphics modes. Many monitors also feature *degaussing buttons* for removing magnetic-field buildup on the picture tube. Read the monitor's documentation and adjust the controls to find out if you can improve the picture. Also, check your monitor's location—a strong magnetic field from another monitor or other source can distort the picture.

If you do not think the monitor is responsible for the picture problems, check your AutoCAD graphics-card configuration. Most AutoCAD drivers enable you to eliminate the menu bar, command-prompt area, and status line from the display. (Perhaps someone inadvertently changed your configuration settings!)

Interrupt Conflicts

By default, AutoCAD communicates with ADI drivers through an interrupt called 7Ah or 78h. Other programs also use this interrupt. If you have other memory-resident programs installed while you run AutoCAD, and strange behavior occurs or the computer locks up before entering the drawing editor, an interrupt conflict may exist in your system. You can buy programs (such as Manifest from Quarterdeck) that tell you which system interrupts are used by each device and program on your computer. The easiest way to find an interrupt conflict is to use one of these programs.

Digitizer Problems

You can recognize a digitizer problem when the crosshairs behave strangely in the drawing editor (they move crazily or not at all). The most common cause of this problem is that the digitizer was configured to use the wrong serial port. Check AutoCAD's configuration, and then check the port into which you plugged the digitizer. Make sure, for example, that if you told AutoCAD that you installed the digitizer in COM1, you actually installed it there. Enable detailed configuration from AutoCAD's main menu, and then run through the digitizer's configuration to see which COM port you chose.

Incorrectly manufactured cables are another common source of digitizer problems. If your serial port's configuration seems correct, check the cable's pinouts against the *AutoCAD Interface, Installation and Performance Guide* diagram for your digitizer's cable. If they do not match, you may need a new cable. Confer with whoever gave you the cable before making any changes.

Some digitizers use ADI drivers. To see how to solve ADI driver-related problems, check the preceding section about using ADI drivers with graphics cards. The same rules hold for digitizer ADI drivers as for graphics card ADI drivers.

If you use AutoCAD 386, and the crosshairs seem to pause frequently in the drawing editor, you are seeing an effect of the DOS 386 Extender's virtual-memory manager.

 For information about alleviating this problem, see the discussion of the VSCAN switch in Appendix E of the *DOS 386 Interface, Installation and Performance Guide*.

Plotter and Printer-Plotter Problems

Most plotter and printer-plotter problems are caused by the same factors that cause digitizer problems; that is, the wrong serial port has been specified, the wrong cable has been used, or an ADI-driver interrupt conflict has occurred. Read the previous sections on digitizers and graphics cards for more information.

B Step Chips: Errata 17 and 21

Some 16MHz, 20MHz, and 25MHz 80386 CPUs that were manufactured in 1985 and 1986 are called *B step chips*. These CPUs contain two errata (17 and 21) that may cause problems for users of AutoCAD 386. You can identify B step chips by the following codes, which should be stamped on the chip's face:

- A80386-16 S40343
- A80386-16 S40344
- A80386-20 S40362
- A80386-25 SX050

In these codes, the letters DX are not appended to the A80386 in the first line, and either S40343, S40344, S40362 or SX050 appears in the second line; the "S" codes identify a B step chip. Note that some manufacturers of IBM clones increased the internal clock speed of the 20MHz CPU to 25MHz, and installed them in their 25MHz computers. These computers contain errata 17 and 21, even though they are identified as 25MHz computers.

Erratum #17 can be solved by setting the DOS extender switch -errata17. To set this switch, enter this text at the DOS command line:

```
C:\ACAD>CFIG386 ACAD.EXE -ERRATA17
```

If this procedure does not solve the problem, you may have an Erratum #21 problem. The Erratum #21 chip must be replaced with a good 80386 CPU.

Summary

In this chapter, you learned about ways to troubleshoot AutoCAD and your hardware. Corruption deduction was discussed, and you learned how to use AutoCAD as a full-screen application in Windows.

AutoCAD Error Messages

This chapter explains some common error messages displayed by AutoCAD. Even when you know exactly what an error message means, you usually only have a starting place for solving the problem. This chapter also suggests some strategies you can use to discover the cause of an error message so that you can recover from the error and avoid it in the future.

AutoCAD's error messages are cryptic, but Autodesk has written the messages that way for a purpose. In some rare instances, fatal errors may be caused by problems in AutoCAD. The Autodesk programmers reasoned that if error messages were cryptic enough, people would report them to Autodesk. The company could then investigate the cause of an error, perhaps uncovering flaws in the software. This reasoning still applies.

If you encounter fatal errors for which neither you nor your dealer can find a cause, report the errors directly to Autodesk. Use the bug-report forms found in the *AutoCAD Installation and Performance Guide*. If you cannot find the forms, write a description of the problem, describe your system's configuration (including the amount of RAM installed and a list of the peripheral devices you use), and include copies of your AUTOEXEC.BAT file, CONFIG.SYS file, and any batch files you use to start AutoCAD. Send the information to:

> Bug Report
> Autodesk, Inc.
> 2320 Marinship Way
> Sausalito, CA 94965

This chapter addresses five categories of error messages:

- Error messages generated by AutoCAD
- Error messages generated by the Phar Lap DOS Extender used in 386 versions of AutoCAD
- DOS error messages that may affect AutoCAD
- Windows error messages that may affect AutoCAD
- Errors generated by AutoLISP and ADS

As an error message is described, the text also provides information that can help you determine the nature of your problem and solve it.

Understanding AutoCAD Error Messages

AutoCAD contains thousands of error messages, most of which you probably will never see. The messages described in the following sections are the most common.

Errors Encountered During Drawing Initialization

You encounter the following error messages as you try to load a drawing into AutoCAD's drawing editor. The loading process begins, and suddenly AutoCAD switches to text mode, displays the error message in capital letters, lists the memory addresses that it was using when it encountered the error, and returns you unceremoniously to the DOS prompt (experienced AutoCAD users often call this process "being dumped"). Although drawing-file corruption causes most of these errors, errors also can result from software conflicts, hardware failure, or software bugs.

EREAD

EREAD (Entity Read) is the error message that AutoCAD users encounter most often. This error usually occurs while a drawing is loading. The EREAD message signifies that data in the drawing file used to describe a particular entity is corrupt, rendering it unreadable by AutoCAD. Corrupted drawings cause the vast majority of EREAD errors. File corruption of the EREAD variety has many causes, such as a hardware error, power surge, abnormal termination of an AutoCAD session, or faulty storage media (particularly bad floppy disks).

In rare instances, software bugs cause EREAD errors. In such cases, the error occurs in more than one drawing file, and can be reproduced reliably by a repeatable command sequence.

Occasionally, software conflicts cause EREAD errors without causing file corruption. These conflicts usually arise from a clash between AutoCAD and an ADI driver, or from the faulty transfer of a file across a network. If you encounter an EREAD error while loading a file on a particular workstation, but you can load the file successfully with a different configuration on that station or from another workstation, a software conflict may be the source of the problem.

SMIO

The **SMIO** (Symbol Table I/O) error message indicates that the drawing file's symbol table, which contains the Layer, Linetype, Style, View, Ucs, and Vport entries, has been corrupted. (Some say that SMIO stands for "Sorry Mate, It's Over.") SMIO errors are caused by the same kinds of corruptions that cause EREAD errors. Another fatal error, GETSM, also indicates that the symbol table has been corrupted.

LTINIT

The **LTINIT** (Linetype Initialization) error message indicates that AutoCAD encountered a file-corruption error while reading and initializing the linetype section of the drawing file. You may be able to recover from this type of error. If you encounter an LTINIT error message, press Ctrl-C as soon as the drawing editor begins to regenerate the drawing file, and then use the DXFOUT command to write a DXF file. You can examine the DXF file in a text editor for invalid linetype descriptions or entries.

EREGEN

The **EREGEN** (Entity Regen) message means that AutoCAD encountered an error while generating a specific entity. When loading a drawing file, AutoCAD reads an entity's definition from the file and then generates the entity on-screen. If the entity's parameters result in an error, AutoCAD stops loading the drawing. An example of such an error is an out-of-context entity, such as a vertex encountered while no polyline entity was being generated.

HMATH

The **HMATH** (High Precision Math) message indicates that one of AutoCAD's mathematical library functions generated an error. Examples of causes of these errors include negative circle radii (caused by a corrupted database) and invalid rotation angles.

TCODE

When AutoCAD encounters a bad header record, this message appears. As with **LTINIT**, you may be able to press Ctrl-C while the drawing loads, and use DXFOUT to write a DXF file. You then can examine the DXF file's header section for any data that does not make sense.

Errors Encountered in the Drawing Editor

These errors occur while you are editing a drawing in AutoCAD. In appearance, they resemble the drawing-initialization errors that were discussed in the last section. With these errors, however, AutoCAD offers to save any changes you made up to the time the error occurred, before the program exits to DOS.

CVFIO

The **CVFIO** (Compressed Vector File I/O) message indicates that AutoCAD encountered an error while reading or writing to its temporary files during the routine that generates vectors for a plot or printer-plot sequence.

SCANDR

AutoCAD generates the **SCANDR** (Scan Database Record) message if it encounters an error while updating temporary files during an editing session. AutoCAD often notes changes and new additions to the temporary files that form the present state of the drawing database. If AutoCAD fails in any attempt to update the drawing database or to update the files referenced by the drawing editor, the program may abort with the **SCANDR** error.

RFSUBS

RFSUBS (Refresh File Subroutines) signifies that AutoCAD's attempts to read or write to the temporary refresh file failed. The *refresh file* describes the present state of the graphics screen. AutoCAD refers to this file during redraw, zoom, and pan operations.

AutoCAD divides detected LIM expanded memory and conventional extended memory into *pages* for use as extended I/O page space. As the drawing editor generates data that do not fit in 640K of RAM, AutoCAD's paging routines store data in these pages. AutoCAD also routes subsequent read requests to this data cache. If AutoCAD cannot read or write successfully to this chained set of data pages, the program generates the **XPAGEIO** error.

Errors Specific to the MS-DOS Environment

You should encounter the following error messages only if you use AutoCAD on DOS-based computers. These errors occur because of malfunctions in structures that are unique to DOS.

FMTOUT

The **FMTOUT** (Format Output) error indicates a problem with the math coprocessor. Make sure that the coprocessor's motherboard switches are set correctly, and that the coprocessor is seated properly in its sockets. If the switches and seating appear to be correct, you may need to replace the coprocessor.

CHECKFD

The **CHECKFD** (Check File Descriptor) message appears when AutoCAD's file-descriptor table encounters an error during bookkeeping. AutoCAD may be trying to close a file that already has been closed.

FREE

The **FREE** (Free Memory Block) message displays when AutoCAD attempts to release a block of memory. This error can be caused by an improper operating environment or by a software conflict between AutoCAD and memory-resident programs, such as real-mode ADI drivers and TSRs.

Miscellaneous Errors

You may encounter the following error messages at any time while you are entering or working in AutoCAD's drawing editor. These errors cannot be associated with a particular drawing file and, except in the case of the `Not a string record` error message, they cannot be attributed to file corruption.

SHELL: Insufficient memory

This message appears when the AutoCAD shell handler detects insufficient free memory prior to invoking a DOS program. Although the lack of sufficient free memory can be caused by an incorrect entry in a Release 11 ACAD.PGP file for the program, it also can be caused by the presence of a TSR program or a device driver that has been loaded and is fielding an interrupt that points back to the heart of AutoCAD's code space. Release 12 does not expect memory allocations in the ACAD.PGP file.

AutoCAD expects to "own" all such interrupts (those interrupts that point back to AutoCAD). To prevent destabilizing the machine, AutoCAD does not swap to DOS when one of AutoCAD's interrupts is used. Network drivers and interrupt-driven mouse drivers are common culprits.

SHELL: Error swapping temp file

This error occurs when you use AutoCAD's SHELL command to run a DOS command. Generally, a hardware error occurs when AutoCAD attempts to page to extended memory or to your hard disk.

Phar Lap DOS Extender Messages

AutoCAD 386 users often encounter the following error messages. Like AutoCAD itself, the AutoCAD 386 Phar Lap DOS Extender contains many error messages. The following sections discuss the most common messages.

Paging File Full

This message appears when the swap file, in which the Phar Lap Virtual Memory Manager stores its code pages, grows large enough to fill the available disk space. Depending on the way you use AutoCAD, VMM's swap files can grow to many times the size of the drawing file itself. (In one extreme case, an AutoCAD user generated a swap file 44 times larger than the drawing file.)

 Even if you believe that you have adequate space for swapping, you must take this message at its word.

Stack Pointer in Unmapped Pages

This message appears when the DOS Extender looks to a particular memory address for some specific information, but it does not find the information. Essentially, the DOS Extender got lost. Although usually keyed by a software conflict, this message can be caused by a number of problems, including hardware failure and 32-bit software incompatibility. (The latter occurs most often on lesser-known clone computers.) The message is generic; if you encounter it often, you may need to do some snooping to find its cause.

Error Reading (Or Writing) Swap File

This message appears when something corrupted the disk-based *swap file*, which stores information that cannot be stored in RAM. This error usually is caused by conflicts between software programs.

DOS Error Messages

DOS sometimes passes error messages to AutoCAD. Although you may see them while you are working in the AutoCAD drawing editor, these error messages are generated by the operating system.

Divide Overflow

The most commonly encountered DOS error message, `Divide Overflow`, indicates that the system is attempting to divide by zero. Because it is a generic message, it can be a result of several things. If you encounter this error message while AutoCAD is running, the error may be due to one of the following four factors:

- A corrupted drawing file
- A software bug
- A conflict between AutoCAD and another piece of memory-resident software
- A malfunctioning math coprocessor

The first two causes can be deduced easily. If the error is caused by a corrupt drawing file, you always will see the message in the same drawing file. If a software bug is causing the error, the message appears whenever you issue the same specific command sequence.

Out of Environment Space

DOS displays this message if you try to set more environment variables than can be contained in the amount of memory that has been set aside for them. AutoCAD uses many environment variables; if you set too many of them, you may see this message. See your DOS manual for instructions on how to use the COMMAND and SHELL commands to create a larger environment space in your operating system.

Program Too Big To Fit in Memory

If you use DISKCOPY to make backups of your AutoCAD 386 disks, and the DISKCOPY command is interrupted prematurely, this message appears when you try to run the AutoCAD installation program. Make new copies of the disks and run the installation program again.

Cannot Load COMMAND, System Halted

AutoCAD users see this message only occasionally, but almost always when they exit from AutoCAD. The error usually can be attributed to a program (an ill-behaved real-mode ADI driver, for example) that has overwritten the memory area inhabited by the DOS COMMAND.COM program and corrupted the COMMAND.COM file. Reboot your computer to get going again.

Error Reading (or Writing) Drive Letter

DOS displays this message if you try to access a disk for some I/O purpose, such as saving your drawing or loading an AutoLISP program, and the disk is flawed. If the drive letter identifies your hard drive, shut off your computer immediately. Do not use it again until a qualified technician looks at it—you may lose data permanently if you try to operate the computer.

General Failure Error Reading (or Writing) Drive Letter

This message is similar to the preceding message, but indicates a more serious problem with the disk. You also see this message when you try to write to an unformatted disk (one that has not been prepared to accept data). If you are positive that the disk is unformatted, you may want to format it. If you encounter this error when you try to access a formatted hard drive, shut off the computer immediately and have it serviced. You may be able to recover the data on your disk.

Not Ready Error Reading (or Writing) Drive Letter

This message signifies that you are trying to write to or read from a disk drive that does not contain a disk, or to a drive whose latch is open.

Errors Specific to Windows

Windows is a delicate operating environment that must be finely tuned to achieve its maximum potential. Errors can originate from either AutoCAD or the Windows operating environment.

Errors Specific to Windows

One of the most common Windows errors is the Out of Memory message. When AutoCAD has used all available RAM, the Window memory manager pages out to your swap file, which reserves space on your hard disk for Windows to use for temporarily storing information. If you are working on a large AutoCAD drawing and you receive this error message, it means that not enough virtual memory is available to run the application. To remedy this problem, do the following:

- Increase the size of your permanent swap file to accommodate large files.
- Add more physical memory (RAM) to your machine

- Free up disk space by eliminating applications that are not often used.

To estimate the size of your swap file, enter **STATUS** to see how much free space is available on the hard disk partition. If it is less than the drawing-file size, increase the swap-file size accordingly.

Understanding the ERRNO System Variables

AutoCAD provides sophisticated macro and programming capability through AutoLISP and the ADS. Good programming requires user-friendly techniques of input control and error-handling procedures. This is accomplished through the ERRNO system variables.

AutoLISP

Besides the error messages you receive during programming or debugging, such as a syntax error, system variables exist that can be built into the program for error control.

When AutoLISP encounters an error during evaluation, it prints the following message:

```
Error:text (a description of the text)
```

Along with this error message is a code that is saved in the AutoCAD system variable ERRNO. This code value is retrieved by using the GETVAR function, and it can be used to return the appropriate error message to the user. If a function has not been defined by the user, or it is nil, the standard error handler stops the AutoLISP evaluation, prints an error message, and displays a traceback of the calling function and its callers, up to 100 levels deep.

There are 84 error codes generated by AutoLISP that can be inspected with (getvar"ERRNO"). Descriptions for these codes are found in the

AutoLISP Programmer's Reference Manual. It is good practice to clear the error code immediately after an AutoLISP function has reported an error. Otherwise, the error value may be misleading. Inspect the variable setting, upon returning to the drawing editor, to automatically clear the variable.

ADS

ADS is a set of functions that are written in the C programming language for developing AutoCAD applications. These functions are called by the AutoLISP interpreter, much like AutoLISP macros, and they provide you with a powerful means of accessing the external software resources of your operating environment. To provide a smooth, interactive operating environment, ADS has several error-handling procedures that are similar to the ERRNO system variables of AutoLISP.

The values of the ERRNO variables are defined in the header file OL_ERRNO.H that accompanies the ADS program. The ERRNO system variable is set to one of these values whenever an ADS library function call causes an error that AutoCAD detects. ADS applications can inspect the current value of ERRNO by calling the ads_getvar() function.

As in AutoLISP, values for these variables must be cleared to receive an accurate message. ADS variables are cleared whenever a new drawing is opened.

There are 84 error codes listed in the *AutoCAD Development System Programmer's Reference Manual.* For more information on the ERRNO system variable, AutoLISP, and ADS, see the *AutoLISP Programmmer's Reference Manual*, and *AutoCAD Development System Programmer's Reference Manual.*

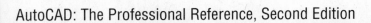
Summary

In this chapter, you learned about common AutoCAD error messages, what they mean, and how to correct them. The chapter also discussed some common operating-system errors and the ERRNO system variable.

Part Five:
AutoCAD Command
Reference

AutoCAD
Command Reference

ABOUT

? ,

Screen **[UTILITY] [next] [ABOUT:]**

Pull down **[File] [About AutoCAD]**

The ABOUT command displays the AutoCAD information banner and
the ACAD.MSG file in the AUTOCAD dialog box shown in figure
ABOUT.1. Because the ACAD.MSG file can be deleted or customized,
the contents of the list box may vary from system to system. If the
ACAD.MSG file is longer than the list box in which it is displayed, a
slider bar is present on the right side of the list box. If the ACAD.MSG
file has been deleted, the dialog box still displays, but the list box is
empty. You can issue the ABOUT command transparently if you preface it with an apostophe.

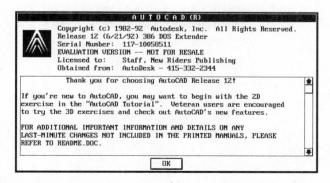

Figure ABOUT.1:
The AUTOCAD dialog box.

437

ALIGN

Pull down **[Modify] [Align]**

The ALIGN command moves and reorients selected objects to align with points you specify, regardless of the current UCS. You may enter two or three pairs of points for ALIGN to consider in calculating a transformation for the new location of the entities to align. Two pairs of points are required for 2D alignment; three pairs allow either a 2D or 3D alignment.

ALIGN is especially useful when you need to both move and rotate objects in two or three axes. Repeated uses of the ALIGN command can replace several executions of MOVE and ROTATE.

Prompts and Options

- **Select objects:**

  Select the objects to align in a new location by any object selection method.

- **1st, 2nd, 3rd source point:**

  You enter a point relative to the selected objects to align with its corresponding destination point chosen in the following prompt. Enter first and second source points to perform 2D transformations. Enter a third source point in a different plane than the first two source points to perform 3D transformations.

- **1st, 2nd, 3rd destination point:**

  You enter a point at the destination location where you want the selected objects aligned by the corresponding source point. Enter first and second destination points to perform 2D transformations. Enter a third destination point in a different plane than the first two destination points to perform 3D transformations.

- **`<2d> or 3d transformation:`**

  At this prompt, you specify either a 2D or 3D transformation. This prompt is issued only if you entered three source and destination points at the previous prompts. If you entered only two source and destination points, a 2D transformation is performed by default because AutoCAD has insufficient information to perform a 3D transformation.

Example

The following example uses ALIGN to move and rotate an object-selection set (see fig. ALIGN.1) in two dimensions so that it aligns with other objects.

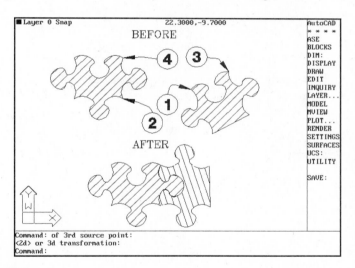

Figure ALIGN.1:
Objects moved and rotated in one step with ALIGN.

Command: **ALIGN** ↵
Select objects: *Select the objects to align*
Select objects:
1st source point: *Pick point* ①
1st destination point: *Pick point* ②
2nd source point: *Pick point* ③

```
2nd destination point: Pick point ④
3rd source point: ↵
<2d> or 3d transformation: ↵
```

Related Commands

MOVE
ROTATE
ROTATE3D

APERTURE

Screen **[SETTINGS] [APERTUR:]**

The APERTURE command sets the size of the *object snap selection target*, which is the box-like target that appears at the intersection of the crosshairs when you use object snap selection. The aperture's size refers to its width and height in pixels (see fig. APERTURE.1). The value must be a whole number between 1 and 50 pixels, which is the distance from the center of the crosshairs to the edge of the aperture box.

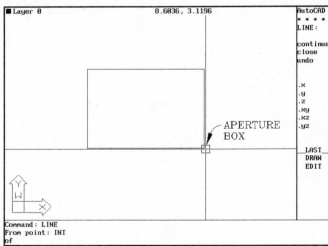

Figure APERTURE.1:
The object snap selection box.

The APERTURE command can be executed transparently by preceding the command name with an apostophe ('APER-TURE).

Aperture size directly affects the number of possible points AutoCAD must check to find the best qualified match. A small setting speeds object snap selection. A large setting is easier to see and requires less pointing accuracy. Experiment with various settings to find the ones that work best for you.

Prompts and Options

- **Object snap target height (1-50 pixels)/<current>:**

  You can specify a new target height at this prompt to assign a new value to the APERTURE system variable. This value, which is stored in the AutoCAD configuration file, is used in all subsequent editing sessions until you change it. The default value for APERTURE is 10. If you press Enter, the current object snap value remains unchanged.

 The DDOSNAP dialog box contains a scroll bar and example graphic for dynamically adjusting the size of the APERTURE box.

Example

The following example shows the way different values affect the size of the aperture box (see fig. APERTURE.1):

```
Command: APERTURE ↵
Object snap target height (1-50 pixels) <10>: 30 ↵
Command: LINE ↵
From point: NEA ↵
to Press Ctrl-C
```

441

Related Commands

DDOSNAP
OSNAP
DDSELECT

Related System Variables

APERTURE
PICKBOX

APPLOAD

The APPLOAD command enables you to selectively list and load
AutoLISP and ADS applications. You also can unload ADS applications.
APPLOAD displays the Load AutoLISP and ADS Files dialog box. The
user-defined list of applications can be saved and redisplayed each time
the APPLOAD command is issued. By maintaining a list of commonly
used applications, you can save time loading them. APPLOAD saves
the default settings in APPLOAD.DFS. APPLOAD can be issued transparently if you precede it with an apostrophe.

Do not edit the APPLOAD.DFS file. Make your changes
through the APPLOAD command.

Prompts and Options

The Load AutoLISP and ADS Files dialog box has the following
options:

- **Files to Load.** You select the application(s) you want to load,
  unload, or remove from the list. If the list of applications is longer
  than the list box, a slider bar is displayed on the right side of the
  list box. The MAXSORT system variable controls how many items
  in the list box can be sorted.

- **File.** The File option displays the Select LISP/ADS Routine dialog box, from which you can select an application to put in the Files to Load list box.

- **Remove.** The Remove option deletes all selected applications from the Files to Load list box.

- **Load.** The Load option lists all selected AutoLISP and ADS applications in the Files to Load dialog box. If all the listed files are loaded, AutoCAD disables the Load button.

- **Unload.** This option unloads all selected ADS applications. If all the selected applications cannot be unloaded, AutoCAD disables the Unload button. Unloading an ADS application frees memory.

 AutoLISP applications cannot be unloaded. Therefore, in order to save memory, you should avoid loading unnecessary applications.

- **Save List.** If this box is checked, the APPLOAD.DFS file is updated when you select Load, Unload, or Exit. To prevent updates to the APPLOAD.DFS file, be sure Save List is unchecked.

Example

The following example loads one AutoLISP and ADS program, and unloads the ADS program. See figure APPLOAD.1.

Command: **APPLOAD** ↵
Click on File *and display the SAMPLE directory*
Double-click on ALIAS.LSP in the Files: *list box*
Click on File
Double-click on AMELINK.EXP in the Files: *list box*
Click on ALIAS.LSP and AMELINK.EXP in the Files to Load *list box to select them*
Click on Load
Command: ↵
Select ALIAS.LSP from the Files to Load *list box and click on* Remove
Select AMELINK.EXP from the Files to Load *list box and click on* Unload

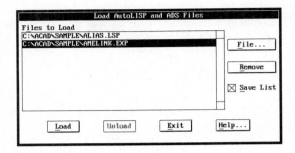

Figure APPLOAD.1:
The Load AutoLISP and ADS Files dialog box.

Related Command

LOAD

Related System Variable

MAXSORT

ARC

Screen **[DRAW] [ARC]**

Pull down **[Draw] [Arc >]**

The ARC command creates arcs of any length or radius. By using this command, you can draw an arc with eight basic options. You can use different combinations to create the various arcs shown in figures ARC.1 and ARC.2. This command also includes an option for continuing an arc that is tangent to the preceding arc or line segment.

Prompts and Options

- **<Start point>:**

    At this prompt, pick the starting point of the arc. Press Enter to continue an arc that is tangent to the preceding arc or line segment.

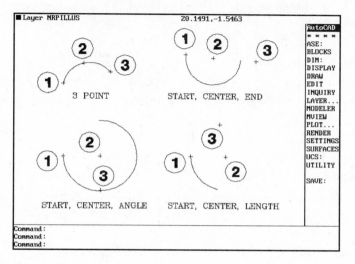

Figure ARC.1:
The basic arc-creation options.

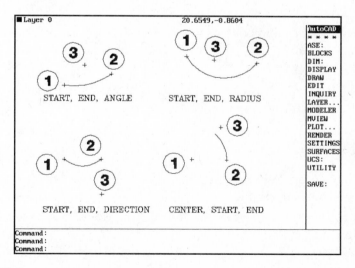

Figure ARC.2:
More arc-creation options.

- **Center:**

  At this prompt, pick the center of the arc.

- **<Second point>:**

  When you are creating an arc by specifying three points, pick the second point at this prompt. This point is a point through which the arc will pass.

- **End point:**

  This option prompts you to specify the end of the arc.

- **Angle:**

  The Angle option enables you to specify the interior angle of the arc. A negative value draws the arc clockwise; a positive value draws the arc counterclockwise.

- **Length of chord:**

  The Length of chord option is used to specify a length for the arc's chord segment (the distance between the arc endpoints).

- **Radius:**

  The Radius option enables you to specify the radius for the arc you wish to create.

- **Direction:**

  The Direction option is used to define a direction from which the arc will be drawn tangent.

Preset Features

- **Start, Center, End.** Specify the starting point, center of the arc's radius, and endpoint.
- **Start, Center, Angle.** Specify the starting point, center of the arc's radius, and angle of the arc.
- **Start, Center, Length.** Specify the starting point, center of the arc's radius, and length of the arc's chord.
- **Start, End, Angle.** Specify the starting point, endpoint, and ending angle.

- **Start, End, Radius**. Specify the starting point, endpoint, and arc's radius.
- **Start, End, Direction**. Specify the starting point, endpoint, and arc's direction.
- **Center, Start, End**. Specify the center of the arc's radius, starting point, and endpoint. This option is the same as the Start, Center, End option, but the points are selected in a different order.
- **Center, Start, Arc**. Specify the center of the arc's radius, starting point, and arc's angle.
- **Center, Start, Length**. Specify the center of the arc's radius, starting point, and length of the arc's chord.

Example

This example illustrates how to create arcs by using different arc options (see fig. ARC.3):

```
Command: ARC ⏎
Center/<Start point>: Pick point ①
Center/End/<Second point>: Pick point ②
End point: Pick point ③
Command: ARC ⏎
Center/<Start point>: C ⏎
Center: Pick point ④
Start: Pick point ⑤
Angle/Length of chord/<End point>: A ⏎
Included angle: 90 ⏎
```

Related Commands

PLINE
FILLET
VIEWRES

Related System Variable

LASTANGLE

447

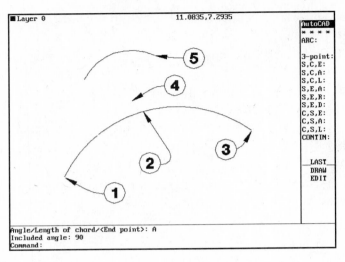

Figure ARC.3:
Arcs created by using the three-point and the center, start, and end options.

AREA

?

Screen **[INQUIRY] [AREA:]**

Pull down **[Assist] [Area]**

The AREA command calculates the area of an entity (such as a 2D polyline or circle), or a group of points. AREA also can be used for calculating the perimeter, line length, or circumference of an object. The area of an open polyline is calculated as if a straight segment existed between the start and endpoints. You also can use AREA to create a running total area by adding and subtracting areas.

To define a boundary for measurement, you must pick three or more nonlinear, coplanar points. Use the same method when selecting polylines for measurement; the polyline must contain three or more nonlinear, coplanar points. Figure AREA.1 illustrates correct and incorrect selection sets.

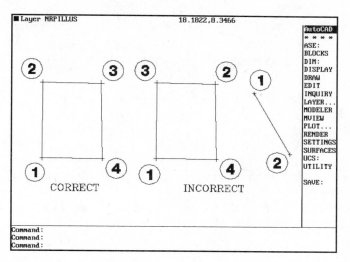

Figure AREA.1:
Correct and incorrect boundary selections.

Prompts and Options

- **<First point>:**

  Use this option to calculate the area defined by a group of points selected on the fly. At this prompt, enter or pick the first point of the group.

  After you enter the first point, the Next point: prompt appears. This prompt is repeated so you can enter any additional points to the group. After you enter all the points, press Enter to end the area-selection process.

- **Entity:**

  Use this option to select a polyline, polygon, or circle to define the boundary of the area to be calculated.

- **Add:**

  Use this option to keep a running total area by adding successive object areas or point-set areas to previous ones.

- **Subtract:**

  Use this option to subtract the area of the selected polyline, poly-gon, circle, or defining points from the running total area.

Many third-party applications create temporary polyline boundaries to simplify area calculation and ensure accurate results. You can do the same. By using ENDpoint and INTersection object snap modes, draw a polyline around the area you want to calculate, or use the BPOLY command to have AutoCAD automatically generate a polyline around a complex area. Use the AREA command's Entity option to select the temporary polyline. After you receive your calculations, you can erase the polyline or store it on a layer that is turned off. You can incorporate this technique into a menu macro.

Example

This example uses the AREA command's Add option to illustrate the way this option performs. The entity shown in figure AREA.2 is a polyline. You use the Entity option to calculate the polyline's area first, then pick a few points to define an additional area to calculate.

```
Command: AREA ↵
<First point>/Entity/Add/Subtract: A ↵
<First point>/Entity/Subtract: E ↵
(ADD mode) Select circle or polyline: Pick point ①
    Area = 12.6287, Perimeter = 16.4473
    Total area = 12.6287
(ADD mode) Select circle or polyline: ↵
<First point>/Entity/Subtract: Pick point ②
(ADD mode) Next point: Pick point ③
(ADD mode) Next point: Pick point ④
(ADD mode) Next point: Pick point ⑤
(ADD mode) Next point: Pick point ↵
    Area = 9.4770, Perimeter = 12.5722
    Total area = 22.1058
<First point>/Entity/Subtract: ↵
```

When you add or subtract areas, AutoCAD does not recognize overlapping boundaries. Make selections carefully to obtain accurate results.

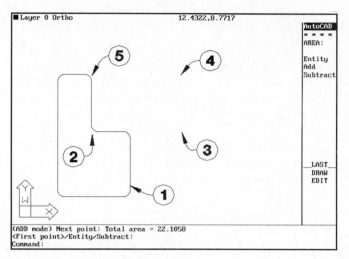

Figure AREA.2:
Using AREA's add option.

Related Command

BPOLY

Related System Variables

AREA
PERIMETER

ARRAY

Screen [EDIT] [ARRAY:]

Pull down [Construct] [Array]

The ARRAY command creates multiple copies of objects that repeat at regularly spaced intervals. The ARRAY command can work in the X direction (columns), Y direction (rows), or both, each with its own spacing. ARRAY can also place multiple copies around an imaginary circle or arc.

451

You can array objects in a positive or negative direction in relation to the origin of the source object(s).

If you are creating a rectangular array, you can specify the X and Y spacing with just two screen picks. The X and Y difference between the two points determines the row and column spacing.

If the array you are creating is not parallel to the current X and Y axes (if it is rotated at 60 degrees, for example), you can use the Snap Angle option in the DDRMODES command dialog box. This option rotates the crosshairs and the direction for the X and Y axes, thus allowing you to create a rotated array.

ARRAY creates copies within the X and Y axes of the current User Coordinate System (UCS). If you need to create arrays within 3D space, use the 3DARRAY.LSP routine supplied in the SUPPORT directory when you installed AutoCAD Release 12. 3DARRAY can be found on the Construct pull-down menu as Array 3D.

Prompts and Options

- **Select objects:**

  This prompt asks you to select the objects to be arrayed. You can select any type or number of AutoCAD entities, including 3D surfaces and solids. After you select an object, the prompt repeats, so you can select additional objects. Press Enter to end the selection process.

- **Rectangular or Polar Array (R/P) <R>:**

  The default option is to create a rectangular array. If you wish to create a polar array instead, enter **P**.

- **Number of rows (—) <1>:**

  At this prompt, three hyphens remind you that rows are horizontal along the X axis of the current User Coordinate System (UCS). Enter the number of copies you wish to make along the X axis. You must make at least one row (the default).

- **Number of columns (|||) <1>:**

  The three vertical bars in this prompt remind you that columns are vertical along the Y axis of the current UCS. You enter the number of copies you wish to make along the Y axis. The default value, 1, is also the minimum value.

- **Distance between rows (—):**

  This prompt requests the vertical spacing between rows. A negative value creates an array in a negative direction from the origin of the source objects. This prompt appears only during rectangular arrays with two or more rows.

- **Distance between columns (|||):**

  This prompt requests the horizontal spacing between columns. Negative column-spacing values are created in the same way as negative row-spacing values. When creating bidirectional arrays, you can use a combination of negative and positive values for row and column spacing. This prompt appears only during rectangular arrays with two or more columns.

- **Center point of array:**

  You see this prompt when you create polar arrays. The center point refers to the polar reference point, about which the selected objects are arrayed.

- **Number of items:**

  This prompt refers to the number of copies of your selected objects.

- **Angle to fill (+=ccw, -=ccw) <360>:**

  The angle you supply at this prompt determines the portion of a circle to be "filled" during a polar array. The default value, 360, is for a full circle. You cannot enter values greater than 360.

- **Rotate objects as they are copied? <Y>**

  If you answer **Y** (the default), objects are rotated relative to the center point of the array. If you answer **N,** the objects maintain the orientation of the source objects.

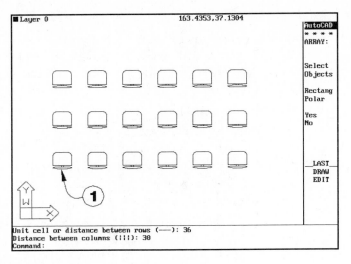

Figure ARRAY.1:
Creating a rectangular array.

Example

This example demonstrates both the rectangular and polar options of the ARRAY command. Figures ARRAY.1 and ARRAY.2 illustrate how the ARRAY command can be used to arrange seating within a room.

```
Command: ARRAY ⏎
Select objects: Select the objects to array at ①
Select objects ⏎
Rectangular or Polar array (R/P) <R>: ⏎
Number of rows (—) <1>: 3 ⏎
Number of columns (||||) <1>: 6 ⏎
Distance between rows (—): 36 ⏎
Distance between rows (—): 30 ⏎
Command: ARRAY ⏎
Select objects: Select the objects to array at ①
Select objects ⏎
Rectangular or Polar array (R/P) <R>: P ⏎
Center point of array: Pick point ②
Number of items: 15
Angle to fill (+=ccw, -=ccw) <360>: ⏎
Rotate objects as they are copied? <Y> ⏎
```

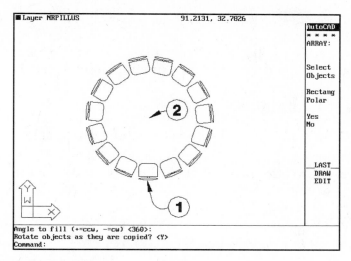

Figure ARRAY.2:
Creating a polar array.

Related Commands

COPY
MINSERT

Related System Variable

SNAPANG

ASCTEXT

Pull down **[Draw] [Text] [Import Text]**

The ASCTEXT command is an AutoLISP function that enables you to place text from an ASCII file into your drawing. ASCTEXT is useful when you want to insert large amounts of text into a drawing. You can use your word processing, database, or spreadsheet program to enter the text, perform spell-checking and basic formatting, and then save the text as an ASCII file.

ASCTEXT provides you with a great deal of flexibility in determining how the text you are importing will look. You can set character height, justification, style, rotation, and line spacing. The ASCTEXT command also enables you to import text into columns to form data tables.

Prompts and Options

- **File to read (including extension) <*default*>:**

  At this prompt, you enter the full path and file name, with an extension, to locate the ASCII text file you want to insert in your drawing. This prompt appears only if the FILEDIA system variable is set to 0. If FILEDIA is set to 1 (the default), use the File to Read dialog box to choose a file to import.

- **Start point or Center/Middle/Right/?:**

  At this prompt, you specify a starting point for the default (left) justification, or enter an alignment option for inserting the text. As you can with the TEXT and DTEXT commands, you can specify any of AutoCAD's text alignments, in addition to those shown in the prompt. AutoCAD's alignment types are shown in the following table. You can view this table by entering a question mark (**?**) at the prompt.

  ```
  Alignment Options
  TLeft    TCenter   TRight
  MLeft    MCenter   MRight
  BLeft    BCenter   BRight
  Left     Center    Right
  Aligned  Middle    Fit
  ```

- **Height <*default*>:**

  At this prompt, you specify the height for the text. This prompt does not appear if the current style has a fixed height.

- **Rotation Angle <0>:**

  You enter the angle at which the inserted text is rotated.

- **Change text options? <N>:**

  You specify the way the text is inserted in your drawing. If you enter **Y** at this prompt, you receive all of the following prompts. If you press Enter or enter **N** at the prompt, ASCTEXT uses its default parameters and draws the text.

- **Distance between lines/<Auto>:**

  You specify a distance that you want to maintain between the lines of imported text. If you do not specify a value here, the default (Auto) line spacing specified by the text style is used.

- **First line to read/<1>:**

  By default, ASCTEXT imports text, starting with the first line of the file you specified. If you want to start importing text after a certain line, specify that line number here.

- **Number of lines to read <All>:**

  By default, ASCTEXT imports the full ASCII file into your drawing. If you want to insert only a certain portion of the lines in the ASCII file, specify the number of lines here.

- **Underscore each line? <N>:**

  You can underline each line of text as it is imported. The command does this by placing the %%U underline-character code at the start of each line of text.

- **Overscore each line? <N>:**

  You can overscore each line of text as it is imported. The command does this by placing the %%O overscore-character code at the start of each line of text.

- **Change text case? Upper/Lower/<N>:**

  You can import all of the characters in the text file in either upper- or lowercase. The default is to import all text exactly as it appears within the ASCII file. You can enter a **U** to force all characters to uppercase, or enter an **L** to force all to lowercase.

- **Set up columns? <N>**

  You can import the text in your ASCII file as a set of columns, which makes it easy to set up tables in AutoCAD. ASCTEXT formats columns by assigning a specified number of text lines to each column. (If you want characters within each column to align, use a text style that specifies a monospace font, such as MONOTXT.SHX.)

- **Distance between columns:**

  At this prompt, you specify the spacing between each column of text.

- **Number of lines per column:**

  At this prompt, you enter the number of lines you want placed in each column as the text is imported. The text file should be preformatted to match the number of lines per column. The first *n* lines are placed in the first column, the next *n* lines are in the second column, and so on.

 ASCTEXT does not enable you to set the style to use for the imported text. You should use the TEXT, DTEXT, or STYLE commands to ensure that the style is set correctly, then run ASCTEXT and import your text.

Example

The following example uses the ASCTEXT command to import an ASCII file. The file used is the ACAD.PGP file that comes with AutoCAD, and is automatically installed in the same directory with the AutoCAD support files. This example assumes that ACAD.PGP is in the \ACAD\SUPPORT directory.

```
Command: ASCTEXT ↵
Choose the \ACAD\SUPPORT\ACAD.PGP file from the dialog box
Start point or Center/Middle/Right/?: 1,8↵
Height <0.2000>: .125↵
Rotation Angle <0>: ↵
Change text options? <N>: ↵
```

Related Commands

DTEXT
TEXT

Related System Variables

FILEDIA
TEXTSIZE
TEXTSTYLE

ASEADDROW

Pull-down [**File**] [**ASE**] >[**Row**] > [**Add...**]

Screen [**ASE**] [**ROW**] [**ADD:**]

The ASEADDROW command adds a row of information into the current table of the currently linked database file (a *row* is a record of information within the database). This command enables you to add text information directly into the database without having to run an additional external database program.

The addition of information to the current database is controlled by the current database driver. This may affect your ability to create rows of duplicate data, or even to add information to the current database at all. The AutoCAD SQL Extension ensures that any information you attempt to enter matches the types of fields into which you are entering data.

If the CMDDIA system variable is set to a value of 1, AutoCAD uses the Add Row dialog box shown in figure ASEADDROW.1 for the entry of information.

Prompts and Options

- **Edit:** This edit box displays the value of the currently high-lighted field. The list box above this field contains all available

459

columns from the linked database. The values that are initially placed here are from the current database row. To change any of these values, highlight the field, and then modify the value displayed in the edit box. Highlighting another field saves the current modifications and presents the next value for editing.

Example

The following example displays the simplicity of adding a row of information to the current database (see fig. ASEADDROW.1).

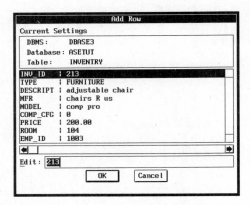

Figure ASEADDROW.1:
The Add Row dialog box before default values are changed.

Command: **ASEADDROW** ↵
Change the value of the INV_ID *field to*
214.
Highlight the DESCRIPT *field, click on*
the box and change the value to Drafting
table.
Click on the OK *button.*

Related Commands

ASEDELROW
ASEEDITROW

ASECLOSEDB

Pull-down [**File**] [**ASE**] > [**Utility**] > [**Close DB**]

Screen [**ASE**] [**UTILITY**] [**CLOSEDB:**]

The ASECLOSEDB command closes any currently open databases. This command is useful if the database driver you use only allows one database to be open at a time.

If the CMDDIA system variable is set to a value of 1, AutoCAD uses the dialog box shown in figure ASECLOSEDB.1 to select the database for closing.

Prompts and Options

- **Database:** This edit box is used for typing in the name of an open database that needs to be closed. You can also choose from the databases displayed in the Attached Databases list box above this field. When you press the OK button, ASE asks if you want to close the selected database. This is a precautionary measure to ensure that a database is not closed by accident.

Example

The following example describes how to close a database file and exit out of the command before actually performing the closure (see fig. ASECLOSEDB.1).

461

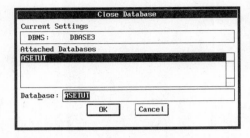

Figure ASECLOSEDB.1:
The Close Database dialog box.

Command: **ASECLOSEDB** ↵
Highlight a database.
Click on the OK button.
In the confirmation dialog box,
click on the NO button.

Related Command

ASESETDB

ASEDELLINK

Pull-down [**File**] [**ASE**] > [**Link**] > [**Delete**]

Screen [**ASE**] [**LINK**] [**DELETE:**]

The ASEDELLINK command removes any links between graphic AutoCAD entities and rows of database information created by ASE.

Prompts and Options

- **All/DBMS/dataBase/Table/<Row>:**

  You define the extent of links that need to be deleted from the current entities.

- **All**. Deletes all database links to the selected entities.
- **DBMS**. Only deletes the links to the current database driver in the selected entities.
- **dataBase**. Deletes any links between the current open database file and the selected entities.
- **Table**. Deletes any links between the current database table and the selected entities.
- **Row**. Deletes the links between the current row of database information and the selected entities.
- **Select objects:**

  Choose the entities that will have their links deleted. A warning box then appears, telling you it will be modifying the specified links. The dialog box expects you to confirm by pressing the Yes button. If you click on the No button, your changes will not go into effect.

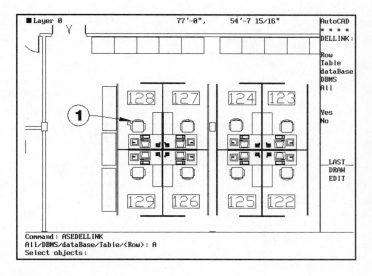

Figure ASEDELLINK.1:
The entity whose database links will be deleted.

Example

The following example shows the steps necessary to delete the database link between an AutoCAD entity and a database row. The entity selected is shown in figure ASEDELLINK.1.

```
Command: ASEDELLINK ↵
All/DBMS/dataBase/Table/<Row>: ALL ↵
Select objects: ①
```
Press the Yes *button in the confirmation dialog*
box to delete the link.

Related Commands

ASEMAKELINK
ASEQLINK

ASEDELROW

Pull-down [**File**] [**ASE**] >[**Row**] > [**Delete**]

Screen [**ASE**] [**ROW**] [**DELETE:**]

The ASEDELROW command deletes a row of information from the current table of the currently linked database file, which enables you to remove text information from the database without having to run an additional database program.

This command displays a dialog box, which asks you to confirm your decision. If you still wish to delete the database information, press OK. Otherwise, press Cancel or Esc.

Related Command

ASEADDROW

ASEEDITLINK

Pull-down [**File**] [**ASE**] > [**Link**] > [**Edit...**]

Screen [**ASE**] [**LINK**] [**EDIT:**]

The ASEEDITLINK command modifies the link between a row of database information and an entity within the drawing.

Prompts and Options

- **All/DBMS/dataBase/Table/<Row>:**

  You define which link information needs to be edited. The following options define which link information will be modified:

- **All**. Edits all database links to the selected entity.

- **DBMS**. Modifies the link to the current database driver in the selected entity.

- **dataBase**. Modifies the link between the current open database file and the selected entity.

- **Table**. Modifies the link between the current database table and the selected entity.

- **Row**. Modifies the link between the current row of database information and the selected entity.

- **Select object:**

  Choose the entity whose link to database information is to be modified.

If you choose an entity that has several links to database information, the Edit Link dialog box, shown in figure ASEEDITLINK.1, is displayed. The dialog box enables you to select which particular links need to be modified.

Figure ASEEDITLINK.1:
The Edit Link dialog box.

- **Next.** Displays the next link of the selected object.
- **Previous.** Displays the previous link of the selected object.
- **First.** Displays the first linked element of the selected object.
- **Last.** Displays the last linked element of the selected object.
- **Proceed.** Enables you to define search criteria for locating the new row to link the object to. This brings up the new dialog box, shown in figure ASEEDITLINK.2.

In this dialog box, you must define key values or search criteria that ASE uses to locate a row in the current database.

Figure ASEEDITLINK.2:
The Edit Link Options dialog box.

- **Key.** If you press the Key button, you see the dialog box shown in ASEEDITLINK.3.

This dialog box enables you to select key columns and the value to search for among those columns. To use this dialog box, highlight the key column you want to use, and place a value in the Edit list box. When you press OK, ASE attempts to locate a row of data that matches your key values in each of the columns.

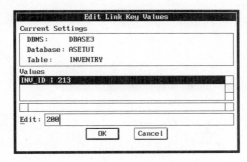

Figure ASEEDITLINK.3:
The Edit Link Key Values dialog box.

- **Search.** The search option is handled in two ways. If you enter a search criteria in the Criteria edit box, the search function attempts to match that criteria. If that edit box is empty, all records in the database are chosen, and a second dialog box enables you to narrow down your choice to a single row.

The dialog box in figure ASEEDITLINK.4 displays if the search criteria is too broad. The buttons that are part of that dialog box allow you to move through the rows of the database to select to which row the selected entity will be linked. When the row is shown in the list box, pressing OK will create the link.

- **Next.** Displays the next row of information in the database.
- **Previous.** Displays the previous row of information in the list box.
- **First.** Places the first row of the database in the list box and makes that row current.

- **Last.** Places the last row of the database in the list box and makes that row current.
- **Highlight.** Highlights any graphic entities within the drawing that are linked to this row of information.
- **Unhighlight.** Removes the highlighting applied to the graphic entities that are linked to this row of information.

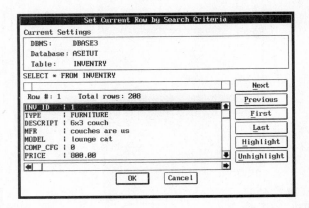

Figure ASEEDITLINK.4:
The Set Current Row by Search Criteria dialog box.

Example

The following example uses ASEEDITLINK to change the row of information that an entity is linked to (see fig. ASEEDITLINK.4).

```
Command: ASEEDITLINK ↵
All/DBMS/dataBase/Table/<Row>: ALL ↵
Select object: Select a linked entity
Click on the Search button.
Select the Next button to locate a new
record.
Click on the OK button to set the new
link.
Click on the OK button again to end the
command.
```

Related Commands

ASEDELLINK
ASESETROW

ASEEDITROW

Pull-down [**File**] [**ASE**] >[**Row**] > [**Edit...**]

Screen [**ASE**] [**ROW**] [**EDIT:**]

The ASEEDITROW command edits the information contained in a row of the current table of the currently linked database file. This command enables you to modify information in the database that has to be updated, possibly based on the modification of information within your drawing.

Prompts and Options

The dialog box contains the following field for editing row information:

- **Edit:** Displays the value of the currently highlighted field. The list box above this field contains all the available columns from the linked database. The values initially placed here are from the current database row. To change any of these values, highlight the field, and then modify the value displayed in the edit box. Highlighting another field saves the current modifications and presents the next value for editing.

After you finish modifying the information in a row of the database, ASE makes sure that all of your entries are the proper types for the fields you are changing. If you change a field containing a key record, you are asked to confirm your decision to change the key value. If the key column is linked to an entity, changing this value causes the link to become invalidated. You need to re-establish the link by using the ASEEDITLINK command.

469

Example

The following example uses ASEEDITROW to modify the value in the Price field of the current database record.

Command: **ASEEDITROW** ↵
Highlight the Price *field.*
Change the value in the Edit *box to* 225.
Click on the OK *button.*

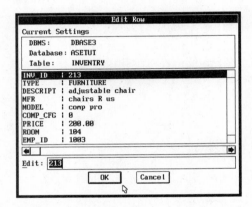

Figure ASEEDITROW.1:
The Edit Row dialog box before editing.

Related Commands

ASEADDROW
ASEEDITLINK

ASEERASEALL

Pull-down [**File**] [**ASE**] > [**Utility**] > [**Erase**] > [**All**]

Screen [**ASE**] [**UTILITY**] [**ERASE**] [**ALL:**]

The ASEERASEALL command destroys the control database within the current drawing. This control database maintains information about databases that are used by the drawing file and links between graphic entities and database information. This command should be used with extreme caution.

Prompts and Options

This command displays a dialog box, asking you to confirm your decision. If you still want to delete the control database information, press OK. Otherwise, press Cancel or Esc.

Related Command

ASEINIT

ASEERASEDB

Pull-down [**File**] [**ASE**] > [**Utility**] > [**Erase**] > [**DB...**]

Screen [**ASE**] [**UTILITY**] [**ERASE**] [**DB:**]

The ASEERASEDB command erases reference information in the control database. This reference information may contain links between the drawing file and the currently opened databases. If this information is removed, there is no way to undo this command—links between database rows and graphic entities will need to be re-established manually.

Prompts and Options

- **Attached Databases:**

  Contains the names of any currently attached databases. To erase the reference information relating to a certain database, highlight that database in this list and press OK. You are asked to confirm your decision by another dialog box. If you press OK, the reference information is deleted.

Example

The following example details the steps used to erase the reference information for a database (see fig. ASEERASEDB.1).

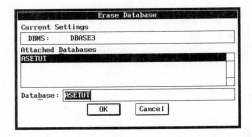

Figure ASEERASEDB.1:
The Erase Database dialog box.

```
Command: ASEERASEDB ↵
```
Highlight a database to erase.
Click on the OK button.
In the confirmation dialog box, click on
the NO button.

Related Command

ASESETDB

ASEERASEDBMS

Pull-down [**File**] [**ASE**] > [**Utility**] > [**Erase**] > [**DBMS...**]

Screen [**ASE**] [**UTILITY**] [**ERASE**] [**DBMS:**]

The ASEERASEDBMS command erases DBMS reference information in the control database. This reference information contains the database drivers that are currently loaded with the drawing file. If this information is removed, there is no way to undo this command. Any databases loaded using this particular driver will need to be reloaded and relinked to drawing information.

Prompts and Options

- **Attached Databases:**

  This list box, shown in figure ASEERASEDBMS.1, contains the names of any currently attached database drivers. To erase the reference information relating to a certain driver, highlight the driver name in this list and press the OK button. You are asked to confirm your decision by another dialog box. If you press OK again, the reference information is deleted.

Example

The following example details the steps used to erase the reference information for a database driver from the control database (see fig. ASEERASEDBMS.1).

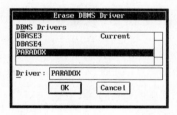

Figure ASEERASEDBMS.1:
The Erase DBMS Driver dialog box.

Command: **ASEERASEDB** ↵
Highlight a database driver to erase.
Click on the OK *button.*
In the confirmation dialog box, click on
the NO *button.*

473

Related Command

ASESETDBMS

ASEERASETABLE

Pull-down [**File**] [**ASE**] > [**Utility**] > [**Erase**] > [**Table...**]

Screen [**ASE**] [**UTILITY**] [**ERASE**] [**TABLE:**]

The ASEERASETABLE command erases table information from the control database (a *table* is a certain group of information pulled from the currently loaded database, or a whole database). Erasing the table causes any links between graphic entities and the database to be removed.

Prompts and Options

- **Attached Tables:**

    This list box, shown in figure ASEERASETABLE.1, contains the names of any tables in the currently attached database. To erase the reference information relating to a certain table, highlight the table name in this list and press OK. You are asked to confirm your decision by another dialog box. If you press OK again, the table is deleted.

Example

The following example details the steps used to erase the reference information for a database table (see fig. ASEERASETABLE.1).

Command: **ASEERASETABLE** ↵
Highlight a database table to erase.
Click on the OK *button.*
In the confirmation dialog box, click on
the NO *button.*

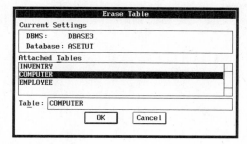

Figure ASEERASETABLE.1:
The Erase Table dialog box.

Related Command

ASESETTABLE

ASEEXPORT

Pull-down [**File**] [**ASE**] > [**Utility**] > [**Export**]

Screen [**ASE**] [**UTILITY**] [**EXPORT:**]

The ASEEXPORT command exports link information to a text file. This information discusses the way graphic entities are linked to a DBMS driver, a specific database, or a certain database table. The information is written in a format that is readable by other database programs.

Prompts and Options

- **All/DBMS/dataBase/<Table>:**

  This option line enables you to define the extent of links to be exported from the current entities. The options presented export the following link information:

- **All**. Exports all database links for all selected entities.

- **DBMS**. Only exports the link information between the database driver and the selected entities.
- **dataBase**. Exports all link information between a database file and the selected entities.
- **Enter name of file for <*DBMS/Database/Table*>:**

  You must enter the name of the database object that you wish link information exported from.
- **SDF/CDF/<*Current DBMS*>:**

  Enter the type of text file output format for the link information. You may export in the Comma Delimited Format, Space Delimited Format, or in a format readable by the current database.
- **Select objects:**

  Choose the entities to have their link information exported.

Example

The following example selects a single entity within the drawing for exporting link information. The entity, shown in figure ASEEXPORT.1, is linked to only one database table. Using the All option, however, ASEEXPORT attempts to export any information on the entity from all of the attached database tables.

```
Command: ASEEXPORT ↵
Select objects: ①
Select objects: ↵
All/DBMS/dataBase/<Table>: T ↵
Enter name of file for DBASE3/ASETUT
/INVENTRY: CHAIR.TXT ↵
SDF/CDF/<Native>: SDF ↵
Command: TYPE ↓
File to list: CHAIR.TXT ↵
             37              71E
```

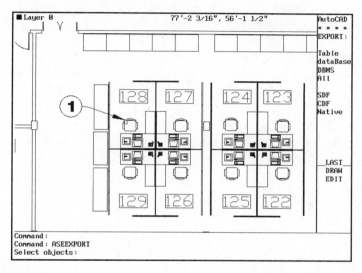

Figure ASEEXPORT.1:
The entity, selected for exporting link information.

Related Commands

ATTEXT
DDATTEXT
ASEMAKEREP

ASEINIT

Pull-down [**File] [ASE] > [Initialize]**

Screen [**ASE] [InitASE]**

The ASEINIT command initializes ASE, and it makes the current drawing ready to receive database-link information. This command creates the control database used to store the link data on a layer in the drawing called ACADASE.

Prompts and Options

This command has no prompts, it simply executes once you have selected it from the screen or pull-down menus. If you do not use the menus to start ASE, enter the following commands at the Command: prompt:

```
(XLOAD "ASE")
(LOAD "ASE")
ASEINIT
```

Related Command

ASETERM

ASEMAKEDA

Pull-down [**File**] [**ASE**] > [**Make DA...**]

Screen [**ASE**] [**MAKE DA:**]

The ASEMAKEDA command creates a displayable attribute of the database information to be placed within the current drawing. This command enables you to show text information stored in the database next to a graphic entity to which it may relate. These attributes are similar to other AutoCAD attributes, which enables you to locate them in a position that best displays the information they contain. The information displayed by the attribute comes from the currently selected row of the current database.

Prompts and Options

The first prompts for the ASEMAKEDA command are similar to the TEXT command, requiring information used to draw the displayable attributes.

- Justify/Style/<Start point>:

These options relate to the way that the attributes will be displayed. Similar to the TEXT command, you are asked to select a text justification, text style, or the starting point for the first displayable attribute.

- **Height <*Current*>:**

  Enter a value for the height to be used for the displayable attribute.

- **Rotation angle <*Current*>:**

  Enter a value for the rotation angle to be used for the displayable attribute.

Once all entity-rendering information is answered, the Make Displayable Attribute dialog box, shown in figure ASEMAKEDA.1, appears. This dialog box contains a list of the current table columns in the currently opened database. The information that you display in the attributes is taken from the columns you choose to display.

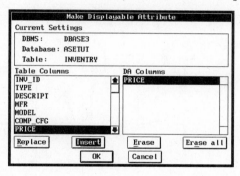

Figure ASEMAKEDA.1:
The Make Displayable Attribute dialog box.

The following buttons aid you in choosing which data to show:

- **Replace.** Replaces the currently highlighted column in the DA Columns list box with a field selected from the Table Columns list box.

- **Insert.** Inserts a new column field into the DA Columns list box from the Table Columns list box.

- **Erase.** Erases the selected column name from the DA Columns list box.
- **Erase all.** Erases all column names from the DA Columns list box, clearing it for a different selection.

Once the column names have been selected, pressing OK causes the data for the current row that is stored under the select column names to be placed in the drawing file. The data is rendered by using the information you supplied to the first set of prompts.

Example

The following example selects a linked entity from the drawing (see fig. ASEMAKEDA.2) to create a displayable attribute.

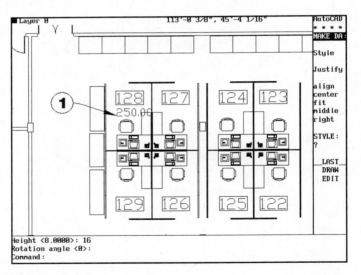

Figure ASEMAKEDA.2:
The selected entity and displayable attribute.

```
Command: ASEMAKEDA ↵
Justify/Style/<Start point>: ①
```

```
Height <8.000>: 16↵
Rotation angle <Current>: ↵
```
From the dialog box, select the Price
column name, and click on the Insert
button.
Click on the OK *button.*

Related Command

ASEQMAKEDA

ASEMAKELINK

Pull-down [**File**] [**ASE**] > [**Make Link**]

Screen [**ASE**] [**MK LINK:**]

The ASEMAKELINK command creates a link between an entity within
the current drawing and a row of the current database. This link does
not alter the entity properties, but it enables you to display the information linked to the entity. You can also edit any information linked to the
entity, create reports containing the information, or use a database
query to select entities that are linked to certain types of data.

Prompts and Options

- **Select objects:**

  Choose the entities to be linked to the current database row. If you
  need to, use the ASESETROW command to first set the database to
  the proper row before performing the linking operation.

Related Commands

ASEEDITROW
ASESETROW
ASEQMAKELINK

ASEMAKEREP

Pull-down [**File**] [**ASE**] > [**Utility**] > [**Make Report**]

Screen [**ASE**] [**UTILITY**] [**MAKERP:**]

The ASEMAKEREP command creates a customized report of the data contained in a currently loaded database. The report is contained in a program outside of AutoCAD, and it is selected when you issue this command. The report must be written to match the commands used by the native database driver program in order to run properly. This command requires you to have the actual database program on your hard disk in order to execute the report program.

Prompts and Options

The dialog box, shown in figure ASEMAKEREP.1, displays the current DBMS driver and open database. Your options within this dialog box are the following:

- **Execute:**

  Enter the name of the custom reporting program that you wish to run in this edit box. This field may need to contain the full drive and path, as well as the program file name, if it is not located in the current directory.

- **History.** Displays a second dialog box that contains a list of all previous reports that have been issued using this particular database.

- **Execute.** Shell out the operating system and run the named report program using the database program specified by the DBMS driver.

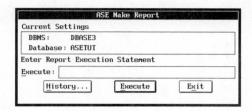

Figure ASEMAKEREP.1:
The ASE Make Report dialog box.

 The exact text entered in the **E**xecute edit box depends on your platform and database software.

Related Command

ASEEXPORT

ASEPOST

Pull-down [**File**] [**ASE**] > [**Utility**] > [**Post**]

Screen [**ASE**] [**UTILITY**] [**POST:**]

The ASEPOST command ensures that any drawing entities in the current drawing are correctly linked to actual data in the current open database. This command does not affect any graphic entities within your drawing, but if entities are linked to columns that have been deleted, that link is invalid. This command reports any of these discrepancies and enables you to repair the invalid links.

483

Prompts and Options

- `Fix/<Report>:`

  This command prompt enables you to automatically generate a report detailing any conflicts between entity links and database information. If you choose Fix the links, ASEPOST removes information from the control database to properly synchronize the drawing file and the database.

Example

The following example shows a possible error message given when using ASEPOST to analyze the database/entity links:

```
Command: ASEPOST ↵
Fix/<Report>: ↵
Please wait ...
1 link(s) to entities for DBASE3/ASETUT
INVENTRY invalid
```

ASEQEDIT

Pull-down [**File**] [**ASE**] > [**Quick Edit...**]

Screen [**ASE**] [**Q-EDIT:**]

The ASEQEDIT command combines the ASESETROW and ASEEDITROW commands to enable you to edit a row of database information by choosing an entity within your drawing linked to the database. If there is no link between the chosen entity and the database, ASEQEDIT enables you to select another entity graphically, or based on a key value in the database.

Prompts and Options

- `Select object:`

  Choose the entity whose database information you wish to edit.

- `Key values/Search criteria/<Select object>:`

  If the entity you initially chose had no links to the database, you will receive this additional command prompt. You have the option of choosing another entity, selecting a database row using a value from the database key column, or specifying other search criteria. This is the same prompt as presented by the ASESETROW command. Please refer to that command for explanations of how to set key-value and search-criteria searches.

Example

The following example shows how easy it is to edit the row information of a selected entity (see fig. ASEQEDIT.1).

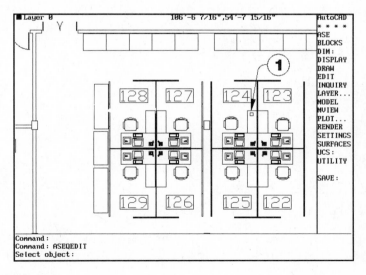

Figure ASEQEDIT.1:
The entity whose database information will be edited.

485

```
Command: ASEQEDIT ↵
Select objects: ①
```
In the dialog box, change the Price
information to **450,** *as shown in figure ASEQEDIT.2.*
Click on the OK *button.*

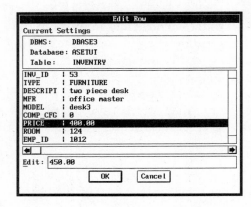

Figure ASEQEDIT.2:
Modifying the price information for the selected entity.

Related Commands

ASEEDITROW
ASESETROW

ASEQLINK

Pull-down [**File**] [**ASE**] > [**Quick Link...**]

Screen [**ASE**] [**Q-LINK:**]

The ASEQLINK command combines the ASESETROW and
ASEMAKELINK commands to enable you to quickly link a graphic

AutoCAD entity with a row of database information. You have the option of first setting the row of data to be linked, or automatically linking the current row to a selected entity.

Prompts and Options

- **Key values/Search criteria/<Select object>:**

  You can set the current database row by choosing a key value for a database column, using specific search criteria to select a row, or choosing a graphic entity that is currently linked to the database.

   This is the same prompt presented by the ASESETROW command; refer to that command for explanations of how to set key-value and search-criteria searches.

- **Select objects:**

  Choose the entities that you want to link to the current row of database information.

Example

The following example demonstrates the speed of linking an AutoCAD entity to the current row of database information:

```
Command: ASEQLINK ↵
Key values/Search criteria/<Select
object>: ↵
Select object: Select an entity to link
to the current row.
```

Related Commands

ASEMAKELINK
ASESETROW

ASEQMAKEDA

Pull-down [**File**] [**ASE**] > [**Quick Make DA...**]

Screen [**ASE**] [**Q-MK DA:**]

The ASEQMAKEDA command combines the ASESETROW and ASEMAKEDA commands to enable you to quickly create a displayable attribute from the information in the current database row. You must select an entity within the drawing that is linked to the database, otherwise you must manually set the database row before the displayable attribute is created.

Prompts and Options

- **Select object:**

  Choose an entity linked to the current database for which you want a displayable attribute created. If the object you select is not linked to a database, you see the following prompt line:

- **Key values/Search criteria/<Select object>:**

  You can set the current database row by choosing a key value for a database column, using specific search criteria to select a row, or choosing a different graphic entity that is currently linked to the database. If you choose an entity that contains multiple database links, you will be asked which link is to be used for creating the displayable attribute.

This is the same prompt as presented by the ASESETROW command. Please refer to that command for explanations of how to set key-value and search-criteria searches.

Example

The following example uses ASEQMAKEDA to easily insert a displayable attribute showing the price of a linked AutoCAD entity.

The two pick points described in the example are shown in figure
ASEQMAKEDA.1.

```
Command: ASEQMAKEDA ↵
Select object: ①
Justify/Style/<Start point>: ②
Height <8.0000>: ↵
Rotation angle <0>: 90 ↵
```
Select the Price *column name, and click*
on the Insert *button.*
Click on the OK *button.*

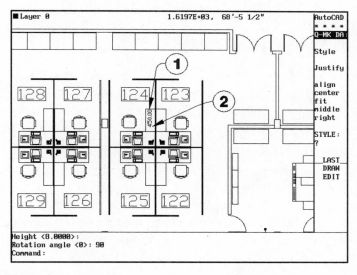

Figure ASEQMAKEDA.1:
The selected entity and location for a displayable attribute.

Related Commands

> **ASEMAKEDA**
> **ASESETROW**

ASEQVIEW

Pull-down [**File**] [**ASE**] > [**Quick View...**]

Screen [**ASE**] [**Q-VIEW:**]

The ASEQVIEW command combines the ASESETROW and ASEVIEWROW commands to enable you to quickly view the information linked to a selected drawing entity. You must select an entity within the drawing that is linked to the database; otherwise, you need to manually set the database row before the information can be displayed.

Prompts and Options

- **Select object:**

  Choose an entity linked to the current database for which you want to view the information. If the object you select is not linked to a database, you see the following prompt line:

- **Key values/Search criteria/<Select object>:**

  You can set the current database row by choosing a key value for a database column, using specific search criteria to select a row, or choosing a different graphic entity that is currently linked to the database. If you choose an entity that contains multiple database links, you are asked which link is to be used for viewing database information.

Example

The following example demonstrates the speed of viewing the database information for an entity that is linked to the current database. The entity selected is shown in figure ASEQVIEW.1.

```
Command: ASEQVIEW ↵
Select object: ①
```
Press the OK button when finished viewing the information.

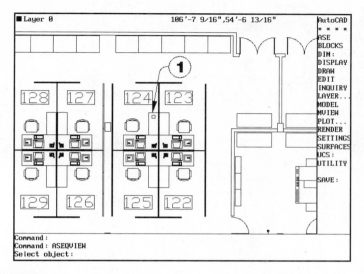

Figure ASEQVIEW.1:
The entity whose information will be viewed.

Related Commands

ASESETROW
ASEVIEWROW

ASERELOADDA

Pull-down [**File**] [**ASE**] > [**Reload DA**]

Screen [**ASE**] [**RELD DA:**]

The ASERELOADDA command regenerates any displayable attributes within the current drawing file. This command is typically used after you have edited the database information and need the new values reflected within the drawing file.

Prompts and Options

- `Select objects:`

  Choose the entities whose displayable attributes need to be re-loaded. ASE looks back at the database and updates any values that have changed within the displayable attributes.

Example

The following example shows an easy way to make sure all the displayable attributes have up-to-date information.

```
Command: ASERELOADDA ↵
Select object: All ↵
Select object: ↵
```

Related Commands

ASEMAKEDA
ASEEDITROW

ASESELECT

Pull-down [**File**] [**ASE**] > [**Select**]

Screen [**ASE**] [**SELECT:**]

The ASESELECT command selects entities within a drawing by using graphical or textual means. The entities can then be placed in a normal AutoCAD selection set for editing.

Prompts and Options

- **Export/<Selection Set>:**

  This command prompt enables you to define where entities are placed after being selected. You can choose to export any selected entities to an external file, or simply build a selection set that AutoCAD can access.

- **Union/Subtract/<Intersection>:**

  This prompt enables you to define, in Boolean terms, the way entities that match both the graphical and textual search criteria are selected. By default, the Intersection option includes any graphic entity that contains a link to the specified textual-selection criteria.

  The results of the Subtraction option are determined by your choice of Graphical or Textual search criteria at the next prompt. If your selection is Graphical, the created selection set is based on the removal of any entities that meet the non-graphic search criteria. If you select Textual, your selection set removes any graphic entities that do not meet the non-graphic search criteria.

  The Union option creates a selection set that includes the results of both the graphic and non-graphic searches.

- **Graphical/<Textual>:**

  You are asked both of these prompts; only the order of your answers affects the Subtract option. The Textual option enables you to define an SQL criteria for matching database information; the Graphical option presents you with the Select Objects: prompt.

Example

The following exercise shows how you can combine graphic and text searches to retrieve only a certain group of entities. The selection points and entities retrieved using ASESELECT are shown in figure ASESELECT.1.

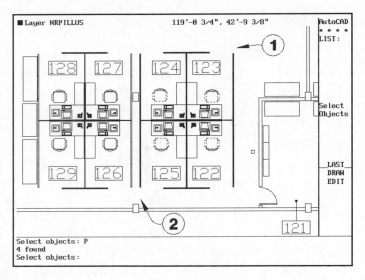

Figure ASESELECT.1:
The selection points and entities retrieved by using ASESELECT.

Command: **ASESELECT** ↵	Issues the ASESELECT command.
Export/<Selection set>: ↵	Accept the default.
Union/Subtract/<Intersection>: ↵	Accept the default.
Graphical/<Textual>: **G** ↵	Start with a graphical search.
Select objects: **W** ↵	Place a window around the entities.
First corner: *Pick point at* ①	
Other corner: *Pick point at* ②	
55 found	
Select objects: ↵	Finish selecting.
Enter search criteria for	Enter a value to
DBASE3/ASETUT/INVENTRY: **PRICE=200** ↵	search for.
Command: **LIST** ↵	Use the LIST command to display the entities selected.
Select objects: **P** ↵	
4 found	
Select objects: ↵	

494

Related Command

SELECT

ASESETDB

Pull-down [**File**] [**ASE**] > [**Set**] > [**DB...**]

Screen [**ASE**] [**SET**] [**DB:**]

The ASESETDB command selects the current database.

Prompts and Options

- **Data**b**ase:**

  Enables you to enter the name of a database file you wish to make current. The names of any currently loaded files are displayed in the list box above this field. To select one of the other files, double-click on its name in the Attached <u>D</u>atabases list box (see fig. ASESETDB.1).

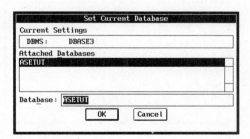

Figure ASESETDB.1:
The Set Current Database dialog box.

On DOS computers, you need to use a SET statement to tell AutoCAD the name of the database you want to load and its location. This needs to be in the following form:

SET *database=path*

In this statement, *database* is the name you are calling the file at the ASESETDB command, and *path* is the full path location to the database file.

- **Username:**

    If you are opening a new database, ASE presents a second dialog box, shown in figure ASESETDB.2, asking for your user name and a password. This information is not typically necessary on single-user DOS systems because only one person at a time uses a file. In a networked environment, however, there may be restrictions on the use of data contained within the file.

- **Password:**

    If necessary to access the information, enter a correct password in this dialog box. After this information is correctly entered, the database will open for viewing and linking (see fig. ASESETDB.2).

Figure ASESETDB.2:
The Set Database Please Enter dialog box.

Example

The following example describes the steps necessary to make a database active within the current drawing session. Keep in mind that paths to the database files must be set before they are recognized by this command.

Command: **ASESETDB** ↵
*Type in the name of a new database to
load at the E̲dit: box.*
Press the OK button.
*At the password/username dialog box,
press the OK button.*

Related Command

ASESETDBMS

ASESETDBMS

Pull-down [**File**] [**ASE**] > [**Set**] > [**DBMS...**]

Screen [**ASE**] [**SET**] [**DBMS:**]

The ASESETDBMS command selects the current database driver. ASE enables you to use several databases, but only one DBMS driver at a time. This limits your access, at any given time, to databases that use the same driver.

Prompts and Options

- D̲river:

  This edit box enables you to enter the name of a database driver you wish to make current. The names of all currently available drivers are displayed in the list box above this field. To select one of the drivers in this list, double-click on its name in the DBMS Drivers list box.

Example

The following example describes the steps necessary to make a new database driver active within the current drawing session (see fig. ASESETDBMS.1):

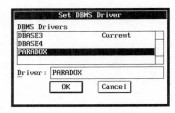

Figure ASESETDBMS.1:
The Set DBMS Driver dialog box.

Command: **ASESETDBMS** ↵
*Highlight the name of a new database
driver to load.*
Press the OK *button.*

Related Commands

> **ASESETDB**
> **ASETERMDBMS**

ASESETROW

Pull-down [**File**] [**ASE**] > [**Set Row...**]

Screen [**ASE**] [**SET ROW:**]

The ASESETROW command selects a row in the current database to make current. This row can be chosen using key values, search criteria, or graphical methods. Once a row is made current, its information can be viewed, edited, and linked to entities within the AutoCAD drawing. The initial dialog box displayed when you issue this command is shown in figure ASESETROW.1.

Figure ASESETROW.1:
The Set Row Options dialog box.

Prompts and Options

- **Criteria:**

  This edit box allows you to define the criteria which will be used to select a row from the current database. This criteria can be an SQL statement such as COST=1000 or FIRSTNAME='BILL'. If you want, you can use one of the other buttons to define your search in a different manner.

- **Key.** If you press this button, you see the dialog box shown in ASESETROW.2. This dialog box allows you to select key columns and the value to search for among those columns. To use this dialog box, highlight the key column you wish to use, and place a value in the Edit list box. When you press the OK button, ASE attempts to locate a row of data that matches your key values in each of the columns.

- **Search.** This option is handled in two ways. If you enter a search criteria in the Criteria edit box, the search function attempts to match that criteria. If that edit box is empty, all records in the database are chosen, and a second dialog box enables you to narrow down your choice to a single row.

499

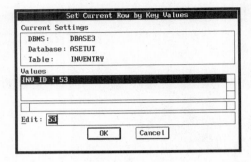

Figure ASESETROW.2:
The Set Current Row by Key Values dialog box.

The dialog box in figure ASESETROW.3 is displayed if the search criteria is too broad. The buttons allow you to move through the rows of the database to select which row should be current. When the row is shown in the list box, pressing the OK button will make it current.

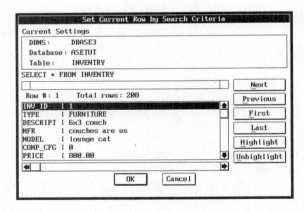

Figure ASESETROW.3:
The Set Current Row by Search Criteria dialog box.

- **Next.** This button will display the next row of information in the database.

- **Previous.** This button will display the previous row of information in the list box.

- **First.** Pressing this button places the first row of the database in the list box and makes that row current.

- **Last.** Pressing this button places the last row of the database in the list box and makes that row current.

- **Highlight.** Use of this button highlights any graphic entities within the drawing that are linked to this row of information.

- **Unhighlight.** Use of this button removes the highlighting applied to the graphic entities that are linked to this row of information.

- **Graphical.** This button allows you to choose a single entity within the drawing that contains links to rows in the database. If more than one link exists, a Selection Link dialog box appears. This box, shown in figure ASESETROW.4, allows you to choose which particular row needs to be made current. The buttons shown in this box perform the same functions as the buttons in the Set Current Row by Search Criteria dialog box.

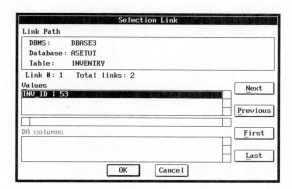

Figure ASESETROW.4:
The Selection Link dialog box.

Example

The following example uses an entity within the current drawing session to set the current database row.

Command: **ASESETROW** ↵
Click on the G*raphical*< *button.*
Select object: *Pick an entity in the*
drawing linked to the database.

Related Commands

> **ASEQEDIT**
> **ASEQLINK**
> **ASEQMAKEDA**
> **ASEQVIE**

ASESETTABLE

Pull-down [**File**] [**ASE**] > [**Set**] > [**Table...**]

Screen [**ASE**] [**SET**] [**TABLE:**]

The ASESETTABLE command makes a table for the current database active (a *table* is a database that is indexed on a certain column). Multiple tables can be defined, each one based on a different key column. If there are no currently defined tables within the control database, this command allows you to choose the key columns that will make up the named table.

Prompts and Options

- **Table:** When using this command, the Set Current Table dialog box, shown in figure ASESETTABLE.1, is displayed. This dialog box contains an edit box in which you can type the name of a table

to make active. You can also choose from any previously defined
tables shown in the Attached Tables list box.

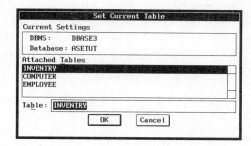

Figure ASESETTABLE.1:
The Set Current Table dialog box.

If the table you enter is not currently defined, the Select Key Columns
dialog box, shown in figure ASESETTABLE.2, displays. This dialog box
allows you to define the columns used to index the current database,
which makes searches for particular rows of information much quicker.

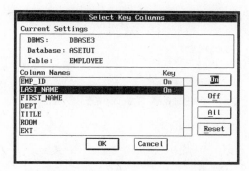

Figure ASESETTABLE.2:
The Select Key Columns dialog box.

- **On.** This button makes the highlighted column name in the
  Column Names list the key column for the table you are defining.

- **O̲f̲f.** This button turns off the highlighting of the column names in the Column Names list box.
- **A̲ll.** This button selects all of the database columns to be key columns for the table you are defining.
- **R̲eset.** This button clears all key-column settings from the Column Names list box, allowing you to choose different columns to serve as keys for this table.

Example

The following exercise changes to a different current table using ASESETTABLE:

```
Command: ASESETTABLE ↵
```
Highlight the name EMPLOYEE *in the table list.*
Click on the OK *key.*

Related Command

ASESETDB

ASESQLED

Pull-down [**File**] [**ASE**] > [**SQL Edit...**]

Screen [**ASE**] [**SQLEDIT:**]

The ASESQLED command is unique because it allows you to execute actual SQL statements directly on your database. All SQL statements that you use must be supported by ASE.

Before using ASESQLED, remember the following restrictions. Any characters in a search string must be enclosed within single quote marks. Information contained within a column of the database is case-sensitive, so you must correctly spell a value in order for the SQL editor to locate the appropriate row. SQL and ASE do not allow you to use SQL keywords as identifiers. Make sure you know the names of all SQL keywords to avoid confusion.

Prompts and Options

- **SQL.** When you use the ASESQLED command, you see the dialog box shown in figure ASESQLED.1. This dialog box allows you to enter a valid SQL statement within the SQL edit box to execute upon your database. Once you have entered an SQL statement, press Execute.

Figure ASESQLED.1:
The SQL Editor dialog box.

- **File.** This button allows you to select a text file containing SQL statements to be executed from a standard File Open dialog box. This file must meet the same criteria as entering single SQL statements with the following additions. If a line of the file begins with a dollar sign, it is a comment. If a line ends with an ampersand, the SQL statement extends to the next line.

- **History.** This button displays the dialog box shown in figure ASESQLED.2, which displays a history of SQL statements that have been executed. You can place any of these statements in the SQL edit box of the SQL Editor dialog box by highlighting the line in the list box and pressing OK.

505

- **Execute.** This button runs the SQL statement in the SQL edit box against the current database file.

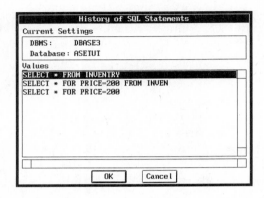

Figure ASESQLED.2:
The History of SQL Statements dialog box.

If the SQL statement to be executed contains the SELECT SQL statement, you see the dialog box shown in figure ASESQLED.3. This box contains all database rows that match the SQL query. You can edit any of the values in each row.

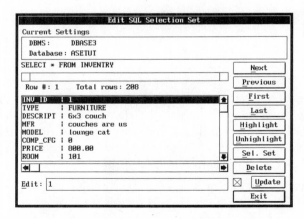

Figure ASESQLED.3:
The Edit SQL Selection Set dialog box.

- **Next.** This button displays the next row of information in the SQL selection set.
- **Previous.** This button displays the previous row of information in the list box.
- **First.** This button places the first row of the selection-set information in the list box for editing.
- **Last.** This button places the last row of the selection-set information in the list box for editing.
- **Highlight.** This button highlights any graphic entities within the drawing that are linked to this row of information.
- **Unhighlight.** This button removes the highlighting applied to the graphic entities that are linked to this row of information.
- **Sel. Set.** This button adds any entities that are linked to the row of information to the selection set.
- **Delete.** This button removes the row of information from the database table and deletes any links to graphic entities.
- **Update.** This button and check box combination keeps you from accidentally modifying values in the key column. If the check box is not active, the Update button is grayed out. Any changes you make to a key column automatically are written out to the database file. If the check box is activated, you must click on Update for any of your edits to take effect in the database.

Example

The following example uses the SQL editor to select all of the records in the current database:

Command: **ASEQLED** ↵
*Enter SELECT * from INVEN at the* Execute *edit box.*
Click on the Execute *button.*
Click on the Exit *button in the Edit SQL*
Selection Set dialog box.

ASETERM

Pull-down [**File**] [**ASE**] > [**Terminate**]

Screen [**ASE**] [**TERMNTE:**]

The ASETERM command closes down ASE. This command is typically used to reduce the memory overhead required by ASE when the connections to the databases and drivers are not needed.

Prompts and Options

A dialog box asking you to confirm your decision displays. If you press the Yes button, ASE closes the control database and saves it to the drawing file. ASE drivers are unloaded from memory, and all ASE commands are disabled within the drawing editor.

Related Command

ASEINIT

ASETERMDBMS

Pull-down [**File**] [**ASE**] > [**Utility**] > [**Term DBMS**]

Screen [**ASE**] [**UTILITY**] [**TERMDBM:**]

The ASETERMDBMS command removes a loaded database driver from memory. This allows you to free up memory that may currently be used by an inactive database driver.

Prompts and Options

- **Driver:** This edit box, shown in figure ASETERMDBMS.1, allows you to choose a database driver you wish to remove from memory. The names of all currently available drivers are displayed in the list box above this field. To select one of the drivers

in this list, double-click on its name in the DBMS Drivers list box.
You are asked to confirm your decision in a second dialog box. If
you still want to remove the driver, press Yes.

Figure ASETERMDBMS.1:
The Terminate DBMS Driver dialog box.

Related Command

ASESETDBMS

ASEVIEWLINK

Pull-down [**File**] [**ASE**] > [**Link**] > [**View...**]

Screen [**ASE**] [**LINK**] [**VIEW:**]

The ASEVIEWLINK command shows any links between AutoCAD
graphic entities and database information.

Prompts and Options

When you choose an entity linked to database information, the
View Link dialog box, shown in figure ASEVIEWLINK.1, displays.
If the chosen entity has more than one link to database information,
this dialog box allows you to scroll through the various rows of information.

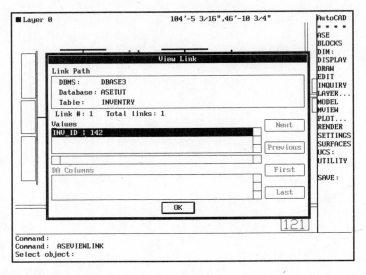

Figure ASEVIEWLINK.1:
The View Link dialog box.

- **Select object:**

  Choose an entity linked to the current database for which you wish to view the link information.
- **Next.** This button displays the next row of linked information.
- **Previous.** This button displays the previous row of linked information.
- **First.** Displays the first row of linked information for the selected object.
- **Last.** Displays the last linked element of the selected object.

Example

The following exercise demonstrates the steps necessary to view the link information for a drawing entity:

Command: **ASEVIEWLINK** ⏎
Select object: *Select a linked entity.*

Related Commands

> **ASEEDITLINK**
> **ASEQVIEW**

ASEVIEWROW

Pull-down [**File**] [**ASE**] > [**Row**] > [**View...**]

Screen [**ASE**] [**ROW**] [**VIEW:**]

The ASEVIEWROW command shows the contents of the current row of the database. This information is then displayed in the dialog box shown in figure ASEVIEWROW.1.

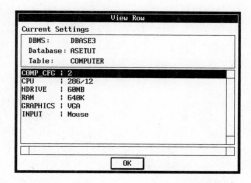

Figure ASEVIEWROW.1:
The View Row dialog box.

Related Command

ASEEDITROW

ATTDEF

Screen [BLOCKS] [ATTDEF:]

Screen [DRAW] [ATTDEF:]

The ATTDEF command, which stands for ATTribute DEFinition, creates attributes for inclusion in block definitions and insertion into drawings. ATTDEF is primarily a tool for building non-graphical intelligence into symbol libraries. During block insertion, the attribute definitions take on their final forms.

Attributes are alphanumeric data attached to a block. An unlimited number of attributes can be attached to any block definition. You can control the appearance of attributes individually through the use of text style, height, color, and layer. You also can control the visibility, default values, user prompts, and preset values of attributes. Attribute data can be extracted for further processing, and is commonly used for schedule and bill-of-material generation.

The ATTDEF command is designed to work from the AutoCAD Command: prompt. An easier method of creating attributes is to use the DDATTDEF command's dialog box.

Prompts and Options

* Invisible:

  This option controls attribute visibility. Invisible attributes can be combined with visible attributes within the same block, as can all other attribute modes.

- **Constant:**

  This option sets a fixed value for the attribute that cannot be changed. A constant value is used, rather than a variable, when it is important that the attribute value not change.

- **Verify:**

  This option ensures that you are asked to confirm all responses to attribute prompts.

- **Preset:**

  Use this option to establish editable, default values for attributes.

- **Attribute tag:**

  Use this option to define the name of the tag used to store attribute data that the user enters.

- **Attribute prompt:**

  This option sets the prompt AutoCAD uses to ask you for the attribute's value when the attribute is inserted.

- **Default attribute value:**

  Use this option so that each attribute can have a default value that is used if the user chooses not to enter another value.

After you set the preceding options, ATTDEF prompts you for text options: justification, insertion point, height, and rotation. Like the TEXT command, ATTDEF uses the current text style.

Example

This example creates a simple attribute definition using the default modes options (see fig. ATTDEF.1):

```
Command: ATTDEF ↵
Enter (ICVP) to change, RETURN when done: ↵
Attribute tag: COST ↵
Attribute prompt: Enter item cost ↵
Default attribute value: $100 ↵
Justify/Style/<Start point>: Pick point ①
Height <0.2000>: .5 ↵
Rotation angle <0>: ↵
```

513

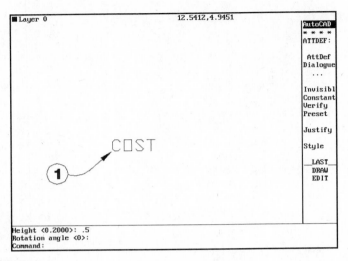

Figure ATTDEF.1:
A basic attribute created with ATTDEF.

Related Commands

ASEMAKEDA
ASEQMAKEDA
ATTDISP
ATTEDIT
ATTEXT
BLOCK
DDATTDEF
DDATTE
DDATTEXT

Related System Variables

ATTDIA
ATTMODE

ATTDISP

Screen **[DISPLAY] [ATTDISP:]**

The ATTDISP command controls attribute visibility of inserted blocks. This command overrides the visibility mode used during attribute definition with the ATTDEF command. ATTDISP is useful for viewing attributes that normally are invisible and for turning off the visibility of all attributes.

The ATTDISP command can be executed transparently by preceding the command name with an apostophe (**'ATTDISP**).

Prompts and Options

- **Normal:**

  This option is the default; it uses the attribute's defined visibility mode (visible or invisible).

- **ON:**

  This option turns on the visibility of all attributes, regardless of defined visibility mode. The defined visibility mode is retained, and you can restore it by using the Normal option.

- **OFF:**

  This option turns off the visibility of all attributes, regardless of defined visibility mode. Use the Normal option to restore the defined visibility mode.

Example

This example displays a block with attributes in both viewports. When you use the ATTDISP command, the cost attribute is displayed (see fig. ATTDISP.1).

```
Command: ATTDISP ↵
Normal/ON/OFF <Normal>: ↵
```
Once the ATTDISP command is used to force attribute display to ON, both attributes become visible.

515

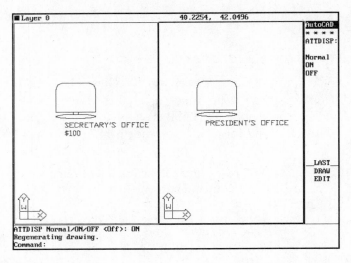

Figure ATTDISP.1:
Viewing attributes with ATTDISP.

Related Commands

ATTDEF
ATTEDIT
ATTEXT
DDATTDEF
DDATTE
DDATTEXT

Related System Variable

ATTMODE

ATTEDIT

Screen **[EDIT] [ATTEDIT:]**

ATTEDIT, which stands for ATTribute EDIT, edits the characteristics of inserted attributes. You can edit an attribute's value, position, height, angle, style, layer, or color. You also can edit attributes individually or globally.

Note that AutoCAD does not highlight attributes when you select them. The attributes are highlighted during editing.

 You also can edit attributes more easily from the DDATTE dialog box.

Prompts and Options

- **Edit attributes one at a time? <Y>**

  If you answer **Y**, you can edit each attribute individually. If you answer **N**, you can edit the attributes globally.

- **Block name specification <*>:**

  This prompt requests the block name to search for attributes. You can use wild cards at this prompt.

- **Attribute tag specification <*>:**

  This prompt requests the attribute tag name for editing. You can use wild cards at this prompt.

- **Attribute value specification <*>:**

  This prompt enables you to edit attributes with specific values only. This prompt often is used for globally updating one value to another across multiple blocks.

- **Select attributes:**

  You select attributes individually at this prompt. Attributes must be visible to be selected. If the attributes were not originally set to be visible, you must set ATTDISP to ON before selecting attributes at this prompt.

- **Value:**

  Use this option to change attribute values.

517

- **Position:**

  This option enables you to change the position of inserted attributes.

- **Height:**

  This option enables you to change the text height of inserted attributes.

- **Angle:**

  This option enables you to change the angle of inserted attributes' text.

- **Style:**

  This option enables you to change the text style of inserted attributes.

- **Layer:**

  This option enables you to change the layer assignment of inserted attributes.

- **Color:**

  This option enables you to change the color assignment of inserted attributes.

- **Next <N>:**

  This option enables you to edit the next attribute in the selection set.

Example

This example uses the attribute created and inserted with the ATTDISP command. It alters the value of the ITEM attribute to call the item a couch (see fig. ATTEDIT.1):

```
Command: ATTEDIT ↵
Edit attributes one at a time? <Y> ↵
Block name specification <*>: ↵
Attribute tag specification <*>: ↵
Attribute value specification <*>: ↵
Select Attributes: Pick point ①
    1 attributes selected.
Value/Position/Height/Angle/Style/Layer/Color/Next <N>: V ↵
```

```
Change or Replace? <R>: R ↵
New attribute value: PERSONNEL OFFICE ↵
Value/Position/Height/Angle/Style/Layer/Color/Next <N>: ↵
```

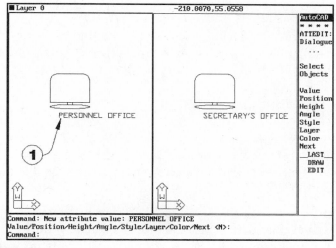

Figure ATTEDIT.1:
The new attribute value.

Related Commands

> **ATTDEF**
> **ATTDISP**
> **ATTEXT**
> **DDATTDEF**
> **DDATTE**
> **DDATTEXT**

ATTEXT

Screen **[UTILITY] [ATTEXT:]**

ATTEXT, which stands for ATTribute EXTraction, extracts attribute information contained in the block insertions of the current drawing. You can extract this information in several standard ASCII-file formats so the data can be placed in database or spreadsheet programs for further processing and analysis.

One example of an ATTEXT application is schedule building. With proper planning and setup, you can extract attributes to build material lists, door schedules, and for a variety of other purposes.

Prompts and Options

- **CDF:**

    CDF, which stands for Comma Delimited Format, requires a template file. This option enables you to extract the attribute information from the entire drawing.

- **SDF:**

    SDF, which stands for Space Delimited Format, requires a template file. This option enables you to extract the attribute information from the entire drawing.

- **DXF:**

    DXF, which stands for Drawing Interchange Format, enables you to extract the attribute information from the entire drawing.

- **Entities:**

    This option enables you to select specific entities for attribute extraction using one of the above formats.

Template Files

To extract attribute information to an external file, you need to create a template file first. This file provides the ATTEXT command with the types of information you want to extract (attribute values) and with the formatting to be used in the output file for storing the attribute information. Template files are only used during CDF or SDF information extractions.

For example, the block shown in figure ATTEDIT.1 has an attribute called Location, which is used to store the location of the chair in a furniture plan. To extract the information stored within the attribute, you can create a template file with the following line:

```
LOCATION        C040000
```

This tells the ATTEXT command the attribute to extract information from within the drawing and the type of information to be extracted (C for character data, or N for numeric). The six numbers after the data type are used to set the length of the field to extract the data to, as well as its decimal accuracy. The first three numbers indicate how large a value can be extracted from the attribute (in the above example, 40 characters). The last three digits relate to decimal accuracy. For character fields, this value defaults to 0. If you are extracting numeric data, you can tell how many decimal places of information will be placed in the extract file.

Related Commands

ASEMAKEREP
ATTDEF
ATTDISP
ATTEDIT
DDATTDEF
DDATTE
DDATTEXT

AUDIT

Screen **[UTILITY] [AUDIT:]**

The AUDIT command, available following Release 11, verifies the integrity of your drawings. When you invoke AUDIT from the drawing editor, AutoCAD can correct any errors in the drawing file automatically if the program detects them, or it can leave all errors uncorrected (the default)—but recommend specific corrective action.

Prompts and Options

- **Fix any errors detected? <N>**

  If you answer **No** (the default), AutoCAD creates a report that documents any errors found and recommends corrective action.

  If you answer **Yes**, AutoCAD creates a report and automatically performs the recommended corrective action.

AUDIT works only on drawings saved with Release 11 or 12. AUDIT does not correct all damaged drawings. In cases where AUDIT is unable to recover damaged information, try using the RECOVER command also.

Related Command

RECOVER

BASE

Screen **[BLOCKS] [BASE:]**

The BASE command defines the insertion point of the current drawing. The results of this command are evident only when you insert the drawing or use the drawing as an external reference.

You can execute the BASE command transparently by preceding the command name with an apostrophe ('BASE).

Prompts and Options

- **Base point <0.0000,0.0000,0.0000>:**

  This prompt requests a base point that can be defined by picking a point on the screen or by entering the point's coordinates. (To specify a 3D point, you must enter the coordinates.) If you supply a 2D point, AutoCAD assumes that the Z value is equal to the current elevation.

The numbers shown in brackets, $<0.0000,0.0000,0.0000>$, show the current coordinate location of the base point. In this case, 0,0,0 is the default for a new drawing. The value shown may be different if you used the BASE command previously on the current drawing, or if you initially created the drawing by using the WBLOCK command.

Related Commands

BLOCK
INSERT
XREF
WBLOCK

Related System Variable

INSBASE

BHATCH

Screen **[DRAW] [BHATCH:]**

Pull down **[Draw] [Hatch...]**

BHATCH draws crosshatching within a boundary area that you select. Unlike the HATCH command, BHATCH creates a closed polyline boundary object automatically by intelligently tracing over existing intersecting objects surrounding the point you pick. You can elect to retain the boundary for later use or for creating additional drawing geometry.

A dialog box enables you to specify the hatch pattern name, angle, style, and scale. You can define your own simple hatch patterns, specify certain objects to consider for boundary calculations,

523

experiment by selecting and viewing boundary selection sets, pre-explode the hatch block, and preview hatches before proceeding. Figure BHATCH.1 shows the main BHATCH dialog box.

```
┌─────────────────────────────────────────┐
│             Boundary Hatch               │
│ Pattern:      No hatch pattern selected. │
│       ┌──────────────┐                   │
│       │ Hatch Options...│                 │
│       └──────────────┘                   │
│ Define Hatch Area                        │
│    ┌──────────────────┐                  │
│    │   Pick Points <  │                  │
│    └──────────────────┘                  │
│  ┌──────────────────┐ ┌────────────────┐ │
│  │ Select Objects < │ │ View selections <│ │
│  └──────────────────┘ └────────────────┘ │
│  ┌──────────────────┐ ┌────────────────┐ │
│  │  Preview Hatch < │ │ Advanced Options...│ │
│  └──────────────────┘ └────────────────┘ │
│  ┌─────┐ ┌──────┐ ┌───────┐ ┌──────┐    │
│  │Apply│ │Cancel│ │Another│ │Help...│   │
│  └─────┘ └──────┘ └───────┘ └──────┘    │
└─────────────────────────────────────────┘
```

Figure BHATCH.1:
The primary BHATCH dialog box.

Prompts and Options

BHATCH displays no command-line prompts. Instead, you make selections from the following dialog boxes and options.

The Boundary Hatch dialog box (see fig. BHATCH.1) offers the following options:

- **Hatch Options.** Click on this button to display the Hatch Options dialog box (see fig. BHATCH.2).
- **Pick Points.** Click on this button to pick a point inside the area(s) you want to hatch. After you pick a point, AutoCAD analyzes the current object-selection set to create a hatch boundary. You can control the objects considered for boundary creation by selecting specific entities or by using the Advanced Options button.
- **Select Objects.** Click on this button to select the objects on-screen to be considered for the hatch boundary.
- **Preview Hatch.** Click on this button to see a temporary example of how the hatch would appear if created with the current settings.

524

- **View selections.** Click on this button to highlight the objects selected for boundary calculation.
- **Advanced Options.** Click on this button to display the Advanced Options dialog box (see fig. BHATCH.4).
- **Apply.** Click on this button to apply the hatch pattern to the selected area with the current settings.
- **Another.** Click on this button to apply the hatch pattern to another selected area. The Boundary Hatch dialog box reappears so that you can perform additional BHATCH operations.

The Hatch Options dialog box (see fig. BHATCH.2) offers the following options:

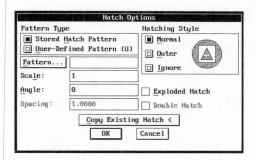

Figure BHATCH.2:
The Hatch Options dialog box.

- **Pattern Type.** The radio buttons in this group enable selection of either a hatch pattern definition stored on disk or specification of a user-defined pattern. If **U**ser-Defined Pattern is chosen, the following spacing and double hatch options are enabled.
- **Pattern.** Clicking on this button displays the Choose Hatch Pattern dialog box, which displays pages of names and graphic examples of hatch patterns stored in the specified disk file (see fig. BHATCH.3). Use the **P**revious and **N**ext buttons to browse through the various patterns. Click on the desired pattern icon to make your selection. Alternatively, you can enter a known pattern name in the edit box.

- **Scale.** You enter a hatch pattern scale factor. You may need to experiment to produce the desired results.

- **Angle.** You enter a hatch pattern angle.

- **Spacing.** You enter the inter-line spacing in drawing units for user-defined hatch patterns.

- **Hatching Style.** Click on one of the radio button options: Normal, Outer, or Ignore. Normal style hatches alternating interior areas within the current boundary. Outer style hatches only the outermost area. Ignore style hatches any inner boundaries indiscriminately.

- **Exploded Hatch.** If this box is checked, the resulting hatch pattern block is inserted as exploded. Individual hatch entities may then be edited.

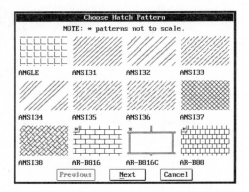

Figure BHATCH.3:
The Choose Hatch Pattern dialog box.

- **Double Hatch.** If this box is checked, the user-defined hatch pattern is mirrored perpendicularly to produce double hatching.

- **Copy Existing Hatch.** Click on this button to select an existing hatch for which you want to use the same settings. In Release 12, hatch options are saved with the inserted hatch block. This makes for a simple reuse of hatch settings.

The Advanced Options dialog box (see fig. BHATCH.4) offers the following options:

Figure BHATCH.4:
The Advanced Options dialog box.

- **Define Boundary Set.** You specify the way boundary entities are calculated. Clicking on the Make New Boundary Set button enables you to pick entities on-screen. If a selection set is already active, the From Existing Set radio button is enabled, and you can add or remove entities. The From Everything on Screen radio button causes all visible entities to be considered.

- **Ray Casting.** This option specifies the direction in which AutoCAD first searches to find boundary entities. You can choose one direction from the positive and negative X and Y axes by selecting a method from the drop-down list box.

- **Retain Boundaries.** When this box is checked, it creates a new closed polyline object from the calculated boundary.

Example

The following example uses BHATCH to hatch an area bounded by various intersecting and non-intersecting objects (see fig. BHATCH.5). BHATCH performs this operation much faster than the HATCH command does.

```
Command: BHATCH ↵
```
Click on the Hatch Options *button.*
Click on the **P**attern *button.*
Click on the ANSI31 *icon.*
Click on the OK *button in the* Define Hatch Pattern *dialog box.*
Click on the **P**ick Points *button.*
```
Select internal point Pick ①
Select internal point ↵
```
Click on the Apply *button to finish hatching (see fig. BHATCH.6).*

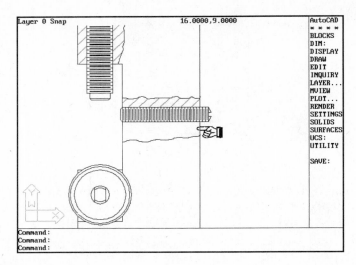

Figure BHATCH.5:
The area to hatch.

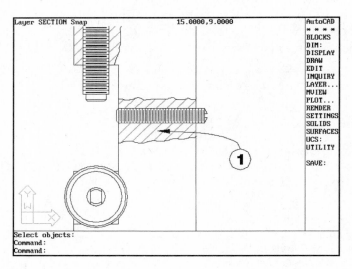

Figure BHATCH.6:
Completed hatch and boundary pick point.

Related Commands

BPOLY
HATCH

Related System Variables

HPANG
HPDOUBLE
HPNAME
HPSCALE

BLIPMODE

Screen **[SETTINGS] [BLIPS:]**

The BLIPMODE command controls the creation of blips when you pick points on-screen. A *blip* is a small plus sign (+) that appears at the exact pick point. Blips are not entities; you can clear them from the screen by using the REDRAW command. If you do not want to use blips, use BLIPMODE to turn off blip generation.

 BLIPMODE can be toggled on and off from within other AutoCAD commands by issuing the transparent 'DDRMODES command.

Prompts and Options

- **ON/OFF <On>:**

  When BLIPMODE is on (the default), blips appear at pick points. When BLIPMODE is off, AutoCAD does not generate blips when you pick points.

529

Example

This example shows how AutoCAD draws entities with BLIPMODE turned on and off (see fig. BLIPMO.1):

```
Command: BLIPMODE ↵
ON/OFF <On>: ↵
Command: LINE ↵
From point: Pick point ①
To point: Pick point ②
Command: BLIPMODE ↵
MODE ON/OFF <On>: OFF ↵
Command: LINE ↵
From point:Pick point ③
To point: Pick point ④
```

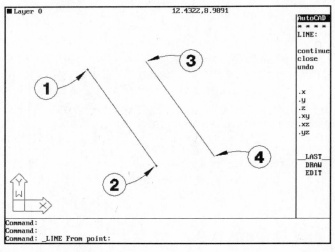

Figure BLIPMO.1:
Using BLIPMODE.

Related Command

'DDRMODES

Related System Variable

BLIPMODE

BLOCK

Screen **[BLOCKS] [BLOCK:]**

The BLOCK command groups entities together to form a single object called a *block*. Blocks aid in organizing and drawing repetitive entities, reduce the size of the drawing, reduce drawing time, and enable the use of attributes.

When you create a block, you give it a name. You can then insert the block by its name. A block can be inserted as many times as needed. Inserting a block, rather than duplicating entities, adds only one entity to the drawing—thus reducing the size of the drawing database. Blocks also can be inserted at any X, Y, and Z scale.

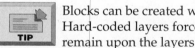 Blocks can be created with *hard-coded* or *soft-coded* layers. Hard-coded layers force a block's individual entities to remain upon the layers on which they were created. Soft-coded layers enable a block's individual entities to be placed on the layer on which the block is inserted and take on that layer's properties. You can create soft-coded layers by creating blocks that use entities on layer 0.

Prompts and Options

- **Block name (or ?):**

  At this prompt, you specify a block name that is not more than 31 characters in length. Letters, numbers, the dollar sign, the hyphen, and the underscore are valid characters for block names. The ? option lists the blocks currently defined within the drawing.

- **Block(s) to List <*>:**

  You can press Enter at this prompt to list all blocks currently defined within the drawing. You can use wild-card combinations to create more specific lists. (Note that the lists are presented in alphanumeric order.)

- **Insertion base point:**

  This prompt requests the point, relative to the block itself, that will be used to insert the block. You can select this point from the screen by using an object snap mode. You also can type the point's coordinates, use XYZ point filters, or use a combination of screen and keyboard input. If you specify the point 0,0, the block will insert in the same relative position in other drawings as it appears in the current drawing.

- **Select objects:**

  This prompt is the standard prompt for selecting objects. The selected objects make up your block. You can use any standard object-selection method.

  After you have selected objects and the block has been created, the original entities are erased from the screen. You can use the OOPS command to restore the entities back into the drawing.

Example

This example demonstrates both the creation of a block as well as its re-insertion into the drawing using the INSERT command. The objects shown in figure BLOCK.1 are both the original chair and the block after its insertion.

```
Command: BLOCK ↵
Block name (or ?): CHAIR ↵
Insertion base point: Pick point ①
Select objects: Select the objects to make up the block
Select objects: ↵
Command: OOPS ↵
Command: INSERT ↵
Block name (or ?) <>: CHAIR ↵
Insertion point: Pick point ②
X scale factor <1>/Corner/XYZ: ↵
Y scale factor (default=X): ↵
Rotation angle <0>: 45 ↵
```

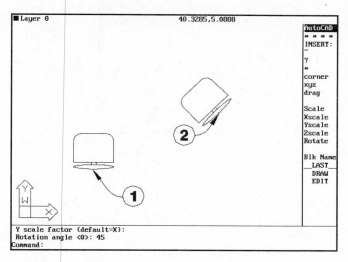

Figure BLOCK.1:
The entities that form the chair block.

Related Commands

ATTDEF
DDATTDEF
DDINSERT
EXPLODE
INSERT
OOPS
WBLOCK
XREF

BPOLY

The BPOLY command creates a new polyline object that outlines an area defined by existing entities. BPOLY performs a subset of the functions of the BHATCH command, but it does not hatch the enclosed area. Figure BPOLY.1 shows the BPOLY dialog box.

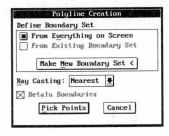

Figure BPOLY.1:
The BPOLY dialog box.

BPOLY is especially useful for creating irregular closed
polylines from construction lines, arcs, circles, and other
entities.

Prompts and Options

BPOLY displays no command-line prompts. Instead, you make selections from the following dialog box options.

The Polyline Creation dialog box (see fig. BPOLY.1) offers the following options:

- **Define Boundary Set.** Options in this group specify the way boundary entities are calculated. Clicking on the Make **N**ew Boundary Set button enables you to pick entities on-screen. If a selection set is already active, the From Existing Boundary Set radio button is enabled, and you can add or remove entities. The From **E**verything on Screen radio button causes all visible entities to be considered.

- **Ray Casting.** This option specifies the direction that AutoCAD first searches to find boundary entities. You can choose one direction from the positive and negative X and Y axes by selecting a method from the drop-down list box.

- **Pick Points.** Click on this button to pick a point on-screen to define the area from which you want a polyline to be made.

- **Retain Boundaries.** When this box is checked, it creates a new closed polyline object from the calculated boundary.

Example

The following example uses BPOLY to create a closed polyline boundary out of various construction objects (see fig. BPOLY.2).

Command: **BPOLY** ↵
Click on the **P**ick Points *button*
Select internal point *Pick point* ①
Select internal point ↵

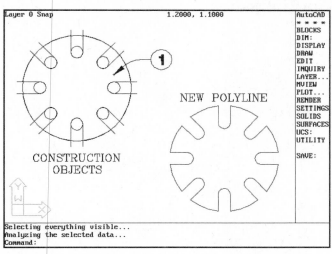

Figure BPOLY.2:
Boundary polyline created by BPOLY.

Related Command

BHATCH

BREAK

Screen **[EDIT] [BREAK:]**

Pull down **[Modify] [Break >]**

The BREAK command removes a portion of a line, arc, polyline, or circle. This command prompts you to select the target object and specify the first and second points of the break. You can break only one entity at a time. If the first and second break points are identical, the entity is divided into two pieces.

Prompts and Options

- **Select object:**

  Select the line, arc, circle, or polyline to break. By default, the point by which you pick the object is considered the first point of the segment to remove. Only one entity can be selected at one time.

- **Enter second point (or F for first point):**

  Select another point on the line, arc, circle, or polyline to break between. The original object-selection point becomes the opposite end of the break, and the portion of the entity between the two points will be removed.

- **Enter first point:**

  You specify a first point of the break that is different from the original object-selection point.

- **Enter second point:**

  The second point determines the portion of the entity to remove.

Example

This example demonstrates how you can use the BREAK command to remove a section of an entity. Figure BREAK.1 shows both the original entities and the result of using the command.

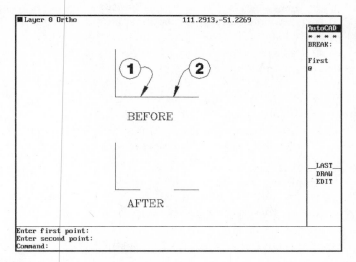

Figure BREAK.1:
The entities before and after using BREAK.

```
Command: BREAK ↵
Select object: Pick point ①
Enter second point (or F for first point): F ↵
Enter first point: Pick point ①
Enter second point: Pick point ②
```

Related Command

TRIM

CAL

Pull down **[Assist] [Calculator]**

The CAL command is an on-line calculator that evaluates points, vectors, or real and integer expressions. Calculations can use object snap modes to access existing geometry, and 'CAL can be issued transparently within another command to provide a point or number. CAL can also be used in AutoLISP functions.

NOTE If you use the AutoCAD object snap modes in your expressions, enter the three-character abbreviations of the object snap modes. You must pick entities—you cannot use the object-selection methods.

CAL follows the standard mathematical order of precedence for evaluating expressions. Vectors and points are entered as a set of points or distance and angles. When you enter points in the WCS, use the * prefix, as in [*2,3,4]. Use the * for Scalar products of vectors and the & for Vector products of vectors. Numbers can be entered in scientific notation or a general number format. You can add ' and " for feet and inches on distances. Angles default to degrees; however, you can use the r suffix for radians or the g suffix for gradians. All angles will be converted to degrees. See the *AutoCAD Release 12 Extras Manual* for a complete list of the CAL functions and modes.

Example

The following examples use CAL and 'CAL to solve equations and to return points and vectors to other commands. See figure CAL.1.

```
Command: CAL ↵
>> Expression: A=(5.25+10.5)/1.5^2 ↵
7.0
Command: ↵
CAL >> Expression: B=3*(14-7) ↵
21
Command: ↵
CAL >> Expression: B/A ↵
3.0
Command: ↵
CAL >> Expression: CVUNIT(DIST(END,INT),INCH,CM) ↵
>> Select entity for END snap: Pick point ①
>> Select entity for INT snap: Pick point ②
5.08
Command:CIRCLE ↵
3P/2P/TTR/<Center point>:'CAL ↵
>> Expression: MEE ↵
>> Select one endpoint for MEE: Pick point ③
>> Select another endpoint for MEE: Pick point ①
Diameter/ <Radius>:'CAL ↵
>> Expression: DIST(END,END)/3 ↵
```

```
>> Select entity for END snap: Pick point ③
>> Select entity for END snap: Pick point ①
```

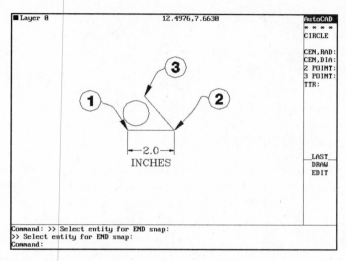

Figure CAL.1:
Entities and pick points for CAL.

Related Commands

DIST
ID
LIST
OSNAP
ROTATE
SOLMASSP

CHAMFER

Screen **[EDIT] [CHAMFER:]**

Pull down **[Construct] [Chamfer]**

The CHAMFER command creates a bevel, called a *chamfer*, between
two nonparallel lines or on continuous segments of 2D polylines.

CHAMFER extends or trims lines as necessary and adds a line to create the beveled edge. With 2D polylines, it adds vertices and a new segment representing the bevel.

You must supply the distance for the start of the bevel from the intersection of the two segments. You can set different distances for each side of the chamfer to create custom bevels. If you set the chamfer distance to 0, CHAMFER trims or extends the two lines to end neatly at their intersection. (This effect is also possible with the FILLET command.)

Prompts and Options

- **Polyline/Distances/<Select first line>:**

  If you press **P** at this prompt, you can select a 2D polyline for chamfering. The Distances option enables you to preset the chamfer distances applied to both sides of the entities' intersection. The default choice at this prompt is to select the first of two lines for chamfering. The first chamfer distance is applied to this line.

- **Select second line:**

  If you choose the default option, you are prompted for a second line. Your selection completes the CHAMFER command. The second chamfer distance is applied to this line.

- **Enter first chamfer distance <current>:**

  If you select the Distances option at the first prompt, you are prompted for the first chamfer distance. You can type a distance, or you can pick two points on the screen and let AutoCAD calculate the distance between them.

- **Enter second chamfer distance <current>:**

  After you enter the first chamfer distance, you are prompted for the second one. This value defaults to be the same distance as the value for the first chamfer distance.

- **Select 2D polyline:**

  The Polyline option requires you to choose a 2D polyline for modifying. The CHAMFER command attempts to bevel each vertex of the selected polyline using the current chamfer distances.

Example

This example demonstrates the differences between beveling two lines and a single polyline with the CHAMFER command. Figure CHAMFER.1 shows the results of using the CHAMFER command on both types of entities.

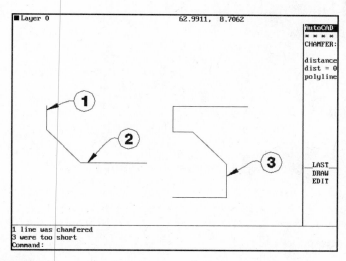

Figure CHAMFER.1:
Using the CHAMFER command.

```
Command: CHAMFER ↵
Polyline/Distances/<Select first line>: D↵
Enter first chamfer distance <0.0000>: 24 ↵
Enter second chamfer distance <24.0000>: ↵
Command: CHAMFER ↵
Polyline/Distances/<Select first line>: Pick point ①
Select second line: Pick point ②
Command: CHAMFER ↵
Polyline/Distances/<Select first line>: P ↵
Select polyline: Pick point ③
```

541

Related System Variables

CHAMFERA
CHAMFERB

Related Commands

FILLET
TRIM

CHANGE

Screen **[EDIT] [CHANGE:]**

Pull down **[Modify] [Change] [Points]**

The CHANGE command changes existing entities' properties, including color, linetype, layer, and text style. You can use CHANGE whenever you want to modify the properties of selected entities, edit text, or change a point's location.

Prompts and Options

- **Select objects:**

  At this prompt, you can choose objects individually or by using one of the other entity selection options. The prompt repeats until you press Enter to end the object-selection process.

Change Point Option

This option acts in different ways, depending on entity type, as shown in the following table:

Table CHANGE.1

Change Point Option Functions

Entity Type	Function of Change Point Option
Lines	Enables you to move the end points of selected lines. If Ortho mode is turned on, the selected lines are drawn horizontally or vertically, depending on the new point selected. If Ortho mode is turned off, the selected lines converge at the new point.
Text	Edits each text entity in your selection set. You can change the text style, height, rotation angle, or text string.
Circle	Resizes the circle's radius. The circle's center point remains stationary.
Block	Changes the insertion point or the rotation angle of selected blocks.
Attribute Definition	Edits attribute definitions just like text, with a few additional options. You also can change the attribute tag, prompt, and default value.

Change Properties Options

- **Change what property (Color/Elev/LAyer/LType/ Thickness) ?:**

  At this prompt, you can change various properties of the objects you have selected. The first option, Color, changes the color of selected objects. Entities with an explicit color assignment do not take on the color characteristics of the parent layer. To force entities to assume the parent layer's color, assign the special BYLAYER color property.

  The Elev option sets the base elevation of the entities selected.

  The LAyer option changes the layer on which the selected entities reside. The target layer must already exist.

TIP If you specify a layer that does not exist, AutoCAD displays the message `Layer not found` and prompts you for another layer name. Use the transparent 'DDLMODES command, which enables you to create a new layer, and then return to the CHPROP command.

The LType option changes the linetype of selected objects. Entities with an explicit linetype assignment do not take on the linetype characteristics of the parent layer. To force entities to assume the parent layer's linetype, assign the special BYLAYER linetype property.

The Thickness option changes the thickness, or extrusion value, of selected objects.

TIP The CHANGE command forces you to do a lot of typing when entering entity properties. The DDCHPROP command allows you to use dialog boxes to select the new entity properties you want to set.

Example

This example shows how to use CHANGE on various types of entities:

```
Command: CHANGE ↵
Select objects: Pick point ①
1 found
Select objects: Pick point ②
1 found
Select objects: ↵
Properties/<Change point>:
Pick point ③ (see fig. CHANGE.1)
```

Related Commands

CHPROP
COLOR
DDCHPROP
'DDEDIT
DDMODIFY

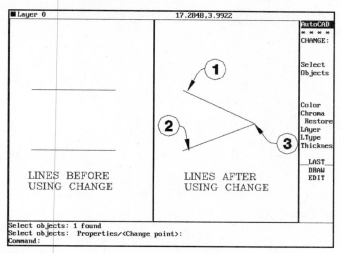

Figure CHANGE.1:
Two lines with changed end points.

Related System Variables

CECOLOR
CELTYPE
CLAYER
ELEV
ELEVATION
LINETYPE
ORTHO
THICKNESS

CHPROP

Screen **[EDIT] [CHPROP:]**

CHPROP, which stands for CHange PROPerties, offers a simple, direct method for modifying the properties of existing entities. It also modifies the properties of all the objects in a selection set at the same time. CHPROP performs a subset of the editing options available with the CHANGE command.

Prompts and Options

- **Select objects:**

  At this prompt, you can choose objects individually or by using one of the other entity-selection options. The prompt repeats until you press Enter to end the object-selection process.

- **Change what property (Color/LAyer/LType/Thickness) ?:**

  At this prompt, you can change various properties of the objects you select. The first option, Color, changes the color of selected objects. Entities with an explicit color assignment do not take on the color characteristics of the parent layer. To force entities to assume the parent layer's color, assign the special BYLAYER color property.

  The prompt's second option, LAyer, changes the layer on which the selected entities reside. The target layer must already exist.

 If you specify a layer that does not exist, AutoCAD displays the message Layer not found and prompts you for another layer name. Use the transparent 'DDLMODES command, which enables you to create a new layer, and then return to the CHPROP command.

The LType option changes the linetype of selected objects. Entities with an explicit linetype assignment do not take on the linetype characteristics of the parent layer. To force entities to assume the parent layer's linetype, assign the special BYLAYER linetype property.

The Thickness option changes the thickness, or extrusion value, of selected objects.

Example

This example shows how the CHPROP options enable you to perfom most of the same types of entity editing as the CHANGE command. Figure CHPROP.1 shows both the original and new versions of the line entities modified with this command.

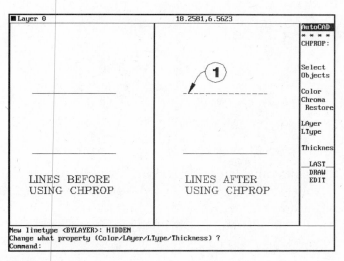

Figure CHPROP.1:
A line entity modified by the CHPROP command's LType option.

```
Command: CHPROP ↵
Select objects: Pick point ①
1 found
Select objects: ↵
Change what property (Color/LAyer/LType/Thickness) ? LT ↵
New linetype <BYLAYER>: HIDDEN ↵
Change what property (Color/LAyer/LType/Thickness) ? ↵
```

Related Commands

CHANGE
COLOR
DDCHPROP

547

DDMODIFY
LINETYPE

Related System Variables

CECOLOR
CELTYPE
CLAYER
THICKNESS

CIRCLE

Screen **[DRAW] [CIRCLE]**

Pull down **[Draw] [Circle >]**

The CIRCLE command draws circles. Circles are created at the current elevation, parallel to the current UCS. By setting the ELEV command's THICKNESS option to a non-zero value, you also can create 3D cylinders. These cylinders are simply extruded circles, which do not actually have a top or bottom.

Prompts and Options

- **3P/2P/TTR/<Center point>:**

  The 3P option enables you to define a circle by specifying three points on the circle's circumference.

  The 2P option enables you to create a circle by selecting two points defining the diameter.

  The TTR option enables you to specify two points on an existing line, circle, or arc that will be tangent to the new circle, and then supply the new circle's radius.

  <Center point>, the default, enables you to specify the center point.

- **Diameter/<Radius>:**

  You specify the circle's radius (the default option) or enter **D** and specify the diameter. You can enter a value from the keyboard or pick two points on the screen to specify the distance.

- **Diameter:**

  At this prompt, you enter a value for the circle's diameter. You can enter a value from the keyboard or pick two points on the screen to specify the distance.

- **First point on diameter:**

  At this prompt, you enter the first point for creating a circle with the 2P method.

- **Second point on diameter:**

  At this prompt, you specify the second point for creating a circle with the 2P method.

- **First point:**

  At this prompt, you specify the first point for creating a circle with the 3P method.

- **Second point:**

  At this prompt, you enter the second point for creating a circle with the 3P method.

- **Third point:**

  At this prompt, you enter the third point for creating a circle with the 3P method.

- **Enter Tangent spec:**

  At this prompt, you enter the first tangency point used to draw the circle. The tangent object snap override enables you to choose your point.

- **Enter second Tangent spec:**

  At this prompt, you enter the second tangency point used to draw the circle. The tangent object snap override will be enabled to enable you to choose your point.

- **Radius <current>:**

  After choosing the two tangent points, you enter a value for the circle's radius.

Example

This example demonstrates two of the common methods for creating circles, as shown in figure CIRCLE.1.

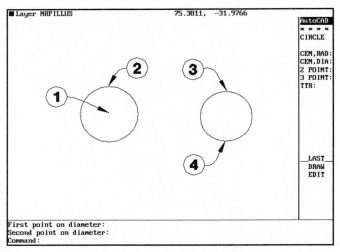

Figure CIRCLE.1:
Circles created using the Center/Radius and 2 point options.

```
Command: CIRCLE ↵
3P/2P/TTR/<Center point>: Pick point ①
Diameter/<Radius>: Pick point ②
Command: CIRCLE ↵
3P/2P/TTR/<Center point>: 2P ↵
First point on diameter: Pick point ③
Second point on diameter: Pick point ④
```

Related Commands

DONUT
ELLIPSE

Related System Variables

CIRCLERAD
VIEWRES

COLOR

Screen **[SETTINGS] [COLOR:]**

The COLOR command controls the color of new entities. If you explicitly set the color value instead of using the BYLAYER option, you can override the layer's default color assignment.

You can use the COLOR command transparently by preceding the command name with an apostrophe ('COLOR).

Prompts and Options

- **New entity color <BYLAYER>:**

    If you enter **BYLAYER**, the most commonly used color setting, the entity color defaults to the color assigned to the layer of insertion.

    You also can enter **BYBLOCK** at the prompt. The BYBLOCK option creates new entities, in the color white, until they are saved and inserted as a block. When inserted, the entities take on the color value currently set with the COLOR command.

    You also can enter a color number or name at the prompt. By naming a color, you assign new entities a specific color value that overrides the color assigned to the current layer. The COLOR command accepts a number from 1 to 255, but what displays on your screen depends on the video board and monitor you are using. You can assign the first seven colors by number or name, as follows:

Color Number	Color
1	Red
2	Yellow
3	Green
4	Cyan
5	Blue
6	Magenta
7	White

 For best results, keep the color value specified by the COLOR command set to BYLAYER. Use the LAYER command's default color to control entity color, which helps to easily identify different layers in your drawing and to redefine colors.

 For a graphical color selection, use 'DDEMODES' color option to choose a color.

Example

This example shows how the value of COLOR can affect any new entities that you create. In the example shown in figure COLOR.1, the color has been changed from its current default of BYLAYER to the color red (1).

```
Command: COLOR ↵
New entity color <BYLAYER>: 1 ↵
Command: LINE ↵
From point: Pick point ①
To point: Pick point ②
To point: ↵
```

 Plotter pen assignments usually are made by color. To achieve different line widths (or types), use a different color for each pen—even if you are using a monochrome monitor.

Related Commands

CHPROP
CHANGE

'DDEMODES
LAYER

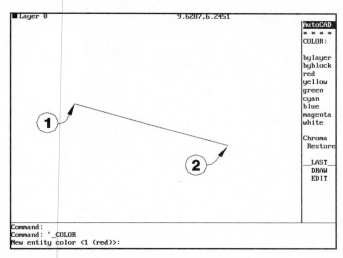

Figure COLOR.1:
A line entity drawn in the color red.

Related System Variable

CECOLOR

COMPILE

R12

Pull down **[File] [Compile...]**

The COMPILE command compiles shape and font definition files into
SHP files before they can be used by AutoCAD. Shape files can contain
definitions of symbols for use by the LOAD and SHAPE commands.
The STYLE command uses shape files that contain text-character definitions to create styles for use by the dimensioning, TEXT, and DTEXT
commands. Besides AutoCAD's native shape source-file format (SHX),
COMPILE also compiles Adobe Type 1 font files (PFB) into SHP files.

553

When you execute the COMPILE command, AutoCAD displays a
general file dialog box with SHP and PFB files listed for the current
directory. Select the desired source file name; AutoCAD compiles it into
a SHP file. If successful, COMPILE displays a notice message noting the
size and name of the file produced. COMPILE responds with an error
message if it encounters errors in the source file.

Related Commands

DTEXT
LOAD
SHAPE
STYLE
TEXT

CONFIG   R12

Pull down **[File] [Configure]**

The CONFIG command enables you to configure the devices that
AutoCAD uses and the various parameters that control the way
AutoCAD works. You can configure AutoCAD any time the program is
active, even with a drawing loaded. See your *AutoCAD Interface, Installation, and Performance Guide* for details on choices available on your
particular computer platform.

Prompts and Options

When you first execute the CONFIG command, it displays your current
hardware configuration. A configuration menu is then displayed. It
offers the following choices:

- **Exit to drawing editor.** This option returns to the drawing—you are prompted to save any changes made.
- **Show current configuration.** This option displays a list of
  the current hardware configuration choices.

- **Allow detailed configuration.** This option enables prompting for advanced configuration information by the other configuration options.

- **Configure video display.** This option enables selection of a different video display.

- **Configure digitizer.** This option enables selection of a different pointing device.

- **Configure plotter.** This option enables selection of a different hard-copy output device.

- **Configure system console.** This option enables selection of platform-specific console options.

- **Configure operating parameters.** This option enables configuration of various directories, files, and data integrity, and networking features. This selection presents the following options:

  ```
  Exit to configuration menu
  Alarm on error
  Initial drawing setup
  Default plot file name
  Plot spooler directory
  Placement of temporary files
  Network node name
  Automatic-save feature
  Full-time CRC validation
  Automatic Audit after IGESIN, DXFIN, or DXBIN
  Login name
  Select Release 11 hidden line removal algorithm
  Server authorization and file-locking
  ```

- **Enter selection <0>.** You enter the number corresponding to your choice and follow the prompts displayed.

Related Command

REINIT

555

Related System Variables

PLOTID
PLOTTER
POPUPS
SCREENBOXES
SCREENMODE
TABMODE

COPY

Screen   **[EDIT] [COPY:]**

Pull down   **[Construct] [Copy]**

The COPY command makes single or multiple copies of as many existing objects as you want. The original selection set remains unchanged after the copy is made.

Prompts and Options

* **Select objects:**

  At this prompt, you can choose objects individually or by using one of the other entity-selection options. The prompt repeats until you press Enter to end the object-selection process.

* **<Base point or displacement>/Multiple:**

  The Base point or displacement option, which is the default, specifies the point from which you are copying the entities. You can specify a 2D or 3D point. If you use a 2D point, the COPY command uses the current elevation setting for the Z value.

  The Multiple option enables you to make multiple copies of the selection set, repeating the following prompt until you press Enter or Ctrl-C.

* **Second point of displacement:**

  You specify the point to which you are copying the entities. (You can specify a 2D or 3D point.) If you use a 2D point, the COPY command uses the current elevation setting for the Z value.

Example

The entities shown in figure COPY.1 represent a window, which you can duplicate by using the COPY command.

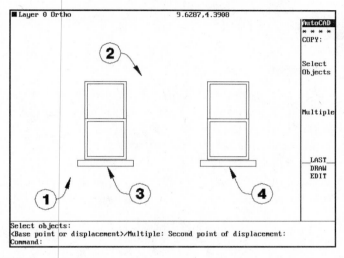

Figure COPY.1:
Using the COPY command to duplicate a group of entities.

```
Command: COPY ↵
Select objects: W ↵
First corner: Pick point ①
Other corner: Pick point ②
7 found
Select objects: ↵
<Base point or displacement>/Multiple: Pick point ③
Second point of displacement: Pick point ④
```

 Use Ortho mode, Snap mode, and object snap settings to simplify the copying process. Ortho mode enables you to copy orthogonally to (0, 90, 180, and 270 degrees) the original. Snap mode enables you to copy at precise increments. Object snap overrides enable you to copy in relation to other existing entities.

Related Commands

ARRAY
OFFSET

DBLIST

Screen **[INQUIRY] [DBLIST:]**

DBLIST (Data Base LIST) provides detailed information on every entity in a drawing. DBLIST switches your display to the text screen and then lists the drawing's entities. To pause the list, you can press Ctrl-S or the Pause key; press any key to continue. To cancel the list, press Ctrl-C.

To print the listing on an attached printer, toggle the printer echo on by pressing Ctrl-Q before issuing the DBLIST command.

Example

This example demonstrates the type of information returned by the DBLIST command.

```
Command: DBLIST ↵
                CIRCLE      Layer: 0
                            Space: Model space
        center point, X= -56.3069  Y= -46.4808  Z=   0.0000
            radius    20.1769
    circumference  126.7754
            area 1278.9694
                CIRCLE      Layer: 0
                            Space: Model space
        center point, X=  25.2901  Y= -48.2497  Z=
0.0000
            radius    18.0497
    circumference  113.4099
            area 1023.5092
```

Related Commands

LIST
SOLLIST

DDATTDEF

Screen   [DRAW] [ATTDEF:] [AttDef Dialogue]

Pull down   [DRAW] [TEXT] [ATTRIBUTES] [DEFINE...]

The DDATTDEF command creates *attribute definitions*—text entities included in blocks that can be assigned different values with each insertion. An attribute definition contains three parts: a tag that defines the type of information conveyed by the attribute, a prompt at which you supply a value when you insert the block, and a default value. Attributes appear on your screen as AutoCAD text; indeed, you will find that part of the attribute definition process involves specifying height, justification, style, rotation and position just as with AutoCAD's TEXT command.

AutoCAD also enables you to assign one or more modes to your attribute definitions: Invisible, so that AutoCAD renders attributes invisible on the screen; Constant, so that inserted attributes maintain a fixed, uneditable value; Verify, so that AutoCAD allows you to check and further edit a value you typed before inserting it; and Preset, so that AutoCAD automatically assigns the attribute's default value upon insertion. You can edit preset attributes with the ATTEDIT or DDATTE commands after you insert them.

 To reduce drawing clutter, make your attribute definitions invisible if you intend to insert a lot of them and do not need to see them on screen.

Figure DDATTDEF.1:
The DDATTDEF dialog box.

Prompts and Options

The DDATTDEF dialog box contains four areas in which you supply information about the attribute's definition (see fig. DDATTDEF.1):

- **Mode**. Click in one or more of the check boxes to make the attribute invisible, constant, verifiable or preset.

- **Attribute**. The Attribute section of the dialog box provides three edit boxes in which you type the attribute's Tag, Prompt, and default Value.

- **Insertion Point**. You supply a point at which AutoCAD draws the attribute. You can click on the **P**ick Pt. < button to pick a point on the screen with your digitizer or mouse, or you can click on the **X**, **Y** and **Z** edit boxes to type explicit coordinates.

- **Text Options**. In the text options area, you detail your attribute's appearance. Choose a desired justification and text style by clicking on the **J**ustification and **T**ext Style pop-up list boxes and selecting from the displayed lists. You can set text height and rotation by clicking on the **H**eight and **R**otation buttons and pointing with your mouse or digitizer, or you can click on the edit boxes that accompany the buttons and type specific values.

If you have defined other attributes and you want the one you are currently creating to be aligned under the most recently created attribute, click on the check box beside the phrase that reads **A**lign below previous attribute. Click on the OK button to create the attribute.

Related Command

ATTDEF

DDATTE

Screen **[EDIT] [DDATTE:]**

DDATTE (Dynamic Dialog ATTribute Edit) enables you to edit attribute string values by using a dialog box. You can edit strings character by character or overwrite an entire line. If all of a block's attributes do not fit in a single dialog box screen, you can use the buttons in the dialog box to move through the various attributes.

Prompts and Options

- **Select block:**

    At this prompt, you choose a block that contains attributes you want to edit.

After a block with attributes is selected, a dialog box appears (see fig. DDATE.1). Each attribute is displayed along with an edit box that enables you to modify the attribute's value. In addition to the standard dialog box buttons, the following buttons appear within the dialog box:

- **Previous.** This button displays the previous group of attributes.
- **Next.** This button displays the next group of attributes.

Related Commands

ATTDEF
ATTEXT

561

BLOCK
DDATTDEF
DDATTEXT
INSERT

```
+-------------------------------------------------+
|                 Edit Attributes                 |
|                                                 |
| Block name: CHAIR                               |
|                                                 |
| Enter furniture cost      [$300            ]    |
| Enter furniture fabric    [Cloth           ]    |
| Enter furniture manufac   [Loth            ]    |
| Enter office number       [220             ]    |
|                           [                ]    |
|                           [                ]    |
|              ▷            [                ]    |
|                           [                ]    |
|                           [                ]    |
|                           [                ]    |
|                                                 |
|   [ OK ] [Cancel] [Previous] [Next] [Help...]   |
+-------------------------------------------------+
```

Figure DDATTE.1:
Using DDATTE to edit attributes within a drawing.

Related System Variable

ATTDIA

DDATTEXT

Screen   [UTILITY] [ATTEXT:] [Att Ext Dialogue]

Pull down   [DRAW] [TEXT] [ATTRIBUTES] [EXTRACT...]

The DDATTEXT command extracts attribute information from your drawing and stores it in a text file. You can analyze the extracted attribute data in a spreadsheet program, catalog it in a database program, or print it as a text report. DDATTEXT extracts information in one of three formats: Comma Delimited Format (CDF), Space Delimited Format (SDF), or Drawing Interchange Format (DXF). Use the format that is accepted by the program in which you want to use the extracted information.

Before you can extract attribute information, you must create a template file that tells AutoCAD how to format the information that it extracts. Each line in the template file defines a field. The template file contains two columns. The left column contains attribute tag names and information about the blocks from which AutoCAD extracts the attribute data. Block information can include block name, nesting level, rotation angle, counter, insertion layer, X, Y, and Z insertion point coordinates, scaling factors and extrusion directions, and entity handles.

The right column of the template file contains format information for the data that AutoCAD extracts. It takes the form Xwwwddd, where X can be N for numeric data or C for character data, www specifies the field's width, and ddd specifies the number of decimal places for numeric data. A sample template file might look like this:

```
BL:NAME   C008000
BL:X      N007001
BL:Y      N007001
BL:NUMBER       N020000
OFFICE    N010000
FLOOR     N015000
NAME      C025000
```

Use an ASCII text editor to create the template file as a plain ASCII text file.

WARNING When you extract attribute data, AutoCAD prompts for the name of the template file to use and the name of the attribute extract file. You must use different file names for the template and extract files, or AutoCAD overwrites the template file.

Prompts and Options

At the top of the DDATTEXT dialog box (see fig. DDATTEXT.1), you see a group of three radio buttons, labeled File Format, with which you select the format for your attribute extract file: Comma Delimited File (CDF), Space Delimited File (SDF), or Drawing Interchange File (DXF).

- The Select **O**bjects button allows you to choose only those blocks from which you want attribute data to be extracted.

- Beneath the Select **O**bjects button, two buttons with companion edit boxes provide the means to specify or select template and output files. You may click on the edit boxes and type filenames, or you may click on the **T**emplate File or Output **F**ile buttons to select files from a list.

- `Template File` and `Output File`. When you click on the **T**emplate File or Output **F**ile button, a second dialog box appears (see fig. DDATTEXT.2). From this box, you may search for and select existing template or output files.

- `Pattern`. In the **P**attern edit box at the top of the **T**emplate/ Output File dialog box, you can enter a file-search pattern using alphanumeric characters and DOS wild-card characters like *.

  Beneath the Pattern edit box, AutoCAD displays the current drive and directory. Beneath the Directory display lie two list boxes from which you can select a different drive or directory or a specific file. Beneath the list boxes, the **F**ile edit box allows you to type a file name. When you select a file from the **F**iles list box, the file name automatically appears in the **F**ile edit box.

Figure DDATTEXT.1:
The DDATTEXT dialog box.

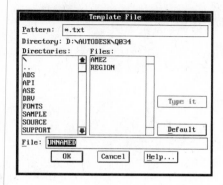

Figure DDATTEXT.2
The Template File dialog box.

Related Command

ATTEXT

DDCHPROP

Pull down **[Modify] [Change] [Properties]**

The DDCHPROP command allows you to change drawing entities'
color, layer, linetype, and thickness properties. When you issue the
DDCHPROP command, AutoCAD prompts you to pick the objects you
wish to modify. Only after selecting these objects do you see the
DDCHPROP dialog box (see fig. DDCHPROP.1).

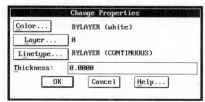

Figure DDCHPROP.1:
The DDCHPROP dialog box.

Prompts and Options

The Change Properties dialog box contains three buttons and an edit box. The buttons display dialog boxes with which to change color, layer, or linetype.

- **Color.** Clicking on the Color button displays the Select Color dialog box (see fig. DDCHPROP.2). The Select Color box contains four palette boxes from which to pick a new color. Click on one of the colored squares to pick a new color, or click on the BY**L**AYER or **B**YBLOCK buttons to set color by one of those methods. You may also click on the Color edit box and type a specific color name.

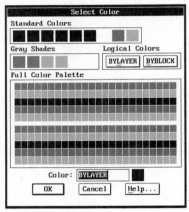

Figure DDCHPROP.2:
The Select Color dialog box.

- **Layer.** To change an entity's layer, click on this button to see the Select Layer dialog box, which features a list box containing the names of all of the layers in the drawing (see fig. DDCHPROP.3). A scroll bar appears on the list box if not all the layer names will fit on screen. To select a new layer, double-click on a layer name, or type a layer name in the **S**et Layer Name edit box.

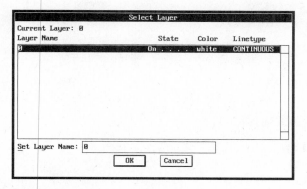

Figure DDCHPROP.3:
The Select Layer dialog box.

- **Linetype.** The Select Linetype dialog box that appears when you click on the Linetype button contains a list box that shows the currently loaded linetypes (see fig. DDCHPROP.4). If not all linetypes fit on screen, a scroll bar allows you to view and select from all of the loaded linetypes. To select a linetype, double-click on one of the linetype names in the list box or click on the Linetype edit box and type a linetype name.

Figure DDCHPROP.4:
The Select Linetype dialog box.

- **Thickness.** To change an entity's thickness, click on the Thickness edit box and type a new thickness.

567

Related Commands

CHPROP
CHANGE
DDMODIFY

Related Variables

CECOLOR
CELTYPE
CLAYER
THICKNESS

DDEDIT

Screen **[EDIT] [DDEDIT:]**

DDEDIT (Dynamic Dialog EDIT) is AutoCAD's easy-to-use text editor.
With DDEDIT, you can add or replace characters, or even overwrite an
entire string—all within a dialog box. DDEDIT enables you to edit
existing text strings or attribute definitions.

TIP

DDEDIT is good for editing text strings, but stops short of
editing all of a text object's attributes. An AutoLISP-defined
command, CHTEXT, allows you to change text justification,
perform search and replace abilities, change text height, width, style, and
so on.

Prompts and Options

- **<Select a TEXT or ATTDEF object>/Undo:**

  The default option edits either text strings or attribute definitions.
  If you choose an attribute definition, you can change the attribute
  tag, prompt, and default values.

Select the Undo option by entering **U**. DDEDIT undoes the edits performed on the previous text string.

After you select a text string or attribute definition, a dialog box, shown in figure DDEDITR.1, appears. The dialog box contains an edit box that enables you to modify the text string or attribute definition.

Figure DDEDITR.1:
The Edit Text dialog box.

Related Commands

DDATTE
CHANGE

DDEMODES

Screen **[SETTINGS] [DDEMODES]**

Pull down **[Settings] [Entity Modes...]**

The DDEMODES command displays the Entity Creation Modes dialog box. From this dialog box you can set the color, linetype, elevation, text style, and thickness for any new entity. The DDEMODES command is also useful for checking the status of these entity-creation settings during an editing session.

Prompts and Options

DDEMODES issues no command-line prompts. Instead, this command provides a dialog box that features a number of buttons.

This dialog box's options perform the following functions:

- **Color.** This option controls the colors of new entities. When you select this option, AutoCAD displays a dialog box containing only color options. To select a new color, you can click on one of the colors in the dialog box or enter a valid AutoCAD color number from 1 to 255. If you select any color other than BYLAYER, you override the default entity color assigned to the current layer with the LAYER command.

- **Layer.** This option displays the Layer Control dialog box, which contains the names of all the currently defined layers and enables you to modify their properties. Refer to the dialog box description for the DDLMODES command for explanations of all the dialog box's options.

- **Linetype.** This option button displays a dialog box, which contains all currently loaded linetypes. You can select the linetype you want to use for all new entities from this dialog box.

- **Text Style.** This option is used to change the current text style. You choose your new text style from a dialog box that lists the currently defined text styles.

- **Elevation.** This option requires you to enter a valid Z value. By default, new entities are drawn in the X,Y plane of the current UCS.

- **Thickness.** This option requires you to enter a valid extrusion thickness. Applicable new entities are drawn with the new thickness.

Practice using the various DDEMODES options in an existing drawing. Note the differences between the capabilities of these options and the options of their more full-featured relatives.

Example

This example uses the TOOLPOST sample drawing to illustrate how the DDEMODES command works. The sequence uses the DDEMODES command to change the default linetype (see fig. DDEMODES.1), and then draw a line, which is shown in figure DDEMODES.2.

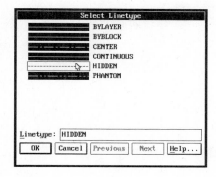

Figure DDEMODES.1:
Setting the default linetype to hidden.

```
Command: DDEMODES ↵
Press the Set Ltype button
Select the HIDDEN linetype
Click on the OK button
Click on the OK button
Command: LINE ↵
From point: Pick point ①
To point: Pick point ②
To point: ↵
```

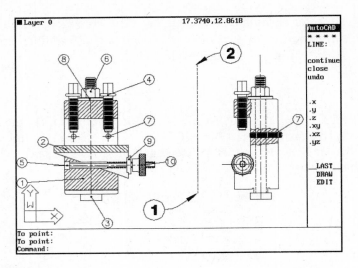

Figure DDEMODES.2:
Drawing a line after setting the default linetype.

Related Commands

COLOR
DDLMODES
ELEV
LAYER
LINETYPE

Related System Variables

CECOLOR
CELTYPE
CLAYER
ELEVATION
THICKNESS

DDGRIPS

Pull down **[Settings] [Grips...]**

Drawing entities in Release 12 might display *grips*, small squares located at strategic points on the entities. You can enable grips with the DDGRIPS command or by setting the GRIPS system variable to 1. With grips enabled, the drawing editor crosshairs snap automatically to a grip when the crosshairs pass over the grip box. You can stretch, move, rotate, scale, or mirror the gripped entity by selecting the grip point. In addition to enabling or disabling grips, the DDGRIPS command also enables you to set the grips' color and size (see fig. DDGRIPS.1).

You can execute the DDGRIPS command transparently by preceding the command name with an apostrophe (**'DDGRIPS**).

Figure DDGRIPS.1:
The DDGRIPS dialog box.

Prompts and Options

At the top of the DDGRIPS dialog box, you see two check boxes. **E**nable Grips enables or disables grips on primitive entities. Enable Grips Within **B**locks enables or disables grips on entities contained within blocks.

- **Select Color.** Beneath the check boxes, the <u>U</u>nselected and <u>S</u>elected buttons display the Select Color dialog box (see fig. DDCHPROP.2, in the DDCHPROP listing), from which you can select colors for unselected and selected grips.

At the bottom of the DDGRIPS dialog box, a scroll bar enables you to adjust the grips' size dynamically. The small square to the right of the scroll bar grows and shrinks as you drag the scroll box, indicating the grips' size.

Related System Variables

GRIPS
GRIPBLOCK
GRIPCOLOR
GRIPHOT
GRIPSIZE

DDIM

Pull down **[Settings] [Dimension Style...]**

The DDIM dialog box (see fig. DDIM.1) provides access to all of AutoCAD's dimensioning system variables. Here you can also create custom system variable settings and save them under unique dimension style names for later recall.

 You can execute the DDIM command transparently by preceding the command name with an apostrophe ('DDIM).

Prompts and Options

The DDIM dialog box contains, on the left side, a Dimension Styles list box that shows the names of currently defined dimension styles. Double-click on a name to set its style. If not all defined styles fit on the current screen, a scroll bar appears with which you can display additional styles.

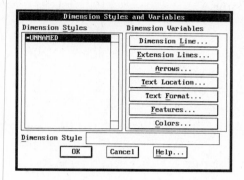

Figure DDIM.1:
The DDIM dialog box.

The **D**imension Style edit box at the bottom of the dialog box provides a place to type a dimension style name for recall. On the right side of the DDIM dialog box, the Dimension Variables series of buttons provides access to various categories of dimension variables through the following dialog boxes:

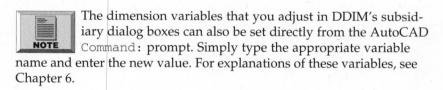

The dimension variables that you adjust in DDIM's subsidiary dialog boxes can also be set directly from the AutoCAD Command: prompt. Simply type the appropriate variable name and enter the new value. For explanations of these variables, see Chapter 6.

- **Dimension Line.** The Dimension **L**ine dialog box allows you to change the dimension line's appearance (see fig. DDIM.2). At the top of the dialog box, you see the name of the current dimension style.
- **Feature Scaling**. The **F**eature Scaling edit box lets you set the global dimension scaling factor.
- **Use Paper Space Scaling**. Clicking on the check box labeled Use **P**aper Space Scaling tells AutoCAD to compute an appropriate global dimension scaling factor based on the scaling between the current model space viewport and paper space, ignoring the value in the Feature Scaling box.

575

- **Dimension Line Color**. In the Dimension **L**ine Color edit box, you can enter a color number for the dimension line.

- **Force Interior Lines**. Beneath the Line Color box, the Force **I**nterior Lines check box forces AutoCAD to draw a dimension line between the two extension lines even when the dimension text is placed outside the extension lines.

- **Basic Dimension**. If you check the **B**asic Dimension box, AutoCAD will draw a box around the dimension's text.

- **Text Gap**. The number that you type in the Text **G**ap edit box beneath the Reference Dimension box sets the spacing around the dimension text when AutoCAD breaks the dimension line to contain the dimension text.

- **Baseline Increment**. The **B**aseline Increment edit box specifies the distance to offset consecutive baseline dimensions, so that they do not overlap one another.

Figure DDIM.2:
The Dimension Line dialog box.

- **Extension Lines**. The **E**xtension Lines dialog box controls the appearance of extension lines in much the same way that the Dimension Line box controls dimension lines (see fig. DDIM.3). Indeed, the first three lines you see in the Extension Line box are identical to those in the Dimension Line box. The fourth line contains an edit box in which you set the extension lines' color, as opposed to dimension line color. The rest of the box diverges from the Dimension Line box.

- **Extension Above Line**. In the **E**xtension Above Line edit box, you can type the distance that you want the extension lines to extend past the dimension line.

- **Feature Offset**. The value entered in the Feature **O**ffset edit box specifies the gap between the dimensioned entity and the beginning of the extension line.

- **Visibility**. The Visibilit**y** pop-up list box controls suppression of extension lines, whether both, only one, or neither.

- **Center Mark Size**. Beneath the Visibility box lies the **C**enter Mark Size edit box, where you set the size of center marks drawn by the CENTER, DIAMETER, and RADIUS dimensioning commands.

- **Mark with Center Lines**. If you click on the **M**ark with Center Lines check box, AutoCAD draws center marks rather than center lines.

```
Extension Lines
Style: *UNNAMED
Feature Scaling          1.00000
[ ] Use Paper Space Scaling
Extension Line Color  BYBLOCK    [ ]
Extension Lines
  Extension Above Line  0.1800
  Feature Offset        0.0625
  Visibility  Draw Both            [▼]
  Center Mark Size      0.0900
  [ ] Mark with Center Lines
  [  OK  ]  [ Cancel ]  [ Help... ]
```

Figure DDIM.3:
The Extension Lines dialog box.

- **Arrows**. The Arrows dialog box (see fig. DDIM.4) controls how arrowheads are drawn at the ends of dimension lines. The first four lines are identical to those in the Dimension Lines dialog box (see fig. DDIM.2). At the top of the Arrows section of the dialog box, a row of four radio buttons specifies what kind of arrowheads are drawn: **A**rrow, Tic**k**, **D**ot or **U**ser.

- **Arrow Size**. Beneath the radio buttons, the Arrow Si**z**e edit box provides a place to enter the arrowheads' size.

- **User Arrow**. In the User Arro<u>w</u> edit box, you type the name of the block to use as the user customized arrowhead. The box is highlighted only if you have depressed the User radio button.

- **Separate Arrows**. If you click on the <u>S</u>eparate Arrows check box, the <u>F</u>irst Arrow and Seco<u>n</u>d Arrow edit boxes highlight so that you may enter the names of separate customized arrowheads for each end of the dimension line.

- **Tick Extension**. If you had selected the Tick radio button, the Tick E<u>x</u>tension edit box highlights, enabling you to enter the distance which you want the dimension line to extend past the tick mark.

```
╔══════════════════════════════════╗
║              Arrows              ║
╠══════════════════════════════════╣
║ Style: *UNNAMED                  ║
║ Feature Scaling      [1.00000]   ║
║ ☐ Use Paper Space Scaling        ║
║ Dimension Line Color [BYBLOCK][ ]║
║ Arrows                           ║
║ ┌──────────────────────────────┐ ║
║ │ ■ Arrow ▣ Tick ▣ Dot ▣ User  │ ║
║ │ Arrow Size       [0.1800]    │ ║
║ │ User Arrow       [<default>] │ ║
║ │ ☐ Separate Arrows            │ ║
║ │ First Arrow      [<default>] │ ║
║ │ Second Arrow     [<default>] │ ║
║ │ Tick Extension   [0.0000]    │ ║
║ └──────────────────────────────┘ ║
║    [  OK  ] [ Cancel ] [Help...] ║
╚══════════════════════════════════╝
```

Figure DDIM.4:
The Arrows dialog box.

- **Text Location**. The <u>T</u>ext Location dialog box governs the appearance of dimension text (see fig. DDIM.5). Again, the first four lines in the dialog box name the current style, set the global dimension scale factor, tell AutoCAD to use paper space scaling, and set dimension line color. Below the fourth line, you find the text settings. In the first two edit boxes, you set the height of dimension text and the height of tolerance text, respectively. The editing features in the rest of the dialog box, three pop-up list boxes and an edit box, govern dimension text placement in relation to the dimension line.

- **Horizontal**. The first pop-up list box, labeled **H**orizontal, controls the text's horizontal placement. This box offers three choices: Default, Force text inside, and Text, arrows inside. If you choose Default, AutoCAD places the text for Linear and Angular dimensions inside the extension lines, provided enough room exists. If not, AutoCAD places the text outside the extension lines. For Radius and Diameter dimensions, AutoCAD places the text outside of the arc or circle. If you choose the Force text inside option, AutoCAD places the text inside the extension lines regardless of the amount of space available. The Text, arrows inside option tells AutoCAD to place text and arrowheads inside the extension lines.

  If not enough room exists for both the arrowheads and the text (in which case AutoCAD normally places the arrowheads and dimension lines outside the extension lines), AutoCAD omits the arrowheads and dimension lines entirely, leaving only the dimension text inside the extension lines.

- **Vertical**. The second Text Placement pop-up list box, labeled **V**ertical, controls the dimensions text's vertical placement in relation to the dimension line. It, too, offers three choices: Centered, Above, and Relative. The Centered option causes AutoCAD to center the text on the dimension line, splitting the line in the process. The Above option tells AutoCAD to place the text above the dimension line a distance equal to the text's height, leaving the dimension line whole. The Relative option causes text to be placed some distance above or below the dimension line based upon the value in the Relative **P**osition edit box (the box is greyed out until you choose the Relative option in the Vertical pop-up list box).

  AutoCAD calculates the relative distance by dividing the relative position value by the text height value. A positive relative position value causes AutoCAD to place the text above the dimension line; a negative value causes text to be placed below the dimension line.

579

- **Alignment.** The third pop-up list box, titled Alignment, governs the text's alignment (or lack thereof) with the dimension line. The box provides four choices: Orient Text Horizontally, Align With Dimension Line, Align When Inside Only, and Align When Outside Only. When you choose to orient text horizontally, AutoCAD always draws the text horizontally, regardless of the dimension line's angle. Align With Dimension Line always causes AutoCAD to align the text at the dimension line's angle. The last two options cause AutoCAD to align text only when it places the text inside or outside of the extension lines, respectively.

```
┌─────────────────────────────────────┐
│           Text Location              │
│ Style: *UNNAMED                      │
│ Feature Scaling      │1.00000 │      │
│ ☐ Use Paper Space Scaling            │
│ Dimension Text Color │BYBLOCK│  │    │
│ Text Position                        │
│  Text Height         │0.1800 │       │
│  Tolerance Height    │0.1800 │       │
│  Text Placement                      │
│  Horizontal │Default          │ ⬇   │
│  Vertical   │Centered         │ ⬇   │
│  Relative Position   │0.0000 │       │
│  Alignment                           │
│  │Orient Text Horizontally     │ ⬇  │
│   ┌──────┐  ┌────────┐  ┌───────┐   │
│   │  OK  │  │ Cancel │  │Help...│   │
│   └──────┘  └────────┘  └───────┘   │
└─────────────────────────────────────┘
```

Figure DDIM.5:
The Text Location dialog box.

- **Text Format.** The Text Format dialog box controls the way that AutoCAD displays dimension text (see fig. DDIM.6). The first three lines in the box display the current style name, let you set the global dimension scale factor, and let you choose to allow AutoCAD to calculate an appropriate scaling factor based on the scaling between the current model space viewport and paper space. The remainder of the dialog box consists of four groups that each govern a different aspect of dimension text formatting.

  Basic Units. The first area, titled Basic Units, contains four edit boxes and a check box. AutoCAD multiplies all linear dimensions by the value stored in the Length **S**caling edit box. If you want the length scaling factor applied to only dimensions created in paper space, click on the Scale in Paper Space **O**nly check box. In the **R**ound Off edit box, enter a value by which all dimensions should be rounded. Text strings entered in the Text Pre**f**ix and Te**x**t Suffix edit boxes will appear before and after, respectively, the dimension text.

The four check boxes in the Zero Suppression group of the Text Format dialog box allow you to suppress various parts of the dimension text. When you click on the 0 **F**eet check box, AutoCAD suppresses the feet portion of a feet-and-inch dimension. The **0** Inches box, when checked, causes AutoCAD to delete the inches portion of a feet-and-inch dimension. When checked, the L**e**ading check box tells AutoCAD to suppress leading zeros in decimal dimensions. The **T**railing check box causes AutoCAD to suppress trailing decimal zeros.

- **Tolerances**. In the Tolerances portion of the Text Format dialog box, you choose how AutoCAD displays dimension tolerances. If you click on the **V**ariance radio button, AutoCAD appends the values entered in the **U**pper Value and Lo**w**er Value edit boxes. If the lower value equals the upper value, AutoCAD displays the tolerances as ±value appended to the dimension text. If the upper value does not equal the lower value, AutoCAD displays the tolerances as +upper value above -lower value. If you selected the **L**imits radio button, AutoCAD adds the upper value to the dimension and subtracts the lower value and displays both calculated values one above the other.

- **Alternate Units**. The Alternate Units group of the Text Format dialog box governs the display of alternate dimension units. If you click on the Show **A**lternate Units? check box, AutoCAD displays alternate as well as standard units in your dimensions. When you click on the check box, the **D**ecimal Places, S**c**aling, and S**u**ffix edit boxes highlight, allowing you to enter values in these boxes. In the **D**ecimal Places box, type the number of decimal places with which you want the alternate units displayed. If you want alternate units in linear dimensions scaled, enter the scaling factor in the Scaling edit box. If you want a suffix appended to the alternate units, type it into the Suffix edit box.

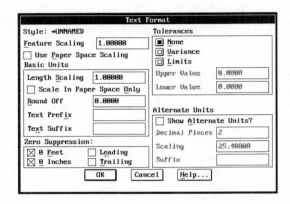

Figure DDIM.6:
The Text Format dialog box.

- **Features.** In the Features dialog box, you can edit the settings for dimension lines, extension lines, arrows, and text location, as discussed above for the individual dialog boxes that deal with these entities. Please see the respective discussions and figures for those dialog boxes for explanation.

- **Colors.** The Colors dialog box lets you set individual colors for dimension lines, extension lines and dimension text. You can also set the global dimension scale factor and instruct AutoCAD to calculate a scale factor based on the scaling in the current model space viewport and paper space. To set an entity color, click on that entity's edit box and type in a color name or number , or click on the adjacent color square to pick a color from the Colors dialog box (see fig. DDIM.7).

Colors		
Style: *UNNAMED		
Feature Scaling	1.00000	
☐ Use Paper Space Scaling		
Dimension Line Color	BYBLOCK	
Extension Line Color	BYBLOCK	
Dimension Text Color	BYBLOCK	
OK	Cancel	Help...

Figure DDIM.7:
The Colors dialog box.

DDINSERT

R12

Pull down **[DRAW] [INSERT...]**

The DDINSERT command (see fig. DDINSERT.1) displays a dialog box for inserting blocks and drawing files into the current drawing.

Prompts and Options

The first two lines in the DDINSERT dialog box contain buttons and companion edit boxes with which you select the block or file to insert. In the edit boxes you can type specific names. A click on one of the buttons reveals further dialog boxes with which you may select blocks or files for insertion. These subsidiary boxes are discussed at length in the following section.

In the bottom group of the dialog box, you specify the insertion point, scale and rotation angle of the inserted block or file. At the top of this group, the check box labeled **S**pecify parameters on screen lets you toggle between entering insertion point, scale and rotation values in the dialog box, or on the screen with your mouse or digitizer. The box is checked by default, leaving the edit boxes greyed out. If you elect to enter the insertion parameters in the dialog box, click on the check box. The edit boxes become active.

583

In the Insertion Point group, click on the **X**, **Y**, or **Z** edit boxes and enter the insertion point coordinates. Do the same in the Scale group to select X, Y and Z scale factors. Click on the **A**ngle edit box in the rotation group and type a rotation angle, in degrees. Below the Options group, a check box lets you specify whether to insert the block exploded into its constituent entities, or as a single block entity. As in previous versions of AutoCAD, you cannot insert a block exploded if you have specified unequal X, Y, or Z scale factors.

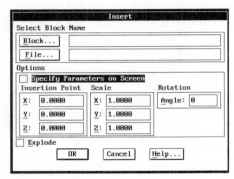

Figure DDINSERT.1:
The DDINSERT dialog box.

As mentioned earlier, the first two buttons in the DDINSERT dialog box summon subsidiary dialog boxes. From these you can select insertion blocks that you defined in the current drawing, or other drawing files.

- **Block.** To select a block defined in the current drawing, click on the Block button. The dialog box displayed (see fig. DDINSERT.2) contains, at the top, the **P**attern edit box, into which you may type a text pattern which the block name you are searching for may contain. Typing **F***, for example, lists all block names beginning with the letter F. Below the **P**attern box, a list box contains the names of all blocks currently defined in the drawing. If they do not all fit on a single screen, a scroll bar on the left side of the list box lets you scroll through the list until you find the needed block. Below the list box, the **S**election edit box provides a place where you may enter a block name directly.

Figure DDINSERT.2:
The DDINSERT Select Block dialog box.

- **File.** To select a drawing file for insertion, click on the File button in the DDINSERT dialog box. The Select Drawing File dialog box (see fig. DDINSERT.3) also begins with a **P**attern edit box where you may type a text pattern that the file you seek may contain. The pattern here, however, must end with the extension DWG, as only AutoCAD drawing files can be inserted. Beneath this edit box, AutoCAD informs you of the current directory, where the file search will take place. Next come two list boxes, equipped with scroll bars, if necessary. The list box on the left enables you to change to a different search directory. The box on the right lists drawing files contained in the current directory. You may select a directory on the left, or a drawing file on the right by double-clicking on the desired name, or by highlighting with the keyboard's arrow cursor keys and pressing Enter. To the right, the Type it and Default buttons remain greyed out, as they do not apply to this operation. Below the two list boxes, the **F**ile edit box allows you to type in a specific filename.

Related Commands

> INSERT
> MINSERT

585

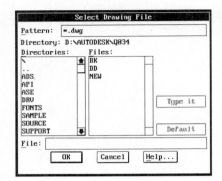

Figure DDINSERT.3:
The DDINSERT Select File dialog box.

Related System Variables

INSBASE
INSNAME

DDLMODES

Screen **[LAYER...]**

Pull down **[Settings] [Layer Control...]**

The DDLMODES (Dynamic Dialog Layer MODES) command uses the Layer Control dialog box to manage layer settings. DDLMODES also provides an easy way for you to check layer status. You can use the DDLMODES dialog box to turn layers on or off, lock or unlock layers, freeze or thaw layers, change color or linetype settings, and set a new current layer (see fig. DDLMODES.1).

Prompts and Options

DDLMODES provides no command-line prompts. When the Layer Control dialog box appears, it contains a list of the layers in the current drawing and a group of option buttons. These option buttons perform the following actions:

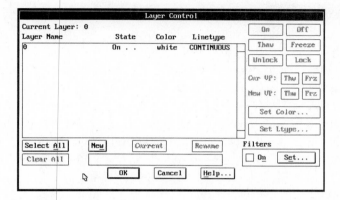

Figure DDLMODES.1:
The DDLMODES dialog box.

- **On.** This option turns selected layers on or off in the current viewport.
- **Off.** This option turns selected layers off in all viewports.
- **Thaw.** The Thaw option changes the status of selected layers from Frozen to Thawed. Layers that are thawed can be turned on and displayed on the screen.
- **Freeze.** This option changes the status of selected layers to Frozen. When a layer is frozen, it cannot be displayed on the screen.
- **Unlock.** Unlocking a layer reverses the Lock setting and enables editing of entities on the selected layer(s).
- **Lock.** Locking a layer prevents any editing of entities on the selected layer(s), as well as preventing any new entities from being placed upon the locked layer.
- **Cur VP Thw.** This option thaws the selected layers in the current viewport only. This option applies only to paper-space viewport entities.
- **Cur VP Frz.** This option freezes the selected layers in the current viewport. This option applies only to paper-space viewport entities.

587

- **New VP Thw.** This option controls whether the currently selected layers will be thawed in new viewports. This option applies only to paper-space viewport entities.

- **New VP Frz.** This option controls whether the currently selected layers will be frozen in new viewports. This option applies only to paper-space viewport entities.

- **Color.** Use this option to change a layer's color. When this option is selected, AutoCAD displays a dialog box containing color options. Any changes made to the color settings of external reference layers are not saved with the drawing.

- **Linetype.** Use this option to change a layer's linetype. When you select this option, AutoCAD displays a dialog box containing linetype options. Any changes made to the linetype settings of external reference layers are not saved with the drawing.

- **Select All.** This option highlights every layer in the layer list box, which is useful for making changes globally across all drawing layers.

- **Clear All.** This option dehighlights any layer that is currently highlighted in the layer list box.

- **New.** This option creates a new layer using the name you entered into the edit box below this button. If no name has been entered AutoCAD responds `Null entry in edit box`; or, if the layer exists, AutoCAD responds `1 layer name is duplicated`.

- **Current.** This option makes the currently highlighted layer the current drawing layer. All new entities are drawn on this layer. Note that you cannot freeze the current layer from this dialog box, and you cannot make a frozen layer the current drawing layer.

- **Rename.** You can rename a layer by clicking on its existing name and then editing the name. You cannot rename a layer to an existing name, and you cannot rename external reference layer names.

- **Filters.** The Filters option controls which particular layers will be displayed in the Layer Control layer list box. This option has two controls, which perform the following actions:

On. This checkbox controls whether the layer name list box displays all the layers within the drawing or only those that match the selected filter set.

S<u>e</u>t. This button displays the Set Layer Filters dialog box (see fig. DDLMODES.2). This dialog box narrows down the number of layers to be displayed in the Layer name list box. You can select only the layers that match a certain layer state (On/Off, Frozen/ Thawed, Locked/Unlocked, etc.) or layer name/color/linetype.

Figure DDLMODES.2:
The Set Layer Filters dialog box.

 The COLOR and LINETYPE commands can override the values of layer color and linetype settings, respectively.

Example

This example uses the TROL1 sample drawing to illustrate how the DDLMODES command works.

```
Command: DDLMODES ↵
```
Click on the Select All *button*
Click on the Off *button*
Click on the Clear All *button*
Select the WHEEL-PH-2 layer
Click on the On *button*

Click on the Set Ltype *button*
Select the CENTER linetype
Click on the OK *button*
Click on the OK *button*

Related Commands

LAYER
VPLAYER

Related System Variable

CLAYER

DDMODIFY

Screen **[EDIT] [DDMODFY:]**

Pull down **[MODIFY] [ENTITY...]**

The DDMODIFY command enables you to change the characteristics of AutoCAD entities. At the top of the DDMODIFY dialog box, three buttons give you access to subsidiary dialog boxes, where you can change the chosen entity's color, layer and linetype (see figs. DDCHPROP.2, DDCHPROP.3, and DDCHPROP.4 in the DDCHPROP command summary). In this top section of the dialog box, you also find an edit box into which you can type a new entity thickness.

The rest of the DDMODIFY dialog box varies depending on the type of entity that you choose to modify. Figure DDMODIFY.1 shows the DDMODIFY dialog box that appears when you modify a line.

In the From point and To point edit boxes, you can specify new endpoints. Click on the **P**ick Point button to pick a point on the screen with your pointing device, or click on the **X**, **Y**, or **Z** edit boxes to type explicit coordinates. You can modify the following properties of AutoCAD entities by using DDMODIFY:

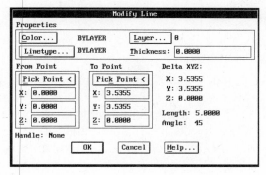

Figure DDMODIFY.1:
The DDMODIFY dialog box for modifying a line.

- **Blocks.** Insertion point; X, Y, and Z scale factors; rotation angle; number of columns and rows, and column and row spacing for blocks inserted with MINSERT.
- **Arcs.** Center point; radius; start angle and end angle.
- **Attdefs.** Tag; prompt; default value; origin point; height; rotation; width; obliquing angle; justification; style; upside down and/or backwards; invisible, constant, preset, and/or verify.
- **Circles.** Center point; radius.
- **Text.** Edit text; other properties same as for Attdefs.
- **Polylines.** Vertex locations; smoothing method; mesh structure; open or closed; application of linetypes.
- **Points.** Location.
- **Shapes.** Origin; size; rotation; width factor; obliquing angle.
- **Solids.** Corner locations.
- **Traces.** Corner locations.
- **3DFaces.** Corner locations, edge visibility.

Related Commands

CHANGE
CHPROP

DDOSNAP

Pull down **[Settings] [Object Snap]**

The DDOSNAP command enables you to set AutoCAD's running object-snap modes. Object snaps enable you to manipulate objects and draw accurately by letting you specify points corresponding to the geometric features of a selected entity. To enter a point with object snap, you need only specify an object snap mode and pick any point on an existing entity. AutoCAD calculates the precise point coordinates according to the mode you specified and the object selected. You may set one or more modes to be applied to all point entry, or enter them on the fly at AutoCAD's command option prompts. AutoCAD provides the following object snap modes:

- **Endpoint**. Snaps to the endpoint of a line or arc.
- **Midpoint**. Snaps to the midpoint of a line or arc.
- **Center**. Snaps to the center of an arc or circle (you must pick the arc or circle on its circumference).
- **Node**. Snaps to a point entity.
- **Quadrant**. Snaps to the nearest 0, 90, 180, or 270 degree quadrant point of an arc or circle.
- **Intersection**. Snaps to the intersections of lines, arcs, and circles.
- **Insertion**. Snaps to the insertion point of a block, shape, attribute or text entity.
- **Perpendicular**. Snaps to the point on a line, circle, or arc that is perpendicular from that object to the last point.
- **Tangent**. Snaps to the point on a circle or arc that is tangent to that object from the last point.
- **Nearest**. Snaps to the point on a line, arc, or circle or to a point entity that is visually closest to the crosshairs.
- **Quick**. Snaps to the first point found that corresponds to one of the set of currently selected object snap modes.

Prompts and Options

The DDOSNAP dialog box contains a check box for each object snap
mode (see fig. DDOSNAP.1). Click on one or more of the boxes to
select the modes that you wish to remain active. At the bottom of the
box, a horizontal scroll bar allows you to dynamically set the size of the
pickbox, a small square that appears at the intersection of the crosshairs
when you activate an object snap mode. An entity to which you want
to snap must cross the boundary of the pickbox when you select the
entity for the object snap to take affect.

> **TIP** DDOSNAP is a transparent command. You may run it by
> typing 'DDOSNAP while using another command. This
> feature is convenient for setting object snap modes on the fly,
> when you do not know ahead of time which ones will be the most useful.

Figure DDOSNAP.1:
The DDOSNAP dialog box.

Related Command

OSNAP

Related System Variable

OSMODE

DDPTYPE

Pull-down [**Setttings**] [**Point Style...**]

Screen [**DRAW**] [**next**] [**POINT:**] [**Type**]

The DDPTYPE command displays a dialog box of point types that can be selected for rendering point entities. This dialog box sets the PDMODE system variable, and it also allows you to set the size of the point entities, which are controlled by the PDSIZE variable.

Prompts and Options

This command has no direct prompts. The dialog box shown in figure DDPTYPE.1 displays when you enter the command. The areas of the dialog box perform the following functions:

- **Point Style**. This upper area of the dialog box contains graphics depicting each of the possible styles for point entities. To set the point style, click on one of the graphics.

- **Point Size:** Enables you to define the size used to represent point entities. The point size varies, depending on which radio button is checked below this edit box. If the Set Size Relative to Screen radio button is checked, the point size is a percentage of the screen resolution. If the Set Size in Absolute Units radio button is checked, the point size is measured in drawing units.

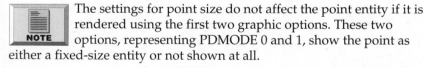

The settings for point size do not affect the point entity if it is rendered using the first two graphic options. These two options, representing PDMODE 0 and 1, show the point as either a fixed-size entity or not shown at all.

Example

The following example uses the DDPTYPE command to set the point display before issuing a POINT command.

Command: **DDPTYPE** ↵
*Select the graphic showing a circle with
an "X" through it.*

Click on the OK button.

Command: **POINT** ↵

Point: *Choose a location for a point.*

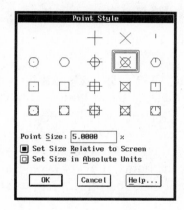

Figure DDPTYPE.1:
The Point Style dialog box.

Related Command

POINT

Related Variables

PDMODE
PDSIZE

DDRENAME

Screen **[Utility] [Rename:] [Rename Dialogue]**

With the DDRENAME dialog box, you can rename blocks, dimension styles, layers, linetypes, text styles, UCS configurations, views, and viewport configurations.

Prompts and Options

At the top of the DDRENAME dialog box (see fig. DDRENAME.1) are two list boxes.

- **Named Objects**. On the left side, the **N**amed Objects list box shows the categories of objects you can rename.
- **Items**. On the right side, the **I**tems list box displays the name of each item in that category that the current drawing holds. For example, when you click on Layer in the Named Objects box, the Items box shows the name of every layer in the drawing. If the layer names do not all fit on one screen, use the scroll bar to view others.

  To rename an item, first pick the kind of item you want to rename from the Named Objects list box. Then pick a specific item from the Items list box. The name of the item that you just picked appears in the **O**ld Name edit box below the two list boxes. Click on the **R**ename To edit box and type the item's new name. AutoCAD accepts item names up to 31 characters in length, and their names may contain letters, digits, $ (dollar sign), - (hyphen), and _ (underscore).

You can rename groups of items that contain the same text pattern with a single DDRENAME command. If, for example, your drawing contained a series of text styles called SIM-PLEX-1, SIMPLEX-2, SIMPLEX-3, SIMPLEX-4, and SIMPLEX-5, and you wanted to rename them all to ROMANS-1...ROMANS-5, you would type SIMPLEX* in the **O**ld Name edit box and ROMANS* in the **R**ename To edit box.

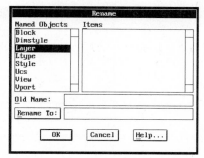

Figure DDRENAME.1:
The DDRENAME dialog box.

Related Command

RENAME

DDRMODES

Screen **[SETTINGS] [DDRMODES]**

Pull down **[Settings] [Drawing Aids...]**

DDRMODES (Dynamic Dialog dRawing MODES) controls drawing mode settings—snap, grid, blips, ortho, axis, and isoplane—by using a dialog box (see fig. DDRMODES.1). DDRMODES also is useful when you need to check the current status of the various drawing-mode settings.

Prompts and Options

DDRMODES provides no command-line prompts. Instead, you make selections from the following dialog box options:

- **Ortho.** This checkbox is used to turn Ortho mode on or off.
- **Solid Fill.** This checkbox is used to notify AutoCAD whether solids and thickened polylines are filled or only their edges are shown.

597

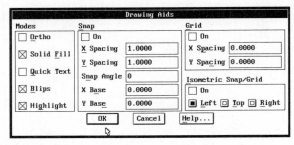

Figure DDRMODES.1:
The DDRMODES dialog box.

- **Quick Text**. This checkbox notifies AutoCAD to display text normally or as a boundary box showing the limits of the text. If the box is not checked, text displays normally.
- **Blips.** This checkbox is used to notify AutoCAD to place "blips" at every point where a point is picked in the drawing editor.
- **Highlight.** This checkbox is used to notify AutoCAD to display the entities chosen for selection sets with a temporary dashed linetype.
- **Snap.** The Snap options are used to turn Snap mode on or off, and to change the snap spacing (the default is 1), snap angle (default 0), and snap base (default 0,0).
- **Grid.** This option turns the drawing grid on or off (the default is off) and changes the grid spacing (the default is 0).
- **Isometric.** This option turns isometric drawing mode on or off and determines which isometric plane is currently in use. The default value is off.

Example

This example uses the TABLET-A sample drawing to illustrate how the DDRMODES command works.

```
Command: DDRMODES ↵
Press the Quick Text button
Press the OK button
Command: REGEN ↵
```

Related Commands

BLIPMODE
GRID
ORTHO
SNAP

Related System Variables

BLIPMODE
COORDS
GRIDMODE
GRIDUNIT
ORTHOMODE
SNAPANG
SNAPBASE
SNAPISOPAIR
SNAPMODE
SNAPSTYL
SNAPUNIT

DDSELECT

Pull down **[SETTINGS] [SELECTION SETTINGS...]**

The DDSELECT dialog box enables you to tell AutoCAD which entity selection modes to use when forming a selection set (see fig. DDSELECT.1).

Prompts and Options

At the top of the DDSELECT dialog box, four check boxes appear beside the four entity selection options that AutoCAD offers. You may pick one, all, or any combination of these options.

- **Noun/Verb Selection**. If you pick the first option, **N**oun/Verb Selection, you can select entities in the drawing, and then select the command with which you wish to edit the entities.

- **Use Shift to Add**. **U**se Shift to Add dictates how additional entities are added to the selection set after you have chosen the first entity or entities. With Use Shift to Add selected, you hold down the Shift key to add more entities to the selection set. To remove entities from the selection set, hold down the Shift key and pick already selected entities. If you do not choose Use Shift to Add, you select entities as in previous versions of AutoCAD, although you can still use the Shift key method to remove entities from the selection set.

- **Click and Drag**. If you pick **C**lick and Drag, you can draw entity selection windows and crossing boxes by picking one corner and then dragging the mouse while continuing to depress the pointing device's button. When you have drawn the desired window, release the button and the entities contained within the window or that cross the window's boundaries are selected. With Click and Drag deactivated, you must make two picks with your pointing device to select the opposite corner of the window or crossing box.

With Click and Drag activated, you can easily clear a selection set by clicking once on a blank area of the screen.

- **Implied Windowing**. If you activate **I**mplied Windowing, you can create either an entity selection window or crossing box at a `Select objects:` prompt. After you pick the first corner, drag the pointing device from left to right to form a window, or from right to left to form a crossing box. With Implied Windowing turned off, you must type a **w** or a **c** at the `Select objects:` prompt to initiate a window or a crossing box.

Beneath these four options, the button labeled **D**efault Selection Mode resets the modes to their default: Use Shift to Add and Implied Windowing selected. Beneath the default button, a horizontal scroll bar lets you dynamically adjust the size of the pickbox, from one to 20 pixels. Beneath the pickbox size scroll bar, the button labeled **E**ntity Sort Method displays a subsidiary dialog box where you may select the situations under which AutoCAD sorts entities in the order in which they appear in the drawing's database.

The **E**ntity Sort Method dialog box contains seven check boxes in which you may click to tell AutoCAD when to sort entities: **O**bject Selection, Object **S**nap, **R**edraws, S**l**ide Creation, R**e**gens, **P**lotting, and PostS**c**ript Output (see fig. DDSELECT.2).

Figure DDSELECT.1:
The DDSELECT dialog box.

Figure DDSELECT.2:
The Entity Sort Method dialog box.

Related Command

SELECT

Related System Variables

SORTENTS
TREEDEPH
TREEMAX

DDSOLMAT

Pull-down [**Model**] [**Utility**] >[**Material...**]

Screen [**MODEL**] [**UTILITY**] [**DDSOLMAT**]

The DDSOLMAT command reviews the material types used by AME within your drawing, adds new material types, modifies material properties, and sets the current material used for new solid entities. This command is the dialog box version of the SOLMAT command.

Prompts and Options

This command has no direct prompts. The dialog box shown in figure DDSOLMAT.1 displays when you enter the command. The name of the current material used for solids is shown in the upper-right area of the dialog box.

- **File.** This button allows you to select the materials file used by AME. The default file, ACAD.MAT, contains material definitions for the most common material types. This button calls the standard File Open dialog box, which enables you to select a different material file.

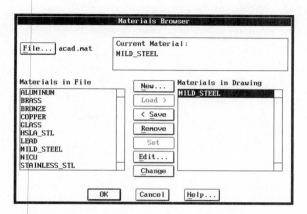

Figure DDSOLMAT.1:
The Materials Browser dialog box.

- **Materials in File**. This list box displays the names of all materials in the current materials file.

- **Materials in Drawing**. This list box displays the names of all materials in the current drawing that have been loaded from the materials file.

- **New.** This button brings up the dialog box shown in figure DDSOLMAT.2. In this dialog box, you define new materials by supplying specific properties of the material.

- **Material Name**. This edit box allows you to enter the name of the new material you are defining. This name can be no longer than 32 characters.

- **Description**. This edit box allows you to enter a short description for the material you are creating.

- **Value**. By highlighting the material properties in the Properties list box, you can enter the associated property value here.

- **Load >**. This button copies materials located in the material file into the current drawing. You must highlight the name of the material you want to load into the drawing, and then click on this button.

603

```
                          Materials Browser
                     Material Properties - New
 Material Name   ┌──────────────────────────────┐
                 └──────────────────────────────┘
 Description     ┌──────────────────────────────┐
                 └──────────────────────────────┘
 Properties
 Density:                          0 kg/cu_m
 Young's modulus:                  0 GN/sq_m
 Poisson's ratio:                  0
 Yield strength:                   0 MN/sq_m
 Ultimate strength:                0 MN/sq_m
 Thermal conductivity coeff.:      0
 Linear expansion coefficient:  0.00e+00
 Specific heat:                    0 kJ/(kg deg_C)
                Value  ┌─┐         kg/cu_m
                       │0│
 Material name required
                  ┌─────────┐  ┌────────┐
                  │   OK    │  │ Cancel │
                  └─────────┘  └────────┘
      ┌─────────┐  ┌──────────┐  ┌─────────┐
      │   OK    │  │  Cancel  │  │ Help... │
      └─────────┘  └──────────┘  └─────────┘
```

Figure DDSOLMAT.2:
The Material Properties—New dialog box.

- **< Save**. This button copies modified or new materials back into the materials file. You must highlight the name of the material you want to save from the drawing, and then click on this button.

- **Remove**. Use this button to remove materials that are loaded in the current drawing. You cannot remove materials from the materials file using this button.

- **Set**. This button allows you to set the current material for use when creating solids. You must highlight the material name you want made current before pressing this button.

- **Edit**. This button brings up the dialog box shown in figure DDSOLMAT.3. In this dialog box, you modify existing materials by changing specific properties of the material. The areas of this dialog box perform the same functions as the Material Properties—New dialog box. The only item that cannot be changed is the material name.

- **Change**. This button substitutes one material type used for solids within the drawing with another material type.

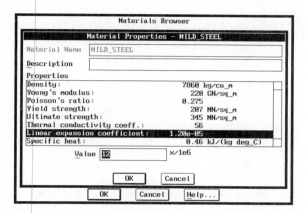

Figure DDSOLMAT.3:
The Material Properties—Material dialog box.

Example

The following example shows how to load a new material into the drawing and make it the current material.

Command: **DDSOLMAT** ↵
Select the COPPER *material from the*
Materials in File *list box and click on*
the Load> *button.*

Highlight the COPPER *material in the*
Materials in Drawing *list box and click*
on the Set *button.*

Click on the OK *button.*

Related Command

SOLMAT

Related Variable

SOLMATCURR

DDSOLPRM

Pull-down [**Model**] [**Primitives...**]

Screen [**MODEL**] [**DDSOLPRM**]

The DDSOLPRM command displays a dialog box that shows the solid primitives you can create by using AME.

Prompts and Options

This command has no direct prompts. The dialog box shown in figure DDSOLPRM.1 is displayed when you enter the command.

Figure DDSOLPRM.1:
The AME Primitives dialog box.

- **Box**. This graphic button executes the SOLBOX command for creating a solid box primitive.
- **Sphere**. This graphic button executes the SOLSPHERE command for creating a solid spherical primitive.
- **Wedge**. This graphic button executes the SOLWEDGE command for creating a solid wedge-shaped primitive.

- **Cone**. This graphic button executes the SOLCONE command for creating a solid cone primitive.
- **Cylinder**. This graphic button executes the SOLCYL command for creating a solid cylinder primitive.
- **Torus**. This graphic button executes the SOLTORUS command for creating a solid torus primitive.
- **Baseplane**. This group of buttons allows you to define the baseplane used by the solid primitives commands. When turned off, the current UCS is used for the base of the primitives; when turned on, you can select a different UCS to serve as the base for the primitive.
- **Object Snap Mode.** This button allows you to select an object snap mode to aid in selecting points to define the solid primitives.

Related Commands

CP
DDOSNAP
OSNAP
SOLBOX
SOLCONE

SOLCYL
SOLSPHERE
SOLTORUS
SOLWEDGE

DDUCS

Screen   **[UCS:] [DDUCS:]**

Pull down   **[Settings] [UCS >] [Named UCS...]**

Pull down   **[Settings] [UCS >] [Preset...]**

DDUCS (Dynamic Dialog User Coordinate Systems) controls User Coordinate Systems (UCSs) through a dialog box. You can change the current UCS, rename a previously defined UCS, list the specifications of a UCS, and delete a UCS through the DDUCS dialog box (see fig. DDUCS.1).

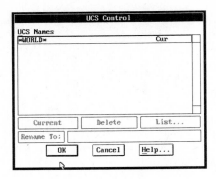

Figure DDUCS.1:
The DDUCS dialog box.

Prompts and Options

This command provides no command-line prompts. When the dialog box appears, it displays a list of currently defined user coordinate systems and several option buttons. The dialog box buttons perform the following options:

- **Current.** The currently highlighted UCS in the list box becomes the current UCS.
- **Delete.** Click on the Delete button to delete the currently highlighted UCS. Note that you cannot delete the *WORLD* or *PREVIOUS* coordinate systems.
- **List.** This option displays the coordinate system's origin and the direction of the X, Y, and Z axes in relation to the current UCS.
- **Rename To.** This option renames the currently highlighted UCS to the name you enter into the adjacent edit box. You cannot rename the *WORLD* or *PREVIOUS* coordinate systems.

Related Commands

UCS
DDUCSP

Related System Variables

UCSFOLLOW
UCSICON
UCSNAME.
UCSORG
UCSXDIR
UCSYDIR
WORLDUCS

DDUCSP

Pull-down [**Settings**] [**UCS**] >[**Presets...**]

The DDUCSP command displays a dialog box that allows you to select a UCS direction.

Prompts and Options

The dialog box shown in figure DDUCSP.1 contains graphics that show the most common UCS directions. To select a UCS, click on the graphic, and then press OK. The radio buttons at the bottom of the dialog box determine whether the UCS is set relative to the current UCS or with respect to the WCS.

Example

The following example uses the DDUCS dialog box to set to a different user-coordinate system.

Command: **DDUCSP** ↵
Select the graphic showing RIGHT UCS.

Click on the OK *button. The UCSicon changes to a broken pencil.*

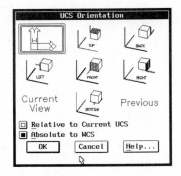

Figure DDUCSP.1:
The UCS Orientation dialog box.

Related Commands

DDUCS
UCS

Related System Variables

UCSFOLLOW
UCSICON
UCSNAME
UCSXDIR
UCSYDIR
WORLDUCS

DDUNITS

Screen **[SETTINGS] [next] [UNITS:] [DDUNITS]**

Pull down **[Settings] [Units Control...]**

AutoCAD allows for the display of coordinates, distances, and angles in several formats, so that, depending upon your trade, you can measure and notate in the most appropriate format. You set the format with the DDUNITS command. The main features of the DDUNITS dialog box (see fig. DDUNITS.1) are two sets of radio buttons. On the left, the Units buttons set the format used for distances and measurement. AutoCAD provides the following options:

- **Scientific.** Format 0.0000E+01, showing decimal distances with exponent.
- **Decimal.** Format 0.0000, showing distances in decimal with no associated units of measure.
- **Engineering.** Format 0'-0.0000", showing feet and decimal inches.
- **Architectural.** Format 0'-0/0", showing feet and fractional inches.
- **Fractional.** Format 0 0/0, showing fractional distances with no associated units of measure.

Beneath the radio buttons, a pop-up list box enables you to set your desired level of precision.

The radio buttons on the right of the dialog box enable you to choose how AutoCAD measures angles. AutoCAD offers the following choices:

- **Decimal Degrees.** Format 0.0000, simple decimal numbers.
- **Deg/Min/Sec.** Format 0d0'0.0000', with 'd' indicating degrees, ''' indicating minutes, and '"' indicating seconds.
- **Grads.** Format 0.0000g, decimal numbers with the appended 'g' indicating grads.
- **Radians.** Format 0.0000r, decimal numbers with the appended 'r' indicating radians.
- **Surveyor.** Format N or S 0d0'0.0000" E or W. The angle between N/S and E/W indicates the distance east or west from north or south. When the angle points in a cardinal direction, AutoCAD shows only the compass point, for example E for 0°.

As with the units section of the dialog box, a pop-up list box beneath the radio buttons enables you to set the precision of the angle's measurement.

611

Figure DDUNITS.1:
The DDUNITS dialog box.

Prompts and Options

At the bottom of the dialog box, the **D**irection button causes AutoCAD to display a subsidiary dialog box from which you choose the direction that equals angle 0 (see fig. DDUNITS.2). You may choose from **E**ast (default), **N**orth, **W**est, **S**outh, or **O**ther. If you choose Other, the **A**ngle edit box and **P**ick < button highlight. You may type an angle in the edit box, or show an angle with your pointing device by picking two points on-screen. Beneath the Pick < button, two additional radio buttons enable you to choose whether AutoCAD measures angles in the **C**ounter-Clockwise or C**l**ockwise direction.

Figure DDUNITS.2:
The Direction Control dialog box.

The angle specified for object rotations is measured independently of the angle zero base. An unrotated object always has a zero rotation. Orientation angles are always measured from the angle zero base. If you choose angle zero to point south, a horizontal line of text is considered to be oriented to 180°.

Related Command

UNITS

Related System Variables

ANGDIR
AUNITS
AUPREC
ANGBASE
LUNITS
LUPREC

DDVIEW

Screen [DISPLAY] [VIEW] [View Dialogue]

Pull down [View] [Set View] [Named View...]

AutoCAD provides the means to save particular drawing views for later recall. This feature enables you to restore a precise display of a drawing or 3D viewpoint that you intend to use frequently. The DDVIEW command enables you to restore, create, delete, and obtain information about views.

Prompts and Options

The top of the dialog box (see fig. DDVIEW.1) contains a list box showing the names of all of the drawing's saved views. If not all views will

AutoCAD: The Professional Reference, Second Edition

fit on a single screen, a scroll bar appears with which you can see other view names.

Beneath the list box, the Restore View: line tells which view AutoCAD restores when you click on the **R**estore button. To restore a view, click on a view name in the list box. Then click on Restore, and, finally, click OK. You also can delete a saved view by clicking on the view name in the list box and then clicking on the **D**elete button. You are not warned before AutoCAD deletes the view, so be sure that you want the view deleted before you click on the button. The other two buttons in the dialog box display subsidiary dialog boxes in which you can create new views and view information about saved views.

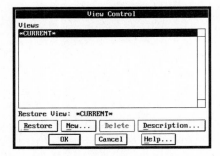

Figure DDVIEW.1:
The DDVIEW dialog box.

- **New.** In the dialog box that appears when you click on the New button, you configure and save new views. At the top of the dialog box, you type the name of the new view in the **N**ew Name edit box. Beneath the edit box, two radio buttons, **C**urrent Display and **D**efine Window, provide the choice to save the current drawing editor display as the new view, or to specify a window that constitutes the view. When you click on **D**efine Window, the **W**indow < button and the First Corner and Other Corner boxes highlight. Click on the button to define the view's window. AutoCAD temporarily removes the dialog boxes so that you can draw the window. After the dialog boxes return, the First Corner and Other Corner boxes display the X and Y coordinates of the two corners. Click on **S**ave View to save the view (see fig. DDVIEW.2).

614

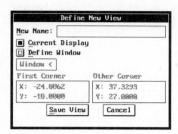

Figure DDVIEW.2:
The Define New View dialog box.

- **Description.** When you click on the display button, an information dialog box appears showing information about the currently selected view (see fig. DDVIEW.3). This box shows the view name and the X, Y, and Z coordinates of the width, height, and twist values of the view's centerpoint and the view direction. Also displayed are the status of perspective, front clipping and back clipping, and the current lens length and the offset values for the front and back clipping planes.

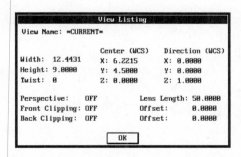

Figure DDVIEW.3:
The View Listing dialog box.

Related Command

VIEW

Related System Variables

VIEWCTR
VIEWDIR
VIEWMODE
VIEWSIZE
VIEWTWIST

DDVPOINT

Pull-down [**View**] [**Set View**] [**Viewport**] [**Presets**]

Screen [**DISPLAY**] [**VPOINT**] [**View Pt.**]

The DDVPOINT command is used to set the current drawing viewpoint. This is the dialog box version of the VPOINT command.

Prompts and Options

This command displays the dialog box shown in figure DDVPOINT.1. The two graphics in this dialog box allow you to set the direction for the X axis and the angle from the X,Y plane. If you pick in the segment of either graphic, the X-axis or X,Y-plane values are set to the number shown for that area. If you pick within the circular area showing the dial, the exact value is determined by the pick point.

The buttons in this dialog box perform the following actions:

- **Absolute to W̲CS**. This radio button ensures that the values set in the X A̲xis and XY P̲lane edit boxes are applied in relation to the world coordinate system.

- **Relative to U̲CS**. This radio button ensures that the values set in the X A̲xis and XY P̲lane edit boxes are applied relative to the user coordinate system.

- **X A̲xis:** This edit box enables you to enter an absolute angle in the X axis.

616

- **XY Plane:** This edit box enables you to enter an absolute angle in the XY plane.
- **Set to Plan View**. This button sets the UCS to the same values that are used for the current plan view.

Example

This example uses the DDVPOINT dialog box to change the way the current drawing is viewed.

Command: **DDVPOINT** ⏎
*Click on the segment showing 270 degrees
in the X Axis graphic.*

*Click on the segment showing 90 degrees
in the XY Plane graphic.*

Click on OK. The drawing regenerates to show the new viewpoint.

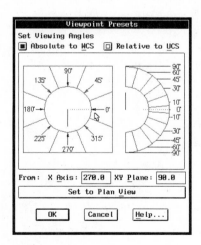

Figure DDVPOINT.1:
The Viewpoint Presets dialog box.

Related Command

VPOINT

Related Variables

VIEWDIR
WORLDVIEW

DELAY

DELAY is a special command for use with AutoCAD script files. DE-LAY programs a delay (measured approximately in milliseconds) in a script. You can cancel the delay by pressing any key.

Use the DELAY command as part of an AutoCAD script. Use the following command syntax:

```
DELAY number
```

In this generic syntax, **number** is the approximate length of the delay in milliseconds. The maximum delay number you can specify is 32,767.

For more information on DELAY, see the SCRIPT command, later in the Reference Guide.

Related Commands

SCRIPT

DIM/DIM1

Screen   **[DIM:]**

Pull down   **[Draw] [Dimensions>]**

The DIM and DIM1 commands enable you to enter AutoCAD's dimensioning mode, which is distinguished from the regular command mode by the `Dim:` prompt. Dimensioning mode is used to draw dimensions in your drawings.

When you use the DIM command, you enter dimensioning mode and remain there until you issue the Exit dimensioning command or press Ctrl-C. When you use the DIM1 command, you remain in dimensioning mode only for a single dimensioning command and then immediately return to normal command mode. In dimensioning mode, AutoCAD's non-dimensioning commands (except for transparent commands, such as 'ZOOM and 'PAN) are not available.

While AutoCAD is in dimensioning mode, you can use any of AutoCAD's 27 dimensioning subcommands. The following pages of this Command Reference describe each dimensioning command in detail:

```
ALIGNED    HOMETEXT    RADIUS    TEDIT
ANGULAR    HORIZONTAL  REDRAW    TROTATE
BASELINE   LEADER      RESTORE   UNDO
CENTER     NEWTEXT     ROTATED   UPDATE
CONTINUE   OBLIQUE     SAVE      VARIABLES
DIAMETER   ORDINATE    STATUS    VERTICAL
EXIT       OVERRIDE    STYLE
```

If you issue a single UNDO command at AutoCAD's `Command:` prompt after you exit dimensioning mode, you will cancel *all* the commands issued during a single dimensioning session. Therefore, if you enter dimensioning mode, draw several dimensions with dimensioning commands, exit from dimensioning mode, and issue the UNDO command, all the dimensions are undone. Similarly, you can issue a single REDO command to restore all the undone dimensions.

A few of the dimensioning commands have the same names as regular AutoCAD commands. You should be careful not to confuse these dimensioning commands with the general AutoCAD commands, such as REDRAW, SAVE, STATUS, STYLE, and UNDO. Some of the commands, such as REDRAW and UNDO, perform similar or identical functions in normal drawing mode and dimensioning mode. Others, however, are noticeably different.

AutoCAD creates dimensions in two types, *associative* and *non-associative*. Associative dimensions are special blocks that are linked to the entities in your drawing. If you stretch, scale, or modify dimensioned elements, the dimensions are automatically updated to reflect the new dimension value. Associative dimensions are enabled by setting the value of the DIMASO variable to 1 (ON). Non-associative dimensions are simply arrowheads, lines, and text, and they do not reflect any changes you make to the entities in your drawing. Non-associative dimensions are created when the DIMASO variable is set to 0.

 When using paper space, you should keep associative dimensions in model space. No link exists between entities across the two areas of the drawing. Therefore, if your model changes, dimension entities created in paper space will not be updated along with your model.

Prompts and Options

After you issue the DIM or DIM1 command, the following prompt appears:

- `Dim:`

  At this prompt, enter the name of the DIM subcommand you want to use.

The Dimension Elements

Each dimension that is created by a dimension command contains certain elements. This is independent of whether the dimension is created as associative (DIMASO is set ON) or normal. As shown in figure DIM.1, there are four distinctive parts of a dimension. These parts are as follows:

① **Dimension Text.** Typically, this is the value measured by the dimension command. This text can be overridden by entering a different value, or it can be supplemented with prefix and suffix text. You can add prefix or suffix text by entering a new value and

the characters "<>". These characters are used to indicate the
dimension value retrieved by the dimension command.

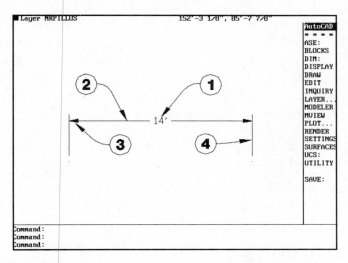

Figure DIM.1:
The basic dimension and its component parts.

② **Dimension Line.** This line, or an arc for angular dimensions,
delineates the extents of the distance.

③ **Dimension Arrow.** These are placed at both ends of the dimension
line. You also can use a specialized block or a tick mark for your
dimension arrows.

④ **Extension Line.** These lines lead from the points you choose to
dimension, and extend beyond the dimension line.

Related Command

DDIM

Related System Variables

For a list of AutoCAD's dimensioning variables, see Chapter 6.

Dim: ALIGNED

Screen [DIM:] [Aligned]

Pull down [Draw] [Dimensions >] [Linear >] [Aligned]

This dimensioning command draws a linear dimension parallel to a selected entity or parallel to two extension line origin points. Use this command when you need to dimension a feature that is not orthogonal and you want extension lines of equal length. When you pick an entity to dimension or two origin points, the ALIGNED command places the dimension line parallel to the entity or points and through a third point that you specify. You can abbreviate the ALIGNED command as AL.

To create angled dimensions with unequal extension lines or for dimensions at specific angles, use the ROTATED command to specify a dimension line angle.

Prompts and Options

- **First extension line origin or RETURN to select:**

  Pick a point at one end of the entity or feature that you want to dimension. AutoCAD prompts for the Second extension line origin. The extension lines are drawn perpendicular to the angle between the first and second extension line origins.

- **Select line, arc, or circle:**

  This prompt appears if you press Enter at the First extension line origin or RETURN to select: prompt. Select a line, polyline, arc, or circle; extension lines are located for you. If you select a line, polyline segment, or arc, AutoCAD dimensions the end points. If you select a circle, the diameter is dimensioned from the pick point to the diameter point on the opposite side. AutoCAD dimensions only the selected segment of a polyline.

- **Second extension line origin:**

  Pick a point at the opposite end of the entity or feature. The extension lines are drawn perpendicular to the angle between the first and second extension line origin points.

- **Dimension line location (Text/Angle):**

  Pick the point through which you want the dimension line to pass. AutoCAD uses the point to determine the offset distance between the selected object or pick points and the dimension line.

  If you use either of the (Text/Angle) options, one of the following prompts appears:

- **Enter text angle:**

  Your response to this prompt modifies the angle at which the dimension text is drawn. If you press Enter at this prompt, the text is drawn at the default text angle.

- **Dimension text <default>:**

  AutoCAD calculates the distance between the two extension line origin points you pick or between the two points derived from the object you select. AutoCAD then offers the distance (in the current drawing units and precision) as the default dimension text value. You can accept this value (press Enter), specify a new value, suppress any text by typing a space, or apply prefix or suffix text to the value (see the DIM/DIM1 command).

Example

AutoCAD offers two ways to create an aligned dimension: you can select an entity or pick both extension line origins. This example demonstrates both of these methods using the drawing shown in figure ALIGNED.1.

```
Command: DIM⏎
Dim: ALIGNED⏎
First extension line origin or RETURN to select:⏎
Select line, arc, or circle: Pick entity pointed to by ①
Dimension line location (Text/Angle): Pickpoint pointed to by ②
Dimension text <15'-4 1/4">:⏎
Dim: ALIGNED⏎
First extension line origin or RETURN to select: Pickpoint ③
Second extension line origin: Pick point ④
Dimension line location (Text/Angle): A⏎ Pickpoint ⑤
Enter text angle: END of ③
Second point: END of ④
Dimension line location(Text/Angle):
Dimension text <15'-4 1/4">:⏎
```

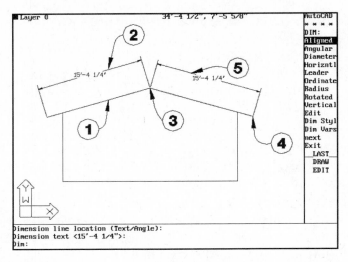

Figure ALIGNED.1:
The selection points used to create the aligned dimensions.

Related Commands

> DDIM
> Dim: ROTATED

Dim: ANGULAR

Screen **[DIM:] [Angular]**

Pull down **[Draw] [Dimensions >] [Angular]**

The ANGULAR dimensioning command dimensions the angle between two non-parallel lines, the angle swept by an arc or around part of a circle, or the angle between any three points (one of which is a vertex of the angle to be dimensioned). The ANGULAR command creates a dimension arc instead of a dimension line, with non-parallel extension lines as needed. You can dimension either the inside or outside of major, minor, or complementary angles. You can abbreviate the ANGULAR command as AN.

Prompts and Options

- **Select arc, circle, line, or RETURN:**

  Pick an arc, circle, line, or polyline segment for AutoCAD to dimension. If you select an arc, AutoCAD automatically locates the end points for the origin of the extension lines. If you select a circle, the point by which you picked the circle becomes the first extension line origin, and then the Second angle end point: prompt appears. If you select a line, AutoCAD considers the line to be one side of an angle you want to dimension and prompts with Second line: for you to pick the second line of the angle to dimension.

  Press Enter at the Select arc, circle, line, or RETURN prompt to tell AutoCAD that you want to specify three points describing an angle for dimensioning. The three points do not need to be on existing geometry.

- **Angle vertex:**

  If you want to dimension an angle by three points, this prompt asks you to enter a point for the vertex of the angle.

- **First angle endpoint:**

  This prompt displays when you dimension an angle by three points. Pick a point along one side of the angle to dimension.

- **Second angle endpoint:**

  This prompt displays when you dimension an angle by three points or when you pick a circle at the initial prompt. Pick a point along the second side of the angle to dimension.

- **Second line:**

  If you pick a line at the initial prompt, this prompt asks you for the second line to describe the angle for dimensioning.

- **Dimension arc line location (Text/Angle):**

  For all angular dimension methods, pick the point through which you want the dimension line arc to pass. AutoCAD uses the point you pick to calculate the offset distance between your selected object or feature and the dimension line arc.

  You can dimension the angle between two lines or the complementary angle (180 degrees, less the angle between the lines), or the inside (minor—under 180 degrees) or outside (major—over 180 degrees) angle of an arc, three points, or points on a circle. The point you pick for the dimension arc location controls which angle is dimensioned.

  If you use either of the (Text/Angle) options, you will see one of the following prompts:

- **Dimension text <default>:**

  AutoCAD calculates the distance between the two extension line origin points you pick or between the two points derived from the object you select. AutoCAD then offers the distance (in the current drawing units and precision) as the default dimension text value. You can accept this value (press Enter), specify a new value, suppress any text by typing a space, or apply prefix or suffix text to the value (see the DIM/DIM1 command).

- **Enter text angle:**

  This prompt modifies the angle at which the dimension text is drawn. If you press Enter, the text is drawn at the default text angle.

- **Enter text location (or RETURN):**

  You can locate the text along the dimension arc or place it inside or outside the dimension arc. This prompt enables you to position the text as you require. If you press Enter, the text is placed along the dimension arc.

Example

This example demonstrates the steps needed to perform common angular dimensioning tasks. The drawing in figure ANGULAR.1 shows the points you pick to create an angular dimension by choosing line entities and by selecting three points that define an angle.

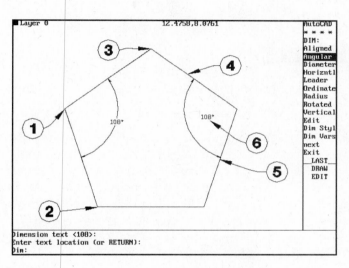

Figure ANGULAR.1:
Dimensioning inside a minor angle between two lines.

```
Command: DIM ↵
Dim: ANGULAR ↵
Select arc, circle, line, or RETURN: ↵
Angle vertex: END of ①
First angle endpoint: END of ②
Second angle endpoint: END of ③
Dimension arc line location (Text/Angle): MID of
```
Pick line between ① and ②
```
Dimension text <108>: ↵
Enter text location: ↵
Dim: ANGULAR
Select arc, circle, line, or RETURN: ④
Second line: ⑤
```

```
Dimension arc line location (Text/Angle): ⑤
Dimension text <108>: ↵
Enter text location: ⑥
```

Related Command

DDIM

Dim: BASELINE

Screen   [DIM:] [next] [Baseline]

Pull down   [Draw] [Dimensions >] [Linear >] [Baseline]

The BASELINE dimensioning command enables you to use one existing linear dimension as the basis for one or more new dimensions. All new dimensions are based on the first extension line of the existing dimension. Each new dimension is created by specifying a new second extension line origin point. The BASELINE command offsets the new dimension line from the previous one and draws a new extended first extension line over the existing first extension line. You can abbreviate the BASELINE command as B.

Baseline dimensions can be created at any time after an initial linear dimension is created. You can select an existing linear dimension for the basis of new baseline dimensions. You must pick the dimension nearest to the end with the extension line you want used as the first extension line. The BASELINE command offsets each new dimension line by the dimension line increment value stored in the DIMDLI dimension variable. Changing the value of DIMDLI or updating existing dimensions with the UPDATE command has no effect on dimensions already placed in your drawing.

Prompts and Options

- **`Second extension line origin or RETURN to select:`**

  This prompt displays if the last dimension you created was a linear dimension or after you select a base dimension. The first extension line of the last dimension is considered the first extension line of subsequent dimensions unless you press Enter to select another extension line. Press Enter if you want to select a dimension other than the last one created.

- **`Select base dimension:`**

  This prompt displays if the last dimension created was not a linear dimension. To select the dimension to use as the base for subsequent dimensions, select it near the end that you want to use for the first extension line.

- **`Dimension text <default>:`**

  AutoCAD calculates the distance between the two extension line origin points you pick or between the two points derived from the object you select. AutoCAD then offers the distance (in the current drawing units and precision) as the default dimension text value. You can accept this value (press Enter), specify a new value, suppress any text by typing a space, or apply prefix or suffix text to the value (see the DIM/DIM1 command).

Example

This example demonstrates the steps necessary to create baseline dimensions from an existing horizontal dimension. The points used to create the dimensions are shown in figure BASELINE.1.

```
Command: DIM↵
Dim: HORIZONTAL↵
First extension line origin or RETURN to select: INT of ①
Second extension line origin: INT of ②
Dimension line location: ③
Dimension text <15'-4">: ↵
Dim: BASELINE ↵
Second extension line origin or RETURN to select: INT of ④
Dimension text <27'-4">: ↵
```

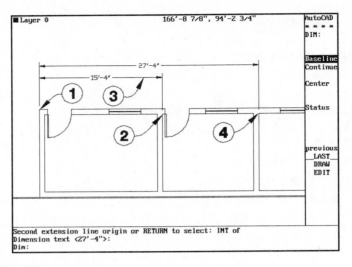

Figure BASELINE.1:
Baseline dimensions created using the BASELINE command.

Related Commands

Dim:CONTINUE
DDIM

Dim: CENTER

Screen   [DIM:] [next] [Center]

Pull down [Draw] [Dimensions >] [Radial >] [Center Mark]

The CENTER dimensioning command creates center marks or center lines at the center points of circles, arcs, or polyline arc segments. You can abbreviate the CENTER command as CE.

Center marks or lines created by the CENTER command are individual line entities. Center marks are drawn twice the length of the positive value of the dimension variable DIMCEN. If DIMCEN is set to a negative number, center lines are also drawn, extending the length of DIMCEN beyond the circle or arc. If DIMCEN is set to 0, AutoCAD disables center marks or center lines.

Prompts and Options

- **Select arc or circle:**

  Select the arc or circle to be dimensioned at any point.

Examples

The following example demonstrates the CENTER command for adding center marks to an arc or circle. The mark created for a typical circle is shown in figure CENTER.1.

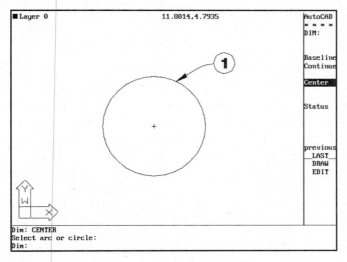

Figure CENTER.1:
The center mark created using the CENTER command.

```
Command: DIM ↵
Dim: CENTER ↵
Select arc or circle: Pick the circle
```

Related Commands

Dim: DIAMETER
Dim: RADIUS
DDINI

Related System Variable

DIMCEN

Dim: CONTINUE

Screen   [DIM:] [next] [Continue]

Pull down   [Draw] [Dimensions >] [Linear >] [Continue]

The CONTINUE dimensioning command enables you to use one existing linear dimension as the basis for a set of dimensions aligned end-to-end (otherwise known as continuous dimensions). The CONTINUE command can be abbreviated as CO.

You can create continuous dimensions at any time after creating an initial linear dimension. If you start the CONTINUE command immediately after completing a linear dimension, AutoCAD treats the second extension line origin point of the previous dimension as the second extension line origin point of each new dimension. If you select an existing linear dimension for the basis of new continuous dimensions, you must pick the dimension nearest to the end with the extension line you want to use as the first extension line of subsequent dimensions.

In most cases, the CONTINUE command aligns each new dimension line with the last. If the dimension's text would otherwise overwrite the previous continued dimension's text, the CONTINUE command offsets the new dimension line by the dimension line increment value stored in the DIMDLI dimension variable.

Prompts and Options

- **`Second extension line origin or RETURN to select:`**

  This prompt displays if the last dimension you created is a linear dimension or after you select a base dimension. The second extension line of the last dimension becomes the first extension line of subsequent dimensions, unless you press Enter to select a different extension line. Press Enter also if you want to select a dimension other than the last one you created.

- **`Select continued dimension:`**

  This prompt displays if the last dimension you create is not a linear dimension. Select the dimension to use as the basis for subsequent dimensions near the end that you want to use for the first extension line.

- **`Dimension text <default>:`**

  AutoCAD calculates the distance between the two extension line origin points you pick or between the two points derived from the object you select. AutoCAD then offers the distance (in the current drawing units and precision) as the default dimension text value. You can accept this value (press Enter), specify a new value, suppress any text by typing a space, or apply prefix or suffix text to the value (see the DIM/DIM1 command).

Examples

This example demonstrates the steps necessary to create continuous dimensions (see figure CONTINUE.1).

```
Command: DIM↵
Dim: CONTINUE↵
Second extension line origin or RETURN to select: ↵
Select continued dimension: Pick point ①
Second extension line origin or RETURN to select: INT of ②
Dimension text <12'>: ↵
```

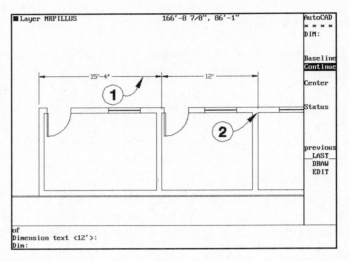

Figure CONTINUE.1:
Using the CONTINUE command.

Related Commands

BASELINE
DDIM

Related System Variable

DIMDLI

Dim: DIAMETER

Screen [DIM:] [Diameter]

Pull down [Draw] [Dimensions >] [Radial >] [Diameter]

The DIAMETER dimensioning command dimensions the diameters of circles, arcs, and polyline arc segments. You can abbreviate the DIAMETER command as D.

AutoCAD can produce several variations of dimensions for diameters. These variations depend on the value of the system variables DIMTIX (Text Inside eXtension lines), DIMTOFL (Text Outside, Force dimension Line inside), and DIMCEN (CENter marks and lines). If both the DIMTOFL and DIMTIX variables are set to 0 (off), a leader is drawn to the dimension text from the point by which you picked the entity. The leader is drawn dynamically so that you can place the text for best readability. When DIMTOFL alone is on (1), AutoCAD places the dimension text outside the arc or circle, as in the previous style, and draws a dimension line through the diameter of the entity. When both DIMTOFL and DIMTIX are on, AutoCAD omits the leader and places the dimension text within the dimension line.

If the dimension variable DIMCEN is positive, a center mark is placed at the center point; if it is 0, no mark is placed; and if it is negative, center lines and marks are drawn. If the dimension text is placed at the center of the arc or circle, the center marks and lines are not drawn.

Dimension text for the DIAMETER command always begins with the diameter symbol (equivalent to %%c) by default.

Prompts and Options

- **Select arc or circle:**

   Pick the arc or circle to dimension. The point you pick determines the location of the dimension line or leader.

- **Dimension text <default>:**

   AutoCAD calculates the distance between the two extension line origin points you pick or between the two points derived from the object you select. AutoCAD then offers the distance (in the current drawing units and precision) as the default dimension text value. You can accept this value (press Enter), specify a new value, suppress any text by typing a space, or apply prefix or suffix text to the value (see the DIM/DIM1 command).

635

- **Enter leader length for text:**

  If dimension text is placed outside the circle or arc (as defined by the DIMTIX variable), you can drag the length of the dimension leader into place or enter a length at the keyboard. If you press Enter instead of dragging, AutoCAD draws a minimum length leader.

Examples

The following example demonstrates the three styles of diameter dimensioning. The dimensions that these examples produce are shown in figure DIAMETER.1.

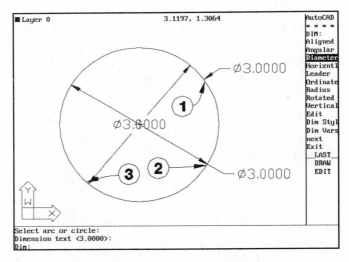

Figure DIAMETER.1:
Dimensioning with the DIAMETER command.

```
Command: DIM ↵
Dim: DIMTIX ↵
Current value <Off> New value: OFF
Dim: DIMTOFL
Current value <Off> New value: OFF
Dim: DIAMETER ↵
Select arc or circle: Pick point ① (see fig. DIAMETER.1)
```

```
Dimension text <3.00>: ↵
Enter leader length for text: ↵
Dim: DIMTOFL ↵
Current value <Off> New value: ON
Dim: DIAMETER ↵
Select arc or circle: Pick point ② (see fig. DIAMETER.1)
Dimension text <3.00>: ↵
Enter leader length for text: ↵
Dim: DIMTIX ↵
Current value <Off> New value: ON ↵
Dim: DIAMETER ↵
Select arc or circle: Pick point ③ (see fig. DIAMETER.1)
Dimension text <3.00>: ↵
```

Related Commands

Dim:CENTER
DDIM
Dim:RADIUS

Related System Variables

DIMTIX
DIMTOFL
DIMCEN

Dim: EXIT

Screen **[DIM:] [Exit]**

The EXIT dimensioning command terminates the dimensioning mode and restores command mode. You can also enter Ctrl-C at the DIM: prompt to terminate the dimensioning mode. The EXIT command can be abbreviated as E.

Example

The following example demonstrates how to use the EXIT command to return to AutoCAD's command mode.

```
Dim: EXIT↵
Command: ↵
```

Dim: HOMETEXT

Screen [DIM:] [Edit] [HOMETEXT]

Pull down [Modify] [Edit Dims >] [Dimension Text >] [Home Position]

The HOMETEXT dimensioning command restores one or more associative dimension text entities to their default (home) positions after they have been altered by the TEDIT, TROTATE, or STRETCH commands. If the dimension was not created with a named dimension style, AutoCAD updates the dimension with the current dimension variable settings. The HOMETEXT command can be abbreviated as HOM.

Prompts and Options

- **Select objects:**

    Select the dimension(s) to restore text to the default position(s). You can pick dimensions by any selection method and by any dimension component: extension lines, dimension line, arrowheads, or text.

Example

The following example takes the text of an associative dimension and return it to its original position. Figure HOMETEXT.1 shows the dimension text before using the HOMETEXT command (in the upper frame) and after using HOMETEXT.

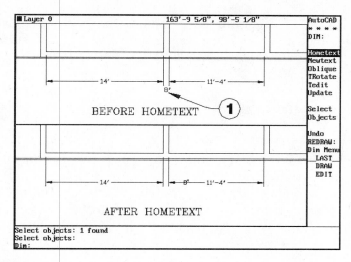

Figure HOMETEXT.1:
Dimension text being returned to its home position.

```
Command: DIM ↵
Dim: HOMETEXT ↵
Select objects: Pick point ①
Select objects: ↵
```

Related Command

Dim:NEWTEXT

Related System Variables

DIMASO
DIMSTYLE

Dim: HORIZONTAL

Screen [DIM:] [Horizntl]

Pull down [Draw] [Dimensions >] [Linear >] [Horizontal]

639

The HORIZONTAL dimensioning command draws dimensions with a horizontal dimension line. The extension line origin points need not have the same Y coordinates. The HORIZONTAL command can be abbreviated as HOR.

Prompts and Options

- **First extension line origin or RETURN to Select:**

  Pick a point at one end of the entity or feature to be dimensioned. AutoCAD prompts for the `Second extension line origin:`. The extension lines are offset from the points you pick by the current value of the dimension variable DIMEXO. The extension lines are drawn vertically, regardless of the angle between the first and second extension line origin points.

- **Select line, arc, or circle:**

  This prompt appears if you press Enter at the `First extension line origin or RETURN to select:` prompt. Pick a line, polyline, arc, or circle; extension lines are located for you. If you select a line, polyline segment, or arc, AutoCAD dimensions its end points. If you select a circle, the diameter is dimensioned between the 0- and 180-degree quadrant points. AutoCAD dimensions only the selected segment of an open polyline.

- **Second extension line origin:**

  Pick a point at the opposite end of the entity or feature to be dimensioned. AutoCAD offsets the second extension line from this point by the current value of the dimension variable DIMEXO. The extension lines are drawn vertically, regardless of the angle between the first and second extension line origin points.

- **Dimension line location (Text/Angle):**

  Pick the point through which you want the dimension line to pass. AutoCAD uses this point to determine the offset distance between the selected object or pick points and the dimension line.

640

If you use either of the (Text/Angle) options, you will see one of the following prompts:

- **Dimension text <default>:**

  AutoCAD calculates the distance between the two extension line origin points you pick or between the two points derived from the object you select. AutoCAD then offers the distance (in the current drawing units and precision) as the default dimension text value. You can accept this value (press Enter), specify a new value, suppress any text by typing a space, or apply prefix or suffix text to the value (see the DIM/DIM1 command).

- **Enter text angle:**

  This prompt modifies the angle at which the dimension text is drawn. If you press Enter, the text is drawn at the default text angle.

- **Dimension text <default>:**

  AutoCAD determines the distance between the two extension line origin points you picked or between the two points derived from the object you selected. Then AutoCAD offers this distance (in the current drawing units and precision) as the default dimension text value. You can accept this value by pressing Enter, enter a new value, suppress any text by typing a space, or apply prefix or suffix text to the value.

Example

This example demonstrates how to use the HORIZONTAL command. The drawing in figure HORIZONTAL.1 shows the dimensions that are created in this example.

```
Command: DIM ↵
Dim: HORIZONTAL ↵
First extension line origin or RETURN to select: ↵
Select line, arc, or circle: Pick point ①
Dimension line location: Pick point ②
Dimension text <14'>: ↵
Dim: HORIZONTAL ↵
First extension line origin or RETURN to select: END of ③
```

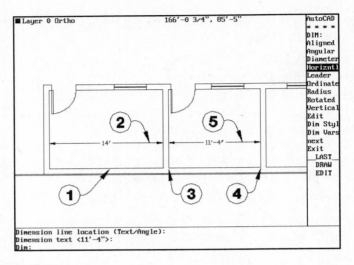

Figure HORIZONTAL.1:
Using the HORizontal command.

```
Second extension line origin: END of ④
Dimension line location (Text/Angle): ②
Dimension text <11'-4">: ↵
```

Related Commands

> **DDIM**
> **Dim: ALIGNED**
> **Dim: VERTICAL**

Dim: LEADER

Screen **[DIM:] [Leader]**

Pull down **[Draw] [Dimensions >] [Leader]**

The LEADER dimensioning command makes *callout notes* or *leader dimensions*, which are dimension lines leading from a line of text to a single arrowhead, which points at the feature to be described. You can abbreviate the LEADER command as L.

Horizontal leaders are made up of a single leader segment. Vertical or angled leader lines that are greater than 15 degrees automatically add a single horizontal segment (one arrowhead long) to the leader line adjacent to the dimension text. You draw a leader by picking an end point of the arrowhead and then dragging and picking any number of leader line segments, followed by pressing Enter. The leader text is then automatically middle-justified to the left or right depending upon the direction the last leader was drawn.

 LEADER dimensions are not associative, but consist of individual line and text entities and arrowheads (solid entities).

Prompts and Options

- **Leader start:**

  Pick the point where you want the leader to point. This point becomes the end point of the leader's arrowhead.

- **To point:**

  Pick any number of points for leader line segments. The first leader segment must be at least two arrowhead lengths long or the arrowhead is omitted. A leader can have any number of segments, although three is the traditional maximum. As with the LINE command, a rubber-band line stretches dynamically from each chosen point to the cursor to indicate the next segment's location. You can enter a **U** at this prompt to undo a leader segment. If you press Enter at this prompt after you enter one or more points, a final leader segment, one arrowhead long, is added automatically if the last segment was not within 15 degrees of horizontal.

- **Dimension text <default>:**

  Enter a single line of text for the leader. The dimension text of the last dimensioning command is presented as the default. You can

643

add prefixes and suffixes to the default text, as with the other dimensioning commands.

Example

The following example demonstrates how simple it is to create callout notes in a drawing. The drawing shown in figure LEADER.1 shows the points used to create a note for the drawing.

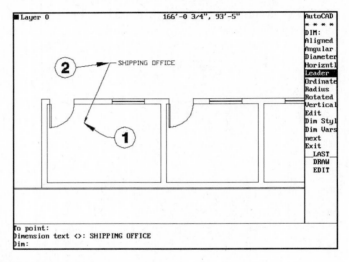

Figure LEADER.1:
A callout created using the LEADER command.

```
Command: DIM ↵
Dim: LEADER ↵
Leader start: Pick point ①
To point: Pick point ②
To point: ↵
Dimension text <>: SHIPPING OFFICE ↵
```

Related Command

DDIM

Dim: NEWTEXT

Screen   [DIM:] [Edit] [Newtext]

Pull down   [Modify] [Edit Dims] [Dimension Text]
[Change Text]

The NEWTEXT dimensioning command assigns a new text string to
one or more existing associative dimensions. The current dimension
variable settings are also applied, unless the selected dimensions were
created with named dimension styles. Non-associative dimensions are
not affected. The NEWTEXT command can be abbreviated as N.

Prompts and Options

- **Enter new dimension text:**

  At this prompt, you enter a new text string for the dimension. You can
  apply prefixes and suffixes or you can suppress text by entering a
  space character. If you press Enter without entering text, AutoCAD
  restores the default text strings of the selected associative dimension(s).

- **Select objects:**

  Select any part of an associative dimension or any number of
  associative dimensions by using AutoCAD's standard object-
  selection methods. If you choose more than one dimension, the
  text of each dimension is changed to the new value.

Example

The following example demonstrates how to use the NEWTEXT command to
change existing associative dimension text. Figure NEWTEXT.1 shows the
effects of using this command.

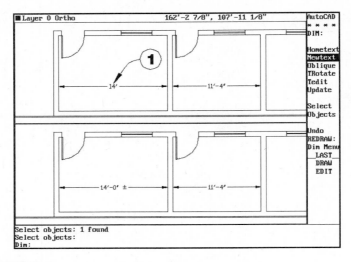

Figure NEWTEXT.1:
Dimension text modified using the NEWTEXT command.

```
Command: DIM ↵
Dim: NEWTEXT ↵
Enter new dimension text: 14'-0" %%P ↵
Select objects: Pick point ①
1 selected, 1 found
Select objects: ↵
```

Related Commands

DDIM
Dim:HOMETEXT
Dim:TEDIT
Dim:TROTATE
Dim:UPDATE

Dim: OBLIQUE

Pull down **[Modify] [Edit Dims >] [Dimension Text >] [Oblique Dimension]**

The OBLIQUE dimensioning command makes the extension lines of existing associative dimensions oblique with respect to their dimension lines. The OBLIQUE command is useful when dimensions in a dense drawing begin to interfere with one another, or for special effects such as isometric dimensioning. The OBLIQUE command can be abbreviated as OB.

Prompts and Options

- **Select objects:**

  Use AutoCAD's normal object-selection methods to select the dimensions to edit. You can use the OBLIQUE command only with associative dimensions.

- **Enter obliquing angle (RETURN for none):**

  At this prompt, you enter the new obliquing angle for extension lines of the selected dimensions. This angle is measured in relation to the angle of the existing extension lines—positive in the counterclockwise direction. The current dimension variable settings are applied to the selected dimension(s) unless the dimension(s) were created with a named dimension style. Pressing Enter gives the same result as entering an angle of zero degrees. The angle you enter does not affect subsequently created dimensions.

Example

This example demonstrates how to use the OBLIQUE command to apply an extension line angle to an existing vertical dimension. Figure OBLIQUE.1 shows the effects of using the OBLIQUE command.

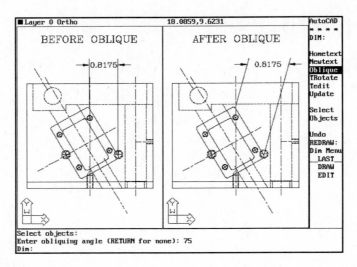

Figure OBLIQUE.1:
Dimension modified with the OBLIQUE command.

```
Command: DIM ↵
Dim: OBLIQUE ↵
Select objects: Pick point ①
1 selected, 1 found
Select objects: ↵
Enter obliquing angle (RETURN for none): 75 ↵
```

Related Commands

> DDIM
> Dim: TEDit
> Dim: TROtate

Dim: ORDINATE

Screen   **[DIM:] [ORDINATE]**

Pull down   **[Draw] [Dimensions >] [Ordinate >] [Automatic]**

The ORDINATE dimensioning command creates ordinate dimensions, also called datum dimensions. The ORDINATE command can be abbreviated as OR.

Ordinate dimensions denote either the X or Y distance from a common origin (0,0) point. This point is established by reorienting the current UCS origin. Ordinate dimensions consist of dimension text and a leader (without arrowhead) pointing to the feature dimensioned. If the angle between the first point (`Select Feature:`) and the second point (`Leader endpoint...`) is closest to the angle of the X axis, then the distance along the Y axis is dimensioned. If the angle between the points is closest to the angle of the Y axis, then the distance along the X axis is dimensioned. You can override the ORDINATE command's choice of axes by specifying the axis to dimension with the Xdatum or Ydatum options. The leader and dimension text are aligned perpendicular to the axis being dimensioned. You can enter ordinate dimension leaders more easily if Ortho mode is on.

Prompts and Options

- **`Select Feature:`**

  Pick the point you want to dimension. This becomes the start point of the ordinate dimension leader, offset by the current value of DIMEXO.

- **`Leader endpoint (Xdatum/Ydatum):`**

  Pick an end point for the leader or enter an **X** or **Y** to specify the dimension type. With Ortho off, if you can drag and pick the leader end point diagonally, an orthogonal break is automatically drawn in the middle of the leader. If you enter the Xdatum or Ydatum options, the corresponding dimension types are drawn, regardless of the direction or location of the leader end point.

- **`Dimension text <default>:`**

  AutoCAD calculates the distance between the two extension line origin points you pick or between the two points derived from the object you select. AutoCAD then offers the distance (in the current drawing units and precision) as the default dimension text value. You can accept this value (press Enter), specify a new value, suppress any text by typing a space, or apply prefix or suffix text to the value (see the DIM/DIM1 command).

Example

The following example uses the ORDINATE command to dimension the part shown in figure ORDINATE.1.

```
Command: DIM ↵
Dim: ORDINATE ↵
Select Feature: CEN of Pick point ①
```

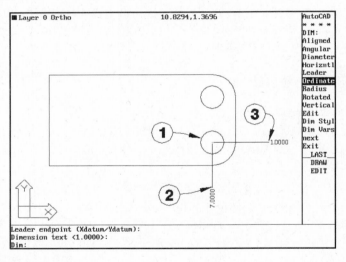

Figure ORDINATE.1:
Ordinate (datum dimensions) used to locate a part feature.

```
Leader endpoint (Xdatum/Ydatum): Pick point ②
Dimension text <7.0000>: ↵
Dim: ORDINATE ↵
```

```
Select Feature: CEN of ①
Leader endpoint (Xdatum/Ydatum): Pick point ③
Dimension text <1.0000>: ↵
```

Related Commands

DDIM
UCS

Dim: OVERRIDE

Screen `[DIM:] [Dim Styl] [Override]`

The OVERRIDE dimensioning command modifies selected dimensions
to use new values for one or more dimension variables. The OVERRIDE
command differs from the UPDATE command, in that it updates
specific dimension variables; the UPDATE command applies all the
current dimension variable settings to the selected dimension(s). The
OVERRIDE command can be abbreviated as OV.

Prompts and Options

- **Dimension variable to override:**

  You enter the name of a dimension variable to change.

- **Current value <*default*> New value:**

  You enter a new value for each dimension variable specified. Press
  Enter to proceed with object selection. The variables you override
  affect only selected dimensions; they do not affect the current
  dimension style or subsequently created dimensions.

- **Select objects:**

  Use any of AutoCAD's object-selection methods to select the
  existing associative dimensions you want to override. The settings
  you specified above are applied to each.

651

- **Modify dimension style "current"? <N>**

  If a selected dimension was defined with a named style, you can enter **Y** to update the style or press Enter to leave the style unchanged. If you enter **Y**, the selected dimension is modified and retains the named style. If you enter **N** or press Enter, the dimension is modified and its style becomes *UNNAMED.

Example

This example demonstrates how the OVERRIDE command can be used to adjust selected dimensions within a drawing. Figure OVERRIDE.1 shows the original dimension and its appearance after overriding its original settings.

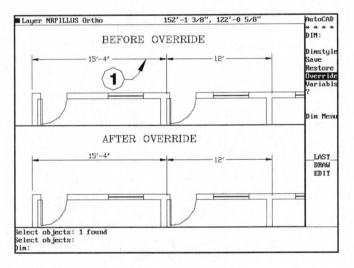

Figure OVERRIDE.1:
Linear dimension before and after overriding DIMTAD.

```
Command: DIM ↵
Dim: OVERRIDE ↵
Dimension variable to override: DIMTAD ↵
Current value <Off> New value: ON
Dimension variable to override: ↵
```

Pick point ①
```
Select objects: 1 selected, 1 found
Select objects: ↵
```

Related Commands

> DDIM
> Dim: UPDATE

Dim: RADIUS

Screen **[DIM:] [Radius]**

Pull down **[Draw] [Dimensions >] [Radial >] [Radius]**

The RADIUS dimensioning command is used to dimension the radius of circles, arcs, and polyline arc segments. You can abbreviate the RADIUS command as RA.

AutoCAD can produce several variations of dimensions for radii. These variations depend on the value of the system variables DIMTIX (Text Inside eXtension lines), DIMTOFL (Text Outside, Force dimension Line inside), and DIMCEN (CENter marks and lines). If both the DIMTIX and DIMTOFL variables are set to 0 (off), a leader is drawn to the dimension text from the point by which the entity was picked. The leader is drawn dynamically so you can place the text for best readability. When DIMTOFL alone is on (1), AutoCAD places the dimension text outside the arc or circle, as in the previous style, and draws a dimension line from the center of the entity. When both DIMTOFL and DIMTIX are on, AutoCAD omits the leader and places the dimension text within the dimension line.

If the dimension variable DIMCEN is positive, a center mark is placed at the center point; if DIMCEN is 0, no mark is placed; and if DIMCEN is negative, center lines are drawn.

Dimension text for the RADIUS command always begins with the symbol R (for RADIUS) by default.

653

Prompts and Options

- `Select arc or circle:`

  Pick the arc or circle to dimension. The point by which you pick the entity determines the end point of the dimension line or leader and the general location of dimension text.

- `Dimension text < default >:`

  AutoCAD calculates the distance between the two extension line origin points you pick or between the two points derived from the object you select. AutoCAD then offers the distance (in the current drawing units and precision) as the default dimension text value. You can accept this value (press Enter), specify a new value, suppress any text by typing a space, or apply prefix or suffix text to the value (see the DIM/DIM1 command).

- `Enter leader length for text:`

  If dimension text is forced outside the arc or circle by the DIMTIX variable, you can drag the length of the dimension leader or enter a length at the keyboard. If you press Enter at this prompt, AutoCAD draws a minimum length leader.

Example

This example creates several types of radial dimensions. Each one is different, due to changes in the three key dimensioning variables. Figure RADIUS.1 shows each type of dimension.

```
Command: DIM ↵
Dim: RADIUS ↵
Select arc or circle: Pick point ①
Dimension text <5.9300>: ↵
Enter leader length for text: Pick point ②
Dim: DIMTOFL ↵
Current value <Off> New value: ON ↵
Dim: RADIUS ↵
Select arc or circle: Pick point ③
Dimension text <5.9300>:
```

```
Enter leader length for text: Pick point ④
Dim: DIMTIX ↵
Current value <Off> New value: ON ↵
Dim: RADIUS ↵
Select arc or circle: Pick point ⑤
Dimension text <5.9300>: ↵
```

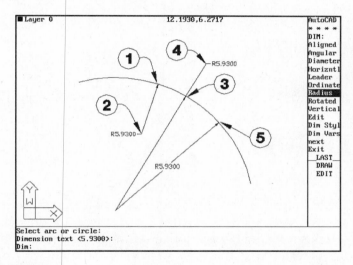

Figure RADIUS.1:
Dimensioning with the RADIUS command.

Related Commands

DDIM
Dim: CENTER
Dim: DIAMETER

Related System Variables

DIMTIX
DIMTOFL
DIMCEN

Dim: REDRAW

The REDRAW dimensioning command repaints the current viewport in the same fashion as the normal REDRAW command does. Any blips are removed and all entities are redrawn. The REDRAW command can be abbreviated as RED.

Related Commands

REDRAW
REDRAWALL

Dim: RESTORE

Screen   [DIM:] [Dim Styl] [Restore]

The RESTORE dimensioning command restores the dimension variable settings saved as a named dimension style, making it the current style. The new settings remain in effect until a setting is changed or until another style is restored. If an existing associative dimension has a named style, you can quickly restore the settings used by that dimension by picking that dimension at the first prompt. The RESTORE command can be abbreviated as RES.

Prompts and Options

- `Current dimension style: NAME`
  `?/Enter dimension style name or RETURN to select`
  `dimension:`

  This prompt lists the current dimension style name. If a named style is not current, the style is listed as *UNNAMED.

You can enter a question mark to display named dimension styles in the current drawing or enter a style name to restore. To select an existing associative dimension entity, press Enter and AutoCAD prompts with `Select dimension:`. If you enter a dimension style name preceded by a tilde (~), AutoCAD displays the differences in values of dimension variables between the specified style and the current settings.

- **Dimension style(s) to list <*>:**

  If you entered a question mark at the previous prompt, this prompt displays. Enter the names of dimension styles for listing (separated by commas) or use wild-card characters to match. If you press Enter or enter an asterisk, AutoCAD lists all the named styles within the current drawing.

- **Select dimension:**

  If you press Enter at the `?/Enter dimension style name or RETURN to select dimension:` prompt, this prompt displays. Select a dimension by using AutoCAD's object-selection methods. If the dimension is defined with a named dimension style, that style is restored as the current style. If the dimension is not defined with a named style, the RESTORE command terminates without affecting the current style.

Example

This example demonstrates the options of the RESTORE command to list, compare, and restore dimension styles.

```
Dim: RESTORE ↵
Current dimension style: *UNNAMED
?/Enter dimension style name or RETURN
to select dimension: ? ↵
Dimension style(s) to list <*>: ↵
Named dimension styles:
  DIM-16
  DIM-8
?/Enter dimension style name or RETURN to select dimension: ~DIM-
8 ↵
Differences between DIM-8 and current settings:
```

```
            DIM-8                   Current Setting
DIMASZ    0.0625                    0.1800
DIMBLK    ARCARROW
DIMDLE    0.0625                    0.0000
DIMDLI    0.0000                    0.3800
DIMEXE    0.0313                    0.1800
DIMGAP    0.0000                    0.0900
DIMSCALE  96.0000                   1.0000
DIMTAD    On                       Off
DIMTIH    Off                      On
DIMTIX    On                       Off
DIMTXT    0.0938                   0.1800
DIMZIN    1                        0
?/Enter dimension style name or RETURN to select dimension: DIM-8↵
```

Related Commands

DDIM
Dim: OVERRIDE
Dim: SAVE
Dim: STATUS
PURGE

Related System Variable

DIMSTYLE

Dim: ROTATED

Screen **[DIM:] [Rotated]**

Pull down **[Draw] [Dimensions >] [Linear >] [Rotated]**

The ROTATED dimensioning command draws a dimension line at a specified angle, regardless of the angle of the feature or object dimensioned. Extension lines are drawn perpendicular to the dimension line. Otherwise, the ROTATED command operates in the same way as the other linear dimensioning commands, such as HORIZONTAL and VERTICAL. The ROTATED command can be abbreviated as RO.

Prompts and Options

- **`Dimension line angle <0>:`**

  You enter an angle for the dimension line. AutoCAD measures the angles with its standard method, counterclockwise 0 degrees in the east direction. You can show AutoCAD an angle by picking two points.

- **`First extension line origin or RETURN to select:`**

  Pick a point at one end of the entity or feature to be dimensioned. AutoCAD prompts for the `Second extension line origin:` . The extension lines are offset from the points you pick by the current value of the dimension variable DIMEXO. The extension lines are drawn perpendicular to the dimension line angle.

  If you press Enter, the following prompt appears.

- **`Select line, arc, or circle:`**

  This prompt appears if you press Enter at the `First extension line origin or RETURN to select:` prompt. Pick a line, polyline, arc, or circle; extension lines are located for you. If you select a line, polyline segment, or arc, AutoCAD dimensions its end points, projecting extension lines to the specified dimension line angle. If you select a circle, the diameter is dimensioned at the dimension line angle specified. AutoCAD dimensions only the selected segment of a polyline.

- **`Second extension line origin:`**

  Pick a point at the opposite end of the entity to be dimensioned. AutoCAD automatically offsets the second extension line from this point by the current value of the dimension variable DIMEXO. The extension line is drawn perpendicular to the dimension line.

- **`Dimension line location (Text/Angle):`**

  Pick the point through which you want the dimension line to pass. AutoCAD uses the point to determine the distance between your selected object, feature, or pick points and the dimension line.

  If you use either of the (Text/Angle) options, the following prompt appears:

- **Enter text angle:**

    This prompt modifies the angle at which the dimension text is drawn. If you press Enter, the text is drawn at the default text angle.

- **Dimension text <*default*>:**

    AutoCAD determines the distance between the two extension line origin points you picked or between the two points derived from the object you selected. AutoCAD then offers this distance in the current drawing units and precision as the default dimension text value. You can accept this value by pressing Enter, enter a new value, suppress any text by typing a space, or apply prefix or suffix text to the value (see Chapter 5).

Example

This example demonstrates the two methods of creating a rotated dimension. Figure ROTATED.1 illustrates the points chosen for this example.

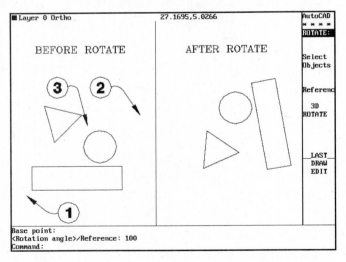

Figure ROTATED.1:
Dimensions created using the ROTATED command.

```
Command: DIM ↵
Dim: ROTATED ↵
Dimension line angle <0>: 30 ↵
First extension line origin or RETURN to select: INT of Pick point ①
Second extension line origin: INT of Pick point ②
Dimension line location (Text/Angle): Pick point ③
Dimension text <5.7956>: ↵
Dim: ROTATED ↵
Dimension line angle <0>: 60 ↵
First extension line origin or RETURN to select: ↵
Select line, arc or circle: Pick point ④
Dimension line location (Text/Angle): A ↵
Enter text angle: 60 ↵
Dimension line location (Text/Angle): Pick point ⑤
Dimension text <5.7956>: ↵
```

Related Commands

DDIM
Dim: ALIGNED
Dim: OBLIQUE

Dim: SAVE

Screen **[DIM:] [Dim Styl] [Save]**

The SAVE dimensioning command stores the current settings of all dimension variables in the current drawing as a named dimension style. This named style remains current until you change a dimension variable, save it under another name, or restore another named style with the RESTORE command. You can abbreviate the SAVE command as SA.

Prompts and Options

- **?/Name for new dimension style:**

  You enter a name for the current style. The name must conform to the general AutoCAD rules for named objects: it can contain as many as 31 letters or digits and it can include dollar signs ($), hyphens (-), or underscore characters (_). If you enter a question mark, AutoCAD produces a listing of the named dimensioned styles in the current drawing.

- **Dimension style(s) to list <*>:**

  If you enter a question mark at the previous prompt, this prompt appears. Enter the names of dimension styles for listing (separated by commas) or use wild-card characters to match. If you press Enter or enter an asterisk, AutoCAD lists all the named styles within the current drawing.

- **That name is already in use, redefine it? <N>**

  This prompt displays if the specified style name already exists. If you answer **N**, the first prompt repeats; if you answer **Y**, the existing style is overwritten and all associative dimensions defined with that style regenerate to reflect any changes in variable values.

Example

The following example demonstrates the SAVE command options. To save a new dimension style, proceed as follows:

```
Command: DIM↵
Dim: SAVE ↵
?/Name for new dimension style: TEST ↵
Dim: SAVE↵
?/Name for new dimension style: TEST That name is already in
use, redefine it? <N> Y↵
Dim: SAVE↵
?/Name for new dimension style: ?↵
Dimension style(s) to list <*>:↵
Named dimension styles: TEST↵
?/Name for new dimension style:
Press Ctrl-C
*Cancel*
```

Related Commands

DDIM
OVERRIDE
RESTORE

Related System Variable

    DIMSTYLE

Dim: STATUS ?

The STATUS dimensioning command lists the current settings of all
dimension variables with a short description of each variable. The
STATUS dimensioning command is not the same as the normal STA-
TUS command, which displays other drawing parameters. The STATUS
command can be abbreviated as STA.

Example

```
Command: DIM
Dim: STATUS
DIMALT     Off                    Alternate units selected
DIMALTD    2                      Alternate unit decimal places
DIMALTF    25.4000                Alternate unit scale factor
DIMAPOST                          Suffix for alternate text
DIMASO     On                     Create associative dimensions
DIMASZ     0.1800                 Arrow size
DIMBLK                            Arrow block name
DIMBLK1                           First arrow block name
DIMBLK2                           Second arrow block name
DIMCEN     0.0900                 Center mark size
DIMCLRD    BYBLOCK                Dimension line color
DIMCLRE    BYBLOCK                Extension line & leader color
DIMCLRT    BYBLOCK                Dimension text color
DIMDLE     0.0000                 Dimension line extension
DIMDLI     0.3800                 Dimension line increment for
DIMEXE     0.1800                 Extension above dimension line
DIMEXO     0.0625                 Extension line origin offset
DIMGAP     0.0900                 Gap from dimension line to text
DIMLFAC    1.0000                 Linear unit scale factor
- Press RETURN for more -
```

You can press Enter to continue the listing or press Ctrl-C to cancel.

663

Related Commands

DDIM
Dim: RESTORE

Dim: STYLE

Screen   **[DIM:] [Dim Style] [Dimstyle]**

The STYLE command changes the current text style in use for dimension text. The STYLE command can be abbreviated as STY.

The style you set affects dimensioning, as well as the TEXT, DTEXT, and ATTDEF commands. The STYLE dimensioning command is not the same as the normal STYLE command. Both commands set the current text style, but the normal STYLE command can also list defined text styles and create new text styles. Do not confuse text styles with dimension styles, which are created with the SAVE and DDIM dimensioning commands.

Prompts and Options

* **New text style <default>:**

   You enter the name of an existing text style to make it the style for new dimensions. The current text style is presented as the default.

Example

The following example demonstrates changing text styles with the STYLE command. ROMANC becomes the current text style upon completion of the example.

```
Command: DIM ↵
Dim: STYLE ↵
New text style <STANDARD>: ROMANC ↵
```

Related Commands

DDIM
STYLE

Related System Variables

DIMSCALE
DIMTXT

Dim: TEDIT

Screen [DIM:] [Edit] [TEDIT]

Pull down [Modify] [Edit Dims >] [Dimension Text >]
[Move Text]

The TEDIT command edits the location or angle of the text of a single existing associative dimension entity. The TEDIT command can be abbreviated as TE.

The TEDIT command includes options to:

- Shift dimension text as far to the left or right as possible along its associated dimension line (only for linear, radius, or diameter dimensions)
- Restore its default position (similar to the HOMETEXT command)
- Alter the text angle (similar to the TROTATE command)

If the dimension was created with a named dimension style, it is regenerated with the dimension variable settings of that style. If the dimension was not created with a named dimension style, the current dimension variable settings are applied to the dimension.

665

Prompts and Options

- **`Select dimension:`**

  Select the dimension to edit with any of AutoCAD's general object-selection methods.

- **`Enter text location (Left/Right/Home/Angle):`**

  Drag the dimension text into the desired position or specify one of the options. If the dimension variable DIMSHO is on (1), the text displays dynamically as you drag it.

- **`Left.`** The Left option moves the dimension text as far to the left along the dimension line as possible with a two-arrowhead length leader to the left of the text.

- **`Right.`** The Right option moves the dimension text as far to the right along the dimension line as possible with a two-arrowhead length leader to the right of the text.

- **`Home.`** The Home option returns the dimension text to its home position, centered along the length of the dimension line.

- **`Angle.`** The Angle option prompts for a new dimension text angle. If you select this option, the `Text angle:` prompt displays:

- **`Enter text angle:`**

  You enter a new text angle or pick two points to show the angle. The text is rotated about its center point. Angles are measured counterclockwise, according to the standard AutoCAD orientation of 0 degrees in the east direction. If you enter **0**, AutoCAD restores the text to its default angle; if you press Enter, the current angle is unchanged.

Example

This example demonstrates each of the TEDit options. Figure TEDIT.1 shows a series of typical horizontal dimensions relocated by using TEDIT.

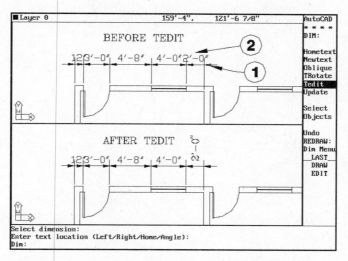

Figure TEDIT.1:
Crowded horizontal dimensions.

```
Command: DIM ↵
Dim: TEDIT ↵
Select dimension: Pick point ①
Enter text location (Left/Right/Home/Angle): A ↵
Enter text angle: 90 ↵
Command: DIM ↵
Dim: TEDIT ↵
Select dimension: Pick point ②
```

Related Commands

> **Dim: HOMETEXT**
> **Dim: TROTATE**

Related System Variables

> **DIMSHO**
> **DIMTAD**

DIMTVP
DIMTIH
DIMTOH

Dim: TROTATE

Pull down **[Modify] [Edit Dims >] [Dimension Text >]
[Rotate Text]**

The TROTATE dimensioning command alters the rotation angle of
dimension text for selected existing associative dimensions. TROTATE
functions like the Angle option of the TEDIT command. The TROTATE
command can be abbreviated as TR.

If a selected dimension was created with a named dimension style, it is
regenerated with the dimension variable settings of that style. If a
selection dimension was not created with a named style, the current
dimension variable settings are applied to that dimension.

Prompts and Options

- **Enter text angle:**

  You enter a new angle for dimension text, either from the keyboard or by picking two points. If you enter **0**, AutoCAD restores
  the dimension text to its default angle. AutoCAD measures the
  angle counterclockwise, according to its standard of 0 degrees in
  the east direction.

- **Select objects:**

  Use AutoCAD's normal object-selection methods to select all the
  dimensions to receive the new dimension text angle setting. Only
  associative dimensions are affected.

Example

This example rotates the dimension text shown in figure TROTATE.1, so that it fits better between the extension lines.

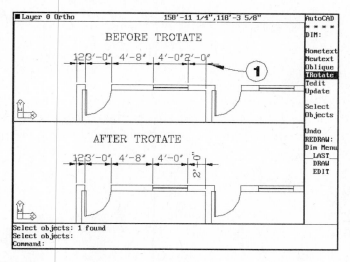

Figure TROTATE.1:
Dimension text before and after rotation.

```
Command: DIM ↵
Dim: TROTATE ↵
Enter text angle: 90 ↵
Select objects: Pick point ①
1 selected, 1 found
Select objects: ↵
```

Related Commands

> **Dim: HOMETEXT**
> **Dim: TEDIT**

Related System Variables

DIMTIH
DIMTOH

Dim: UNDO

Screen   [DIM:] [Edit] [Undo]

The UNDO dimensioning command undoes the last dimension operation. The command can be repeated back to the beginning of the current dimensioning session. No redo command exists for Dim mode. The UNDO command can be abbreviated as U.

Related Commands

REDO
UNDO

Dim: UPDATE

Screen   [DIM:] [Edit] [Update]

Pull down   [Modify] [Edit Dims >] [Update Dimension]

The UPDATE dimensioning command regenerates selected existing associative dimensions using the current dimension style, units parameters, and text style. UPDATE overrides any dimension style reference a dimension may have, redefining it with the current dimension style. If the current dimension style is *UNNAMED, the dimensions lose their style and are regenerated with the current dimensioning variable settings. The UPDATE command can be abbreviated as UP.

Prompts and Options

- `Select objects:`

  Use AutoCAD's normal object-selection methods to select existing associative dimensions to be updated.

Example

This example modifies an existing dimension with UPDATE to reflect a change in the DIMTAD variable. Figure UPDATE.1 shows the effects of the UPDATE command.

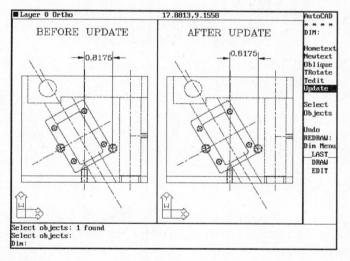

Figure UPDATE.1:
The original horizontal dimensions.

```
Dim: UPDATE ↵
Select objects: Pick the dimension at ①
Select objects: ↵
```

Related Commands

Dim: HOMETEXT
Dim: NEWTEXT
Dim: OBLIQUE
Dim: TEDIT
Dim: TROTATE
SCALE
STRETCH

Dim: VARIABLES

Screen   [DIM:] [Dim Styl] [Variabls]

The VARIABLES dimensioning command lists all dimension variable settings for a specified named style or compares the differences between a named style and the current style. You cannot change dimension variables or make a style current with this command. The desired style may be specified by name or by picking a dimension defined with that style. The VARIABLES command can be abbreviated as VAR.

Prompts and Options

- `Current dimension style: CURRENT`
  `?/Enter dimension style name or RETURN to select`
  `dimension:`

  You enter a question mark to display named dimension styles in the current drawing or to enter a style name to list. To select an existing associative dimension created with the desired style, press Enter and AutoCAD prompts with `Select dimension:`. Enter a dimension style name preceded by a tilde (~) to view the differences in values of dimension variables between the specified style and the current settings.

- **Dimension style(s) to list <*>:**

  This prompt appears if you enter a question mark at the ?/Enter dimension style name prompt. Enter the names of dimension styles for listing (separated by commas), or use wild-card characters to match. If you press Enter or enter an asterisk, AutoCAD lists all the named styles within the current drawing.

- **Select dimension:**

  Use AutoCAD's normal object-selection methods to select a dimension created with the dimension style you want to list or compare. The selected dimension need not be defined with a named style for its variables to be listed.

Example

This example demonstrates the steps for displaying the variables stored within a named style.

```
Command: DIM ↵
Dim: VARIABLES ↵
Current dimension style: *UNNAMED
?/Enter dimension style name or RETURN to select dimension: ?
↵
Dimension style(s) to list <*>: ↵
Named dimension styles: ↵
  ARCH
?/Enter dimension style name or RETURN to select dimension:
ARCH ↵
Status of ARCH:
DIMALT    Off                    Alternate units selected
DIMALTD   0                      Alternate unit decimal places
DIMALTF   25.4000                Alternate unit scale factor
DIMAPOST                         Suffix for alternate text
DIMASO    On                     Create associative dimensions
DIMASZ    0.0625                 Arrow size
DIMBLK    ARCARROW               Arrow block name
DIMBLK1   ARCARROW               First arrow block name
DIMBLK2   ARCARROW               Second arrow block name
DIMCEN    0.0900                 Center mark size
```

```
DIMCLRD   1 (red)         Dimension line color
DIMCLRE   1 (red)         Extension line & leader color
DIMCLRT   BYBLOCK         Dimension text color
DIMDLE    0.0000          Dimension line extension
DIMDLI    0.0000          Dimension line increment for
continuation
DIMEXE    0.0313          Extension above dimension line
DIMEXO    0.0625          Extension line origin offset
DIMGAP    0.0000          Gap from dimension line to text
DIMLFAC   1.0000          Linear unit scale factor
- Press RETURN for more -
```

Related Commands

DDIM
Dim: RESTORE
Dim: SAVE

Dim: VERTICAL

Screen   [DIM:] [Vertical]

Pull down   [Draw] [Dimensions >] [Linear >] [Verti-cal]

The VERTICAL dimensioning command draws dimensions with a vertical dimension line. The extension line origin points need not have the same X coordinates. The VERTICAL command can be abbreviated as VE.

Prompts and Options

- **First extension line origin or RETURN to Select:**
  Pick a point at one end of the entity or feature to be dimensioned. AutoCAD prompts for the Second extension line origin:. The extension lines are offset from the points by the current value

of the dimension variable DIMEXO. The extension lines are drawn horizontally, regardless of the angle between the first and second extension line origin points.

If you press Enter, the following prompt appears.

- `Select line, arc, or circle:`

    This prompt appears if you press Enter at the `First extension line origin or RETURN to select:` prompt. Pick a point to select a line, polyline, arc, or circle; extension lines are located for you. If you select a line, polyline segment, or arc, AutoCAD dimensions its end points. If you select a circle, the diameter is dimensioned between the 90- and 270-degree quadrant points. AutoCAD dimensions only the selected segment of an open polyline.

- `Second extension line origin:`

    Pick a point at the opposite end of the entity or feature to be dimensioned. AutoCAD offsets the second extension line from this point by the current value of the dimension variable DIMEXO. The extension lines are drawn horizontally, regardless of the angle between the first and the second extension line origin points.

- `Dimension line location (Text/Angle):`

    Pick the point through which you want the dimension line to pass. AutoCAD uses this point to determine the offset distance between your selected object, feature, or pick points and the dimension line.

    If you use either of the (Text/Angle) options, the following prompt appears:

- `Enter text angle:`

    This prompt modifies the angle at which the dimension text is drawn. If you press Enter, the text is drawn at the default text angle.

- `Dimension text <default>:`

    AutoCAD calculates the distance between the two extension line origin points you pick or between the two points derived from the object you select. AutoCAD then offers the distance (in the current drawing units and precision) as the default dimension-text value. You can accept this value (press Enter), specify a new value, suppress any text by typing a space, or apply prefix or suffix text to the value (see the DIM/DIM1 command).

Example

This example uses the VERTICAL command to dimension a part using various options. Figure VERTICAL.1 illustrates the points used in this example.

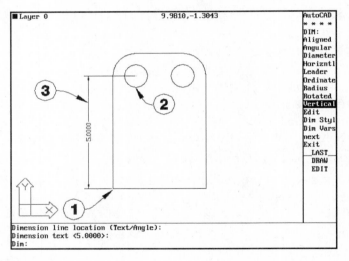

Figure VERTICAL.1:
Dimensioning with the VERTICAL command.

```
Command: DIM ↵
Dim: VERTICAL ↵
First extension line origin or RETURN to select: END of
Pick point ①
Second extension line origin: CEN of Pick point ②
Dimension line location (Text/Angle): A ↵
```

```
Enter text angle: 90 ↵
Dimension line location (Text/Angle): Pick point ③
Dimension text <5.0000>: ↵
```

Related Commands

DDIM
Dim: HORIZONTAL

DIST

Screen   **[INQUIRY] [DIST:]**

Pull down   **[Assist] [Inquiry >] [Distance]**

DIST measures the distance between two 2D or 3D points. You can enter the coordinates of the points at the keyboard or choose them on screen with a pointing device. The DIST command also provides information about the angle in the X,Y plane, the angle from the X,Y plane of an imaginary line between the two points, and the difference in X, Y, and Z values between the two points.

R12   You can execute the DIST command transparently by preceding the command name with an apostrophe ('**DIST**).

Prompts and Options

- **First point:**

  At this prompt, specify the first point.

- **Second point:**

  At this prompt, specify the second point.

Example

The following example uses the DIST command to measure the distance between two points:

```
Command: DIST ↵
First point: 1,1 ↵
Second point: 5,5 ↵
```

AutoCAD displays the following information:

```
Distance = 5.6569, Angle in XY Plane = 45, Angle from XY Plane = 0
Delta X = 4.0000, Delta Y = 4.0000, Delta Z = 0.0000
```

 Use the object snap modes to help measure the distance between specific points on existing entities.

Related System Variable

DISTANCE

DIVIDE

Screen **[EDIT] [DIVIDE:]**

Pull down **[Construct] [Divide]**

The DIVIDE command places points or blocks along the length of an entity, dividing it into a specified number of equal segments. You can divide lines, circles, arcs, and polylines. The divided entity, however, is not actually broken into individual segments.

Prompts and Options

* **Select object to divide:**
  When AutoCAD displays this prompt, you can use the standard object-selection methods to pick a line, circle, arc, or polyline.

- **<*Number of segments* >/Block:**

  At this prompt, you can either enter the number of equal segments to create, or select the Block option. The Block option enables you to insert a block at the dividing points. Note that you must define the block in the current drawing prior to selecting the Block option.

  When you select the Block option, the following prompts appear:

- **Block name to insert:**

  Enter the name of a block already defined in the current drawing.

- **Align block with object? <Y>:**

  If you accept the default answer of **Y**, the block is aligned with the divided entity. An aligned block is rotated around its insertion point parallel with the divided entity. If you answer **N**, the block is inserted with a rotation angle of 0.

- **Number of segments:**

  At this prompt, enter the number of equal segments to create.

Example

This example shows how the DIVIDE command is typically used in a real-world situation. Figure DIVIDE.1 shows a wall line that needs to be broken into seven even sections for placement of windows.

```
Command: DIVIDE ↵
Select object to divide: Pick point ①
<Number of segments>/Block: 7 ↵
```

Related Command

MEASURE

DLINE

Pull down **[Draw] [Line>] [Double Lines]**

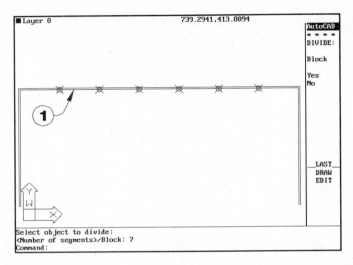

Figure DIVIDE.1:
A wall line, showing the locations for a few windows.

The DLINE command draws double lines and arcs. DLINE is defined by AutoLISP in the file DLINE.LSP, and it is loaded by the default AutoCAD menu. With DLINE, you can choose to snap double-line starting points to other objects, break intersecting objects, and cap double-line segments automatically. DLINE gives you complete control over the width of double lines and how they are drawn from a center line used to locate segment end points.

Prompts and Options

The following prompt appears when DLINE is first executed and before a start point is specified:

```
Break/Caps/Dragline/Offset/Snap/Undo/Width/<start point>:
```

This prompt is displayed after a start point is specified:

```
Arc/Break/CAps/CLose/Dragline/Snap/Undo/Width/<next point>:
```

In Arc mode, you are presented with a slightly different prompt:

```
Break/CAps/CEnter/CLose/Dragline/Endpoint/Line/Snap/Undo/
Width/<second point>:
```

Descriptions for each of DLINE's options follow. The options available depend on which of the DLINE prompts you just received.

- **Arc.** After you enter a start point, you can enter Arc mode with this option. DLINE draws double arcs through combinations of Start point, Center point, Endpoint or Start point, Second point, Endpoint.

- **Break.** The Break option causes DLINE to remove a section of the entity between double-line endpoints when the Snap option is used. The Break option issues the prompt `Break Dline's at start and end points? OFF/<ON>:`

- **Caps.** The Caps option causes DLINE to close the specified ends of double-line segments automatically. The Caps option issues the prompt `Draw which endcaps? Both/End/None/Start/ <Auto>:` The Both option caps both endpoints, End caps only the ending segment, None disables capping, Start caps only the beginning segment, and Auto caps segments not snapped to other objects with the Snap option.

- **Center.** The Center option enables you to specify the center point of double-line arcs when in Arc mode.

- **Close.** The Close option closes double lines or arcs created during the current invocation of DLINE with double lines or double arcs, respectively. Two double-line segments or one double-arc segment must exist before closing.

- **Dragline.** The Dragline option sets the location of double lines with respect to the rubber band line used to specify points. The Dragline option issues the prompt `Set dragline position to the Left/Center/Right/<Offset from center = default>:` The Left and Right options set the dragline to the left or right edge of the double line from the perspective of looking from the start point toward the end point. Center places the double lines equidistant from the dragline. Offset allows specification of an offset distance.

- **Endpoint.** You specify an endpoint for double line arcs with this option.

- **Line.** The Line option returns to Line mode from Arc mode.

- **Offset.** The Offset option begins double lines in a specified direction and distance from a base point. This option issues the prompt `Offset from:` to request the base point. At the `Offset toward:` prompt, specify a point to define the direction of the new double lines. The `Enter offset distance:` prompt accepts a distance from the base point, in the direction previously specified, to begin double lines. The distance between the base point and the point specified as the direction is offered as the default offset distance.

- **Second point.** The Second point option appears only during Arc mode and accepts a second point through which DLINE draws double arcs.

- **Snap.** When Snap is on, DLINE searches near pick points for objects to attach its double lines or arcs similar to Osnap. DLINE issues the prompt `Set snap size or snap On/Off. Size/ OFF/<ON>:` The On and Off options enable or disable Snap, respectively. You can control the distance (in pixels) that Snap searches with the Size option, which prompts `New snap size (1-10)<default>:`. If the Break option (above) is on, objects found by Snap will be broken and intersections with DLINE segments will be cleaned up automatically.

- **Start point.** This option, which is the default, asks you to specify a starting point for double lines or arcs.

- **Undo.** The Undo option voids the last picked point in Line or Arc mode.

- **Width.** This option prompts `New DLINE width <default>:`. You enter a distance or pick two points to specify the distance between double lines.

Example

The following example uses DLINE in several steps to draw shapes using some of the available options and defaults. The results are shown in figure DLINE.1

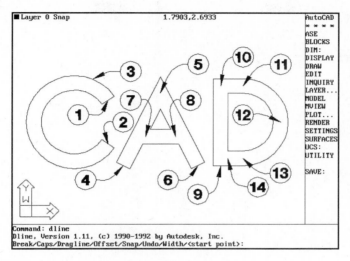

Figure DLINE.1:
Shapes created with DLINE.

Command: **DLINE** ↵
Dline, Version 1.11, (c) 1990-1992 by Autodesk, Inc.
Break/Caps/Dragline/Offset/Snap/Undo/Width/<start point>:
Pick point ①
Arc/Break/CAps/CLose/Dragline/Snap/Undo/Width/<next point>:
A ↵
Break/CAps/CEnter/CLose/Dragline/Endpoint/Line/Snap/Undo/
Width/<second point>: **E** ↵
Endpoint: *Pick point* ②
Angle/Direction/Radius/<Center>: **D** ↵
Tangent direction: *Pick point* ③
Break/CAps/CEnter/CLose/Dragline/Endpoint/Line/Snap/Undo/
Width/<second point>: ↵
Command: ↵
Dline, Version 1.11, (c) 1990-1992 by Autodesk, Inc.
Break/Caps/Dragline/Offset/Snap/Undo/Width/<start point>:
Pick point ④
Arc/Break/CAps/CLose/Dragline/Snap/Undo/Width/<next point>:
Pick point ⑤
Arc/Break/CAps/CLose/Dragline/Snap/Undo/Width/<next point>:
Pick point ⑥
Arc/Break/CAps/CLose/Dragline/Snap/Undo/Width/<next point>: ↵

683

```
Command: ↵
Dline, Version 1.11, (c) 1990-1992 by Autodesk, Inc.
Break/Caps/Dragline/Offset/Snap/Undo/Width/<start point>:
Pick point ⑦
Arc/Break/CAps/CLose/Dragline/Snap/Undo/Width/<next point>:
Pick point ⑧
Command: ↵
Dline, Version 1.11, (c) 1990-1992 by Autodesk, Inc.
Break/Caps/Dragline/Offset/Snap/Undo/Width/<start point>: Pick
point ⑨
Arc/Break/CAps/CLose/Dragline/Snap/Undo/Width/<next point>:
Pick point ⑩
Arc/Break/CAps/CLose/Dragline/Snap/Undo/Width/<next point>:
Pick point ⑪
Arc/Break/CAps/CLose/Dragline/Snap/Undo/Width/<next point>: A ↵
Break/CAps/CEnter/CLose/Dragline/Endpoint/Line/Snap/Undo/
Width/<second point>: Pick point ⑫
Endpoint: Pick point ⑬
Break/CAps/CEnter/CLose/Dragline/Endpoint/Line/Snap/Undo/Width/
<second point>: L ↵
Arc/Break/CAps/CLose/Dragline/Snap/Undo/Width/<next point>:
Pick point ⑭
```

Related Commands

> **ARC**
> **BREAK**
> **EXTEND**
> **LINE**
> **OFFSET**
> **PLINE**
> **SNAP**
> **TRIM**
> **UNDO**

DONUT or DOUGHNUT

Screen **[DRAW] [DONUT:]**

Pull down **[Draw] [Donut]**

The DONUT command draws filled rings and circles by using wide-polyline-arc segments. You must provide the inside diameter, outside diameter, and center point for the polyline.

Prompt and Options

- **`Inside diameter <0.5000>:`**

  This prompt requires you to enter a value or two points for the size of the donut's hole. The default value is 0.5 units.

- **`Outside diameter <1.0000>:`**

  This prompt requires you to enter a value or two points to create the donut's outer diameter. The outside diameter must be greater than the inside diameter. The default value is 1.0 units.

- **`Center of doughnut:`**

  At this prompt, specify the donut's center point. You can enter the point's coordinates or pick the point on-screen. This prompt repeats until you press Enter, enabling you to make multiple donuts of the same size.

Example

The following example creates two donut objects with the DONUT command.

```
Command: DONUT ↵
Inside diameter <0.5000>: 3 ↵
Outside diameter <1.0000>: 4 ↵
Center of doughnut: Pick a point ①
Center of doughnut: ↵
```

Related Commands

FILL
PLINE
PEDIT

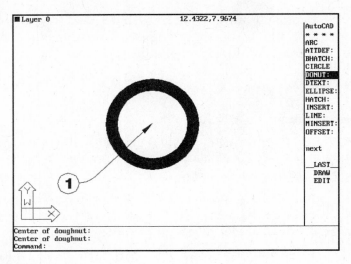

Figure DONUT.1:
The polyline entity created by the DONUT command.

Related System Variables

DONUTID
DONUTOD

DRAGMODE

Screen **[SETTINGS] [DRAGMOD:]**

The DRAGMODE command controls dragging when you draw or move objects. Some drawing commands (such as CIRCLE, ARC, INSERT, and SHAPE) enable you to drag objects so that you can see the size, shape, or position of the entity. Some editing commands, such as MOVE, COPY, and STRETCH, also take advantage of this dragging capability.

You can execute the DRAGMODE command transparently by preceding the commmand name with an apostrophe ('DRAGMODE).

 Most of the time, you will want to take advantage of AutoCAD's dragging capabilities to make drawing and editing easier. If you use DRAGMODE during large selection-set manipulations, however, such as when moving or copying complex blocks, screen performance may suffer. Turn off DRAGMODE temporarily during such operations for smoother cursor movement on slower systems.

You can control DRAGMODE's default setting in new drawings by modifying the state of DRAGMODE in the default prototype drawing. You also can use the DRAGMODE system variable to control dragging.

Prompts and Options

- ON:

  This option enables object dragging when requested by the user or by a menu macro, and the keyword **drag** is used at the appropriate prompts.

- OFF:

  This option disables object dragging.

- Auto:

  This option initiates object dragging automatically for all commands that allow object dragging.

Related System Variables

DRAGMODE
DRAGP1
DRAGP2

DTEXT

Screen **[DRAW] [DTEXT:]**

Pull down **[Draw] [Text] [Dynamic]**

DTEXT (Dynamic TEXT) enables you to enter text strings into your drawing. DTEXT produces the same results as the TEXT command but offers several advantages:

- You can see the text in the drawing as you type.
- You can move the cursor to a different part of the screen to begin a new text line.
- When starting a second line of text, you press Enter only once. With the TEXT command, you must press Enter twice to start a second line of text.

Prompts and Options

- **Justify/Style/<Start point>:**

  At this prompt, you have three choices. First, you can select Justify to change the text justification. The default value is left justification. Second, you can select Style to change the current text style. Note that the style must already be defined using the STYLE command. Third, you can enter the starting point of a left-justified text string, which is the default choice at this prompt. If you know the justification option you want to use, you can enter it at this prompt without selecting Justify first. The DTEXT justification options are described later.

- **Height:**

  At this prompt, specify the text's height. You see this prompt only when the current style does not have a predefined text height.

- **Rotation angle:**

  At this prompt, enter the text's rotation angle.

- **Text:**

  At this prompt, type the text string. This prompt is repeated so that you can type additional text strings. Press Enter at a blank `Text:` prompt to end the DTEXT command.

  If you press Enter, AutoCAD highlights the last text entered and prompts for a new string. The new string is placed directly below the highlighted text and has the same text style, height, and rotation as the highlighted text.

Justification Options

You can choose among the following justification options for your text:

- **Align.** You specify the start point and endpoint of the text string. AutoCAD adjusts the text's height so that the text fits between the two points.
- **Fit.** You specify the start point, endpoint, and height of the text string. AutoCAD fits the text between the two points by adjusting the width factor.
- **Center.** You specify the center of the text string horizontally and the base of the text string vertically.
- **Middle.** You specify the center of the text string horizontally and vertically.
- **Right.** You specify the right endpoint of the text string at the base.
- **TL.** Text justification is at the top left corner of the first character's text cell. A *text cell* is the rectangular area into which all characters of a font fit. You can visualize this area by imagining a character with both ascenders and descenders, or an uppercase letter with a descender.
- **TC.** Text-justification is at the top of a string's text cells; the string itself is centered horizontally.
- **TR.** Text-justification is at the top right corner of the last text cell of a string.
- **ML.** Text-justification is at the vertical middle of an uppercase text cell and at the left of the first character. Regardless of the text

string's composition, ML justification is calculated as if the first character is uppercase without descenders.

- **MC.** Text-justification is at the vertical middle of an uppercase text cell and at the horizontal center of the text string. Regardless of the text string's composition, MC justification is calculated as if the entire string were uppercase without descenders.
- **MR.** Text-justification is at the vertical middle of an uppercase text cell and at the horizontal right of the last character. Regardless of the text string's composition, MR justification is calculated as if the last character were uppercase without descenders.
- **BL.** Text-justification is at the bottom left of the first character's text cell.
- **BC.** Text-justification is at the bottom of a string's text cells; the string itself is centered horizontally.
- **BR.** Text-justification is at the bottom right corner of the last text cell of a string.

Example

This example shows the simplicity of using the DTEXT command. The text entity that is drawn is shown in figure DTEXT.1, along with the box that shows the position of all new letters before you type them.

```
Command: DTEXT↵
Justify/Style/<Start point>: Pick point ①
Height <0.2000>: .5↵
Rotation angle <0>: ↵
Text: THIS IS A LINE↵
Text: OF TEXT↵
Text: ↵
```

Related Commands

CHANGE
DDEDIT
QTEXT
STYLE
TEXT

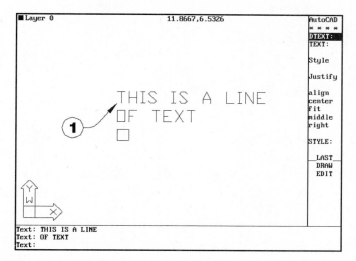

Figure DTEXT.1:
The text string entered with the DTEXT command.

Related System Variables

TEXTSIZE
TEXTSTYLE

DVIEW

Screen **[DISPLAY] [DVIEW:]**

Pull down **[View] [Set View >] [Dview]**

DVIEW, which stands for Dynamic VIEW, is used to set up views of three-dimensional models interactively from any point in space. The DVIEW command uses a camera-and-target metaphor to help you visualize and set up a view.

DVIEW also creates perspective projections of three-dimensional models. In perspective mode, objects that are close to the camera appear larger than objects that are farther away. The default projection mode is parallel projection. In parallel-projection mode, objects appear to be their true size regardless of their distance from the camera.

Prompts and Options

- `Select objects:`

  The objects selected for DVIEW are used to give you a preview of how the entire three-dimensional model will look in the new view. Selected objects are dragged on the screen as the view is dynamically changed. Be careful not to select too many objects to drag. Depending on your graphics system and the speed of your computer, dragging of objects may become sluggish and awkward.

  If you press Enter at this prompt, AutoCAD utilizes a user-defined block named DVIEWBLOCK as the view indicator. DVIEWBLOCK must be scaled to fit into a one-unit cube. DVIEWBLOCK is shown aligned with the X, Y, and Z axes of the current UCS. If DVIEWBLOCK does not exist, AutoCAD uses a small house as the view indicator.

- `CAmera/TArget/Distance/POints/PAn/Zoom/TWist/CLip/Hide/Off/Undo/<eXit>:`

- `CAmera.` The CAmera option rotates the camera about the target. When you select this option, AutoCAD prompts for the angle from the Z,Y plane and the angle in the X,Y plane from the X axis, relative to the target point.

- `TArget.` The TArget option rotates the target about the camera. When you select this option, AutoCAD prompts for the angle from the X,Y plane and the angle in the X,Y plane from the X axis, relative to the target point.

- `Distance.` The Distance option switches from parallel to perspective view and changes the camera's distance from the target along the current line of sight. When you select this option, AutoCAD prompts for the camera-to-target distance.

- **POints.** The POints option sets the camera and target points. These are the points you are looking from and to. When you select this option, AutoCAD prompts for camera and target points.

- **PAn.** The PAn option moves both the camera and target points parallel to the current view plane. When you select this option, AutoCAD prompts for a displacement-base point and the second point of displacement.

- **Zoom.** The Zoom option zooms the image in and out but does not change the perspective. This option works in much the same manner as a camera's zoom lens. When you select this option, AutoCAD prompts for a zoom-scale factor in parallel projection mode and lens length in perspective-projection mode.

- **TWist.** The TWist option rotates a view about the line of sight. When you select this option, AutoCAD prompts for a view twist angle.

- **CLip.** The CLip option moves a cutting plane, which removes objects from the view. The back-cutting plane removes objects behind the plane; the front-cutting plane removes objects in front of the plane. The front- and back-cutting planes may be independently moved in relation to one another. When you select this option, AutoCAD prompts for front or back clipping and then prompts for the distance from the target to place the cutting plane.

- **Hide.** The Hide option removes hidden lines from the selected objects while within the DVIEW command.

- **Off.** The Off option turns off perspective-projection mode and turns on parallel-projection mode.

- **Undo.** The Undo option undoes the effects of the other DVIEW command options, one at a time.

- **eXit.** The default option, eXit, returns you to the Command: prompt and regenerates the view based on the settings of the other options.

Example

This example shows how the DVIEW command is used to dynamically view the house in the DHOUSE drawing. Figure DVIEW.1 shows the selection points for choosing the entities in the drawing. Figure DVIEW.2 displays the house model in its dynamic view.

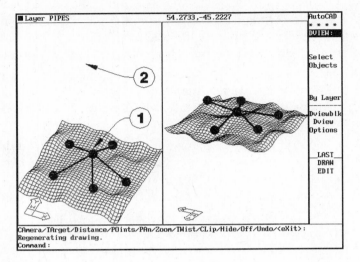

Figure DVIEW.1:
The selection points for choosing the house entities.

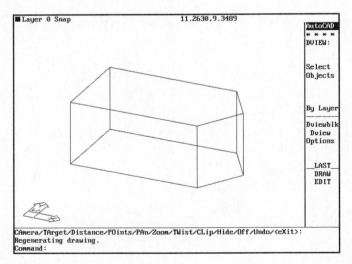

Figure DVIEW.2:
The house model after the dynamic view options have been set.

```
Command: DVIEW ↵
Select objects: W
First corner: Pick point ①
Other corner: Pick point ②
20 found
Select objects: ↵
CAmera/TArget/Distance/POints/PAn/Zoom/TWist/CLip/Hide/Off/Undo/
<eXit>: D↵
New camera/target distance <1.0000>: 50↵
CAmera/TArget/Distance/POints/PAn/Zoom/TWist/CLip/Hide/Off/Undo/
<eXit>: CA↵
[T]oggle angle in/Enter angle from XY plane <90.00>: 25↵
[T]oggle angle from/Enter angle in XY plane from Xaxis <-90.00>:
-100↵
CAmera/TArget/Distance/POints/PAn/Zoom/TWist/CLip/Hide/Off/
Undo/<eXit>: ↵
Regenerating drawing.
```

Related Commands

> VIEW
> VPOINT
> DDVPOINT

Related System Variables

> BACKZ
> FRONTZ
> LENSLENGTH
> TARGET
> VIEWDIR
> VIEWMODE
> VIEWSIZE
> VIEWTWIST
> WORLDVIEW

DXBIN

Screen **[UTILITY] [DXF/DXB] [DXBIN:]**

Pull down **[File] [Import/Export >] [DXB In...]**

The DXBIN command imports DXB files, which are binary drawing-exchange files. DXB files are limited in the types of entities and other drawing data they can contain. Unlike binary DXF files, binary DXB files are not a complete representation of the AutoCAD drawing file. DXB files are used by programs such as AutoShade to export simple drawing data, which then can be imported by the AutoCAD DXBIN command.

DXB files are useful for creating flat drawings of three-dimensional models created (pre-4.1) in the CONFIG command. To create a DXB file, configure your plotter for file output format, selecting the AutoCAD DXB file-output option. A DXB file contains only line entities. In a DXB plot file, circles, arcs, and text are composed of many short lines.

Prompts and Options

When you execute the DXB command, it displays a file selection dialog box for you to specify the file to import.

Related Commands

CONFIG
DXFIN
DXFOUT
FILMROLL
IGESIN
IGESOUT
PSIN
PSOUT

DXFIN

Screen **[UTILITY] [DXF/DXB] [DXFIN:]**

Pull down **[File] [Import/Export] [DXF In...]**

The DXFIN command imports a file—which conforms to the Drawing Interchange File (DXF) standard—into the current drawing. DXF files often are used to transfer drawing files between CAD packages.

The DXFIN command imports some or all of a DXF file into the current drawing, depending on whether any entities exist in the current drawing. If you want to import a complete DXF file, including defined layers, linetypes, text styles, blocks, and so on, the current drawing must be new and completely empty.

You can create a new and empty drawing file by using two methods. First, you can enter the new drawing name at the OPEN command's File edit box as *filename=*, in which *filename* is the name of the new drawing. This sets the new drawing equal to no prototype, which begins it as an empty drawing. Second, you can check the No Prototype box of the Create New Drawing dialog box. Regardless of the way you create the new and empty drawing file, you must use DXFIN before any command that creates entities or defines named layers, linetypes, text styles, and so on. When the DXFIN command successfully imports a complete DXF file, AutoCAD automatically performs a ZOOM All command.

If a drawing file is not new and empty, DXFIN will import only the entities section of a DXF file, ignoring all named objects in the DXF file, such as layers, linetypes, text styles, and blocks. A DXF file, however, does not need to be a complete drawing file containing named definitions; it can be as simple as a single entity. Some third-party AutoCAD application programs create new entities as DXF files and use DXFIN to insert them into a drawing.

The following prompt appears if you use DXFIN in a drawing that is not new and empty:

    Not a new drawing — only ENTITIES section will be input.

Prompts and Options

When you execute the DXFIN command, it displays a file-selection dialog box listing files with the extension DXF. Select a file or enter the path and file name of an existing file to import.

Related Commands

DXBIN
DXFOUT
FILMROLL
IGESIN
IGESOUT
PSIN
PSOUT

Related System Variable

FILEDIA

DXFOUT

Screen **[UTILITY] [DXF/DXB] [DXFOUT:]**

Pull down **[File] [Import/Export] [DXF Out...]**

The DXFOUT command creates a file in the Drawing Interchange File (DXF) standard. This file standard directly represents your drawing. It often is used to convert AutoCAD files to other CAD-related packages and prepare it for machine-tool devices, rendering packages, or other CAD programs that support the DXF format.

The DXFOUT command enables you to adjust the precision of the DXF file, write-only entities, or create a binary version of the DXF file. AutoCAD automatically attaches the extension DXF to the file name you specify.

A DXF file typically takes two to three times more disk space than the original drawing file. Whereas the default format created by DXFOUT is an ASCII file, the binary format is more compact, efficient, and precise; it also loads several times faster. Do not confuse the Binary DXF file with a Drawing Interchange Binary (DXB) file used in the DXBIN command.

By default, the DXFOUT command creates a complete ASCII DXF file, which fully describes the drawing, including all named definitions such as layers, linetypes, text styles, and blocks. The default precision is six decimal places, which often is sufficient. You can specify the accuracy between 0 and 16 places. The more decimal places you instruct AutoCAD to use, the larger your DXF file will be. Binary DXF files are created with the full precision of the AutoCAD drawing and are not affected by the precision you specify.

If you want to write specific entities to the DXF file, use the DXFOUT command's Entity option. You then are prompted to specify the desired accuracy.

Prompts and Options

When you execute the DXFOUT command, it displays the Create DXF File dialog box listing files with the extension DXF. Select an existing file to overwrite or specify a new path and file name.

- **Enter decimal places of accuracy (0 to 16)/Entities/Binary <6>:**

  Accept the default or enter the number of decimal places of accuracy if you want AutoCAD to write a full ASCII DXF file.

  The Entities option issues the standard `Select Objects:` prompt, then reprompts for the number of decimal places of accuracy and again offers the binary option.

  The Binary option creates a smaller, yet more precise, file than the standard ASCII format. This binary file has the same DXF extension as the ASCII format. After the Binary option is specified, AutoCAD immediately begins writing the DXF file.

- **Select objects:**

  Use any of AutoCAD's standard object-selection methods to select the entities to write in the DXF file.

Related Commands

DXBIN
DXFIN
FILMROLL
IGESIN
IGESOUT
PLOT
PSIN
PSOUT

Related System Variable

FILEDIA

EDGESURF

Screen **[DRAW] [next] [3D Surfs] [EDGSURF:]**

Pull down **[Draw] [3D Surfaces >] [Edge Defined Patch]**

The EDGESURF command is one of six commands that create a 3D polygon mesh. EDGESURF creates a four-sided mesh that can be defined by arcs, lines, and open polylines (either 2D or 3D).

The EDGESURF command creates a *Coons surface patch* between the four edge entities. To picture this form of mesh, envision a fishing net. The net can be a four-sided shape of virtually any size, and its holes can be any size.

The two axes of the mesh are called the M and N directions of the surface. The AutoCAD system variables SURFTAB1 and SURFTAB2 define the number of tabulation lines along the M and N directions of the surface.

Large SURFTAB settings create smoother surfaces at the expense of file size, entity regeneration, and hidden-line removal. When you are setting the variables, consider the application of the mesh. If large settings are needed for the final product, construct two meshes with the same boundaries: a temporary mesh with a moderate number of faces and a final mesh (kept on a frozen layer until needed) that has more faces. By using the temporary mesh, you can save time during the drawing and editing stages of your project. Replace the temporary mesh with the final mesh before final plotting and presentation.

As with other polygon meshes, you can edit the completed mesh by using most of AutoCAD's editing commands. These include the PEDIT command for fitting smooth curves through each vertex. If you use the EXPLODE command to break the mesh apart, the mesh is replaced with 3Dface entities.

The endpoints of boundary entities must intersect, and the entities must form a closed region. If not, AutoCAD returns the following message:

```
Edge n does not touch another edge.
```

In this message, the *n* signifies the number of the entity that does not coincide with the next.

Prompts and Options

- **Select edge** *n*:

  Select each of the four boundary edges for the polygon mesh in any order. Remember that the first edge selected determines the *M* direction of the mesh, and that the endpoints of each edge must intersect. The end of the first edge nearest the pick point is the origin of the mesh, with the M direction extending toward the opposite end of the edge. The other axis of the mesh is the *N* direction. The number of tabulation lines in the *M* and *N* directions is determined by the value of the variables SURFTAB1 and SURFTAB2. The default values for SURFTAB1 and SURFTAB2 create a 6×6 mesh.

Example

This example creates a mesh between four entities in 3D space. The entities shown in figure EDGESURF.1 are a combination of arcs and lines positioned in 3D space.

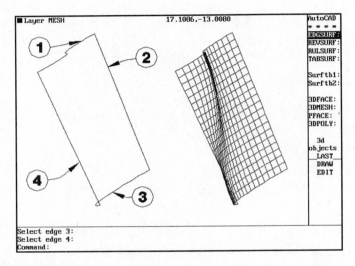

Figure EDGESURF.1:
The edgesurf edges and the polygon mesh created using EDGESURF.

```
Command: EDGESURF ⏎
Select edge 1: ①
Select edge 2: ②
Select edge 3: ③
Select edge 4: ④
```

Related Commands

> PEDIT
> PFACE
> REVSURF
> RULESURF

TABSURF
3DFACE
3DMESH

Related System Variables

SURFTAB1
SURFTAB2

ELEV

Screen   [SETTINGS] [ELEV:]

The ELEV command sets the elevation of the current *construction plane* for subsequently created drawing entities. This elevation is a distance along the Z axis above or below the current User Coordinate System (UCS) origin. The construction plane is a plane located at the specified elevation above or below the X,Y plane of the current UCS. The Z coordinates of points and new entities default to lie in the construction plane, unless otherwise specified when the points are input or the entities are created.

The ELEV command also sets the *extrusion* thickness for subsequently drawn entities. The term *extrusion* refers to the distance an entity is projected along the Z axis. An extruded circle, for example, resembles a cylinder when viewed from an oblique viewpoint.

The DDEMODES command dialog box has edit boxes for setting the elevation and thickness of all new entities, and it can be used transparently within other commands.

The use of the ELEV command is not recommended. Setting elevation to a nonzero height is confusing and can lead to errors when combined with a UCS located above or below the WCS origin. It is easier and less confusing to leave the elevation set to zero and to use the UCS to control the location of the construction plane.

Use the THICKNESS system variable or the DDEMODES dialog box to control extrusion thickness. The ELEV command will probably be deleted in a future release of AutoCAD.

Entities not affected by the current thickness setting are meshes, 3D faces, 3D polylines, viewports, dimensions, and text. You can assign a thickness to text after it has been created, however, by using the CHANGE or CHPROP command.

Prompts and Options

- **New current elevation <0.0000>:**

  At this prompt, you enter a value or pick two points to show a distance to define the new elevation. A negative value specifies an elevation below the current UCS. If you pick a point at this prompt, AutoCAD prompts for a second point.

- **New current thickness <0,0000>:**

  You can enter a value or pick two points to show a distance to define the extrusion value for entities. A negative value extrudes entities along the negative Z axis. If you pick a point at this prompt, AutoCAD prompts for a second point.

Example

This example shows the effects of elevation and thickness on the creation of new entities. The result is shown in figure ELEV.1.

```
Command: ELEV↵
New current elevation <0.0000>: 2↵
New current thickness <0.0000>: 2↵
```

Related Commands

CHANGE
DDEMODES
DDUCS
UCS

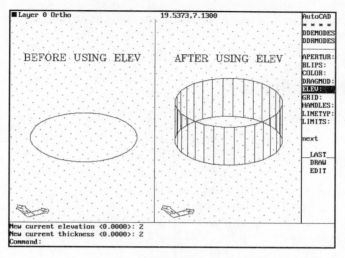

Figure ELEV.1:
An extruded circle at an elevation of 2 above the UCS.

Related System Variables

ELEVATION
THICKNESS

ELLIPSE

Screen **[DRAW] [ELLIPSE:]**

Pull down **[Draw] [Ellipse >]**

The ELLIPSE command draws an ellipse. This ellipse is constructed of polyline arcs and is a single closed polyline. You can use the PEDIT command to modify an ellipse.

You can specify ellipses by any one of several combinations of axis endpoints (the default), axis distances, rotation, or a center point. If the Snap Style option is set to isometric mode, the ELLIPSE prompt includes an isometric option, which creates an isometric circle in the current isometric plane. See the SNAP command for details on isometric mode.

Prompts and Options

- **`<Axis endpoint 1>/Center/Isocircle:`**

  The default option is to specify one endpoint of the first axis. If you enter **C** for the Center option, ELLIPSE displays the `Center of ellipse:` prompt. If Snap mode is set to isometric, you can enter **I** for the Isocircle option and ELLIPSE prompts `Center of circle:` and `<Circle radius>/Diameter:`. The Isocircle option draws a 2D ellipse that looks like a circle drawn in the current isometric plan.

- **`Axis endpoint 2:`**

  You enter the second endpoint of the first axis.

- **`<Other axis distance>/Rotation:`**

  After you specify the major axis, you enter a distance value or pick a point to show a distance for the half width of the ellipse. If you enter **R** for the Rotation option, the ELLIPSE command displays the `Rotation around major axis:` prompt.

- **`Rotation around major axis:`**

  At this prompt, you enter an angle value or pick a point to show the angle to rotate the ellipse around the first axis. The Rotation option is similar to specifying the second axis endpoint by rotating a perfect circle around the first axis in 3D. The Rotation option, however, does not actually rotate the ellipse in 3D. The ellipse is drawn as a two-dimensional oval in the current UCS. An angle of 0 degrees creates an ellipse that looks like a circle in plan view.

- **`Center of ellipse:`**

  The Center option displays this prompt. You specify a point for the center of the ellipse. The ELLIPSE command then prompts for the endpoint of the first axis.

- **`Axis endpoint:`**

  If you specify a center point for the ellipse, this prompt displays. You specify a point for one end of the first axis. The point defines the length of the axis from the center point. AutoCAD then displays the `<Other axis distance>/Rotation:` prompt.

Figure ELLIPSE.1 shows an example of the three points selected by the preceding method and the axes they define.

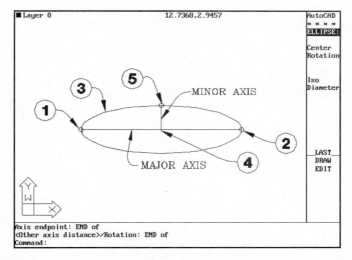

Figure ELLIPSE.1:
The ellipse axes and the three points.

Example

This example demonstrates two common methods for creating an ellipse. The first method defines the major and minor axes of the ellipse. The second method specifies the ellipse center, and then defines its axes. The results are shown in figure ELLIPSE.1.

```
Command: ELLIPSE ↵
<Axis endpoint 1>/Center: Pick point ①
Axis endpoint 2: Pick point ②
```

```
<Other axis distance>/Rotation: Pick point ③
Command: ELLIPSE ↵
<Axis endpoint 1>/Center: C ↵
Center of ellipse: Pick point ④
Axis endpoint: Pick point ⑤
<Other axis distance>/Rotation: Pick point ①
```

Related Commands

CIRCLE
ISOPLANE
PEDIT
SNAP

Related Variables

PLINEWIND
PLINEGEN

END

Screen **[UTILITY] [next] [END:]**

The END command finishes your drawing session by saving your work. If you have an existing drawing in the same directory as the current drawing, and that file has the same name as the current drawing, the existing drawing file is renamed with a BAK extension. If a file with the same name as the current drawing and a BAK extension already exists in the same directory as the current drawing, that file is deleted.

Related Commands

QUIT
SAVE

ERASE

Screen **[EDIT] [ERASE:]**

Pull down **[Modify] [Erase >]**

The ERASE command deletes selected entities from a drawing.

Prompts and Options

- **Select objects:**

  Use any of AutoCAD's standard object-selection methods to select the objects that you want this command to erase. Press Enter to terminate object selection and erase the selected entities.

Example

The following example shows how the ERASE command deletes entities from a drawing. Figure ERASE.1 shows the results of the ERASE command.

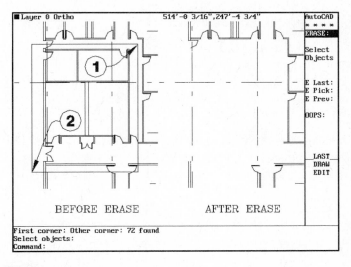

Figure ERASE.1:
Selecting the entities to be erased.

```
Command: ERASE ↵
Select objects: W ↵
First corner: Pick point ①
Other Corner: Pick point ②
Select objects: ↵
```

Related Commands

UNDO
OOPS

EXPLODE

Screen **[EDIT] [EXPLODE:]**

Pull down **[Modify] [Explode]**

The EXPLODE command reduces a *complex entity* (inserted blocks, polylines, associative dimensions, and meshes) into its component parts. Complex entities are made up of simpler entities, such as lines, arcs, text, 3Dfaces, and other entities.

When polylines are exploded, they are reduced into lines and arcs. Polylines that are curve-fit or spine-fit lose their original geometry and are exploded into lines and arcs that approximate the curve or spline. Tangent and width information also is lost when polylines are exploded.

Polygon meshes are exploded into three-dimensional faces. Polyface meshes are exploded into three-sided faces, lines, and points. If a polyline or mesh contains component parts with differing layers, colors, or linetypes, all component parts receive the layer, color, and linetype of the first component part in the polyline or mesh when exploded. Associative dimensions are exploded into lines, text, and points, and their arrowheads are exploded into blocks or solids.

Block references (inserted blocks) are exploded into the entities contained in their block definitions. You cannot explode external references (xrefs) and their dependent blocks, mirrored blocks, or blocks with unequal X, Y, or Z scales. Attributes in exploded blocks are deleted and replaced with their original attribute-definition entities.

 To explode an xref, first load it into the drawing with the XBIND command.

 To set a block's x, y, and z scale factors to the same value, use the DDMODIFY command.

If complex entities are nested, such as a block containing other blocks or other complex entities, only the outer entity is exploded. After you explode the outer block, you can select and explode the entities that were contained within it.

Prompts and Options

• **Select objects:**
Use any of AutoCAD's standard object-selection methods to select the objects that you want to explode. You can press Enter to terminate object selection and explode the selected entities into their component parts.

Example

The following example shows how to use the EXPLODE command to explode the polyline shown in figure EXPLODE.1 into lines and arcs.

```
Command: EXPLODE ↵
Select objects: Pick point ①
Select objects: ↵
```

Related Commands

BLOCK
DDMODIFY
INSERT
UNDO
XBIND

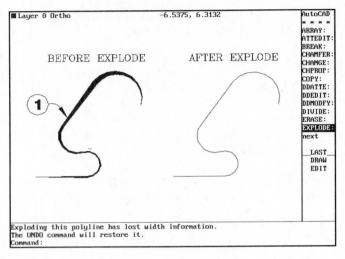

Figure EXPLODE.1:
A polyline that has been exploded.

EXTEND

Screen **[EDIT] [EXTEND:]**

Pull down **[Modify] [Extend]**

The EXTEND command increases the length of lines, open polylines, and arcs so that they intersect a boundary edge. The edge may be any entity, such as a line, circle, arc, sketch line, viewport entity, or an open or closed polyline (both 2D and 3D). You also can extend associative dimensions; when you extend an associative dimension, it updates automatically. Hatch entities cannot be extended, nor can you select a hatch as a boundary edge. Other entities that cannot be extended or used as a boundary edge include blocks, shapes, meshes, 3D faces, text, traces, and points.

AutoCAD enables you to select multiple boundary edges, but you can choose entities to be extended only one at a time. The EXTEND command offers an Undo feature, which returns the most recently extended entity to its former length.

 The EXTEND command can be used only on entities that are parallel to the current UCS. You can easily overcome this restriction, however, by setting the UCS to Entity, invoking the EXTEND command, and then setting the UCS to Previous.

Prompts and Options

- `Select boundary edge(s)...`
  `Select object(s):`

  Select the boundaries to which you want to extend the entities. Boundaries can be lines, arcs, circles, open or closed polylines, viewport borders, or sketched lines.

- `<Select object to extend>/Undo:`

  Pick the entities you want to extend. The point at which you pick the entity determines the direction of the extension. AutoCAD extends the entity from the endpoint that is closest to the picked location.

  If you wish to reverse the effects of the EXTEND command on the last entity, enter **U** to return the previously extended entity to its original length.

Example

The following example demonstrates the EXTEND command with lines and arcs (see fig. EXTEND.1). Note that the line pointed to by ④ will not be extended because it does not intersect the EXTEND command boundary.

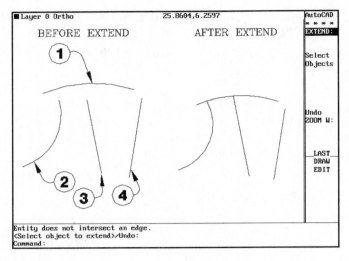

Figure EXTEND.1:
The lines and arcs before and after using the EXTEND command.

```
Command EXTEND ↵
Select boundary edge(s)...
Select object(s): ①
Select object(s): ↵
<Select object to extend>/Undo: ②
<Select object to extend>/Undo: ③
<Select object to extend>/Undo: ④
The entity does not intersect an edge.
<Select object to extend>/Undo:
```

Related Commands

CHAMFER
CHANGE
FILLET
STRETCH
TRIM

FILES

Screen **[UTILITY] [FILES:]**

Pull down **[File] [Utilities...]**

The FILES command enables you to perform file maintenance from within AutoCAD. You can list drawing files, list other files, delete files, rename files, copy files, and unlock files.

The FILEDIA system variable controls the method of file specification with the FILES command. If FILEDIA is set to 1, each of the command options is performed through dialog boxes (see fig. FILES.1). If the FILEDIA variable is set to 0, AutoCAD issues the text-only prompts.

 You can execute the FILES command transparently by preceding the command name with an apostrophe (**'FILES**).

Figure FILES.1:
The FILES command dialog box.

 You should be careful not to delete any files in use or delete AutoCAD's temporary files when you are using the FILES command. Temporary files are designated with the extensions $A, $AC, and AC$. Files used for file-locking are given an extension of *??*K. AutoCAD may crash if you delete temporary files. If lock files are deleted, anyone can access the file in use on a network system. A loss of data is inevitable when two people edit the same file on two different machines.

715

Prompts and Options

If the FILEDIA variable is set to 1, each of the five FILES command options (List files, Copy file, Rename file, Delete file, and Unlock file) displays a second dialog box. This dialog box, shown in figure FILES.2, displays available files and the standard dialog box buttons OK, Cancel, and Help. The FILES command options perform the following operations:

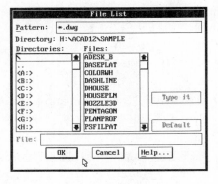

Figure FILES.2:
The typical FILES command dialog box.

- **List files...** The File List dialog box appears, listing all the drawing files in the current directory. To change the file types that are displayed in the list box, change the wild-card pattern to the files you want to see. For example, you could change the pattern to *.* to see all the files in the current directory.

- **Copy file...** Initially, the Source File dialog box appears. You should select the file to copy from by navigating the Directories: and Files: list boxes. When the file appears, highlight it in the Files: list box and click on the OK button. You can also type the full path and name of the source file in the File: edit box.

  After selecting the source file, you need to supply a location and name for the copy. The Destination File dialog box appears and requests this information. You can navigate the Directories: list box to choose a location for the file. To change the destination file's name, type in a new name, including extension, into the File: edit box. Click on the OK button when you are finished. AutoCAD displays the status of the copy at the bottom of the dialog box.

- **Rename files.** The Old File Name dialog box appears, requesting the name of the original file. You can select the file name from the Directories: and Files: list boxes or type in the full path and name from the File: edit box. Click on the OK button when you are finished.

  The New File Name dialog box appears next, requesting the new name for the file. You may select the file name from the Directories: and Files: list boxes, or type the full path and name in the File: edit box. If you select an existing file name, you are prompted to verify that you want to replace the existing file. Press the OK button when you are finished. The success or failure of the operation is reported at the bottom of the dialog box.

- **Delete files.** The File(s) to Delete dialog box appears, requesting the names of the files you want erased from your disk. You may select the file names from the Directories: and Files: list boxes, or type the full path and name in the File: edit box. If you want to list a specific group of files, such as all of the backup drawing files, you can enter the appropriate pattern at the Pattern edit box.

  When the files you want to erase are displayed in the Files: list box, you must highlight each file you want to delete. To delete all listed files, click on the Select All button. To dehighlight a group of files, click on the Clear All button. Click on the OK button when you are finished. AutoCAD displays the number of files that it deletes at the bottom of the dialog box. Any files that are currently locked by AutoCAD are not deleted.

- **Unlock files.** This option is used to remove the file locks set by AutoCAD in any configuration with file-locking enabled. The Files to Unlock dialog box displays, requesting the names of the files you want to unlock. You specify the names of the actual files you want to unlock, not the names of lock files (#.??K) themselves. You can list specific files by using the Pattern: edit box (such as

717

any file matching the *.DWG template). Select the files individually from the Directories: and Files: list boxes, use the Select all button, or type the names of the exact files you want to unlock.

AutoCAD attempts to unlock any locked files you specify. If a file is already in use by someone, a message appears at the bottom of the dialog box, informing you that the file is in use, and inquiring if you still want the file to be unlocked. When files are unlocked, AutoCAD displays the total number at the bottom of the dialog box.

- **E̲xit**. This option returns you to the drawing editor.

If the FILEDIA variable is set to 0, the FILES command presents the following prompts and options:

- **Exit File Utility Menu**

  When you select this option, you return to the drawing editor.

- **List Drawing files:**

  AutoCAD presents a list of all files with the extension DWG in the specified drive or directory. (The list is similar to the results of the DOS command DIR *.DWG /W/P.) After you select this option, AutoCAD displays the following prompt:

      Enter drive or directory:

  Press Enter if you want to see a list of the drawing files in the current directory. Otherwise, you can enter an alternative drive or directory.

- **List user specified files:**

  When you select this option, AutoCAD lists files according to a file-name specification you supply. Wild cards are allowed. You can restrict the list to just the backup files (*.BAK), for example, or to all the drawings with file names beginning with the letter F (F*.DWG). When you select this option, AutoCAD displays the following prompt:

      Enter file search specification:

  You should enter a valid file-search specification for your operating system. Include a drive and path prefix if necessary.

- **Delete files:**

  When you select this option, AutoCAD erases files from a disk. The following prompt appears, asking you to specify the files to be deleted:

  ```
  Enter file deletion specification:
  ```

  You can enter a drive, path, and file-name specification. Wild cards are allowed. If you specify a file that is locked, AutoCAD displays the following messages:

  ```
  Deletion denied, file: filename was locked by
  login name at time on date

  0 files deleted.

  Press RETURN to continue:
  ```

  If the file is not in use, you can unlock the file and then delete it.

- **Rename files:**

  By selecting this option, you can rename existing files from within AutoCAD. This option does not accept wild-card characters. AutoCAD displays the following prompt:

  ```
  Enter current filename:
  ```

  Now you enter the name of the file to rename. Include a drive and path prefix if necessary. AutoCAD then prompts for the file's new name, as follows:

  ```
  Enter new filename:
  ```

  You should enter a new name for the file. Do not include a drive or path. If you specify a file that is locked, AutoCAD displays the following messages:

  ```
  Rename denied, file: filename was locked by login
  name at time on date

  0 files renamed.

  Press RETURN to continue:
  ```

  If the file is not in use, you can unlock the file and then rename it.

- **Copy files:**

  When you select this option, you can make a copy of one or more specified files from within AutoCAD. The original file is called *source*, and the copy is called *destination*. You can place the copy on a separate drive or in a different directory. AutoCAD displays the following prompts:

  ```
  Enter name of source file:
  Enter name of destination:
  Copied xxxxxx bytes.
  Press RETURN to continue:
  ```

  The *xxxxxx* will be replaced with a number that represents the size of the file copied.

  If you specify a file that is locked, AutoCAD displays the following message:

  ```
  Copy denied, file: filename was locked by login
  name at time on date
  0 files copied.
  Press RETURN to continue:
  ```

  If the file is not in use, you can unlock the file, and then copy it.

- **Unlock files:**

  If you try to open a file that is locked, you receive the following message:

  ```
  Waiting for file: filename.dwg
  Locked by user: login name at time on date
  Press Ctrl-C to Cancel
  ```

  If you press Ctrl-C, or if 12 attempts to retrieve the file have failed, AutoCAD displays the following prompt:

  ```
  Access denied: filename.dwg is in use.
  Press Return to Continue:
  ```

These prompts indicate that the file is locked. (If a user turns off his computer or if it crashes while editing a locked file, the file remains locked.) If you select the Unlock files option of the Files command, the following prompt appears:

```
Enter locked file(s) specification:
```

You enter the locked drawing's name with the extension DWG, and AutoCAD responds with the following prompt:

```
The file: filename.dwg was locked by login name
at time on date.
Do you wish to unlock it <Y>
```

After you verify that the file is not actually in use, press Enter to accept the default of Yes, and the following messages appear:

```
Lock was successfully removed.
1 files unlocked.
Press RETURN to continue:
```

If the drawing file has been deleted, and the lock file still exists, the following messages appear:

```
ORPHAN lock file filename was locked by login
name at time on date.
Do you still wish to unlock it? <Y>
```

Example

This example demonstrates how to use the FILES command to remove all backup files in the current directory.

Command: **FILES**↵
Click on the Delete file... *button*
Double-click in the Pattern *edit box and enter* ***.BAK**, *then press the OK button. All files matching the selected pattern are shown in the* Files: *list box*
Click on the Select all *button to highlight the files*

Press the OK *button to delete the selected files and return you to the FILES command dialog box*
Press the Exit *button*

Related Commands

SH
SHELL

Related System Variable

FILEDIA

FILL
 9

Screen **[DRAW] [PLINE:]** *or* **[SOLID:]** *or* **[TRACE:]**

then **[FILL ON]** *or* **[FILL OFF]**

The FILL command controls the display of wide polylines, solids, and traces. The default, On, displays these entities filled in. When FILL is turned off, AutoCAD displays only the outlines of these entities (see fig. FILL.1). This setting affects both the screen display and the printed or plotted output. Solid filled entities also display only as outlines when hidden lines are removed with the HIDE command.

Filled entities are regenerated faster when the FILL command is off. A regeneration is necessary in order to see the results of changing the Fill mode setting on existing entities.

R12   You can execute the FILL command transparently by preceding the command name with an apostrophe ('**FILL**).

Prompts and Options

- ON/OFF <*default*>
- ON:

  When you specify the ON option, AutoCAD displays wide polylines, solids, and traces as solid (filled in). Existing entities are not affected until the next regeneration.

- OFF:

  When the OFF option is specified, AutoCAD displays wide polylines, solids, and traces as outlines.

Related Commands

DDRMODES
PLINE
SOLID
TRACE

Related System Variable

FILLMODE

FILLET

Screen [EDIT] [next] [FILLET:]

Pull down [Construct] [Fillet]

The FILLET (pronounced FILL-it) command joins the closest endpoints of two entities with an arc. The two entities are trimmed or extended so that the arc fits precisely between them. The arc is placed on the current layer if the two entities are on different layers. Otherwise, the arc is placed on the same layer as the filleted entities.

The FILLET command can be used only with line, arc, circle, or polyline entities. Filleting occurs only when enough distance exists between vertices or endpoints to accommodate the full fillet radius. When used with a fillet radius of 0, the FILLET command is useful for joining entities at their intersection.

You can fillet an entire polyline or two straight 2D-polyline segments. Segments must be contiguous or separated by another segment, which is removed to produce the fillet. You cannot fillet one polyline segment with another entity.

Prompts and Options

- **Polyline/Radius/<select first object>:**

  The default option—select first object—immediately fillets two entities, which can be lines, circles, or arcs. Circles and arcs must be selected by picking or by coordinate entry, and are filleted depending on the points you supply. Circles are not trimmed. You can select multiple objects by a window or crossing-selection set, but only two objects will be filleted, sometimes with unexpected results. If you select a polyline without first using the Polyline option, AutoCAD displays an error message. When the first entity is chosen, it is highlighted.

- **Select second object:**

  You select the second entity to be filleted. The two entities are trimmed or extended until they intersect the fillet arc. Lines that are parallel to each other cannot be filleted.

- **Select 2D polyline:**

  This option fillets all the valid vertices of a 2D polyline. The fillet radius is applied to each vertex. Vertices that have enough distance between the following and preceding vertices are filleted with the set radius. The command reports the number of vertices that could or could not be filleted.

- **Enter fillet radius <0.000>:**

   You enter the radius of the arc to join the selected entities. A value of **0** forces the entities' endpoints to intersect each other. A positive value joins the chosen entities with an arc.

Example

The following example shows you how the FILLET command can be used on lines and polylines (see fig. FILLET.1).

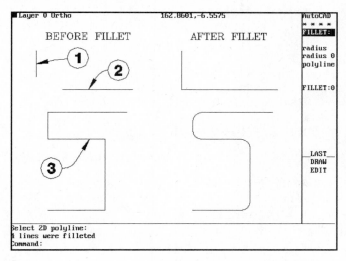

Figure FILLET.1:
The entities before and after using the FILLET command.

```
Command: FILLET ↵
Polyline/Radius/<Select first object>: R ↵
Enter fillet radius <0.0000>: 0 ↵
Command: FILLET ↵
FILLET Polyline/Radius/<Select first object>: Pick point ①
```

```
Select second object: Pick point ②
Command: FILLET ↵
Polyline/Radius/<Select first object>: R ↵
Enter fillet radius <0.0000>: 6 ↵
Command: FILLET ↵
FILLET Polyline/Radius/<Select first object>: P ↵
Select 2D polyline: Pick point ③
4 lines were filleted
```

Related Command

CHAMFER

Related System Variable

FILLETRAD

FILMROLL

Screen **[RENDER] [RMAN] [FILMROL:]**

Pull down **[File] [Import/Export >] [Filmroll]**

The FILMROLL command creates a file for use by AutoShade or 3D Studio, which are Autodesk programs that render three-dimensional models. The file is given the extension FLM. After the filmroll file is created, you can load it into AutoShade or 3D Studio for rendering and animating. This file contains information about all surfaces within the drawing, independent of the current UCS or view, the last view used in the drawing, and data stored in any AutoShade or Autodesk RenderMan blocks placed in the drawing (lights, cameras, scenes, and surface finishes). The filmroll-file format is described in more detail in the *AutoShade User Guide*.

Prompts and Options

If the FILEDIA variable is set to 0, the FILMROLL command presents the following prompts and options:

- **Enter the filmroll file name < *default*>:**

  You enter a valid name for the file, including a drive and path specification, if necessary. AutoCAD assumes the current drawing's name as the default. The extension FLM is automatically added to the file name.

  After the filmroll file's name is entered, the following messages report the progress of the command:

  ```
  Creating the filmroll file
  Filmroll file created
  ```

If the FILEDIA variable is set to 1, the FILMROLL command presents a dialog box, requesting the name to be given to the filmroll file. You can choose the exact location at which you want the file to be stored by navigating the Directories: and Files: list boxes. Enter a valid file name in the File: edit box and click on the OK button. The filmroll file is created, and AutoCAD displays a message to let you know that the file is created.

Related System Variable

FILEDIA

FILTER

Screen **[EDIT] [next] [SELECT:] [Filters]**

Pull down **[Assist] [Object Filters]**

The FILTER command displays the Entity Selection Filters dialog box (see fig. FILTER.1), and enables you to create filters to aid in creating select sets. FILTER can be used at the Command: prompt to create select sets for later use, or it can be used transparently at a Select objects: prompt to select objects for the current command. FILTER creates a list of properties that an entity must have to be selected. Entity properties include color, linetype, layer, entity type, coordinates, and so forth.

For the FILTER command to work, entity color and linetype must be assigned directly to an entity with the COLOR, LINETYPE, or CHPROP commands. Entities with properties set to BYLAYER are not filtered.

The Entity Selection Filters dialog box is divided into three groups of options: the Entity Selection Filter List Box, the Select Filter group, and the Named Filters group. FILTER enables you to use relational operators (<,>,and !=) and Boolean operators (AND, OR, XOR, and NOT) when defining filters.

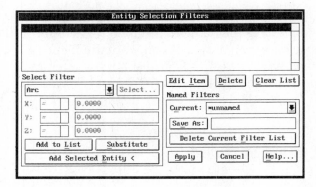

Figure FILTER.1:
The Entity Selection Filters dialog box.

Prompts and Options

- **Select Objects:**

    You select the objects to which you want to apply the filter. This prompt appears after you click on **A**pply in the Entity Selection Filters dialog box.

You can use the following options with the FILTER command.

- **Edit Item.** This option moves the filter highlighted in the Filters List Box to the Select Filter group for editing.
- **Delete.** This option deletes the filter highlighted in the Filters List Box.

- **Clear List**. This option deletes all of the filters in the Filters List Box.

- **Select Filter Drop-down list box**. This option displays a list of all of the filter types available. If you are editing an existing filter, this option shows the current filter's type.

- **Select**. This option displays a dialog box with all the available items of the filter type being edited. Valid types for the select are Xdata ID, Block Name, Color, Dimension Style, Layer, Linetype, or Text Style Name.

- **X:** This option displays the relational operators from which you can choose. The relational operators are =, !=, <, <=, >, >=, *. X displays an X value in the edit box when working with coordinates, such as the starting point of a line. X displays the selected attribute when working with types such as the color of layer.

- **Y:** Y displays the relational operators from which you can choose. The relational operators are =, !=, <, <=, >, >=, *. This option displays a Y value in the edit box when working with coordinates.

- **Z:** Z displays the relational operators from which you can choose. The relational operators are =, !=, <, <=, >, >=, *. This option displays a Z value in the edit box when working with coordinates.

- **Add to List**. This option adds the current Select Filter settings to the Filters list box above the highlighted filter.

- **Substitute**. This option replaces the filter highlighted in the Filter List Box with the Select Filter settings.

- **Add Selected Entity**. This option adds the properties of a selected entity to the Filter List Box.

- **Current**. This option displays a drop-down list box of the available named filter lists.

- **Save as**. This option saves the current set of filters in the Filter List Box to the name entered in the Save As edit box. This creates a named filter list.

- **Delete Current Filter List**. This option deletes the current filter from the list of available named filters.

- **Apply**. This option exits the Entity Selection Filters dialog box, and performs the filter on all items you select.

729

Example

The following example uses FILTER transparently to select entities to
ERASE. See figure FILTER.2.

```
Command: ERASE ↵
Select Objects: 'FILTER ↵
```
Click on the Select Filter *pop-up list*
Select Color
Click on Select
Type **Blue** *or* **5** *and click on* OK
Click on the X: *pop-up list and select* !=
Click on Add to List
Click on Add selected Entity *and pick the line at* ①
Highlight Color = BYLAYER *in the Filters List Box*
Click on Delete
Highlight Line Start *and click on* Edit Item
Set the X: *and* Y: *pop-up lists to* >= *and click on* Substitute
Delete the Line End *filter*
Delete the Normal Vector *filter*
Type **FILTER1** *in the* Save As *edit box and click on* Save As
Click on Apply *and select all of the entities*
```
6 found
4 were filtered out
Select objects: ↵
```

Once an item is selected using a filter, you can change the
filter without affecting the selected entities.

Related Command

SELECT

FINISH

Pull down **[Render] [Finishes]**

Screen **[RENDER] [FINISH]**

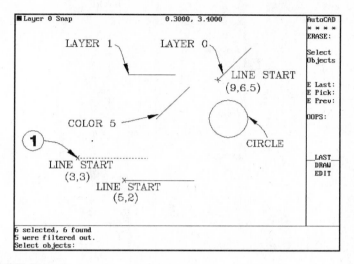

Figure FILTER.2:
Objects selected by using the FILTER command.

The FINISH command enables you to assign and control surface-finish characteristics of three-dimensional objects for rendering. The surface-finish characteristics you can control with the FINISH command are name, color, ambiance, diffusion, shininess, and roughness. The FINISH command also enables you to share finishes between drawings with the import and export options.

A finish is assigned to an object in one of two ways. The first way is to assign a finish directly to an object. The second way assigns the finish to an AutoCAD Color Index (ACI). All objects with the same ACI share the same finish.

The FINISH command has four dialog boxes. The dialog boxes are Finishes, New/Modify Finish, Import Preset Finish, and Attach by AutoCAD Color Index.

Prompts and Options

The Finishes dialog box is the main dialog box for the FINISH command; all other FINISH dialog boxes and options are accessed through this dialog box. The Finishes dialog box is shown in figure FINISH.1.

Figure FINISH.1:
The Finishes dialog box.

The Finishes Dialog Box

- **Finishes.** The Finishes list box shows the currently defined finishes. A period or a number appears after the name of the finish in the list box. The number is an AutoCAD Color Index (ACI). Finishes with an ACI number after them are attached to that ACI, and all objects with that ACI share the attached finish.

  The *GLOBAL* finish is the default finish template. If you want to define several new finishes with common values for specific finish characteristics, set the *GLOBAL* finish to the common values shared between finishes. All new finishes will have the values defined in the *GLOBAL* finish.

  To modify, delete, export, or attach a finish, first highlight it in the Finishes list box and then pick the appropriate button.

- **New.** The New button displays the New Finish dialog box in which you can define a new finish. The *GLOBAL* finish defines the default characteristics for new finishes. The New Finish and the Modify Finish dialog boxes are identical in appearance and features.

- **Modify.** The Modify button displays the Modify Finish dialog box in which you can change the characteristics of a finish. Highlight the finish you want to modify in the Finishes list box, then click on the Modify button.

- **Delete**. The **D**elete button deletes a highlighted finish from the list of defined finishes.

- **Import**. The **I**mport button displays the Import Preset Finish dialog box, enabling you to select a predefined finish from a list box for import into the current drawing. You can also preview the finish before importing it by highlighting a finish and then clicking on the Preview Finish icon. The predefined finishes are stored in the NULLSURF.SP3 file.

- **Export**. The E**x**port button writes the highlighted finish to the NULLSURF.SP3 file. Only exported finishes can be imported into other drawings.

 Currently, AutoCAD does not offer a way to delete a preset finish from within the AutoCAD program. However, the NULLSURF.SP3 file is an ASCII text file, and it can be modified with any ASCII text editor. Use your text editor to delete any unwanted finishes.

- **Pick**. The **P**ick button enables you to pick the finishes block in your drawing to modify, delete, export, or attach. The Finishes dialog box disappears momentarily to let you pick the block, and reappears after you pick, highlighting the finish name in the Finishes list box.

- **Entities**. The **E**ntities button in the Attach group assigns a highlighted finish to a specific entity. When the Finishes dialog box disappears, pick the object to assign the finish.

- **ACI**. The **A**CI button in the Attach group displays the Attach by AutoCAD Color Index dialog box, enabling you to assign a highlighted finish to an AutoCAD Color Index (ACI). The ACI is the same as the AutoCAD color number. All objects that have the same ACI will also have the same finish.

  The color of the finish can be set independently from the actual entity color. This means that you do not need to know the rendering color at the time the object is drawn, and you do not need a display device that is capable of displaying all AutoCAD colors in order to draw objects that will be rendered later.

The ACI method for attaching a finish is more efficient when there are many objects sharing the same finish because you do not have to pick each object requiring the same finish.

To assign a color to an ACI, highlight a finish in the Finishes dialog box, and then click on ACI. When the Attach by AutoCAD Color Index dialog appears, pick an index number. The ACI that you pick will be removed from the list; therefore, it cannot be used more than once.

New and Modify Finish Dialog Boxes

Finish characteristics are set in the New and Modify Finish dialog boxes. You can name a finish, change the name of a finish, specify a specific color for the finish, alter a finish's settings, or preview a finish. Both the New Finish and Modify Finish dialog boxes are explained here because their features are identical. The Modify Finish dialog box is shown in figure FINISH.2.

Figure FINISH.2:
The Modify Finish dialog box.

- **Finish Name:** The Finish **N**ame edit box is used to assign or alter the name of a finish. You cannot change the name of the *GLOBAL* finish. The name of the finish is limited to eight characters.

- **Use Entity Color.** The Use **E**ntity Color button in the Color group causes objects to be rendered with the color of the entities in the AutoCAD drawing. When a finish uses the entity's color, Current Color in the color group will display <entity color>.

- **Set Color.** The Set **C**olor button in the Color group displays the color dialog box, allowing you to explicitly specify the color of a finish. The explicit color setting overrides the entity color. You can set the color numerically by specifying the color by red, green, and blue (RGB) values or hue, luminance, and saturation (HLS) values. You also can set the color visually by picking the color from the color wheel. Current Color in the Color group displays the RGB or HLS values of the specified color.

- **Ambient:** The **A**mbient edit box in the Settings group adjusts the amount of ambient light that is reflected by a finish. *Ambient light* is light that does not have a source or direction and illuminates everything evenly. Values must range from zero to one.

- **Diffuse:** The **D**iffuse edit box in the Settings group specifies the amount of light hitting an object that is dispersed in all directions by a finish. Values must range from zero to one.

- **Specular:** The **S**pecular edit box in the Settings group specifies the shininess of a finish. The shinier a finish is, the more pronounced the highlights become. Values must range from zero to one.

- **Roughness:** The **R**oughness edit box in the Settings group specifies the size of the specular highlight. The roughness setting will only have an effect if Specular is greater than zero. Values must range from 0 to one.

- **Preview Finish.** The **P**review Finish button in the Preview group shows you the approximate effects of the settings and color characteristics. You can also click on the Preview Finish icon to preview the finish.

735

Example

This example of the FINISH command uses a 3D torus and a single point light to create and apply a gold finish to the torus, as in figure FINISH.3.

Choose Render, *then* Finish
Click on **N**ew, *and then in the* Finish **N**ame *edit box, enter* **GOLD**
Click on Set **C**olor *in the* Color *group*
In the Color *dialog box, set* Red *to 1,* Green *to .83, and* Blue *to 0, and then click on* OK
Set **A**mbient *to .40,* **D**iffuse *to .53,* **S**pecular *to .93, and* **R**oughness *to .02*
Click on the preview finish icon
Note the effects of the settings on the sphere. The actual finish will appear slightly different, depending on lighting conditions.

Click on OK
```
Enter New Finish location <current>:
```
Pick any point
Click on Entities *in the Attach group*
```
Gathering objects...
Select objects to attach "GOLD" to:
```
Pick the torus
```
1 found
Select objects: ↵
Updating drawing...done.
```
Click on OK in the Finishes dialog box
Use the RENDER command to render the torus and view the new finish

Related Commands

LIGHT
RPREF

GIFIN

R12

The GIFIN command imports a Graphics Interchange Format raster file into AutoCAD. AutoCAD scans the raster image and creates a block consisting of a rectangular colored solid for each pixel in the GIF file. Once a raster image is imported into AutoCAD, you can trace over the raster image with AutoCAD geometry to create an AutoCAD drawing of the raster image. When you are through, you can erase the raster image. Raster images can be scaled, mirrored, and rotated like regular entities.

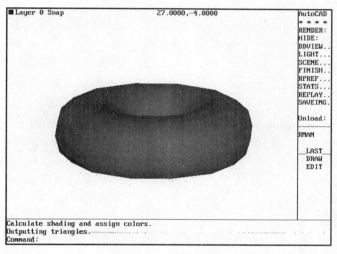

Figure FINISH.3:
The rendered torus with a gold finish.

 Do not explode the block representation of a raster file. If you do, the resulting entities will use large quantities of disk space and memory.

 The system variable GRIPBLOCK should be set to 0 to avoid highlighting all the solid entities in the block.

Prompts and Options

- `GIF file name:`

  At this prompt, you enter the name of the GIF file you want to import (you do not need to include the extension).

- **Insertion point <0,0,0>:**

  At this prompt, you enter the X, Y, and Z coordinates or pick the insertion point for the raster file.

- **Scale Factor:**

  You enter a number or drag the crosshairs to scale the raster file from the insertion point.

- **New length:**

  If you press Enter at the Scale Factor prompt, you will be prompted to pick a point to specify the scale factor.

The following options actually function as separate commands that control how a raster file will be imported. (These same options are also available under the PCXIN and TIFIN commands.)

- **RIASPECT.** You enter a real number to control the aspect ratio of the raster image.

 To display VGA or MCGA images in 320×200 mode, use an RIASPECT of 0.8333.

- **RIBACKG.** This command sets the background color of the raster image. Areas of the raster image that are the same color as RIBACKG are not converted to solid entities in a block.

 To reduce the size of an imported image, set RIBACKG to the most common color in your raster image.

- **RIEDGE.** RIEDGE controls the amount of the image imported. Enter **0** (the default) to disable edge detection; enter **1** to **255** to increase edge detection. The higher the RIEDGE number, the more prominent an image must be to be imported.

 Use RIEDGE to import just the edges of an image if you want to trace over it with vectors.

- **RIGAMUT.** RIGAMUT controls the number of colors that are imported from a raster image. The value reflects the number of colors starting with 0 (black) through 256. If you enter **3**, you import the black, red, and yellow areas of the raster file. Use RIEDGE and RITHRESH to control importing on a monochrome display.
- **RIGREY.** If RIGREY is set to a non-zero number, the raster file is imported in shades of grey. The default is 0.
- **RITHRESH.** RITHRESH controls the amount of raster image imported based on the brightness of the image area. The default is 0. Enter a number to import only pixels with a brightness over the number.

Example

The following example imports a GIF file called TEST.GIF into AutoCAD at 3,3,0.

```
Command: GIFIN ↵
GIF file name: TEST ↵
Insertion point <0,0,0>: 3,3,0 ↵
Scale factor: 2 ↵
```

Related Commands

PCXIN
TIFFIN

Related System Variable

GRIPBLOCK

GRAPHSCR

Enter **GRAPHSCR** *or* **'GRAPHSCR**

The GRAPHSCR command switches a single-screen AutoCAD system from the text screen to the graphics screen. On systems with windowing environments, the switch is between the graphics window and the text window. You can press F1 to switch between the two types of screen display. This command has the opposite effect of the TEXTSCR command. Neither of these commands affects an AutoCAD system with dual screens. The GRAPHSCR command often is used to return to the drawing editor after commands such as LIST, STATUS, TIME, or TYPE are invoked. The GRAPHSCR command can be used transparently.

Related Command

TEXTSCR

Related System Variable

SCREENMODE

GRID

Screen   [SETTINGS] [GRID:]

The GRID command displays a rectangular array of reference points, which are aligned with the current UCS. You can turn the grid on or off by pressing F7 or Ctrl-G. You can change the grid's spacing in both axes, set the spacing so that it is equal to the current Snap increment, and adjust the grid-aspect ratio for special needs (such as isometric drafting). You also can turn the grid on and off and alter its appearance for each viewport. The grid is a visual tool on the display and, therefore, is not plotted.

Prompts and Options

- Grid spacing(X) or ON/OFF/Snap/Aspect <0.0000>:

  The default option is to enter a number at this prompt. AutoCAD sets the grid spacing to that number of drawing units. If you enter a number followed by an **X**, the grid spacing is adjusted to a multiple of the current snap spacing. If you set the snap, for example, to a spacing of one drawing unit, you can display a grid point at every 10 snap points by entering **10X**. If the grid is turned on but cannot be seen because the spacing between dots is not great enough, you see the following prompt: Grid too dense to display.

On and Off. The On and Off options are used to set the display of the grid. The most recent settings for spacing and aspect are used. You can toggle the grid on and off by pressing Ctrl-G or F7.

Snap. The Snap option sets the grid spacing to the current snap-increment value.

Aspect. The Aspect option enables you to display a grid that has different X and Y spacing. This feature is detailed in the following example.

Example

In this example, a grid is displayed with an X (horizontal) spacing value of .5 drawing units and a Y (vertical) spacing of 1 drawing unit. The grid that AutoCAD draws is shown in figure GRID.1.

```
Command: GRID ↵
Grid spacing(x) or ON/OFF/Snap/Aspect <0.0000>: A ↵
Horizontal spacing(x) <0.0000>: .5 ↵
Vertical spacing(x) <0.0000>: 1 ↵
```

Related Commands

DDRMODES
LIMITS
SNAP

Related System Variables

GRIDMODE
GRIDUNIT

741

```
■Layer 0 Snap                        7.0000,4.0000
                                                              AutoCAD
                                                              * * * *
                                                              GRID:

                                                              grd=snap

                                                              ON
                                                              OFF
                                                              Aspect


                                                              DrawMode
                                                              Dialogue
                                                              ...

                                                              LAST
                                                              DRAW
                                                              EDIT



Horizontal spacing(X) <0.0000>: .5
Vertical spacing(X) <0.0000>: 1
Command:
```

Figure GRID.1:
The grid set so that the X and Y aspects have different values.

HANDLES

Screen   **[SETTINGS] [HANDLES:]**

The HANDLES command enables and disables the assigning of entity handles. When an entity is added to a drawing, it is given an entity name and, if handles are enabled, it is given a unique entity identifier called an *entity handle*. The entity names change from session to session in the drawing editor, but the entity handle always remains the same. This ensures continuity between entities within the drawing editor and external programs that reference them.

Entity handles are used by external programs to directly access drawing entities. When a program needs information about an entity, it can use the entity handle to refer to the entity state. The PTEXT AutoLISP program, which comes with Release 12, uses entity handles to keep track of the correct text entities as it performs text entry and editing.

Prompts and Options

- **ON/DESTROY:**

  The only two options are to turn on the entity handles or to destroy all the handles that are associated with existing entities. At this prompt, type the entire keyword **On** or **Destroy**. The Destroy process also causes AutoCAD to discontinue assigning handles to new entities.

- **Proceed with handle destruction <NO>:**

  Due to the severity of destroying entity handles, AutoCAD displays a prompt to confirm your intention. You can type **No** or press Enter to abort the handle-destruction process; otherwise, enter the key phrase shown to complete the destruction of the entity handles. The *key phrase* is one of five possible phrases that is randomly chosen to complete the destruction process. After you correctly type in the key phrase, all handles are removed from the drawing database.

Example

The following example shows how to destroy the entity handles within a drawing. The warning text and key phrase are shown in figure HANDLE.1.

```
Command: HANDLES ↵
ON/DESTROY: DESTROY ↵
Proceed with handle destruction <NO>: DESTROY HANDLES ↵
```

Related System Variable

HANDLES

HATCH

Screen **[DRAW] [HATCH:]**

Pull down **[Draw] [Hatch]**

```
***** WARNING *****

Completing this command will destroy ALL
database handle information in the drawing.
Once destroyed, links into the drawing from
external database files cannot be made.

If you really want to destroy the database
handle information, please confirm this by
entering 'GO AHEAD' to proceed or 'NO'
to abort the command.

Proceed with handle destruction <NO>: GO AHEAD
Database handles removed.

Command:
```

Figure HANDLE.1:
The warning message and key phrase for entity-handle destruction.

The HATCH command fills areas of your drawing with patterns. In the crosshatching process, you select a boundary that AutoCAD fills with the pattern you specify. The resulting hatch region is saved as an unnamed block definition that can be moved, copied, colored, and manipulated in much the same manner as other blocks. Hatches, like all other AutoCAD 2D entities, can be created in any definable construction plane. This versatility makes hatches very desirable for adding textures to three-dimensional models such as buildings.

AutoCAD offers more than 50 predefined hatch patterns in the file ACAD.PAT. These patterns include brick, stone, wood, grass, and other textures. The HATCH command also enables you to create simple patterns directly at the Command: prompt.

Prompts and Options

- `Pattern (? or name/U,style)< `*`default`*`>:`

  At this prompt, you enter a pattern name or type **?** to see a list of available patterns. The default is the current pattern. If no pattern has yet been used, you can enter its name with an optional style, or you can use the U option to create a user-defined pattern. Hatch-pattern styles are explained later in this section.

The specified hatch pattern must be defined in the file ACAD.PAT or stored in a file with the pattern name and a PAT extension. If you want to use a hatch pattern named GLASS, for example, it must be in the ACAD.PAT file or in a file named GLASS.PAT.

- **Pattern(s) to list <*>:**

  You enter the names of patterns you want to list, using wild cards if desired. All hatch-pattern definitions stored in the ACAD.PAT file are listed. This option does not list patterns that are defined in other files.

  To view examples of the supplied hatch patterns, use the new BHATCH command.

- **Angle for crosshatch lines <0>:**

  The U option, for defining a user-specific hatch pattern, presents this prompt. This pattern is a simple repeating-line pattern with a set distance between each line. You can enter a value for the pattern angle or pick two points that describe the angle of the pattern.

- **Spacing between lines <1>:**

  You enter the number of drawing units for the spacing between each line in the user-defined pattern.

- **Double hatch area? <N>:**

  The user-defined hatch is a single series of repeating lines. This option adds another set of repeating lines drawn perpendicular to the first set of lines using the same spacing.

- **Scale for pattern <1>:**

  This prompt is displayed after you enter a valid pattern name at the first HATCH command prompt. You enter a scale factor to be applied to the pattern definition to enlarge or reduce the hatch drawn.

- **Angle for pattern <0>:**

  At this prompt, you enter an angle to rotate the pattern. Note that some hatch patterns are angled by default.

- **Select objects:**

  You select the entities to form the hatch boundary. The boundary forms the limits within which the pattern will be created. The boundary objects chosen affect the accuracy of the hatching. If the entities do not form a closed area (their endpoints do not meet), the hatch may be incomplete (see fig. HATCH.1).

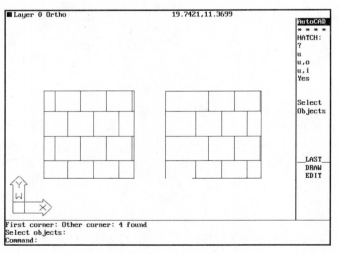

Figure HATCH.1:
Incomplete and complete boundaries for hatch patterns.

To hatch a region bounded by entities that extend beyond the desired area, you can use the PLINE command to create a temporary hatch boundary. Hatch the closed polyline, and then delete it. The hatch block remains within the drawing.

To re-create the boundary for a hatch pattern semi-automatically, use the new BPOLY command. To create boundaries, preview hatches, and better control hatching, use the BHATCH command.

Hatching Styles

Hatching styles, which you specify by placing a comma and the style letter after the pattern name, affect the manner in which hatching occurs. The hatch boundary forms the limits within which the hatch will fill. If entities are within the outermost boundary that is chosen, and those entities form another boundary, the hatching stops at that inner boundary. Hatch styles determine how AutoCAD regards these inner boundaries.

The first hatch style, N (*N*ormal), tells the HATCH command that all boundaries found are valid. AutoCAD fills every other closed region found within the selected boundary objects. This style has the same effect as using no style name at all. The second style type, O (fill *Outer*most), fills only the area defined by the outermost set of boundaries. The final hatch style, I (ignore *I*nternal boundaries), completely fills the area defined by the outermost boundary, regardless of any other possible boundaries found.

Finally, different entities are hatched differently by the HATCH command. Text, attributes, and shape entities have a rectangular boundary that follows the outline of the letters or the shape. AutoCAD recognizes solids and trace entities, and does not perform hatching within their boundaries. Blocks are hatched according to the arrangement of entities within the blocks. If the entities form boundaries, those boundaries are treated as normal entity boundaries. Paper-space viewports are considered valid boundaries, so the HATCH command fills the viewport with the selected pattern.

Example

This example shows how to use the HATCH command to fill in the wall shown in figure HATCH.2.

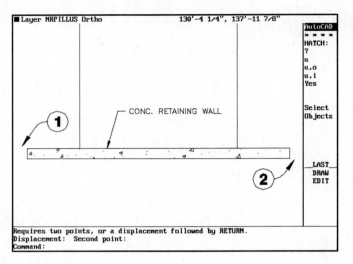

Figure HATCH.2:
Filling a wall with the concrete hatch pattern.

```
Command: HATCH ↵
Pattern (? or name/U,style): AR-CONC ↵
Scale for pattern <1>: 5 ↵
Angle for pattern <0>: ↵
Select objects: W ↵
First corner: Pick point at ①
Second corner: Pick point at ②
```

Related Commands

BHATCH
BPOLY

Related System Variables

HPANG
HPDOUBLE
HPNAME
HPSCALE

HPSPACE
SNAPBASE

HELP

Screen **[INQUIRY] [HELP:]**

Screen **[* * * *] [HELP]**

Pull down **[Assist] [Help!]**

The HELP command provides information on the commands available within the AutoCAD program. You can issue the HELP command transparently by preceding the command with an apostrophe ('**HELP**). A question mark (**?**) also invokes help. If HELP is used transparently, it provides information about the command that is currently in process.

When you enter **HELP** at the Command: prompt, AutoCAD displays the Help dialog box shown in figure HELP.1. This dialog box displays help for the current command in use, as well as providing a comprehensive index from which you can select other commands. The Help information is cross-referenced to the *AutoCAD Reference Manual*.

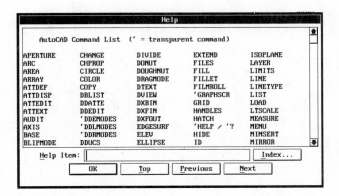

Figure HELP.1:
The AutoCAD Help dialog box.

749

Prompts and Options

The HELP command dialog box has an edit box in which you can type the particular command about which you want information. In addition to standard dialog-box buttons, the dialog box also contains buttons that perform the following functions:

- **Index.** This button displays an alphabetized list of all items about which you may request help. If you pick one of the items, its help information will be displayed.
- **Top.** This button displays lists of AutoCAD commands and system variables.
- **Previous.** This button displays the previous item of help information in relation to the information shown in the dialog box.
- **Next.** This button displays the next item of help information in relation to the information shown in the dialog box.

HIDE

Screen   **[DISPLAY] [HIDE:]**

Pull down   **[Render] [Hide]**

The HIDE command temporarily suppresses the display of any lines or edges that are hidden behind a surface. A *surface* can be a circle, solid, trace, wide polyline, polygon mesh, extruded edge, or 3D face. The HIDE command gives an opaque top and bottom face to extruded circles, solids, traces, and wide polylines. This command typically is used to present a three-dimensional model. HIDE also is useful for verifying the accuracy of a model's surfaces.

The command is completely automatic unless issued from the screen or pull-down menus, in which case you are prompted to confirm the hide operation. A hidden-line removal may take time, depending on the complexity of the model. You can reduce this time by using the ZOOM command to fill the display with only the desired geometry. AutoCAD hides only the information that appears within the boundaries of the current display. The HIDE command also works more quickly if un-needed layers are frozen.

After hidden lines are removed, the entire drawing can be displayed only after a regeneration of the drawing, caused by using any display command. To save a hidden-line view for later display, use the MSLIDE command.

The HIDE command affects only the current viewport, and you can hide only one viewport at a time. Also, only entities on layers that are turned on and thawed will be used for hidden-line removal. Displays made by the command are lost after the drawing session ends or the viewport is regenerated. The SHADE command performs similar results by filling the faces with color. The SHADE command is quicker than the HIDE command, but it is not always as accurate. The HIDE command does not affect plotting. The PLOT command includes an option for hiding entities.

Example

This example demonstrates the effects of the HIDE command in two viewports. Figure HIDE.1 shows the objects in the right-hand viewport after the HIDE command .

```
Command: HIDE ↵
Regenerating Drawing.
Hiding lines: done nn%
Removing Hidden Lines: xxx
```

Related Commands

   RENDER
   SHADE

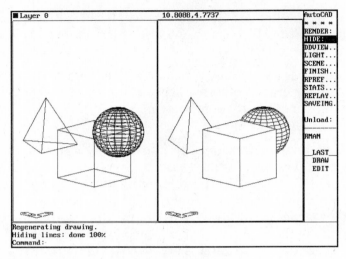

Figure HIDE.1:
The right viewport displays entities of the left viewport after hidden lines are removed.

ID

Screen   **[INQUIRY] [ID:]**

Pull down   **[Assist] [Inquiry >] [ID Point]**

The ID command identifies the absolute X,Y,Z coordinates of a single point within 3D space. You pick a point within the drawing editor, and AutoCAD displays the point's coordinates. The ID command is useful for finding the location of points along entities that do not lie parallel to the WCS.

R12   You can execute the ID command transparently by preceding the command name with an apostrophe ('**ID**).

Prompts and Options

- **Point:**

  You specify a point in the drawing editor for which you want to retrieve the coordinates. You can use object snap overrides or any other method of point selection.

Example

This example illustrates how to use the ID command. The ID command displays the coordinates of the point shown in figure ID.1.

```
Command: ID ↵
Point: INT of Pick point ①
```

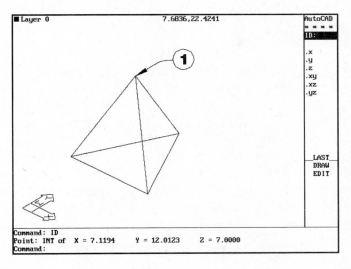

Figure ID.1:
Coordinates retrieved by the ID command.

Related System Variable

LASTPOINT

IGESIN

Screen **[UTILITY] [IGES] [IGESIN:]**

Pull down **[File] [Import/Export >] [IGES In]**

The IGESIN command imports drawing information from a file that conforms to the *Initial Graphics Exchange Specification* (IGES). IGES enables the accurate exchange of data between CAD systems that support the IGES specification. IGES is an international standard that is used by many larger CAD systems as well as PC-based CAD systems, such as AutoCAD. When you register your AutoCAD software, you receive a copy of the current IGES Interface Specification, which details the features of AutoCAD which are supported in the most recent release of the IGES specification.

Prompts and Options

By default, IGESIN displays a dialog box for you to select the IGES file you want to import. If the FILEDIA variable is set to 0, you will instead receive the `File name:` prompt, at which you enter the path and file name of a valid IGES file. The Select IGES File dialog box (see fig. IGESIN.1) initially displays the names of any files with an IGS extension. If the file you want to import is in the list, you can highlight it and click on the OK button. You also can navigate the Directories list box if the file is in a different drive or directory. In addition to the standard OK, Help, and Cancel buttons, the dialog box presents the following buttons:

- **Type it.** This dialog box button produces a prompt in the AutoCAD command line area for you to manually enter the name of the IGES import file.
- **Default.** This button resets the default options such as file-name pattern and directory location if they have been changed.

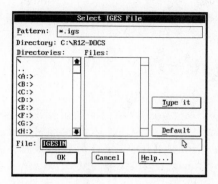

Figure IGESIN.1:
The dialog box for importing an IGES file.

Related Commands

DXFIN
DXFOUR
IGESOUT

Related System Variable

FILEDIA

IGESOUT

Screen　**[UTILITY] [IGES] [IGESOUT:]**

Pull down　**[File] [Import/Export >] [IGES Out]**

The IGESOUT command exports AutoCAD drawing information to a file that conforms to the Initial Graphics Exchange Specification. Other CAD programs that support the IGES interface then can read in the entity information created by AutoCAD. When you register your AutoCAD software, you receive a copy of the current IGES Interface

Specification that details which features of AutoCAD are supported in the most recent release of the IGES specification.

Prompts and Options

By default, the IGESOUT command displays a dialog box that enables you to name the IGES file you want to create. If the FILEDIA variable is set to 0, you instead see the `File name:` prompt, on which you enter a valid file name. The Create IGES File dialog box (see fig. IGESOUT.1) initially displays the name of the current drawing file. To use this name for the export file, click on the OK button. You may also navigate the Directories list box if you want to store the file in a different drive or directory. In addition to the standard OK, Help, and Cancel buttons, the dialog box has the following buttons:

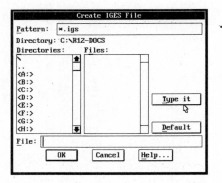

Figure IGESOUT.1:
The dialog box for exporting an IGES file.

- **Type it.** This dialog box button produces a prompt in the AutoCAD command line area for you to enter the name of the IGES export file.
- **Default.** This button resets the default options such as file-name pattern and directory location if they have been changed.

Related Commands

DXFIN
DXFOUT
IGESIN

Related System Variable

FILEDIA

INSERT

Screen   **[DRAW] [INSERT:]**

Screen   **[BLOCKS] [INSERT:]**

Pull down   **[Draw] [Insert]**

The INSERT command places blocks created with the BLOCK command into the current drawing. INSERT enables you to specify the way blocks are located, scaled, and rotated when added to your drawing. If a block name that you specify is not currently defined in the drawing, INSERT attempts to load the block from disk.

 For a more intuitive method of inserting blocks, use the DDINSERT command.

Prompts and Options

- **Block name (or ?) <default>:**

  At this prompt, you enter a block name to insert, or accept the default name of the last block inserted. If the name you supply is not a block defined in the current drawing, the program attempts to find a file with a matching name along the AutoCAD search path. If no match is found, the command is aborted, and you receive an error message. To see a list of the blocks defined in the current drawing, enter a question mark at this prompt. If you want to enter a drawing file from disk, enter a tilde (~) to display the Select File dialog box.

 If you type an asterisk before the name of the block to insert, AutoCAD automatically explodes the block when it places the block into your drawing.

- **Insertion point:**

  You specify an insertion point for the block. This *insertion point* is used to place, scale, and rotate the block in the drawing editor.

  Until you specify a point for the block you insert, the block is highlighted so you can drag it on-screen and have an idea of how the block will look when placed. If you know in advance the various insertion parameters (X, Y, and Z scales and rotation), you can preset the parameters so that the highlighted image is more accurate before being inserted. You can enter these preset parameters at this prompt before you choose the insertion point. A description of each parameter option follows:

- **Scale**. The Scale option presets the scale in each axis (X, Y, and Z) to the same value. The highlighted block is updated, and then you can choose its insertion point. After the block is located in the drawing, you are not prompted to enter a value for the scale factors.

- **Xscale.** The Xscale option presets the scale in the X axis only. Insertion then proceeds as with Pscale (see note following).

- **Yscale.** The Yscale option presets the scale in the Y axis only. Insertion then proceeds as with Pscale.

- **Zscale--.** The Zscale option presets the scale in the Z axis only. Insertion then proceeds as with Pscale.

- **Rotate.** The Rotate option presets the block rotation value. The highlighted block is updated, and insertion can proceed. After the block is located, this angle is used, and you are not prompted to supply this value.

The following five options enable you to preset the high-lighted block's values, but then you must answer the INSERT command's usual prompts about scale factors and rotation.

- **Pscale.** The Pscale option presets all three axes' scales, but after the block is located, you still are prompted for a block scaling factor.
- **Pxscale.** The Pxscale option presets the block's X-axis scale factor, but after the block is located, you still are prompted for the scale along this axis.
- **Pyscale.** The Pyscale option presets the block's Y-axis scale factor, but after the block is located, you still are prompted for the scale along this axis.
- **Pzscale.** The Pzscale option presets the block's Z-axis scale factor, but after the block is located, you still are prompted for the scale along this axis.
- **Protate.** The Protate option presets the highlighted block's rotation. After the block is located in the drawing editor, you again are prompted for a final rotation angle.
- **X scale factor <1>/Corner/XYZ:**

  You enter a number for the X-scale factor, accept the default value, or enter an option. You receive this prompt when none of the scale factors is preset. A positive scale factor creates an inserted block in the same orientation as the original block definition. If you enter a negative value, the block appears mirrored about the Y axis. You also can specify a scale factor by dragging your pointing device or by using the Corner option. For either of these choices, the distance between the two specified points is used as the scale factor for both the X and Y axes.
- **Y scale factor (default=X):**

  You enter a number for the Y-scale factor or accept the default. By default, this value is the same as the X-scale factor.
- **Rotation angle <0>:**

  At this prompt, you enter a number for the rotation angle to be used when inserting the block. You can specify a point, either by coordinates or by dragging the pointing device, and the angle between this point and the insertion point will be used as the rotation angle.

- **X scale factor <1>/Corner:**

  This prompt appears if you use the XYZ option. You will be prompted for scale factors for each of the three axes, beginning with the X axis. The corner option works the same as in the first prompt.

- **Y scale factor (default=X):**

  This second prompt of the XYZ option enables you to specify a scale factor for the Y axis. By default, this value is set to the same scale as the one for the X axis.

- **Z scale factor (default=X):**

  This last prompt of the XYZ option enables you to specify a scale factor for the Z axis. By default, this value is set to the same scale as that for the X axis.

To change the scale factors of a block after it is inserted, use the DDMODIFY command. You cannot use the EXPLODE command to explode blocks with unequal X, Y, and Z scale factors.

Example

The following example uses the INSERT command to insert a block of a chair as illustrated in figure INSERT.1. This exercise demonstrates the effects that uneven scale factors can have upon a block.

```
Command: INSERT ↵
Block name (or ?): CHAIR ↵
Insertion point: Pick point ①
X scale factor <1> / Corner / XYZ: ↵
Y scale factor (default=X): ↵
Rotation angle <0>: ↵
Command: INSERT ↵
Block name (or ?): CHAIR ↵
```

```
Insertion point: Pick point ②
X scale factor <1> / Corner / XYZ: 3 ↵
Y scale factor (default=X): 1 ↵
Rotation angle <0>: 315 ↵
```

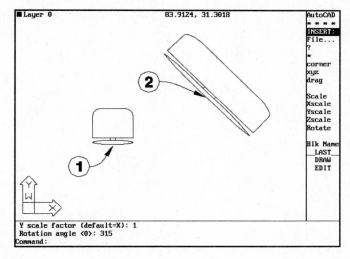

Figure INSERT.1:
A chair block, inserted with various scaling and rotation factors.

Related Commands

> **DDINSERT**
> **DDMODIFY**
> **EXPLODE**
> **MINSERT**
> **XREF**

Related System Variables

> **INSBASE**
> **INSNAME**

ISOPLANE

The ISOPLANE command is used in conjunction with the STYLE option of the SNAP command to create isometric drawings that resemble 3D objects. The ISOPLANE command is a drawing aid (similar to the GRID, SNAP, and ORTHO commands) that enables you to draw in the three isometric drafting planes.

Setting the Style option of the SNAP command to Isometric forces the crosshair cursor to align with the 30-, 90-, and 150-degree axes used in isometric drafting. If Grid mode is turned on, it too will display as isometric. When Ortho mode is on in Isometric mode, lines can be drawn only in the two axes of the current isometric plane.

Figure ISOPLANE.1 demonstrates how a 2D isometric drawing appears to be three-dimensional. The figure contains three distinct isometric planes at 30, 90, and 150 degrees. The ISOPLANE command enables you to specify which plane to work in, and should be used in conjunction with the ORTHO command to restrict drawing to a single plane at one time. When you are drawing in one of the isometric planes, the crosshairs align parallel to that plane.

Use the Ctrl-E control-key sequence to quickly switch between the three isometric planes.

Prompts and Options

- `Left/Top/Right/<Toggle>:`

  The Left option sets the current isometric plane to the left plane (see fig. ISOPLANE.1). After you select this or any other option at this prompt, the crosshairs are rotated to reflect the plane you chose.

  The Right option sets the current isometric plane to the right plane.

  The Top option sets the current isometric plane to the top plane.

Accepting the default option, Toggle, cycles among the left, top, and right isometric planes. If your current plane is top, it is changed to right, and so on. After pressing Enter at the prompt, you return to AutoCAD's `Command:` prompt.

Example

This example demonstrates how to use the ISOPLANE and SNAP commands to prepare to draw in the left isometric plane. The drawing shown in figure ISOPLANE.1 shows the crosshairs aligned to the left plane.

```
Command: SNAP ↵
Snap spacing or ON/OFF/Aspect/Rotate/Style <1.0000>: S ↵
Standard/Isometric <S>: i↵
Vertical spacing <1.0000>: ↵
Command: ISOPLANE ↵
Left/Top/Right/<Toggle>: ↵
Current Isometric plane is: Top
```

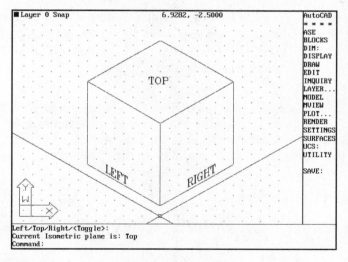

Figure ISOPLANE.1:
A sample of 2D entities that appear to be three-dimensional.

Related Commands

DDRMODES
ELLIPSE
SNAP

Related System Variable

SNAPISOPAIR

LAYER

The LAYER command enables you to control layers used for the drawing, displaying, and plotting of entities. Layers enable you to group similar types of information in a drawing for easier editing and creation. Layers, similar to sheets of mylar used for overlay drafting, ease the burden of keeping track of the various elements in your drawing. The LAYER command enables you to set the color, linetype, and visibility of each layer, make new layers, set the current layer, freeze or thaw layers, or lock and unlock layers.

> **TIP** You also can use the DDLMODES command to modify layer properties. Instead of working from the command line, as the LAYER command works, the DDLMODES command uses a dialog box to display all layers and modify their properties.

Prompts and Options

- `?/Make/Set/New/ON/OFF/Color/Ltype/Freeze/Thaw/`
  `LOck/Unlock:`

  This prompt presents all of the LAYER command's options. The following paragraphs explain each option.

  The ? option lists all of the layers defined within the current drawing. This list contains the full name of the layer, its color and linetype, and its state of visibility. When using this option, you get an additional prompt, `Layer name(s) to list <*>:`, that enables you to specify which layer name(s) you want listed. The default lists all the layers. If you are looking for information about particular layers only, you can type each layer's name, separated by commas, or use wild-card searches to narrow down the layers listed.

- **New current layer <default>:**

  Both the Make and Set options use this prompt. Enter the name of a layer to set as the current layer. The Make option creates a new layer with the name entered and then sets it as the current layer. Set establishes the layer name as the current layer only if that layer already exists. The current layer is where new entities that you draw are placed. These new entities take on the color and linetype characteristics of the layer on which they reside.

- **New layer name(s):**

  The New option prompts you to enter the names of new layers that you want to add to the current drawing. If you want to enter more than one layer name, separate each name with a comma. The layer name can be up to 31 characters in length and can include numbers, letters, and special characters, such as $, -, and _.

- **Layer name(s) to turn Off:**

  The Off option affects the visibility of layers, which governs how they are considered during screen redraws. A layer that is turned off is not visible on-screen, but the layer's entities are calculated during any screen regenerations. To have layers ignored during screen regenerations, use the Freeze option. The Layer command warns you if you attempt to turn off the current layer.

- **Layer name(s) to turn On:**

  Enter the names of layers to turn on. As with the other LAYER options, if you need to turn on more than one layer, separate each layer name with a comma.

- **Color:**

  The Color option is used to assign the color to display entities. Enter a color number or name for layers you specify. Then, at the

`Layer name(s) for color` *number* `<default>:` prompt,
enter the name(s) of the layers you want that color assigned to.
Any entity whose color is set to BYLAYER (the default for new
entities) assumes the color assigned to the layer on which it resides. The color you enter can be any valid color number for your
graphics card or the name of one of the first seven colors: red,
yellow, green, cyan, blue, magenta, or white.

- **`Linetype (or ?) <CONTINUOUS>:`**

  Enter a linetype name to set for layers you specify. This linetype is
  applied to all entities on the specified layers. If you use the ?
  option, a list of the linetypes currently loaded in the current
  drawing is displayed. Any entity whose linetype is set to
  BYLAYER (the default for new entities) assumes the linetype of the
  layer on which it resides. The linetype you enter can be any valid
  linetype defined within the drawing or within the ACAD.LIN file,
  used for storing linetype definitions.

  After you specify a linetype, you must indicate which layers that
  linetype is to be used for at the `Layer name(s) for linetype`
  name `<default>:` prompt. The default sets the current layer to
  the new linetype, but you also can enter other layer names as
  needed. You may need to regenerate the drawing to see the change
  take effect.

- **`Layer name(s) to Freeze:`**

  Enter the name(s) of layers to freeze. *Freezing* a layer is similar to
  turning off a layer, except that entities on frozen layers are not
  calculated during regenerations. Therefore, regenerations can
  proceed faster than with layers that are only turned off. Frozen
  layers also are not displayed, but they can be turned on. Note that,
  unlike the Off option, the current layer cannot be frozen.

- **`Layer name(s) to Thaw:`**

  Enter the name(s) of layers to thaw. *Thawing* a layer reverses the
  freezing process. Layers that have been thawed are not necessarily
  turned on; whether the layers are turned on depends on the
  On/Off state of the layer. If the layer is turned on, you may need
  to perform a regeneration before the thawed entities become
  visible on-screen.

- **`Layer name(s) to Lock:`**

  Enter the name(s) of layers to lock. The locking process prevents any changes to entities on layers designated as locked.

- **`Layer name(s) to Unlock:`**

  Enter the name(s) of layers to unlock. Layers that are currently locked are unlocked, and you can then make changes to the entities that reside upon those layers.

Example

This example uses the LAYER command to change the linetype of the entities on the LINES layer, which is shown in the figure LAYER.1.

```
Command: LAYER ↵
?/Make/Set/New/ON/OFF/Color/Ltype/Freeze/
Thaw/LOck/Unlock: LT ↵
Linetype (or ?) <CONTINUOUS>: HIDDEN ↵
Layer name(s) for linetype HIDDEN
<0>: LINES ↵
?/Make/Set/New/ON/OFF/Color/Ltype/Freeze/
Thaw/LOck/Unlock: ↵
Regenerating drawing.
```

Related Commands

> CHANGE
> COLOR
> DDEMODES
> DDLMODES
> LINETYPE
> REGEN
> REGENALL
> VPLAYER

Related System Variables

> CECOLOR
> CELTYPE

CLAYER
PLINEGEN

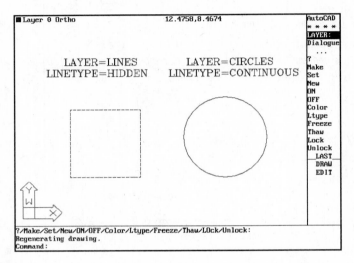

Figure LAYER.1:
Using the LAYER command to set the linetype of a layer.

LIGHT

Screen **[RENDER] [LIGHT]**

Pull down **[Render] [Lights]**

The LIGHT command enables you to specify, place, and control lighting for rendering. The three types of lights you can place anywhere in model space are point, distant, and spot. You also can control the amount of ambient light that shines on all surfaces.

You can control the position and intensity of all types of lighting. However, to control the color of lights and render spotlights, AutoShade Version 2 must be installed and operational.

Prompts and Options

The LIGHT command has four dialog boxes. They are Lights, New Light Type, New and Modify Light, and New Spotlight.

The Lights Dialog Box

The Lights dialog box (see fig. LIGHT.1) is the main dialog box for the LIGHT command. All other LIGHT dialog boxes and options are accessed through this dialog box. You can select the following options from this dialog box:

- **Lights.** The Lights list box shows the names of the lights in the current drawing.

- **New.** The New button displays the New Light Type dialog box, enabling you to select a new light type and add it to a drawing. You can choose one of three types of lights to add to your drawing: point, distant, and spotlight. After a new light type is chosen, the New Light dialog box appears. New lights are positioned at the current viewpoint and, in the case of distant lights and spotlights, are parallel to the current line of sight.

  A *point* light emits beams uniformly in all directions. A point light is analogous to a bare light bulb.

  A *distant* light emits parallel beams from a plane at the light source. A distant light behaves similar to sunlight. Distant lights do not have fall-off parameters.

  A *spot* light emits beams in the shape of a cone originating at the light source. The spread of the beam, as well as other beam parameters, can be changed to alter the characteristics of the spot. Although you can define spotlights with AVE Render (if RMan Prompting is turned on in the Rendering Preferences dialog box), spotlights can be rendered only with AutoShade Version 2 with Autodesk RenderMan.

- **Modify.** The Modify button displays the Modify Light dialog box, enabling you to change parameters of a light highlighted in the

Lights list box. If you double-click on a light name in the Lights list box, the Modify Light dialog box automatically appears, enabling you to edit the selected light.

- **Delete.** The **D**elete button enables you to delete a light from the drawing. Highlight the light you want to delete, and then click on **D**elete.

- **Pick.** The **P**ick button causes the Lights dialog box to disappear, enabling you to pick a light icon to modify from the drawing.

- **Ambient Light.** The **A**mbient Light edit box specifies the amount of background light that shines on all object surfaces. The value range for ambient light is from zero (off) to one (brightest). Use the slider bar to interactively specify a value.

- **None.** The N**o**ne option of the Point Light Fall-off group causes a light's intensity to illuminate all objects uniformly, regardless of the distance from the point-light source. Normally, the intensity of light reaching an object decreases as the distance from the light source increases. This phenomenon is called *fall-off*.

- **Inverse Linear.** The **I**nverse Linear option of the Point Light Fall-off group causes a point light's intensity to fall off inversely to the distance from the light source. This means that an object that is 10 units from a point light source will be illuminated at 1/10 the intensity of the source.

- **Inverse Square.** The Inverse **S**quare option of the Point Light Fall-off group causes a point light's intensity to fall off inversely to the square of the distance from the light source. This means that an object that is 10 units from a point light source will be illuminated at 1/100 the intensity of the source.

The New and Modify Light Dialog Boxes

The New and Modify Light dialog boxes enable you to specify light characteristics. In the New and Modify dialog boxes, you can name or rename a light, position it, set its intensity, alter its color, and control its shadows.

Figure LIGHT.1:
The Lights dialog box.

Because many of the New and Modify Light dialog options are common to all light types, each option that follows applies to all light types. Specific differences are discussed where appropriate. The Modify Point Light dialog box is shown in figure LIGHT.2.

The dialog box offers the following options:

- **Light Name**. The Light **N**ame edit box is used to assign or change the name of a light. Light names are limited to eight characters.

Figure LIGHT.2:
The Modify Point Light dialog box.

- **Intensity**. The Intensity edit box specifies the brightness of the light. Distant lights have a maximum intensity of one because they do not have a fall-off parameter. Use the slider bar to interactively specify a value.

- **Modify**. The Modify button in the Position group allows repositioning of the light. For point lights, you are prompted to enter the light location. For distant lights and spotlights, you are prompted for the light target in addition to the light location. Specify a 3D point or pick a new point.

- **Show**. The Show button in the Position group displays the X, Y, and Z location of the light position (if applicable), and target.

- **Modify Light Color**. The Modify Light Color button displays the Color dialog box and allows you to specify a color for a light. This button is enabled only if RMan Prompting has been turned on in the Rendering Preferences dialog box. You can specify the color of the light by its red, green, and blue (RGB) values; specify hue, luminance, and saturation (HLS) values; or pick the color visually.

- **Depth Map Size**. The Depth Map Size edit box allows you to specify how shadows from lights are rendered in AutoShade Version 2 with Autodesk RenderMan. Enter a value between zero and six. Zero produces no shadows; a value of six produces sharp-edged shadows. Use the slider bar to interactively specify a value.

The following three parameters are for spotlights only:

- **Cone Angle**. The Cone Angle edit box specifies the angle from the spotlight's line of sight to the outer edge of the beam cone. Use the slider bar to interactively specify a value.

- **Cone Delta Angle**. The Cone Delta Angle edit box specifies the angle from the edge of the beam cone to the outer edge of the fall-off cone. This area is also known as the area of rapid decay. Use the slider bar to interactively specify a value.

- **Beam Distribution**. The Beam Distribution edit box specifies the rate of rapid decay fall-off.

Example

The following example uses the LIGHT command to create a new point-light source in the PINS2.DWG that is located in \ACAD\TUTORIAL. If you do not have this drawing, you can install it from your AutoCAD distribution disks by installing the AVE Render tutorial files. Render the PINS2 drawing before and after adding the new light.

Choose Render, *then* Lights
Click on the New *button in the* Lights *dialog box,*
then click on OK *in the* New Light Type *dialog box*
In the Light **N**ame *text box, enter* **P1** ↵
Set Intensity *to 10.00*
Click on Modify *in the* Position *group*
`Enter light location <current>: 4.5,-3` ↵
`Click on OK in the two consecutive dialog boxes`
`to return to the AutoCAD command prompt`

Related CommandPoint

FINISH

LIMITS

`Screen` **[SETTINGS] [LIMITS:]**

`Pull down` **[Settings] [Drawing Limits]**

The LIMITS command defines a rectangular boundary within which you can draw. You can exceed or redefine the boundary at any time. The boundary limits have a lower left corner and an upper right corner in the X-Y plane, but no limit in the Z axis.

The drawing's limits also are used for displaying the extent of the grid when Grid mode is turned on, and as an area specification for plotting. Model space and paper space each have their own drawing limits, and when you issue the ZOOM command's All option, ZOOM displays the drawing's limits or extents, whichever is greater.

Prompts and Options

- **ON/OFF/<Lower left corner><0.0000,0.0000>:**

  The On option turns on limits-checking. While turned on, any coordinate entry that does not fall within the drawing limits is not accepted. If you try to enter coordinates outside of these boundaries, the following message appears:

  **Outside limits.

  Note that this checking is not absolute. For example, you can define a circle whose perimeter exceeds the drawing's limits.

  The Off option disables limits checking. Limits checking is off by default, even after you set the drawing's limits.

  The Lower left corner option is the default and defines the lower left corner of a rectangular area that represents the drawing's limits. Enter a 2D coordinate or pick a point on-screen. The default is 0,0, unless otherwise specified in a prototype drawing.

- **Upper right corner<12.0000,9.0000>:**

  After specifying the lower left corner of the drawing's limits, you are prompted for the upper right corner. This point represents the opposite corner of the rectangular area of the drawing's limits. The default setting is governed by the prototype drawing.

Example

This example demonstrates the effects of setting a drawing's limits with the LIMITS command. The points describing the drawing's limits are shown in figure LIMITS.1.

```
Command: LIMITS ↵
ON/OFF/<Lower left corner><0.0000,0.0000>: Pick ①
Upper right corner<12.0000,9.0000>: Pick ②
```

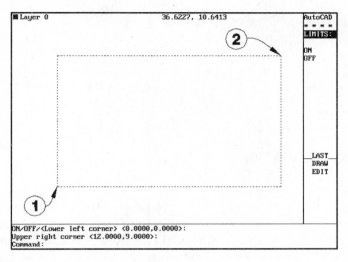

Figure LIMITS.1:
The grid turned on to show the drawing limits.

Related Commands

> GRID
> PLOT
> ZOOM

Related System Variables

> LIMCHECK
> LIMMAX
> LIMMIN

LINE

Screen   **[DRAW] [LINE:]**

Pull down   **[Draw] [Line >]**

The LINE command draws straight lines between two specified points. These points may have any 2D- or 3D-coordinate location. The command repeats, enabling many lines to be created, until you press Enter or type Ctrl-C. After lines have been drawn, you can type **C** to create a closed polygon. You can draw lines at right angles by using Ortho mode. You also can use the TRACE or POLYLINE commands for wide lines.

Prompts and Options

- **From point:**

  Specify a starting point for the line segment. The point may have any X, Y, and Z coordinates and can be preceded with any object-snap overrides or point filters. If you press Enter at this prompt, AutoCAD begins the line by using the endpoint of the last line or arc created.

- **To point:**

  Enter an endpoint for the segment, and a line is drawn. This prompt repeats until you press Enter or Ctrl-C.

- **Close**. Enter **C** at any **To point:** prompt to connect the end of the last line with the beginning of the first line and complete the command. You must have drawn at least two previous lines to use the Close option.

- **Undo**. Enter **U** while within the command to remove the last end-point specified. You can use the Undo option to remove previous line segments back to the initial **From point:** location.

Example

This example shows the simplicity of using the LINE command. The lines drawn are shown in figure LINE.1.

```
Command: LINE ↵
From point: Pick ①
To point: Pick ②
To point: Pick ③
To point: C ↵
```

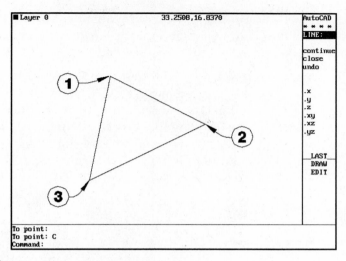

Figure LINE.1:
Simple shape drawn with the LINE command.

Related Commands

    PLINE
    TRACE
    UNDO
    3DPOLY

Related System Variable

    LASTPOINT

LINETYPE

Screen **[SETTINGS] [LINETYP:]**

The LINETYPE command is used to load and list the linetypes available in the current drawing. You also can create new linetypes with this command and chose a new linetype for subsequent entities. The default linetype is BYLAYER, which new entities display in the linetype assigned to the layer on which they are created.

Linetype definitions supplied with AutoCAD are stored in the support file ACAD.LIN and must be loaded into AutoCAD before they can be used in a drawing. Once a linetype is used in the current drawing, its definition is stored with the drawing file. You can define your own linetypes within the AutoCAD drawing editor and store them in ACAD.LIN, save them in a different file with the extension LIN, or modify the ACAD.LIN file directly.

Prompts and Options

- **?/Create/Load/Set:**

  Presents all the choices available with the LINETYPE command. An explanation of each option follows.

- **File to list <ACAD>:**

  When you choose the ? option, the Select Linetype File dialog box appears. By default, the ACAD.LIN file is highlighted. Pressing Enter lists all of the linetypes in the ACAD.LIN file. If you want, you can use the Directories and Files list boxes to select another file to list. By default, AutoCAD considers any file with an LIN extension to contain linetype definitions.

- **Name of linetype to create:**

  Choosing the Create option enables you to create a linetype definition from within the AutoCAD drawing editor. Enter the name you want to give the linetype. The name can be up to 31 characters long but cannot contain any spaces.

  After entering the name of the linetype you want to create, the Create or Append Linetype File dialog box appears. It enables you to add the linetype to the ACAD.LIN file or create a new file for storing the linetype.

- **Descriptive text:**

  Enter up to 47 characters and spaces to describe the linetype you are about to create. Dashes, underscores, periods, and spaces are used semi-graphically to depict what the linetype actually looks like. This text is displayed next to the linetype name when you list linetypes.

- **Enter pattern (on next line) A,**

  The linetype pattern is a series of dashes or spaces of different lengths and dots that make up one complete linetype pattern. It is repeated between the line endpoints, according to the current linetype scale. A positive number indicates the length of a line segment; a negative number indicates a space. If you want a dot in the linetype definition, use the value zero (0). For example, the definition 2,-.5,0,-.5 produces a line segment of two units, a space of one-half unit, a dot, and then another space of one-half unit before repeating.

- **Linetype(s) to load:**

  This prompt appears when you choose the Load option. At this prompt, enter the name of the linetype you want added to the drawing. By default, the Select Linetype File dialog box selects the ACAD.LIN file from which to load linetypes.

- **Linetype *linetype name* is already loaded. Reload it? <Y>**

  If the linetype name you specified is already loaded in the drawing, you receive this prompt. The only time you need to reload a linetype definition is if it has been changed and the drawing needs to be updated.

- **New entity linetype <default>:**

  If you choose the Set option, enter the name of a linetype currently loaded into the drawing. This linetype is used when you create any new entities with commands such as LINE, ARC, and CIRCLE. Setting the value to BYLAYER causes new entities to assume the linetype assigned to the layer on which they are created.

Example

This example shows the process for loading a new linetype from the ACAD.LIN file and making it the default linetype used for drawing new entities. The various linetypes are shown in figure LINETYPE.1.

```
Command: LINETYPE ↵
?/Create/Load/Set: L ↵
Linetype(s) to load: DASHDOT ↵
```

Make sure that ACAD.LIN is highlighted in the dialog box and click on the OK button.

```
Linetype DASHDOT loaded.
?/Create/Load/Set: S ↵
New entity linetype (or ?) <BYLAYER>:
DASHDOT ↵
?/Create/Load/Set: ↵
```

```
Linetypes defined in file H:\ACAD12\SUPPORT\ACAD.lin:

    Name            Description
_____     _____

BORDER          __ __ . __ __ . __ __ . __ __ . __ __ .
BORDER2         _ _ . _ _ . _ _ . _ _ . _ _ . _ _ . _ _
BORDERX2        ____ ____  .  ____ ____  .  ____ ____  .
CENTER          ____ _ ____ _ ____ _ ____ _ ____ _ ____
CENTER2         ___ _ ___ _ ___ _ ___ _ ___ _ ___ _ ___

CENTERX2        _____ __ _____ __ _____ __ _____ __
DASHDOT         __ . __ . __ . __ . __ . __ . __ . __ .
DASHDOT2        _._._._._._._._._._._._._._._._._._._._
DASHDOTX2       ____  .  ____  .  ____  .  ____  .  ____
DASHED          __ __ __ __ __ __ __ __ __ __ __ __ __ __

DASHED2         _ _ _ _ _ _ _ _ _ _ _ _ _ _ _ _ _ _ _ _
DASHEDX2        ____ ____ ____ ____ ____ ____ ____ ____
DIVIDE          ____ . . ____ . . ____ . . ____ . . ____
DIVIDE2         _ . . _ . . _ . . _ . . _ . . _ . . _ .
DIVIDEX2        _____ . . _____ . . _____ . . _____
- Press RETURN for more -
```

Figure LINETYPE.1:
Linetypes loaded from the ACAD.LIN file.

Related Commands

CHANGE
CHPROP
DDCHPROP
DDEMODES
DDMODIFY

Related System Variables

CELTYPE
FILEDIA
LTSCALE
PSLTSCALE
PLINEGEN

LIST
?

Screen **[INQUIRY] [LIST:]**

Pull down **[Utility] [List]**

The LIST command displays information about entity properties stored in the drawing database. The properties include information such as line lengths, the layer in which an entity resides, or scaling factors of blocks. If the information is too lengthy and begins to scroll off the screen, press Ctrl-S to pause scrolling and then press any key to resume. Press Ctrl-C to cancel the command. You can turn on the printer echoing by pressing Ctrl-Q, and all entities listed on-screen also are printed.

Prompts and Options

- **Select objects:**
  Choose the entities about which you want information displayed.

Example

This example invokes the LIST command to view the properties of a line.

```
Command: LIST ↵
Select objects:

    LINE            Layer: 0
                    Space: Model space
    from point, X=  16.6089   Y=    4.4457   Z=    0.0000
      to point, X=  -7.9727   Y=   -8.1630   Z=    0.0000
```

```
Length =  27.6267,  Angle in XY Plane  =    207
     Delta X = -24.5816, Delta Y = -12.6087, Delta Z = 0.0000
```

 To view and modify entity properties, use the new
DDMODIFY command.

Related Commands

AREA
DBLIST
DDMODIFY
DIST
ID
SOLLIST

Related System Variables

AREA
PERIMETER

LOAD

Screen **[DRAW] [next] [SHAPE:] [LOAD:]**

The LOAD command is used to load compiled shape-definition files
into the drawing editor from disk for use with the SHAPE command.
Note that, unlike blocks, shape definitions are not stored in the drawing. The shape files must be accessible every time you load a drawing
for editing.

Prompts and Options

- When the FILEDIA variable is set to 1, this command presents no
  prompts. Instead, the Select Shape File dialog box appears. In the

`Files:` list box are listed any files that have an SHX extension. Select one of these files, and its shapes are then available from the SHAPE command. If the FIELDIA variable is set to 0, you receive the `Name of shape file to load (or ?):` prompt. Enter the name of the shape-definition file containing the shapes you want to use within the drawing.

Example

The following example demonstrates using the LOAD command to load a shape file, and then uses the SHAPE command to determine what shapes are available.

Command: **LOAD** ↵

Choose the PC.SHP file that comes with the AutoCAD software.

Command: **SHAPE** ↵
Shape name (or ?): **?** ↵

Available shapes:
File: PC.SHX
  FEEDTHRU   DIP8
  DIP14   DIP16
  DIP18   DIP20
  DIP24   DIP40

Related Commands

COMPILE
SHAPE

Related System Variables

FILEDIA
SHPNAME

LTSCALE

Screen **[SETTINGS] [next] [LTSCALE:]**

The LTSCALE command controls the display of noncontinuous linetypes. Each linetype is a pattern of dashes, dots, and spaces; and the pattern has a fixed size. By setting the LTSCALE value, you may adjust the scale of the pattern so that it matches the scale at which you are plotting. Typically, you set the value of LTSCALE equal to the scale of your drawing.

In a large drawing, if the linetype scale is set to a low number, screen regeneration can be slow. You can improve screen regeneration speed by assigning a high value to the linetype scale until you are ready to plot the drawing.

Prompts and Options

- **New scale factor <1>:**

  The current linetype scale factor is shown in angle brackets. Enter any positive number at the prompt. Decimal fractions are enabled. After the next screen regeneration, the display reflects the new linetype scale.

Example

This example displays the difference in linetypes by using two different LTSCALE factors (see fig. LTSCALE.1).

```
Command: LTSCALE ↵
New scale factor <1>: ↵
Command: LTSCALE ↵
New scale factor <1>:5 ↵
```

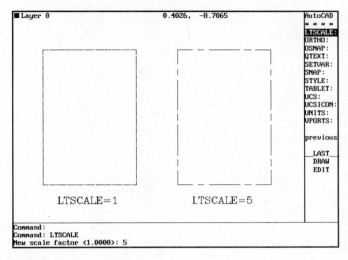

Figure LTSCALE.1:
The Center linetype at a LTSCALE factor of 1 and 5.

Related Commands

LINETYPE
REGENAUTO

Related System Variables

LTSCALE
PSLTSCALE

MEASURE

Screen   **[EDIT] [next] [MEASURE:]**

Pull down   **[Construct] [Measure]**

The MEASURE command places equally spaced points along an entity
at a specified distance. Blocks can be substituted for points if the blocks

are already defined within the drawing with the BLOCK command. You can measure arcs, circles, lines, and 2D or 3D polylines.

 The MEASURE command is useful for generating smooth camera and target points in two or three dimensions when making animations. Draw a 3D polyline, line, or arc to depict the camera path and use MEASURE or DIVIDE to place points along this path at even intervals for each frame of the animation.

Prompts and Options

- **Select object to measure:**

  Pick the entity to mark at equal distances. The MEASURE command works with only one entity at a time. The starting location for the placement of points or blocks is the endpoint closest to the point used to pick the entity. From the endpoint, measure points are calculated at equal intervals until no more will fit. You can use the Previous selection-set option to select all the points or blocks that are placed along the entity. Use the PDMODE and PDSIZE variables to alter the visual appearance of the points.

- **<Segment length>/Block:**

  At this prompt, specify a distance or pick two points to show a distance for measuring the entity. If you enter **B** to invoke the Block option, you must enter a block name already defined within the drawing. If you enter a block name, the following prompt appears:

- **Align block with object? <Y>:**

  Answer **Y** to rotate the inserted blocks about their insertion points so that they are aligned with the entity being measured.

Example

This example shows how the MEASURE command draws points at even spacings along a polyline. The entity shown in figure MEASURE.1 contains points placed at three-inch intervals.

```
Command: MEASURE ↵
Select object to measure: Pick point ①
<Segment length>/Block: 3 ↵
```

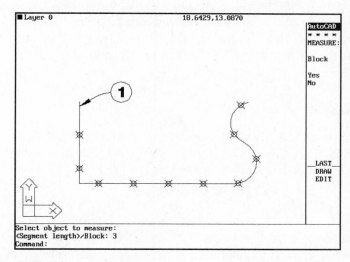

Figure MEASURE.1:
Points placed along a polyline with the MEASURE command.

Related Commands

DIVIDE
OSNAP
POINT

Related System Variables

PDMODE
PDSIZE

MENU

Screen **[UTILITY] [MENU:]**

The MENU command enables you to load alternative menu files into the AutoCAD drawing editor. AutoCAD is supplied with the menu ACAD.MNU, which includes menu selections for each command supplied with the software, as well as additional selections for running packages such as the Advanced Modeling Extension, AutoSHADE, and Autodesk Renderman. Typically, add-on packages that increase the functionality of AutoCAD have a customized menu for accessing their functions.

Prompts and Options

By default, the MENU command displays a dialog box that allows you to select the menu file you want to use. If the FILEDIA variable is set to 0, you see instead the `Menu File name or . for none <ACAD>:` prompt, at which you enter the name of a valid menu file. The Select Menu File dialog box initially displays the names of any files with either a MNU or MNX extension. If the file you want to load is in the list, you can highlight it and click on the OK button. You also can navigate the Directories: list box if the file is in a different drive or directory.

Related System Variables

MENUECHO
MENUNAME

MINSERT

Screen **[BLOCKS] [MINSERT:]**

Screen **[DRAW] [MINSERT:]**

The MINSERT (Multiple INSERT) command inserts a block multiple times in a regular pattern. This command combines the INSERT and ARRAY commands into a single command. After the MINSERT command has been used, the array of blocks becomes a single entity that cannot be exploded. As a single entity, these blocks take up less space in the drawing database. If you need to modify any of the individual blocks, use the INSERT and ARRAY commands instead.

Prompts and Options

- **Block name (or ?):**

  At this prompt, you enter the name of a block defined in the current drawing or in the AutoCAD library search path. You cannot precede a block with an asterisk (*) to insert it as preexploded, as you can with the INSERT command. You can enter a question mark to display a list of defined blocks, or enter a tilde (~) to display the Select Block dialog box to insert a drawing from disk.

- **Insertion point:**

  You specify the insertion point for the multiple arrayed block. This point is the location where the first block will be inserted in the array.

- **X scale factor <1.000>:**

  At this prompt, you enter a scale factor for the block in the current X axis.

- **Y scale factor (default=X):**

  You enter a scale factor for the block in the current Y direction. By default, the Y axis scale factor is set to the same value as the X axis scale factor.

- **Rotation angle:**

  At this prompt, you enter a nonzero number to rotate the array. This has the same effect as using the ROTATE command on an array of blocks.

- **Number of rows (--):**

  At this prompt, you enter any positive, nonzero number for the number of rows of the array.

- **Number of columns (|||):**

  At this prompt, you enter any positive, nonzero number for the number of columns of the array.

- **Unit cell or distance between rows (--):**

  You enter a number for the distance between rows of the block array. A positive number will create rows along the positive Y axis; a negative value will create rows along the negative Y axis. Specify a point to indicate that you want to show AutoCAD both the distance between rows and the distance between columns by defining a unit cell rectangle. The width of the rectangle becomes the column spacing; the height of the rectangle specifies the row spacing.

- **Other corner:**

  You specify a unit cell rectangle corner point opposite the point specified above.

- **Distance between columns (|||):**

  You enter a number for the distance between columns of the array.

Example

This example demonstrates how to create an arrayed insertion of a chair block, as shown in figure MINSERT.1.

```
Command: MINSERT ↵
Block name (or ?) <ARROW>: CHAIR ↵
Insertion point: Pick point ①
X scale factor <1> / Corner / XYZ: ↵
Y scale factor (default=X): ↵
Rotation angle <0>: ↵
Number of rows (--) <1>: 2 ↵
Number of columns (|||) <1>: 4 ↵
Unit cell or distance between rows (--): 60 ↵
Distance between columns (|||): 30 ↵
```

Related Commands

ARRAY
BLOCK
INSERT
ROTATE

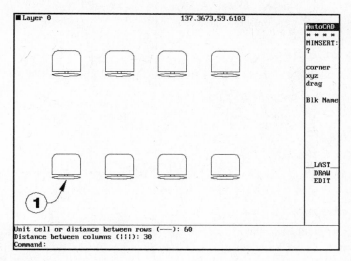

Figure MINSERT.1:
A 2 x 4 array of the chair block.

MIRROR

Screen **[EDIT] [next] [MIRROR:]**

Pull down **[Construct] [Mirror]**

The MIRROR command creates copies of selected entities symmetrically about a temporary mirror line. You can opt to remove the original entities from the drawing after the mirrored entities are created or leave the original entities intact.

Text, attribute, and attribute-definition entities specified in a MIRROR selection set are literally mirrored to create new copies; they read backwards or upside-down, depending on the angle of the mirror line. Associative dimension text is not affected. To mirror text, attributes, and attribute definitions so that the text reads correctly, set the MIRRTEXT system variable to 0. Text and constant attributes within a block will be inverted, regardless of the value of MIRRTEXT. Note that you cannot explode a mirrored block.

791

Prompts and Options

- **Select objects:**

  You select the entities to be mirrored.

- **First point of mirror line:**

  You specify one endpoint of a rubber-band line, which can be of any length.

- **Second point:**

  You specify the second endpoint of the mirror line. The entities selected will be mirrored after you select this point.

- **Delete old objects? <N>**

  If you press Enter at this prompt, the original entities will remain in the drawing. If you answer **Y** to this prompt, the original entities will be erased after your mirrored entities are created.

For easier editing, use the Grip Edit Mirror mode. See Chapter 4 for details.

Example

This example demonstrates the effects of using the MIRROR command on both line and text entity types. The points used to create the mirror line, and the new entities created, are shown in figure MIRROR.1.

```
Command: MIRROR ↵
Select objects: W ↵
First corner: Pick point ①
Other corner: Pick point ②
7 found
Select objects: ↵
First point of mirror line: Pick point ③
Second point: Pick point ④
Delete old objects? <N> ↵
```

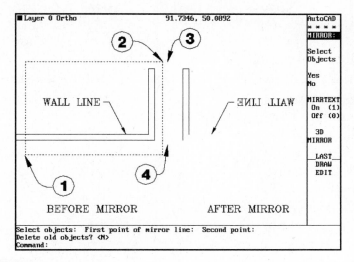

Figure MIRROR.1:
The mirrored entities.

Related System Variable

MIRRTEXT

MIRROR3D

Screen **[EDIT] [next] [MIRROR:] [3D MIRROR]**

Pull down **[Construct] [Mirror 3D]**

MIRROR3D enables you to mirror entities about any plane in three dimensions.

Prompts and Options

- **Select objects:**

  You select the object you want to mirror. You can use any of the AutoCAD entity-selection modes.

- **Delete old objects <N>:**

  You can enter **Y** to delete the object in its current location; enter **N** to duplicate the entity in its mirrored location.

- **Plane by Entity/Last/Zaxis/View/XY/YZ/<3points>:**

  At this prompt, you choose a method for specifying the plane about which to mirror. You can use the following options with the MIRROR3D command.

- **Entity.** The Entity option specifies the construction plane of a 2D entity as the mirroring plane. Entity displays the following prompt:

  `Pick circle, arc or 2D-polyline segment:` You select the entity or segment to define the plane for mirroring.

- **Last.** The Last option specifies the last mirroring plane. If there is no last plane, you are warned and reprompted with the original prompt.

- **Zaxis.** The Zaxis option specifies the mirroring plane as a point on a plane and a point on the Z axis of the plane. Zaxis displays two prompts.

  `Point on plane:` You enter a point on the current plane.

  `Point on Z-axis (normal) of the plane:` You enter a point to define the Z axis of the plane.

- **View.** The View option aligns the mirroring plane with the current viewing plane through a selected point. View has one prompt:

  `Point on view plane <0,0,0>:` You enter a point for the mirroring plane to pass through.

- **XY.** The XY option aligns the mirroring plane with the XY plane that passes through a selected point. XY has one prompt:

  `Point on XY plane <0,0,0>:` You enter a point for the mirroring plane to pass through.

- **YZ.** The YZ option aligns the mirroring plane with the YZ plane that passes through a selected point. YZ has one prompt:

  `Point on YZ plane <0,0,0>:` You enter a point for the mirroring plane to pass through.

- **ZX.** The ZX option aligns the mirroring plane with the ZX plane that passes through a selected point. ZX has one prompt:

  `Point on ZX plane <0,0,0>:` You enter a point for the mirroring plane to pass through.

- **<3points>.** This option specifies a mirroring plane that passes through three selected points. The 3points option has three prompts:

  `1st point on plane:` You enter the first point of the mirroring plane.

  `2nd point on plane:` You enter the second point of the mirroring plane.

  `3rd point on plane:` You enter the third point of the mirroring plane.

Example

The following example mirrors a solid about a plane using the Z option.

```
Command: MIRROR3D ↵
Select objects: Pick point ①
Select objects: ↵
Plane by Entity/Last/Zaxis/View/XY/YZ/ZX/<3points>: Z ↵
Point on plane: Pick point ②
Point on Z-axis (normal) of the plane: Pick point ③
Delete old objects? <N> ↵
```

Related Commands

> **MIRROR**
> **ROTATE**
> **ROTATE3D**

MOVE

Screen **[EDIT] [next] [MOVE:]**

Pull down **[Modify] [Move]**

The MOVE command relocates entities to another position in a drawing. The MOVE command works both in 2D or 3D; nothing but the position of the entities changes.

Prompts and Options

- **Select objects:**

  You select the entities to be moved using AutoCAD's standard object selection methods.

- **Base point or displacement:**

  You specify a base point for the move in the current User Coordinate System (UCS). The base point need not be on any selected entity. Or, enter an XYZ distance to move the current selection set. You may specify a 2D or 3D point, and the point's XYZ values will be considered the displacement for the selected entities in each of those axes.

- **Second point of displacement:**

  After you have specified a base, enter a second point to move the entity or entities towards. You can enter a location by picking the point, entering a relative location, or giving an absolute XYZ location.

For easier editing, use the Grip Edit Move mode. See Chapter 4 for details.

Example

This example shows a typical application of the MOVE command. The selected entities shown in figure MOVE.1 are moved to a new location, as displayed in the figure.

```
Command: MOVE ↵
Select objects: Pick point ①
1 found
Select objects: ↵
Base point or displacement: Pick point ②
Second point of displacement: Pick point ③
```

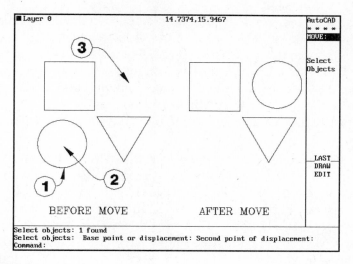

Figure MOVE.1:
An object being relocated with the MOVE command.

Related Command

COPY

MSLIDE

Screen **[UTILITY] [SLIDES] [next] [next] [MSLIDE:]**

The MSLIDE command creates slide files. Slides are snapshot images of the current screen display. Although slides cannot be edited like normal drawing files, they have the advantages of taking up little space on your disk and loading quickly. You can use slide files for icon items in icon menus, for referencing other drawings, and for creating presentations of your work.

Prompts and Options

- **Slide file <default>:**

By default, the MSLIDE command displays a dialog box that allows you to enter the name of the slide file to create. If the FILEDIA variable is set to 0, you receive instead the `Slide file <default>:` prompt, where you should enter the name to give the slide file. The Create Slide File dialog box initially displays the names of any current slide files. You can navigate the Directories: list box if you want to save the slide in a different drive or directory.

The slide file is given the extension SLD. After you enter a valid file name, AutoCAD redraws the screen and creates the image file. Slides made in model space contain only the current viewport. Slides made in paper space include all visible viewport entities and their contents. To make a slide, adjust your screen display with the AutoCAD display commands ZOOM, PAN, VIEW, and so on to achieve the view you want. Then execute the MSLIDE command. The command line area, screen menu area, status line, crosshairs, and UCS icon are not included in the slide image.

 You can create an automated slide show by using a script in AutoCAD. See the SCRIPT and DELAY commands for more information.

Related Commands

SCRIPT
DELAY
VSLIDE

MSPACE

Screen **[MVIEW] [MSPACE]**

Pull down **[View] [Model Space]**

The MSPACE command switches from paper space to model space and works only when paper space is active and at least one viewport has been created in paper space. Model space is active when the normal UCS icon is visible (if the UCSICON command is On) in each viewport and the crosshairs are constrained within the current viewport. The MSPACE command is not allowed if TILEMODE is set to 0.

Related Commands

MVIEW
PSPACE

Related System Variable

TILEMODE

MULTIPLE

MULTIPLE is a command modifier for issuing another command many times in succession. Enter **MULTIPLE** at the Command: prompt, followed by the name of the command to be repeated. The command is repeated until you cancel it by pressing Ctrl-C. You can use MULTIPLE with any command except PLOT, QUIT, and END.

MULTIPLE does not remember any of the specified command's options. If you select MULTIPLE INSERT, for example, you must answer all the INSERT command's prompts each time the command is repeated.

Example

The following example places many points in the drawing using MULTIPLE to repeat the POINT command (see fig. MULTIPLE.1).

```
Command: MULTIPLE POINT ↵
POINT Point:
POINT Point:
POINT Point:
```

799

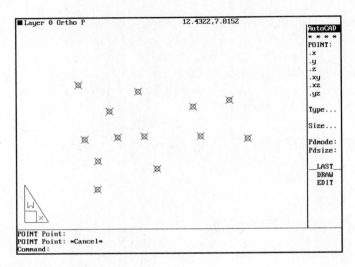

Figure MULTIPLE.1:
Using MULTIPLE to execute the POINT command repeatedly.

Related Command

COPY

MVIEW

Screen **[MVIEW]**

Screen **[DISPLAY] [MVIEW:]**

Pull down **[View] [Mview >]**

The MVIEW command controls the creation and display of viewpoints in paper space. MVIEW controls the size, number, and location of viewports as they are created in paper space. If model space is active, AutoCAD automatically switches to paper space to perform the MVIEW command's options. As with any paper space commands, you must set the TILEMODE system variable to 0 (off) in order to use the

MVIEW command. The maximum number of active viewports cannot exceed 16 on MS-DOS systems.

Prompts and Options

- **ON:**

  The ON option enables the display of entities within a selected viewport. You must first select the viewports by picking the viewport boundary. The entities within the selected viewports are then displayed.

- **OFF:**

  The OFF option disables the display of all entities within a selected viewport.

- **Hideplot:**

  Hideplot controls whether hidden lines are removed or not removed in the selected viewport when paper space is plotted. After you specify this option, you see the ON/OFF: prompt, at which you can specify whether hidden lines are removed during plotting of the viewport (ON) or not.

- **Fit:**

  The Fit option fills the current display with a single viewport.

- **2:**

  This option creates two equal size paper space viewports either side by side or one directly over the other, as directed by the Horizontal/<Vertical>: prompt. Horizontal creates a horizontal division between the two viewports; Vertical (the default) creates a vertical division. After you choose either horizontal or vertical orientation, you will receive the Fit/<First Point>: prompt. This prompt directs you to define the area used to create the two viewports.

- **3:**

  This option creates three viewports, one large, two small, with the orientation defined by the Horizontal/Vertical/Above/Below/Left/<Right>: prompt. After you choose an orientation, you will receive the `Fit/<First Point>:` prompt to specify the area used to create the three viewports.

- **4:**

  This option divides the screen into four equal size paper space viewports.

- **Restore:**

  This option creates a paper space viewport configuration equivalent to a model space viewport configuration saved with the VPORTS command. The Restore option is an effective way to transfer views created for modeling purposes to paper space for hard copy output. After choosing to restore a viewport configuration, you will receive the `Fit/<First Point>:` prompt, to specify the area used to restore the viewports within.

- **?/Name of window configuration to insert <default>:**

  Type **?** to list the saved viewport configurations within the current drawing or enter the name of the viewport configuration for retrieval into paper space.

- **<First point>:**

  You specify a point for one corner of a single paper space viewport.

- **Other corner:**

  You specify a point for the opposite corner of the viewport. After you enter a point, the current model space viewport is displayed in the newly created paper space viewport.

Example

The following example uses MVIEW to create three viewports within paper space (see fig. MVIEW.1).

```
Command: MVIEW ↵
ON/OFF/Hideplot/Fit/2/3/4/Restore/<First Point>: 3 ↵
Horizontal/Vertical/Above/Below/Left/<Right>: B ↵
Fit/<First Point>: Pick point ①
Second point: Pick point ②
Regenerating drawing.
```

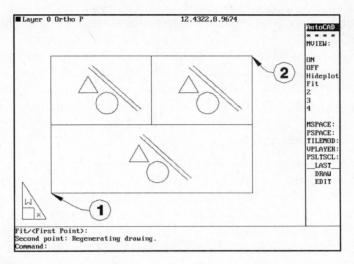

Figure MVIEW.1:
Three viewports created with the MVIEW command.

Related Commands

MSPACE
PSPACE
VPLAYER
VPORTS

Related System Variables

MAXACTVP
PSLTSCALE
TILEMODE
VISRETAIN

MVSETUP

Pull down **[View] [Layout] [MV Setup]**

The MVSETUP AutoLISP program provides automated drawing setup for AutoCAD. It supports both paper space and model space. If you want to use only model space, the MVSETUP routine performs the drawing setup as the SETUP command did in versions of AutoCAD prior to Release 11. If you want to use both paper space and model space, however, MVSETUP enables you to define, align, and scale viewports, as well as place a title block in paper space within which the model space viewports can be arranged.

The MVSETUP program has two options to the setup routine. The first option executes the setup routine that AutoCAD used in pre-Release 11 versions. This routine is limited to setting the proper units and scale and to inserting a border scaled to the paper size on which you will be plotting. The second option invokes the setup routine that places a drawing border in paper space and enables you to define viewports to display your model space entities. To use the pre-Release 11 setup option, answer No at the `Enable Paper/Modelspace? <Y>:` prompt.

Prompts and Options

- **`Enable Paper/Modelspace? <Y>:`**

  The type of setup performed depends on whether or not paper space is activated. If you answer **N**, the setup routine described following is used. If you activate paper space, the paper space setup routine is performed. AutoCAD displays this prompt only if TILEMODE is set to 1; the paper space setup routine is executed if TILEMODE is set to 0 when the MVSETUP command is issued.

The Model Space Setup Routine

- **`Select the Units from the screen menu:`**

  The screen menu displays a list of five different types of units available in AutoCAD. Select the unit system with which you will create your drawing. This sets the AutoCAD UNITS command to the proper value.

- **Select the Scale from the screen menu:**

    The screen menu displays a list of common drawing scales (1=1, 1/8"=1'0", 1"=20', and so on). Select the scale that you want to use when you plot your drawing. If that scale is not listed, select the OTHER option. When you enter a value for the scale, that value should be equal to the number of drawing units to plot within each one plotting unit. This value is used to set the LTSCALE system variable.

- **Select the Paper size from the screen menu:**

    The screen menu displays a list of common paper sizes ranging from A to E size. Select one that fits the size of paper on which you will plot your drawing. If the paper size you need does not appear in the list, use the OTHER option to specify the horizontal and vertical size of the paper.

The Paper Space Setup Routine

The paper space setup routine is executed if you answer yes to the `Enable Paper/Modelspace? <Y>:` prompt or if the TILEMODE system variable is set to 0 when the MVSETUP command is issued. When paper space is activated, the MVSETUP command automates the process of inserting a title block, creating paper space viewports, scaling paper space viewports, and aligning the views of paper space viewports.

- **Align viewports/Create/Scale viewports/Options/ Titleblock/Undo:**

    This prompt is the first of many that appear when you use the paper space setup routine. Each of these options has its own set of prompts, which are discussed in the following paragraphs. The only prompt not discussed is the Undo option, which appears here and in each of the options prompts. The Undo option is similar to the AutoCAD Undo command; it reverses any steps that have been performed thus far by MVSETUP.

- **Align viewports.** You receive the following prompt after you specify the Align viewports option:

- **Angled/Horizontal/Vertical alignment/Rotate view/ Undo:**

  The Angled option enables you to pan a view in a paper space viewport to a specific distance and angle from a base point. If you specify Angled, you receive the following prompts:

- **Basepoint:**

  You specify a point in the viewport that will remain stationary and be used as a reference point for the pan.

- **Other point:**

  You enter a point in the viewport to be panned. This point will be moved so that it is the specified distance and angle away from the basepoint of the first viewport.

- **Distance from basepoint:**

  You enter the distance that the two points will be located apart from each other.

- **Angle from basepoint:**

  You enter the desired angle between the two points chosen. After you enter this value, the second viewport is panned by this angle and the distance.

 The angled alignment of viewports is sometimes difficult to use. You might find it easier to exit the MVSETUP command and use the AutoCAD PAN command to move around the viewport.

If you specify the Horizontal or Vertical alignment options, you receive two prompts. Horizontal alignment pans one viewport up or down to align two points that you specify. Vertical alignment pans one viewport left or right to align two points that you specify.

- **Basepoint:**

  You enter a point in the viewport that will remain stationary and be used as a reference point.

- **Other point:**

  You enter a point in the viewport that you want to line up with the basepoint that was chosen. The viewport is then panned so that the two points line up with each other.

  If you specify the Rotate view option from the Align viewports prompt, you receive the following prompts:

- **Basepoint:**

  You enter a point around which the view within the viewport will be rotated by the value entered at the following prompt.

- **Angle from basepoint:**

  You enter a value to rotate the view. It is always measured from 0 degrees, so if you want to have the viewport rotated from a current value of 15 degrees to 60 degrees, you enter **60** at this prompt. If you enter 0 at this prompt, the view returns to its non-rotated state.

- **Create.** You receive the following prompt after you specify the Create option at the first MVSETUP paper space prompt:

- **Delete objects/Undo/<Create viewports>:**

  If you specify the Delete objects option, you receive the following prompt:

- **Select the objects to delete:**

  Pick any entities you want to delete.

  If you specify the default option, Create, you receive the following prompt:

- **Redisplay/<Number of entry to load>:**

  The Redisplay option redisplays the currently available viewport configurations. The four supplied viewport configurations are the following:

- **None.** No viewports are created, and you return to the previous prompt.

- **Single.** A single viewport is created. You must define the area of the viewport by specifying two points.

- **Std. Engineering.** A group of four viewports is created in a rectangular area that you define. Each of the viewports is set with a different view into your model space drawing. These views are the top view (XY plane of the UCS); isometric view (Viewport rotated to -45 degrees in the XY plane and elevated 30 degrees in the Z axis); front view (XZ plane of the UCS); and right side view (YZ plane of the UCS).

- **Array of viewports.** A rectangular array of viewport entities is created. You can define the quantity by entering the number of viewports along the X and Y axes.

 Only 16 active viewports are permitted in the DOS versions of AutoCAD. If you need more than 16 viewports, you must turn off some viewports to allow others to be turned on. Use the MVIEW command to turn on and off viewports.

If you specify the Single, Std. Engineering, or Array of viewports options, you receive the following prompts:

- **Bounding area for viewports... First point:**

You specify the first corner point of a rectangular area that will hold the viewports to be created.

- **Other point:**

You specify the opposite corner of the area to hold the viewports.

If you specify the Array of viewports option, you receive the following prompts.

- **Number of viewports in X. <1>:**

You enter the number of viewports in the X direction (columns).

- **Number of viewports in Y. <1>:**

You enter the number of viewports in the Y direction (rows).

If you specify the Std. Engineering or Array of viewports options, you receive the following prompts.

- **Distance between viewports in X. <0.0>:**

You enter a distance between adjacent viewport edges in the X direction.

- **Distance between viewports in Y. <0.0>:**

You enter a distance between adjacent viewport edges in the Y direction.

- **Scale viewports.** You receive the following prompts after you specify the Scale viewports option from the first MVSETUP paper space prompt:

- **Select the viewports to scale:**

Pick each of the viewports that you want to specify a scale for.

- **Set zoom scale factor for viewports. Interactively/<Uniform>:**

If you selected more than one viewport at the preceding prompt, you are presented with this prompt. You can scale all of the viewports at once (uniform) or specify separate scales (interactively) for each viewport.

- **Number of paper space units. <1.0>:**

For each viewport that you scale, you must define the ratio of paper space units to model space units. The default of one unit is adequate for most drawings.

- **Number of model space units. <1.0>:**

You enter the number of model space units to plot within the number of paper space units specified in the last prompt. To create a 1/4"=1'-0" scale viewport, for example, enter **1** at the previous prompt and **48** here.

- **Options.** You receive the following prompt after you select the Options option from the first paper space MVSETUP prompt.

- **Set Layer/LImits/Units/Xref:**

If you specify the Set Layer option, you receive the following prompt:

- **Layer name for title block or . for current layer:**

You enter the name of the layer on which the title block created by the Title block option of the first paper space MVSETUP prompt should be placed. You can enter a period to place the title block on the current layer.

If you specify the LImits option, you receive the following prompts.

- **Set drawing limits? <N>:**

  You can enter **Y** at this prompt to automatically set the paper space limits to the size of the title block.

  If you specify the Units option at the Options prompt, you receive the following prompt.

- **Paperspace units are in Feet/Inches/ MEters/Millimeters? <in>:**

  You enter the unit type for paper space units. The default is inches.

  If you specify the Xref option at the Options prompt, you receive the following prompt.

- **Xref Attach or Insert title block? <Insert>:**

  You enter the placement method for the title block. If you specify Insert, the title block will be inserted as a block in your drawing. If you specify Xref, the title block will be attached as an external reference.

- **Title block.** You receive the following prompt after you select the Title block option from the first MVSETUP paper space prompt:

- **Delete objects/Origin/Undo/<Insert title block>:**

  If you specify the Delete objects option, you receive the following prompt.

- **Select objects:**

  Pick any existing entities that you do not want in your drawing.

  If you select the Origin option from the Title block option prompt, you receive the following prompt:

- **New origin point for this sheet:**

  You specify a new insertion point for the title block.

  If you select the default option, Insert title block, from the Title block option prompt, you receive the following prompts:

- **Add/Delete/Redisplay/<Number of entry to load>:**

  A numbered list of the available title blocks is displayed on the screen. If you select one of these numbers, that title block is drawn in paper space. The Redisplay option displays the list of available title blocks on the screen again.

- **Title block description:**

  The Add option displays this prompt. You also can add your own title blocks to the list. When adding a new title block, you must provide a brief description to differentiate it from the other title blocks.

- **Drawing to insert:**

  After you have described the new title block to add, you need to specify its name and location to have it added to the MVSETUP information file. Type in the full path name and file name of the drawing. The drawing will be inserted into paper space and the description and location of the file are saved to a file named MVSETUP.DFS.

- **Number of entry to delete from list:**

  When you want to delete an entry from the title block list, enter its number at this prompt after specifying the Delete option at the previous prompt.

- **Create a drawing named *drawing name*? <Y>:**

  The default title blocks created by the MVSETUP command do not exist as drawing files. They are stored as a series of drawing instructions within the MVSETUP.DFS file. When you insert one of these title blocks (the ANSI-? title blocks in the title block list), AutoCAD then asks if you want the title block saved as a drawing file. If you plan to use any of the title blocks often, you can save it as a drawing file so that the title block is reloaded faster the next time it is needed. Also, in order for the title block to be inserted as a block or an external reference (XREF), you must create a drawing file.

Example

The following example uses the MVSETUP command to set up a title block in paper space, display the drawing in multiple scaled viewports, and then align the object between viewports.

```
Command: MVSETUP ↵
Paperspace/Modelspace is disabled.
The pre-R11 setup will be invoked unless it is enabled.
Enable Paper/Modelspace?  <Y>: ↵
Entering Paper space.
Use MVIEW to insert Model space viewports.
Regenerating drawing.
MVSetup, Version 1.15, (c) 1990-1992 by Autodesk, Inc.
Align/Create/Scale viewports/Options/Title block/Undo: O ↵
Set Layer/LImits/Units/Xref: LI ↵
Set drawing limits? <N>: Y ↵
Set Layer/LImits/Units/Xref: X ↵
Xref Attach or Insert title block? <Insert>: X ↵
Set Layer/LImits/Units/Xref: ↵
Align/Create/Scale viewports/Options/Title block/Undo: T ↵
Delete objects/Origin/Undo/<Insert title block>: ↵
Available title block options:
0: None
1: ISO A4 Size(mm)
2: ISO A3 Size(mm)
3: ISO A2 Size(mm)
4: ISO A1 Size(mm)
5: ISO A0 Size(mm)
6: ANSI-V Size(in)
7: ANSI-A Size(in)
8: ANSI-B Size(in)
9: ANSI-C Size(in)
10: ANSI-D Size(in)
11: ANSI-E Size(in)
12: Arch/Engineering (24 x 36in)
13: Generic D size Sheet (24 x 36in)
Add/Delete/Redisplay/<Number of entry to load>: 9
Create a drawing named ansi-c.dwg? <Y>: ↵
Align/Create/Scale viewports/Options/Title block/Undo: C ↵
Delete objects/Undo/<Create viewports>: ↵
Available Mview viewport layout options:
0: None
1: Single
2: Std. Engineering
3: Array of Viewports
Redisplay/<Number of entry to load>: 2 ↵
Bounding area for viewports.  Default/<First point >: 2,2 ↵
Other point: 15,14 ↵
```

```
Distance between viewports in X. <0.0>: ↵
Distance between viewports in Y. <0.0>: ↵
Align/Create/Scale viewports/Options/Title block/Undo: S ↵
Select the viewports to scale:
Select objects: Pick point at ① (see fig. MVSETUP.1)
Other corner: Pick point at ②
4 found
```

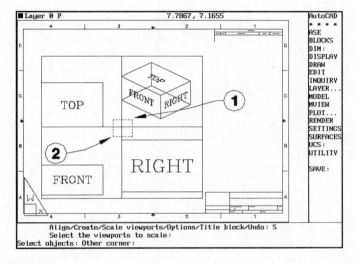

Figure MVSETUP.1:
The pick points for scaling the viewports.

```
Select objects: ↵
Set zoom scale factors for viewports.
Interactively/<Uniform>: ↵
Enter the ratio of paper space units to model space units...
Number of paper space units.  <1.0>: ↵
Number of model space units.  <1.0>: ↵
Align/Create/Scale viewports/Options/Title block/Undo: A ↵
Angled/Horizontal/Vertical alignment/Rotate view/Undo? H ↵
Basepoint: INT ↵
of Pick point ③
Other point: INT ↵
of Pick point ④
Angled/Horizontal/Vertical alignment/Rotate view/Undo? V ↵
Basepoint: INT ↵
```

```
of Pick point ④
Other point: INT ↵
of Pick point ⑤
```

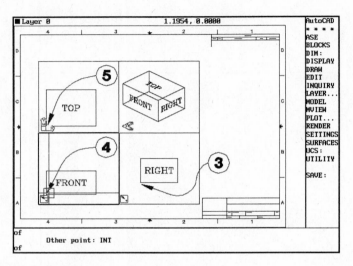

Figure MVSETUP.2:
The pick points for aligning the viewports.

```
Angled/Horizontal/Vertical alignment/Rotate view/Undo? ↵
Align/Create/Scale viewports/Options/Title block/Undo: ↵
```
The completed setup appears in figure MVSETUP.3.

Related System Variables

LTSCALE
PSLTSCALE
TILEMODE

NEW

R12

Pull down **[File] [New...]**

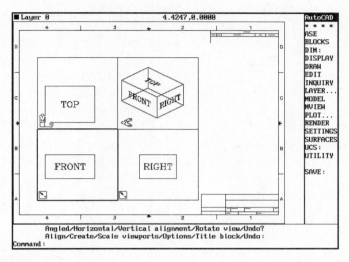

Figure MVSETUP.3:
The results of the MVSETUP example.

The NEW command begins and initializes a new drawing in the drawing editor. If you have made any modifications to the current drawing, you can save them, discard them, or cancel the NEW command. The Create New Drawing dialog box displays for you to specify a new file name and prototype drawing (see fig. NEW.1).

Figure NEW.1:
The Create New Drawing dialog box.

Prompts and Options

NEW displays no command-line prompts. Instead, you make selections from the following dialog boxes and options.

The Create New Drawing dialog box offers the following options:

- **Prototype.** This button is enabled if the No Prototype button below it is not checked. Clicking on the Prototype button displays the Prototype Drawing File dialog box, where you can select a prototype for the new drawing (see fig. NEW.2). Alternatively, you can enter the name of a known file in the text box to the right of the button. The new drawing inherits all of the entities and settings of the prototype. When a prototype drawing has been selected, its name appears in the text box. If no prototype file is selected, AutoCAD uses defaults from the configured default prototype drawing file.

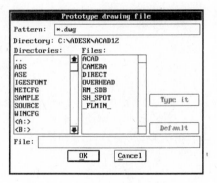

Figure NEW.2:
The Prototype Drawing File dialog box.

- **No Prototype.** If this box is checked, the new drawing uses no prototype file, and AutoCAD's default settings, as shipped, are used.
- **Retain as Default.** Checking this box causes AutoCAD to store the name of the prototype drawing file selected above as the default for subsequent new drawings.
- **New Drawing Name.** Clicking this button displays the Create Drawing File dialog box (see fig NEW.3). You can use this dialog box to select a destination directory and specify a file name for the new drawing. After you have selected a directory and file name, they appear in the text box to the right of the button. Alternatively,

you can simply enter a new file name in the text box and the drawing is placed in the default directory. By entering a new file name followed by the equal sign (=) and the name of an existing file, you can specify both the new name and the prototype AutoCAD should use. For example, entering WIDGET=GADGET would create a new drawing named WIDGET with all of the objects and settings from a drawing named GADGET. You can also omit the prototype name in this method to specify no prototype.

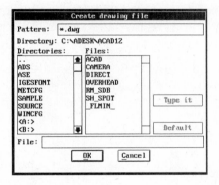

Figure NEW.3:
The Create Drawing File dialog box.

Related Commands

END
OPEN
QUIT
SAVE
SAVEAS

Related System Variables

ACADPREFIX
DBMOD

817

OFFSET

Screen **[DRAW] [OFFSET:]**

Screen **[EDIT] [next] [OFFSET:]**

Pull down **[Construct] [Offset]**

The OFFSET command creates a copy of an entity parallel to the original entity. You can offset arcs, circles, lines, and two-dimensional polylines. When used on circles and arcs, the new entity has the same center point as the original. If the OFFSET command is used to copy a polyline, the new polyline has the same width(s) as the original, and the vertices of the polyline is offset in the direction selected.

The OFFSET command works only on one entity at a time. To offset a single entity many times, use the Array command. When you offset entities that have an extrusion distance, the results are unpredictable if the current UCS is not the same as the UCS in which the entity was created.

Prompts and Options

- **Offset distance or Through: <Through>**

  You enter a distance to offset the entity that you select at the next prompt. You can pick two points that define the distance you want to use, or select the Through (default) option, which instructs AutoCAD to offset the entity through a chosen point.

- **Select object to offset:**

  You pick the entity to be offset.

- **Through point:**

  This prompt appears if you specified the Through option at the first prompt. The point supplied at this prompt provides AutoCAD with the direction and offset distance for the new entity.

- **Side to offset?**

  If a distance is supplied for the OFFSET command, AutoCAD asks on which side of the original to place the new entity.

Example

The following example offsets polyline and circle entities shown in figure
OFFSET.1.

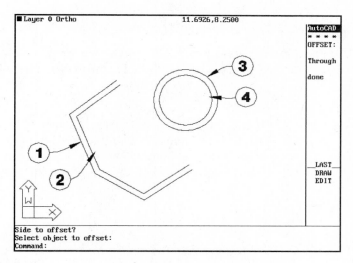

Figure OFFSET.1:
Duplicate entities created by the OFFSET command.

```
Command: OFFSET ↵
Offset distance of Through <Through>: .25 ↵
Select object to offset: Pick point ①
Side to offset? Pick point ②
Select object to offset: Pick point ③
Side to offset? Pick point ④
```

Related Commands

    ARRAY
    COPY

Related System Variable

    OFFSETDIST

OOPS

Screen [BLOCKS] [BLOCK:] [OOPS]

Screen [EDIT] [ERASE:] [OOPS:]

Pull down [Modify] [Erase] [Oops!]

The OOPS command restores entities that have been removed from the drawing by the ERASE, BLOCK, or WBLOCK commands. The OOPS command only restores the last set of entities removed.

 The OOPS command provides a function not available with the UNDO command. If you have problems selecting the correct entities for an edit command, erase the troublesome entities and then perform the edit on the remaining entities. You can then use the OOPS command to restore the erased entities back to their original condition.

 The OOPS command does not restore entities deleted before you use the PLOT command. Instead, you must use the UNDO command in order to restore deleted entities.

Related Commands

UNDO
U

OPEN

Pull down [File] [Open...]

The OPEN command loads a drawing into the drawing editor. If you have made any modifications to the current drawing, you can save them, discard them, or cancel the OPEN command. The Open Drawing dialog box displays to enable you to specify a file name (see fig. OPEN.1).

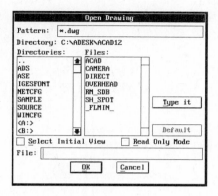

Figure OPEN.1:
The Open Drawing dialog box.

Prompts and Options

The OPEN command does not display command-line prompts. Instead, you can make selections from the following options available in the Open Drawing dialog box.

- **Pattern.** This edit box contains the pattern specification for files to appear in the Files list box below. The wild cards ? and * can be used to refine the list to desired file names.

- **Directories.** This list box contains a listing of the subdirectories available from the current directory, displayed following Directory above. Use the scroll bar to display more file names and drive letters. Double-click on a directory name or drive letter to change the current directory.

- **Files.** This list box contains a listing of the files available in the current directory. Use the scroll bar to display more file names. Double-click on a file name, or click on it once and click on the **O**K button to proceed.

- **Select Initial View.** Checking this box permits you to select a view defined in the selected drawing to be displayed when the drawing loads. A simple dialog box appears when you enter the drawing editor for you to make your selection.

821

- **Read Only Mode.** When this box is checked, AutoCAD does not allow any modifications to the selected drawing to be saved in the drawing file.
- **File.** Displays the name of the file selected above in an edit box. You may type the name of a desired file here or edit an existing name.

Use Read Only mode to open drawings for viewing that may need to be edited concurrently by others on a network. When drawings are opened in Read Only mode, AutoCAD does not create a lock, and the drawing may be opened by other users.

Related Commands

NEW
QUIT
SAVE
SAVEAS

Related System Variables

DWGWRITE
ACADPREFIX

ORTHO

Screen **[SETTINGS] [ORTHO]**

The ORTHO command is a drawing aid that constrains points chosen by the cursor to right angles from each other. You can press Ctrl-O or F8 to turn Ortho on or off. When Ortho mode is on, the word Ortho is displayed on the left end of the status bar. Ortho is affected by the current UCS and Snap style. Any coordinate entry from the keyboard overrides Ortho mode. You can turn Ortho mode on or off through a radio button in the DDRMODES dialog box.

You can execute the ORTHO command transparently by preceding the command name with an apostrophe ('ORTHO).

Prompts and Options

- **ON/OFF<Off>:**

  Turns orthogonal mode on or off.

Example

The following example demonstrates how to set the Ortho mode to ON, and Ortho mode's effects on a command such as the LINE command.

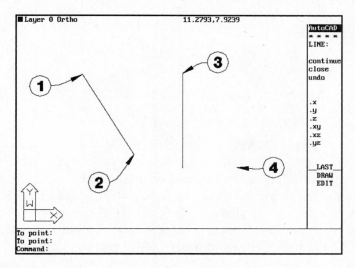

Figure ORTHO.1:
Lines drawn with Ortho mode turned on.

```
Command: LINE ↵
From point: Pick point ①
To point: Pick point ②
```

```
To point: Pick point ⑩
Command: ORTHO ↵
ON/OFF <Off>: ON ↵
Command: LINE ↵
From point: Pick point ③
To point: Pick point ④
To point: ↵
```

Related Command

DDRMODES

Related System Variable

ORTHOMODE

OSNAP

Screen **[* * * *]**

Screen **[SETTINGS] [next] [OSNAP:]**

Pull down **[Assist [Object Snap]**

The OSNAP (Object SNAP) command causes AutoCAD to use a specific geometric point on an existing entity when a command requests point entry. Twelve different geometric modes are available, and are described in the following section. The OSNAP command can be set to one or more running object snap settings. You can also temporarily activate any of the object snap modes within a command by entering the first three letters of the snap mode before you pick a point. This is known as *Object Snap Override*, and is active only for the single point selection.

You can execute the OSNAP command transparently by preceding the command name with an apostrophe ('OSNAP).

Prompts and Options

- **Object snap modes:**

  You can specify one or more object snap modes by typing the first three letters of the mode. More than one mode can be requested by separating each mode with a comma. The following mode options are available:

- **CENter.** Snaps to the center point of the picked arc or circle.

- **ENDpoint.** Snaps to the nearest endpoint of an arc, line, polyline, mesh, or 3dface vertex. Endpoint object snap also snaps to the end points of extruded edges.

- **INSertion.** Snaps to the insertion point of text, attributes, blocks, or shapes.

- **INTersection.** Snaps to the nearest intersection of any combination of lines, polylines, arcs, or circles. The intersection point is only found if the objects intersect in three-dimensional space. Intersection also snaps to the corners of solid entities, lines, and extruded polyline segments, or the intersecting edge of two wide entities.

- **MIDpoint.** Snaps to the middle point of a line or arc. Midpoint also snaps to the midpoint of all four edges of an extruded line or polyline segments and the midpoint of an arc's extruded edge.

- **NEArest.** Snaps to the point on an entity that is nearest to the crosshairs.

- **NODe.** Snaps to a point entity.

- **PERpendicular.** Snaps to a point that is perpendicular from the previous point to the selected entity. The resulting point does not have to be located on the selected entity.

- **TANgent.** Snaps to a point that forms a tangent between the arc or circle and the previous point.

- **QUAdrant.** Snaps to the nearest point on an arc or circle that is located at 0, 90, 180, or 270 degrees.

- **QUIck, <osnap>.** Forces all object snap modes to accept the first point that satisfies the current mode(s), not necessarily the most accurate. Quick generally finds the snap point on the most recently drawn entities within the aperture box. Intersection object snap ignores the Quick object snap modifier.

- **NONe.** Nullifies any running object snap.

Example

The following example uses object snap overrides to choose specific points on the entities shown in figure OSNAP.1.

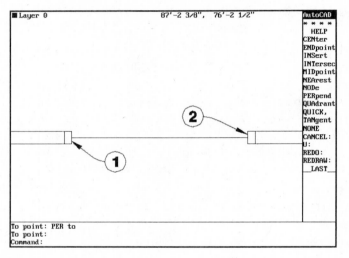

Figure OSNAP.1
A line drawn with the help of object snap overrides.

```
Command: LINE ↵
From point: MID of Pick point ①
To point: PER of Pick point ②
To point: ↵
```

Related Commands

APERTURE
DDOSNAP

Related System Variables

APERTURE
OSMODE

PAN

Screen **[DISPLAY] [PAN:]**

Pull down **[View] [Pan]**

The PAN command shifts the view of your drawing that is currently on-screen to another location. The PAN command is typically used to view adjacent areas of your drawing without changing the zoom scale. You can use the PAN command transparently (preceded by an apostrophe) if the requested view does not require a screen regeneration.

Prompts and Options

- **Displacement:**

  At this prompt, you select a starting point that serves as a reference to shift the view of the current drawing.

- **Second point:**

  At this prompt, you enter the second point for moving the display. If you press Enter at this prompt, a relative displacement is used based on the point you enter at the Displacement: prompt.

Example

Figure PAN.1 shows the result of using the PAN command in two viewports, one before the command and one after.

```
Command: PAN ↵
Displacement: Pick point ①
Second point: Pick point ②
```

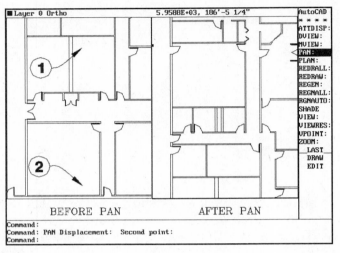

Figure PAN.1:
Using the PAN command to view other portions of a drawing.

Related Command

ZOOM

PCXIN

PCXIN imports a Zsoft PCX raster file into AutoCAD. AutoCAD scans the raster image and creates a block consisting of a solid for each rectangular colored pixel in the PCX file. After you have imported a raster image into AutoCAD, you can trace over the raster image with AutoCAD geometry to create an AutoCAD drawing of the raster image. When you are through, you can erase the raster image. Raster images can be scaled, mirrored, and rotated like regular entities.

 Do not explode the block representation of a raster file—the resulting entities use large quantities of disk space and memory.

The system variable GRIPBLOCK should be set to 0 to avoid highlighting all of the solid entities in the block.

Prompts and Options

- **PCX file name:**

  You enter the name of the PCX file you want to import. You do not need to include the extension.

- **Insertion point <0,0,0>:**

  You enter the X, Y, and Z coordinates or pick the insertion point for the raster file.

- **Scale Factor:**

  You enter a number or drag the crosshairs to scale the raster file from the insertion point.

- **New length:**

  If you press Enter at the Scale Factor prompt, you are prompted to pick a point to specify the scale factor.

See the listing in the GIFIN command summary for the description of a series of options that control how a raster file is imported (RIASPECT, RIBACKG, RIEDGE, RIGAMUT, RIGREY, and RITHRESH).

Example

The following example imports a PCX file called TEST.PCX into AutoCAD at 3,3,0.

```
Command: PCXIN ↵
PCX file name: TEST ↵
Insertion point <0,0,0>: 3,3,0 ↵
Scale factor: 2 ↵
```

Related Commands

GIFIN
TIFIN

Related System Variable

GRIPBLOCK

PEDIT

Screen **[EDIT] [next] [PEDIT:]**

Pull down **[Modify] [PolyEdit]**

The PEDIT command edits 2D and 3D polylines and polygon meshes. Each of these entities is a variation of the basic polyline entity; thus, the PEDIT command performs a variety of manipulations of these entities. Each type of polyline produces a different response from the PEDIT command. The next section explains how each form of editing works.

Prompts and Options

- **Select polyline:**

  At this prompt, select a polyline for editing by using any of the standard AutoCAD object selection methods. If the selected entity is not a polyline or mesh, the following message appears:

  `Entity selected is not a polyline`

  If the selected entity is a line or an arc, it will be highlighted and you will receive the following prompt:

- **Do you want to turn it into one? <Y>**

  The PEDIT command can change a "normal" line into a 2D polyline. If you decide not to transform the entity, the PEDIT command terminates.

2D Polylines

The following prompts and options appear when you use the PEDIT command to edit 2D polyline entities:

- **Close/Join/Width/Edit vertex/Fit/Spline/Decurve/ Ltype gen/Undo/eXit <X>:**

  After a 2D polyline has been selected or created, you see these options.

- **Close.** The Close option creates a closing polyline segment from the end of the polyline back to its beginning. If the ending segment is an arc, the Close option creates a closing arc segment. After the polyline is closed, this option changes to Open. The Open option removes closing polyline segments.

- **Join.** When you specify the Join option, you see the Select objects: prompt. You can select line, arc, and polyline segments to add to the current polyline, each segment chosen must meet the adjacent segment at its endpoint, forming a continuous chain. After performing the join operation, the Pedit command reports how many segments were added.

- **Width.** The Width option enables you to set a constant width for all segments of the polyline. If individual segments have tapered widths, this value will override the previous width information. When you choose the Width option, you receive the following prompt:

  Enter new width for all segments:

- **Edit vertex.** The Edit vertex option presents this new prompt line of options. These options are used to edit a polyline on a vertex-by-vertex basis. When you edit vertices, the PEDIT command marks the current vertex with an X. Each of the options that has additional prompts are described with their prompts. The options without additional prompts are described in the following paragraphs.

- **Next/Previous/Break/Insert/Move/Regen/Straighten/ Tangent/Width/eXit <X>:**

- **Next.** The Next option enables you to move the vertex marker (the X) to the next polyline vertex. The Previous option moves the vertex marker to the preceding vertex.

- **Regen.** When you make vertex edits, you can easily obscure the current shape of the polyline. The Regen option forces a regeneration of only the polyline so that you can view it in its current form.

- **Break** and **Straighten.** If you select either the Break or Straighten options, you are presented with the prompt `Next/ Previous/Go/eXit <N>:`. The Break option removes the section of the polyline between the specified vertices. The Straighten option removes all of the vertices between the two specified vertex points and replaces them with one polyline segment. With either option, the current position of the vertex marker is considered the starting point for breaking or straightening.

- **Next, Previous, Go,** and **eXit.** The Next or Previous options locate the ending vertex for your edit. After that vertex is located, use the Go option to execute the break or straighten actions. The eXit option returns to the previous prompt without performing any editing.

- **Insert.** The Insert option allows you to specify the coordinates of a new polyline vertex to be created. The Insert option issues this prompt: `Enter location of new vertex:`.

- **Move.** The Move option enables you to alter the location of the current polyline vertex by supplying a new location for the current vertex. The Move option issues the following prompt: `Enter new location:`.

- **Tangent.** The Tangent option enables you to determine the tangent direction used by fitted curves at the current vertex. The Tangent option issues the prompt: `Direction of tangent:`. The tangent direction is indicated by an arrow through the Edit vertex mode's X's.

- **Fit.** The Fit option creates a continuous smooth curve composed of arcs among all of the polyline's vertices. If you specify any tangent directions for vertices (under the Edit vertex option), the directions are used to compute the curve direction at the vertices. If you explode a curve-fit polyline or use the BREAK or TRIM commands on the polyline, a pair of arcs will appear between each vertex.

- **Spline.** The Spline option uses the existing polyline vertices to form the frame for fitting either a quadratic B-spline or a cubic B-spline curve (based on the value of the SPLINETYPE variable) along the polyline. The resolution (number of lines or arcs between each pair of vertices) is set by the value of the SPLINESEGS system variable. If SPLINESEGS is positive, the spline uses lines; if negative, the spline uses arcs to create the B-spline.

- **Decurve.** The Decurve option removes any curve-fitting or spline-fitting arc segments from the polyline.

- **Ltype gen.** By default, when AutoCAD displays polylines with noncontinuous linetypes, the pattern begins and ends at each vertex. Setting Ltype gen ON forces linetypes to be rendered between endpoints, ignoring intermediate vertices.

- **Undo.** The Undo option reverses the last action performed on the polyline. If you make many changes in the Edit vertex option, all the changes can be reversed by a single undo.

- **eXit.** The eXit option terminates the polyline editing and returns you to the `Command:` prompt.

- **Width.** The Width option enables you to vary the width of the polyline segment between the current vertex and next vertex. The Width option displays the following prompt: `Enter starting width <default>:`. Enter a value to be used for the starting width and the ending width. If the polyline has a width currently assigned, that width appears as the default. The polyline does not show the effects of the change in width until you use the Regen option, or if you exit to the main PEDIT prompt line.

3D Polylines

The following prompt and options appear when you use the PEDIT command to edit 3D polyline entities:

- `Close/Edit vertex/Spline curve/Decurve/Undo/eXit <X>:`
- **Close.** The Close option creates a closing polyline segment from the end of the polyline back to its beginning. When the polyline is

closed, this option changes to Open in the prompt line. The Open option removes a closing polyline segment.

- **Spline curve.** The Spline curve option works the same as for 2D polylines except that the curve is generated in 3D space and consists of straight line segments only, regardless of the value of SPLINESEGS.

- **Decurve.** The Decurve option removes any spline-fitting and restores the polyline to its original state.

- **Undo** and **Regen.** The Undo and Regen options function the same as for 2D polylines.

- **Edit vertex.** The Edit vertex option displays the following prompt. Each option edits vertices in the same manner as in 2D polyline editing, except that now you can supply a 3D location for the polyline's vertices.

      Next/Previous/Break/Insert/Move/Regen/Straighten/
      eXit <X>:

Polygon Meshes

The following prompt appears when you use the PEDIT command to edit polygon meshes:

- **Edit vertex/Smooth surface/Desmooth/Mclose/Nclose/ Undo/eXit <X>:**

- **Edit vertex.** The Edit vertex option displays the following prompt, which enables you to relocate the position of each of the vertices of the polygon mesh. The prompt displays the current position of the vertex you are editing in both the M and N directions.

- **Vertex (m,n). Next/Previous/Left/RIght/Up/Down/ Move/REgen/eXit <X>:**

  For meshes generated by commands affected by the SURFTAB1 and SURFTAB2 system variables, the M direction corresponds to the SURFTAB1 setting, and the N direction corresponds to the SURFTAB2 setting. The options Next, Previous, Left, Right, Up, and Down all move the current vertex X marker through the mesh.

- **Move.** The Move option of Edit vertex enables you to relocate the current polyline vertex by specifying a new coordinate anywhere within 3D space. The Move option displays the prompt: `Enter new location:`.

- **Smooth surface.** The Smooth Surface option fits a smooth surface to the framework of the mesh by using one of three smoothing options based on the value of the SURFTYPE variable. If the variable is equal to 5, quadratic B-spline surface smoothing occurs. If its value is 6, a cubic B-spline smoothing routine is used. If the variable value is 8, the surface is smoothed with a Bezier curve equation. The density of the smoothed surface is controlled by the SURFU system variable in the M direction and by the SURFV system variable in the N direction. The surface does not pass through the vertex (control) points of the mesh, but is controlled by them—as in spline-fitting a 2D or 3D polyline.

- **Desmooth.** The Desmooth option reverses any smoothing and restores the original polygon mesh.

- **Mclose** and **Nclose.** The Mclose and Nclose options close the polygon mesh in the M or N directions. If the polygon mesh is currently closed in either the M or N direction, the close option for that direction is replaced with Mopen or Nopen.

- **Undo.** The Undo option reverses the previous action performed on the mesh. If you make many changes in the Edit vertex option, all the changes can be reversed by a single undo.

- **Exit.** The Exit option terminates editing and returns to the `Command:` prompt.

Example

The following example uses the PEDIT command to edit a 2D polyline, shown in figure PEDIT.1, by inserting a vertex, relocating another vertex, and then creating a spline-fit polyline. In order to see the original polyline, set the SPLFRAME variable to 1 before beginning the command sequence.

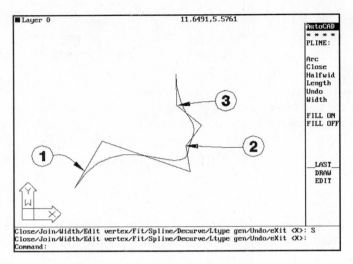

Figure PEDIT.1:
The polyline and the new splined shape.

```
Command: PEDIT ↵
Select polyline: Pick point ①
Close/Join/Width/Edit vertex/Fit/Spline/Decurve/Ltype gen/
Undo/eXit <X>: E ↵
Next/Previous/Break/Insert/Move/Regen/Straighten/Tangent/
Width/eXit <N>: ↵
Move to the next vertex
Next/Previous/Break/Insert/Move/Regen/Straighten/Tangent/
Width/eXit <N>: ↵
Move to the next vertex   .
Next/Previous/Break/Insert/Move/Regen/Straighten/Tangent/
Width/eXit <N>: I ↵
Enter location of new vertex: Pick point ②
Next/Previous/Break/Insert/Move/Regen/Straighten/Tangent/
Width/eXit <N>: ↵
Move to the next vertex
Next/Previous/Break/Insert/Move/Regen/Straighten/Tangent/
Width/eXit <N>: ↵
Next/Previous/Break/Insert/Move/Regen/Straighten/Tangent/
Width/eXit <N>: ↵
Next/Previous/Break/Insert/Move/Regen/Straighten/Tangent/
Width/eXit <N>: M ↵
Enter new location: Pick point ③
```

```
Next/Previous/Break/Insert/Move/Regen/Straighten/Tangent/
Width/eXit <N>: X↵
Close/Join/Width/Edit vertex/Fit/Spline/Decurve/Ltype gen/
Undo/eXit <X>: S↵
Close/Join/Width/Edit vertex/Fit/Spline/Decurve/Ltype gen/
Undo/eXit <X>: ↵
```

Related Commands

EDGESURF
LASTPOINT
PFACE
PLINE
REVSURF
RULESURF
TABSURF
3DFACE
3DMESH
3DPOLY

Related System Variables

PLINEGEN
SPLFRAME
SPLINESEGS
SPLINETYPE
SURFTAB1
SURFTAB2
SURFTYPE
SURFU
SURFV

PFACE

Screen [DRAW] [next] [3D Surfs] [PFACE:]

The PFACE command creates a polygon mesh by first locating points in 3D space and then connecting these points to form a face. Virtually any number of points (called vertices) can be defined. Many different faces can be created from these vertices. The polyface entity that is created can be modified in the same manner as any other polygon mesh. This command was designed for use with AutoLISP programs and ADS applications, so input for this command can be quite complicated.

No matter how many faces are created, they are linked together as one entity. Each face can be given a separate color or can be placed on a different layer as it is created. The edges of a face can be made invisible. If a frozen layer contains one of the polyfaces, the entire polyface is invisible until the layer is thawed.

Prompts and Options

- **`Vertex x:`**

  At this prompt, you enter a point, either 2D or 3D. The prompt continues until you press Enter, signifying the end of the vertex definition.

- **`Face x, Vertex x:`**

  This prompt defines the edges of each face. As you define the first face, enter each vertex (by the number defined) as they connect to form the face. After all vertices for the face are identified, press Enter to define the next face. Pressing Enter at the first vertex prompt of any face instructs AutoCAD to complete the command and create the polyfaces. If you want an edge of the face to be invisible, precede the vertex number with a minus sign, such as -3.

  You also can enter **Color** and **Layer** at this prompt. These two options enable you to create a polyface that has individual faces of different colors and are located on different layers.

Example

This example creates a simple polyface entity, shown in figure PFACE.1, using the PFACE command.

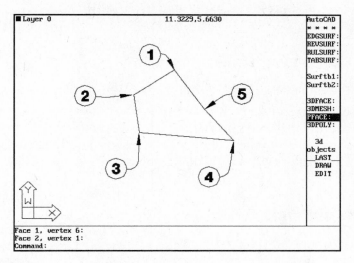

Figure PFACE.1:
A simple polygon mesh created with the PFACE command.

```
Command: PFACE ↵
Vertex 1: Pick point ①
Vertex 2: Pick point ②
Vertex 3: Pick point ③
Vertex 4: Pick point ④
Vertex 5: Pick point ⑤
Vertex 6: ↵
Face 1, vertex 1: 1 ↵
Face 1, vertex 2: 2 ↵
Face 1, vertex 3: 3 ↵
Face 1, vertex 4: 4 ↵
Face 1, vertex 5: 5 ↵
Face 1, vertex 6: ↵
```

Related Commands

PEDIT
REVSURF
RULESURF
TABSURF
3DFACE
3DMESH

PLAN

Screen   **[DISPLAY] PLAN:]**

Pull down   **[View] [Set View >] [Plan View >]**

The PLAN command sets the view to the plan view of one of three possible coordinate systems. When you are working in model space, the plan view is parallel to the X-Y plane of the coordinate system. The PLAN command provides a quick method of setting your viewport to 0,0,1.

Prompts and Options

- **<Current UCS>/UCS/World:**

  The default option, <Current UCS>, changes the view to the plan of the current UCS. The UCS option changes the view to the plan of a previously saved UCS. If you select the World option, the drawing regenerates and you can view your drawing from the WCS.

- **?/Name of UCS:**

  At this prompt, you enter the name of a saved User Coordinate System. You can use the **?** option to display a list of currently saved User Coordinate Systems.

- **UCS name(s) to list <*>:**

  At this prompt, you enter the name of a UCS to list, or press Enter to view a list of all defined User Coordinate Systems.

Example

This example shows how to restore the plan view of a named UCS. Figure PLAN.1 shows, in two viewports, the difference in the display.

```
Command: PLAN ↵
?/Name of UCS: FACE1 ↵
<Current UCS>/UCS/World: U ↵
```

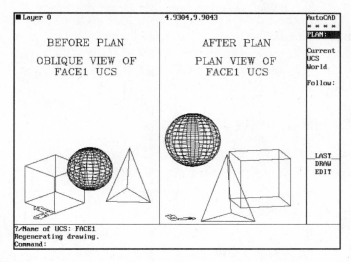

Figure PLAN.1:
The initial SITE-3D drawing before setting the plan view.

Related Commands

DDUCSP
DDVPOINT
DDVIEW
VPOINT
UCS

Related System Variables

UCSFOLLOW
UCSNAME

PLINE

Screen   **[DRAW] [next] [PLINE:]**

Pull down   **[Draw] [Polyline >] [2D]**

The PLINE command draws polyline entities. Polylines are complex entities that are a combination of line and arc segments, but are treated by AutoCAD as a single entity. As a complex entity, 2D polylines have great flexibility to meet special needs in an AutoCAD drawing—from custom leader lines to hatch boundaries.

Prompts and Options

- **From point:**

  At this prompt, you enter the starting point of the polyline.

- **Arc/Close/Halfwidth/Length/Undo/Width/<Endpoint of line>:**

  This prompt contains all of the major options of the PLINE command.

- **Arc.** This option presents this additional prompt:

- **Angle/CEnter/CLose/Direction/Halfwidth/Line/ Radius/Second pt/Undo/Width/<Endpoint of arc>:**

  Each of the possible polyline arc options is discussed in the following paragraphs.

- **Angle.** This option asks you to enter the included angle of the arc. The Angle option issues the `Included angle:` prompt. After you have entered the value for the included angle, you receive this prompt: `Center/Radius/<Endpoint>:`. Enter the center point for the arc, the arc's radius, or use the default option to specify an endpoint for the arc.

- **CEnter.** This option displays the prompt `Center point:`, at which you enter the arc's center point. By default, the PLINE command draws arcs tangent from the last segment and automatically locates the arc's center point. This option enables you to override the default action of the PLINE command.

- **Angle/Length/<End point>:**

  If you used the Center option displayed previously, enter the additional information needed to create the arc. You can enter the included angle, a value for the chord length, or simply specify the arc's endpoint (the default option).

- **Close**. This option draws a polyline arc segment back to the beginning of the polyline.
- **Direction.** This option enables you to specify the direction that the arc will be drawn from the arc's starting point. The Direction option issues the Direction from starting point: prompt. The PLINE command draws the arc tangent to the starting point by default. If you want to override this default, pick a point in the drawing editor to indicate the arc's new direction.
- **End point:**

  After the polyline arc direction has been entered, locate the end point of the arc by specifying a point.
- **Halfwidth.** This option enables you to enter a value for the width of a polyline segment based on the width from the center of the polyline to its edge. The actual width of the polyline segment will be double the value you enter at the prompt below.

  Starting half-width <0.000>:
- **Ending half-width <0.000>:**

  The ending polyline half-width is the same as its starting half-width by default. This gives the polyline segment a uniform width. If you want the width tapered from the beginning to the end, enter an ending half-width that differs in value from the starting half-width.
- **Line**. This option returns you to the Line mode prompt.
- **Radius.** This option accepts a value for the radius of an arc.
- **Angle/<End point>:**

  After you enter the radius, locate an ending point at the prompt above to create the arc or enter a value for the arc's included angle.
- **Second point.** Polyline arc segments can be created similar to a standard three-point arc with this option. Enter the second of three points that will describe the arc.
- **End point:**

  After the second point of the polyline arc is located, specify the end point at this prompt to properly create the polyline arc.

843

- **Undo.** This option undoes individual segments one at a time.
- **Width.** The Width option works in the same manner as the half-width option. It enables you to assign a width at the Starting with <0.000> prompt for the current polyline segment. The difference is that the width is measured from the edges of the polyline, not from the center to the edge.
- **Ending width <0.000>:**

  The ending polyline width is the same as its starting width by default. This gives the polyline segment a uniform width. If you want the width to taper from beginning to end, enter an ending width at the above prompt that differs from the starting width.
- **Endpoint of arc.** The default option, enables you to select the endpoint for an arc that is drawn tangent to the last segment.

Following are the remaining PLINE Line mode options:

- **Close.** This option works in the same manner as the Close option of Arc mode, except that it draws a straight segment back to the beginning of the polyline.
- **Halfwidth, Undo,** and **Width.** These options work the same as when you draw polyline arc segments.
- **Length.** You enter a value for the length of the next segment. The segment will be drawn at the same angle as the previous segment. If no segment exists, an angle of 0 degrees is used to draw the next segment.
- **Endpoint of line.** This option, which is the default, enables you to specify the location for another segment endpoint.

Example

This example demonstrates using some of the PLINE command's options to create the polyline shown in figure PLINE.1.

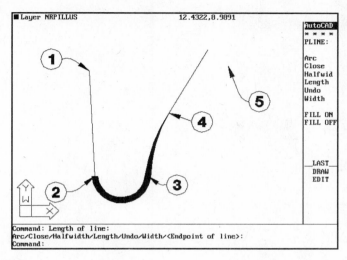

Figure PLINE.1:
A polyline created with various PLINE options.

```
Command: PLINE ↵
From point: Pick point ①
Arc/Close/Halfwidth/Length/Undo/Width/<Endpoint  of  line>: Pick
point ②
Arc/Close/Halfwidth/Length/Undo/Width/<Endpoint of line>: W↵
Starting width <0.0000>: .25 ↵
Ending width <0.2500>: ↵
Arc/Close/Halfwidth/Length/Undo/Width/<Endpoint of line>: A↵
Angle/CEnter/CLose/Direction/Halfwidth/Line/Radius/Second pt/
Undo/Width/<Endpoint of arc>: Pick point ③
Angle/CEnter/CLose/Direction/Halfwidth/Line/Radius/Second pt/
Undo/Width/<Endpoint of arc>: W ↵
Starting width <0.2500>: ↵
Ending width <0.2500>: 0 ↵
Angle/CEnter/CLose/Direction/Halfwidth/Line/Radius/Second pt/
Undo/Width/<Endpoint of arc>: ④
Angle/CEnter/CLose/Direction/Halfwidth/Line/Radius/Second pt/
Undo/Width/<Endpoint of arc>: L ↵
Arc/Close/Halfwidth/Length/Undo/Width/<Endpoint of line>: L ↵
Length of line: ⑤
Arc/Close/Halfwidth/Length/Undo/Width/<Endpoint of line>: ↵
```

Related Commands

FILL
PEDIT
TRACE

Related System Variables

PLINEGEN
PLINEWID

PLOT

R12

Screen   **[PLOT...]**

Pull down   **[File] [Plot...]**

The PLOT command produces a hard copy of your drawing on an installed and configured plotting device. The PLOT command outputs only the current drawing. You can specify one of several different drawing areas to plot, including the most recent display view, the extents of the drawing, the limits as established by the LIMITS command, a named view, or a user-specified window. Each plot may be directed either to the configured plotter or to a file on disk.

Prompts and Options

In AutoCAD Release 12, the plotting facility has been completely renovated to work from a comprehensive dialog box. The Plot Configuration dialog box, shown in figure PLOT.1, displays each of the plotting options in a series of radio buttons, check boxes, and option buttons, divided into logical groups. The functions of each of these groups are described in the following paragraphs.

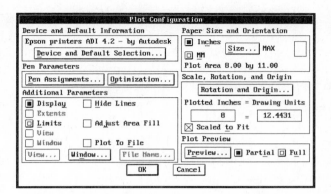

Figure PLOT.1:
The Plot Configuration dialog box.

The Plot Configuration dialog box is controlled by the CMDDIA system variable. If CMDDIA is set to 0, then no dialog box will be shown and the prompts used in previous versions of AutoCAD will be displayed. This setting is most useful if you need to perform plotting from a script file.

The Device and Default Information group has a single button that performs the following function:

- **Device and Default Selection.** This button allows you to choose from up to 29 predefined plotter configurations that you can use to plot your drawing. Because the PRPLOT command has been removed in Release 12, both printer plotter and pen plotter configurations can be placed in this list to use as your output device.

  This button displays the Device and Default Selection dialog box. This dialog box contains a list box of the defined plotter configurations. You must use the CONFIG command to create plotter configurations. To make one of the configurations active, highlight it and click on the OK button. If you click on the Cancel button, any modifications you have made in the dialog box will be removed. This dialog box also contains the following buttons:

- **Save Default To File.** This button allows you to save all the plotting parameters you have chosen from the Configuration Plot dialog box, to a plot configuration file. This file can be used at a later time to restore all the defaults you have chosen. Plot configuration files have an extension of PCP.

- **Get Default From File.** This button retrieves any previously saved plotter configuration file and updates the current plot parameters.

- **Show Device Requirements.** This option displays additional configuration information about the plotter. If this button is greyed, there are no additional requirements for this particular plotting device.

- **Change Device Requirements.** This option enables you to change plotter configuration values if the selected plotter has any additional possible values. If this button is greyed, no other values are possible.

The Pen Parameters group is used to specify information that is specific to the type of plotter you have selected. This group has two buttons:

- **Pen Assignments.** This button is used to assign AutoCAD color numbers to plotter pens. This button displays the Pen Assignments dialog box, which is used to define which AutoCAD color is assigned to each plotter pen number, and also assign such attributes as hardware linetype, pen speed, and pen width. Click on the Feature Legend. button to display which of these attributes may be assigned using the current plotter.

- **Optimization.** At plot time, AutoCAD optimizes the plot information so that your plotter does not waste time.

TIP You can configure the types of optimization you want by selecting one of the radio buttons provided in the Optimizing Pen Motion dialog box. Some plotters perform optimization, and if you modify any of these options, you may instead increase your plot time.

The Additional Parameters group determines what information in your drawing gets sent to the plotter. The group of radio buttons allows you to plot out the current display, the drawing's extents, the drawing's limits, a named view, or a windowed area of your drawing. You can also choose to hide lines that may be obscured in a 3D drawing, adjust the fill area based on the width of the pen in use, or send all the plot information to a file. The buttons in this group perform the following functions:

- **View.** If you choose to plot a view, this button displays the View Name dialog box. This box contains a list of all the named views within the current drawing. To plot one of the views, highlight the name in the list box, and click on the OK button.

- **Window.** If you choose to plot a windowed area of your drawing, this button displays the Window Selection dialog box. This box allows you to enter the absolute X and Y locations for the window's corners, or you pick the window by clicking on the Pick button.

- **File Name.** You can choose to plot the drawing to a file, instead of the plotter. Typically, the default plot file name is set with the CONFIG command, but you can use this button to select a different file name for the plot file.

The Paper Size and Orientation buttons are used to tell AutoCAD the size of the output for your plot. The radio buttons in this group determine which type of units, Inches or Millimeters, are used for displaying the size of the plot. The final button, **Size**, performs the following action:

- **Size.** The Size button allows you to choose the size of plotted output for the current plot. The Paper Size and Orientation dialog box displays a list of possible paper sizes based on the current plotter configuration. You can also specify custom plot sizes by filling in the User edit boxes. You may also choose to have the plot oriented normally in landscape mode, or rotated 90 degrees and placed in portrait mode.

The Scale, Rotation, and Origin group is used to determine the final plot parameters before output. You can directly enter the scale for the plot in the supplied edit boxes, or you may choose to fit the plot within the boundaries of the paper you have chosen by checking the Scaled to Fit check box. The only button in this group performs the following actions:

- **Rotation and Origin.** This button allows you to rotate the plotted output and locate the starting point on the paper where the plot will begin.

The final group of plot options is the Plot Preview group. It allows you to perform an on-screen preview before any information gets sent to the plotter. This has the advantage of displaying any possible problem with the plot before actually putting any information down on paper. The two options, Partial or Full, determine the amount of detail shown when you click on the Preview button.

When you perform a partial preview, you will see an accurate rendering of the paper size you are plotting to, along with an indicator of the amount of space needed to plot the drawing. This preview shows no drawing geometry and is quick. A full preview, on the other hand, shows exactly what will plot in the area that is assigned. This method takes longer to preview due to the greater amount of detail required.

Example

This example of the PLOT command shows you how to set plot parameters and perform a full plot preview. When shown in preview mode, the drawing looks similar to figure PLOT.2.

Command: **PLOT** ↵
Click on the Extents *radio button*
Click on the Size *button*
Select "C" size from the list box, then press the OK button
Set the scale to 1=1
Click on the Full *button, then click on the* Preview *button*
Click on the End Preview *button*
Click on the Cancel *button*

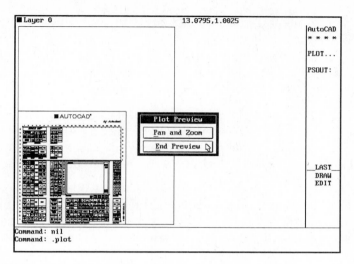

Figure PLOT.2:
The Plot Configuration dialog box.

Related Commands

CONFIG
FILL
QTEXT

Related System Variables

CMDDIA
PLOTID
PLOTTER

POINT

Screen **[DRAW] [next] [POINT:]**

Pull down **[Draw] [Point]**

The POINT command creates a point entity in your drawing. You can enter a point coordinate from the keyboard, or you can pick a point on the screen. If you enter 2D coordinates, the Z elevation defaults to the current construction plane. Point entities can be used for object snap points when you use the NODe object snap mode.

You can alter the style and size of point display by using the PDMODE and PDSIZE system variables. After you change these variables, all subsequently created points reflect the new settings. Existing points do not display in the new style and size until the drawing is regenerated.

AutoCAD also creates points when you create associative dimensions. These points are placed on a layer named DEFPOINTS. If you move these points, AutoCAD automatically updates the associated dimension. These dimension points are not affected by the settings of the PDMODE and PDSIZE variables.

Prompts and Options

- `Point:`
  At this prompt, you specify the new point entity's location.

Related Commands

DIVIDE
MEASURE

Related System Variables

PDMODE
PDSIZE

POLYGON

Screen **[DRAW] [next] [POLYGON:]**

Pull down **[Draw] [Polygon]**

The POLYGON command creates a multisided regular polygon as a polyline entity. Each entity has sides of equal length and spacing around the center. Polygons are closed polyline entities made up of at least three segments (up to 1,024 segments).

Prompts and Options

- **Number of sides <4>:**

  At this prompt, you specify the number of sides for the polygon. Enter any number from 3 to 1,024. The default creates a square.

- **Edge/<Center of polygon>:**

  When you specify an edge, you draw one side of the polygon. The other edges are drawn using the same length. If you want to draw the polygon by using a circle as a guide, specify the circle's center point.

- **First endpoint of edge:**

  This Edge option's first prompt requests the starting point for the polygon face.

- **Second endpoint of edge:**

  At this prompt, you specify a point to define the end point of the polygon's first edge.

- **Inscribed in circle/Circumscribed about circle (I/C) <I>:**

  This prompt appears after you specify the polygon's center point.

  You enter **I** if you want to specify the polygon using a circle to inscribe it. When the polygon is inscribed in the circle, the circle's radius defines the distance from the center to the corners of the sides.

853

You enter **C** if you want to specify the polygon by using a circle to circumscribe it. If the entity is circumscribed by the circle, the radius measures the distance from the center perpendicular to one of the edges. This distance is often referred to as the distance across the flats, as you measure the head of a bolt.

- **Radius of circle:**

  At this prompt, you enter a distance for the radius, and the polygon is created with the first side aligned with the X axis. Pick a point to indicate the radius, and the polygon is created using that point to set its size and orientation.

Example

This example creates a polygon with eight sides. The results are shown in figure POLYGON.1.

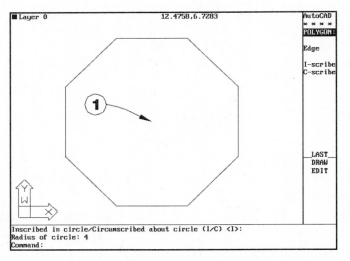

Figure POLYGON.1:
An octagon drawn with the POLYGON command's Circumscribed option.

```
Command: POLYGON ↵
Number of Sides <4>: 8 ↵
```

```
Edge/<Center of polygon>: Pick point ①
Inscribed in circle/Circumscribed about circle (I/C) <I>: C↵
Radius of circle: 4 ↵
```

PSDRAG

PSDRAG controls the display of PostScript images while they are placed and scaled by the PSIN command.

Prompts and Options

- **`PSIN drag mode <0>:`**

  You can enter **0** (the default) or 1. Enter **0** to display just the boundary of PostScript images while dragging. Enter **1** to display the rendered PostScript image (see fig. PSDRAG1).

If you are importing a complex postscript graphic, you can reduce the redraw time by setting PSDRAG to 0.

The PSIN drag mode has no effect if the PSQUALITY system variable is set to 0; only boundaries are displayed.

Related Commands

PSIN
PSFILL

Related System Variable

PSQUALITY

855

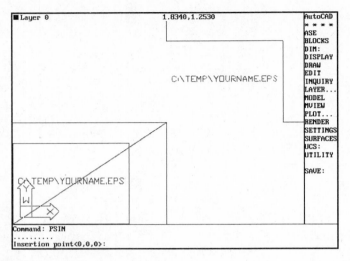

Figure PSDRAG.1:
A PostScript font with PSDRAG set to 1.

PSFILL

The PSFILL command fills areas that are enclosed by 2D polylines. PSFILL uses a pattern defined in the AutoCAD PostScript support file ACAD.PSF. The fill pattern is visible only on hard-copy output and is not drawn on-screen in the drawing editor.

Prompts and Options

- `Select polyline:`

  You pick the polyline for which you want to specify a PostScript fill pattern. The new pattern is assigned to the area within the polyline.

- `PostScript fill pattern (. = none) <.>/?:`

  You enter the name of a fill pattern to assign to the selected area. The default for this prompt is none. You can enter a question mark to list the names of available fills. You can precede the pattern name with an asterisk to prevent printing of the solid polyline outline on hard copy; only the fill pattern is plotted. Fill patterns included with Release 12 include Grayscale, RGBcolor, AIlogo, Lineargray, Radialgray, Square, Waffle, Zigzag, Stars, Brick, and Specks.

Related Commands

FILL
PEDIT
PLINE

Related System Variables

FILLMODE
PLINEWID
PLINEGEN

PSIN

Pull down **[Draw] [Import/Export] [PostScript In]**

The PSIN command imports an existing Encapsulated PostScript (EPS) file into the current drawing. You can drag the image on screen and place it by picking. Before the image is placed, it appears as a box outlining the size and shape of the image. The file name of the image appears within the box. After the EPS image has been imported, it becomes an anonymous (unnamed) AutoCAD block. The original PostScript data is appended to the block as extended entity data in case the image is output back to an EPS file with the PSOUT command.

Prompts and Options

- **File:**

At this prompt, you enter the name of an existing EPS file without the extension or select a file with the Select PostScript File dialog box.

- `Insertion point <0,00>:`

  You enter an insertion point for the lower left corner of the image or accept the default.

- `Scale factor:`

  You enter a scale factor for the imported image.

Example

This example uses PSIN to import an EPS file into the current drawing (see fig. PSIN.1).

```
Command: PSIN↵
Insertion point <0,00>: ↵
Scale factor: 1 ↵
```

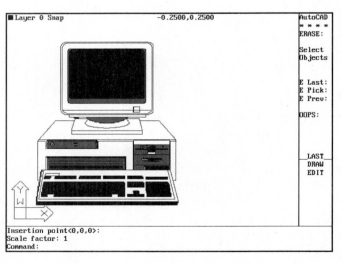

Figure PSIN.1:
Encapsulated PostScript image imported into AutoCAD with PSIN.

Related Commands

DXBIN
DXFIN
IGESIN
PSOUT
PSQUALITY

PSOUT

Screen **[UTILITY] [PSOUT:]**

Pull down **[File] [Import/Export] [PostScript Out]**

The PSOUT command exports the current drawing as an Encapsulated PostScript (EPS) file. The file is given the same name as the current drawing, with the extension EPS. The EPS file can then be imported into another graphics or desktop publishing program. A user-selectable resolution screen image may be included for previewing the file within other programs. If any blocks exist in the drawing with PostScript information in extended entity data, such as created by PSIN, that information is output to the EPS file as well.

Prompts and Options

- **File:**

  Use the Create PostScript File dialog box to enter the output file name or specify an existing file to overwrite.

- **What to export — Display, Extents, Limits, View, or Window <D>:**

  At this prompt, you enter an option for the area of the current drawing to export. The initial default is Display.

  - **Display.** This option exports an area equivalent to the visible drawing area.

- **Extents.** This option exports an area containing all the entities in the current space.
- **Limits.** This option exports an area equivalent to the current drawing's limits as set by the LIMITS command.
- **View.** This option exports an area defined by an existing view created by the VIEW command.
- **Window.** This option exports an area bounded by a window you draw on-screen.
- **Include a screen preview image in the file? (None/EPSI/TIFF) <None>:**

  You enter the type of screen preview to include within the EPS file or accept the default, None. EPSI-type preview images are predominantly used by the Macintosh platform. TIFF previews are usually necessary for DOS. If you specify a preview image type, the following prompt appears.
- **Screen preview image size (128x128 is standard)? (128/256/512) <128>:**

  You enter a number for the resolution of the screen preview image. Smaller sizes display faster than larger ones. Higher-resolution images display with more detail.

Example

The following example creates an EPS file of the current display and includes a TIFF-format screen preview image.

```
Command: PSOUT↵
File: Enter the file name in the edit box
What to export — Display, Extents, Limits, View or Window <D>: ↵
Include a screen preview image in the file? (None/EPSI/TIFF)
<None>: T↵
Screen preview image size (128x128 is standard)? (128/256/512)
<128>: ↵
Effective plotting area: 7.50 wide by 5.43 high
```

Related Commands

DXFOUT
DXBOUT
IGESOUT
PSIN
PSQUALITY

Related Variable

PSPROLOG

PSPACE

Screen **[MVIEW] [PSPACE:]**

Pull down **[View] [Paper Space]**

The PSPACE command switches the active drawing space from model space to paper space. This command works only when the TILEMODE system variable is set to 0 (off). The MVIEW command pull-down menu item sets TILEMODE to 0, which activates paper space. You must make paper space active to create or edit paper-space entities.

When paper space is active, the UCS icon appears only in paper space (as a triangle), a P appears on the status line, and the crosshairs are active over the entire drawing screen (see fig. PSPACE.1). Model space must be active if you want to work on model-space entities or to pan, zoom, or modify the viewport contents. When model space is active, a normal UCS icon appears in each mview viewport, and the crosshairs are active only in the current mview viewport. You use the MSPACE command to make model space active.

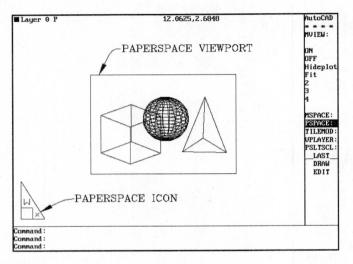

Figure PSPACE.1:
The drawing editor in paper space.

Prompts and Options

Although the PSPACE command does not have any options, it issues two informational prompts:

- **** Command not allowed unless TILEMODE is set to 0 ****

  If TILEMODE is not 0 (off), this message reminds you that it must be set to 0 before you can use paper space.
- **Already in paper space.**

  If paper space is the active drawing space, this prompt appears.

Related Commands

MSPACE
MVIEW

Related System Variable

TILEMODE

PURGE

Screen **[UTILITY] [PURGE:]**

The PURGE command selectively removes from the drawing unreferenced definitions of blocks, dimension styles, layers, linetypes, shapes, and text styles. By using the PURGE command to remove unused definitions, you can reduce the size of the drawing and speed up the loading of drawings.

The PURGE command must be used before you use any drawing or editing command or any command that creates named definitions, such as blocks, layers, and so on. If you need to use the PURGE command to remove unused entities, you should do this immediately after you enter the drawing editor.

Named definitions that are nested, such as blocks, are purged only one level per session. Therefore, you must purge the highest level first, end the drawing, and then re-enter the drawing to purge the nested items. You may have to do this procedure several times to purge all unused items if they are deeply nested.

Prompts and Options

- **Purge unused Blocks/Dimstyles/LAyers/LTypes/ SHapes/STyles/All:**

  At this prompt, you enter the capital letter(s) of the definition type to purge. Enter an **A** to purge unreferenced definitions of all types.

- **Purge *item NAME?* <N>**

  If any unreferenced definitions of the specified type exist (listed in the prompt), the PURGE command displays each unreferenced definition's name (in the prompt) and asks if you want to remove it. PURGE continues to prompt for all unreferenced items of that type. If you specify the All option, PURGE prompts for all unreferenced definitions of each of the types.

Example

This example uses the PURGE command to remove a block definition from the drawing.

```
Command: PURGE ↵
Purge unused Blocks/Dimstyles/LAyers/LTypes/SHapes/STyles/
All: B↵
Purge block CHAIR? <N> Y ↵
```

QSAVE

Pull down **[File] [Save]**

The QSAVE command works the same way as the SAVE command, saving any changes to the current drawing to disk without exiting the drawing editor. The difference between QSAVE and SAVE is that QSAVE does not prompt for a file name; the current drawing is saved to the default file name without hesitation. If the current drawing has not yet been named, the Save Drawing As dialog box appears so that you can specify a file name.

Use the QSAVE command to save your work periodically. It saves changes to the default drawing quickly.

Related Commands

END
NEW
QUIT
SAVE
SAVEAS

Related System Variables

DBMOD
DWGNAME
DWGPREFIX
SAVETIME

QTEXT

Screen **[SETTINGS] [next] [QTEXT:]**

The QTEXT command turns quick text mode on and off. When quick text mode is on, any text entity is regenerated as boxes that indicate the approximate size of the text entity, instead of text characters. The screen regenerates and redraws much faster with quick text mode on, especially if the drawing contains much text or uses a complex font. New text displays as text characters until the next screen regeneration. Quick text mode does not affect the text editing commands CHANGE, DDATTE, and DDEDIT.

Prompts and Options

- **ON/OFF:**

  You enter **ON** to turn quick text mode on. After the next regeneration, the display shows all existing text as boxes.

  You enter **OFF** to disable quick text mode. After the next regeneration, all text displays normally.

Example

The following example shows the effect of quick text mode on existing text in a drawing (see fig. QTEXT.1).

```
Command: QTEXT↵
On/Off <Off>: ON↵
Command: REGEN↵
```

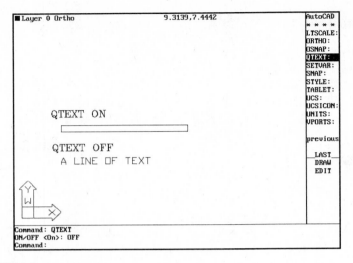

Figure QTEXT.1:
Text as it appears normally, and with QTEXT on.

Related Commands

DDRMODES
REGEN

Related System Variable

QTEXTMODE

QUIT

Screen **[UTILITY] [next] [QUIT:]**

Pull down **[File] [Exit AutoCAD]**

The QUIT command terminates AutoCAD without saving the current drawing.

Prompts and Options

R12 In Release 12, the QUIT command uses a comprehensive dialog box that prevents you from mistakenly exiting an editing session before you have saved your drawing. The new QUIT dialog box has the following buttons:

- **Save Changes**. This button is automatically highlighted, and enables you to save your work before exiting the AutoCAD program.
- **Discard Changes.** This button immediately exits to the operating system without saving any changes you have made to your drawing.
- **Cancel Command.** This button cancels the QUIT command and places you back in the drawing editor to continue drawing.

Example

The following example describes how to quit the drawing without saving your changes.

Command: **QUIT** ↵
Press Tab
Press Enter

Related Commands

END
SAVE
SAVEAS

Related System Variable

DBMOD

RCONFIG

Pull down **[Render] [Preferences] [Reconfigure]**

The RCONFIG (ReCONFIGure) command enables you to change the configured display and hard-copy rendering devices used by the RENDER command. All other AutoCAD display and output are through devices configured by the CONFIG command. After the RCONFIG command is issued, AutoCAD switches focus to the text display and then displays the current rendering device configuration. The configuration menu has four options.

Prompts and Options

- **Enter selection <0>:**

  You enter one of the four configuration menu options at this prompt.

- **0. Exit to drawing editor**

  This option prompts you to save your configuration changes and then returns you to the drawing editor.

- **1. Show current configuration**

  This option redisplays the opening screen of the RCONFIG command, showing the current configuration.

- **2. Configure rendering device**

  This option displays the currently available rendering and combined rendering/display devices and enables you to configure them. The prompts and options vary depending on the device. Consult the *Interface, Installation, and Performance Guide* and your rendering driver's documentation for more information.

- **3. Configure hard copy rendering device**

  This option displays the currently available hard-copy rendering devices and enables you to configure them. The prompts and options vary depending on the device. Consult the *Interface, Installation, and Performance Guide* and your rendering driver's documentation for more information.

Related Commands

CONFIG
RENDER
RPREF

RECOVER

Pull-down **[File] [Recover]**

Screen (This command is not in screen menu)

The RECOVER command salvages a damaged drawing file. Available with Release 11, AutoCAD now includes drawing recovery information in each drawing file, which makes the process of recovering damaged file information very accurate.

Prompts and Options

This command has no direct prompts. You initially see the File Open dialog box, which indicates the drawing file that needs recovery. The RECOVER analyzes each section of the drawing file, looks for errors, and then displays a final dialog box that indicates whether a drawing recovery is possible. The following listing shows the drawing recovery for a file that is still in good shape:

```
Drawing recovery log.
Drawing header read successfully.
Recovering Block definition table.
No errors in Block definition table.
Recovering Text font and shape table.
No errors in Text font and shape table.
Recovering Linetype table.
No errors in Linetype table.
Recovering Layer table.
No errors in Layer table.
Recovering View table.
No errors in View table.
Recovering Coordinate system table.
```

869

```
No errors in Coordinate system table.
Recovering Viewport table.
No errors in Viewport table.
Recovering Dimension style table.
No errors in Dimension style table.
Recovering Registered application table.
No errors in Registered application table.
```

 When you use the OPEN command to load a file into the drawing editor, AutoCAD makes a quick check to see whether it can spot any problems with the file. If it detects any errors, a message appears at the bottom of the dialog box, stating that the file needs recovery.

You should attempt to run RECOVER to salvage any usable drawing information. If this step does not work, try to rename the backup file to give it a DWG file extension. This older copy of the drawing may still contain valid drawing information.

Related Command

> **AUDIT**

Related Variable

> **AUDITCTL**

RECTANG

Pull down **[Draw] [Rectangle]**

RECTANG allows you to draw orthogonal rectangles by picking any two opposing corners. The rectangle is a closed polyline, and as such, can be edited with the PEDIT command, solidified, or extruded.

Prompts and Options

- **First corner:**

  You specify the first corner of the rectangle. You can enter coordinates, pick a point, or use the object snap modes.

- **Other corner:**

  You specify the second corner of the rectangle. You can enter coordinates, pick a point, or use the object snap modes.

Example

The following example draws a rectangle (see fig. RECTANG.1).

```
Command: RECTANG ↵
First corner: 4,3 ↵
Second corner: 8.5,6 ↵
```

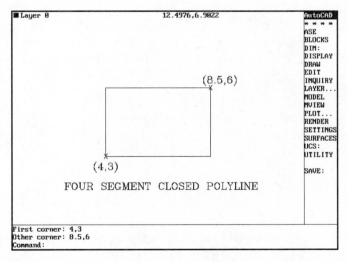

Figure RECTANG.1:
A rectangle created with the RECTANG command.

Related Commands

PEDIT
POLYGON
POLYLINE

Related System Variables

PLINEGEN
PLINEWID

REDEFINE

The REDEFINE command reverses the UNDEFINE command by restoring an AutoCAD command to its original action. The UNDEFINE command disables AutoCAD commands so that they cannot be used. You also can use AutoLISP or ADS to define a custom command to replace an undefined command. For example, you can change the END command so that it asks you to confirm that you really want to exit the drawing editor before you exit.

If you do not want to redefine the command, but you still need to use it with its original actions, you can enter the command name preceded by a period at the Command: prompt. For example, if END is undefined, you can still use it by typing **.END** at the Command: prompt.

Prompts and Options

- Command name:

  You enter the name of the AutoCAD command to restore.

Example

The following example uses the UNDEFINE command to disable the ELEV command. The REDEFINE command is then used to restore the ELEV command back to its original action.

```
Command: UNDEFINE ↵
Command name: ELEV↵
Command: ELEV↵
Unknown command
Type ? for list of Commands.
Command: ELEV↵
New current elevation <0.0000>: *Cancel* Press Ctrl-C
Command: REDEFINE↵
Command name: ELEV↵
Command: ELEV↵
New current elevation <0.09000>: Press Ctrl-C
*Cancel*
```

Related Command

UNDEFINE

REDO

Screen **[* * * *] [REDO:]**

Pull down **[Assist] [Redo]**

The REDO command reverses the effects of a single UNDO command. REDO only works if the immediately preceding command was UNDO (or U).

Example

The following example creates a line and uses the UNDO command to remove the line. The REDO command reverses the UNDO command, which restores the line.

```
Command: LINE↵
From point: 1,1↵
To point: 5,5↵
To point: ↵
Command: U ↵
Command: REDO ↵
```

Related Commands

OOPS
PLOT
UNDO

REDRAW

Screen   **[DISPLAY] [REDRAW:]**

Screen   **[* * * *] [REDRAW:]**

Pull down   **[View] [Redraw]**

The REDRAW command redisplays the image in the current viewport.
You can use this command as a transparent command within another
command by entering **'REDRAW**. Blips are removed from the display.

Use this command to refresh the display after you erase entities that
overlap, or to return to the current drawing after viewing a slide with
the VSLIDE command.

REDRAW is substantially faster than the REGEN command, which also
refreshes the displayed image. The REGEN command, however, regenerates the current view in addition to redrawing it.

The current viewport automatically redraws when a layer is turned on
or off, or the grid is turned off. Note that the grid's density affects the
speed of the redraw. Entities on layers that are turned off add to the
time that REDRAW takes. However, entities on frozen layers do not
take additional time to redraw. You can stop a redraw operation by
pressing Ctrl-C. In this case, you can select only displayed entities until
a complete redraw takes place.

Related Commands

REDRAWALL
REGEN
REGENALL

REDRAWALL

Screen **[DISPLAY] [REDRALL:]**

Pull down **[View] [Redraw All]**

The REDRAWALL command is similar to the REDRAW command, except that it redisplays the images in all active viewports on the screen, not just the current viewport. You can use this command transparently by entering '**REDRAWALL**.

Related Commands

REDRAW
REGEN
REGENALL

REGEN

Screen **[DISPLAY] [REGEN:]**

The REGEN command regenerates the geometry of all entities within the drawing and redisplays the image in the current viewport. You cannot use this command transparently. If you make modifications to a drawing, you may need to issue the REGEN command to ensure that the modifications are displayed correctly.

A regeneration occurs automatically when the drawing is loaded into memory with the OPEN command. Certain command options, such as ZOOM All and LAYER Freeze/Thaw, always regenerate the drawing automatically. Other actions, such as redefining a block or text style, or resetting linetype scale, automatically regenerate the drawing unless automatic regenerations have been turned off. Automatic regeneration by such commands is controlled by the REGENAUTO command. The REGEN command also smooths out arcs and circles that look segmented due to the current zoom factor.

To speed up the regeneration process, you should freeze out layers that are not in use. You can stop the screen regeneration by pressing Ctrl-C. In this case, any entities not displayed may not be selected or redrawn until a completed regeneration takes place.

Related Commands

REDRAW
REDRAWALL
REGENALL
REGENAUTO

REGENALL

Screen **[DISPLAY] [REGNALL:]**

The REGENALL command regenerates the entire drawing and redisplays the current views in all active viewports. The REGENALL command differs from the REGEN command in that REGENALL regenerates every active viewport. If you have only one active viewport, the REGENALL command works exactly the same as the REGEN command.

Related Commands

REDRAW
REGEN
REDRAWALL
REGENAUTO

REGENAUTO

Screen **[DISPLAY] [RGNAUTO:]**

The REGENAUTO command controls automatic screen regenerations caused by commands such as BLOCK, STYLE, LTSCALE, LAYER, and ZOOM, which automatically cause a screen regeneration.

 You can execute the REGENAUTO command transparently by preceding the command name with an apostrophe ('REGENAUTO).

Prompts and Options

- **ON/OFF <On>:**

  When REGENAUTO is on, AutoCAD executes a screen regeneration when certain commands require it.

  If REGENAUTO is off, AutoCAD disables automatic regeneration caused by certain actions. With some commands, this forces AutoCAD to prompt you to verify that you want a screen regeneration. If you execute such a command, the following prompt appears:

      About to regen, proceed? <Y>

  Note that you can suppress this prompt by setting the EXPERT system variable to a value of 1 or more.

Related Commands

REGEN
REGENALL

Related System Variables

EXPERT
REGENMODE

REINIT

R12

Screen **[UTILITY] [next] [REINIT:]**

877

The REINIT command reinitializes the peripherals with which AutoCAD communicates. Use REINIT when operation of your display, digitizer, or plotter has been lost or interrupted by another program, or by disconnecting and reconnecting the peripheral. You also can use REINIT to reload the ACAD.PGP file after changes have been made in the current editing session.

Prompts and Options

This command issues no prompts. All options are selected from the Re-initialization dialog box (see fig. REINIT.1).

I/O Port Initialization

The following options re-initialize communications with your system's input and output ports. Selecting an option may not necessarily re-establish communications with the peripheral attached to the specified port. See the Device and File Initialization options below.

- **Digitizer.** Checking this box initializes the port specified for the digitizer during AutoCAD configuration.
- **Plotter.** Checking this box initializes the port specified for the plotter during AutoCAD configuration.

Device and File Initialization

The following options attempt to re-initialize communications directly with peripherals attached to your system.

- **Digitizer.** Checking this box initializes the configured digitizer. If the I/O port itself, to which the digitizer is connected, has been reset by other software, I/O port initialization may need to be performed. See the I/O Port Initialization options above.
- **Display.** Checking this box initializes the configured display. Both the AutoCAD graphics screen and text screen are completely redrawn. Use this option if another program executed from within AutoCAD does not restore the screen contents upon exiting.

- **PGP File.** Checking this box reloads the ACAD.PGP file. Any changes made to ACAD.PGP will not take effect until the file is loaded by the REINIT command or when AutoCAD is started.

Figure REINIT.1:
The REINIT command dialog box.

Related Command

CONFIG

Related System Variable

REINIT

RENAME

Screen **[UTILITY] [RENAME:]**

The RENAME command changes the names of named items such as dimension styles, layers, views, and text styles. You cannot rename an item, however, to an existing name used by the same type of item, nor can you rename colors. In addition, the linetypes BYLAYER, BYBLOCK, CONTINUOUS, the layer 0, and anonymous blocks such as those created by the HATCH command cannot be renamed.

  The new DDRENAME dialog box is much easier to use than the RENAME command when you are renaming defined items.

879

Prompts and Options

- **Block/Dimstyle/LAyer/LType/Style/Ucs/VIew/VPort:**

  This prompt contains a list of the named items that you can rename. Type the uppercase letter(s) for the item type you want to rename.

- **Old item name:**

  At this prompt, you enter the current name of the item that you want to rename. If the name you enter does not belong to a current item, the command exits and the prompt `Old item NAME not found` appears.

- **New item name:**

  At this prompt, you enter a new name for the item. The new name is subject to the standard limitations on name length and valid characters used by AutoCAD for all other item names. When you rename a linetype, the new name applies only to the current drawing. The linetype name in the ACAD.LIN file remains the same. When a block that was inserted from an external drawing file is renamed, the external file remains unaffected.

Example

The following example renames a layer named DOOR-2 to UNUSED_DOORS.

```
Command: RENAME ↵
Block/Dimstyle/LAyer/LType/Style/Ucs/VIew/VPort: LA↵
Old layer name: DOOR-2 ↵
New layer name: UNUSED_DOORS ↵
```

Related Command

DDRENAME

RENDER

Screen   **[RENDER] [RENDER:]**

Pull down **[Render] [Render]**

The RENDER command creates a realistically shaded image of three-dimensional surface or solid objects within AutoCAD. Finish, lighting, scene, and rendering preference information is used to produce the shaded image. The rendered image can be output to the full AutoCAD screen, a viewport, a hard-copy device, or a file.

 Make sure AME is loaded before rendering any solids created with AME. The AME entities are translated into meshes before rendering and thus produce a better rendering.

Related Commands

> **FINISH**
> **HIDE**
> **LIGHT**
> **RPREF**
> **SCENE**
> **SHADE**

RENDSCR

The RENDSCR (RENDering SCRreen) command redisplays the last rendered image on single-monitor systems. After an image is displayed on the full screen, you can press any key to return to the current drawing. The F1 key continues to work normally, flipping between the drawing editor and text display.

Related Commands

> **RCONFIG**
> **RENDER**
> **VSLIDE**

Related System Variable

SCREENMODE

REPLAY

Pull down **[Render] [Files] [Replay Image]**

Screen **[RENDER] [REPLAY]**

The REPLAY command enables you to display raster image files on the configured rendering display. You can display GIF, TGA, TIFF, and RND files.

Any rectangular area of a GIF, TGA, or TIFF file can be displayed by specifying an XY image offset (in pixels) and an image size (in pixels). The area can then be placed anywhere on the rendering screen by specifying an XY screen offset (in pixels). This process is useful if the image file was created by a system with a different rendering display resolution. The REPLAY command can only display entire RND files on rendering displays for which they were created.

The REPLAY command displays the REPLAY file dialog box, which displays the Image Specifications dialog box when you specify a valid file name. The REPLAY dialog box operates like any other file dialog box. However, the Image Specifications dialog box appears only with files with GIF, RND, TGA, or TIF file extensions.

 The REPLAY command can be used for crude bitmap tracing. Just scan your line drawing into a TIFF, TGA, or GIF file and use the REPLAY command to display it in an AutoCAD viewport. Then trace over the image with lines, circles, and other elements. The image remains on-screen until the screen is redrawn. You must use a rendering display driver capable of rendering to a viewport to use this technique.

Prompts and Options

- **Image Name.** The Image Name edit box shows the path and name of the image file to be loaded.

- **IMAGE Size.** The IMAGE icon enables you to specify visually the area of the image file to display. To specify the image area, pick two points on the icon for the opposite corners of the image area rectangle. The size of the image file is displayed next to the icon title.

- **SCREEN Size.** The SCREEN icon enables you to specify visually the position of the specified image area on the rendering screen. Pick a point on the icon for the center of the image area rectangle, to position it on the rendering screen. The size of the screen is displayed next to the icon title.

- **Image Offset.** In the X and Y Image Offset edit boxes, you specify the size of the specified image area rectangle in pixels. Values for the X and Y image offset must be positive and cannot exceed the entire image size.

- **Image Size.** In the X and Y Image Size edit boxes, you specify the number of pixels the upper left corner of the image area rectangle is located from the X and Y image offset. Values for the X and Y image size must be positive and cannot exceed the entire image size.

- **Screen Size.** The X and Y values displayed show the actual size of the image area that will be displayed. The values will be equal to the Image Size up to a maximum of the value displayed in SCREEN.

- **Screen Offset.** The X and Y Screen Offset edit boxes specify the number of pixels the lower left corner of the image area rectangle is from 0,0 of the AutoCAD rendering screen. Values for the X and Y screen offset must be positive and cannot exceed the size of the rendering screen.

- **Reset.** The Reset button sets all parameters back to the defaults.

Related Commands

RCONFIG
RENDER
RENDSCR
VSLIDE

RESUME

The RESUME command continues a script file that has been halted. If you stop a script file by pressing Backspace, enter **RESUME** at the Command: prompt to restart it at the next line of the script. If you stop the script with Ctrl-C as it executes a command, you can use the RESUME command transparently by entering **'RESUME**.

Related Commands

DELAY
RSCRIPT

REVSURF

Screen [DRAW] [next] [3D Surfs] [REVSURF:]

Pull down [Draw] [3D Surfaces >] [Surface of Revolution]

The REVSURF command is one of six commands that create 3D polygon meshes. This command creates a mesh defined by rotating a profile entity (path curve) around an axis of rotation. The REVSURF command is useful for creating objects that are radially symmetrical about one axis, such as a wine goblet. This command can create surfaces that are open like a vase, closed like a spindle, or hollow like a tire. The SURFTAB1 and SURFTAB2 system variables are used to control the M and N densities of the mesh.

Prompts and Options

- `Select path curve:`

  The path curve may be an arc, circle, line, 2D polyline, or 3D polyline. You can pick only one entity as the path curve. The path curve defines the N direction of the mesh. If the path curve is a circle or closed polyline, the 3D polygon mesh produced by the REVSURF command will be closed in the N direction. If you select an invalid entity for the path curve, the error message `Entity not usable to define surface of revolution` appears.

- `Select axis of revolution:`

  The axis of revolution may be a line, 2D polyline, or 3D polyline. When a curved or multisegmented polyline is selected as the axis of revolution, the vector from the first vertex to the last vertex defines the actual axis of revolution. The axis of revolution defines the M direction of the 3D polygon mesh. The pick point used to select the axis of rotation influences the rotation angle. See the following discussion about the direction of revolution.

  If you choose an entity other than a line or an open polyline, the error message `Entity not usable as rotation axis` appears. The same entity cannot be both the curve path and the axis of revolution. If you attempt to connect the two entities, the error message `Entity has already been selected` displays.

- `Start angle <0>:`

  The default of 0 degrees for the start angle begins creating the mesh at the location of the path curve. If you specify an angle other than 0 degrees, the mesh is offset from the path curve by that angle.

- `Included angle (+=ccw, -=cw)<Full circle>:`

  The included angle specification determines the extent to which the path curve sweeps around the axis of revolution. If the default Full circle option is used, the resulting mesh is closed in the M direction. A positive included angle causes the mesh to be generated in a counterclockwise direction. The mesh generates with respect to the pick point that you used to select the axis of revolution.

Direction of Revolution

The direction of revolution is determined by the pick point used for selecting the axis of revolution and included angle specification. The end point of the axis of revolution closest to the pick point becomes the base of the vector that defines the axis of revolution. The opposite end becomes the top. If you look from the top of the vector to the base, a positive included angle constructs the polygon mesh in the counter-clockwise direction, offset by the start angle.

The method in which meshes generate can be visualized easily by using the right-hand rule. Imagine placing your thumb along the axis of revolution with the top of your thumb pointing to the top of the axis of revolution vector. Next, curl your fingers around the axis of revolution vector. The curl of your fingers indicates the direction of revolution for a positive included angle. The start angle direction can be visualized in the same manner.

Example

The following example uses the REVSURF command to construct a polygon mesh, as shown in figure REVSURF.1. The left viewport shows the original path curve and axis of revolution, while the right viewport displays the completed mesh.

```
Command: REVSURF↵
Select path curve: Pick point ①
Select axis of revolution: Pick point ②
Start angle <0> Pick point ↵
Included angle (+=ccw, -=cw)<Full circle>: ↵
```

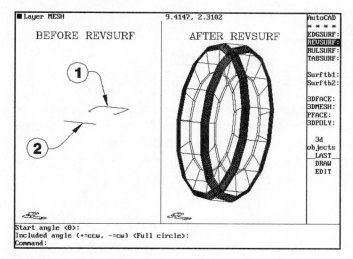

Figure REVSURF.1:
The surface of revolution.

Related Commands

EDGESURF
PFACE
RULESURF
TABSURF
3DFACE
3DMESH

Related System Variables

SURFTAB1
SURFTAB2

ROTATE

Screen **[EDIT] [next] [ROTATE:]**

Pull down **[Modify] [Rotate]**

The ROTATE command rotates selected entities about a fixed point in the current construction plane. After you choose the fixed point, AutoCAD asks you for the amount, in degrees, that you want to rotate the entities. The new orientation of the entities is based on the rotation value entered.

Prompts and Options

- **Select objects:**

  You can use any object selection method to choose all the entities you want to rotate.

- **Base point:**

  The base point is the location about which the entities are rotated. After you enter the rotation value, the chosen entities are rotated about the Z-axis of the base point.

- **<Rotation angle>/Reference:**

  At this prompt, you enter a value with which to rotate the entities. A positive number changes the entities' orientation in a counter-clockwise direction. A negative number rotates the entities in a clockwise direction. A rubber-band line appears between the base point and the crosshairs. The entities that are being rotated are highlighted and dragged as you move the crosshairs.

- **Reference angle <0>:**

  The Reference option enables you to define the angle of rotation by specifying a reference angle and a new angle.

- **New angle:**

  The selected entities are rotated by the difference between the reference angle and the new angle that you specify at this prompt.

Example

This example demonstrates how to use the ROTATE command to change the orientation of a group of entities shown in figure ROTATE.1.

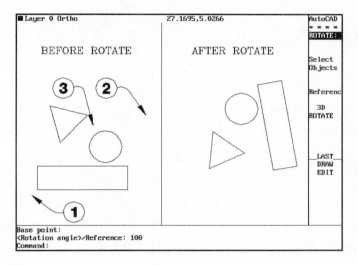

Figure ROTATE.1:
Rotating a group of entities.

```
Command: ROTATE ↵
Select objects: W ↵
First corner: Pick point ①
Other corner: Pick point ②
Base point: Pick point ②
<Rotation angle>/Reference: 100 ↵
```

Related Command

DDMODIFY

Related System Variables

DRAGMODE
HIGHLIGHT

ROTATE3D

Screen **[EDIT] [next] [ROTATE:] [3D ROTATE]**

Pull down **[Modify] [Rotate 3D]**

ROTATE3D enables you to rotate an object about a 3D axis. The axis of rotation is defined by selecting one of the options below.

Prompts and Options

- **Select objects:**

  You select the objects you want to rotate about a 3D axis.

- **<Rotation angle>/Reference:**

  You enter the degree of rotation about the 3D axis or specify the Reference option to enter the current angle and a new angle. Reference displays the prompts below:

- **Reference angle <0>:**

  Enter the current degree of rotation of the selected entities.

- **New angle:**

  Enter the new angle of the selected entities.

- **Axis by Entity/Last/View/Xaxis/Yaxis/Zaxis/ <2point>:**

  You specify the desired method of defining the 3D axis of rotation. The prompt's options are described below.

  You can use the following options with the ROTATE3D command.

- **Entity.** This option aligns the axis of rotation with an existing entity. The Entity option displays the following prompt:

- **Pick a line, circle, arc, or 2D-polyline segment**

  Select the entity to define the 3D axis of rotation. The circle and arc options use the 3D axis of the circle or arc.

- **Last.** This option uses the last axis of rotation. If there is no last axis, you are warned and reprompted with the Axis prompt.

- **View.** This option aligns the axis of rotation with the current view passing through a selected point. The View option displays the following prompt:

- **Point on view direction axis <0,0,0>:**
  Enter a point that the axis of rotation passes through.

- **Xaxis.** Aligns the axis of rotation with the X axis, passing through a selected point. The Xaxis option displays one prompt:

- **Point on X axis <0,0,0>:**
  Enter the point on the X axis that the axis of rotation passes through.

- **Yaxis.** Aligns the axis of rotation with the Y axis, passing through a selected point. The Yaxis option displays one prompt:

- **Point on Y axis <0,0,0>:**
  Enter a point on the Y axis that the axis of rotation passes through.

- **Zaxis.** Zaxis aligns the axis of rotation with the Z axis, passing through a selected point. The Zaxis option displays one prompt:

- **Point on Z axis <0,0,0>:**
  Enter a point on the Z axis that the axis of rotation passes through.

- **<2points>.** Zpoints specifies two points that define the axis of rotation. 2points displays 2 prompts.

- **1st point on axis:**
  Enter the first point of the axis of rotation.

- **2nd point on axis:**
  Enter the second point of the axis of rotation.

Example

The following example uses ROTATE3D to rotate a solid around a line in three dimensions. See figure ROTATE3D.1.

```
Command: ROTATE3D ↵
Select objects: Pick point ①
Select objects: ↵
Axis by Entity/Last/View/Xaxis/Yaxis/Zaxis/<2points>: 2 ↵
1st point on axis: Pick point ②
2nd point on axis: Pick point ③
<Rotation angle>/Reference: 90 ↵
```

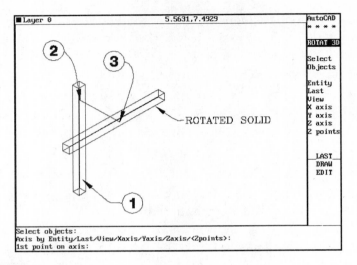

Figure ROTATE3D.1:
A solid rotated in three dimensions about a line.

Related Commands

MIRROR3D
ROTATE

RPREF

Screen **[RENDER] [RPREF]**

Pull down **[Render] [Preferences]**

The characteristics of the image that the RENDER command produces
are controlled by options of the RPREF command. The RPREF command displays the Rendering Preferences dialog box, enabling you to
modify the rendering characteristics. The characteristics that can be
modified include type of rendering, type of shading, finish use, output
destination, black and white or color output, and color separation.

Prompts and Options

Rendering Preferences is the main dialog box for the RPREF command. All other preferences-related dialog boxes and options are accessed through this dialog box.

The Rendering Preferences Dialog Box

- **Full Render.** This option of the Rendering Type group produces the most accurate rendered image. Full Render causes the rendered image to be created using 3D polygons. Full Render also causes edge artifacts and overlapping faces to be considered by the RENDER command.

- **Quick Render.** This option of the Rendering Type group produces the fastest rendered image. Quick Render causes the rendered image to be created in scanlines. A *scanline* is a horizontal row of pixels. Quick Render does not consider edge artifacts or overlapping faces.

  The difference in speed between Full Render and Quick Render increases as the complexity of your model and the amount of memory you have increase. Quick Render slows down for high-resolution output devices.

- **ACAD RenderMan.** This option is not yet available.

- **Smooth Shading.** This option of the Rendering Options group causes the transition between adjacent polygon mesh surfaces to appear smooth when rendered. AutoCAD uses the Gouraud algorithm for smooth shading.

  The *Gouraud algorithm* calculates the color at all vertices of a mesh face and then blends the color across the face. The angle between two face normals must be 45 degrees or less for the Gouraud algorithm to be applied to the faces. A *normal* is an imaginary line that is perpendicular to the center of a polygon mesh face.

- **Merge.** With 24-bit frame buffers, this option of the Rendering Options group enables multiple images to be merged in the frame buffer. This is a time-saving option. If a complex drawing is changed in one area, that area can be rendered and then merged with the original image. Merge only works with full render.

- **Apply Finishes.** This option of the Rendering Options group enables you to control the application of defined finishes. If Apply Finishes is off, all entities are rendered with the default *GLOBAL* finish.

- **More Options.** This button in the Render Options group accesses the Full or Quick Render Options dialog box depending on the current rendering type. The Full/Quick render Options dialog box enables you to control output mode (color or black and white), color separations, and several face parameters.

- **Select Query.** This drop-down list enables you to choose between rendering all objects in the drawing or selecting specific objects. The two options are listed as Select All and Make Selection.

- **Framebuffer.** This option of the Destination group sends rendering output to your rendering video display. Images rendered to the screen can be saved in various raster file formats for input into other programs or recall at a later time. See the SAVEIMG and REPLAY commands for more information.

- **Hardcopy.** This option of the Destination group sends rendering output to your rendering hard-copy device. Images can be saved as encapsulated PostScript (EPS) files for use with other third-party programs such as desktop publishing or vector-based drawing applications. To create an EPS file, configure the hard-copy rendering device for the RHEXPORT.EXP driver.

- **Best Map/No Fold.** This option in the Color Map Usage group maintains a separate color map for each rendering viewport and does not change the AutoCAD colors 9-255 to the closest color in the 1-8 color range. Entity colors in inactive nonrendering viewports are altered according to the color map of the rendering viewport.

- **Best Map/Fold.** This option in the Color Map Usage group maintains a separate color map for each rendering viewport and changes the AutoCAD colors 9-255 to the closest color in the 1-8 AutoCAD color range. This means that all entities with AutoCAD color values above 8 in nonrendering viewports are changed to the closest color in the 1-8 AutoCAD color range. This prevents entity colors from changing after rendering in another viewport.

- **Fixed ACAD Map.** This option in the Color Map Usage group uses the standard AutoCAD color map for both nonrendering and rendering viewports. Results from this option are usually poor renderings and inconsistent results.

The color map options are only available for 256-color display devices.

- **RMan Prompting.** This option of the Settings group in conjunction with Autodesk AutoShade Version 2 enables you to place and render spotlights, add and render colored lights to your drawing, and render with shadows.

- **Icon Scale.** This edit box in the Settings group specifies the scale factor to apply to rendering blocks (lights and finishes). Set the icon scale to the same scale as other symbols in your drawing.

- **Information.** This button displays the AVE Render copyright notice and the current AVE Render display and hard-copy configuration.

- **Reconfigure.** This button executes the RCONFIG command, enabling you to change the AVE Render configuration.

Related Commands

RCONFIG
STATS

RSCRIPT

The RSCRIPT command causes a script to repeat itself from the beginning. You can execute the RSCRIPT command only from a script file. The script continues to repeat until you press Ctrl-C or Backspace.

Related Commands

DELAY
RESUME
SCRIPT

RULESURF

Screen   [DRAW] [next] [3D Surfs] [RULESURF:]

Pull down   [Draw] [3D Surfaces >] [Ruled Surface]

The RULESURF command is one of six commands that create a 3D polygon mesh. This command creates a 2×N mesh defined by a ruled surface between two boundary entities. These boundaries may be arcs, lines, points, and open or closed polylines (either 2D or 3D). If one of the boundaries is a closed entity (a circle or closed polyline), the other boundary must be open. Note that you can use a point for one boundary.

The end of the entity that is closest to the point used to pick the entity becomes the starting point for that end of the mesh. The mesh is then created along the entity, defined by ruling lines spanning the space between each boundary. The SURFTAB1 variable determines the density of the mesh in the N direction.

Prompts and Options

• Select first defining curve:

Pick a point to select the first boundary edge for the polygon mesh. The end point of the entity, closest to the point picked, determines the beginning of the mesh's first end.

- **Select second defining curve:**

  Pick a point to select the second boundary for the mesh. The end point of the entity closest to the point picked determines the beginning of the mesh's second end.

Example

This example creates a ruled surface between two polylines (see fig. RULESURF.1).

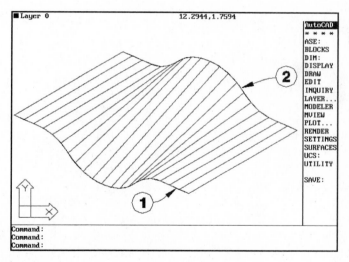

Figure RULESURF.1:
Polygon mesh created with the RULESURF command.

```
Command: RULESURF ↵
Select first defining curve: Pick point ①
Select second defining curve: Pick point ②
```

Related Commands

3DFACE
3DMESH
EDGESURF
PFACE
REVSURF
TABSURF

Related System Variable

SURFTAB1

SAVE

Screen **[SAVE:]**

Pull down **[File] [Save]**

The SAVE command displays the Save Drawing As dialog box, requests a file name, and saves the current drawing as a file with the extension DWG. Entering a tilde (~) at the `Save current changes as:` prompt displays the Save Drawing As dialog box, if the system variable FILEDIA is set to 0. You can enter the drawing name in the File edit box or select a name from the Files list box. Do not include the DWG extension; it is assumed. If the drawing has already been named, SAVE uses that name as a default in the File edit box. Each time you use SAVE, the previous saved drawing is renamed as the backup (BAK) drawing.

Save your drawing regularly during a drawing session to avoid data loss due to system failure or power loss. Use the SAVETIME system variable to set the number of minutes between automatic saves. Setting SAVETIME to 0 disables the autosave feature.

Prompts and Options

- **Save current changes as:**

  If FILEDIA is set to 0, SAVE displays this prompt. Enter the name of the drawing file to save changes, or accept the default file name.

- **Pattern:**

  Enter a pattern to filter files in the Files list box. The pattern can use the * and ? wild-card characters. The pattern defaults to *.DWG.

- **Directories:**

  Pick a drive or directory to list its contents in the Files list box. Double-click on any item in the list to select it. Select the double dot (..) to move back one directory and the backslash (\) to display the root directory. Available drive letters are shown in angle brackets (<>). If the directory list is longer than the Directories list box, a slider bar is displayed on the right side of the list box. The current directory is listed above the Directories list box.

- **Files:**

  Pick a drawing file name in which to save the current changes. Click on any file name to select it. If the list of files is longer than the Files list box, a slider bar is displayed on the right side of the list box. If you pick a file name from the list, an AutoCAD message dialog box displays the warning The specified file already exists. Do you want to replace it?

 The MAXSORT system variable determines how many files or directories are to be sorted. MAXSORT defaults to 200 sorted entries. If the number is fewer than the number of entries in the list box, none are sorted.

- **Type it:**

  Click on the **T**ype it button to enter the drawing file's name at the Command: prompt instead of the dialog box.

- **Default:**

  Click on the **D**efault button to reset the dialog box to its original state. This resets the Pattern edit box, Directories list box, Files list box, and File edit box to their values when the dialog box was displayed. The default is not available until a file name has been entered.

- **File:**

  Enter the name of the file to save or accept the default name. If the current drawing has already been named, the name is displayed in the Files edit box. You can accept the name by clicking on OK or pressing Enter.

Related Commands

END
NEW
OPEN
QSAVE
QUIT
SAVEAS

Related System Variables

DWGNAME
DWGPREFIX
DWGTITLED
DWGWRITE
FILEDIA
MAXSORT
SAVEFILE
SAVETIME
TDUPDATE

SAVEAS

Pull down **[File] [Save as...]**

The SAVEAS command works like the SAVE command—saving any changes to the current drawing to disk without exiting the drawing editor—except that this command asks for a new file name. The Save Drawing As dialog box appears (see fig. SAVEAS.1), and the current drawing name is the default. Clicking on OK accepts your file name choice.

Use the QSAVE command to periodically save your work. QSAVE automatically saves changes to the default drawing name and bypasses the dialog box.

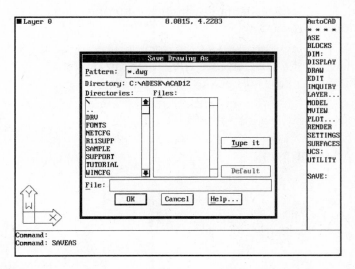

Figure SAVEAS.1:
The Save Drawing As dialog box.

Prompts and Options

SAVEAS displays no command-line prompts unless FILEDIA is set to a value of 0. Instead, you make selections from the following dialog box options:

- **Pattern.** This edit box contains the pattern specification for files to appear in the Files list box. You can use the wild cards ? and * to refine the list to desired file names.
- **Directories.** This list box contains a list of the subdirectories that are available from the current directory. Use the scroll bar to display more names and drive letters. Double-click on a directory name or drive letter to change the current directory.
- **Files.** This list box contains a list of the files available in the current directory. Use the scroll bar to display more file names. Double-click on a file name, or click on it once and click on the OK button to proceed.
- **File.** Displays the name of the default drawing (if it has been named) or of a selected file. You either can type the name of a desired file in the edit box or edit an existing name.
- **Type it.** Click on this button to enter the drawing file's name at the command line instead of in the dialog box.

Related Commands

END
QSAVE
QUIT
SAVE

Related System Variables

DBMOD
DWGNAME
DWGPREFIX
FILEDIA
MAXSORT

SAVEIMG

Screen **[RENDER] [SAVEIMG]**

Pull down **[Render] [Files] [Save Image]**

The SAVEIMG command displays the Save Image dialog box, which enables you to save the current viewport, drawing area, or full-screen image to a TGA, TIFF, GIF, or RND file. You can view saved images by using the REPLAY command and many other programs.

One of two Save Image dialog boxes displays when the SAVEIMG command is executed, depending on the rendering display driver configuration. If you have the rendering display driver configured for rendering in a viewport, the Portion group shows three options for specifying the area of the screen to save. If you have the rendering display driver configured for full-screen rendering, the Portion group displays an icon, enabling you to interactively specify the area of the screen to save. The Save Image dialog box for viewport rendering is shown in figure SAVEIMG.1.

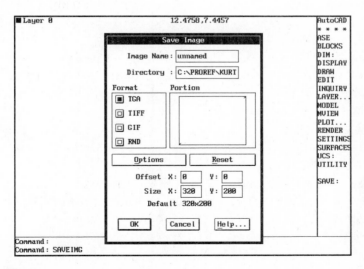

Figure SAVEIMG.1:
The Save Image dialog box.

903

Prompts and Options

- **Image Name.** You can use the Image Name edit box to specify the file name for the rendered image. Do not include a file extension. The default file name is the file name of the current drawing. If the drawing does not have a name, the file name is UNNAMED.

- **Directory.** The Directory edit box shows the directory of the image file. The default directory is the directory that was current when you started your AutoCAD session.

- **TGA.** The TGA option of the Format group causes the image file to be saved in 32-bit RGBA Truevision V2.0 format. TGA files have the TGA extension. The TGA file can be either compressed or uncompressed, depending on the settings of the TGA Options dialog box. The TGA Options dialog box is accessed through the Options button.

- **TIFF.** The TIFF option of the Format group causes the image file to be saved in 32-bit Tagged Image File Format. The TIFF file extension is TIF. The TIFF file can be compressed (using one of two methods), or it can be uncompressed, depending on the settings of the TIFF Options dialog box. The TIFF Options dialog box is accessed through the Options button.

- **GIF.** The GIF option of the Format group causes the image file to be saved in Graphics Interchange Format, which is developed by CompuServe Information Service. The saved GIF file has the GIF extension.

- **RND.** The RND option of the Format group causes the image file to be saved in the RND file format. RND is an Autodesk-defined format. Offset and Size settings are not available for RND files.

- **Portion.** If the rendering driver is configured for full-screen rendering, the Portion group displays an icon, enabling you to interactively choose the area of the rendered image to save. Pick two opposite corner points to define the area to be saved.

- **Active viewport.** The Active viewport option of the Portion group saves only the area of the active viewport.

- **Drawing area.** The Drawing area option of the Portion group saves the drawing area. The drawing area does not include the command area, screen menu, or pull-down menu bar.
- **Full screen.** The Full screen option of the Portion group saves the entire screen including command area, screen menu, and pull-down menu bar.
- **Options.** The Options button either displays the TGA Options or the TIFF Options dialog box, depending on the image file format selection. The TGA Options dialog box enables you to choose between no compression and RLE (run length encoded) compression for TGA files. The TIFF Options dialog box enables you to choose from no compression or PACK (packbits) and LZW (Lempel-Ziv and Welch) compression.

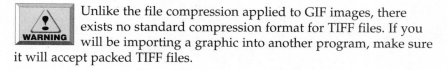 Unlike the file compression applied to GIF images, there exists no standard compression format for TIFF files. If you will be importing a graphic into another program, make sure it will accept packed TIFF files.

- **Reset.** The Reset button sets the saved area offset and size to the defaults.
- **Offset.** The Offset X and Y edit boxes show the distance in pixels from the lower left corner of the screen to the lower left corner of the save area. Values must be positive and cannot be greater than the Size X and Y values. You can change the value by using this edit box.
- **Size.** The Size X and Y edit boxes show the distance in pixels from the lower left corner of the save area to the upper right corner. Values must be positive and cannot be greater than the screen size. You can change the value by using this edit box.
- **Default.** Default displays the maximum save area size in pixels.

Related Commands

HIDE
MSLIDE

RENDER
REPLAY
SHADE

SCALE

Screen **[EDIT] [next] [SCALE:]**

Pull down **[Modify] [SCALE]**

The SCALE command enlarges or reduces selected entities by a specified value. You can specify the new size by entering a numeric scale factor or by specifying an existing object, typically using a new length relative to a reference length.

 Use the Grip edit mode SCALE option to scale an entity without issuing the SCALE command. The Grip edit mode SCALE allows for multiple copies of scaled items.

 You can scale a viewport in paper space to increase or decrease the amount of model space area visible in the viewport.

Prompts and Options

- **Select objects:**

  Choose all the entities you want to enlarge or reduce by means of any of the object selection methods.

 Use the CHANGE command to change the scale, rotation, and size of text.

- **Base point:**

Enter a base point in the current coordinate system around which to scale entities. When the scaling occurs, all points on selected entities move closer to the base point or farther away from the base point as their scale is reduced and enlarged.

 Choose a base point that relates to the entity or entities being scaled and positions them correctly after scaling. You generally pick a corner or the center of the object being scaled.

- **<SCALE factor>/Reference:**

Specify a scale factor by which to scale entities. A number greater than one enlarges the entities; a number between 0 and one reduces the entities. You can enter a number or pick a point to show a distance. If you pick a point, a rubber-band line appears between the base point and the crosshairs. The entities to be scaled are highlighted and dragged as you move the crosshairs.

Enter an **R** for the Reference option if you want to define the scale factor in reference to a length, such as the size of an existing entity.

 You cannot scale the X, Y, or Z values of primitive AutoCAD entities independently.

- **Reference length <1>:**

If you specify the Reference option, the scale factor is defined by the ratio of the two lengths that you specify. You also can pick two points, usually on an existing object, to show the reference length.

- **New length:**

Enter the new length to scale the reference length to. The selected entities are then scaled by the ratio between the reference length and the new length. You also can pick one point to show the new length as a distance from the base point. As you move the cursor to pick the new length, AutoCAD shows a rubber-band line from the base point.

Example

This example uses the SCALE command to enlarge and reduce entities, using both a set scale factor and a reference length. The results are shown in figure SCALE.1.

```
■ Layer 0                        12.4758,8.5109              AutoCAD
                                                             * * *
                                                             SCALE:

                                                             Select
                                                             Objects
         BEFORE SCALE        AFTER SCALE


                                                             Referenc

            TEST            TEST
                                                              _LAST_
                                                              DRAW
                                                              EDIT



Command:
Command: SCALE
Select objects:
```

Figure SCALE.1:
The text before and after the SCALE command.

```
Command: SCALE
Base point: Pick a point near the center of the text
<SCALE factor>/Reference: 2 ↵
Command: SCALE
Select objects: Select the text
Select objects: ↵
Base point: Pick a point in the center of the text
<SCALE factor>/Reference: R
Reference length <1>: .5 Specifies the starting height of the text
New length: .625 Specifies the final text height
```

Related Command

CHANGE

SCENE

Screen **[RENDER] [SCENE]**

Pull down **[Render] [Scenes]**

The SCENE command enables you create, name, restore, modify, and
delete combinations of multiple views and related lighting that produce
a specific image. One or more lights assigned to a single view define a
scene. Lights not associated with a scene are not considered when the
scene is rendered.

Prompts and Options

The SCENE command has three dialog boxes. The first Scenes dialog
box accesses the New Scene and Modify Scene dialog boxes. Figure
SCENE.1 shows the Scenes dialog box.

Figure SCENE.1:
The Scenes dialog box.

The Scenes Dialog Box

- **Scenes.** The Scenes list box displays the currently defined scenes
  and specifies the scene to be modified, deleted, or rendered. If the
  NONE scene is selected, the current view and all lights are used
  for rendering. You can highlight a scene and exit the dialog box
  with OK to specify the scene to be rendered by the RENDER
  command.

- **New.** The <u>N</u>ew button accesses the New Scene dialog box, enabling you to add a new scene to your drawing
- **Modify.** The <u>M</u>odify button accesses the Modify Scene dialog box (see fig. SCENE.2), enabling you to change scene parameters including scene name, view for scene, and associated lights. To modify a scene, highlight a scene name in the Scenes list box and then click on <u>M</u>odify.

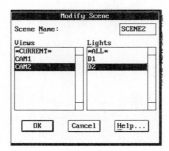

Figure SCENE.2:
The Modify Scene dialog box.

- **Delete.** The <u>D</u>elete button removes a scene from the drawing. To delete a scene, highlight a scene name in the Scenes list box and then click on the <u>D</u>elete button.

The New Scene and Modify Scene Dialog Boxes

Because the New Scene and Modify Scene dialog boxes have identical features, they are discussed together.

- **Scene Name.** The Scene <u>N</u>ame edit box enables you to specify or change the name of the scene. The scene name must be eight characters or fewer; long names are truncated to eight characters.
- **Views.** The Views list box displays all the saved views in the drawing. The highlighted view is the scene view. To change the view for a scene, highlight a different view. The *CURRENT* view is the view in the current active viewport.

- **Lights.** The Lights list box displays all the defined lights in your drawing and enables you to select the lights for the scene. The highlighted lights are selected for the current scene. You can click on an unhighlighted light name to highlight it and add it to the scene. You can click on an highlighted light name to remove that light from the scene. The *ALL* light name uses all the defined lights in the scene.

Example

This example demonstrates how to add a scene to a drawing. Use the PINS2 drawing in the \ACAD\TUTORIAL subdirectory. After the drawing is loaded, change the view with the VPOINT or DVIEW command, and then use the VIEW command to save the new view as CAM2.

Choose Render, *then* Scenes
In the Scene Name *edit box, enter* **SCENE2** ↵
Click on CAM2 *in the* Views *list box*
Click on D2 *in the* Lights *list box*
Click on OK *in the two subsequent dialog boxes*
Restore the CAM1 view
Choose Render, *then* Render
The SCENE2 scene is rendered with the CAM2 view and the D2 light.

Related Commands

LIGHT
RENDER
VIEW

SCRIPT

Screen **[UTILITY] [SCRIPT:]**

The SCRIPT command displays the Select Script File dialog box and invokes the selected script file. If the FILEDIA system variable is set to 0, you are prompted with Script file

<drawing name>: at the command prompt. You can execute the SCRIPT command transparently by preceding the command name with an apostrophe ('SCRIPT).

A *script file* is a set of steps to execute AutoCAD commands and options. You must create this file in ASCII format with the SCR extension. AutoCAD interprets and executes the contents of a script file exactly as if you were entering the characters at the keyboard. Therefore, any extra spaces, returns, blank lines, or typographical errors cause problems. You can undo the effects of the SCRIPT command by issuing a single Undo. You can stop scripts by pressing Ctrl-C. You can use the EXPERT system variable to eliminate conditional prompts in scripts.

You also can execute script files automatically when you load AutoCAD by putting the script's file name after the drawing's file name. For example, you can type the following:

    C:\> **ACAD DRAWING1 SCRIPT1**

If a script file contains a SCRIPT command, the current script is stopped, and the specified script becomes current.

Scripts are often used to display slide shows, plot drawings, and reset system variables. If you change drawing standards and need to update existing drawings, use script files to do the work.

Prompts and Options

- **Script file <drawing name>:**

    If the system variable FILEDIA is set to 0, SCRIPT displays this prompt. Enter the name of the script file you want to run; do not enter the SCR extension. Preface the file name with a drive and a path specification if needed. The default script file name is the same as the drawing name. Enter a tilde (~) to display the dialog box.

- **P**attern:

  Enter a pattern to filter files in the Files list box. The pattern can use the * and ? wild-card characters. The pattern defaults to *.SCR.

- **D**irectories:

  Pick a drive or directory to list its contents in the Files list box. Double-click on any item in the list to select it. Select double dot (..) to move back one directory or backslash (\) to display the root directory. Available drive letters are listed in angle brackets (<>). If the directory list is longer than the Directories list box, a slider bar is displayed on the right side of the list box. The current directory is listed above the Directories list box.

- **F**i**les:

  Pick a script file to execute. Double-click on any file name to select it. If the list of files is longer than the Files list box, a slider bar is displayed on the right side of the list box.

 The MAXSORT system variable determines how many files or directories are sorted. MAXSORT defaults to 200 sorted entries. The value of MAXSORT must exceed the number of entries in the list box in order to have an effect.

- **T**ype it

  Click on the **T**ype it button to enter the script file's name at the `Command prompt:` instead of the dialog box.

- **F**ile:

  Enter the name of the script to execute or accept the default name. If the current drawing has already been named, the drawing name is displayed in the Files edit box as the default script name. You can accept the name by clicking on OK or pressing Enter.

Related Commands

DELAY
GRAPHSCR
RESUME

913

RSCRIPT
TEXTSCR

Related System Variables

EXPERT
FILEDIA
MAXSORT

SELECT

Screen **[EDIT] [next] [SELECT:]**

The SELECT command enables you to create a selection set to use with another command. At the other command's SELECT objects: prompt, you can enter **P** to specify the selection set established with the SELECT command.

To build selection sets based on specific entity properties, use the new FILTER command.

If the PICKFIRST system variable is on, you can select objects with the cursor and then issue the command that will act on the entities. If PICKFIRST is off, you cannot preselect entities; you must issue SELECT, and then select the entities using the options described below. PICKFIRST is new to Release 12.

You cannot select entities from paper space that were created in model space, and vice versa.

Prompts and Options

- **SELECT objects:**

  Select all the entities that you want in your selection set. You can use any of the selection methods described below.

  You can use the following options with the SELECT command:

- **A point.** Picks the entity passing through the specified point.

- **ALL.** Selects all of the entities in the drawing.

- **Add (A).** Adds entities to the selection set.

- **Auto (AU).** If a pick fails to select an object, the selection method becomes the BOX option.

- **BOX.** If you move the crosshairs to the right it becomes a window—to the left it becomes a crossing window.

- **CPolygon (CP).** Selects all entities crossing or enclosed in a user-defined irregular polygon.

- **Crossing.** Selects entities crossing or enclosed in a window area.

- **Ctrl-C.** Cancels the selection process without creating the selection set.

- **Fence.** Selects entities that cross the fence line.

- **Last (L).** Selects the most recently created entity that is currently visible.

- **Multiple (M).** Enables you to pick multiple points on-screen before SELECT searches for entities. Press Enter to proceed.

- **Previous (P).** Selects the previous select set.

- **Remove (R).** Removes specified entities from the selection set.

- **SIngle (SI).** Selects the first object found and completes the selection set.

- **Undo (U).** Removes the last group of selected entities.

- **Window (W).** Selects entities enclosed within a window area.

- **WPolygon (WP).** Selects all entities enclosed in a user-defined irregular polygon.

R12

R12

R12

R12

Example

The following example uses SELECT to create a selection set. See figure SELECT.1

```
Command: SELECT
SELECT objects: W
First corner: Pick point ① of a window
Other corner: Pick point ②
SELECT objects: Include x found message ↵
Command: SELECT
SELECT objects: F
First fence point: Pick point ③
Undo/<Endpoint of line>: Pick point ④
Undo/<Endpoint of line>: Include x found message ↵
```

Related Command

FILTER

Related System Variables

HIGHLIGHT
PICKADD
PICKAUTO
PICKFIRST
PICKDRAG

SETVAR

```
Screen   [* * * *] [SETVAR:]
```

```
Screen   [SETTINGS] [next] [SETVAR:]
```

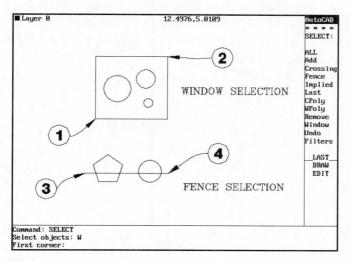

Figure SELECT.1:
Window and fence selection sets.

The SETVAR (SET VARiable) command modifies and lists the settings of AutoCAD system variables. System variables store values used to control the behavior of AutoCAD commands. These values may be text strings, integers, real numbers, or coordinates. Variables that cannot be modified are called *read-only* variables. Almost all string variables are read-only.

You can use SETVAR transparently to modify a variable setting while using another command, by prefacing SETVAR with an apostrophe ('SETVAR). You also can transparently access most system variables while using another command by prefacing the variable name with an apostrophe.

Prompts and Options

- **Variable name or ? <variable name>:**
  Enter the name of the variable you want to modify or enter a question mark (?) to list variables.

- **Variable(s) to list <*>:**

  Enter the name(s) of the variables you want to list. If you press Enter, AutoCAD displays a list of all the variables, one page at a time. You can specify more than one variable by separating each with a comma or by using wild-card characters such as a question mark (?) or an asterisk (*).

- **New value for *VARIABLE* <*current value* >:**

  Enter a new value for the variable or press Enter to leave the current value unchanged. If the specified variable is read-only, the variable is displayed with the current value and the `New value for:` prompt does not display.

Example

The following example demonstrates setting an AutoCAD variable:

```
Command: SETVAR
Variable name or ?: EXPERT
New value for EXPERT <0>: 2
```

Related Commands

SOLVAR
DDSOLVAR

SHADE

Screen   **[DISPLAY] [SHADE] [SHADE:]**

Pull down   **[Render] [Shade]**

The SHADE command generates a shaded rendering of a 3D model by filling every face in the current viewport with a color. The color displayed is based on the entity's color, the distance of the face from the current viewpoint, the setting of the SHADEDGE and SHADEDIF system variables, and your display hardware's capabilities. You cannot select or plot the image, but you can make a slide of it with MSLIDE or save the image to a file with SAVEIMG.

The SHADEDGE system variable controls the color in which edges are drawn. AutoCAD calculates the shading as if the objects were illuminated by a single light source directly behind you as you face the screen. The ratio of diffuse reflection from the light source to ambient (background) light is controlled by the SHADEDIF system variable. Regenerate the drawing to remove shading.

 You can reduce the time required for the SHADE command by freezing unnecessary layers, excluding irrelevant objects from the view, and by minimizing the size of the viewport in which the shading is performed.

Example

The following example shades the 3D entities shown in the viewport of figure SHADE.1.

```
Command: SHADE
Regenerating Drawing.
Shading XX% done.
Shading complete
```

Related Commands

HIDE
RENDER
MSLIDE
SAVEIMG
VSLIDE

919

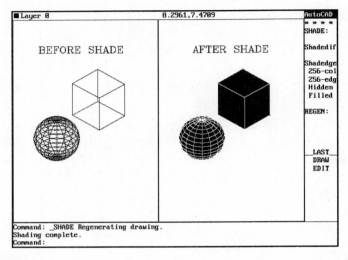

Figure SHADE.1:
The right viewport displays the shaded entities of the left viewport.

Related System Variables

SHADEDGE
SHADEDIF
SOLRENDER

SHAPE

Screen **[DRAW] [next] [SHAPE:]**

The SHAPE command inserts a shape entity into a drawing at a specified location. Shapes are entities that you can define in an actual file (*.SHP) using lines, arcs, and subshapes. Shape entities can be inserted into the drawing similar to blocks. Shape definitions, however, do not become part of the drawing. The actual shape entities that become a part of the drawing contain only the entity's location, size, and a reference to the shape definition file.

Shape definitions must be compiled with the COMPILE command and loaded with the LOAD command before they can be inserted. You can use the Insert object snap mode to snap to a shape's insertion point. When you load a drawing file, AutoCAD loads the compiled definition file corresponding to any inserted shapes.

 If you modify a shape definition file, you must recompile it or AutoCAD continues to use the old shape definition.

In Release 11 and 12, you can use Xrefs instead of shapes if you need the efficiency and automatic updating provided by external definitions. Xrefs are easy to create and modify.

 Shapes that are in an externally-referenced drawing (xref) are not available in the drawing that the xref is attached to.

Prompts and Options

- **Shape name (or ?) <default>:**

  Enter the name of a shape to insert. It must be already loaded into the drawing. Enter a question mark (**?**) to see a list of all currently loaded shapes.

- **Shape(s) to list <*>:**

  Press Enter to list all the shapes currently loaded in the drawing. You also can enter more than one name to list by separating each name with a comma or use a wild-card search string to list only shapes that match the wild-card pattern.

- **Starting point:**

  Enter a point in the drawing to locate the origin of the shape.

- **Height <1.0>:**

  Enter a value to use as a multiplier for the shape's height. The shape's height initially is based on its definition in the shape file. You also can point to define the height.

- **Rotation angle <0.0>:**

  Enter the angle you want to rotate the shape around its starting point. The shape's initial orientation is defined in the shape file. You also can point to define the rotation angle.

Example

This example first loads a shape file from one of AutoCAD's sample shape files. After the shape file is loaded, its shape names are listed and then a shape is inserted into the drawing.

```
Command: LOAD
File: PC
Specify the PC.SHX file in the AutoCAD SAMPLE directory
Command: SHAPE
Shape name (or ?): ?
Shape(s) to list <*>: ⏎
Available Shapes:
File: C:\ACAD\SAMPLE\PC.shx
FEEDTHRU        DIP8
DIP14           DIP16
DIP18           DIP20
DIP24           DIP40
Command: ⏎
SHAPE Shape name (or ?): DIP24
Starting point: Pick any point
Height <1.0>: 2
Rotation angle <0>: 90
```

Related Commands

BLOCK
COMPILE
LOAD
PURGE
XREF

Related System Variable

SHPNAME

SHELL/SH

Screen **[UTILITY] [External Commands] [SHELL:]**

The SHELL command and the less-powerful SH command enable you to run other programs or temporarily exit to the operating system prompt without ending the current drawing session. When you execute either command, AutoCAD suspends the drawing editor, switches focus to the text display, and presents a prompt. After issuing one operating system command, you are returned to the drawing editor and AutoCAD resumes.

You may encounter memory problems with the SHELL command and larger programs. If so, you are prompted with `Shell error: insufficient memory for command`.

The SH command uses less memory but can only execute operating system commands.

 Do not use the SH or SHELL command to perform any of the following tasks:

- Delete any files having extensions of ??K, ac, ac, or $a
- Run the CHKDSK command with a /F option on DOS or OS/2 systems
- Execute programs that reset serial ports (avoid Microsoft BASIC and programs compiled with it) on DOS or OS/2 systems
- Run programs that write to the same graphics memory as AutoCAD
- Swap drawing disks
- Execute TSR (Terminate and Stay Resident) programs on DOS systems unless the programs are loaded before you load AutoCAD

923

 Remember to save your drawing file before you temporarily exit the drawing editor.

Prompts and Options

- **OS Command:**

  Enter the name of the single command or program you want to run, or press Enter and an operating system prompt appears.

  If you press Enter to get an operating system prompt, you can then execute any number of programs or operating system commands. Issue the EXIT command to return to the drawing editor.

 Make sure that you exit the SHELL or SH command from the same directory as you entered.

Example

The following example uses the SHELL command to list the drawing files in the SAMPLE directory, using the DOS DIR command.

```
Command: SHELL
OS Command: DIR C:\ACAD\SAMPLE\*.DWG
```

The list varies depending on the files in your directory and the version of DOS you are running.

SKETCH

Screen **[DRAW] [next] [SKETCH:]**

The SKETCH command creates a contiguous series of lines as you move the cursor. This feature enables you to draw freehand or to trace curves on a paper drawing in tablet mode. If you set the AutoCAD system variable SKPOLY to 1, each group of individual lines converts to a single polyline when the command is completed. A common application of this command is to trace contour lines from a site plan.

If the current thickness is set to a non-zero value, the sketched lines or polylines are not extruded until they are placed in the drawing with the Record or eXit option. The SKETCH command is affected by the current snap, ortho, and tablet settings.

 You cannot turn tablet mode on and off while sketching.

The length on the individual SKETCH lines is controlled by the record increment. If the record increment is set to 0.2 units, a new line is generated each time the cursor moves to more than 0.2 units. The length of the SKETCH lines is also affected by the speed at which the cursor is moved across the screen. If the you move the cursor, the segments created may be longer than the length specified by the record increment.

The SKETCH command creates temporary lines that can be edited before they are placed on the drawing. If you create more temporary entities than can be stored in memory, AutoCAD prompts you to stop sketching entities and writes them to the disk. If you do not pause while AutoCAD writes to disk, input is lost and accuracy suffers.

 You must use the continuous linetype when sketching.

Prompts and Options

- **Record increment** < *value*>:

  Enter the length for each line segment. After the pointing device is moved this distance, the temporary segment is created on-screen. Use the largest value that produces sufficient detail.

- **Sketch. Pen eXit Quit Record Erase Connect.**

  Select one of the options described below. These options control how and when the SKETCH lines are drawn.

  You can use the following options with the SKETCH command:

- **. (period):**

  Draws a single line segment from the last point to the current pointing device location. Record increment does not affect the line length.

- **Pen:**

  This option turns the sketching on and off by placing the pen "up" and "down" on the drawing. When the pen is down, you can record lines.

- **eXit:**

  Records temporary line segments and exits the SKETCH command.

- **Quit:**

  Discards temporary line segments and returns to the Command: prompt.

- **Record:**

  Records temporary line segments and remains in the SKETCH command.

- **Erase:**

  Erases temporary line segments in the opposite order from which they were entered as you move your pointing device back over the line segments.

- **Connect:**

  By moving your pointing device close to the endpoint of the last temporary line segment, you can connect to that endpoint and continue sketching. If you enter **Connect** while the pen is down, you get the prompt Connect command meaningless when pen down. You can abort the connect by pressing Ctrl-C or entering any other option.

Example

The following example shows you how to draw curved polylines using the SKETCH command:

```
Command: SKPOLY
New value for SKPOLY <0>: 1
Command: SKETCH
Record increment <0.1000>: ↵
Sketch. Pen eXit Quit Record Erase Connect . P <Pen down>
```
Begin creating entities at ① by dragging the pointing device to ② (see fig. SKETCH.1)
```
P <Pen up>
Sketch. Pen eXit Quit Record Erase Connect . X
1 polyline with XX edges recorded.
```

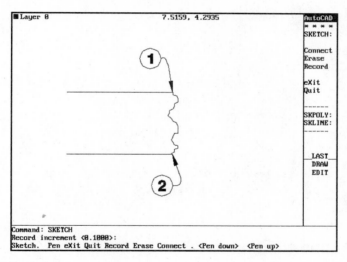

Figure SKETCH.1:
Using SKETCH to draw connecting lines.

Related Commands

LINE
PLINE
PEDIT

Related System Variables

SKETCHINC
SKPOLY

SNAP

Press **^B** *or* **F9**

Screen **[SETTINGS] [next] [SNAP:]**

Pull down **[Settings] [Drawing Aids]**

SNAP restricts the movement of the crosshairs to specified increments enabling you to accurately enter points in the drawing area. You can alter the snap spacing in the X and Y directions, reset the base point of the snap and grid, and rotate the snap and grid about a point in the drawing. You also can use SNAP in Isometric mode to create drawings that appear to be three-dimensional but are actually two-dimensional. Each viewport may have individual snap settings. You can override any snap settings with keyboard input or object snap modes.

R12 You can execute the SNAP command transparently by preceding the command name with an apostrophe ('SNAP).

Prompts and Options

- **Snap spacing or ON/OFF/Aspect/Rotate/Style <1.000>:**

  Enter a new snap increment or enter one of the options described as follows to configure the SNAP command. Enter a number or pick two points to specify the snap increment.

- **ON:**
  This option turns on SNAP. You also can turn it on with the F9 key or Ctrl-B.

- **OFF:**

  This option turns off SNAP. You also can turn it off with the F9 key or Ctrl-B.

- **Aspect:**

  This option enables you to set different X and Y axis values for the snap spacing. The following prompts appear:

- **Horizontal spacing <1.0000>:**

  You can enter a number or pick two points to specify a distance.

- **Vertical spacing <1.0000>:**

  You can enter a number or pick two points to specify a distance.

- **Rotate:**

  This option enables you to rotate the snap and the crosshairs in the drawing. This rotation also affects the grid and Ortho mode. After you specify the Rotation option, the following prompts appear:

- **Base point <0.0000,0.0000>:**

  You can enter coordinates or pick a point.

- **Rotation angle <0>:**

  You can enter an angle of rotation or pick a point to define the angle of rotation.

 Resetting the rotation of the snap and grid does not affect the origin or orientation of the current UCS. It is generally better to use the UCS command than to rotate or offset snap.

 If you want to create an ARRAY at an angle, rotate the snap angle.

- **Style:**

  This option enables you to set the snap style to either Standard (the default) or Isometric. Style displays the following prompt:

- **Standard/Isometric <current>:**

  Standard resets the snap style to the default setting. Isometric enables isometric drafting, based on snap angles of 30, 90, 150, 210, 270, and 330. After you specify Isometric, AutoCAD displays the prompt:

- **Vertical spacing <1.0000>:**

  Specify the distance between the snap points.

 You can check and alter current SNAP settings by using the STATUS and DDRMODES commands.

Example

Follow this example to adjust the horizontal and vertical spacing of the SNAP command and to specify a rotation angle:

```
Command: SNAP
Snap spacing or ON/OFF/Aspect/Rotate/Style <1.000>: A
Horizontal spacing <1.0000>: .5
Vertical spacing: <1.0000> 1
Command: SNAP
Snap spacing or ON/OFF/Aspect/Rotate/Style <A>: R
Base point: <0.0000,0.0000>: Press Enter
Rotation angle <0>: 25
Command: GRID
Grid spacing(X) or ON/OFF/Snap <0.0000>: S
```

Figure SNAP.1 illustrates what your screen should now look like.

Related Commands

> **DDRMODES**
> **GRID**
> **ISOPLANE**
> **OSNAP**
> **STATUS**

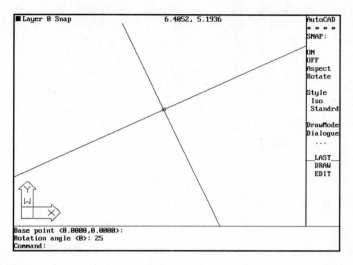

Figure SNAP.1:
The grid and crosshairs after adjusting snap spacing and rotation.

Related System Variables

SNAPANG
SNAPBASE
SNAPISOPAIR
SNAPMODE
SNAPSTYL
SNAPUNIT

SOLAREA

Screen **[MODEL] [INQUIRY] [SOLAREA:]**

Pull down **[Model] [INQUIRY >] [Area Calc.]**

The SOLAREA command calculates the surface area of solid entities. If you select more than one solid entity, SOLAREA reports the total area.

931

The area is calculated by totaling the area enclosed by the boundaries of the selected regions, minus any holes in the regions. Because the calculations are based on region boundaries, the wire mesh density does not affect accuracy. The SOLAREAU system variable determines the unit of measure for the area, the default is square centimeters.

 If you select a region that does not have a surface mesh, SOLAREA adds the mesh based on the SOLSOLIDIFY system variable.

Prompts and Options

- `Select objects:`

  Select the objects you want to include in the calculation. After you finish selecting objects, AutoCAD responds with the following message: `Surface area of solids is value sq cm .`

Example

The following example shows SOLAREA calculating the surface area of a region one drawing unit by one drawing unit:

```
Command: SOLAREA
Select objects: Select a region
Surface area of solids is 1 sq cm.
```

Related Commands

AREA
SOLMASSP
SOLLIST
SOLVAR

Related System Variables

SOLAREAU
SOLSOLIDIFY

SOLBOX

Pull-down [**Model**] [**Primitives...**]

Screen [**MODEL**] [**PRIMS.**] [**SOLBOX:**]

The AME SOLBOX command creates a box-shaped solid primitive. This command is very similar to the 3D command's BOX option, except that this element can be assigned material properties and can be acted upon by the AME editing commands.

Prompts and Options

- **Baseplane/Center/<Corner of box><0,0,0>:**

  This is the initial prompt for the SOLBOX command. At this prompt, you can use the Baseplane option to define the orientation of the base, the center point of the box primitive, or a starting corner for the box. If you press Enter, the first box corner is placed at the coordinate 0,0,0.

- **Baseplane by Entity/Last/Zaxis/View/XY/YZ/ZX/ <3points>:**

  If you choose the Baseplane option in the main SOLBOX option line, you see this next set of prompts. These prompts set the direction and orientation of the plane from which the box primitive is extruded. This command is similar to the UCS command.

When locating points for AME commands, use the Baseplane option to set the orientation of the UCS. You can also use a command called Construction Plane, which is abbreviated as CP or 'CP. When you set the UCS orientation using Baseplane, that UCS remains in effect for the duration of the command. In contrast, you can use 'CP to change the UCS orientation each time you are asked to choose a point. 'CP shares the same choices for locating the UCS as the Baseplane option.

- **Entity.** This option allows you to choose an entity within in the drawing. The baseplane will be aligned to the plane the entity was constructed in.

933

- **Last**. This option sets the baseplane to the last construction plane used to draw objects. If there was no previous construction plane, this command does not alter the current construction plane.
- **Zaxis**. This option defines the baseplane by locating an origin point and a point along the Z axis.
- **View**. This option aligns the construction plane to the current drawing view.
- **XY**. This option uses the X,Y direction of the current UCS to define the construction plane.
- **YZ**. This option uses the Y,Z direction of the current UCS to define the construction plane.
- **ZX**. This option uses the Z,X direction of the current UCS to define the construction plane.
- **3points**. This option allows you to select three points in the drawing editor to define the baseplane origin and directions of the X and Y axes.

When locating points in response to prompts, you can use the ADS Geometry Calculator program. This program is a transparent application that calculates the location of a new point or the value of an entity's direction or size, and supplies that number back to the prompt. Once the program is loaded, it can be called by entering 'CAL at any prompt.

- **Cube/Length/<Other corner>:**

  This prompt line appears after you choose the Center option or after you pick a starting corner for the box primitive. The following options define the remaining dimensions for the box primitive:
- **Cube**. This option allows you to enter a length to be used for all three box dimensions. The resulting box primitive will be a cube.
- **Length**. This option allows you to define each of the box's dimensions: length, width, and height. The box primitive is created by using these values.

- **<Other corner>.** This prompt locates the second corner of the box primitive's footprint, and then asks for a height to apply to the primitive.

Example

The following example creates a single solid box primitive using the SOLBOX command (this entity is shown in fig. SOLBOX.1).

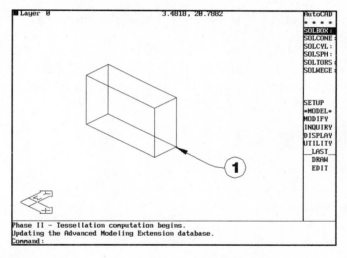

Figure SOLBOX.1:
Creating a box-shaped solid primitive.

```
Command: SOLBOX ↵
Baseplane/Center/<Corner of box>
<0,0,0>: ↵
Cube/Length/<Other corner>: ①
Height: 5
```

Related Command

3D: BOX

Related Variables

SOLDISPLAY
SOLMATCURR
SOLWDENS

SOLCHAM

Pull-down [**Model**] [**Modify**] > [**Chamfer Solids**]

Screen [**MODEL**] [**MODIFY**] [**SOLCHAM:**]

The AME SOLCHAM creates a chamfer along the edge of solid entities. A *chamfer*, also known as a *bevel*, is a primitive element that is subtracted from the solid entity where it is being applied.

Prompts and Options

- **Select base surface:**

  This prompt requires you to select the surface of a solid entity to bevel. Once the solid is selected, you need to define which edges will be chamfered.

- **Next/<OK>:**

  When you select one of the solid's edges, you may actually be selecting a face that you do not want to bevel. This prompt highlights the selected face to make sure that it is the one you want to modify. If you choose Next, the adjoining face is highlighted.

- **Pick edges of this face to be chamfered (press ENTER when done):**

  At this prompt, you select the actual edges to be beveled by the command. Only the edges that are part of the selected base surface are chamfered.

- **Enter distance along base surface <*dist*>:**

  This distance is the distance along the base surface you selected from the edge of the surface to the start of the bevel.

- **`Enter distance along adjacent surface <dist>:`**

  This distance is along the adjacent face, and it is also measured from the current edge to the start of the bevel.

Example

The following example uses the SOLCHAM command to bevel two of the edges of a box primitive. The entity that results from the modifications is shown in figure SOLCHAM.1.

```
Command: SOLCHAM ↵
Pick base surface: ①
Next/<OK>: ↵
Pick edges of this face to be chamfered
(press ENTER when done):
```
Pick the edges at ② and ③.
```
Enter distance along base surface
< 0.00> : .5 ↵
Enter distance along adjacent surface
< 0.50> : ↵
```

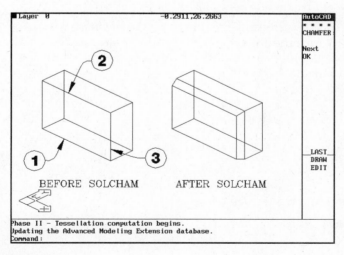

Figure SOLCHAM.1:
Beveling the edges of a box-shaped solid primitive with the SOLCHAM command.

Related Commands

CHAMFER
SOLFILL

SOLCHP

Screen **[MODEL] [MODIFY] [SOLCHP:]**

Pull down **[Model] [Modify] [Change Prim.]**

SOLCHP stands for *SOLid CHange Properties*. SOLCHP edits a solid primitive's properties, even if the primitive is part of a composite.

Any change to a primitive that is part of a composite causes a partial re-evaluation of the composite. This can be time-consuming for complex composite regions.

When creating or editing a composite model, you may accidentally create a region with no area (called a *null region*). If this occurs, AutoCAD identifies the null region with a THETA symbol (ø).

Prompts and Options

- **Select a solid or region:**

  Select the solid or region. You cannot use the AutoCAD window, crossing, previous, or last selection modes. If you select a composite region, you receive the following prompt:

- **Select primitive:**

  Pick a feature on the selected solid. If you cannot pick the primitive you want, use the Next option in the following prompt to cycle through the primitives.

- `Color/Delete/Evaluate/Instance/Move/Next/Pick/`
  `Replace/Size/eXit <N>:`

  Select the type of change you want to make or primitive to edit. These options are described next.

- `Color.` The Color option changes the selected primitive's color. Enter a color number or name.

- `Delete.` The Delete option erases the specified primitive. If the solid was part of a composite solid, AutoCAD displays the `Retain detached primitive? <N>:` prompt, giving you the opportunity to keep it as a separate primitive. Answer **N** to erase the primitive completely; answer **Y** to create a separate solid.

- `Evaluate.` The Evaluate option causes a reevaluation of the composite region and stays in the SOLCHP command. Use Evaluate after performing many edits on an existing composite solid to see your changes.

- `Instance.` The Instance option copies the selected primitive as a separate region at the same coordinates in space as the original primitive. Instance is useful for making copies of a primitive that is part of a composite solid without breaking the composite apart. The copy is drawn on the current layer with the selected primitive's color.

- `Move.` The Move option moves the selected primitive, in the same manner as AutoCAD's MOVE command. You are prompted with `Base point or displacement` and `Second point of displacement`.

- `Next.` The Next option cycles through the solid primitives that make up the selected composite solid. When the desired primitive is highlighted, select one of the other SOLCHP options.

- `Pick.` The Pick option enables you to directly select a solid primitive for editing.

- `Replace.` The Replace option substitutes a specified composite or primitive solid for the currently selected primitive. At the `Select solid to replace primitive...` prompt, pick a new solid to replace the selected primitive. Note that the new solid is not moved to the location of the replaced primitive. If you replace a

primitive that is part of a composite, you are prompted with
`Retain detached primitive?<N>:`. If you answer yes, a copy
of the primitive is placed on the layer on which it was originally
created.

The location of the replacement is not altered during the
replacement. The replacement is made in the CSG tree structure only.

- **Size.** The Size option resizes any user-specified dimensions of the
primitive. The MCS icon is displayed, which represents the
primitive's X, Y, and Z axes. The current dimensions of each axis
are displayed one at a time in the following prompts: `Length
along X axis <`*value*`>:`, `Length along Y axis <
`*value*`>:`, and `Length along the Z axis < `*value*`>:`.
- **Exit.** The Exit option completes the SOLCHP by re-evaluating the
region's CSG tree and exiting to the `Command:` prompt.

Example

The following example demonstrates SOLCHP's options, using the solids
shown in figure SOLCHP.1.

```
Command: SOLCHP
Select a region: Pick the composite solid
Select primitive: Pick the box at ①
Color/Delete/Evaluate/Instance/Move/Next/Pick/
Replace/Size/eXit <N>: C
New color <7 (white)>: 1
Color/Delete/Evaluate/Instance/Move/Next/Pick/
Replace/Size/eXit <N>: ⏎
```

AutoCAD highlights the circle primitive.

```
Color/Delete/Evaluate/Instance/Move/Next/Pick/
Replace/Size/eXit <N>: I
```

AutoCAD creates a copy of the circle in the same location; the copy is not yet
visible.

```
Color/Delete/Evaluate/Instance/Move/Next/Pick/
Replace/Size/eXit <N>: M
```

```
Base point of displacement: Pick the circle's center
Second point of displacement: Pick at point @25<0
Color/Delete/Evaluate/Instance/Move/Next/Pick/
Replace/Size/eXit <N>: S
Radius of circle <0.75>: 1
Color/Delete/Evaluate/Instance/Move/Next/Pick/
Replace/Size/eXit <N>: E
Color/Delete/Evaluate/Instance/Move/Next/Pick/
Replace/Size/eXit <N>: ↵
Color/Delete/Evaluate/Instance/Move/Next/Pick/
Replace/Size/eXit <N>: ↵
Color/Delete/Evaluate/Instance/Move/Next/Pick/
Replace/Size/eXit <N>: R
Select region to replace primitive: Pick the region primitive
Retain detached primitive <N>: ↵
Color/Delete/Evaluate/Instance/Move/Next/Pick/
Replace/Size/eXit <N>: X
```

Note that, although the replacement box did not move to the cylinder's position, it is part of the composite solid.

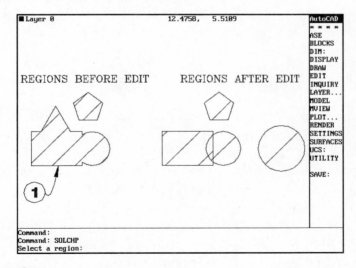

Figure SOLCHP.1:
Composite and primitive solids before and after editing.

941

Related Commands

CHANGE
CHPROP
SOLPURGE

Related System Variable

SOLRENDER

SOLCONE

Pull-down [**Model**] [**Primitives...**]

Screen [**MODEL**] [**PRIMS.**] [**SOLCONE:**]

The AME SOLCONE command creates a cone-shaped solid primitive. This command is similar to the 3D command's CONE option, except that this element can be assigned material properties and can be acted upon by the AME editing commands.

Prompts and Options

- **Baseplane/Elliptical/<Center point><0,0,0>:**

  This is the initial prompt for the SOLCONE command. At this prompt, you can use the Baseplane option to define the orientation of the base, a point on the base of the cone, or the center point for the cone. If you press Enter, the center of the cone is placed at the coordinate 0,0,0.

- **Baseplane by Entity/Last/Zaxis/View/XY/YZ/ZX/<3points>:**

  If you choose the Baseplane option in the main SOLCONE option line, you see this next set of prompts. These prompts set the direction and orientation of the plane from which the cone primitive is extruded. This command is similar to the UCS command.

When locating points for AME commands, you can use the Baseplane option to set the orientation of the UCS. You can also use a command called Construction Plane, which is abbreviated as CP or 'CP. When you set the UCS orientation using Baseplane, that UCS remains in effect for the duration of the command. In contrast, you can use 'CP to change the UCS orientation each time you are asked to choose a point. 'CP shares the same choices for locating the UCS as the Baseplane option.

- **Entity**. This option allows you to choose an entity within the drawing. The baseplane is aligned to the plane in which the entity was constructed.

- **Last**. This option sets the baseplane to the last construction plane used to draw objects. If there is no previous construction plane, this command does not alter the current construction plane.

- **Zaxis**. This option defines the baseplane by locating an origin point and a point along the Z axis.

- **View**. This option aligns the construction plane to the current drawing view.

- **XY**. This option uses the X,Y direction of the current UCS to define the construction plane.

- **YZ**. This option uses the Y,Z direction of the current UCS to define the construction plane.

- **ZX**. This option uses the Z,X direction of the current UCS to define the construction plane.

- **3points**. This option allows you to select three points in the drawing editor to define the baseplane origin and directions of the X and Y axes.

 When locating points in response to prompts, you can use the ADS Geometry Calculator program. This program is a transparent application that can be used to calculate the location of a new point or the value of an entity's direction or size, and supply that number back to the prompt. Once the program is loaded, it can be called by entering **'CAL** at any prompt.

- **Elliptical**. This option from the main prompt line allows you to define the axis endpoints that describe the circular shape of the cone primitive's base. You then see the following prompts:

- **<Axis endpoint 1>/Center:**

    This prompt allows you to locate the endpoint of the major axis or the center of the cone's base.

- **Axis endpoint 2:**

    This prompt requests the other major axis endpoint.

- **Other axis distance:**

    This prompt allows you to define the distance along the minor axis of the ellipse.

- **Center:** If you chose the Center option, you need to locate the center of the cone's base. Once this is done, you are asked to locate two other points along the axes of the base.

- **Apex/<Height>:** Once the base of the cone has been described, you must define how tall the cone is. The Apex option allows you to pick a point that locates the tip of the cone; the Height option allows you to define the height of the cone, with the tip centered within the base.

- **Diameter/<Radius>:** Both of these options are used to size the cone base—either by defining the radius or diameter distance. After answering this prompt, you need to enter the value for the height of the cone.

Example

The following example creates a single solid cone primitive using the SOLCONE command. The cone that is created is shown as a wireframe in figure SOLCONE.1.

```
Command: SOLCONE ↵
Baseplane/Elliptical/<Center point>
<0,0,0>: E ↵
<Axis endpoint 1>/Center: ①
Axis endpoint 2: ②
Other axis distance: ③
Apex/<Height>: 8 ↵
```

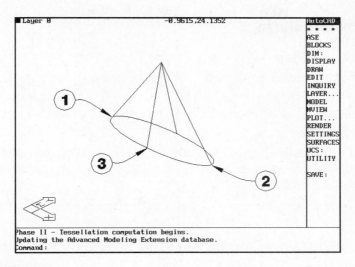

Figure SOLCON.1:
A wireframe representation of a cone primitive.

Related Command

3D: CONE

Related Variables

SOLDISPLAY
SOLMATCURR
SOLWDENS

SOLCUT

Pull-down [**Model**] [**Modify**] > [**Cut Solids**]

Screen [**MODEL**] [**MODIFY**] [**SOLCUT:**]

The AME SOLCUT command cuts through solids, allowing you to view the solid entities in sections. With SOLCUT, you can keep both portions of the cut solid, or you can delete one of the halves.

Prompts and Options

- `Select objects:`

  Choose the solid entities to be sliced be through by using this command.

- `Cutting plane by Entity/Last/Zaxis/View/XY/YZ/ZX/ <3points>:`

  This option allows you to define where the cutting plane slices. These options are similar to the settings for locating the construction plane.

For descriptions of other options, refer to the baseplane options in the SOLBOX command.

- `Both sides/<Point on desired side of the plane>:`

  This prompt asks which side of the solid that was cut should be kept in the drawing. You can pick the side, or choose to keep both sides.

Example

The following example takes a simple solid primitive and defines a cutting plane through the entity. The results are shown in figure SOLCUT.1.

```
Command: SOLCUT ↵
Select objects: ②
Select objects: ↵
Cutting plane by Entity/Last/Zaxis/View
/XY/YZ/ZX/<3points>: ↵
1st point on plane: NEA to ①
2nd point on plane: PER to ②
3rd point on plane: PER to ③
Both sides/<Point on desired side of the
plane>: ③
```

Related Commands

SOLPROF
SOLSECT

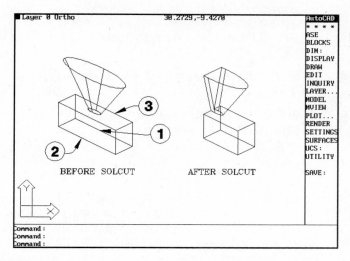

Figure SOLCUT.1:
A solid entity cut along a user-specified plane.

SOLCYL

Pull-down **[Model] [Primitives...]**

Screen **[MODEL] [PRIMS.] [SOLCYL:]**

The AME SOLCYL command creates a cylinder-shaped solid primitive. This command is similar to the 3D command's CONE option, in which both the base and top of the cone have dimensions larger than 0. This element can be assigned material properties and be acted upon by the AME editing commands.

Prompts and Options

- **Baseplane/Elliptical/<Center point><0,0,0>:**

  This is the initial prompt for the SOLCYL command. At this prompt, you can use the Baseplane option to define the orientation of the base, a point on the base of the cylinder, or the center point for the cylinder. If you press Enter, the center of the cylinder is placed at the coordinate 0,0,0.

- **Baseplane by Entity/Last/Zaxis/View/XY/YZ/ZX/ <3points>:**

  If you choose the Baseplane option in the main SOLCYL option line, you see this next set of prompts, which set the direction and orientation of the plane from which the cylinder primitive is extruded. This command is similar to the UCS command.

When locating points for AME commands, you can use the Baseplane option to set the orientation of the UCS. You can also use a command called Construction Plane, which is abbreviated as CP, or 'CP. When you set the UCS orientation using Baseplane, that UCS remains in effect for the duration of the command. In contrast, you can use 'CP to change the UCS orientation each time you are asked to choose a point. 'CP shares the same choices for locating the UCS as the Baseplane option.

- **Entity**. This option allows you to choose an entity within in the drawing. The baseplane will be aligned to the plane the entity was constructed in.
- **Last**. This option sets the baseplane to the last construction plane used to draw objects. If there was no previous construction plane, this command does not alter the current construction plane.
- **Zaxis**. This option defines the baseplane by locating an origin point and a point along the Z axis.
- **View**. This option aligns the construction plane to the current drawing view.
- **XY**. This option uses the X,Y direction of the current UCS to define the construction plane.
- **YZ**. This option uses the Y,Z direction of the current UCS to define the construction plane.
- **ZX**. This option uses the Z,X direction of the current UCS to define the construction plane.

- **3points**. This option allows you to select three points in the drawing editor to define the baseplane origin and directions of the X and Y axes.

 When locating points in response to prompts, you can use the ADS Geometry Calculator program. This program is a transparent application that can be used to calculate the location of a new point, or the value of an entity's direction or size, and supply that number back to the prompt. Once the program is loaded, it can be called by entering 'CAL at any prompt.

- **Elliptical.** This option from the main prompt line allows you to define the axis endpoints that describe the circular shape of the cylinder primitive's base. You receive the following prompts:

- **<Axis endpoint 1>/Center:** This first prompt allows you to locate the endpoint of the major axis or the center of the cylinder's base.

- **Axis endpoint 2:** This prompt requests the other major axis endpoint.

- **Other axis distance:** This prompt allows you to define the distance along the minor axis of the ellipse.

- **Center:** If you choose the Center option, you need to locate the center of the cylinder's base. Once this is done, you are asked to locate two other points along the axes of the base.

- **Center of other end/<Height>:** Once the base of the cylinder has been described, you must define how tall the object is. The Center of other end option allows you to pick a point locating the top plane of the cylinder; the Height option allows you to define the height of the cylinder primitive, with the top centered above the base.

- **Diameter/<Radius>:** Both of these options are used to size the cylinder base and the top, either by defining the radius or diameter distance. After answering this prompt, you need to enter the value for the height of the cylinder.

Example

The following example demonstrates how to create a solid cylindrical primitive by using the SOLCYL command. In this example, you use a top cylinder point that is shifted from the bottom of the center point. When you choose the points in this manner, the command creates the cylinder aligned to the points you choose. You can see the results of this example in figure SOLCYL.1.

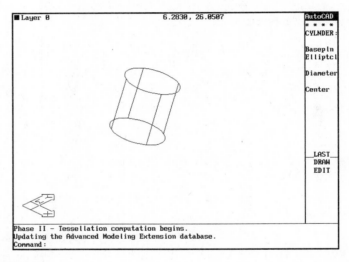

Figure SOLCYL.1:
A cylinder created with the SOLCYL command and aligned with our pick points.

```
Command: SOLCYL ↵
Baseplane/Elliptical/<Center point>
<0,0,0>: ↵
Diameter/<Radius>: 4 ↵
Center of other end/<Height>: C ↵
Center of other end: .XY of 1,2 ↵
(need Z): 8 ↵
```

Related Command

3D: CONE

Related Variables

SOLDISPLAY
SOLMATCURR
SOLWDENS

SOLDISP

The SOLDISP command changes a solid or region display to a mesh or wireframe representation. Regions and solids are drawn as wireframes by default. If you are rendering your regions or solids, use SOLDISP to create a mesh representation before rendering to get the best results from RENDER. If AME is loaded, it automatically transforms its entities into meshes before rendering.

You can set the SOLDISPLAY system variable to mesh or wireframe. SOLDISPLAY affects all new entities. Use SOLDISP to modify existing entities.

Prompts and Options

- `Mesh/<Wire>:`

  Specify Mesh to display the selected entities as mesh representations. Specify Wire (the default) to display selected entities as wireframe representations.

- `Select objects:`

  Select the objects to represent as meshes or wireframes. You can use all of AutoCAD's selection modes.

951

Example

The following example uses the SOLDISP command to change a wireframe region to a mesh representation (see fig. SOLDISP.1).

```
Command: SOLDISP
Mesh/<Wire>: M
Select objects: Pick the region
Select objects: ↵
1 region selected
```

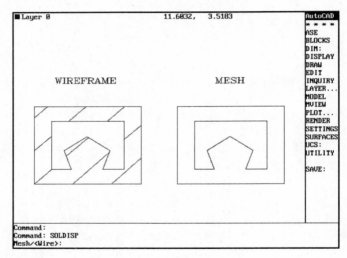

Figure SOLDISP.1
A wireframe region before and a mesh region after using SOLDISP.

Related System Variable

SOLDISPLAY

SOLEXT

Pull-down [**Model**] [**Extrude**]

Screen [**MODEL**] [**SOLEXT:**]

The AME SOLEXT command extrudes AutoCAD entities and regions in order to create new solid entities.

Prompts and Options

- **Select objects:**

  Select the regions, polylines, or circles that you want to extrude. The polylines you select must contain fewer than 500 vertices and more than three vertices. Polyline segments should also not cross over each other. Polyline widths or entity thicknesses are ignored by the extrusion process.

- **Height of extrusion:**

  This value defines how tall the extrusion face is.

- **Extrusion taper angle<0>:**

  This value defines the slant of the extrusion face as it is created. This value must be greater than 0, but less than 90 degrees.

 Be careful about assigning an extrusion taper angle. Coupling the height value with a taper angle can cause the entities to close to a point before reaching the assigned height.

- **Extrude loops to different heights?<N>:**

  If the selected objects include region primitives, you see this prompt. You have the option to extrude the regions to different heights than the other entities.

- **Pick loops for new height. (press ENTER when done):**

  If you choose to assign different heights to region primitives, you see this prompt. You can select which particular primitives are given the selected heights.

- **PMESH region. Change it to WIREFRAME for feature selection?<Y>:**

  If you choose a region that is a mesh, you see this prompt. You must convert the mesh to a wireframe before it can be extruded.

953

Example

In the following example, you take a polyline and use the SOLEXT command to extrude the entity into a solid. The results appear in figure SOLEXT.1.

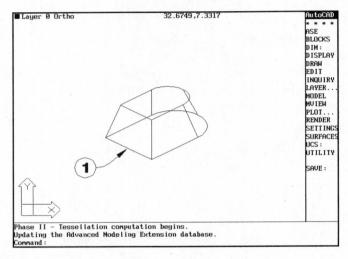

Figure SOLEXT.1:
A polyline transformed into an extruded solid with the SOLEXT command.

```
Command: SOLEXT ↵
Select objects: ①
Height of extrusion: 6 ↵
Extrusion taper angle<0>: 15 ↵
```

Related Variables

SOLDELENT
SOLSOLIDIFY

SOLFEAT

Screen **[MODEL] [DISPLAY] [SOLFEAT:]**

Pull down **[Model] [Display] [Copy Feature]**

The SOLFEAT (SOLid FEATure) command makes a 2D copy of a 3D edge or face of a solid object. The SOLFEAT command creates an anonymous block containing the lines, arcs, polylines, and circles that represent the selected edge or face. This block is inserted at the same location as the current edge or face, on the current layer. You use this command primarily to create 2D elevations from 3D solid models.

> **TIP** To select the block created by SOLFEAT, use the Last object-selection option available with most AutoCAD editing commands.

Prompts and Options

Depending on your initial selection, you receive different prompts requesting further information. These prompts provide the following options:

- **Edge/<Face>:**

  The Edge option enables you to create a block by copying the geometry of the selected edge of a solid. After you select Edge, the following prompt appears:

- **All/<Select>:**

- **All.** This option creates a new block for every edge in the selected solid.

- **Select.** This option creates a block for each edge you select. You are prompted with `Select an edge:`. You must pick the edges individually; you cannot use the AutoCAD entity selection options.

  You can pick an entity only if it is a wireframe representation. If you pick a mesh, AutoCAD displays the following prompt:

955

- **PMESH region. Change it to WIREFRAME for feature selection? <Y>:**

  If you answer yes, the entity is converted to a wireframe representation and you are reprompted to select an edge. If you answer no, the entity is ignored, and you are prompted to select a new entity.

- **Face.** The default option, Face, creates a block by copying the geometry of the selected face of a solid. After you specify Face, the following prompt appears:

- **All/<Select>:**

- **All.** This option creates a new block for every face in the selected region.

- **Select.** This option creates a block for each face you select. You are prompted with `Select a face:`, and you must pick the faces individually. You cannot use the AutoCAD entity selection options.

  You can pick an entity, only if it is a wireframe representation. If you pick a mesh, AutoCAD displays the following prompt:

- **PMESH region. Change it to WIREFRAME for feature selection? <Y>:**

  If you answer yes, the entity is converted to a wireframe representation and you are reprompted to select an edge. If you answer no, the entity is ignored, and you are prompted to select a new entity.

Use the SOLDISP command and the SOLDISPLAY system variable to create wireframe representations of entities, before using SOLFEAT.

Example

The following example demonstrates use of the SOLFEAT command to copy a solid edge and face.

```
Command: SOLFEAT
Edge/<Face> : E
All/<Select>: ↵
```

```
Pick an edge: Pick ① (see fig. SOLFEAT.1)
Pick an edge: ↵
Command: SOLFEAT
Edge/<Face> : ↵
All/<Select>: ↵
Pick a face... Pick ①
```

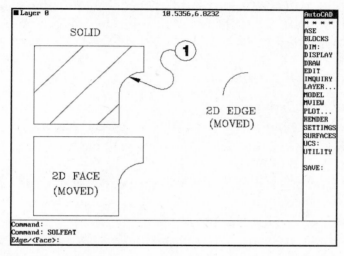

Figure SOLFEAT.1:
Solid selected by the SOLFEAT command, and 2D edge and face blocks moved away from the Solid.

Related Command

SOLDISP

Related System Variable

SOLDISPLAY

SOLFILL

Pull-down [**Model**] [**Modify**] > [**Fillet Solids**]

Screen [**MODEL**] [**MODIFY**] [**SOLFILL:**]

The AME SOLFILL command creates a fillet along the edge of solid entities. A *fillet* is a rounded corner; it is considered a primitive element that is subtracted from the solid entity where it is being applied.

Prompts and Options

- **Select objects:**

  Choose the solid entity that will have its edges filleted.

- **Select edges of solids to be filleted (press ENTER when done):**

  This prompt requires you to select the edges of the solid entity that will be rounded.

- **Diameter/<Radius> of fillet:**

  This value determines the amount that the edge you selected will be filleted.

Example

The following example uses the SOLFILL command to round the edges of a box primitive (the entity that results is shown in figure SOLFILL.1).

```
Command: SOLFILL ↵
Select object: ①
Select edges of solids to be filleted
(press ENTER when done): pick ①,
②, and ③
Diameter/<Radius> of fillet: .25 ↵
```

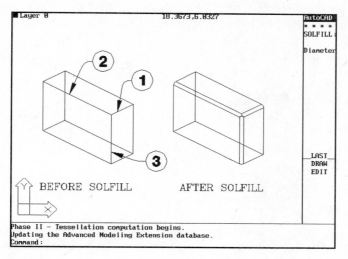

BEFORE SOLFILL   AFTER SOLFILL

Figure SOLFILL.1:
Using SOLFILL to round the edges of a solid primitive.

Related Commands

FILLET
SOLCHAM

SOLID

Screen **[DRAW] [next] [SOLID:]**

SOLID draws solid-filled areas. These areas can be defined by three or four points. The points are entered in an edge-to-edge order. The first two points are the endpoints of a starting edge. The next point defines the third point of a triangle, or you can enter a fourth point to define an ending edge. If FILL or the system variable FILLMODE is on, the areas are filled.

To save time during regenerations and redraws, turn FILL off. To see the results of turning FILL on or off, regenerate the drawing.

Prompts and Options

- **First point:**

  Specify the first point of the solid entity.

- **Second point:**

  Specify the next point of the entity.

- **Third point:**

  The direction in which you select the third point determines the appearance of the solid. If points are selected in a clockwise or counterclockwise direction, the solid appears as a bow tie. See figure SOLID.1 for an example.

- **Fourth point:**

  You do not have to specify a point at this prompt. If you pick a point, AutoCAD draws a four-sided solid. If you press Enter at this prompt, AutoCAD creates a three-sided solid. In either case, the command continues with a prompt for the next solid. The next solid uses the last two points that you picked as the first and second points of the new solid. The new prompt asks you for the new solid's third point.

Example

The following example illustrates the method for creating solid entities.

```
Command: SOLID
First point: Pick point ① (see fig. SOLID.1)
Second point: Pick point ②
Third point: Pick point ③
Fourth point: Pick point ④
Third point: Pick point ⑤
Fourth point: ↵
Third point: ↵
```

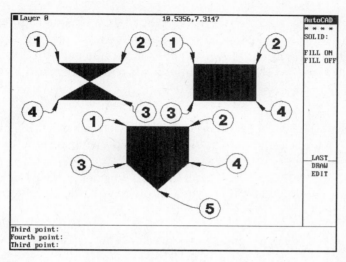

Figure SOLID.1:
Creating solids with FILL on.

Related Command

FILL

Related System Variable

FILLMODE

SOLIDIFY

Screen **[MODEL] [SOLIDIFY]**

Pull down **[Model] [Solidify]**

The SOLIDIFY command converts 2D entities into solid regions. Valid 2D entities include polylines, polygons, circles, ellipses, traces, donuts, and AutoCAD 2D solid entities. Open polylines must have at least two segments and are solidified as though they had a closing segment connecting their end points. They cannot have any crossing segments. Entities with a negative thickness value cannot be solidified without the optional AME software. Polylines with width information are solidified from their center line.

 The SOLDELENT system variable determines whether or not the selections are deleted from the drawing file after they are extruded.

The SOLSOLIDIFY system variable controls whether or not other solid commands solidify 2D entities when encountered.

 You can assign a thickness before entity creation, change an entity's thickness with CHANGE or CHPROP before using SOLIDIFY, or use the SOLEXT command—all with the same results.

Prompts and Options

- **`Select objects:`**

  Select the objects you want to solidify. You can use any of AutoCAD's entity selection options.

Example

The following example uses the SOLIDIFY command to create solid regions from different 2D AutoCAD entities. Figure SOLIDIFY.1 illustrates the entities before and after conversion.

```
Command: SOLIDIFY
Select objects: ALL
```

Related Commands

SOLEXT
SOLMESH
ELEV

Related System Variables

SOLDELENT
SOLSOLIDIFY
THICKNESS

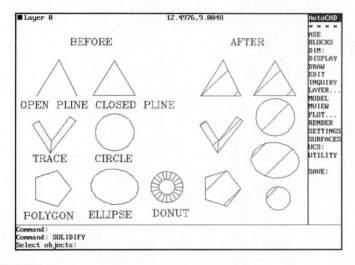

Figure SOLIDIFY.1:
2D objects before and after conversion by the SOLIDIFY command.

SOLIN

Pull-down [**Model**] [**Utility**] > [**ASM In...**]

Screen [**MODEL**] [**UTILITY**] [**SOLIN:**]

The AME SOLIN command is used only to provide a link between the old AutoDESK AutoSolid program and AME v2.1. This command is the only method available for loading solid primitives from that package into AME version 2.1. This command reads an *assembly file* that contains definitions of the solid elements that can be loaded by AME.

963

Prompts and Options

- **File name <*file*>:**

  A dialog box displays, asking for the name of the assembly file containing elements created with the AutoSolid command or using the AME SOLOUT command.

Related Commands

DXFIN
SOLOUT

SOLINT

Screen **[MODEL] [SOLINT:]**

Pull down **[Model] [Intersect]**

The SOLINT command creates a composite region from the intersection of two or more regions. If you select an object that is not a region, it is solidified according to the current setting of the SOLSOLIDIFY system variable. Selected objects that are not regions and cannot be solidified are rejected, and the command proceeds. If an intersection would result in a region with no area (null region), the entities are rejected, and the command is terminated.

Prompts and Options

- **Select objects:**

  Select the objects you want to use to create the new composite solid. To end the selection process, press Enter. The program then creates the new composite solid. If the regions are not solid and cannot be solidified, you are prompted with **n non-region objects ignored.**

If the selected regions or solids result in a null region, you are prompted with `Null intersection encountered`.

Be careful to avoid creating a null solid by using SOLINT on nonintersecting solids. You cannot see the null solid, but you can purge it using the SOLPURGE command.

Example

The following example shows you how to create an intersection region from two overlapping regions. (see fig. SOLINT.1)

```
Command: SOLINT
Select objects: Select the cylinder and box
Select objects: ↵
```

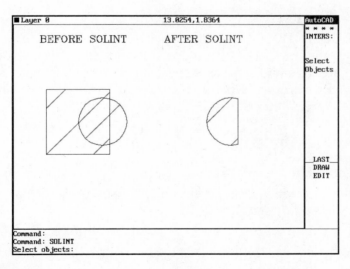

Figure SOLINT.1:
The circle and box, before and after using the SOLINT command.

Related Commands

SOLPURGE
SOLSUB
SOLUNION

Related System Variable

SOLSOLIDIFY

SOLINTERF

Pull-down [**Model**] [**Inquiry**] > [**Interference**]

Screen [**MODEL**] [**INQUIRY**] [**INTERF:**]

The AME SOLINTERF command is used to check a group of solids to determine interference. *Interference* occurs when two or more solid entities share the same volume of space within the drawing editor. SOLINTERF determines whether these solids are overlapping:if so, it displays the area of interference.

Prompts and Options

- `Select the first set of solids...Select objects:`

  At this prompt, you must select the first solid or group of solids to be checked for interference.

- `Select the second set of solids...Select objects:`

  This prompt asks you to select the second solid or group of solids, which will be checked for interference with the first set. Once these entities are chosen, SOLINTERF analyzes the volumes of space that the two groups inhabit. If there is no interference, the command ends.

- **Create interference solids?<N>:**

  At this prompt, you are asked if a new solid should be created in the area where the solids interfere with each other. If you answer Yes, a new solid is created and the command terminates.

- **Highlight pairs of interfering solids?<N>:**

  This prompt allows you to highlight the areas in which the two groups of solids interfere with each other. If there is more than one point of interference, an additional prompt enables you to step through and highlight one interference area at a time.

Example

This example uses two primitives that share a volume of space in order to illustrate how the SOLINTERF command operates. The area shared by both entities is shown in figure SOLINTERF.1.

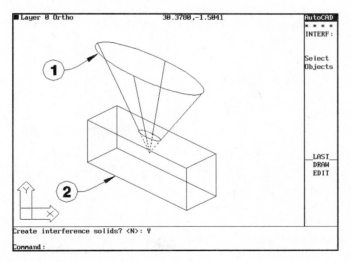

Figure SOLINTERF.1:
The volume of spcae taken up by both solid entities.

```
Command: SOLINTERF ↵
Select the first set of solids...
Select objects: ①
Select objects: ↵
Select the second set of solids...
Select objects: ②
Create interference solids? <N>: Y↵
Highlight pairs of interfering solids?
<N>: Y ↵
eXIT/<Next pair>: X ↵
```

SOLLIST

Screen **[MODEL] [INQUIRY] [SOLLIST:]**

Pull down **[Model] [Inquiry >] [List Objects]**

SOLLIST displays information about a region, an edge, a face, or a region's CSG (Constructive Solid Geometry) tree. Set the SOLPAGELEN system variable to control the number of lines per page of the list.

Prompts and Options

- **Edge/Face/Tree/<Object>:**

   Select an option. Each of the options are described below.

- **Edge.** Enter **E** to receive information about the edge of a solid object. If you select a mesh region, you are prompted with the following:

   ```
   PMESH region. Change it to WIREFRAME for feature
   selection? <Y>:
   ```

- **Face.** Enter **F** to receive information about the face of a solid object.

- **Tree.** Enter **T** to receive information on components at all levels of a solid model's CSG tree.

- **Object.** Press Enter or enter **O** to receive information on only the primitive or composite at the first level of a solid's CSG tree.

- **Pick an edge:**

  You receive this prompt if you specify the Edge option. Carefully select an edge of the solid model. The information displayed varies depending on the type of edge you select.

- **Select a face:**

  You receive this prompt if you specify the Face option. Select a visible edge of the face you want to list.

- **Select objects:**

  This prompt appears after you specify the Tree or Object options. You can select multiple solid objects at this prompt. The prompt is repeated until you press Enter. The Tree option then displays information for the entire CSG tree for the selected solids. With Object, you receive the information about the composite solid at the top of the selected solid's CSG tree only.

- **Select objects:**

  If you specify the Object option, you receive this prompt, which enables you to select multiple solid objects. The prompt is repeated until you press Enter.

Example

The following example shows the list for an edge and for the entire tree of the region shown in figure SOLLIST.1.

```
Command: SOLLIST
Edge/Face/Tree/<Object>: E
Pick an edge: Pick point ①
Circular edge, length = 1.570596,
radius = 1, center: (4, 4, 0)
Command: SOLLIST
Edge/Face/Tree/<Object>: T
```

```
Select objects: Pick point ①
Select objects: ↵
Object type = REGION (6)    HANDLE =E9
     Area not computed    Material = MILD_STEEL
     Representation= WIREFRAME    Render type CSG
```

Related System Variable

SOLPAGELEN

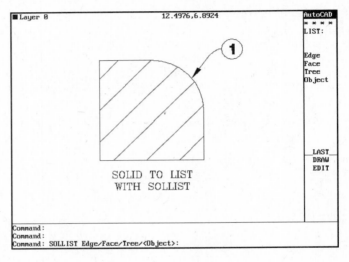

Figure SOLLIST.1:
The composite solid to list.

SOLMASSP/DDSOLMASSP

Screen **[MODEL] [INQUIRY] [SOLMASP:]**

Screen **[MODEL] [INQUIRY] [DDSOLMSP:]**

Pull down **[Model] [Inquiry >] [Mass Property]**

SOLMASSP is an inquiry command that reports the mass properties of selected regions. These properties include the area, perimeter, bounding box, and centroid (center of area). If the X,Y plane of the selected regions is coplaner with the current UCS, SOLMASSP also calculates moment of inertia, product of inertia, radius of gyration, and principal moments and directions about the centroid. You can save the information to a file. Use the SOLMASS system variable to control the unit of measure.

 Use the File button from the DDSOLMASSP dialog box or the `File name <current drawing name>:` prompt from the SOLMASSP command, to save the calculations to a file.

DDSOLMASSP delivers the same information in a dialog box. You can enter DDSOLMASSP at the `Command:` prompt or select Mass Property from the Inquiry option of the Model pull-down menu.

Prompts and Options

- **`Select objects:`**

  Select the objects you want to use. The prompt is repeated for you to select multiple objects; press Enter to end the selection process. Any solids or regions that are not coplaner with the first selection are ignored. If you select an object that is not a region, it is solidified according to the current SOLSOLIDIFY settings.

- **`Write to a file? <N>:`**

  Enter **Y** to save the calculations to a file for later use. Enter **N** or accept the default to terminate the command.

- **`File name < `*`default`*`>:`**

  Enter a valid file name to save calculations. If the system variable FILEDIA is set to 0, this prompt appears. Otherwise, a file dialog box appears. The default extension is MPR.

 If you want to list several objects at once, make sure that they are all coplaner with the first object selected.

Example

The following example uses the DDSOLMASSP dialog to display the properties of a square region inserted at 4,4,0 with the other corner at 6,6,0 (see fig. DDSOLMASSP.1).

```
Command: DDSOLMASSP
Select objects: Select the box
Select objects: ↵
```

Related System Variables

PDMODE
PDSIZE
SOLAREAU
SOLDECOMP
SOLLENGTH
SOLSOLIDIFY
SOLSUBDIV
SOLMASS
SOLVOLUME

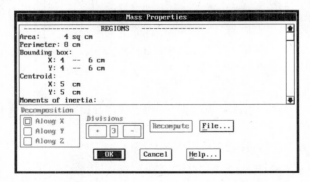

Figure DDSOLMASSP.1:
The Mass Properties calculations displayed by DDSOLMASSP.

SOLMAT

Pull-down [**Model**] [**Utility**] > [**Material...**]

Screen [**MODEL**] [**UTILITY**] [**SOLMAT:**]

The AME SOLMAT command loads, views, and edits materials used by solids within the current drawing file. This is the command line version of the DDSOLMAT command, and it performs the same functions as that command.

For a more interactive approach to setting and modifying materials, use the DDSOLMAT command.

Prompts and Options

- **Change/Edit/LIst/LOad/New/Remove/SAve/SEt/?/ <eXit>:**

  This prompt for the SOLMAT command enables you to choose which of the many options you need to execute.

- **Material name:**

  If you choose the Change option, this prompt asks you to select the name of a material currently loaded in the drawing whose properties you want to modify. When you enter a valid name, you are presented with a numbered list of the properties to change. Select the number of the property to edit, and supply a new value. When you are done, enter **0** to save the modifications you have made.

- **Material to list <*Material name*>/?:**

  This option enables you to list the properties of any material loaded into the drawing.

- **Load material:**

  This prompt enables you to load in new materials from the material definition file. Enter the name of a material stored within the

973

ACAD.MAT file. This file contains names and properties of most common materials used for solid modeling. If the file does not contain the material name you supplied, you are asked to choose another file containing material definitions.

- **Material Name:**

  If you choose to define a new material, this prompt requests the name you want the material called. If the name does not belong to a currently loaded file, you are presented with a list of material properties that is used to describe the material. These values need to be set in order for proper material calculations to be performed.

  Save the material to a file?<N>:

  Once a new material has been defined, you can use this option to save it to the ACAD.MAT file.

- **Material to remove<*Current material*>/?:**

  If a material is no longer used by solids within your drawing, you can remove its definition from the drawing. Enter the name of the material to remove at this prompt. If you choose the question mark, you can list all materials within the drawing.

- **Material to save<Current material>/?:**

  The SAve option allows you to save the material properties of the named material to the ACAD.MAT file.

- **New default material name<Name>/?:**

  The SEt option allows you to tell AME which material currently loaded in the drawing will be used for new solids.

- **List materials from file<ACAD>:**

  The ? option allows you to list any material names defined within the current drawing file and the current materials file.

Example

The following example illustrates how to change the value of the property of a material and make it the current material within the drawing.

```
Command: SOLMAT ↵
Change/Edit/LIst/LOad/New/Remove/SAve
```

```
/SEt/?/<eXit>: LO ↵
Load Material: COPPER ↵
```
Material COPPER loaded in drawing.
```
Change/Edit/LIst/LOad/New/Remove/SAve
/SEt/?/<eXit>: E ↵
```
Material name: **COPPER** ↵

Material COPPER

1. Density, kg/cu_m   8940
2. Young's modulus, GN/sq_m   117.5
3. Poisson's ratio   0.345
4. Yield strength, MN/sq_m   330
5. Ultimate strength, MN/sq_m 380
6. Thermal conductivity coeff   386
7. Linear expansion coeff., x/1e6 16.7
8. Specific heat, kJ/(kg deg_C)   0.383

Enter the number of a value you want to
change, or press ENTER to exit: **5** ↵
```
Enter ultimate strength in MN/sq_m <380>
...... 350 ↵
```
Enter the number of a value you want to
change, or press Enter to exit: ↵
```
Save the material to a file? <N>: ↵
Change/Edit/LIst/LOad/New/Remove/SAve
/SEt/?/<eXit>: SE ↵
New default material <MILD_STEEL>/?:
COPPER ↵
Change/Edit/LIst/LOad/New/Remove/SAve
/SEt/?/<eXit>: ↵
```

Related Command

DDSOLMAT

Related Variable

SOLMATCURR

SOLMESH

Screen **[MODEL] [DISPLAY] [SOLMESH:]**

Pull down **[Model] [Display] [Mesh]**

The SOLMESH command converts solids from a wireframe representation to a surface-mesh representation. A mesh represents solids as a series of faces that approximate the curves and surfaces. Meshed solids explode into polyface mesh (polyline) entities. A mesh representation is required for hidden-line removal or shaded images. Although the mesh and wireframe blocks may exist for a region, only one can be displayed at a time; the other is hidden on the AME_FRZ layer.

You can convert a mesh to a wireframe using the SOLWIRE command.

You cannot use the tangent, quadrant, or center object snap modes on a meshed arc or circle.

Prompts and Options

- **Select objects:**

  Select the objects you want to convert to a mesh representation. After you complete your selection set, press Enter to mesh the solids and complete the command. If you select an object that is not a region, it is converted according to the current setting of the SOLSOLIDIFY system variable.

Example

The following example shows you how to convert a solid from a wireframe representation to a mesh representation. See figure SOLMESH.1

```
Command: SOLMESH
Select objects: Select the region
Select objects: ↵
```

Using xref is an easy way to build complex models, but be careful when using external files that include solids. After you use xref, you cannot edit the solids while they are part of an xref, and the solids can be shaded only if they already are converted to a mesh representation.

 Because a mesh approximates solid surfaces, complex surfaces might be distorted with too small a SOLWDENS setting. Thin shells (two parallel, curved surfaces a small distance apart) also might be represented improperly. If this situation occurs, increase the dimension between the surfaces, or set SOLWDENS to a higher value.

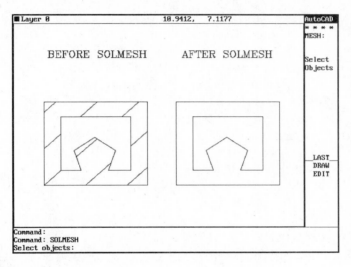

Figure SOLMESH.1
A region before and after SOLMESH

Related Commands

SOLDISP
SOLWIRE

977

Related Variables

SOLWDENS
SOLDISPLAY

SOLMOVE

Screen **[MODEL] [MODIFY] [SOLMOVE:]**

Pull down **[Model] [Modify] [Move Object]**

The SOLMOVE command combines into one command the functions of AutoCAD's MOVE and ROTATE commands. SOLMOVE creates a temporary Motion Coordinate System (MCS) in which you move and rotate your selected objects (see fig. SOLMOVE.1); all movement is relative to the MCS. The MCS origin is the intersection of the X, Y, and Z axes. The MCS icon is placed oriented to the current UCS by default. The MCS also can be oriented to the WCS, any face, or any edge. If the MCS is set to an edge of the solid being moved, the MCS moves with the solid. The X axis of the MCS has one arrow, the Y axis has two arrows, and the Z axis has three arrows.

Prompts and Options

- **Select objects:**

  Select the solids you want to move or rotate. If the object selected is not a region, it is converted to the current settings of the SOLSOLIDIFY system variable.

- **?/<Motion description>:**

  Enter the desired motion description code for the selected objects. (Note that you can combine motion description codes.) The ? option lists the motion description codes. Press Enter at this prompt to exit SOLMOVE.

  You can choose from among the following motion-description codes.

- **A[efuw].** Aligns objects with the selected coordinate system; to use this code, enter **A**, followed by one of the letters in brackets: **e** = edge, **f** = face, **u** = UCS, or **w** = WCS.
- **R[xyz]** *degrees.* Rotates objects about the selected axis; to use this code, enter **R** followed by the axis letter and the number of degrees.
- **T[xyz]** *degrees.* Translates objects along the selected axis; enter **T** followed by the axis letter and the distance to move.
- **E.** Sets MCS to an edge coordinate system.
- **F.** Sets MCS to a face coordinate system.
- **U.** Sets MCS to the UCS (User Coordinate System).
- **W.** Sets MCS to the WCS (World Coordinate System).
- **O.** Restores objects to their original orientations and positions.

In the following example, you flip and move a region with the SOLMOVE command (see fig. SOLMOVE.1). This maneuver requires both a rotation of the region and a translation of the region.

```
Command: SOLMOVE
Select objects: Pick the region
1 found
Select objects: ↵
1 solid selected.
<Motion description>/?: RX180
<Motion description>/?: TY3
<Motion description>/?: ↵
```

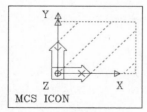

Figure SOLMOVE.1
The MCS icon during the SOLMOVE command.

You can combine several SOLMOVE motion description codes on one line, separated by commas. This procedure enables you to move and rotate a solid in one step. You can combine all the steps from the preceding command sequence into one command, for example, by typing **RXI180,TY3** at the `<Motion de-scription>/?:` prompt.

Related Commands

MOVE
ROTATE
UCS

Related System Variables

SOLAXCOL
SOLSOLIDIFY

SOLOUT

Pull-down [**Model**] [**Utility**] > [**ASM Out...**]

Screen [**MODEL**] [**UTILITY**] [**SOLOUT:**]

The AME SOLOUT command is used only to provide a link between the old AutoDESK AutoSolid program and AME v2.1. This command creates an assembly file, which contains definitions of the solid elements in the drawing.

Elliptical cones, cylinders, and some fillets and chamfers are not supported by the assembly-file format.

All extrusions are saved straight extrusions, even if they are tapered.

Prompts and Options

- **File name** *<file>*: A dialog box displays, asking for the name of an assembly file you want to create. An assembly file will be created that is compatible with the AutoSolid program. This command does not support all solid features of AutoCAD AME (such as elliptical cones and cylinders, some types of fillets and chamfers, and tapered extrusions).

Related Commands

DXFOUT
SOLIN

SOLPROF

Pull-down [**Model**] [**Display**] > [**Profile Solids**]

Screen [**MODEL**] [**DISPLAY**] [**SOLPROF:**]

The AME SOLPROF command creates a profile of a group of solids as they are viewed in the current UCS. This profile is similar to a silhouette, which contains only an outline of the objects selected. This command requires that the TILEMODE variable be set to 0. You must create a viewport and be in model space (by entering the MSPACE command) to select entities within the drawing.

Prompts and Options

- **Select objects:**

  Select the solids, or objects that can be solidified, to create a profile.

- **`Display hidden profile lines on separate layer<Y>:`**

  This option allows you to define whether edges hidden by an object (such as a back face) have lines created for the profile. When the profile is created, it is placed on a layer that has either a PV- (Profile Visible) prefix or a PH- (Profile Hidden) prefix, and the entity handle of the current viewport.

- **`Project profile lines onto a plane?<Y>:`**

  At this prompt, you define whether the profile image is created with normal line entities or 3D entities. If you answer Yes, the profile is created by projecting the solids selected onto the current UCS plane. If you select No, the profile creates all visible and hidden lines with 3D entities.

- **`Delete tangential edges?<Y>:`**

  This prompt allows you to determine whether edges between two tangent surfaces, such as an arc and a line, have a line drawn at the meeting point.

Example

The following example creates a profile of the composite solid shown in figure SOLPROF.1. The original entity on the left is shown in wireframe mode. Once the profile is created, the edges of the cone become visible.

```
Command: SOLPROF ↵
Select objects: ①
Select objects: ↵
Display hidden profile lines on separate
layer? <Y>: ↵
Project profile lines onto a plane? <Y>:
↵
Delete tangential edges? <Y>: ↵
```

Related Command

SOLCUT

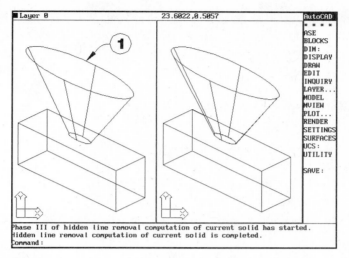

Figure SOLPROF.1:
A profile of a solid entity.

SOLPURGE

Screen **[MODELS] [UTILITY] [SOLPURG:]**

Pull down **[Model] [UTILITY >] [Purge Objects]**

The SOLPURGE command erases information stored with solid objects and releases that memory. More memory and less information to hold can improve performance and reduce the size of drawing files. If purged information is needed later, it is recalculated which causes some commands to take longer to perform. Use the SOLPURGE command on solids that are not likely to change.

Prompts and Options

- **Memory/2dtree/Bfile/Pmesh/<Erased>:**

  Enter an option, or accept the default which purges secondary solid entities which remain after a solid has been erased. Memory associated with erased solids also is released. This option is the default because it is the safest and most commonly used option. The following are the other options for the SOLPURGE command:

- **Memory.** This option releases memory associated with solids and regions. You specify which solids to release from memory at the **All/<Select>:** prompt.

- **All/<Select>:**

  The All option releases memory used by all the solid entities in your drawing.

  The Select option releases memory for specified solid entities. Nonsolid entities are ignored.

 - **2dfile.** Organizes a region's structure to reduce its size and complexity.

- **Bfile.** Removes boundary files from solids. This can significantly reduce the size of a drawing.

 Purging Bfile entities can slow AME operations requiring those entities because AME must re-create them on the fly.

- **Pmesh.** The Pmesh option removes selected Pmesh entities. If the selected solids are currently viewed as a mesh, AutoCAD switches them back to wireframe representations before purging the mesh.

 If you do not have much memory on your computer, use the Erased option frequently to keep memory free and minimize paging to disk.

Related Command

PURGE

SOLREV

AME

Pull-down [**Model**] [**Revolve**]

Screen [**MODEL**] [**SOLREV.**]

The AME SOLREV command is similar to the normal AutoCAD REVSURF command. It creates a solid entity by revolving an outline composed of normal AutoCAD entities about a set axis.

Prompts and Options

- **Select region, polyline or circle for revolution...Select objects:**

    This prompt clearly states the types of entities that can be used for this command. Choose one of the entities to begin the process of creating a revolved surface.

- **Axis of revolution - Entity/X/Y/<Start point of axis>:**

    This prompt allows you to define which axis the selected entity will be turned about to create the new entity. You have several choices.

> **TIP** When locating points in response to prompts, you can use the ADS Geometry Calculator program. This program is a transparent application that calculates the location of a new point or the value of an entity's direction or size, and supplies that number back to the prompt. Once the program is loaded, it can be called by entering **'CAL** at any prompt.

- **Entity**. This option allows you to select line or single-segment polylines that form the center of the revolution path.
- **X**. This option uses the positive X axis of the current UCS as the center point of the revolution path.
- **Y**. This option uses the positive Y axis of the current UCS as the center point of the revolution path.

985

- **<Start point of axis>**. This option allows you to define the two points that describe the center of the path of revolution.
- **Angle of revolution<full circle.>:**

    This prompt defines whether the entity creates a closed circular path or an open path. You can then input the number of degrees that the entity is to be revolved about the axis.

Example

In this example, you create a path of revolution of the polyline shown in figure SOLREV.1. This new entity is shown as a wireframe in order to shorten the time required to display the entity.

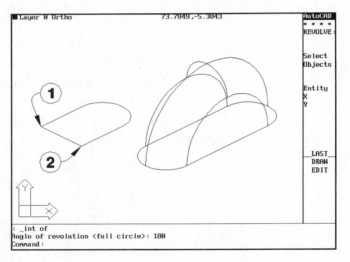

Figure SOLREV.1:
A wireframe representation of a polyline path of revolution.

```
Command: SOLREV ↵
Select objects: ①
Select objects: ↵
Axis of revolution - Entity/X/Y/<Start
point of axis>: INT of ①
End point of axis: INT of ②
Angle of revolution <full circle>:
180 ↵
```

Related Command

REVSURF

Related Variables

SOLDELENT
SOLDISPLAY
SOLSOLIDIFY
SOLWDENS

SOLSECT

Pull-down [**Model**] [**Display**] > [**Section Solids**]

Screen [**MODEL**] [**DISPLAY**] [**SOLSECT:**]

The AME SOLSECT command creates a cross-section through a selected group of solids. The plane that passes through the solids can be defined in any location, giving you great flexibility in the cross-section image that is created.

Prompts and Options

- **Select objects:**
  Choose the solid entities whose section will be shown.

- **Cutting plane by Entity/Last/Zaxis/View/XY/YZ/ZX/ <3points>:**
  This option allows you to define where the section plane through the selected entities is shown. These options are similar to the settings for locating the construction plane.

- **Entity.** This option allows you to choose an entity within in the drawing. The section plane will be aligned to the plane in which the entity was constructed.

987

- **Last**. This option sets the section plane to the last construction plane used to draw objects. If there is no previous construction plane, this command does not alter the current construction plane.
- **Zaxis**. This option defines the section plane by locating an origin point and a point along the Z axis.
- **View**. This option aligns the section plane to the current drawing view.
- **XY**. This option uses the XY direction of the current UCS to define the section plane.
- **YZ**. This option uses the YZ direction of the current UCS to define the section plane.
- **ZX**. This option uses the ZX direction of the current UCS to define the section plane.
- **3points**. This option allows you to select three points in the drawing editor to define the section-plane origin and directions of the X and Y axes.

Example

This example takes a simple combined solid entity and creates a section plane through the entity. The results are shown in figure SOLSECT.1.

```
Command: SOLSECT ↵
Select objects: ②
Select objects: ↵
Cutting plane by Entity/Last/Zaxis/View
/XY/YZ/ZX/<3points>: ↵
1st point on plane: NEA to ①
2nd point on plane: PER to ②
3rd point on plane: PER to ③
```

Related Commands

SOLCUT
SOLPROF

Related Variables

SOLHANGLE
SOLHPAT
SOLHSIZE
SOLSECTYPE

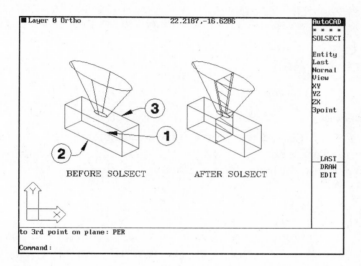

Figure SOLSECT.1:
The section plane created at the selected location.

SOLSEP

Screen **[MODEL] [MODIFY] [SOLSEP:]**

Pull down **[Model] [Modify] [Separate]**

The SOLSEP command separates solids used in a composite solid. SOLSEP breaks down solids into their components until the solid primitive level is reached. The SOLSEP command reverses any SOLINT, SOLUNION, and SOLSUB commands that have been performed. The resulting solids are placed on the layers on which they were originally created.

 You cannot separate solid primitives. They already are at the lowest possible level on the CSG tree.

 SOLSEP sometimes returns unexpected results, depending on how the composite solids were created originally. If you mistakenly separate the wrong solids, use the UNDO command to return them to their original composite form.

Prompts and Options

- `Select objects:`

  Select one or more composite solids for separating.

- `Only booleaned regions can be separated. Primitives ignored.` This warning message appears when one or more of the solids selected is a solid primitive.

Example

The following example applies the SOLSEP command to the composite solid shown in figure SOLSEP.1. This solid was generated by applying the SOLUNION command to a box and a cylinder.

```
Command: SOLSEP
Select objects: Pick the region
Select objects: ↵
1 solid selected.
```

Related Commands

SOLUNION
SOLINT
SOLSUB

SOLSPHERE

Pull-down [**Model**] [**Primitives...**]

Screen [**MODEL**] [**PRIMS.**] [**SOLSPH:**]

The AME SOLSPHERE command creates a spherical solid primitive. This command is similar to the 3D command's SPHERE option, except that this element can be assigned material properties and be acted upon by the AME editing commands.

Prompts and Options

- **Baseplane/<Center of sphere><0,0,0>:**

  This is the initial prompt for the SOLSPHERE command. At this prompt, you can use the Baseplane option to define the orientation of the base or define the center point of the sphere. If you press Enter, the center of the sphere is placed at the coordinate 0,0,0.

- **Baseplane by Entity/Last/Zaxis/View/XY/YZ/ZX/ <3points>:**

  If you choose the Baseplane option in the main SOLSPHERE option line, you see this next set of prompts. These set the direction and orientation of the plane in which the sphere primitive is created. This command is similar to the UCS command, the options allow you to define the baseplane.

TIP When locating points for AME commands, you can use the Baseplane option to set the orientation of the UCS. You can also use a command called Construction Plane, abbreviated as CP or 'CP. When you set the UCS orientation using Baseplane, that UCS remains in effect for the duration of the command. In contrast, you can use 'CP to change the UCS orientation each time you are asked to choose a point. 'CP shares the same choices for locating the UCS as the Baseplane option.

- **Entity**. This option allows you to choose an entity within the drawing. The baseplane will be aligned to the plane in which the entity was constructed.
- **Last**. This option sets the baseplane to the last construction plane used to draw objects. If there is no previous construction plane, this command does not alter the current construction plane.
- **Zaxis**. This option defines the baseplane by locating an origin point and a point along the Z axis.
- **View**. This option aligns the construction plane to the current drawing view.
- **XY**. This option uses the XY direction of the current UCS to define the construction plane.
- **YZ**. This option uses the YZ direction of the current UCS to define the construction plane.
- **ZX**. This option uses the ZX direction of the current UCS to define the construction plane.
- **3points**. This option allows you to select three points in the drawing editor to define the baseplane origin and directions of the X and Y axes.

> **TIP**
>
> When locating points in response to prompts, you can use the ADS Geometry Calculator program. This program is a transparent application that can calculate the location of a new point, calculate the value of an entity's direction or size, and supply that number back to the prompt. Once the program is loaded, it can be called by entering **'CAL** at any prompt.

- **Diameter/<Radius>:**

  This prompt line appears after you choose the Center option or after you pick a starting corner for the sphere primitive. With this prompt, you define the size of the sphere by either specifying a value for the radius of the sphere or by defining the size of the sphere's diameter.

Example

This example creates a spherical primitive solid using the SOLSPHERE command. The entity is displayed as a meshed object in figure SOLSPHERE.1.

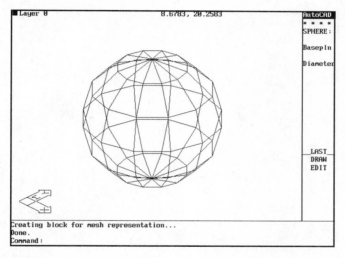

Figure SOLSPHERE.1:
The sphere created by using the SOLSPHERE command.

```
Command: SOLSHERE ↵
Baseplane/<Center of sphere><0,0,0> ↵
Diameter/<Radius>: 10 ↵
```

Related Command

3D: SPHERE

Related System Variables

SOLDISPLAY
SOLMATCURR
SOLWDENS

SOLSUB

Screen **[MODEL] [SOLSUB:]**

Pull down **[Model] [Subtract]**

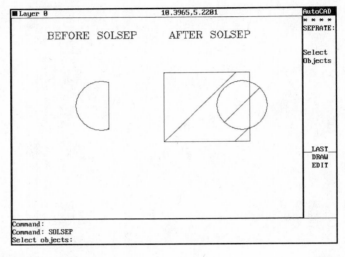

Figure SOLSEP.1:
The composite region, before and after separating.

The SOLSUB command performs a Boolean subtraction operation. SOLSUB uses two selection sets. The first selection set defines the source object(s). If more than one solid object is selected, they are all combined with a union operation. The second selection set defines the object(s) that are to be subtracted from the first selection set. If you select more than one solid for this set, they are combined with a union operation. Any solids contained in both selection sets are ignored in the second selection set. Any intersecting area is subtracted and a new composite solid results.

Prompts and Options

- **Source objects...**
  Select objects:

  Pick the solids you want to subtract from at this prompt. If you select an object that is not a region, it is solidified according to the current setting of the SOLSOLIDIFY system variable.

- **Objects to subtract from them...**
  Select objects:

  Pick the solids you want to subtract from the first selection set. A *null solid* (a solid without volume) can result by subtracting too much of a solid. The following message is displayed as the command is reversed:

  `Null solid encountered. Automatically separating.`

If there are no regions in the select set to subtract that are coplaner with a source selection set, the source selection set is rejected.

Example

The following example uses the SOLSUB command to subtract a circle from a box (see fig. SOLSUB.1).

```
Command: SOLSUB
Source objects...
Select objects: Pick the box
Objects to subtract from them...
Select objects: Pick the circle
```

Related Commands

SOLINT
SOLUNION

Related System Variable

SOLSOLIDIFY

SOLTORUS

Pull-down [**Model**] [**Primitives...**]

Screen [**MODEL**] [**PRIMS.**] [**SOLTORS:**]

The AME SOLTORUS command is used to create a donut-shaped solid primitive. This command is very similar to the 3D command's TORUS option, except that this element can be assigned material properties and be acted upon by the AME editing commands.

Prompts and Options

- **Baseplane/<Center of torus><0,0,0>:**

  This is the initial prompt for the SOLTORUS command. At this prompt, you can use the Baseplane option to define the orientation of the base or define the center point of the torus primitive. If you press Enter, the center of the torus is placed at the coordinate 0,0,0.

- **Baseplane by Entity/Last/Zaxis/View/XY/YZ/ZX/ <3points>:**

  If you choose the Baseplane option in the main SOLTORUS option line, you see this next set of prompts, which set the direction and orientation of the plane in which the torus primitive is created. This option is similar to the UCS command.

When locating points for AME commands, you can use the Baseplane option to set the orientation of the UCS. You can also use a command called Construction Plane, abbreviated CP, or 'CP. When you set the UCS orientation using Baseplane, that UCS will remain in effect for the duration of the command. In contrast, you can use 'CP the change the UCS orientation each time you are asked to choose a point. 'CP shares the same choices for locating the UCS as the Baseplane option.

> **Entity.** This option allows you to choose an entity within in the drawing. The baseplane will be aligned to the plane the entity was constructed in.
>
> **Last.** This option will set the baseplane to the last construction plane used to draw objects. If there was no previous construction plane, this command will not alter the current construction plane.
>
> **Zaxis.** This option will define the baseplane by locating an origin point and a point along the Z axis.
>
> **View.** This option will align the construction plane to the current drawing view.
>
> **XY.** This option uses the XY direction of the current UCS to define the construction plane.
>
> **YZ.** This option uses the YZ direction of the current UCS to define the construction plane.
>
> **ZX.** This option uses the ZX direction of the current UCS to define the construction plane.
>
> **3points.** This final option allows you to select 3 points in the drawing editor to define the baseplane origin and directions of the X and Y axes.

When locating points in response to prompts, you can use the ADS Geometry Calculator program. This program is a transparent application that calculates the location of a new point or the value of an entity's direction or size, and supplies that number back to the prompt. Once the program is loaded, it can be called by entering **'CAL** at any prompt.

- **Diameter/<Radius> of torus:**

   This prompt defines the size of the torus entity by either entering a value for its radius or diameter.

- **`Diameter/<Radius> of tube:`**

  This prompt defines the size of the tube that forms the torus entity by either entering a value for its radius or diameter.

Example

This example creates a torus-shaped primitive solid using the SOLTORUS command. The entity is displayed as a meshed object in figure SOLTORUS.1.

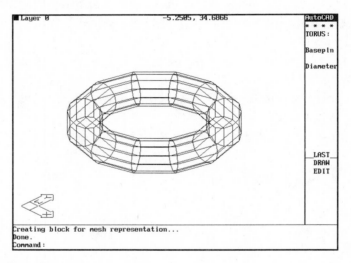

Figure SOLTORUS.1:
The torus entity created using the SOLTORUS command.

```
Command: SOLTORUS ↵
Baseplane/<Center of torus><0,0,0> ↵
Diameter/<Radius> of torus: 10 ↵
Diameter/<Radius> of tube: 2.5 ↵
```

Related Command

3D: TORUS

Related Variables

SOLDISPLAY
SOLMATCURR
SOLWDENS

SOLUCS

Screen   **[MODEL] [UTILITY] [SOLUCS:]**

Pull down   **[Model] [UTILITY >] [SolUCS]**

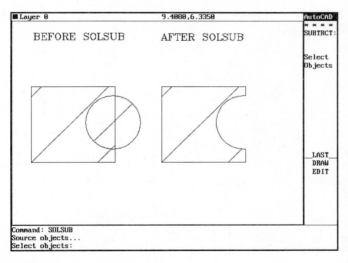

Figure SOLSUB.1:
The regions before and after the SOLSUB command.

The SOLUCS command aligns the UCS with either an edge or a face of a
solid entity. This cannot be done with solids using the UCS command.

Prompts and Options

- **Edge/<Face>:**

  Specify the option corresponding to the solid feature you want to align the UCS with. Press Enter to accept the default option, Face.

- **Pick an edge...**

  Pick an edge with which to align the UCS.

- **Pick a face...**

  Pick a face to align the UCS with by picking an edge. Edges are created by the boundaries of two faces, so you must indicate which face you want to align the UCS with at the next prompt.

- **<OK>/Next:**

  If the highlighted face is the one you want to align with, press Enter. Otherwise, enter **N** to select the adjacent face.

Example

The following example demonstrates aligning the UCS with the face of a solid using the SOLUCS command (see fig. SOLUCS.1).

```
Command: SOLUCS
Edge/<Face>: ↵
Select a face... Pick the region
Next/<OK>: N
Next/<OK>: ↵
```

Related Command

UCS

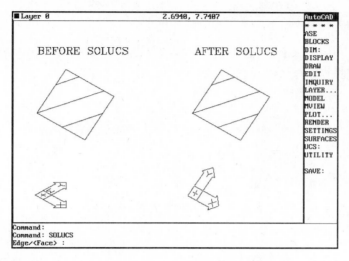

Figure SOLUCS.1:
UCS icon before and after aligning with a region.

SOLUNION

Screen   **[MODEL] [SOLUNON:]**

Pull down   **[Model] [Union]**

The SOLUNION command combines two or more solid objects with a Boolean union operation to create a single composite solid. The selected objects need not intersect.

Prompts and Options

- **Select objects:**

  Pick the solids you want to unite using AutoCAD's general object selection methods. If a selected object is not a region, it is solidified according to the current settings of the SOLSOLIDIFY system variable.

Example

The following example uses the SOLUNION command to combine a solid box and a solid cylinder.

```
Command: SOLUNION
Select objects: Pick the box and circle
```

Figure SOLUNION.1 shows the regions before and after the SOLUNION command.

Related Commands

> **SOLINT**
> **SOLSUB**

Related System Variable

> **SOLSOLIDIFY**

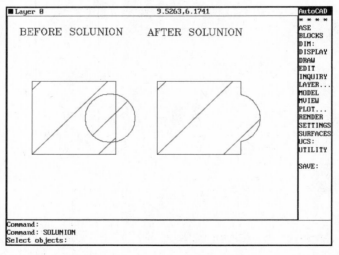

Figure SOLUNION.1:
Solids before and after the SOLUNION command.

SOLVAR/DDSOLVAR

Screen [MODEL] [UTILITY] [SETUP] [SOLVAR:]

Pull down [Model] [Setup] [Variables]

The DDSOLVAR command provides access to the solid modeling system variables, much like the SETVAR command does for AutoCAD system variables. You also can type the name of the solid system variables at the Command: prompt and bypass the DDSOLVAR command. The DDSOLVAR command displays the AME System Variables dialog box, which enables you to graphically set the solid system variables.

Prompts and Options

- **Variable name or ?:**

  Enter the name of a valid solid variable you want to change. Type **?** to list all of the solid variables with a brief description of their purpose. You can omit the SOL prefix from the variable name, and most variables can be further abbreviated.

 You can enter the variable name directly at the Command: prompt

Example

The following example changes the value of the solid variables that control units.

Command: **DDSOLVAR**
Click on Units
Enter **INCH** *in the Length edit box (see Fig. DDSOLVAR.1)*
Turn Consistent Units *on by clicking on the check box*
Click on OK twice

Figure DDSOLVAR.1:
The Region System Variables dialog box.

Related Command

SETVAR

SOLWEDGE

Pull-down [**Model**] [**Primitives...**]

Screen [**MODEL**] [**PRIMS.**] [**SOLWEGE:**]

The AME SOLWEDGE command is used to create a wedge-shaped solid primitive. This command is very similar to the 3D command's WEDGE option, except that this element can be assigned material properties and be acted upon by the AME editing commands.

Prompts and Options

- **Baseplane/Center/<Corner of box><0,0,0>:**

  This is the initial prompt for the SOLBOX command. At this prompt, you can use the Baseplane option to define the orientation of the base, the center point of the box primitive, or the starting corner for the box. If you press Enter, the first box corner is placed at the coordinate 0,0,0.

- **Baseplane by Entity/Last/Zaxis/View/XY/YZ/ZX/ <3points>:**

  If you choose the Baseplane option in the main SOLBOX option line, you see this next set of prompts. These prompts set the direction and orientation of the plane from which the box primitive extrudes. This command is similar to the UCS command.

  TIP When locating points for AME commands, you can use the Baseplane option to set the orientation of the UCS. You can also use a command called Construction Plane, abbreviated CP, or 'CP. When you set the UCS orientation using Baseplane, that UCS will remain in effect for the duration of the command. In contrast, you can use 'CP the change the UCS orientation each time you are asked to choose a point. 'CP shares the same choices for locating the UCS as the Baseplane option.

- **Entity**. This option allows you to choose an entity within in the drawing. The baseplane is aligned to the plane in which the entity was constructed.

- **Last**. This option sets the baseplane to the last construction plane used to draw objects. If there is no previous construction plane, this command does not alter the current construction plane.

- **Zaxis**. This option defines the baseplane by locating an origin point and a point along the Z axis.

- **View**. This option aligns the construction plane to the current drawing view.

- **XY**. This option uses the XY direction of the current UCS to define the construction plane.

- **YZ**. This option uses the YZ direction of the current UCS to define the construction plane.

- **ZX**. This option uses the ZX direction of the current UCS to define the construction plane.

- **3points**. This option allows you to select three points in the drawing editor to define the baseplane origin and directions of the X and Y axes.

> **TIP** When locating points in response to prompts, you can use the ADS Geometry Calculator program. This program is a transparent application that calculates the location of a new point, the value of an entity's direction or size, and supplies that number back to the prompt. Once the program is loaded, it can be called by entering **'CAL** at any prompt.

- **Length/<Other corner>:**

  This prompt line appears after you choose the Center option or after you pick a starting corner for the wedge primitive. These final options define the remaining dimensions for this entity.

- **Length**. This option allows you to define each of the wedge's dimensions: length, width, and height. The wedge primitive will be created using these values.

- **<Other corner>:**

  This prompt locates the second corner of the wedge primitive's footprint, and then asks for a height to apply to the primitive.

Example

In the following example, you create a single wedge primitive using the SOLWEDGE command. The entity that you create is shown in figure SOLWEDGE.1.

```
Command: SOLWEDGE ↵
Baseplane/Center/<Corner of wedge>
<0,0,0>: ↵
Length/<Other corner>: ①
Height: 8
```

Related Command

3D: WEDGE

Related Variables

SOLDISPLAY
SOLMATCURR
SOLWDENS

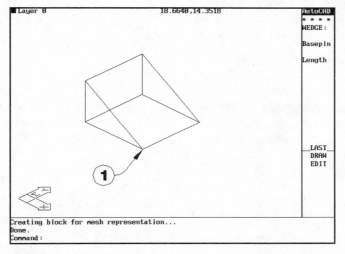

Figure SOLWEDGE.1:
Creating a wedge-shaped solid primitive.

SOLWIRE

Screen [MODEL] [DISPLAY] [SOLWIRE:]

Pull down [Model] [Display] [Wireframe]

The SOLWIRE command changes the display of selected solids from mesh to wireframes. A wireframe display enables you to use object snaps, which are not possible with mesh displays. Both the wireframe and mesh blocks of a solid can exist in a drawing at the same time but only one can be displayed. The other block is hidden on the frozen AME_FRZ layer.

1007

You can switch between wireframes and meshes as often as you want using the SOLWIRE and SOLMESH commands.

A solid must have a mesh representation to be properly shaded or rendered.

Prompts and Options

- `Select objects:`

  Pick solid objects to display as wireframe blocks. If the selected object is not a region, it is converted according to the current settings of the SOLSOLIDIFY command.

Example

The following example shows you how to use the SOLWIRE command to wire a cylinder (see fig. SOLWIRE.1).

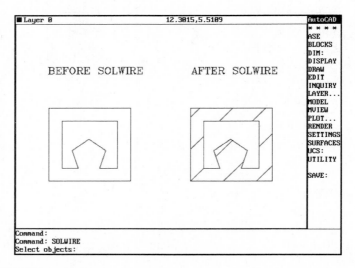

Figure SOLWIRE.1:
A region before and after SOLWIRE.

```
Command: SOLWIRE
Select objects: Pick the region
Select objects: ↵
```

Related Command

SOLMESH

Related System Variables

SOLDISPLAY
SOLSOLIDIFY
SOLWDENS

STATS

Screen **[RENDER] [STATS]**

Pull down **[Render] [Statistics]**

The STATS command displays statistical information about the last rendering and enables you to save the statistics as a file.

Prompts and Options

- **Scene name.** Scene name displays the name of the last scene rendered. If no scene was current at the time, (none) is displayed.
- **Last rendering type.** Last rendering type shows what rendering type was used to create the rendered image. The possible values are Full Render or Quick Render.
- **Rendering time.** Rendering time displays how much time the last rendering took to complete.
- **Total faces.** Total faces displays the number of faces rendered in the last rendering.
- **Total triangles.** Total triangles displays the number of triangles rendered in the last rendering.

- **Cyclic overlaps corrected.** If the last rendering was a full render, this value is the number of cyclic overlaps corrected. A cyclic overlap occurs when face A overlaps face B, which overlaps face C, which overlaps face D, which in turn overlaps face A. Cyclically overlapping faces increase rendering time.

- **Triangles chopped.** Triangles chopped displays the number of triangles that intersect after face intersection correction has been applied to the intersecting faces.

- **Original extents.** Original extents displays the minimum and maximum X, Y, and Z coordinates of the drawing extents.

- **Projected extents.** Projected extents displays the minimum and maximum X, Y, and Z coordinates of the drawing after it appears on screen.

- **Save statistics to file.** The Save statistics to file check box and edit box enable you to write the statistical information to a file. First, place a check in the check box, then enter a file name, including the extension, in the edit box. The resulting file is an ASCII file, which you can display by using any text editor or the DOS TYPE command. If the file name you enter already exists, the information is appended to that file.

STATUS

? ,

Screen **[INQUIRY] [STATUS:]**

R12 The STATUS command provides detailed information about the current drawing and AutoCAD's memory usage. (See fig. STATUS.1.) In Release 12 STATUS can be issued transparently if you preface the command name with an apostrophe ('STATUS). Information that STATUS provides includes the number of entities in the drawing; the drawing's limits and whether or not they are being exceeded; the current color, layer, and linetype; and the status of drawing aids, such as Snap and Ortho modes. STATUS also displays information on disk and memory usage. The number format is controlled by the UNITS command.

Use the STATUS command to monitor your free disk space. If
the disk fills up, AutoCAD will probably crash with an
UNABLE TO OPEN PAGING FILE error.

```
0 entities in UNNAMED
Model space limits are X:      0.0000   Y:     0.0000   (Off)
                       X:     12.0000   Y:     9.0000
Model space uses        *Nothing*
Display shows          X:      0.0000   Y:     0.0000
                       X:     12.4867   Y:     9.0000
Insertion base is      X:      0.0000   Y:     0.0000   Z:    0.0000
Snap resolution is     X:      1.0000   Y:     1.0000
Grid spacing is        X:      0.0000   Y:     0.0000

Current space:          Model space
Current layer:          0
Current color:          BYLAYER -- 7 (white)
Current linetype:       BYLAYER -- CONTINUOUS
Current elevation:      0.0000   thickness:    0.0000
Fill on  Grid off  Ortho off  Qtext off  Snap off  Tablet off
Object snap modes:      None
Free disk: 3203072 bytes
Virtual memory allocated to program: 6000 KB
Amount of program in physical memory/Total (virtual) program size: 49%
Total conventional memory: 392 KB      Total extended memory: 2800 KB
-- Press RETURN for more --
Swap file size: 3300 KB
Command:
```

Figure STATUS.1:
Status information regarding the current drawing and system.

Related Command

UNITS

STRETCH

Screen **[EDIT] [next] [STRETCH:]**

Pull down **[Modify] [Stretch]**

The STRETCH command moves and stretches entities by relocating the
points that define the entities. To select objects for STRETCH, you drag
a crossing window. Entities in the window are moved; entities that
cross the edge of the window are stretched. You cannot stretch some
entities, such as circles, shapes, text, blocks, and points. You can move
these entities, however, if their primary definition point is located
within the crossing window.

You can stretch two-dimensional entities only in their construction plane. Before you issue the STRETCH command, set the UCS so that it aligns with the entities.

  Use the Grip Edit Stretch mode for quicker stretching and as a copy option. You can also stretch a circle's radius with the Grip Edit Stretch mode.

Prompts and Options

- **Select object to stretch by window or polygon...**
  Select objects:

  At this prompt, you must use a crossing window to select entities. The prompt repeats until your selection set is complete.

- **First corner:**

  Slect the first point of a crossing window.

- **Other corner:**

  Select the second point to define a crossing window. If you specify more than one crossing window, only the entities selected with the last crossing window are affected by STRETCH.

- **Base point or displacement:**

  Enter the base point of displacement or a coordinate amount of displacement.

- **Second point of displacement:**

  Enter the new endpoint for the stretched entities.

Example

The following example uses STRETCH on the entities shown in figure STRETCH.1.

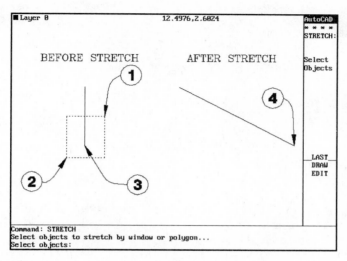

Figure STRETCH.1:
A line before and after STRETCH.

```
Command: STRETCH
Select object to stretch by window or polygon...
Select objects: Pick point ①
Other corner: Pick point ②
1 found
Select objects: ↵
Base point or displacement: Pick point ③
Second point of displacement: Pick point ④
```

Related Commands

CHANGE
EXTEND
MOVE
TRIM

STYLE

Screen **[SETTINGS] [next] [STYLE:]**

The STYLE command loads fonts that you can use with the TEXT, DTEXT, ATTDEF, and dimensioning commands to create text. In addition, STYLE enables you to define the look of a text font in the drawing. In Release 12 you can issue the STYLE command transparently if you preface it with an apostrophe ('STYLE).

 If you change a style, all text created with that style is changed to match the new style. This causes AutoCAD to regenerate the drawing.

Prompts and Options

- **Text style name (or ?) < *current style* >:**

    Enter the desired name for the text style. Each unique text style must have its own name. The default name for the text style is the name of the file that contains the font. Use the question mark option (?) to obtain a list of the currently defined fonts in the drawing.

 The LIST and DDMODIFYcommands display the STYLE settings of a text object.

- **Text style(s) to list <*>:**

    If you choose the question mark option (?), you can specify which style(s) you want to view. If you press Enter, all loaded text styles

are listed. You also can enter a wild-card search string to list only
styles that match the wild-card pattern.

Files with a PFB extension are postscript fonts that are now
supported under Release 12. These are waded and used in
the same manner as normal font files.

- **File:**

  The Select Font File dialog box is displayed (see fig. STYLE.1).
  Enter the name of the file that contains the font definition. This file
  has an SHX extension. (You do not enter the extension.) If you
  press Enter, the style is based on the font file of the current style.

- **Height <0.0>:**

  Specify a height of 0 if you want the TEXT and DTEXT commands
  to prompt for a text height each time you use them. Enter the
  default height for the style if you want all text created with this
  style to have a uniform height.

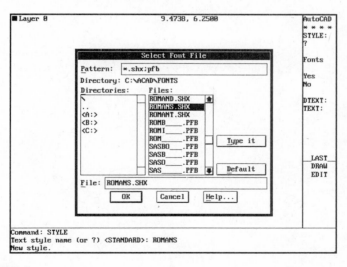

Figure STYLE.1:
The Select Font File dialog box.

1015

- **Width factor <1.0>:**

  The width factor expands or compresses the amount of space taken up by each letter. A default value of 1.0 uses the text as defined in the font file. A value smaller than 1 compresses the text; a value greater than 1 expands the text.

- **Obliquing angle <0>**

  Enter an angle that forces the font to be slanted. A positive value slants the text forward by the specified degree; a negative value slants the text backward.

- **Backwards? <N>**

  A backward font is a horizontal mirror image of normal text.

- **Upside-down? <N>**

  An upside-down font is a vertical mirror image of normal text.

- **Vertical? <N>**

  This prompt appears only if the vertical option is enabled in the font file definition. A font entered vertically is drawn with each letter below the previous one.

 Unlike blocks, font files are stored externally. Unique font files must accompany the drawing file in drawing exchanges.

Example

The following example defines a text style using the ROMANS font file.

```
Command: STYLE ↵
New Style. Text style name (or ?) <STANDARD>:ROMANS ↵
File: ROMANS ↵
Height <0.000>: ↵
Width factor <1.00>: ↵
Obliquing angle <0> ↵
Backwards? <N> ↵
Upside-down? <N> ↵
Vertical? <N> ↵
ROMANS is now the current text style.
```

Related Commands

CHANGE
COMPILE
DIM
DTEXT
PURGE
RENAME
TEXT

Related System Variables

TEXTSTYLE
TEXTSIZE
FILEDIA

TABLET

Screen **[SETTINGS] [next] [TABLET:]**

The TABLET command prepares AutoCAD to receive input from a digitizer tablet. It also prepares a tablet menu to supply command input. The TABLET command enables you to synchronize the drawing editor's coordinate tracking with a paper (or other media) drawing that you want to digitize (trace) accurately into AutoCAD.

Prompts and Options

- **Option (ON/OFF/CAL/CFG)**

    Enter the full two- or three-character option desired. The CAL and CFG options are discussed in the following prompts. The ON and OFF options turn tablet mode on and off. When tablet mode is on (and the tablet has been calibrated), the tablet is used for digitizing a paper drawing. When tablet mode is off, the tablet is used for screen pointing and tablet menu selection. A shortcut is to press F10, which turns tablet mode on or off.

1017

AutoCAD enables you to use up to four points when calibrating AutoCAD's coordinate space with a paper drawing. The location of these points determines the type of coordinate transformation used by AutoCAD when interpreting digitized information.

If only two points are used for the calibration, AutoCAD performs an *Orthogonal* transformation of the information you are digitizing. This is a uniform interpretation of the coordinates entered, and is most useful for drawings that are considered accurate.

For drawings that may have uneven scaling in the two axes, AutoCAD enables you to digitize three points to assign an *Affine* transformation to the coordinates. This type of transformation corrects for the uneven scaling in both axes.

Drawings that are actually two-dimensional perspective images should use four digitizing points. AutoCAD performs a *Projective* transformation of the information entered, and tries to correct for the uneven scaling and lack of parallel lines in any axis.

- **Digitize point # *number*:**

  The CAL option (short for CALibrate) enables you to synchronize a paper drawing—that is attached to a digitizer tablet—with points in the drawing editor. The number of coordinates you use determines the accuracy of the coordinates in the drawing editor. First you pick the point on the paper drawing, and then you are prompted for its coordinates.

- **Enter coordinates point #*number*:**

  Enter the known coordinate for the point you digitized. When you have chosen all the points that you want to digitize, press Enter. AutoCAD reports on the success or failure of establishing a successful coordinate transformation.

- **Select transformation type...**
  Orthogonal/Affine/Projective/<Repeat table>:

  Enter the type of coordinate transformation you want to use when digitizing the current drawing. Press Enter to display the table showing the success or failure of establishing a proper coordinate transformation.

- **Configuration Prompts and Options:**

  If you choose the CFG option (short for ConFiGure), you can define the screen pointing area and the areas used by a tablet menu for entering commands.

- **Enter number of tablet menus desired (0-4) <4>:**

  The default AutoCAD tablet menu uses four separate areas that define executable commands. If the tablet you are using has a different number of areas, enter that number here. The maximum number of tablet menu areas is four.

- **Do you want to realign tablet menu areas? <N>**

  This prompt appears if you currently are using a tablet menu, and you accepted the default number of menu areas at the previous prompt. This prompt enables you to change the location of the areas. If you do not want to change the location, press Enter at this prompt. The following prompts appear for specifying the screen pointing area:

- **Digitize upper left corner of menu area menu #number:**

  For each of the menu areas, you must pick three points that define the pointing area for the menu's commands. The *number* shown in the prompt is a digit from 1 to 4, specifying which tablet menu area you are configuring. This prompt asks for the first point of that area.

- **Digitize lower left corner of menu area #number:**

  Pick the second point to define the tablet menu area.

- **Digitize lower right corner of menu area #number:**

  Pick the final point to define the tablet menu area.

- **Enter number of columns for menu area #number:**

  Each tablet menu is divided into a series of rows and columns. Each box in this array can correspond to a menu item to execute. Enter the number of columns in the tablet menu area (*#number*). AutoCAD's default template has menu areas defined with the following numbers of rows and columns: area 1 is 25×9, area 2 is 11×9, area 3 is 9×13, and area 4 is 25×7.

- **Enter number of rows for menu area #*number*:**

  Enter the number of rows in the tablet menu area shown on the prompt line.

- **Do you want to respecify the screen pointing area?:**

  This option enables you to define an area on the digitizer tablet that corresponds to the drawing area in the drawing editor. This area should not overlap any of the defined menu areas, but otherwise it can be as large or as small as you want.

- **Digitize lower left corner of screen pointing area:**

  Pick the first point of the rectangular area that you want to use for picking points in the drawing editor.

- **Digitize upper right corner of screen pointing area:**

  Pick the second point of the rectangular area that you want to use to pick objects in the drawing editor. After you enter this point, the tablet menu becomes active.

Example

The following example shows you how to configure the supplied AutoCAD tablet menu ACAD.MNU. Use figure TABLET.1 as a guide.

```
Command: TABLET ↵
Option (ON/OFF/CAL/CFG): CFG↵
Enter the number of tablet menus desired (0-4) <0>: 4↵
Digitize the upper left corner of menu area 1: Pick point ①
Digitize the lower left corner of menu area 1: Pick point ②
Digitize the lower right corner of menu area 1: Pick point ③
Enter the number of columns for menu area 1: 25↵
Enter the number of rows for menu area 1: 9↵
Digitize the upper left corner of menu area 2: Pick point ②
Digitize the lower left corner of menu area 2: Pick point ④
Digitize the lower right corner of menu area 2: Pick point ⑤
```

```
Enter the number of rows for menu area 2: 11↵
Digitize the upper left corner of menu area 3: Pick point ⑥
Digitize the lower left corner of menu area 3: Pick point ⑦
Digitize the lower right corner of menu area 3: Pick point ⑧
Enter the number of columns for menu area 3: 9↵
Enter the number of rows for menu area 3: 13↵
Digitize the upper left corner of menu area 4: Pick point ④
Digitize the lower left corner of menu area 4: Pick point ⑨
Digitize the lower right corner of menu area 4: Pick point ⑩
Enter the number of columns for menu area 4: 25↵
Enter the number of rows for menu area 4: 7
Do you want to respecify the screen pointing area (Y) ↵
Digitize lower left corner of screen pointing area: Pick point S-LL
Digitize upper right corner of screen pointing area: Pick point S-UR
```

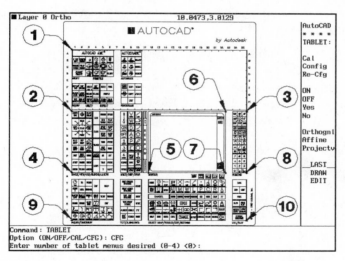

Figure TABLET.1:
Pick points for configuring the standard tablet menu.

TABSURF

Screen **[DRAW] [next] [3D Surfs] [TABSURF:]**

Screen **[SURFACES] [TABSURF:]**

Pull down **[Draw] [3D Surfaces] [Tabulated Cylinder]**

The TABSURF command is one of six AutoCAD commands that create 3D polygon meshes. This command creates a tabulated surface (TABulated SURFace). The surface is a 2 × N mesh, defined by a path curve and direction vector. The mesh projects, in the M direction, to the length and in the direction of the direction vector, from the starting point to the other endpoint.

The path curve may be an arc, circle, line, or an open or closed polyline (either 2D or 3D). The endpoint nearest your pick point becomes the start of the point mesh. The direction vector is defined by the first and the last endpoints of a selected line or open polyline. The endpoint nearest your pick point is the starting point of the direction vector.

The SURFTAB1 variable determines the density of the mesh in the N direction. The mesh projects the distance in the M direction, from the starting point to the other endpoint. The original entities used to define the path curve and direction vector are unchanged by TABSURF. If you use the EXPLODE command on the mesh, the mesh breaks into individual 3D faces.

Prompts and Options

- **Select path curve:**

  At this prompt, select the entity to be projected.

- **Select direction vector:**

  Select the line or open polyline to define the distance and direction of the desired projection. The endpoint that is closest to the pick point of the entity determines the beginning of the mesh. If you select a polyline, AutoCAD uses the first and last vertices to calculate the distance and direction.

Example

The following example creates a TABSURF mesh from a different line and an open polyline. Figure TABSURF.1 shows the entities before and after the command.

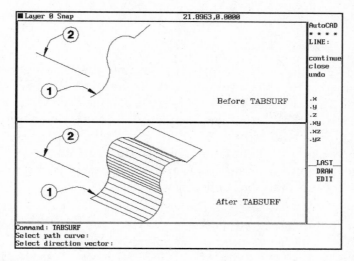

Figure TABSURF.1:
A tabulated surface mesh.

```
Command: TABSURF ↵
Select path curve: Pick point ① (see fig. TABSURF.1)
Select direction vector: Pick point ②
```

Related Commands

>   **EDGESURF**
>   **PFACE**
>   **REFSURF**
>   **RULESURF**
>   **3DFACE**
>   **3DMESH**

Related System Variable

SURFTAB1

TEXT

Screen **[DRAW] [next] [TEXT:]**

The TEXT command adds a single text string to the drawing. Characters display on the screen after you type the string and press Enter at the Text: prompt. This command is similar to the DTEXT command except that the DTEXT command displays the text string on the drawing as you type it and accepts multiple lines of text. You can justify the text string with one of 15 options. You also can enhance the text by underlining it, or include such special characters as degree symbols, plus or minus symbols, or diameter symbols.

NOTE

The effect of MIRROR on a text string is dependent on the MIRRTEXT system variable. If this variable is set to 1 (on), the text string is mirrored. If MIRRTEXT is set to 0, the text is adjusted for the mirror angle so that it is readable.

Prompts and Options

- **Start Point.** The default option asks you to pick the starting point for left-justified text. Press Enter to place new text directly beneath the last text drawn.
- **Height.** Enter the height of the text, adjusted for the intended plot scale. Note that this prompt appears only if the current text style has a height setting of 0. If the defined style has a fixed height, you cannot alter its value.

- **Rotation angle.** Enter the angle at which the text is to be placed. A rotation angle of 180 (degrees) places the text upside down. Common angles are 0 and 90 degrees.
- **Text.** Enter the text string to add to the drawing. You may use spaces in the string. When you press Enter, the string appears in the drawing and the Command: prompt appears.
- **Style.** The second option of the main prompt enables you to specify a text style to become the current style. Note that any text style must first be defined in the drawing with the STYLE command. After you select the Style option, the following prompt appears:
- **Style Name (or ?) <current>:**

  Enter the name of an existing text style. The current style is shown in the angle brackets.
- **?.** If you enter a question mark (?), AutoCAD displays the styles defined in the drawing and the following prompt appears:
- **Text style(s) to list <*>:**

  You can use wild-card characters at this prompt to specify text styles. If you press Enter, all the defined styles are listed.
- **Justify.** This first option at the main prompt for the TEXT command enables you to specify the justification for the text string. One of the following two prompts displays after you select this option:
- **Align/Fit/Center/Middle/Right/TL/TC/TR/ML/MC/MR/ BL/BC/BR:**
- **Align/Center/Middle/Right:**

  If the style you are using is vertically oriented, the latter prompt, Align/Center/Middle/Right: , displays. In all other cases, the former prompt displays. If you are familiar with the justification abbreviations, you can skip the Justify option and enter any of these options at the TEXT command's main prompt. The justification options are discussed next.

- **Align.** The Align option specifies the height and rotation of the text by picking two points. The size of text is adjusted by the Align option to make the entire text string fit between the picked points. After you select this option, you are prompted to select the following points:

  ```
  First text line point:
  Second text line point:
  ```

- **Fit.** Similar to Align, the Fit option asks you to specify two points for the location and orientation of the text string. You are prompted for the text height. The width factor for the text string is adjusted so that the text fits between the picked points. This option is not available for vertically-oriented text. If you choose this option, the following prompts appear:

  ```
  First text line point:
  Second text line point:
  Height <default>:
  ```

- **Center.** The Center option requests a point that is used to center justify the text. The baseline of the text string is centered at the picked point. The prompts for this option are similar to those of the Start point option (for left-justified text).

- **Middle.** The Middle option centers the text horizontally, similar to the Center option, but it also centers the text string vertically. This option center justifies subsequent lines of text at the specified middle point below the previous line of text. The Middle option and the MC option do not work in exactly the same way. If the string has characters with descending elements (for example, the letters "y," "g," and "p") or ascending elements ("b," "h," and "t"), the Middle option calculates the middle point of an imaginary box that represents the extents of these characters. The MC option does not calculate the middle point in the same way. Therefore, the results may differ based on the text string's characters.

- **Right.** The Right option places right-justified text at a point you specify. The prompts for this option resemble those of the Start point option (for left-justified text).

- **TL:**

  (Top Left) AutoCAD prompts you for the top left point. The subsequent prompts for this option are similar to those of the Start point option (for left-justified text).

- **TC:**

  (Top Center) AutoCAD prompts you for the top center point. The subsequent prompts for this option are similar to those of the Center option (for center-justified text).

- **TR:**

  (Top Right) AutoCAD prompts you for the top right point. The subsequent prompts for this option are similar to those of the Right option (for right-justified text).

- **ML:**

  (Middle Left) AutoCAD prompts you for the middle left point. The subsequent prompts for this option are similar to those of the Start point (for left-justified text).

- **MC:**

  (Middle Center) AutoCAD prompts you for the middle center point. The subsequent prompts for this option are similar to those of the Center option (for center-justified text).

- **MR:**

  (Middle Right) AutoCAD prompts you for the middle right point. The subsequent prompts for this option are similar to those of the Right option (for right-justified text).

- **BL:**

  (Bottom Left) AutoCAD prompts you for the bottom left point. The subsequent prompts for this option are similar to those of the Start point option (for left-justified text).

- **BC:**

    (Bottom Center) AutoCAD prompts you for the bottom center point. The subsequent prompts for this option are similar to those of the Center option (for center-justified text).

- **BR:**

    (Bottom Right) AutoCAD prompts you for the bottom right point. The subsequent prompts for this option are similar to those of the Right option (for right-justified text).

For a sample of these options, see figure TEXT.1.

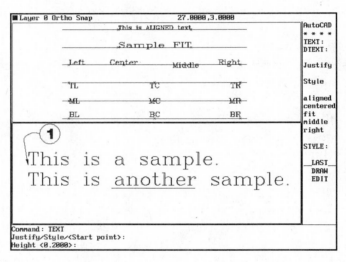

Figure TEXT.1:
Left-justified text strings entered with the Start point option.

You can place any of the following special codes in the text string to create the symbols described in the following list. These codes affect all fonts provided with AutoCAD. Fonts obtained from third-party sources may contain these and more characters:

Code	Character
%%c	The diameter symbol
%%d	The degrees symbol
%%p	The plus/minus symbol
%%o	Overscore (On or Off)
%%u	Underscore (On or Off)
%%%	The percent symbol

Example

The example below demonstrates the procedure for entering multiple lines of text that are left-justified:

```
Command: TEXT ↵
Justify/Style/<Start point>: Pick point ① (see fig. TEXT.1)
Height <0.2000>: .5 ↵
Rotation angle <0>: ↵
Text: This is a sample. ↵
Command: TEXT ↵
Justify/Style/<Start Point>: ↵
Text: This is %%uanother%%u sample. ↵
```

Related Commands

DDEDIT
DTEXT
QTEXT
STYLE

Related System Variables

MIRRTEXT
TEXTEVAL
TEXTSIZE
TEXTSTYLE

TEXTSCR

Enter **TEXTSCR**

Press **F1 (key)**

The TEXTSCR command causes the text screen or windows to display on a single monitor. The purpose of the TEXTSCR command is to provide a method for macros and scripts to flip to the text screen. The TEXTSCR command has the opposite effect of the GRAPHSCR command. You can use the TEXTSCR command transparently by preceding the command with an apostrophe. Neither command has any effect on a system with dual monitors. Pressing the F1 key also flips between the text and graphics screens.

Related Command

GRAPHSCR

TIFFIN

TIFIN imports a Tagged Image File Format raster file into AutoCAD. AutoCAD scans the raster image and creates a block consisting of a rectangular colored solid for each pixel in the TIF file. Once a raster image is imported into AutoCAD, you can trace over the raster image with AutoCAD geometry to create an AutoCAD drawing of the raster image. When you are through, you can erase the raster image. Raster images can be scaled, mirrored, and rotated like regular entities.

Do not explode the block representation of a raster file—the resulting entities will use large quantities of disk space and memory.

The system variable GRIPBLOCK should be set to 0 to avoid highlighting all of the solid entities in the block.

Prompts and Options

- **TIF file name:**

  You enter the name of the TIF file you want to import (you do not need to include the extension).

- **Insertion point <0,0,0>:**

  You enter the X, Y, and Z coordinates or pick the insertion point for the raster file.

- **Scale Factor:**

  You enter a number or drag the crosshairs to scale the raster file from the insertion point.

- **New length:**

  If you press Enter at the Scale Factor prompt, you will be prompted to pick a point to specify the scale factor.

See the listing in the GIFIN command summary for the description of a series of options that control how a raster file will be imported (RIASPECT, RIBACKG, RIEDGE, RIGAMUT, RIGREY, and RITHRESH).

Example

The following example imports a TIF file called TEST.TIF into AutoCAD at 3,3,0.

```
Command: TIFFIN ↵
TIF file name: TEST ↵
Insertion point <0,0,0>: 3,3,0↵
Scale factor: 2 ↵
```

Related Command

GIFIN
PCXIN

1031

Related System Variable

GRIPBLOCK

TIME

Screen **[INQUIRY] [TIME:]**

R12 The TIME command displays information regarding the current time and date, date and time of the last modification to the drawing, total time spent in the drawing editor, elapsed time, and the time until the next automatic save. (The interval between automatic saves is controlled by the system variable SAVETIME.)

The time and date of the last modification to the drawing are updated when the END command or the SAVE command is used. The total time spent in the drawing editor is continuously updated. The current editing session's time, however, is lost if the drawing is quit. The elapsed timer is similar to a stopwatch.

Only the elapsed timer can be turned on, off, or reset to zero. The computer's clock provides the current time and date. All AutoCAD time values display in military, 24-hour format, which is accurate to the nearest millisecond.

R12 You can execute the TIME command transparently by preceding the command name with an apostrophe ('TIME).

Prompts and Options

- **Display:**
  Displays all the current time information.

- **ON:**

  Turns on the elapsed timer. The timer is on by default.
- **OFF:**

  Turns off the elapsed timer.
- **Reset:**

  Resets the elapsed timer.

Example

The following example displays the current time information, resets the elapsed timer to zero, and displays the new time information. (The variable SAVETIME has been set to 15 minutes.)

```
Command: TIME ↵
Current time: 15 Jun 1992 at 11:12:00.352
Times for this drawing:
  Created: 23 Jan 1992 at 09:15:34.453
  Last updated: 14 Jun 1992 at 14:00:34.732
  Total editing time: 0 days 01:42:45.253
  Elapsed timer (on): 0 days 00:10:34.182
  Next automatic time save in: 0 days 00:14:10.190
Display/ON/OFF/Reset: R ↵
Timer reset.
Display/ON/OFF/Reset: D ↵
Current time:  15 Jun 1992 at 11:12:05.352
Times for this drawing:
  Created: 23 Jan 1992 at 09:15:34.453
  Last updated: 14 Jun 1992 at 14:00:34.732
  Total editing time: 0 days 01:42:50.253
  Elapsed timer (on): 0 days 00:00:00.832
  Next automatic time save in: 0 days 00:13:41.040
Display/ON/OFF/Reset: ↵
```

Related System Variables

CDATE
DATE
SAVETIME

1033

TDCREATE
TDINDWG
TDUPDATE
TDUSRTIMER

TRACE

Screen **[DRAW] [next] [TRACE:]**

The TRACE command creates solid filled entities similar to polyline segments with width. TRACE segments are similar to polyline segments in that the endpoints are mitered to meet each other. They are much more limited than polylines, however. The miter angles are calculated for both ends of each segment before it is drawn. Thus, a segment is drawn after the angle of the following segment is known. You cannot use the following editing commands on a trace entity: CHANGE, EXPLODE, EXTEND, OFFSET, and TRIM.

You cannot execute UNDO when you are drawing the trace segments, nor does the TRACE command have a close option. The appearance of the completed trace entity is solid if the FILL mode is on; otherwise, only the outline of the entity displays.

Prompts and Options

- **Trace width:**

  You can alter the default width of .05 units by entering any value you choose. The value becomes the default for the next use of TRACE.

- **From point:**

  This point is the starting location of the trace entity.

- **To point:**

  Enter the second point of the trace. This prompt repeats until you press Enter or Ctrl-C.

Example

The following example illustrates the method for creating a simple TRACE
entity. Notice how the resulting corners are mitered as shown in figure
TRACE.1. (Fill has been turned off in this example.)

```
Command: TRACE ↵
Trace width <0.0500>: .5 ↵
From point: Pick point ①
To point: Pick point ②
To point: Pick point ③
To point: Pick point ④
To point: ↵
```

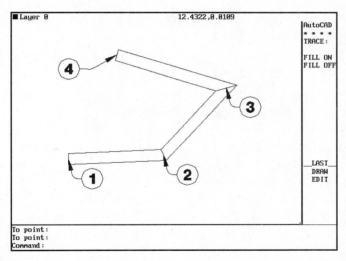

Figure TRACE.1:
A simple application of the TRACE command.

Related Commands

> FILL
> LINE
> POLYLINE

Related System Variables

FILLMODE
TRACEWID

TREESTAT

TREESTAT displays the status of the current drawing's spatial index. The information displayed by TREESTAT can be used to improve system performance. AutoCAD indexes all drawing entities spatially using a tree structure. TREESTAT uses two main branches, a 2D branch for paper space (quad-tree), and a 2D or 3D branch (oct-tree) for model space. The TREESTAT command displays two particularly important pieces of information, the number of nodes and the average entities per node.

Use the TREEDEPTH system variable to increase or decrease the length of the tree to attain the best possible performance. The oct-tree structure is more effective if there are fewer entities per node. Therefore, a deep tree with many nodes is preferable. Each node takes about 80 bytes of memory, so too many nodes will consume memory and force disk swapping. Usually, you do not need to tune AutoCAD's performance unless you are working with an extremely large drawing. The ideal setting depends on your system's configuration and the size of the drawing.

 A negative tree depth makes AutoCAD ignore the Z coordinates of entities and use a quad-tree for model space indexes.

TREESTAT has no prompts or options.

Example

The following example displays and resets the tree depth using the TREESTAT command and the TREEDEPTH system variable. See figure TREESTAT.1.

Command: **TREESTAT** ↵

The resulting display varies depending on your system and drawing. Notice the tree depth. The default in a new drawing is 30 for model space and 20 for paper space.

Command: **TREEDEPTH** ↵
New value for TREEDEPTH <3020>: **4030** ↵
Command: **TREESTAT** ↵

The tree depth is now 40 for model space and 30 for paper space.

```
Model-space branch
------------------
Oct-tree, depth limit = 40
Subtree containing entities with defined extents:
    Nodes: 1    Entities: 0
    Average entities per node: 0.00
    Average node depth: 5.00
    Nodes with population 0: 1
Total nodes: 4    Total entities: 0

Paper-space branch
------------------
Quad-tree, depth limit = 30
Subtree containing entities with defined extents:
    Nodes: 1    Entities: 0
    Average entities per node: 0.00
    Average node depth: 5.00
    Nodes with population 0: 1
Total nodes: 4    Total entities: 0


Command:
```

Figure TREESTAT.1:
The spatial tree with reset tree depths.

Related System Variable

TREEDEPTH

1037

Commands

TRIM

Screen **[EDIT] [next] [TRIM:]**

Pull down **[Modify] [Trim]**

The TRIM command edits the length of lines, open or closed 2D polylines, circles, and arcs to match a cutting edge(s). The cutting edge(s) can be lines, circles, arcs, open or closed 2D polylines, or paper space viewport entities. You cannot trim or use as a cutting edge the following entities: blocks, shapes, meshes, 3D faces, text, traces, shapes, or points. To trim a circle, you must intersect cutting edges in at least two places.

You can select multiple cutting edges. Entities to be trimmed must be picked one at a time. The same entity can be both a cutting edge and an object to trim. You can perform trims only on entities that lie parallel to the current UCS. The TRIM command cuts polylines to the center of the polyline, with the ends remaining squared. If you select an associative dimension to trim, AutoCAD trims and updates the dimension. Note that you may not split a dimension entity in two.

Prompts and Options

- **Select cutting edge(s)...**
  Select objects:

  Select the entities that you want to use as the cutting edges for the command. These may be lines, arcs, circles, open or closed 2D polylines, or paper space viewports.

- **Select object to trim>/Undo:**

  Pick the object to trim. Only one object can be picked at one time. If you specify the Undo option, Undo restores the last trimmed entity to its former appearance. This prompt repeats until you press Enter.

  The following error message is related to this command:

      The entity is not parallel to the UCS.

Example

The following example demonstrates the command by trimming existing entities, as shown in figure TRIM.1.

```
Command: TRIM ↵
Select cutting edge(s)...
Select objects: Select all lines
Select object(s): ↵
<Select object to trim>/Undo: Pick points ① or ② (prompt repeats)
<Select object to trim>/Undo: ↵
```

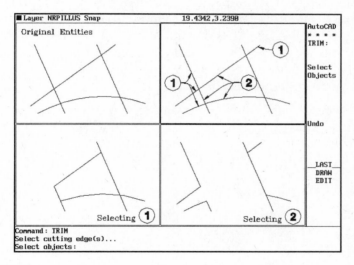

Figure TRIM.1:
Before and after images of entities to be trimmed.

Related Commands

> **BREAK**
> **EXTEND**
> **FILLET**
> **CHANGE**
> **STRETCH**

AutoCAD: The Professional Reference, Second Edition

U

Screen　**[* * * *] [U:]**

Pull down　**[Assist] [UNDO]**

The U command is an abridged version of the UNDO command. This command reverses the effects of the previous command. The U command has no effect if the drawing has just been loaded, or if the previous command was PLOT, SH, or SHELL. You can disable the U command with the UNDO command's Control option. Undo options are available in the entity selection mode; and with the DIM, DIM1, EXTEND, LINE, PLINE, and TRIM commands. You can reverse all of the effects of running a script by executing a single U command. Any transparent commands executed during the previous command are also reversed by executing the U command.

AutoCAD presents the following prompt if the U command cannot be executed:

    Everything has been undone.

Related Commands

> **REDO**
> **UNDO**

Related System Variable

> **UNDOCTL**

UCS

Screen　**[UCS:]**

Pull down　**[Settings] [UCS>]**

The UCS command enables you to define an arbitrary coordinate system. This system can make drafting 3D entities much easier. UCS stands for *User Coordinate System* and is relative to the World Coordinate System (called WCS). AutoCAD uses the current coordinate system when you enter any coordinate locations. You also can set and modify the UCS with a dialog box. See the DDUCS command for more information.

Prompts and Options

- **Origin.** Define a new UCS by specifying a different origin point relative to the current UCS. You can specify a point relative to the WCS by preceding the coordinates with an asterisk (*). The current UCS is moved, but the directions of the existing X, Y, and Z axes are maintained.

- **ZAxis.** The ZAxis option prompts you to select an origin point and then a point along the positive Z axis. If you press Enter at the second prompt, this option has the same effect as the Origin option. The ZAxis option is useful for rotating the UCS to work on a different side of a model.

- **3point.** The 3point option defines the UCS based on three points you select. The first point determines the origin point, the second defines the positive direction along the X axis, and the third point defines the positive direction of the Y axis.

- **Entity.** If an entity exists that was created in a specific UCS, you can return immediately to the UCS by selecting the entity. The type of entity picked determines the origin and X-Y plane. You cannot use certain entities, such as 3D polylines, polygon meshes, and paper space viewports.

- **View.** The View option defines the UCS so that it is parallel to the current view. This option does not modify the origin point.

- **X/Y/Z.** The X, Y, and Z options rotate the UCS around the specified axis. The right rule is used to determine rotation direction. This option is handy for creating a UCS from the existing UCS, such as making a side UCS from the plan view.

- **Previous.** The Previous option restores the previously defined UCS. You can step back up to ten User Coordinate Systems with this option. If the variable TILEMODE is set to 0, the 10 previous UCSs in both paper space and model space are saved. The UCS restored with the Previous option depends on the current space.
- **Restore.** The Restore option works in conjunction with the Save option. Restore retrieves a saved UCS.
- **Save.** The Save option saves the current UCS in the drawing with a specific name. After you save a UCS, you can retrieve it with the Restore option.
- **Delete.** Use the Delete option to remove saved User Coordinate Systems from the drawing.
- **?.** This option lists the User Coordinate Systems that have been saved in the drawing.
- **World.** If you accept the default option of World, AutoCAD restores the World Coordinate System (WCS).

Example

The following example uses the UCS command options to define three User Coordinate Systems and save them (see fig. UCS.1).

```
Command: UCS ↵
Origin/ZAxis/3point/Entity/View/X/Y/Z/Prev/
Restore/Save/Del/?/<World>: O ↵
Origin point <0,0,0>: *3,3,0 ↵
Command: ↵
Origin/ZAxis/3point/Entity/View/X/Y/Z/Prev/
Restore/Save/Del/?/ <World>: S ↵
?/Desired UCS name: TOP ↵
Command: ↵
Origin/ZAxis/3point/Entity/View/X/Y/Z/Prev/
Restore/Save/Del/?/<World>: ZA ↵
Origin point <0,0,0>: ↵
Point on positive portion of Z-axis
<0.0000,0.0000,1.0000>: 0,-1,0 ↵
Command: ↵
Origin/ZAxis/3point/Entity/View/X/Y/Z/Prev/
Restore/Save/Del/?/<World>: S ↵
```

```
?/Desired UCS name: FRONT ↵
Command: ↵
Origin/ZAxis/3point/Entity/View/X/Y/Z/Prev/
Restore/Save/Del/?/<World>: Y ↵
Rotation angle about Y-axis <0>: 90 ↵
Command: ↵
Origin/ZAxis/3point/Entity/View/X/Y/Z/Prev/
Restore/Save/Del/?/<World>: O ↵
Origin point <0,0,0>: 0,0,5 ↵
Command: ↵
Origin/ZAxis/3point/Entity/View/X/Y/Z/Prev/
Restore/Save/Del/?/<World>: S ↵
?/Desired UCS name: SIDE ↵
```

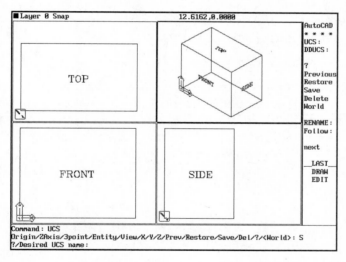

Figure UCS.1:
Viewports with the three different UCSs saved in the example.

Related Commands

DDUCS
PLAN
UCSICON

Related System Variables

UCSFOLLOW
UCSICON
UCSNAME
UCSORG
UCSXDIR
UCSYDIR
WORLDUCS

UCSICON

Screen **[SETTINGS] [next] [UCSICON:]**

Pull down **[Settings] [UCS] Icon>**

The UCSICON command controls the display of the graphical icon for the current coordinate system. The UCS icon indicates the orientation of the current coordinate system and whether the current coordinate system is the World Coordinate System (WCS) or a User Coordinate System (UCS). This icon also indicates whether you are viewing the drawing from above (positive Z) or from below (negative Z) and indicates the current space, model, or paper. Figure UCSICON.1 shows these four icons.

You can turn the UCS icon on or off and set it to display at the origin (when it fits on the screen) or at the lower left corner of the viewport. You can set the icon separately in each viewport.

Prompts and Options

- **ON.** Turns on the display of the UCS icon in the current viewport.
- **OFF.** Disables the display of the icon in the current viewport.
- **All.** Applies the settings made by the current UCSICON command to all active viewports. The prompt repeats.

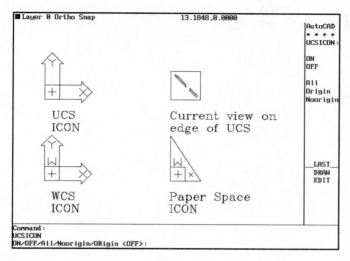

Figure UCSICON.1:
Coordinate system icons.

- **Noorigin.** Sets the current viewport to display the UCS icon in the lower left corner, regardless of the origin of the current coordinate system.
- **ORigin.** Sets the current viewport to display the UCS icon at the current coordinate system's origin point. If this point is located off the screen or if the location of the origin would force part of the icon off the screen, the icon is displayed instead in the lower left corner of the viewport.

Example

This example disables the UCSICON.

```
Command: UCSICON ↵
ON/OFF/All/Noorigin/ORigin <ON>: OFF ↵
```

Related Commands

> DDUCS
> DDUSCP
> UCS

1045

Related System Variable

UCSICON

UNDEFINE

Enter **UNDEFINE**

The UNDEFINE command disables specified AutoCAD commands so that they cannot be executed in the normal manner. You can replace a disabled (undefined) command with an AutoLIS- or ADS-defined command, which then executes in place of the original command. An undefined command still can be executed by prefacing its name with a period as in **.QUIT**. You can use the REDEFINE command to restore undefined commands.

Prompt and Option

- **Command name:**

  At this prompt, enter the name of the AutoCAD command that you want to disable.

Example

This example disables the QUIT command so that it is unusable in the drawing editor. Afterward, this example uses a leading period to execute the command in spite of its being undefined. For this example, the system variable FILEDIA is set to 0.

```
Command: UNDEFINE⏎
Command name: END⏎
Command: END⏎
Unknown command. Type ? for list of commands.
Command: .END⏎
End AutoCAD.
```

Related Command

REDEFINE

UNDO

Screen **[EDIT] [next] [UNDO:]**

The UNDO command reverses the effects of previous commands or groups of commands. You can set markers during the editing session and later automatically undo all the commands back to these markers. The effects of an UNDO can be reversed with the REDO command. The U command is a simpler version of the UNDO command that only reverses the previous single command.

 The following commands and system variables are not affected by the UNDO command:

ABOUT	AREA	ATTEXT	COMPILE	CONFIG
CONFIG	CVPORT	DELAY	DIST	DXFOUT
END	FILES	FILMROLL	GRAPHSCR	HELP
HIDE	ID	IGESOUT	LIST	MSLIDE
NEW	OPEN	PLOT	PSOUT	QSAVE
QUIT	RECOVER	REDRAW	REGEN	REGENALL
REINIT	RESUME	SAVE	SAVEAS	SHADE
SHELL	STATUS	TEXTSCR		

Prompts and Options

- **Auto.** Causes UNDO to interpret menu picks as one command. After you select this option, the following prompt appears:

- **ON/OFF <*default*>:**

  When set to ON, UNDO reverses the effects of a menu selection, no matter how many steps it includes. For example, if a menu selection changes layers, inserts a block, and rotates it as needed, one execution of UNDO treats all these steps as one. If the Auto option is set to OFF, each step is removed individually. The *default* displays the current setting.

- **Back.** Instructs AutoCAD to undo all commands until a mark is found. You can use the Mark option (explained later) to place multiple marks throughout the drawing. If no mark is in the drawing, AutoCAD displays the following prompt:

  ```
  This will undo everything. OK? <Y>
  ```

- **Control.** Enables the normal UNDO, disables it, or limits it to one step or command. If you select this option, the following options appear:

  All. The All option enables the UNDO command fully to operate.

  None. The None option disables completely the UNDO and U commands. If you select this option and then later enter the UNDO command, the `Control:` prompt immediately displays.

  One. This option restricts U and UNDO to a single step. You cannot perform multiple UNDO commands if you select this option. When this mode is active, UNDO displays the following prompt instead of the standard UNDO prompt:

- **Control /<1>:**

  Press Enter to UNDO a single action, or enter **C** to modify the settings.

  AutoCAD may present the following prompt if the U command cannot be executed:

  ```
  Everything has been undone.
  ```

- **End.** This option turns off the Group option.

- **Group.** This option treats a sequence of commands as one command. These commands are usually entered at the keyboard.

Precede the commands with **Group**, finish the set with **End** (as discussed earlier), and then you can use a single U command to undo all the commands.

- **Mark.** This option works in conjunction with the Back option. You can place marks periodically as you enter commands. Then you can use Undo Back to undo all the commands that have been executed since the last mark.

- **Number.** You can enter a number to tell AutoCAD to undo the last *number* of commands issued.

Example

The following example demonstrates several features of the UNDO command.

```
Command: UNDO↵
Auto/Back/Control/End/Group/Mark/<number>: M↵
Command: LINE↵
From point: Pick a point
To point: Pick a point
To point: ↵
Command: MOVE↵
Select objects: L↵
1 found
Select objects: ↵
Base point or displacement: 0,0↵
Second point of displacement: 2,2↵
Command: COPY↵
Select objects: P↵
Select objects: ↵
<Base point or displacement>/Multiple: 2,2↵
Second point of displacement: 4,4↵
Command: UNDO↵
Auto/Back/Control/End/Group/Mark/<number>: 2↵
COPY MOVE
Command: REDO↵
Command: UNDO↵
Auto/Back/Control/End/Group/Mark/<number>: B↵
COPY MOVE LINE
Mark encountered
```

Related Commands

OOPS
REDO
U

UNITS

Screen [SETTINGS] [next] [UNITS:]

The UNITS command specifies the units that AutoCAD uses when it reports and accepts numeric information. You use the UNITS command to tell AutoCAD what type of distance and angle formats to use. If you are drawing a building floor plan, for example, you can use architectural units; if you are designing a printed circuit board, you may want to specify decimal units. The DDUNITS command enables easier operation by means of a dialog box.

 You can execute the UNITS command transparently by preceding the command name with an apostrophe ('UNITS).

Prompts and Options

- **Report Formats:**   (Examples)
  1. Scientific   1.55E+01
  2. Decimal   15.50
  3. Engineering   1'-3.50"
  4. Architectural   1'-3 1/2"
  5. Fractional   15 1/2

  Enter choice, 1 to 5 <*default*>:

  Enter the desired units format number. The type of units you choose also is expected when you enter distances. No matter what type of units you decide to use, you can always enter measurements in decimal units. When you choose engineering units, you can enter distances either in feet and decimal inches or in decimal inches; however, AutoCAD always reports measurements in feet and decimal inches. When you use architectural units, separate the fractional inches from the inches with a hyphen, such as 1'6-3/4".

- **Number of digits to right of decimal point (0 to 8) <*default*>:**

  Enter the number of decimal places to display after the decimal point. AutoCAD rounds distances to the specified accuracy for display, but maintains full precision in the drawing.

- **Denominator of smallest fraction to display (1, 2, 4, 8, 16, 32, or 64) <*default*>:**

  If you work with fractional inches, specify at this prompt the smallest denominator that you intend to use. When you work in architectural units, this value is typically 8 or 16.

- **System of angle measure:**

1. Decimal Degrees	45.5
2. Degrees/minutes/seconds	45d00'0.00"
3. Grads	50.0000g
4. Radians	0.7854r
5. Surveyor's units	N 45d00'0" E

  Enter choice, 1 to 5 <*default*>:

  Requests the units for displaying angles. Enter the desired system number.

- **Number of fractional places for display of angles (0 to 8)<*default*>:**

  Determines the degree of accuracy that AutoCAD uses when it reports angles. If you specify 0 decimal places, AutoCAD reports only the number of degrees. If you previously specified Degrees/minutes/seconds or Surveyor's units and you specify 1 to 2 decimal places, AutoCAD reports degrees and minutes. For 3 to 4 decimal places, AutoCAD reports degrees, minutes, and seconds. For more decimal places, AutoCAD also reports decimal seconds.

- **Direction for angle 0:**

      East   3 o'clock = 0
      North 12 o'clock = 90
      West   9 o'clock = 180
      South   6 o'clock = 270

- **Enter direction for angle 0 <*default*>:**

  AutoCAD usually measures angles using the three o'clock position as the 0 degree direction. You can use this option to specify a different starting direction for 0 degrees.

- **Do you want angles measured clockwise? <N> :**

  AutoCAD typically measures angles counterclockwise. Enter **Y** to change this, so that angles are measured in a clockwise direction.

Example

This example changes the default units system to architectural measurements.

```
Command: UNITS ↵
Report Formats:         (Examples)
    1. Scientific       1.55E+01
    2. Decimal          15.50
    3. Engineering      1'-3.50"
    4. Architectural    1'-3 1/2"
    5. Fractional       15 1/2
With the exception of Engineering and Architectural formats,
these formats can be used with any basic unit of measurement.
For example, decimal mode is perfect for metric units as well
as decimal English units.
Enter choice, 1 to 5 <2>: 4 ↵
Denominator of smallest fraction to display
(1, 2, 4, 8, 16, 32, or 64) <16>: ↵
Systems of angle measure:       (Examples)
    1. Decimal Degrees          45.0000
    2. Degrees/minutes/seconds  45d0'0"
    3. Grads                    50.0000g
    4. Radians                  0.7854r
    5. Surveyor's units         N 45d0'0" E
```

```
Enter choice, 1 to 5 <2>: ↵
Number of fractional places for display of angles
(0 to 8) <4>: ↵
Direction for angle 0d0'0":
  East      3 o'clock   =    0d0'0"
  North    12 o'clock   =   90d0'0"
  West      9 o'clock   =  180d0'0"
  South     6 o'clock   =  270d0'0"
Enter direction for angle 0d0'0" <0d0'0">: ↵
Do you want angles measured clockwise? <N> ↵
```

Related Command

DDUNITS

Related System Variables

LUNITS
LUPREC
AUNITS
AUPREC
ANGBASE
ANGDIR
UNITMODE

VIEW

Screen **[DISPLAY] [VIEW:]**

Pull down **[View] [Set View] [Named View...]**

The VIEW command enables you to save displays of the current drawing under a name that you can later display. This is different from saving the screen's display as accomplished with the MSLIDE command. When AutoCAD saves a view, it stores information about the current view, not the entities in the view. This includes all information needed to restore the view, including 3D viewpoint and perspective (if perspective viewing is on). When you restore the view, AutoCAD uses the information to display that portion of your drawing quickly.

1053

Views can greatly speed the process of moving between different areas of your drawing. Defining a view also can aid in plotting—if the same area of a drawing is plotted often—because the view is retained in the drawing file for future use.

Prompts and Options

- **?:**

  Enter **?** to list the defined views. You then see the following prompt:

- **View(s) to list <*>:**

  If you press Enter, all the view names are listed. You also can enter a wild-card search string to list only view names that match the wild-card pattern.

- **View name(s) to delete:**

  If you no longer need one of the defined views, you can delete it from the list of views. Enter the name of the view you want to delete. If the name you have entered does not match a current view, the VIEW command reports: No matching view names found.

- **View name to restore:**

  Enter the name of a saved view, and AutoCAD displays it in the current viewport. The view is enlarged or shrunk to fit in the current viewport. If you use the VIEW command transparently (by prefixing it with an apostrophe), the named view cannot be one that requires a drawing regeneration. If a view created for paper space is restored while the drawing editor is in model space (and vice versa), AutoCAD switches to the correct space.

- **View name to save:**

  Both the Save and Window options of the VIEW command present this prompt, which asks you to enter a name to assign the current view. After you enter a valid name, the Save option stores the view information for the current viewport. The Window option enables you to define a rectangular area that is stored with the view name. If you specify an existing view name, it is over-written without warning. The following prompts appear:

First corner:

When you use the Window option of the VIEW command, you must define a rectangular area that is saved with the view name. Enter a point for the first corner of the rectangular area.

Other corner:

Enter a point for the opposite corner of the window.

Example

This example defines a view of the current drawing with the Windows option in one viewport and restores it in another. (See figure VIEW.1.)

```
Command: VIEW↵
?/Delete/Restore/Save/Window: W↵
View name to save: DETAIL↵
First corner: Pick①
Other corner: Pick②
Click in another viewport
Command: VIEW↵
?/Delete/Restore/Save/Window: R↵
View name to restore: SCHEDULE ↵
```

Related Command

DDVIEW

Related Variables

VIEWCTR
VIEWSIZE

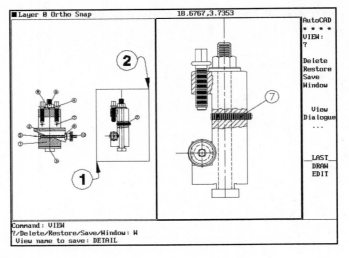

Figure VIEW.1:
The defined view on the left, and the restored view on the right.

VIEWRES

Screen **[DISPLAY] [VIEWRES:]**

The VIEWRES command controls the display resolution of circles and arcs. AutoCAD calculates and displays arcs and circles as series of short, straight line segments. It also controls whether most zooms can be performed at redraw speed instead of requiring a regeneration. If VIEWRES is set for *fast zooms*, most pans and zooms execute at redraw speed. The VIEWRES Circle zoom percent setting controls the resolution of arcs and circles. A setting of 100 always regenerates with sufficient line segments to approximate smooth circles and arcs. As you zoom into the drawing, the line segments become apparent unless you have the fast zoom feature turned off. A higher circle zoom percent enables you to zoom farther in before the line segments become apparent; a lower setting makes them apparent at lower levels of zoom magnification, or even at each regeneration.

The circle zoom percent affects only the displayed image. Any printed or plotted output is created at the highest resolution possible by the printer or plotter.

Prompts and Options

- **Do you want fast zooms? <Y>:**

  If you answer no at this prompt, AutoCAD forces a screen regeneration after any PAN, ZOOM, or VIEW Restore; thus, any attempt at a transparent zoom is useless. If you answer yes, AutoCAD zooms at redraw speed whenever possible. Zooms outside the currently generated area or significantly small zoomed views still require a screen regeneration.

- **Enter circle zoom percent (1-20000) <100>:**

  Your response to this prompt determines the accuracy for the display of circles and arcs, including any arcs in font styles. The higher the number, the more segments are displayed for an arc or circle, and the smoother the arc or circle appears. The disadvantage to a higher number is an increase in screen display time. The default of 100 is sufficient for most purposes. On faster systems with less complicated drawings, you can set the circle zoom percent higher with little loss of performance.

Example

The following example uses the VIEWRES command to initiate fast zooms and to set the circle zoom percent to 16 in one viewport and to 200 in another. The example assumes that two viewports are active, with a circle visible in each, as shown in figure VIEWRES.1.

```
Command: VIEWRES ↵
Do you want fast zooms? <Y>: ↵
Enter circle zoom percent (1-20000) <100>: 16 ↵
Regenerating drawing Click on the right viewport to make it current
Command: VIEWRES ↵
Do you want fast zooms? <Y>: ↵
Enter circle zoom percent (1-20000) <16>: 200 ↵
Regenerating drawing
```

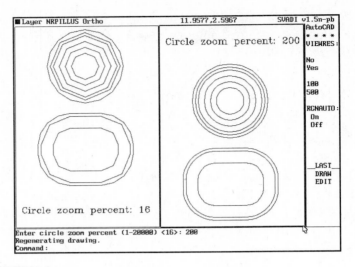

Figure VIEWRES.1:
The effect of different VIEWRES settings on entity appearance.

Related Command

REGEN

VPLAYER

Screen **[MVIEW] [VPLAYER:]**

Pull down **[View] [Mview] [Vplayer]**

The VPLAYER (ViewPort LAYER) command controls the freeze or thaw status of layers within individual viewports. The VPLAYER command works in both paper space and model space, but the TILEMODE system variable must be set to 0. If layers are frozen or turned off with the LAYER command, they are invisible in every viewport, regardless of the settings made in this command.

You may adjust the visibility of layers for all the current viewports. It is more beneficial to quickly freeze a layer in all the viewports, than it is to thaw the same layer in a single viewport.

Prompts and Options

- `?:`

  Lists the status of layers for a given viewport. If you are working within model space, AutoCAD temporarily switches to paper space. You then receive the `Select a viewport:` prompt. Picking a viewport at this prompt lists the layers that are frozen within the selected viewport.

- `Freeze:`

  Freezes one or more layers within a selected viewport. You receive the `Layer(s) to Freeze:` prompt. You can enter more than one layer at the prompt by separating each layer name with a comma. You also can use wild-card characters, after which you are asked to select the viewports within which to freeze the layers by the `All/Select/<Current>:` prompt.

  If you select All, the layer status is modified in all the current viewports, including paper space viewports that are not displayed. The Select option prompts you to select which viewports are to be modified. The default affects the display only in the current viewport.

- `Thaw:`

  Reverses the effect of the Freeze option. Note that if a specific layer is frozen globally with the LAYER command, this command has no effect. You receive the `Layer(s) to Thaw:` prompt. After selecting the layer or layers to thaw, you are prompted to choose which viewports are to be affected. (See the Freeze option for a description.)

- **Reset:**

  Restores the default visibility of a layer as defined by the Vpvisdflt option, discussed in the following paragraphs. You receive the `Layer(s) to Reset:` prompt, and then you are asked to select the viewports to be reset. (See the Freeze option for a description of this prompt.)

- **Newfrz:**

  Creates new layers that are to be frozen in all viewports. This option is most useful for making layers that are intended to be displayed in only one viewport. Thaw the viewport of choice. You receive the `New viewport frozen layer name(s):` prompt. You can enter multiple layer names by separating each one with a comma. The default value for each of the new layers also is set to frozen. This ensures that the layer is frozen in new viewports.

- **Vpvisdflt:**

  Enter **V** to specify the default visibility for a specific layer, or group of layers. This feature affects any viewports created after the command is completed, as well as those currently displayed.

  This feature is useful for modifying layers that contain text or dimensions that should not be displayed in other viewports. You receive the `Layer name(s) to change default viewport visibility:` prompt. More than one layer can be specified by separating each layer name with a comma, or by using wild-card characters. After specifying the layer names, the default visibility is set with the response to the prompt `Change default viewport visibility to Frozen/<Thawed>:`

Example

The following example shows the effects of adjusting the viewport's layer visibility.

```
Command: VPLAYER ↵
?/Freeze/Thaw/Reset/Newfrz/Vpvisdflt: F↵
Layer(s) to Freeze: TEXT,DIMENSION↵
All/Select/<Current>: S↵
```

```
Select Objects: Select the bottom viewport
?/Freeze/Thaw/Reset/Newfrz/Vpvisdflt: ↵
Regenerating drawing.
```

The results are shown in figure VPLAYER.1.

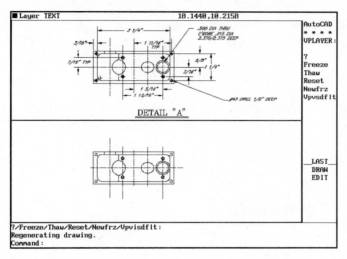

Figure VPLAYER.1:
Layers frozen in one viewport by VPLAYER.

Related Commands

LAYER
DDLMODES

Related System Variables

TILEMODE
VISRETAIN

VPOINT

Screen   **[DISPLAY] [VPOINT:]**

Pull down   **[View] [Set View] [Viewpoint]**

The VPOINT command enables you to look at your drawing from any location in 3D space. You can specify a 3D coordinate for the viewpoint, rotate the current view by specifying two perpendicular angles, or interactively specify a viewpoint by using two graphical aids. After a viewpoint coordinate is supplied, the resulting view is constructed by displaying the extents of the drawing within the current viewport, as seen from the viewpoint looking through the origin point (typically 0,0,0). VPOINT displays images in parallel projection. For the dynamic selection of a 3D view, or for perspective projection, use the DVIEW command.

Prompts and Options

- **Rotate:**

  Enter **R** to rotate the current viewpoint by specifying two rotation angles. The first angle rotates in the X-Y plane of the WCS. The second angle rotates the viewpoint up in the Z direction. All angles are calculated from the 0,0,0 coordinate. The prompts for these two angles are as follows:

  ```
  Enter angle in XY plane from X axis<current>
  Enter angle from XY plane<current>:
  ```

It may be easier to visualize these settings by using the DDVPOINT command.

- **View point:**

  Press Enter to select a new viewpoint interactively with the compass and axes tripod icons (see fig. VPOINT.1). The icon located in the upper right corner symbolizes a flattened globe that represents all possible 3D viewpoints around your model, which is located at the center. The center point of the icon is the north pole (looking down), the middle ring shows the equator, and the outer circle represents the south pole. As the cursor is moved around this globe, the axes move to show the X, Y, and Z axes for this viewpoint.

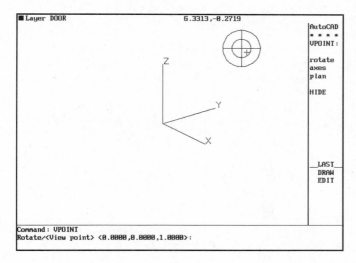

Figure VPOINT.1:
The graphical method of specifying a VPOINT coordinate.

The model can be viewed from below, if the cursor is placed between the "equator" and the "south pole." Pressing Enter while at this screen aborts the option and accepts the previous viewpoint coordinate.

- **<0.0000,0.0000,1.0000>:**

The default setting shows the current viewpoint coordinates are seen in brackets. Enter a new 3D coordinate to view the model from that location.

Example

The following example creates four views: top, front, right side, and isometric by using VPOINT options. Each view is displayed in a viewport, as seen in figure VPOINT.2.

```
Command: Click in the lower right viewport
Command: VPOINT ↵
```
Rotate/<View point> <0.0000,0.0000,1.0000>: ↵ (See fig. VPOINT.1)
```
Command: Click in the lower left viewport
Command: VPOINT ↵
```
Rotate/<View point> <0.0000,0.0000,1.0000>: **0,-1,0** ↵
```
Command: Click in the upper right viewport
Command: VPOINT ↵
```
Rotate/<View point> <0.0000,0.0000,1.0000>: **R** ↵
```
Enter angle in XY plane from X axis <270>: 0 ↵
Enter angle from XY plane <90>: 0 ↵
Regenerating drawing.
```

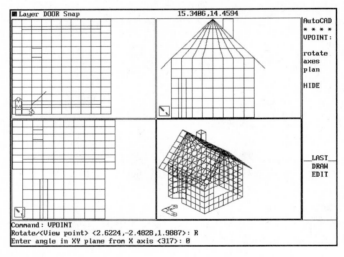

Figure VPOINT.2:
Four views of the sample drawing DHOUSE.DWG obtained with the VPOINT command.

Related Command

> DVIEW
> DDVPOINT

Related System Variables

WORLDVIEW
TARGET
VIEWDIR

VPORTS

Screen **[SETTINGS] [next] [VPORTS:]**

The VPORTS (or Viewports) command enables multiple concurrent views within the AutoCAD drawing editor. This command can create up to either four or 16 viewports, depending on your display. The viewports that you create and control with the VPORTS command are specifically for use within model space. Viewports are tiled; that is, they cannot overlap.

The TILEMODE system variable must be set to 1 (on) to use VPORTS. You cannot use VPORTS within paper space (see the MVIEW command). When using viewports, only the contents of the current viewport can be plotted.

Each viewport presents a view of your drawing. These views are updated automatically as changes to the drawing are made. Only the current viewport is affected by a screen display command such as HIDE, PAN, REDRAW, REGEN, SHADE, and ZOOM. The current viewport is identified by a heavy outline around its border. Only one of the viewports can be current. It is easy, however, to switch between viewports, or even select entities visible in different viewports, while within one command. To change the current viewport, click on the desired viewport.

You can begin almost any command in the current viewport, and alternate between viewports as needed while still within the command. The commands that do not accept a change to another viewport are DVIEW, GRID, PAN, SNAP, VPLAYER, VPORTS, VPOINT, and ZOOM.

The crosshairs are displayed only in the current viewport. When the cursor is moved to any other viewport, the crosshairs become an arrow.

1065

Initially, entities are highlighted and dragged only in the viewport in which they were selected. However, if you click in another viewport to make it current while dragging, entities being dragged are highlighted in the new current viewport as well as each previous current viewport.

Prompts and Options

The prompts and options for this command control the size and location of the viewports, and enable you to save and retrieve their arrangement:

- **Save:**

  The current viewport configuration can be saved with this option. Each viewport configuration stores the number of viewports, size, location, and the views displayed within each viewport. Additional information saved for each viewport is listed as follows:

  2D display information (viewpoint)

  3D display information (viewpoint or dynamic view information)

  Front and back clipping planes (set with the command)

  Grid mode and settings

  Perspective mode (set with the DVIEW command)

  Snap mode and settings

  UCSICON setting

  VIEWRES mode and settings

  A saved viewport configuration can be retrieved with the Restore option (described later in this section) or can be retrieved into paper space with the MVIEW Restore command. After selecting this option, you receive the following prompt:

      ?/Name for new viewport configuration:

  Enter the name of the viewport configuration to save. You also can obtain a list of defined viewports by entering a question mark (?) at this prompt, or at the prompts issued by the Restore or Delete options (see the following paragraphs). You then are prompted for the named viewports to list, and you can use wild-card characters. You can use up to 31 characters for the name when saving viewports.

- **Restore:**

You can redisplay viewports that have been saved previously with the VPORTS command with this option.

?/Name of viewport configuration to restore:
Enter the name of the viewport configuration to restore.

- **Delete:**

You can remove a defined viewport with this option. You are prompted for the name of the viewport to delete. Deleting saved viewports reduces drawing size slightly.

?/Name of viewport configuration to delete:
Enter the name of the viewport configuration to delete.

- **Join:**

You can merge two displayed viewports into one with this option. The boundaries of the two define the new viewport's boundary. The resulting viewport must be rectangular for the join to take effect. Join displays the following prompts:

Select dominant viewport <*current*>:
Click in the viewport that you want to provide the settings (see the list under the Save option) for the combined viewport.

Select viewport to join:
Pick the second viewport, to combine it with the dominant viewport.

- **Single:**

This option returns the display to a single viewport. The screen is filled with the contents of the current viewport, and the drawing settings assume the settings of the current viewport.

- **?:**

This option lists the saved viewport configurations. You receive the following prompt:

Viewport configuration(s) to list <*>:
Wild-card characters are accepted. Pressing Enter displays all the

saved viewport configurations. The data displayed represent the 2D screen coordinates for the lower left corner and upper right corner of each viewport. The screen coordinate values range from 0,0 (lower left) to 1,1 (upper right). When listing the viewports, the current configuration always is displayed first, with the current viewport shown at top. The viewport(s) specified at the prompt follow.

- **2:**

  This option creates two viewports. The following prompt appears:

  > **Horizontal/<Vertical>:**

  Type **V** (or press Enter) or **H** to specify a vertical or horizontal configuration.

- **3:**

  This option creates three viewports. You receive the following prompt:

  > **Horizontal/Vertical/Above/Below/Left/<Right>:**

  Enter the first letter of one of these options to specify the arrangement of viewports. The options operate as follows:

  > **Horizontal:**

  This option divides the current display into three equal-sized viewports, divided horizontally across the screen.

  > **Vertical:**

  This option creates equal-sized viewports that divide the display vertically.

  > **Above, Below, Left or Right:**

  These options determine the location of one larger-sized viewport in relation to two smaller (and equally sized) viewports.

Example

The following example uses the VPORTS command to create three tiled viewports within model space in a left-biased arrangement. (Refer to figure VPORTS.1).

```
Command: VPORTS ↵
Save/Restore/Delete/Join/Single/?/2/<3>/4: 3 ↵
Horizontal/Vertical/Above/Below/Left/<Right>: L ↵
```

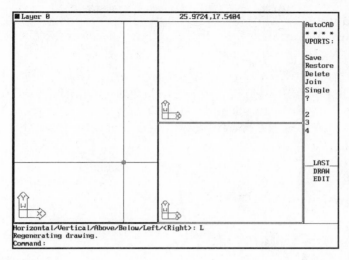

Figure VPORTS.1:
Three tiled (non-overlapping) model space viewports.

Related Command

MVIEW

Related System Variables

CVPORT
MAXACTVP
TILEMODE

VSLIDE

Screen **[UTILITY] [SLIDES] [VSLIDE]**

The VSLIDE command displays previously created slide files. Slide files (extension SLD) can be used to create presentations of your work. Slides are only snap shots; they contain no entity information, so they load much more quickly than drawings. They cannot be edited, however. Slides take up very little space and are therefore excellent for showing highlights of your work.

Multiple slide files can be compiled into a slide library (extension SLB) by using the SLIDELIB.EXE program that accompanies AutoCAD. The ACAD.SLB file contains slides used by icon items in icon menus. When a slide is displayed, the current drawing is concealed but still active.

 You can create an automated slide show by using a script within AutoCAD. See the SCRIPT and DELAY commands for more information.

Prompts and Options

The options for viewing slide images are outlined as follows:

- **Slide file <default>:**

  Enter the name of the slide file (without the extension) you want to display on the screen. If the FILEDIA system variable is set to 1 (on), a file dialog box displays instead of this prompt. If so, use the dialog box to specify the file name.

  The default name for the slide file is the same name as the current drawing. After you enter the appropriate file name, AutoCAD displays the image saved in the slide file in the current viewport. To redisplay your drawing, invoke the REDRAW command.

  The VSLIDE command also can display slides stored in slide file libraries. To view slides stored within slide file libraries, you must put the slide file name in parentheses after the name of the library. To view the file showing the Romans text style out of the ACAD.SLB file, for example, you would enter **ACAD(ROMANS)** as the slide name.

Example

The following example uses VSLIDE to view both an individual slide file and a slide stored within a slide file library. The example assumes that the

COLORWH.SLD and ACAD.SLB files are in the AutoCAD program directory or another directory in AutoCAD's search path (see fig. VSLIDE.1).

```
Command: VSLIDE ↵
Slide file <default>: COLORWH ↵
Command: VSLIDE ↵
Slide file <default>: ACAD(CONE) ↵
```

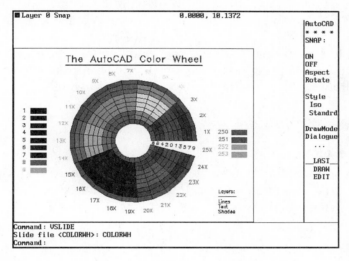

Figure VSLIDE.1:
The COLORWH slide displayed by VSLIDE.

Related Commands

MSLIDE
SCRIPT
DELAY
REPLAY

Related System Variables

FILEDIA
SORTENTS

1071

WBLOCK

Screen **[BLOCKS] [WBLOCK:]**

The WBLOCK command copies a block definition or entity group to an external file. This file can be edited like any other drawing file. The file then can be inserted in another drawing with the INSERT or DDINSERT commands. The file created by the WBLOCK command inherits all the drawing settings and definitions that are used by the selected block or entities in the current drawing. Named views, UCS's, and viewport configurations are not copied. The current UCS in the current drawing becomes the WCS of the new drawing.

Prompts and Options

- **File name:**

  Enter a name for the new file (without the extension). The extension DWG is added for you. If the file already exists, AutoCAD asks whether you want to overwrite the existing file.

- **Block name:**

  Enter the name of the block to copy as a drawing file. If you enter an equal sign (=), AutoCAD looks for, and uses if found, a block name that is the same as the file name given above. If you enter an asterisk (*) here, AutoCAD copies all the entities of the current drawing. If you press Enter at this prompt, you can select the entities that you want copied to a separate file.

If you issue an asterisk (*) for the block name, AutoCAD copies all the entities in the drawing. Unused information such as unreferenced block names, layers, linetypes, text styles, and dimension styles is not included in the new drawing file. This method is an excellent means of reducing file size should the drawing contain additional, unused data. This is especially applicable when you archive completed drawings.

- **Insertion point:**

  This prompt appears if you press Enter at the `Block name:` prompt. Specify the insertion base point for the new drawing file, relative to the entities you select. This method is similar to choosing an insertion point for a block.

- **Select objects:**

  This prompt appears if you press Enter at the `Block name:` prompt. Select each of the entities you want copied to the new file. You can use any appropriate selection method. The selected entities are erased from the current drawing. Use the OOPS or U command to restore them, if desired.

Example

The following example demonstrates how to create a new drawing that contains specific entities.

```
Command: WBLOCK ↵
File name: DETAIL ↵
Block name: Press Enter to select specific entities
Insertion base point: Pick a point for the new drawing's origin (0,0,0) point
Select objects: Select the entities to be placed in the drawing file
```

The entities are copied to the DETAIL drawing file and removed from the current drawing. To restore the entities back to the drawing, use the OOPS or UNDO command.

Related Commands

> BLOCK
> INSERT
> OOPS

Related Variable

> FILEDIA

XBIND

Screen   **[BLOCKS] [XBIND:]**

The XBIND (eXternal BIND) command permanently attaches dependent symbols of an external reference drawing to the current drawing database. Normally, none of the information stored within external references is made a permanent part of the drawing database. If you need to use some of the external reference's dependent symbols, such as dimension styles or blocks, you must add them to the database with XBIND. Otherwise, the external reference might be deleted, and those objects no longer would be available for your use.

Prompts and Options

* **Block/Dimstyle/LAyer/LType/Style:**

   This is the list of dependent symbol types that can be permanently bound into the drawing database from the external reference. Type the capitalized letters of the dependent symbol type you want to bind into the current drawing database.

* **Dependent *symbol* name(s):**

   After you have determined the dependent symbol you want to bind into the drawing database, enter its name at this prompt. The XBIND command scans the external reference for the named symbol. If it is found, that symbol is added to the drawing database. If it is not found, you are so informed. External-reference-named dependent symbols are easy to locate—they have the external reference file name, plus a vertical bar (|), and the named object's name. Once bound, the vertical bar is replaced with $*number*$. For the first occurrence of the bound entity, *number* is set to 0. Each time a symbol with the same name is bound, this number is increased.

When drawing symbols are bound into a drawing, using them is often cumbersome due to their revised symbol names. You can use the DDRENAME command to easily select and revise the names of these symbols.

Example

In the following example, two layers belonging to an external reference file are bound into the TABLET drawing file.

```
Command: LAYER ↵
?/Make/Set/New/ON/OFF/Color/Ltype/Freeze/Thaw/
LOck/Unlock: ?↵
Layer(s) to LIST <*>: ↵
Command: XBIND↵
Block/Dimstyle/LAyer/LType/Style: LA↵
Dependent layer name(s): TABLET-B|OUTLINES,TABLET-B|PLINES↵
Scanning...
2 Layer(s) bound.
Command: LAYER↵
?/Make/Set/New/ON/OFF/Color/Ltype/Freeze/Thaw/
LOck/Unlock: ?↵
Layer(s) to LIST <*>: ↵
```

Related Command

XREF

XREF

Screen **[BLOCKS] [XREF:]**

The XREF (eXternal REFerence) command enables you to insert references to external drawings. An external reference is similar to a block, except that no part of the external reference resides within the drawing database. After an external reference is attached to a drawing, only a reference to the external file is placed in the drawing database.

An external reference has two advantages over a block. It takes up less space within a drawing file, and it cannot be edited from within the drawing into which it was inserted. The external reference is similar to any other drawing file. The next time the file containing the external reference is loaded into the drawing editor, or plotted with the PLOT command, the current version of the external reference is loaded. In contrast, the only way to edit a block is to explode it, modify the entities, and then redefine the block by using the modified entities.

Prompts and Options

The XREF command contains a number of options and suboptions, many of which provide information about current drawing files that are referenced.

- **?.** If you specify the ? option, the external references that are a part of the drawing file are listed.

- **Xref(s) to list <*>:**

  If you press Enter at this prompt, all current external references are listed. You also can enter a wild-card search string to list only external reference names that match the wild-card pattern.

- **Bind.** Binding makes an external reference a permanent part of the current drawing database.

- **Xref(s) to bind:**

  Enter the name or names of external references that you want placed in the drawing database. If you are binding multiple external references, separate each name with a comma. The external reference is stored as a block, and all related dependent symbols (blocks, dimension styles, layers, linetypes, and text styles) are given names that combine the name of the original external reference file, a dollar sign, a number, another dollar sign, and then the name of the original dependent symbol. This procedure ensures that the names used in the external reference are not confused with any similarly-named objects within the current drawing.

If you only want to bind some of the external references' dependent symbols, use the XBIND command.

- **Detach.** Detaching an external reference completely severs it from the current drawing.
- **Xref(s) to detach:**

  Enter the name of an external reference that you want removed from the drawing. If you are removing multiple external references, separate each name with a comma.
- **Path.** If you selected the Path option, you can respecify the path used to find external reference files.
- **Edit path for which Xref(s):**

  Enter the name of the external reference at this prompt. You can change the path for several external reference files with this option.
- **Old path: <current path and filename for XREF >
  New path:**

  The current path for the external reference is displayed, followed by a prompt asking you to enter a new file path. After you enter a valid path and file name, you are returned to the Command: prompt.

 You get an error message if you attempt to edit an existing drawing that has had of one of its referenced files renamed at DOS or with the FILES command. The Path option of the XREF command is most helpful for telling AutoCAD what the new name is. Otherwise, you must use XREF Delete, and then use the Attach option with the new file name.

- **Reload.** The Reload option updates the external reference without having to exit the drawing editor. This option is especially convenient in a network environment in which other users might be making modifications to an external reference that you have inserted into your drawing. After they have completed their changes, you can use the Reload option to update your copy of the external reference.
- **Xref(s) to reload:**

  Enter the name of a referenced file to be reloaded.

- **<Attach>.** The default option of the first external reference prompt inserts an external reference into the drawing file.

- **Xref to attach <current XREF name >:**

  Enter the name of the file you want placed within the drawing. The following prompts are then used to locate and size the external reference in the drawing editor.

- **Insertion point:**

  The base point of an external reference is used to place it within the drawing editor. This point (0,0,0, by default, set by the BASE command) is the insertion point for the external reference when it is placed, scaled, and rotated. This insertion point is similar to the insertion point for blocks.

  Until you specify a point in the drawing editor for the external reference you are inserting, the external reference is shown highlighted. This gives you an idea of the way the external reference appears when placed. If you already know the various insertion parameters (X, Y, and Z scales, and rotation), they can be preset so that the highlighted image is more accurate before you insert it. These preset options are entered at this prompt before specifying the insertion point. Each option is described in the following table.

Parameter	Function
SCALE	Presets the scale in each of the three axes (X, Y, and Z) to the same value. The highlighted external reference is scaled, and then you can specify its insertion point. After the external reference is located in the drawing, you are not asked to enter values for scale factors.
XSCALE	Presets the scale only in the X axis. Insertion then proceeds, and you are not prompted for the remaining scale values.
YSCALE	Presets the scale only in the Y axis. Insertion then proceeds, and you are not prompted for the remaining scale values.
ZSCALE	Presets the scale only in the Z axis. Insertion then proceeds, and you are not prompted for the remaining scale values.

ROTATE   Presets the external reference rotation value. The highlighted entity is rotated, and then insertion can proceed as before. This angle is used after the external reference is located; you are not asked to supply this value, as seen when this command is typically executed.

The following five options enable you to preset the highlighted external reference values, and also to display the normal prompts for scale factors and rotation after insertion. They are primarily used by AutoCAD applications initially to scale and rotate external references for on-screen dragging before permitting user scaling and rotation.

Parameter	Function
PSCALE	Presets all three axis scales. After the external reference is located, you still are asked to enter an external reference scaling factor.
PXSCALE	Presets the scale factor of the external reference's X axis. After the external reference is located, you are asked for the scale along this axis.
PYSCALE	Presets the scale factor of the external reference's Y axis.
PZSCALE	Presets the scale factor of the external reference's Z axis.
PROTATE	Presets the highlighted external reference's rotation.

- **X scale factor <1>/Corner/XYZ:**

    This prompt is displayed if none of the scale factors are preset. Its default value sets the X-axis scale factor for the inserted external reference. A negative value mirrors the external reference that appears about the X axis.

    You also can pick a point within the drawing editor or specify the Corner option. In either case, the distance between this first point and a second point that you select is used to set the scale factors for both the X and Y axes.

- **Y scale factor (*default=X*):**

  Enter a Y-axis scale factor. The default is the same value used in the previous prompt.

- **Rotation angle <0>:**

  Enter a rotation value for the external reference. It is then rotated about its insertion point by this value.

- **X scale factor <1>/Corner:**

  If your external reference needs to be scaled in the Z direction, use the XYZ option. By default, you only enter values for the X- and Y-axis scale when you insert an external reference. The Z axis is then given the same scale factor as the X axis.

- **Y scale factor (*default=X*):**

  Specify a scale factor for the Y axis. By default, this is set to the same scale as used for the X axis.

- **Z scale factor (*default=X*):**

  Specify a scale factor for the Z axis. By default, this is set to the same scale as used for the X axis.

Example

The following example uses the Attach option of XREF to add an external reference. (Note the change from fig. XREF.1 to fig. XREF.2.)

```
Command: XREF ↵
?/Bind/Detach/Path/Reload/<Attach>: A↵
Xref(s) to Attach: ADESK_B↵
Attach Xref ADESK_B: ADESK_B
ADESK_B loaded.
Insertion point: 0,0↵
 X scale factor <1>/corner/XYZ: ↵
 Y scale factor (default=X): ↵
 Rotation angle (0): ↵
Command: XREF ↵
?/Bind/Detach/Path/Reload/<Attach>: ?↵
Xref(s) to list <*>: ↵
Xref Name                                    Path
------------------------------------         --------------------
ADESK_B                                      adesk_b
Total Xref(s): 1
```

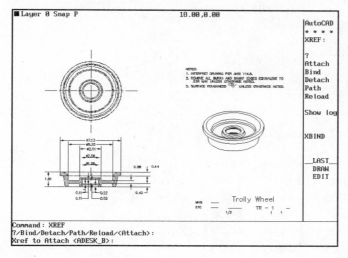

Figure XREF.1:

The trolley wheel, drawing TROL1.DWG with no border.

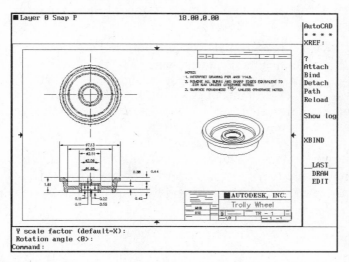

Figure XREF.2:

The same drawing after attaching the external reference for the border.

Related Command

XBIND

ZOOM

Screen **[DISPLAY] [ZOOM:]**

Pull down **[View] [ZOOM] [Window]**
Pull down **[View] [ZOOM] [Dynamic]**
Pull down **[View] [ZOOM] [Previous]**
Pull down **[View] [ZOOM] [All]**
Pull down **[View] [ZOOM] [Extents]**
Pull down **[View] [ZOOM] [Vmax]**

The ZOOM command enlarges or reduces the display of the drawing to aid in drafting and editing. If more than one viewport is active, the display seen in each viewport can be zoomed independently.

R12 You can execute the ZOOM command transparently by preceding the command name with an apostrophe ('ZOOM), so you can use it while other commands are pending. To optimize the ZOOM command, use the VIEWRES command to enable fast zooms and turn automatic screen regenerations off with the REGENAUTO command.

If used in model space with paper space enabled, the ZOOM Scale XP option enables a paper space viewport to be scaled relative to paper space. The Vmax option makes the view as large as possible without causing a screen regeneration.

Prompts and Options

- **All/Center/Dynamic/Extents/Left/Previous/Vmax/ Windows/<Scale (X/XP)>:**

  This is the main ZOOM prompt, at which you enter an option or scale factor.

- **All.** If the current display is the plan view of the World Coordinate System (WCS), this option zooms to the greater of the drawing's extents or limits. If the display shows a view of a 3D model, this option displays the model's extents. The All option always causes a screen regeneration.

- **Center.** Specify the center and magnification of the zoomed view. You receive the `Center point:` prompt, at which you specify the center of the view to be zoomed. AutoCAD then presents the `Magnification or Height <default>:` prompt, at which you enter the height of the view in drawing units. The default value shows the current magnification. Selecting a smaller value increases the screen's magnification. If the number is followed by an X, the new view is based relative to the current display. Type **4** at this prompt, for example, to create a view four units high; type **4X** to create a view four times as large as the current display. You also can type **XP** after a number to scale the current display relative to paper space.

- **Dynamic.** This option enables you graphically to indicate the desired view. The ZOOM Dynamic screen appears after you select the Dynamic option, as shown in figure ZOOM.1. On color displays, the outermost box indicates the drawing limits, the box indicated by the red corner brackets shows the currently generated information, the green dashed box indicates the current view, and the gray box with an X indicates the view to be zoomed.

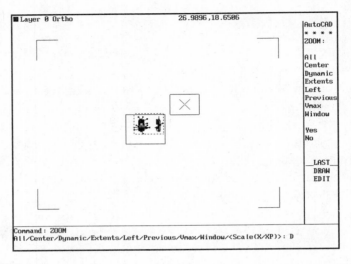

Figure ZOOM.1:
The ZOOM Dynamic screen.

You can resize the X box by pressing the pick button. The X turns into an arrow, indicating that the window can be resized. Press the pick button again to return to the X. Press Enter to accept the new view. If the X box is moved outside the currently generated area, an hourglass appears in the lower left corner of the screen to indicate that a regeneration is taking place.

- **Extents.** ZOOM Extents creates a view that fills the display with the drawing's entities. This is unlike ZOOM Limits (described in following paragraphs) because the limits of a drawing can be far greater than the area used by the entities.

- **Left.** This option is similar to the Center option, which was discussed earlier. Specify a point that is to be the lower left corner of the new view at the `Lower left corner point:` prompt. AutoCAD then prompts for the size of the zoomed view with the `Magnification or Height <default>:` prompt. Enter the number of drawing units for zoom height at this prompt.

- **Previous.** This option zooms to the previous view that was on the display within that specific viewport. This command displays the previous view, whether it was created with the PAN, VIEW, or ZOOM commands. The last ten views are saved for each viewport. The view created with this command may differ from the time it was last seen if the drawing has been modified, but the display shows the same area.

- **Vmax.** This option creates the largest available view that does not require a regeneration. This command usually provides the view needed at a redraw speed. As such, ZOOM All, which forces a regeneration, should be used only after finding that the view created by ZOOM Vmax is undesirable.

R12
- **Window.** If a point is selected or coordinates given, the ZOOM command then defaults to the Window option. Window may also be selected by entering the Window option. The ZOOM Window option is the most common way to create the desired view. You are asked to drag a window around the area to zoom in on with the following prompts:

  ```
  First corner:
  Other corner:
  ```

- **Scale.** This option creates a view when you enter a scale factor number. The drawing is then displayed relative to the drawing's limits. The number given can be any positive number. If the number is less than one, the entities within the display are smaller in the new view. If the number is followed by an X, as in 4X, the created view is scaled relative to the current display. If you want to create a scaled view relative to paper space units, type **XP** after the number, as in **5XP**. If the paper space is to be plotted at 1=1 scale, the view shown in this case is scaled to .2 (five times the scale of the paper space units).

Example

The following example demonstrates the ZOOM command's Window option.

```
Command: ZOOM ↵
All/Center/Dynamic/Extents/Left/
Previous/Vmax/Window/<Scale (X/XP)> Pick ①
(see figure ZOOM.2)
Other corner: Pick ②
```

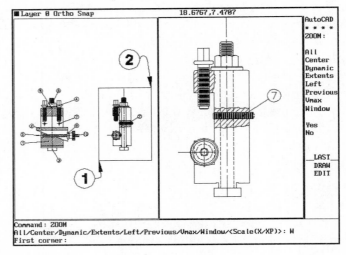

Figure ZOOM.2:
The ZOOM Window in progress.

Related Commands

PAN
VIEW
REGENAUTO
VIEWRES

Related System Variables

    ENTMAX
    EXTMIN
    LIMMAX
    LIMMIN
    VIEWCTR
    VIEWSIZE
    VSMAX
    VSMIN

3D

Screen **[DRAW] [next] [3D Surfs] [3D Objects]**

Pull down **[Draw] [3D Surfaces]**

The 3D command is an AutoLISP program that enables you to create three-dimensional objects, including boxes, spheres, domes, dishes, meshes, pyramids, and wedges. Each object is constructed as a 3Dmesh.

The AutoLISP file that defines this command is loaded the first time you make the screen or pull-down menu selections. You also can load the file by entering **3D** at the Command: prompt. After you enter **3D** at the Command: prompt, the command prompts you to specify which type of object you want to draw. The 3D.LSP file also defines individual commands that you can execute at the Command: prompt to draw specific objects.

The individual object commands are AI_BOX, AI_CONE, AI_DOME, AI_DISH, AI_MESH, AI_PYRAMID, AI_SPHERE, AI_TORUS, and AI_WEDGE. As with all entities within the AutoCAD drawing editor, the points that you enter for the 3D objects are relative to the current UCS. Generally, you can enter values or pick points to show distances and angles at the prompts.

Prompts and Options

- **Box/Cone/DIsh/DOme/Mesh/Pyramid/Sphere/Torus/ Wedge:**

  This is the initial prompt for the 3D command. You specify which three-dimensional object to draw by entering the capital letter(s) shown in the prompt for that type of object. The sections that follow list the prompts and options for each object type.

Box

- **Corner of box:**

  You specify the first corner of the box by entering a coordinate or by picking a point in the drawing editor.

- **Length:**

  You enter the length of the box along the X axis.

- **Cube/<Width>:**

  If you specify the cube option by entering **C**, the distance that you entered for the length is also used for both the width and the height of the box. If you pick a point or enter a different value for the width (Y axis), the box will be rectangular.

- **Height:**

  You specify the height of the box in the Z axis.

- **Rotation angle about Z axis:**

  You specify an angle to rotate the box around its starting corner.

Cone

- **Base center point:**

  You specify the center point of the base of the cone.

- **Diameter/<radius> of base:**

  You specify a value or pick a point to show a distance for the radius of the cone, or enter **D** if you prefer to specify a value for the cone's diameter.

- **Diameter of base:**

  You supply a value or pick a point for the diameter of the cone's base.

- **Diameter/<radius> of top <0>:**

  You can accept the default of 0 for the radius at the top, specify a different radius, or enter **D** to specify the diameter at the top of the cone. To create a cylinder or tube, set the top and bottom radius values to the same number.

- **Diameter of top <0>:**

  You can enter a value or pick a point to specify the diameter of the cone top. A value of zero for the diameter causes the cone to form a point.

- **Height:**

  You specify the height from the base point that you entered to the top of the cone.

- **Number of segments <16>:**

  The cone is created from a series of 3D mesh faces. This prompt enables you to specify the number of faces that should be used. The more segments that you use to create the cone, the smoother the cone looks.

Dish, Dome, and Sphere

Both the dome and dish are hemispheres. The dome is the top half of the sphere, and the dish is the bottom half.

- **Center of dish**, **Center of dome**, or **Center of sphere:**

  You can enter coordinates or pick a point to locate the center of the dish, dome, or sphere.

- **Diameter/<Radius>:**

  You can enter a value or pick a point to show a distance for the dish, dome, or sphere's radius; or enter **D** for the Diameter option.

1089

- **Diameter:**

  If you selected the Diameter option at the previous prompt, specify the value here.

- **Number of longitudinal segments <16>:**

  You enter the number of "wedges" that will be used to approximate the shape of the dish, dome, or sphere. As with the cone, the object is created from a series of 3D mesh faces. The greater the number of faces you use, the smoother is the surface.

- **Number of latitudinal segments <8>:**

  You enter the number of faces that each longitudinal section will be divided into to approximate the shape of the dish, dome, or sphere. As with the longitudinal segments, the greater the number of faces that you use, the smoother is the surface of the object. The default number of latitudinal segments for a sphere is twice that of the dish and dome.

Mesh

- **First corner:**

  You specify the first corner point of the mesh. A *mesh* is a four-sided surface, defined by four arbitrary 3D points at the corners, and divided by vertices in two directions, M and N. After you locate each corner of the mesh area, the surface is created within those points.

- **Second corner:**

  You specify the second corner point of the mesh.

- **Third corner:**

  You specify the third corner point of the mesh.

- **Fourth corner:**

  You specify the fourth and final corner point of the mesh.

- **Mesh M size:**

  You specify the number of vertices in the M direction (from the first to the fourth corner points). When requesting this number, AutoCAD highlights the side representing the M direction.

- **Mesh N size:**

  You specify the number of vertices in the N direction (from the first to the second corner points). When requesting this number, AutoCAD highlights the side representing the N direction.

Pyramid

The Pyramid option creates three- or four-sided pyramids that can meet at a top point or be truncated with a three- or four-sided top. A four-sided pyramid also can terminate in a top ridge, specified by two points.

- **First base point:**

  You specify a point for the first corner of the pyramid base.

- **Second base point:**

  You specify a point for the second corner of the pyramid base.

- **Third base point:**

  You specify a point for the third corner of the pyramid base.

- **Tetrahedron/<Fourth base point>:**

  A pyramid's base can be three- or four-sided. Specify a point to create a four-sided base pyramid or enter a **T** for the Tetrahedron option, which draws a three-sided pyramid.

- **Top/<Apex point>:**

  This prompt appears after you specify the T option at the previous prompt. Specify the shape for the top of the tetrahedron at this prompt. If you specify an apex point, the sides of your pyramid will meet at a single point. If you enter a **T** for the Top option, you are prompted for three points to define the plane of the top.

- **First corner:**, **Second corner:**, and **Third Corner:**

  At these prompts, you specify the corner points of the top of the pyramid. To locate each corner, you must specify the Z coordinate. If you do not, the top of the pyramid probably will lie within the same plane as the base.

- **Ridge/Top/<Apex point>:**

  This prompt appears after you specify a fourth point for the base of the pyramid. Specify an Apex point to create a pyramid in which the sides meet at a single point. The Top option enables you to specify the four corner points that will be used to create a flattened top for the pyramid. The Ridge option enables you to specify the end points of an edge line along which the pyramid's four sides will meet.

- **First corner:**, **Second corner:**, **Third Corner:**, and **Fourth point:**

  You specify the corner points of the top of the pyramid at these prompts. To locate the end corner, you must enter a value for the Z coordinate. If you do not, the top of the pyramid probably will lie within the same plane as the base.

- **First ridge point:**

  You specify the first end point of the ridge edge. The side defined by the first and fourth base points will meet at this point. The sides defined by the first and second base points, and by the third and fourth base points, will meet along the ridge edge.

- **Second ridge point:**

  You specify the second end point to the ridge edge. The side defined by the second and third base points will meet at this point.

When you specify the points used to create the pyramid's ridge or top, always locate the points in the same order and direction as the first two base points. Locating these points out of order results in a twisted pyramid.

Torus

- **Center of torus:**

  You specify the center point of the torus.

- **Diameter/<radius> of torus:**

  You can size the torus by entering a value or picking a point to show a distance for the radius. You also can enter a **D** for the Diameter option.

- **Diameter:**

  If you specified the Diameter option at the previous prompt, enter the diameter value here or pick a point to show a distance for the diameter.

- **Diameter/<Radius> of tube:**

  You can size the tube by entering a value or picking a point to show a distance for the radius. You also can enter a **D** for the Diameter option.

- **Diameter:**

  If you specified the Diameter option at the previous prompt, specify the diameter value here.

- **Segments around tube circumference <16>:**

  You enter the number of segments to use to approximate the cross section of the torus tube. The more segments you use, the smoother the torus appears.

- **Segments around torus circumference <16>:**

  You enter the number of segments used to create the torus. The more wedges you use, the smoother the torus appears.

Wedge

- **Corner of wedge:**

  You can enter a value or pick a point for the first corner of the wedge. A wedge is created in a manner similar to the 3D box.

The only difference is that the top of the wedge slopes down to meet its base.

- **Length:**

  You specify the length along the X axis of the wedge's base.

- **Width:**

  You specify the width along the Y axis of the wedge's base.

- **Height:**

  You specify the height of the wedge in the Z axis.

- **Rotation angle about Z axis:**

  You specify a rotation angle by which to rotate the wedge about its first corner point in the current UCS.

Examples

The following examples show you how to create the 3D objects discussed previously. The examples assume that the 3D.LSP file is automatically loaded by AutoCAD. The examples show the creation of objects in three viewports, one with a plan view, one with a front view, and one with a 3D view.

```
Command: 3D ↵
Box/Cone/DIsh/DOme/Mesh/Pyramid/Sphere/Torus/
Wedge: B ↵ (See fig. 3D.1)
Corner of box: 2,2 ↵
Length: 15 ↵
Cube/<Width>: 8 ↵
Height: 10 ↵
Rotation angle about z axis: 0 ↵

Command: AI_CONE ↵
Box/Cone/DIsh/DOme/Mesh/Pyramid/Sphere/Torus/
Wedge: C ↵ (See fig. 3D.2)
Base center point: 10, 6.5 ↵
Diameter/<radius> of base: 4 ↵
Diameter/<radius> of top <0>: ↵
Height: 15 ↵
Number of segments<16>: 25 ↵
```

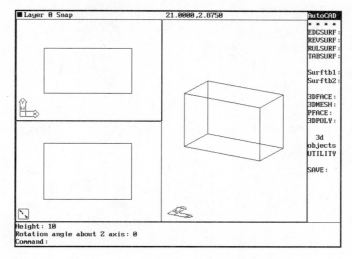

Figure 3D.1:
The 3D box.

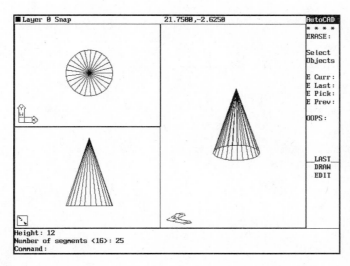

Figure 3D.2:
The 3D cone.

```
Command: 3D ↵
Box/Cone/DIsh/DOme/Mesh/Pyramid/Sphere/Torus/
Wedge: DO ↵ (See fig. 3D.3)
Center of dome: 10,6.5,5 ↵
Diameter/<Radius>: 6 ↵
Number of longitudinal segments<16>: 25 ↵
Number of latitudinal segments <8>: 30 ↵
```

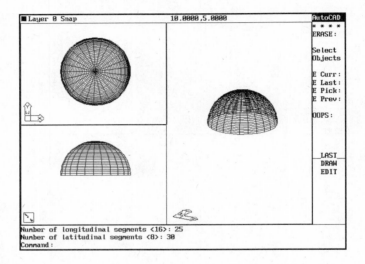

Figure 3D.3:
The 3D dome.

```
Command: 3D ↵
Box/Cone/DIsh/DOme/Mesh/Pyramid/Sphere/Torus/
Wedge: M ↵ (See fig. 3D.4)
First corner: 4,4 ↵
Second corner: 16,10,2 ↵
Third corner: 19.5,4.25,8 ↵
Fourth corner: 4,0,10 ↵
Mesh M size: 25 ↵
Mesh N size: 20 ↵

Command: 3D ↵
Box/Cone/DIsh/DOme/Mesh/Pyramid/Sphere/Torus/
Wedge: P ↵ (See fig. 3D.5)
```

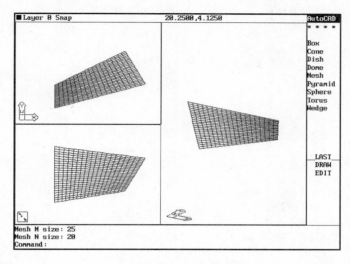

Figure 3D.4:
The 3D mesh with 25 M vertices and 20 N vertices.

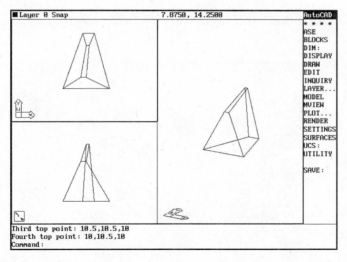

Figure 3D.5:
The 3D four-sided pyramid.

```
First base point: 6,3 ↵
Second base point: @8<0 ↵
Third base point: @10<105 ↵
Tetrahedron/<Fourth base point>: @2<180 ↵
Top/<Apex point>: T ↵
First top point: 9,5,7 ↵
Second top point: 10,5,7 ↵
Third top point: 10.5,10.5,10 ↵
Fourth top point: 10,10.5,10 ↵
```

The following steps create a sphere:

```
Command: 3D ↵
Box/Cone/DIsh/DOme/Mesh/Pyramid/Sphere/Torus/
Wedge: S ↵ (See fig. 3D.6)
Center of sphere: 10,7,4 ↵
Diameter/<radius>: 7 ↵
Number of longitudinal segments <16>: 20 ↵
Number of latitudinal segments <16>: 20 ↵
```

The following steps create a torus:

```
Command: 3D ↵
Box/Cone/DIsh/DOme/Mesh/Pyramid/Sphere/Torus/
Wedge: T ↵ (See fig. 3D.7)
```

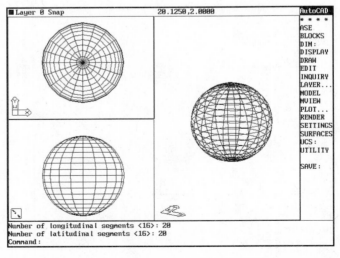

Figure 3D.6:
The 3D sphere.

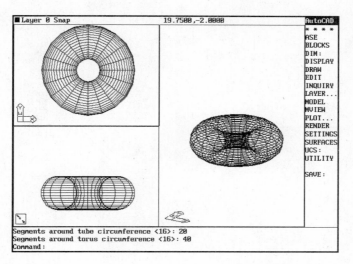

Figure 3D.7:
The 3D torus.

```
Center of torus: 10,7,2 ↵
Diameter/<radius> of torus: 8 ↵
Diameter/<Radius> of tube: 3 ↵
Segments around tube circumference <16>: 20 ↵
Segments around torus circumference <16>:40 ↵
Command: 3D ↵
Box/Cone/DIsh/DOme/Mesh/Pyramid/Sphere/Torus/
Wedge: W ↵ (See fig. 3D.8)
Corner of wedge: 4,4 ↵
Length: 8 ↵
Width: 5 ↵
Height: 10 ↵
Rotation angle about Z axis : 0 ↵
```

3DARRAY

Pull down **[Construct] [Array 3D]**

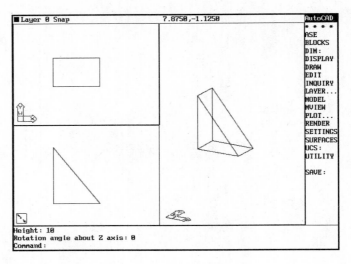

Figure 3D.8:
The 3D wedge.

The 3DARRAY command is an AutoLISP program that enables you to create 3D rectangular and polar arrays in AutoCAD's model space. An array repeats the selected objects in a regularly spaced circular (polar) or rectangular pattern. Rectangular arrays created with this command have rows, columns, and levels in the X, Y, and Z axes, respectively, of the current UCS. Polar arrays created by 3DARRAY are similar to polar arrays created by the ARRAY command. The difference is that the axis of rotation can be at any orientation in space, rather than being restricted to rotating about a point in the current construction plane, perpendicular to the current Z axis.

Prompts and Options

- `Select objects:`

  You can use any of the normal AutoCAD selection methods to select all of the entities that you want arrayed.

- **Rectangular or Polar Array (R/P)?**

  At this prompt, you specify whether you are creating a polar or rectangular array.

- **Number of rows (--)<1>:**

  If you specify a rectangular array, this prompt appears next. As with the ARRAY command, you must enter the number of rows you want to create. The default value of 1 means that you do not want to copy the selected items in the Y direction.

- **Number of columms (||||)<1>:**

  You enter the number of columns in the X direction. The default value of 1 indicates that you want no copies of selected items in the X direction.

- **Number of levels (...)<1>:**

  You enter the number of levels you want made in the Z direction. The default value of 1 indicates that you want no copies of the selected items in the Z direction.

- **Distance between rows (--):**

  This prompt appears if you entered a number other than 1 at the Number of rows (--)<1>: prompt. Enter the distance (in the Y direction) that each of the copies will be spaced between each of the succeeding rows.

- **Distance between columns (||||):**

  This prompt appears if you entered a number other than 1 at the Number of columns (||||)<1>: prompt. Enter the distance (in the X direction) that each copy will be spaced between each of the succeeding columns.

- **Distance between levels (...):**

  This prompt appears if you entered a number other than 1 at the Number of levels (...)<1>: prompt. Enter the distance (in the Z direction) that each of the copies will be spaced between each of the succeeding levels.

1101

- **Number of items:**

  This prompt appears if you create a polar array. Enter the number of copies that you want to create with the polar array.

- **Angle to fill <360>:**

  You enter the portion of a circle, in degrees, in which you want to place the entities. The default value of 360 degrees causes the items that you are copying to be distributed within a full circle.

- **Rotate objects as they are copied? <Y>:**

  When creating polar arrays, you can rotate each copy or maintain their original orientation.

- **Center point of array:**

  You specify the first point of the axis about which the entities will be arrayed.

- **Second point on axis of rotation:**

  You specify the second point of the axis around which the entities are arrayed. They will be copied in a manner similar to a 2D polar array.

Example

The following example shows you how to use the 3DARRAY routine to create a rectangular array in model space. First create a 3D box, using the Box option in the 3D command.

```
Command: 3DARRAY↵
Select objects: Pick the box
Rectangular or Polar Array (R/P)? R↵
Number of rows (--)<1>: 4↵
Number of columns (||||) <1>: 4↵
Number of levels (...)<1>: 3↵
Distance between rows (--)
Distance between columns (||||): 4↵
Distance between levels (...): 4↵
```

After the final prompt, the array of entities is created. Your drawing should resemble figure 3DARRAY.2.

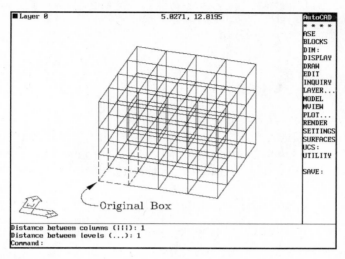

Figure 3DARRAY.1:
The arrayed 3D box.

Related Command

ARRAY

3DFACE

Screen   **[DRAW] [next] [3DFACE:]**

Screen   **[SURFACES] [3DFACE:]**

Pull down   **[Draw] [3D Surfaces] [3D Face]**

The 3DFACE command creates entities that are made of three or four sides. The corners for these faces are entered in either clockwise or counterclockwise direction. 3Dfaces are not filled with color; their vertices can be in different planes. Three-dimensional faces do not have to be flat; the selected points can have different Z coordinates. Three-dimensional faces are colored with the SHADE command and treated

1103

as opaque by the HIDE command. The faces cannot be given a thickness. The edges of the face can be made invisible during the entity creation.

Prompts and Options

- **First/Second/Third/Fourth point:**

  Points are entered in a circular direction; either clockwise or counterclockwise around the face. Three-dimensional faces can be triangular; response to the fourth point is optional. Until you press Enter or Ctrl-C, 3DFACE repeats the third point and fourth point prompts to create adjacent 3D faces.

You may use the following options with the 3DFACE command:

- **Invisible.** If the edge you are defining should be invisible, type **I** or select the Invisible option from the screen menu before specifying the point that begins that edge.
- **ShowEdge.** This screen menu option displays all invisible edges of the face after the next screen regeneration.
- **HideEdge.** This screen menu option makes any hidden edges invisible after the next screen regeneration.

Example

The following example creates two 3Dfaces (see fig. 3DFACE.1). The edge that runs between coordinates 0,3,3 and 6,3,3 is invisible.

```
Command: 3DFACE ↵
First point: 6,0,0 ↵
Second point: 0,0,0 ↵
Third point: I ↵
0,3,3 ↵
Fourth point: 6,3,3 ↵
Third point: 6,6,0 ↵
Fourth point: 0,6,0 ↵
Third point: ↵
```

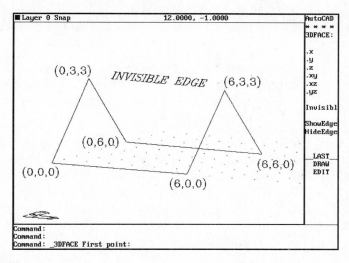

Figure 3DFACE.1:
Three 3Dfaces.

Related Commands

EDGESURF
PFACE
REVSURF
RULESURF
TABSURF
3DMESH

Related System Variable

SPLFRAME

3DMESH

Screen **[DRAW] [next] [3D Surfs] [3DMESH:]**

Screen **[SURFACES] [3DMESH:]**

Pull down **[Draw] [3D Surfaces] [3D Objects...] [Mesh]**

The 3DMESH command creates an M×N three-dimensional mesh, defined by the locations of each of its vertices. The 3DMESH command forms a net-like surface, each face of which is defined by four vertices. You must specify the coordinates for the corners of the faces.

The first step consists of specifying the number of vertices in the two directions of the mesh (known as the M and N directions). Most polygon meshing commands automatically determine these values from the variables SURFTAB1 and SURFTAB2, but the 3DMESH command does not. After you specify the number of vertices in the M and N directions, the 3DMESH command prompts for the location of each vertex, in order.

This command is best suited for use by third-party programs that automate the selection of coordinate points. For most purposes, you should use one of the other 3D surface commands. After the mesh is created, you can edit it with the PEDIT command. If the mesh is exploded, it is replaced with individual 3Dfaces.

You now have the option of drawing the edges of the mesh and then specifying the mesh size in the M and N direction. This option, new to AutoCAD Release 12, makes creating the mesh much faster—and it makes only smooth meshes. This option is accessed by the MESH selection on the pull-down menu. Specifically, you select the X, Y, and Z coordinates for each of the four corners of the mesh, not for each vertex. The intermediate vertices' coordinates are then calculated as they fall between the four corners. As seen in figure 3DMESH.1, many other three-dimensional surfaces are available.

Prompts and Options

The following options appear if you type the command or select 3D Mesh from the screen menu:

- **Mesh M size:**
  Mesh N size:

  You enter the number of vertices in the M and N directions of the mesh. These values can be any positive integer greater than two.

- **Vertex (*m*, *n*):**

  You specify the coordinates for the *m*,*n* vertex, in which *m* and *n* denote the location of the vertex in the mesh. This prompt repeats for each *m*,*n* location in the mesh until all the vertex locations for the mesh are specified.

  The following prompts appear:

- **First Corner:**
  Second Corner:
  Third Corner:
  Fourth Corner:

  You select the locations for the four corners of the mesh.

- **Mesh M size:**
  Mesh N size:

  You enter the number of vertices to be calculated, which determines the appearance of the mesh. The number specified in the N direction divides the mesh between the first and second corners.

Example

The following example creates a simple 3DMESH:

```
Command: 3DMESH ↵
Mesh M size: 4 ↵
Mesh N size: 3 ↵
Vertex (0, 0): 0,0,0 ↵
Vertex (0, 1): 0,1,1 ↵
Vertex (0, 2): 0,2,1 ↵
Vertex (1, 0): 2,0,1 ↵
Vertex (1, 1): 2,2,0 ↵
Vertex (1, 2): 2,3,1 ↵
Vertex (2, 0): 4,0,2 ↵
Vertex (2, 1): 4,1,1 ↵
```

```
Vertex (2, 2): 4,2,0 ↵
Vertex (3, 0): 6,0,0 ↵
Vertex (3, 1): 6,1,0 ↵
Vertex (3, 2): 6,2,2 ↵ (see fig. 3DMESH.1)
```

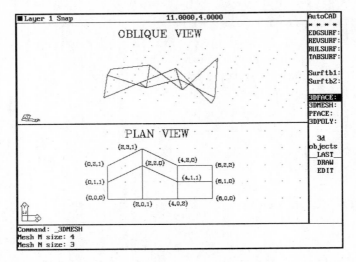

Figure 3DMESH.1:
A 4x3 mesh created with the 3DMESH command.

Related Commands

EDGESURF
MESH
PEDIT
PFACE
REVSURF
RULESURF
TABSURF
3DFACE

3DPOLY

Screen   [DRAW] [next] [3D Surfs] [3DPOLY:]

Screen   [SURFACES] [3DPOLY:]

Pull down   [Draw] [3D Poly]

The 3DPOLY command creates special polylines that can have vertices located anywhere within 3D space. These polylines differ from 2D polylines, in that they cannot contain arcs, tangent information, or widths. The PEDIT command can be used to alter the entities after they are created. Curves can be approximated by spline fitting with multiple short, straight segments. Three-dimensional polylines can only have a continuous linetype.

Prompts and Options

- **From point:**

  You specify the starting point of the 3D polyline.

- **Close:**

  Closes the polyline from the end point of the current segment to the first point of the beginning segment.

- **Undo:**

  Removes the previous segment and redraws the entity.

- **Endpoint of line:**

  You specify an end point for the current segment. This prompt repeats until you press Enter or Ctrl-C to end the command.

Example

The following example demonstrates how to construct a simple three-dimensional polyline.

```
Command: 3DPOLY ↵
From point: 0,0,0 ↵
```

```
Close/Undo/<Endpoint of line>: 2,1,3 ↵
Close/Undo/<Endpoint of line>: 4,0,-1 ↵
Close/Undo/<Endpoint of line>: 5,4,3 ↵
Close/Undo/<Endpoint of line>: 2,5,1↵
Close/Undo/<Endpoint of line>: C ↵
```

The finished 3D polyline is shown in figure 3DPOLY.1. The view also shows the same polyline after it has been edited with the PEDIT Spline Curve command sequence.

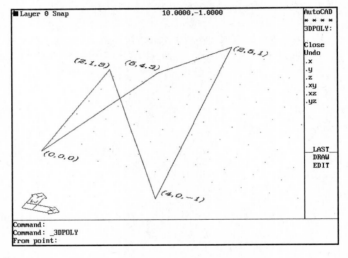

Figure 3DPOLY.1:
A 3D polyline created with the 3Dpoly command.

Related Commands

PEDIT
POLYLINE

VI

Part Six:
AutoCAD System
Variable Reference

AutoCAD System Variable Reference

AutoCAD *system variables* catalog every aspect of the drawing editor's environment, including such details as the current snap increment or whether dialog boxes are activated. Because, by definition, a variable can assume diverse values, you can change the values of AutoCAD's system variables to modify the drawing environment. (Dimensioning and Solid Modeling variables are discussed in their respective chapters.)

Accessing System Variables

Accessing system variables can be done in a general manner by using the SETVAR command, or specifically by using the command that sets the system variable. You also can type the system variable name at the command prompt. You can set a snap increment, for example, by entering **SETVAR** at the AutoCAD Command: prompt and then entering **SNAPUNIT**, which is the system variable that holds the value of the snap increment. You also can issue the SNAP command or type **SNAPUNIT** at the Command: prompt. AutoLISP programmers also can access system variables with the GETVAR and SETVAR AutoLISP functions. ADS programmers can use ADS_GETVAR and ADS_SETVAR. On the rare occasions that a system variable and a command share the same name, you must use SETVAR to directly access the system variable.

AutoCAD defines some system variables as *read-only*, meaning that you cannot directly change their value with SETVAR. Some read-only variables can be set with other AutoCAD commands; others are untouchable. ACADVER, the current AutoCAD version number, is an untouchable variable.

When you use the SETVAR command, AutoCAD first prompts for a variable name. You can enter a name or a question mark (?) to see a list of variables and their current values. If you enter ?, AutoCAD asks which variables to list. You can type an asterisk (*) to list almost all of the variables, a variable name to list a single variable, several names (which must be separated by commas), or a wild-card pattern. If you enter a variable name, AutoCAD either prompts for a new value or, in the case of a read-only variable, shows the variable's current value and informs you of its read-only status.

Although SETVAR enables you to access system variables, some system variables are not listed with the question mark (?) then asterisk (*) option of SETVAR. These variables are ERRNO, MACROTRACE, RE-INIT, USERI1-5, USERR1-5, USERS1-5. To access these system variables, you must either enter the variable name at the `Command:` or SETVAR prompt, or enter the command that sets the system variable, if such a command exists.

The following list of AutoCAD's system variables is set up in five columns. The first column contains each system variable's name. The second column indicates the variable's type. General system variables are categorized into the following types:

Type	Meaning
String	The variable is a text string
Integer	The variable is a whole number

Type	Meaning
Real	The variable is a decimal number
2D Point	The variable is a point specified by X and Y values
3D Point	The variable is a point specified by X, Y, and Z values

The third column tells the AutoCAD command that sets the system variable when such a command exists. The fourth column shows the variable's default value. The fifth column indicates where the system variable is saved.

Most system variables are saved in the ACAD.CFG configuration file. Some variables, however, are saved in the drawing and some are not saved. System variables saved in ACAD.CFG are marked *CFG*, those saved in the drawing are marked *DWG*, and variables that are not saved are marked *NS*. All read-only variables also are marked with an *RO*. System variables that are new for Release 12 are shown in bold. System variables that have been changed in some way for Release 12 are shown in italic. See table SV.1.

Table SV.1

System Variables

Variable Name	Type	Command Name	Default Setting	Saved In
ACADPREFIX	String		C:\ACAD;...	NS, RO
ACADVER	String		12	NS, RO
AFLAGS	Integer	**DDATTDEF**	0 ATTDEF	NS
ANGBASE	Real	**DDUNITS**	0 UNITS	DWG
ANGDIR	Integer	**DDUNITS**	0 UNITS	DWG

continues

Table SV.1
Continued

Variable Name	Type	Command Name	Default Setting	Saved In
APERTURE	Integer	**DDOSNAP** APERTURE	10	CFG
AREA	Real	AREA LIST	0.0000	NS, RO
ATTDIA	Integer		0	DWG
ATTMODE	Integer	ATTDIST	1	DWG
ATTREQ	Integer		1	DWG
AUDITCTL	Integer		0	CFG
AUNITS	Integer	**DDUNITS** UNITS	0	DWG
AUPREC	Integer	**DDUNITS** UNITS	0	DWG
BACKZ	Real	DVIEW	0.0000	DWG, RO
BLIPMODE	Integer	BLIPMODE	1	DWG
CDATE	Real	TIME	19930202.144648898	NS, RO
CECOLOR	String	DDEMODES COLOR	BYLAYER	DWG
CELTYPE	String	**DDEMODES LINETYPE**	BYLAYER	DWG
CHAMFERA	Real	CHAMFER	0.0000	DWG
CHAMFERB	Real	CHAMFER	0.0000	DWG
CIRCLERAD	Real		0.0000	NS
CLAYER	String	DDLMODES DDEMODES LAYER	0	DWG
CMDACTIVE	Integer	CMDACTIVE	0	NS, RO
CMDDIA	Integer		1	CFG

Variable Name	Type	Command Name	Default Setting	Saved In
CMDECHO	Integer		1	NS
CMDNAMES	String		""	NS
COORDS	Integer	^D F6	1	DWG
CVPORT	Integer	VPORTS	2	DWG
DATE	Real	TIME	2448806.36807836	NS, RO
DBMOD	Integer		0	NS, RO
DIASTAT	Integer		1	NS, RO
DISTANCE	Real	DIST	0.0000	NS
DONUTID	Real		0.5000	NS
DONUTOD	Real		1.0000	NS
DRAGMODE	Integer	DRAGMODE	2	DWG
DRAGP1	Integer		10	CFG
DRAGP2	Integer		25	CFG
DWGCODEPAGE	String		ASCII	DWG
DWGNAME	String		UNNAMED	NS, RO
DWGPREFIX	String		C:\ACAD\	NS, RO
DWGTITLED	Integer	NEW	0	NS, RO
DWGWRITE	Integer	OPEN	1	NS
ELEVATION	Real	ELEV DDEMODES	0.0000	DWG
ERRNO	Integer		0	NS
EXPERT	Integer		0	NS
EXTMAX	3D point		-1.000E+20,-1.000E+20	DWG, RO
EXTMIN	3D point		1.0000E+20,1.0000E+20	DWG, RO
FILEDIA	Integer		1	CFG
FILLETRAD	Real	FILLET	0.0000	DWG
FILLMODE	Integer	FILL	1	DWG

continues

Table SV.1
Continued

Variable Name	Type	Command Name	Default Setting	Saved In
FRONTZ	Real	DVIEW	0.0000	DWG, RO
GRIDMODE	Integer	**DDRMODES** GRID F7	0	DWG
GRIDUNIT	2D point	**DDRMODES** GRID	0.0000,0.0000	DWG
GRIPBLOCK	Integer	DDGRIPS	0	CFG
GRIPCOLOR	Integer	DDGRIPS	5	CFG
GRIPHOT	Integer	DDGRIPS	1	CFG
GRIPS	Integer	DDSELECT	1	CFG
GRIPSIZE	Integer	DDGRIPS	3	CFG
HANDLES	Integer	HANDLES	0	DWG, RO
HIGHLIGHT	Integer		1	NS
HPANG	Real	BHATCH HATCH	0	NS
HPDOUBLE	Real	BHATCH HATCH	0	NS
HPNAME	String	BHATCH HATCH	""	NS
HPSCALE	Real	BHATCH HATCH	1.0000	NS
HPSPACE	Real	BHATCH HATCH	1.0000	NS
INSBASE	3D Point	BASE	0.0000,0.0000,0.0000...	DWG
INSNAME	String	DDINSERT INSERT	""	NS
LASTANGLE	Real	ARC	0	NS, RO
LASTPOINT	3D Point		0.0000,0.0000,0.0000	NS

Variable Name	Type	Command Name	Default Setting	Saved In
LENSLENGTH	Real	DVIEW	50.0000	DWG
LIMCHECK	Integer	LIMITS	0	DWG, RO
LIMMAX	2D Point		12.0000,9.0000	DWG
LIMMIN	2D Point		0.0000,0.0000	DWG
LOGINNAME	Sting	CONFIG	""	NS, RO
LTSCALE	Real	LTSCALE	1.0000	DWG
LUNITS	Integer	DDUNITS UNITS	2	DWG
LUPREC	Integer	DDUNITS UNITS	4	DWG
MACROTRACE	**Integer**		**0**	**NS**
MAXACTVP	Integer		16	NS
MAXSORT	Integer		2000	CFG
MENUCTL	**Integer**		**1**	**CFG**
MENUECHO	**Integer**		**0**	**NS**
MENUNAME	String	MENU	ACAD	DWG, RO
MIRRTEXT	Integer		1	DWG
MODEMACRO	**String**		**""**	**NS**
OFFSETDIST	**Real**	**OFFSET**	**-1.0000**	**NS**
ORTHOMODE	Integer	^O F8	0	DWG
OSMODE	Integer	**DDOSNAP** OSNAP	0	DWG
PDMODE	Integer		0	DWG
PDSIZE	Real		0.0000	DWG
PERIMETER	Real	AREA DBLIST LIST	0.0000	NS, RO
PFACEVMAX	Integer		4	NS, RO
PICKADD	**Integer**	**DDSELECT**	**1**	**CFG**

continues

Table SV.1
Continued

Variable Name	Type	Command Name	Default Setting	Saved In
PICKAUTO	Integer	**DDSELECT**	0	**CFG**
PICKBOX	Integer		3	CFG
PICKDRAG	Integer	**DDSELECT**	0	**CFG**
PICKFIRST	Integer	**DDSELECT**	0	**CFG**
PLATFORM	String		Platform Dependent	NS, RO
PLINEGEN	Integer		0	DWG
PLINEWID	Real	**PLINE**	0.0000	**DWG**
PLOTID	String	**PLOT**	""	CFG
PLOTTER	Integer	**PLOT**	0	**CFG**
POLYSIDES	Integer	**POLYGON**	4	NS
POPUPS	Integer		1	NS, RO
PSLTSCALE	Integer		1	**DWG**
PSPROLOG	String		""	**CFG**
PSQUALITY	Integer		75	**CFG**
QTEXTMODE	Integer	QTEXT	0	DWG
REGENMODE	Integer	REGENAUTO	1	DWG
RE-INIT	Integer	**REINIT**	0	**NS**
SAVEFILE	String	**CONFIG**	**AUTO.SV$**	**CFG, RO**
SAVENAME	String	SAVEAS	""	NS, RO
SAVETIME	Integer	**CONFIG**	120	**CFG**
SCREENBOXES	Integer	**CONFIG**	26	**CFG, RO**
SCREENMODE	Integer	**F1** **F2 (WINDOWS)**	0	**CFG, RO**
SCREENSIZE	2D Point		574.0000,414.0000	RO, NS
SHADEDGE	Integer		3	DWG
SHADEDIF	Integer		70	DWG

Variable Name	Type	Command Name	Default Setting	Saved In
SHPNAME	**String**	**SHAPE**	""	**NS**
SKETCHINC	Real	SKETCH	0.1000	DWG
SKPOLY	Integer		0	DWG
SNAPANG	Real	**DDRMODES** SNAP	0	DWG
SNAPBASE	2D Point	**DDRMODES** SNAP	0.0000,0.0000	DWG
SNAPISOPAIR	Integer	**DDRMODES** SNAP ^E	0	DWG
SNAPMODE	Integer	**DDRMODES** SNAP	0	DWG
SNAPSTYL	Integer	**DDRMODES** SNAP	0	DWG
SNAPUNIT	2D Point	**DDRMODES** SNAP	1.0000,1.0000	DWG
SORTENTS	**Integer**	**DDSELECT**	**0**	**CFG**
SPLFRAME	Integer		0	DWG
SPLINESEGS	Integer		8	DWG
SPLINETYPE	Integer		6	DWG
SURFTAB1	Integer		6	DWG
SURFTAB2	Integer		6	DWG
SURFTYPE	Integer		6	DWG
SURFU	Integer		6	DWG
SURFV	Integer		6	DWG
SYSCODEPAGE	**String**		**ASCII**	**DWG, RO**
TABMODE	**Integer**	**TABLET** F10	**0**	**NS**
TARGET	3D Point	DVIEW	0.0000,0.0000,0.0000	DWG, RO
TDCREATE	Real	TIME	2448806.36779607	DWG, RO

continues

1121

Table SV.1
Continued

Variable Name	Type	Command Name	Default Setting	Saved In
TDINDWG	Real	TIME	0.00000000	DWG, RO
TDUPDATE	Real	TIME	2448806.26779607	DWG, RO
TDUSRTIMER	Real	TIME	0.00000000	DWG, RO
TEMPPREFIX	String		""	NS, RO
TEXTEVAL	Integer		0	NS
TEXTSIZE	Real	TEXT	0.2000	DWG
TEXTSTYLE	*String*	*TEXT STYLE*	*STANDARD*	*DWG*
THICKNESS	Real	ELEV DDEMODES	0.0000	DWG
TILEMODE	Integer	TILEMODE	1	DWG
TRACEWID	Real	TRACE	0.0500	DWG
TREEDEPTH	**Integer**	**TREESTAT**	**3020**	**DWG**
TREEMAX	**Integer**		**10000000**	**CFG**
UCSFOLLOW	Integer		0	DWG
UCSICON	Integer	UCSICON	1	DWG
UCSNAME	String	**DDUCS** UCS	""	DWG, RO
UCSORG	3D Point	**DDUCS** UCS	0.0000,0.0000,0.0000	DWG, RO
UCSXDIR	3D Point	**DDUCS** UCS	1.0000,0.0000,0.0000	DWG, RO
UCSYDIR	3D Point	**DDUCS** UCS	0.0000,1.0000,0.0000	DWG, RO
UNDOCTL	**Integer**	**UNSO**	**5**	**NS, RO**
UNDOMARKS	**Integer**	**UNDI**	**0**	**RO, NS**
UNITMODE	Integer		0	DWG

Variable Name	Type	Command Name	Default Setting	Saved In
USERI1 - 5	Integer		0	DWG
USERR1 - 5	Real		0.0000	DWG
USERS1 - 5	**String**		**""**	**NS**
VIEWCTR	2D Point	PAN ZOOM	6.2433,4.5000	DWG, RO
VIEWDIR	3D Point	DVIEW	0.0000,0.0000,1.0000	DWG, RO
VIEWMODE	Integer	DVIEW UCS	0	DWG, RO
VIEWSIZE	Real	VIEW ZOOM	9.0000	DWG, RO
VIEWTWIST	Real	DVIEW	0	DWG, RO
VISRETAIN	Integer		0	DWG
VSMAX	3D Point	PAN VIEW ZOOM	37.4006,27.0000,0.0000	NS, RO
VSMIN	3D Point	PAN	-24.9734,-18.00,0.000	NS, RO
WORLDUCS	Integer	UCS	1	NS, RO
WORLDVIEW	Integer	DVIEW UCS	1	DWG
XREFCTL	Integer		0	CFG

Categorizing System Variables

The remainder of the System Variable Reference groups and describes the system variables according to their use, rather than alphabetically. This method of organization enables you to find a variable by the task that you want to perform, without having to know the variables name.

If you know the system variable name, you can look it up in table SV.2 and get the group number. When appropriate, the possible values of the system variable are listed after the variable description

Table SV.2
System Variable Index

Variable	#	Variable	#	Variable	#
ACADPREFIX	1	HANDLES	2	SHADEDGE	27
ACADVER	1	HIGHLIGHT	2	SHADEDIF	27
AFLAGS	23	HPANG	20	SHPNAME	21
ANGBASE	6	HPDOUBLE	20	SKETCHINC	24
ANGDIR	6	HPNAME	20	SKPOLY	24
APERTURE	2	HPSCALE	20	SNAPANG	10
AREA	18	HPSPACE	20	SNAPBASE	10
ATTDIA	23	INSBASE	21	SNAPISOPAIR	10
ATTMODE	23	INSNAME	21	SNAPMODE	10
ATTREQ	23	LASTANGLE	18	SNAPSTYL	10
AUDITCTL	2	LASTPOINT	18	SNAPUNIT	10
AUNITS	6	LENSLENGTH	26	SORTENTS	11
AUPREC	6	LIMCHECK	4	SPLFRAME	19
BACKZ	26	LIMMAX	4	SPLINESEGS	19
BLIPMODE	2	LIMMIN	4	SPLINETYPE	19
CDATE	43	LOGINNAME	1	SURFTAB1	19
CECOLOR	3	LTSCALE	5	SURFTAB2	19
CELTYPE	3	LUNITS	6	SURFTYPE	19
CHAMFERA	12	LUPREC	6	SURFU	19
CHAMFERB	12	MACROTRACE	33	SURFV	19
CIRCLERAD	12	MAXACTVP	25	SYSCODEPAGE	1
CLAYER	3	MAXSORT	13	TABMODE	13
CMDACTIVE	2	MENUCTL	13	TARGET	26
CMDDIA	13	MENUECHO	13	TDCREATE	24

Variable	#	Variable	#	Variable	#
CMDECHO	2	MENUNAME	13	TDINDWG	24
CMDNAMES	2	MIRRTEXT	7	TDUPDATE	24
COORDS	2	MODEMACRO	33	TDUSRTIMER	24
CVPORT	25	OFFSETDIST	12	TEMPPREFIX	1
DATE	34	ORTHOMODE	2	TEXTEVAL	7
DBMOD	31	OSMODE	2	TEXTSIZE	7
DIASTAT	13	PDMODE	15	TEXTSTYLE	7
DISTANCE	18	PDSIZE	15	THICKNESS	3
DONUTID	12	PERIMETER	18	TILEMODE	2
DONUTOD	12	PFACEVMAX	19	TRACEWID	12
DRAGMODE	8	PICKADD	11	TREEDEPTH	31
DRAGP1	8	PICKAUTO	11	TREEMAX	16
DRAGP2	8	PICKBOX	11	UCSFOLLOW	16
DWGCODEPAGE	2	PICKDRAG	11	UCSICON	16
DWGNAME	30	PICKFIRST	11	UCSNAME	16
DWGPREFIX	30	PLATFORM	1	UCSORG	16
DWGTITLED	30	PLINEGEN	19	UCSXDIR	16
DWGWRITE	30	PLINEWID	19	UCSYDIR	16
ELEVATION	3	PLOTID	28	UNDOCTL	17
ERRNO	35	PLOTTER	28	UNDOMARKS	17
EXPERT	2	POLYSIDES	12	UNITMODE	6
EXTMAX	4	POPUPS	13	USERI1 - 5	32
EXTMIN	4	PSLTSCALE	5	USERR1 - 5	32
FILEDIA	13	PSPROLOG	29	USERS1 - 5	32
FILLETRAD	12	PSQUALITY	29	VIEWCTR	25
FILLMODE	2	QTEXTMODE	7	VIEWDIR	26
FRONTZ	26	REGENMODE	2	VIEWMODE	26
GRIDMODE	9	RE-INIT	35	VIEWSIZE	25
GRIDUNIT	9	SAVEFILE	30	VIEWTWIST	26

continues

Table SV.2
Continued

Variable	#	Variable	#	Variable	#
GRIPBLOCK	11	SAVENAME	30	VISRETAIN	22
GRIPCOLOR	11	SAVETIME	30	VSMAX	25
GRIPHOT	11	SCREENBOXES	13	VSMIN	25
GRIPS	11	SCREENMODE	14	WORLDUCS	16
GRIPSIZE	11	SCREENSIZE	14	WORLDVIEW	26
				XREFCTL	22

WARNING If any of the system variables are reset by an application, they may remain set after the application is completed. To prevent this, the application must specifically reset the variables to their original values. The application also must have a function that runs in the event of an application error that resets the system variables.

1 System-Setting Variables

The *system-setting* variables hold general system information and settings. These variables are used to gather environment information rather than reset the environment. They are all read-only and cannot be changed by any AutoCAD command.

ACADPREFIX

ACADPREFIX stores the directory path set by the ACAD DOS environment variable. The install process for AutoCAD can create a start-up batch file called ACADR12.BAT. The ACAD environment variable is included in the batch file with the paths of the separate AutoCAD modules added as warranted by the installation. You can add directories to the path to increase the area searched for files. Use the DOS SET command to set the ACAD DOS environment variable.

ACADVER

ACADVER stores the release number. This number will vary with each release and update. Release 12 386 for DOS shows 12 as the release number.

LOGINNAME

LOGINNAME stores the user's login name. The login name may be stored in the configuration file or, if AutoCAD is so configured, entered with each startup. Access to the login name is provided for any on-line programs that need to know the name of the current draftsperson.

PLATFORM

PLATFORM stores the name of the hardware AutoCAD is running on. This is used by third-party developers to identify the platform in use and work within its idiosyncrasies. The following are valid responses:

```
Microsoft Windows        Sun4/SPARCstation

386 DOS extender         DECstation

Apple Macintosh          Silicon Graphics Iris Indigo
```

SYSCODEPAGE

SYSCODEPAGE stores the code page, as indicated by the ACAD.XMF file. The *code page* identifies the keyboard character set or language being used. The following are valid responses:

```
ascii      dos860     dos932     iso8859-6
dos437     dos861     iso8859-1  iso8859-7
dos850     dos863     iso8859-2  iso8859-8
dos852     dos864     iso8859-3  iso8859-9
dos855     dos865     iso8859-4  mac-roman
dos857     dos869     iso8859-5
```

TEMPPREFIX

TEMPPREFIX stores the directory configured for placement of AutoCAD's temporary files. The directory defaults to the current drawing directory. In the event of a system crash, you should look for any system files that are stored on the disk as files or file fragments.

2 Drawing-Mode Variables

The *drawing-mode variables* enable you to set the drawing environment's basic modes of operation and activate or deactivate some of Auto-CAD's command responses.

APERTURE

APERTURE controls the height, in pixels, of the snap target. The default value is 10. The target usually is made smaller to aid selection in dense drawings and larger to reduce the need for precise target placement in less dense drawings.

AUDITCTL

AUDITCTL controls the creation of an audit report file (*.ADT). An audit report file contains the results of the AUDIT commands, which checks the drawing database's integrity.

    0 = (the default). Disables the audit report file.
    1 = Enables the audit report file.

BLIPMODE

BLIPMODE controls the placement of pick marks made during cursor selection.

> 0 = No pick marks.
> 1 = (the default). Pick marks on.

CMDACTIVE

CMDACTIVE lists the type of command, if any, that is currently active. This information is useful when writing AutoLISP or ADS applications, and you need to know what the drafter is doing at any given moment.

CMDECHO

CMDECHO controls the echoing of prompts and input to the command line during AutoLISP routines. Developers frequently turn the echo off to speed up, and clean up the appearance of their applications.

> 0 = Command-line echo is off.
> 1 = (the default). Command-line echo is on.

CMDNAMES

CMDNAMES displays, in English, the name of the command, if any, that is currently active. Any transparent commands also are displayed. For example: **CIRCLE'PAN** indicates that the CIRCLE command has been issued, and that the PAN command is now being used transparently during the CIRCLE command. A response of "" (the default) indicates that no command is currently active.

COORDS

COORDS controls the coordinate display in the status line of the graphics screen. By default, the coordinate display is on and updates as the cursor is moved. If the coordinate display is turned off by using F6 or

^D, the coordinate display is updated only if a point is picked by using the cursor. If the coordinate display is turned back on by using F6 or ^D, then the coordinate display is updated as the cursor is moved and after a point is picked, the angle and distance of the cursor from the previous pick point will be shown during second point prompts. A final selection of F6 or ^D returns the coordinate display to its original status.

0 = Coordinate display is updated at pick points only.
1 = Coordinate display is continuously updated with absolute coordinates as the cursor is moved.
2 = Coordinate display is continuously updated with absolute coordinates as the cursor is moved. The coordinate display changes to angle and distance during second point prompts.

DWGCODEPAGE

DWGCODEPAGE stores the drawing-code page. DWGCODEPAGE is set to the value of SYSCODEPAGE when a drawing is started, but otherwise is not maintained. The code page identifies the keyboard character set or language being used. DWGCODEPAGE may be set to any of the values used by SYSCODEPAGE (see group 1 for values).

EXPERT

EXPERT suppresses or enables successive levels of prompts that AutoCAD uses to warn the user in the event of potentially dangerous editing. With each level of EXPERT, a new level of warning, plus all those previous to the level, are suppressed. Because of the far-reaching effects of some editing changes, EXPERT should be used with care.

0 = (the default) All prompts are issued as normal.
1 = Suppresses the regeneration and current layer off warnings.
2 = Suppresses the BLOCK and WBLOCK redefinition and overwrite prompts.

3 = Suppresses the linetype redefinition or reloading prompts.

4 = Suppresses the redefinition of UCS and viewport prompts.

5 = Suppresses the redefinition and override of dimension style prompts.

FILLMODE

FILLMODE controls the appearance of solids, traces, and polylines. With fill on, these entities are shown as solid where applicable. With fill off, the entities are shown as outlines.

0 = Fill is off.

1 = (the default). Fill is on.

HANDLES

HANDLES stores the results of the HANDLE command. If the HANDLES command is never used or is reused to turn drawing handles off, the HANDLES system variable will be 0 (the default). If the HANDLES command is used to turn the drawing handles on, the HANDLES system variable will be 1. *Drawing handles* are a hexidecimal number that is permanently assigned to an entity and remains with that entity even after the drawing is closed. Entity names also are hexidecimal codes that identify drawing entities, but they are not permanently stored with the drawing.

0 = (the default). Handles are disabled.

1 = Handles are enabled.

HIGHLIGHT

HIGHLIGHT controls the highlighting of selected entities.

> 0 = OFF. Highlighting is turned off.
> 1 = ON (the default). Highlighting is turned on.

 Grip-mode editing is not affected by HIGHLIGHT'S setting.

 Some display list drivers affect the appearance of highlighted entities. If HIGHLIGHT does not work consistently, you may be using a Display List Driver that disrupts HIGHLIGHT.

ORTHOMODE

ORTHOMODE controls the orthagonal drafting mode. With ORTHOMODE on, coordinate entry is read from the cursor along the 0, 90, 180, and 270 degree points only. After a point is picked, the rubberband cursor extends horizontally or vertically from the pickpoint to a crosshair line. The rubberband cursor extends to the farther crosshair.

> 0 = (the default). Orthogonal mode is turned off.
> 1 = Orthogonal mode is turned on.

OSMODE

OSMODE sets the object snap mode. The value can be any of the modes shown or a sum of any of the modes to make multiple selections.

> 0 = NONe (the default)   32 = INTersection
> 1 = ENDPoint   64 = INSertion

2 = MIDpoint	128 = PERpendicular
4 = CENter	256 = Tangent
8 = NODe	512 = NEArest
16 = QUAdrant	1024 = QUIck

REGENMODE

REGENMODE controls automatic regeneration. If REGENMODE is set to 1 (the default), AutoCAD performs a regeneration whenever the need arises. If REGENMODE is set to 0, you are prompted before AutoCAD performs a regeneration.

> 1 = ON. Drawing regeneration is automatic.
> 0 = OFF. Drawing regeneration will be prompted.

TILEMODE

TILEMODE controls the availability of paper space to maintain Release 10 compatibility. If TILEMODE is set to 1 (the default), you must work in model space. If you want viewports, use the VPORTS command. If TILEMODE is set to 0, you can go into paper space and use MVIEW to set up your viewports.

> 1 = ON. No paper space, use VPORTS.
> 2 = OFF. Paper space available, use MVIEW.

3 Entity-Mode Variables

The *entity-mode variables* control the attributes of entities drawn after the variables are set. You can reset the variables to apply different attributes, such as color or linetype, to different entities. Each of these variables can be set by using the DDEMODES command.

CECOLOR

CECOLOR sets the color for any entities that are drawn after
CECOLOR is set. The color can be BYLAYER (the default), BYBLOCK,
or, depending on the display driver, a string between 1 and 255.
BYLAYER color means the entity has the same color as the layer.
BYBLOCK means that the entity appears white until it is inserted into a
drawing, then the entity takes on the current color, either explicitly set
or the current layer color.

CELTYPE

CELTYPE sets the linetype for any entities drawn after CELTYPE is set.
The linetype can be provided by AutoCAD, user-defined, BYLAYER
(the default), or BYBLOCK. The 12 linetypes provided by AutoCAD are
stored in ACAD.LIN and, with the exception of continuous and hidden,
must be loaded with the LINETYPE command before they can be used
by the Layer Control dialog box.

CLAYER

CLAYER sets the layer for any entities drawn after CLAYER is set. All
drawings begin with a single layer 0 (the default). Any layers you want
to use after that must be created with the LAYER or DDLMODES
commands.

ELEVATION

ELEVATION sets the height, along the Z axis, of any entities drawn
after ELEVATION is set. The default is 0. No limits are set on the Z axis,
so the elevation has no practical limit. ELEVATION can be set with the
ELEV command or DDEMODES.

THICKNESS

THICKNESS sets the extrusion height, along the Z axis, of any entities drawn after THICKNESS is set. The default is 0. There are no limits set on the Z axis, so the thickness has no practical limit. THICKNESS can be set with the ELEV command, after ELEVATION, or with DDEMODES.

4 Limits and Extents

The *limits and extents variables* control the boundary of your drawing and AutoCAD's behavior in accordance with the boundary.

EXTMAX

EXTMAX is a World Coordinate System point that marks the uppermost right-hand corner of the drawing on the WCS X-Y plane for the current space. As the drawing expands along the positive Y axis or along the positive X axis, EXTMAX is recalculated. If entities are removed, EXTMAX is recalculated to a point closer to the origin when ZOOM All or ZOOM Extents is issued.

EXTMIN

EXTMIN is a World Coordinate System point that marks the lowermost left hand corner of the drawing on the WCS X-Y plane for the current space. As the drawing expands along the negative Y axis or along the negative X axis, EXTMIN is recalculated. If entities are removed, EXTMIN is recalculated to a point closer to the origin when ZOOM All or ZOOM Extents is issued.

LIMCHECK

LIMCHECK sets the limits checking for the current space, either model or paper. If LIMCHECK is on, AutoCAD will not accept points outside of the current limits.

0 = (the default). Limits checking is turned off.
1 = Limits checking turned on.

LIMMAX

LIMMAX is a World Coordinate System point that marks the upper-most right-hand point of the drawing limits on the WCS X-Y plane for the current space.

LIMMIN

LIMMIN is a World Coordinate System point that marks the lowermost left-hand point of the drawing limits on the WCS X-Y plane for the current space.

5 Line-Scale Variables

The *line-scale variables* control the model space and paper space linetype scaling.

LTSCALE

LTSCALE sets the global linetype scale for model space. The linetype scale determines how big the dashes and gaps are, in a line relative to the current drawing. LTSCALE may need to be set differently, depending on whether or not you want to view the drawing or plot it.

 If you wish to view the drawing, try an LTSCALE similar to your drawing scale. If you are going to plot the drawing, try an LTSCALE that is 0.3 to 0.5 times your drawing scale.

PSLTSCALE

PSLTSCALE controls the paper-space scaling of model-space lines. Because paper space is usually set up with a scale factor of 1:1, and you can have multiple viewports with different scales, linetype scaling is very important in paper space. If you want the linetypes in the MVIEW viewport to appear scaled, along with the other entities in the viewport, leave PSLTSCALE at the default setting of 1. If you do not want the linetype scaling to be controlled by the MVIEW viewport scaling, set PSLTSCALE to 0.

> 0 = Linetypes are not scaled, along with the MVIEW viewport.
> 1 = (the default) Linetypes are scaled, along with the MVIEW viewport.

6 Units Variables

The *units variables* control the units and degree of precision that AutoCAD uses. AutoCAD always maintains the same level of internal accuracy for calculations, but you can control the external appearance of the drawings units and precision. With the exception of UNITMODE, all of the variables can be set with the DDUNITS or UNITS commands (see fig. SV.1).

ANGBASE

ANGBASE sets the direction of angle 0 in the current UCS. The value can be anywhere from 0 (the default) to 360.

ANGDIR

ANGDIR sets the direction on angle measure in the current UCS.

> 0 = (the default). Counter-clockwise.
> 1 = Clockwise.

AUNITS

AUINITS sets the unit of measure for angular drawing.

> 0 = Decimal degrees (the default).
> 1 = Degrees/Minutes/Seconds.
> 2 = Grad.
> 3 = Radians.
> 4 = Surveyor's units.

AUPREC

AUPREC sets the precision, in decimal places, of angular measure. AutoCAD maintains the same level of internal accuracy. AUPREC affects the external appearance of angular measures. Valid entries are from 0 (the default) to 8.

LUNITS

LUINITS sets the unit of measure for linear drawing.

> 1 = Scientific.
> 2 = Decimal.
> 3 = Engineering.
> 4 = Architectural.
> 5 = Fractional.

LUPREC

LUPREC sets the precision, in decimal places, of linear measure. AutoCAD maintains the same level of internal accuracy. LUPREC affects the external appearance of linear measures. Valid entries are from 0 to 8; 4 is the default.

UNITMODE

UNITMODE controls the way AutoCAD displays fractional feet and inches and surveyor's angles. Because you cannot enter a space when entering coordinates, fractional feet and inches and surveyor's units use a hyphen or are run together. To make the output easier to read, AutoCAD can alter the input by adding spaces in the appropriate places. UNITMODE determines whether or not AutoCAD alters the input.

0 = (the default). AutoCAD alters the input.
1 = AutoCAD accepts the input and does not add spaces.

To make AutoCAD accept your fractional feet and inches input or surveyor's units as entered, set UNITMODE to 1.

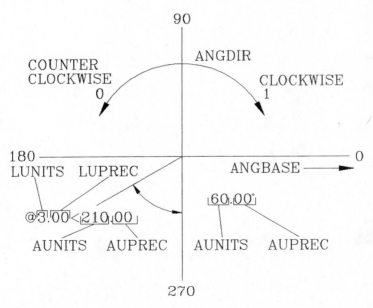

Figure SV.1:
Unit system variables.

7 Text Variables

The *text variables* control AutoCAD's text functions and the way other functions deal with text (see fig. SV.2).

MIRRTEXT

MIRRTEXT controls the results of the MIRROR command on text. By default, text is mirrored along with other entities. Because this can make the text difficult to read, MIRRTEXT enables you to prevent text from being reversed when it is copied with the MIRROR command.

    0 = Text is not reflected when copied by the MIRROR command.
    1 = Text is reflected when copied by the MIRROR command.

Dimension text is not affected by MIRRTEXT. Dimension text is never reflected when copied by the MIRROR command.

QTEXTMODE

QTEXTMODE controls the appearance of text. If QTEXTMODE is off (the default), text appears normally. If QTEXTMODE is on, text is replaced by a rectangle that redraws and regenerates faster than text.

    0 = OFF (the default). Text is shown normally.
    1 = ON. Text is replaced with a rectangle.

If you have a large amount of text in a drawing, and you need to see where it is but not what it says, you can use QTEXTMODE to display the text as rectangles. This will speed up redraws and regenerations of the drawing.

TEXTEVAL

TEXTEVAL controls the way text prompts interpret your entries. If TEXTEVAL is on (the default), all text beginning with "(" or "!" will be interpreted as an AutoLISP expression. If TEXTEVAL is off, all text is taken literally.

0 = OFF. Text is not evaluated for AutoLISP expressions.
1 = ON (the default). Text is evaluated for AutoLISP expressions.

 DTEXT takes all text input as literal, regardless of TEXTEVAL's setting.

TEXTSIZE

TEXTSIZE sets the height of text drawn after TEXTSIZE is set. TEXTSIZE does not affect the current text style's settings. The default value is 0.2000.

 If the current text style has a fixed height, TEXTSIZE is ignored.

TEXTSTYLE

TEXTSTYLE sets the current text style's name. The default is STANDARD. You can enter any defined style. Use the STYLE command to set or create text styles.

8 Drag-Mode Variables

The *drag-mode variables* control where and when AutoCAD redraws a selected image as the image is being dragged across the screen.

TEXTSIZE

TEXT TO MIRROR   TEXT TO MIRROR
TEXT TO MIRROR   TEXT TO MIRROR

MIRRTEXT 1   MIRRTEXT 0

SAMPLE TEXT
WITH QTEXTMODE
SET TO 0

QTEXTMODE 1   QTEXTMODE 0

Figure SV.2:
Text system variables.

DRAGMODE

DRAGMODE controls whether entities are shown as they are dragged into position. An example of this is the CIRCLE command. When you draw a circle, you are prompted for a center point, and then you can drag the circle in and out to set the radius. DRAGMODE can be set to one of three levels. If DRAGMODE is set to 0, all dragging is suppressed. If DRAGMODE is set to 1, dragging is enabled if you enter **DRAG** at the Command: prompt. If DRAGMODE is set to 2 (the default), the dragging is automatic and performed whenever possible.

    0 = OFF. All dragging is suppressed.
    1 = ON. Dragging is enabled when requested with DRAG.
    2 = Automatic (the default). Dragging is done whenever
        possible.

If you are dragging a complex entity, you can set DRAGMODE to 0 or 1 to stop automatic dragging and to speed up placement of the complex entity.

DRAGP1

DRAGP1 determines when an entity being dragged should be regenerated, based on a distance moved. The default is 10.

 If your digitizer has a tendency to twitch, you can set DRAGP1 to a high number to prevent regenerations quickly.

DRAGP2

DRAGP2 determines when an entity being dragged should be regenerated, based on a fast drag-sampling rate. The default is 25.

 If your digitizer has a high, fast motion setting, you can set DRAGP2 high to maintain speed in fast motion jumps.

9 Grid Mode Variables

The *grid-mode variables* control the existence and size of the background grid.

GRIDMODE

GRIDMODE controls the display of the grid. The grid also can be set by pressing F7, and the GRID and DDRMODES commands. The grid is altered only in the current viewport and is aligned with the current UCS.

0 = OFF (the default). The grid is off.
1 = ON. The grid is on.

By turning the grid on and off, or off and on, you can simulate a redraw without issuing the REDRAW command.

GRIDUNIT

GRIDPOINT sets the X and Y spacing for the grid in the current viewport.

10 Snap-Mode Variables

The *snap-mode variables* control the existence, origin, size, angle, and mode of the snap feature. These variables enable you to have a rotated grid plane or three isometric grid planes.

SNAPANG

SNAPANG sets the degree of rotation of the snap/grid, relative to the current UCS in the current viewport. Valid entries are from 0 to 360.

SNAPBASE

SNAPBASE sets the point of origin for the snap/grid in the current viewport with current UCS coordinates.

SNAPISOPAIR

SNAPISOPAIR sets the current isometric plane for the current viewport. The isometric snap style is set with SNAPSTYL, the Style option of the GRID command, or DDRMODES.

0 = Left plane (the default).
1 = Top plane.
2 = Right plane.

SNAPMODE

SNAPMODE turns the snap feature on and off for the current viewport.

0 = OFF (the default). Sets the snap off.
1 = ON. Sets the snap on.

SNAPSTYL

SNAPSTYL sets the snap to the default standard orthagonal mode or isometric mode.

0 = Standard mode.
1 = Isometric mode.

SNAPUNIT

SNAPUNIT sets the X and Y spacing for the current viewport.

11 Grip and Selection Variables

The *grip variables* and *selection variables* control the appearance and behavior of grips, selected entities, and selection modes. Many of these variables are new for Release 12. For additional information see Chapter 4.

GRIPBLOCK

GRIPBLOCK controls the appearance of grips in blocks. If you set GRIPBLOCK to 1, all of the entities in the block will be assigned grips.

0 = OFF (the default). Displays a grip at the block
insertion point only.
1 = ON. Displays a grip for each element in the block.

GRIPCOLOR

GRIPCOLOR sets the color of unselected grips. Unselected grips are
drawn as a box outline. The default color is 5. Valid entries are an
integer from 1 to 255.

GRIPHOT

GRIPHOT sets the color for selected grips. A selected grip is drawn as a
solid box. The default color is 1. Valid entries are an integer from 1 to
255.

GRIPS

GRIPS enables or disables grip mode editing. Grip mode editing enables you to use grips to create a selection set and enter STRETCH,
MOVE, ROTATE, SCALE, and MIRROR edit modes.

0 = OFF. Disables grip-mode editing.
1 = ON (the default). Enables grip-mode editing.

GRIPSIZE

GRIPSIZE controls the size of the grips in pixels. The default value is 3.
Valid entries are an integer from 1 to 255.

PICKADD

PICKADD controls the selection of entities using noun/verb selection.
If PICKADD is set to 0, each selection replaces the last selection set
rather than being added to it. Entities can be added to a selection set if

you press and hold the Shift key while making selections. If PICKADD is set to 1 (the default), each selected entity is added to the selection set. You can use the Shift pick to remove selected entities from the set.

PICKAUTO

PICKAUTO controls automatic windowing when selecting entities. If PICKAUTO is off, you must click directly on an entity at the Select objects: prompt to select it. After you click once, automatic windowing is returned as a selection method. If PICKAUTO is on, you can window objects at the Select objects: prompt without issuing a Window or Crossing option.

> 0 = OFF. Disables automatic windowing at the Select objects: prompt for the first selection.
> 1 = ON (the default). Enables automatic windowing at the Select objects: prompt.

PICKBOX

PICKBOX controls the height of the object-selection target box in pixels.

PICKDRAG

PICKDRAG controls the method used to draw an automatic selection window. If PICKDRAG is 0 (the default), you draw a window by clicking at one corner, moving the digitizer, and clicking at the opposite corner. If PICKDRAG is 1, you draw a window by clicking and holding the digitizer button at one corner, moving the digitizer, and releasing the button at the opposite corner.

> 0 = OFF (the default). Automatic windows are drawn with two separate clicks.
> 1 = ON. Automatic windows are drawn with a click and hold, then move, then release.

PICKFIRST

PICKFIRST controls the noun/verb selection of entities before editing. If PICKFIRST is 0, you must enter an editing command before you begin selecting entities. If PICKFIRST is 1, you can select entities (the noun) and then enter an editing command (the verb). The previously selected entities are automatically selected by the editing command.

> 0 = OFF. Disables noun/verb selection.
> 1 = ON (the default). Enables noun/verb selection.

SORTENTS

SORTENTS controls the order in which the drawing database is sorted. Release 12 uses an *octal tree* to store the entities on the virtual screen. The virtual screen is divided into rectangular regions and subregions. The entities are stored in an eight-level tree based on their region and subregion location. Because entities are stored based on their location, object selection, zooming, regeneration, and redrawing are much faster. If, however, you need the entities to be sorted by their order of creation rather than by their location, you can reset SORTENTS. You can enter one of the following options or the sum of the options you would like to use:

> 0 = Disables SORTENTS, the octal tree sorting is used for every AutoCAD function.
> 1 = Sort for object selection. This turns octal-tree sorting off when selecting objects, so that the most recently drawn item is selected when two or more entities overlap at the selection point.
> 2 = Sort for object snap. This turns octal-tree sorting off when object snaps are in use. This enables the QUIck object snap to find the most recently drawn entity.
> 4 = SOrt for redraws. This turns the octal tree off when the drawing is redrawn. This is done only if it is important that the objects be redrawn in their order of creation.

8 = Sort for MSLIDE slide creation. This turns octal-tree sorting off when a slide is displayed with MSLIDE. This is done when you need the slide to be drawn in the order in which component parts were drawn.

16 = Sort for regeneration. This turns octal-tree sorting off when the drawing regenerates. This is done when it is important that the entities be regenerated in the order of their creation.

32 = Sort for plotting. This turns octal-tree sorting off when plotting. This usually is not a concern because both AutoCAD and most plotters have their own entity-sort routines. This is important if you are plotting to an image file and you need the entities to be drawn in the order of their creation. The default is on.

64 = Sort for PostScript output. This turns octal-tree sorting off when using PostScript output commands. This is done so the entities are drawn in the order of their creation.

The Entity Sort Method button in the Entity Selection Settings dialog box enables you to set SORTENTS with a dialog box.

12 Drawing-Function Variables

The *drawing-function variables* store the default values of the drawing and editing functions, such as radii, diameters, width, and distances. These variables enable AutoCAD to remember your last entry in a drawing command and use it as the default the next time you use the command. Some of these variables are new for Release 12, reflecting AutoCAD's increased flexibility and access to environment settings (see fig. SV.3).

CHAMFERA

CHAMFERA sets the default distance to trim the first line selected when using the CHAMFER command. Each use of CHAMFER resets the value.

CHAMFERB

CHAMFERB sets the default distance to trim the second line selected when using the CHAMFER command. Each use of CHAMFER resets the value.

CIRCLERAD

CIRCLERAD holds the default circle radius. Each use of CIRCLE resets the value. To specify no default, enter **0**.

DONUTID

DONUTID sets the default interior diameter of a DONUT. The value can be 0 to create a solid fill circle.

DONUTOD

DONUTOD sets the default outside diameter of a DONUT. The value must be greater than 0. If the value of DONUTID is greater than DONUTOD, the values are switched and used as defaults for the next DONUT command.

FILLETRAD

FILLETRAD sets the default radius of the FILLET command. To specify no radius, enter **0**.

OFFSETDIST

OFFSETDIST sets the default distance for the OFFSET command. To offset through a point, enter a negative number. The initial default is -1.0000 (for through).

POLYSIDES

POLYSIDES stores the default number of sides to a POLYGON. Valid entries are an integer between three and 1024.

TRACEWID

TRACEWID stores the default width of the TRACE command.

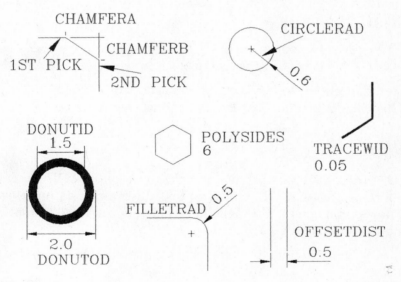

Figure SV.3:
Drawing function system variables

1151

13 Menu and Dialog-Box Variables

The *menu variables* and *dialog-box variables* control the behavior or access to information on, AutoCAD's GUI. About half of them are new for Release 12. You probably will not need to change these variables unless you are developing an application.

CMDDIA

CMDDIA controls whether or not the PLOT command issues a series of prompts or uses dialog boxes.

> 0 = Prompt for PLOT settings.
> 1 = (the default). Use dialog boxes for PLOT settings.

DIASTAT

DIASTAT holds the exit status of the last dialog box. If the dialog box is canceled, DIASTAT is 0. If the dialog box is accepted, DIASTAT is 1.

> 0 = Cancel. The last dialog box was canceled.
> 1 = Ok (the default). The last dialog box was accepted.

FILEDIA

FILEDIA controls the availability of dialog boxes. If FILEDIA is set to 1, dialog boxes is used. If FILEDIA is set to 0, the command prompt is used unless you enter a tilde (~). Then, dialog boxes are used for that prompt or command.

> 0 = OFF. Do not use dialog boxes unless they are requested
> with a tilde (~).
> 1 = ON (the default). Use dialog boxes if they exist.

The PLOT and Enter Attribute dialog boxes are controlled by independent variables. CMDDIA controls the PLOT dialog box; ATTDIA controls the Enter Attributes dialog box.

MAXSORT

MAXSORT holds the maximum number of elements that can be in a list if AutoCAD is to sort the list. If the number of elements in the list is greater than MAXSORT, the list is not sorted at all.

MENUCTL

MENUCTL controls screen menu page-swapping in response to keyboard entry. If MENUCTL is off, the screen menu does not change based on keyboard entry. If MENUCTL is on (the default), the screen menu shows the option menus as keyboard entry is made.

> 0 = OFF. The screen menu does not switch pages to display options based on keyboard entry.
> 1 = ON (the default). The screen menu switches pages to display options based on keyboard entry.

MENUECHO

MENUECHO controls the echoing of menu commands to the Command: prompt. This is used to clean up the display of menus as they run commands, macros, and AutoLISP expressions. You can enter one of the following values or the sum of some of the values to get a combined effect:

> 0 = No suppression (the default).
> 1 = Suppresses echoing of all menu items. ^P turns this setting on and off in individual menus.
> 2 = Suppresses the display of system prompts and some AutoLISP prompts issued by menus.

4 = Prevents ^P from turning menu echo on and off.
8 = Echoes DIESEL input and output for debugging
    DIESEL code.

 If you set MENUECHO to 3, output from the PROMPT
AutoLISP function is not displayed.

MENUNAME

MENUNAME contains the name of the current menu file, as entered
when the menu was loaded.

POPUPS

POPUPS lists the availability of the Advanced User Interface. The
Advanced User Interface consists of dialog boxes, pull-down menus, the
menu bar, and icon menus. This is useful for applications that must
determine the best possible method of user interface.

0 = OFF. The Advanced User Interface is not available.
1 = ON (the default). The Advanced User Interface is available.

SCREENBOXES

SCREENBOXES holds the number of boxes available for menu items in
the screen-menu area. If the screen menu has been removed during
configuration, SCREENBOXES are set to 0. Some AutoCAD platforms
allow the graphics window to be resized, or the screen menu to be
reconfigured, during an editing session. Both of these occurrences may
cause a change in the size of the screen area and thus SCREENBOXES.
The default is 26.

TABMODE

TABMODE controls the use of tablet mode. When tablet mode is on, the screen-pointing area of the tablet performs like a digitizer rather than a screen pointing device. The digitizer is calibrated to the scale of the drawing to be digitized so the drawing created in AutoCAD is drawn in true size. When tablet mode is off (the default), the screen area of the digitizer is not scaled and represents the portion of the drawing on the screen.

  0 = OFF (the default). Turns the tablet off.
  1 = ON. Turns the tablet on.

14 Screen-Mode Variables

The *screen-mode variables* control the size and access to graphic viewports and the text screen.

SCREENMODE

SCREENMODE lists the active screen mode or window. The value is one of the following or the sum of some of the options. SCREENMODE is useful when an application needs to determine which screen the user is currently viewing.

  0 = The text screen is being displayed (the default).
  1 = The graphics screen is being displayed.
  2 = There is a dual screen display.

SCREENSIZE

SCREENSIZE lists the size of the current viewport for the X and Y axis in pixels. SCREENSIZE can be used by an application to determine proper scaling of graphic entities drawn with low-level graphic functions such as GRDRAW.

15 Point Variables

The *point variables* control the size, orientation, and appearance of point entities.

PDMODE

PDMODE controls the appearance of points. The value can be any one of the following:

    0 = A dot (the default).
    1 = Nothing.
    2 = A plus (+).
    3 = An X.
    4 = A short vertical line from the point up 90 degrees.

You can add any one of the following values to those above to draw a figure around the point:

    32 = A circle.
    64 = A square.
    96 = A circle and a square.

PDSIZE

PDSIZE controls the size of points drawn.

    0 = (the default). The point is drawn at 5% of the graphic area's height.
    >0 = The point is drawn at the absolute size specified
    <0 = The point is a percentage of the viewport height.

> **NOTE** If the value of PDSIZE is negative, the point retains its appearance as the viewport is zoomed in and out, provided that the viewport is regenerated. If the viewport does not regenerate, you can enter **REGEN** to make the points adjust their size according to the new zoom factor.

The Point Style dialog box shows all of the available point styles. The top row of points shows the point for the values 0 to 4. The next three rows show the effect of adding 32, 64, and 96 to the point values. The Point Size edit box and the Absolute and Relative radio buttons control the settings for PDSIZE. A positive value for PDSIZE indicates an absolute point size. A negative value for PDSIZE indicates a relative point size.

16 UCS Variables

The *UCS variables* control and store information on the Use Coordinate System. These variables usually are set by AutoCAD commands, as opposed to direct access by the variable's name or by SETVAR. The values stored in these variables are very important to any drafter, but are particularly useful to 3D drafters. Most of these variables can be set by using the UCS command.

UCSFOLLOW

UCSFOLLOW controls AutoCAD's automatic display of the PLAN view when the UCS changes. UCSFOLLOW is stored separately for model space and paper space, but in paper space the value is always treated as if it is 0.

> 0 = OFF (the default). A change in the UCS does not cause AutoCAD to change the display to the PLAN view for the new UCS.
> 1 = ON. A change in the UCS causes AutoCAD to change the display to the PLAN view for the new UCS.

UCSICON

UCSICON controls the display of the UCS icon. The value can be any of the following values or the sum of the desired options:

0 = OFF. The UCS icon is not displayed.
1 = ON (the default). The UCS icon is displayed.
2 = Origin. If UCSICON is on, the UCS icon is placed on the UCS origin, if possible, in the current display.

UCSNAME

UCSNAME holds the name of the current UCS. If the UCS is unnamed, the value is "".

UCSORG

UCSORG holds a World Coordinate System (WCS) point that is the origin of the current UCS.

UCSXDIR

UCSXDIR holds a WCS point. A vector drawn from the WCS origin to the UCSXDIR points in the X direction of the current UCS.

UCSYDIR

UCSYDIR holds a WCS point. A vector drawn from the WCS origin to the UCSYDIR points in the Y direction of the current UCS.

WORLDUCS

WORLDUCS tells whether the current UCS is the same as the WCS.

0 = The current UCS is not the same as the WCS.
1 = (the default). The current UCS is the same as the WCS.

17 Undo Variables

The *undo variables* control the behavior of the UNDO command.

UNDOCTL

UNDOCTL controls how much the UNDO command will undo. The value can be any of the following or the sum of the desired options. The default is 5:

> 0 = OFF. UNDO is disabled.
> 1 = ON. UNDO is enabled.
> 2 = Undo only one command.
> 4 = Each function is considered a single command, no matter how many commands it may contain. For example, a menu item is treated as a single command, even if it performs multiple tasks.
> 8 = The Group option of the UNDO command is currently active.

UNDOMARKS

UNDOMARKS holds the number of marks placed in the command stream being recorded by UNDO. Marks are placed by using the Mark option of the UNDO command. If the Group option of the UNDO command is in use, the Mark and Back options cannot be used.

18 Data and List Variables

The *data variables* and *list variables* store and provide access to information gathered by the inquiry commands. With the exception of LASTPOINT, these variables are all read-only.

AREA

AREA stores the area value calculated by the last AREA, LIST, or DBLIST command. The value is listed in square drawing units.

DISTANCE

DISTANCE stores the value calculated by the last DIST command. The value is listed in linear drawing units.

LASTANGLE

LASTANGLE stores the end angle of the last arc drawn. The *end angle* is relative to the current UCS for the current space (model or paper).

LASTPOINT

LASTPOINT stores the last point selected. The point is listed in current UCS coordinates for the current space (model or paper). The LASTPOINT is accessed by entering an AT sign (@) at the `Command:` prompt.

If you want to establish the coordinates of a specific point in the drawing, use the ID command. LASTPOINT is set to the value returned by ID.

PERIMETER

PERIMETER stores the perimeter value calculated by the last AREA, LIST, or DBLIST command. The value is listed in linear drawing units.

19 Face, Surface, and Polyline Variables

The *face variables*, *surface variables*, and *polyline variables* affect a wide variety of settings, mostly in 3D drawing. While polylines often are used in 2D drawing, their system variables are included here because polylines often are necessary for the 3D entities that the other variables affect (see figs. SV.4, SV.5, and SV.6).

PFACEVMAX

PFACEMAX stores the maximum number of vertices per face allowed in a PFACE.

PLINEGEN

PLINEGEN controls the linetype generation in 2D polylines. If PLINEGEN is set to 0 (the default), each line segment is considered separate when linetypes are applied to the polyline. If PLINEGEN is set to 1, the vertices of the polyline are ignored, and the linetype generation is applied to the entire line from beginning to end.

> 0 = OFF (the default). Each vertex-defined line segment is individually considered as linetypes are applied.
> 1 = ON. The vertices are ignored and the entire polyline is considered when linetypes are applied.

PLINEGEN does not affect polylines with tapered segments.

For smoother overall appearance of a linetype on a polyline, set PLINEGEN to 1.

PLINEWID

PLINEWID sets the default width of a polyline. The default is 0.

SPLFRAME

SPLFRAME controls the appearance of polylines and meshes. If SPLFRAME is 0 (the default), a splined polyline or smoothed mesh is shown without the original lines that define the polyline or mesh. Invisible edges in 3D faces also are left invisible. If SPLFRAME is 1, the original polyline or mesh is retained when a splined polyline of smoothed mesh is generated. Invisible edges of 3D faces are displayed.

SPLINESEGS

SPLINESEGS sets the number of line or arc segments used in each curve of a splined 2D or 3D polyline. If SPLINESEGS is negative, the absolute value of SPLINESEGS is used to determine the number of segments, but arcs are used instead of lines, creating a fit curve. If SPLINESEGS is positive, then line segments are used to generate a spline curve.

A negative value for SPLINESEGS does not create a fit curve on 3D polylines. A spline curve is used instead.

SPLINETYPE

SPLINETYPE sets the type of spline curve applied by the PEDIT command. The value can be one of the following:

    5 = Quadratic B-spline.
    6 = Cubic B-spline (the default).

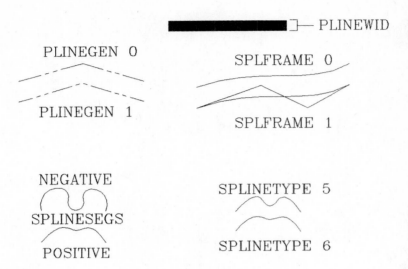

Figure SV.4:
Spline system variables.

SURFTAB1

SURFTAB1 sets the number of tabulated surfaces generated by the RULESURF and TABSURF commands. SURFTAB1 also sets the mesh density along the M axis for the EDGESURF and REVSURF commands.

SURFTAB2

SURFTAB2 sets the mesh density along the N axis for the EDGESURF and REVSURF commands.

The higher the setting you use for SURFTAB1 and SURFTAB2, the smoother your image is. The lower the setting, the faster your drawing regenerates.

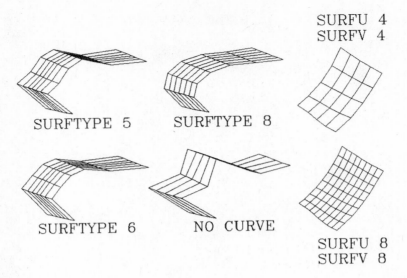

Figure SV.5:
Drawing function system variables.

SURFTYPE

SURFTYPE sets the type of smoothing used by the Smooth option of the PEDIT command when a 3D MESH is selected. The value can be one of the following:

    5 = Quadratic B-spline surface.
    6 = Cubic B-spline surface.
    8 = Beizier surface.

> **NOTE** Quadratic smoothing requires at least three points in each direction on the 3D surface mesh.
>
> Cubic smoothing requires at least four points in each direction on the 3D surface mesh.

Bezier smoothing is limited to meshes with no more than 11 points along the M or N axis.

SURFU

SURFU sets the density in the M direction on 3D MESHES. Valid entries are an integer from 2 to 200. The default is 6.

SURFV

SURFV sets the density in the M direction on 3D MESHES. Valid entries are an integer from 2 to 200. The default is 6.

The higher the setting you use for SURFU and SURFV, the smoother your image is. The lower the setting, the faster your drawing regenerates.

20 Hatching Variables

The hatching variables control the behavior of the HATCH and BHATCH commands. All of these variables are new for Release 12. This reflects the improvements made in hatching by the introduction of the BHATCH command.

HPANG

HPANG sets the default hatch-pattern angle.

HPDOUBLE

HPDOUBLE sets the default for hatch pattern doubling of user-defined hatch patterns. Doubling causes a second set of hatch lines to be drawn at 90 degrees to the original hatch pattern.

HPNAME

HPNAME sets the default hatch-pattern name. To set a default of no pattern name, enter a period (.), and HPNAME will be set to " ". The name can be up to 34 characters long.

HPSCALE

HPSCALE sets the default scale factor for hatch patterns. The value must be non-zero.

HPSPACE

HPSPACE sets the default distance between lines in a user-defined hatch pattern. The value must be non-zero.

21 Insert Variables

The insert variables control the name and location of inserted entities.

INSBASE

INSBASE sets a current UCS 3D point in the current space as the insertion-base point for a drawing file. The default value is the WCS origin 0,0,0.

INSNAME

INSNAME sets the default block name used by the INSERT and DDINSERT commands. The name cannot exceed 31 characters. Valid characters are letters, digits, and the dollar sign ($), hyphen (-), and underscore (_) characters. The name cannot include any eight-bit characters. Eight-bit characters use the character codes from 127 to 255. On DOS platforms, AutoCAD uses the extended IBM character set (DOS 850 code page). On UNIX and Windows systems, AutoCAD uses the ISO 8859/1 code page. To enter a default of no name, enter a period (.), INSNAME will be set to " ". After you enter the name, AutoCAD converts the name to all uppercase.

SHPNAME

SHPNAME sets the default block name used by the SHAPE command. The name cannot exceed 31 characters. Valid characters are letters, digits, and the dollar sign ($), hyphen (-), and underscore (_) characters. The name cannot include any eight-bit characters. Eight-bit characters use the character codes from 127 to 255. On DOS platforms, AutoCAD uses the extended IBM character set (DOS 850 code page). On UNIX and Windows systems, AutoCAD uses the ISO 8859/1 code page. To enter a default of no name, enter a period (.), SHPNAME will be set to " ". After you enter the name, AutoCAD converts the name to all uppercase.

22 Xref Variables

The xref variables control the behavior of external reference drawings.

VISRETAIN

VISRETAIN controls the behavior of the external referenced layer settings ON/OFF, Freeze/Thaw, Color, and Linetype. If VISRETAIN is set to 0 (the default), any changes to externally referenced layer settings are saved in the external reference file. If VISRETAIN is set to 1, any changes to externally referenced layer settings are not saved in the external reference file. These changes are good for the current drawing session only.

> 0 = OFF (the default). Changes to external reference layer settings for ON/OFF, Freeze/Thaw, Color, and Linetype are saved in the externally referenced file.
> 1 = ON (the default). Changes to external reference layer settings for ON/OFF, Freeze/Thaw, Color, and Linetype are not saved in the externally referenced file.

XREFCTL

XREFCTL controls whether external reference log files (XLG) are written. The log file is created and then appended every time the Attach, Detach, and Reload options of the XREF command are used. The log file records the drawing name, the date and time of the operation, and the operation type. The XLG file name will be the same as the drawing.

 AutoCAD continues to append to a log file once it is created. You should be careful to delete old XLG files or edit existing ones to prevent them from becoming too large.

23 Attribute Variables

The attribute variables control the existence of attributes and their display and editing properties. See Chapter 5 for more information on attributes.

AFLAGS

AFLAGS sets the attribute flag for the ATTDEF and DDATTDEF commands. The value can be one of the following or the sum of any of the desired values.

    0 = (the default). No attribute modes are selected.
    1 = The attribute value will be invisible.
    2 = The attribute value will be constant.
    4 = Verify the attribute value by reentering the value.
    8 = The attribute value is preset.

ATTDIA

ATTDIA controls the use of the Enter Attributes dialog box when inserting blocks with attributes.

0 = OFF (the default). Use the `Command:` prompt to prompt for attribute values.

1 = ON. Use the Enter Attributes dialog box when inserting blocks with attributes.

ATTMODE

ATTMODE controls the display of attribute values. The value can be one of the following:

0 = OFF. All attribute values are invisible.

1 = Normal, (the default). Attribute values are displayed according to their definition.

2 = ON. All attribute values are visible.

ATTREQ

ATTREQ controls the prompting for attribute values when a block with attributes is inserted.

0 = OFF. Default values are used for all attributes.

1 = ON (the default). You are prompted for values when a block with attributes is inserted.

24 Sketching Variables

The sketching variables control the behavior of the SKETCH command.

SKETCHINC

SKETCHINC sets the SKETCH record increment.

 If you move the cursor fast enough, you can create sketch segments that are longer than the SKETCH record increment. This will not reset the value of SKETCHINC.

SKPOLY

SKPOLY controls the use of lines versus polylines when the SKETCH command is in use.

> 0 = OFF (the default). Lines are drawn by the SKETCH command.
> 1 = ON. Polylines are drawn by the SKETCH command.

25 View and Viewport Variables

The view and viewport variables control the existence, size, and number of views and viewports.

CVPORT

CVPORT lists the identification number of the current viewport.

MAXACTVP

MAXACTVP sets the maximum number of viewports to regenerate. The default is 16.

VIEWCTR

VIEWCTR holds the center point of the current viewport as a current UCS point.

VIEWSIZE

VIEWSIZE holds the height of the current viewport in drawing units.

VSMAX

VSMAX holds the upper right corner of the current viewport's virtual screen. The point is in the current UCS. This point changes as the view is zoomed and regenerated.

VSMIN

VSMIN holds the lower left corner of the current viewport's virtual screen. The point is in the current UCS. This point changes as the view is zoomed and regenerated.

 To prevent time-consuming drawing regenerations, avoid zooming beyond the edge of the current virtual screen, as defined by VSMAX and VSMIN.

26 Dview Variables

The dview variables control the behavior of the DVIEW command. These variables are all read-only, so they are set by other commands.

BACKZ

BACKZ holds the distance in drawing units from the target plane to the back clipping plane.

 BACKZ will have no effect if VIEWMODE does not include the four-bit code for back plane clipping.

FRONTZ

FRONTZ holds the distance in drawing units from the target plane to the front clipping plane.

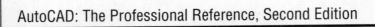

 BACKZ will have no effect if VIEWMODE does not include the two-bit code for front plane clipping and the 16-bit code for front clip not at eye.

LENSLENGTH

LENSLENGTH holds the length of the lens used for perspective viewing with the Distance option of the DVIEW command. The length is expressed in millimeters.

TARGET

TARGET holds the target point of the current viewport as a current UCS 3D point. The target is the point in the viewport you are looking directly at from the camera point.

VIEWDIR

VIEWDIR holds the camera point of the current viewport as a current UCS 3D point. The camera is the point in space from which you look at the target point.

VIEWMODE

VIEWMODE controls the view mode for the current viewport as a result of the DVIEW command. The value can be one of the following or the sum of the desired options.

    0 = OFF (the default). Viewing is normal.
    1 = Perspective mode is active.
    2 = Front clipping is allowed.
    4 = Back clipping is allowed.
    8 = The UCS follow mode is on.

16 = The front clip plane is offset the distance in FRONTZ from the target plane rather than at the camera point stored in VIEWDIR.

VIEWTWIST

VIEWTWIST holds the twist angle for the current viewport. The twist angle enables you to twist the view around the current line of sight from the camera point to the target point. The twist angle is measured in degrees, counter-clockwise from 0, which always begins to the right.

WORLDVIEW

WORLDVIEW controls the automatic changing of the UCS to the WCS during the DVIEW and VPOINT commands. Both commands expect input to be relative to the current UCS so, by default, the current UCS changes to the WCS for ease of use.

0 = OFF. The current UCS is not changed to the WCS when the DVIEW or VPOINT commands are issued.
1 = ON (the default). The current UCS is changed to the WCS when the DVIEW or VPOINT commands are issued.

 If you are more comfortable entering values to the DVIEW and VPOINT commands from the current UCS rather than from the WCS, set WORLDVIEW to 0.

27 Shading Variables

The shading variables control the appearance of objects rendered with the SHADE command.

1173

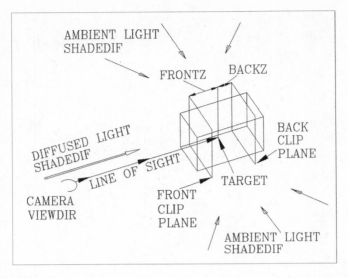

Figure SV.6:
Drawing function system variables.

SHADEDGE

SHADEEDGE controls the appearance of surface edges and faces when using the SHADE command. Valid entries are the following:

> 0 = Faces are shaded; edges are not highlighted.
> 1 = Faces are shaded; edges are drawn in the background color.
> 2 = Faces are not shaded, edges are drawn in the entity color.
> 3 = (the default). Faces are shaded in the entity color; edges are drawn in the background color.

SHADEDIF

SHADEDIF sets the percentage of diffused reflective light versus ambient light in the drawing. Diffused reflective light comes directly from the light source, which is at the camera point. Ambient light has no source, so it lights all surfaces to the same degree. As the diffused reflective light is increased or decreased, the ambient light is decreased or increased so that the light level is maintained at 100%.

28 Plotting Variables

The plotting variables control which plotter is made the default.

PLOTID

PLOTID sets the current plotter, based on its assigned description. Plotter descriptions are set when the plotter is added to the configuration.

PLOTTER

PLOTTER sets the current plotter, based on its assigned ID number. Plotter numbers are set when the plotter is added to the configuration. The value can be from 0 to the highest number of plotters currently configured. The maximum number of plotters is 29.

29 PostScript Variables

PostScript variables control the behavior of the PostScript commands. Both importing and exporting of PostScript images can be affected. For more information on PostScript output, see Chapter 11 on file import and export.

PSPROLOG

PSPROLOG sets which prologue section from the ACAD.PSF file is added to your PostScript output when you use PSOUT. Prologue codes are added to customize your PostScript output.

PSQUALITY

PSQUALITY controls the appearance of PostScript images when they are imported into AutoCAD with the PSIN command.

> 0 = Disables PostScript image generation. PostScript images are shown as a box outline.
>
> Positive = Determines the number of pixels per drawing unit that are used to render the PostScript image. The image will be filled.
>
> Negative = The absolute value of PSQUALITY determines the number of pixels per drawing unit that are used to render the PostScript image. The image is rendered as outlines only; it will not be filled.

30 File-Name and Saving Variables

The file-name and saving variables control the file-access feature of AutoCAD. All of the variables are read-only, so they are set with other commands.

DWGNAME

DWGNAME holds the drawing name entered by the user, including any path the user may have entered. If the drawing has not been named, the default value is UNNAMED.

DWGPREFIX

DWGPREFIX holds the drive and directory prefix for the drawing. This enables you to determine the current working directory.

DWGTITLED

DWGTITLED lists whether or not the drawing has been named.

0 = OFF (the default). The drawing has not been named.
1 = ON. The drawing has been named.

DWGWRITE

DWGWRITE holds the value of the read-only feature of the Open Drawing dialog box.

0 = OFF. Open the drawing for reading only; no editing is allowed.
1 = (the default). Open the drawing for reading and writing.

SAVEFILE

SAVEFILE holds the name of the current file name used by the automatic-save feature. The default is AUTO.SV$.

SAVENAME

SAVENAME holds the name to which you have saved the drawing. The default is " ".

SAVETIME

SAVETIME sets the length of time, in minutes, between automatic saves of the current drawing to the automatic-save file name stored in SAVEFILE. To disable the automatic-save feature, set SAVETIME to 0. The save-time counter begins after a change to the drawing, and is reset when AutoCAD initiates an automatic save or when the user issues a SAVE, SAVEAS, or QSAVE command.

31 Database Variables

The database variables control the structure, and thus the search speed, of the drawing database. They also indicate the level of change in the database as a result of editing.

DBMOD

DBMOD indicates the level of modification to the current drawing. DBMOD will be the sum of following options that are selected:

1 = The entity database has been modified.
2 = The symbol table has been modified.
4 = A database variables has been modified.
8 = A window has been modified.
16 = A view has been modified.

TREEDEPTH

TREEDEPTH sets the maximum number of spatial indexes or levels in the graphic tree. AutoCAD indexes entities based on their graphic location in a two-branch tree. One branch is a quad tree for paper space and the other is a quad (for 2D) or octal (for 3D) tree for model space. The first two characters in TREEDEPTH specify the maximum number of levels in the model-space tree. The second two characters specify the maximum number of levels in the paper-space tree.

The tree performs best when it has more levels because there are fewer entities per level, which speeds searching. Unfortunately, the larger the tree, the more memory it takes that can cause disk-swapping and can negate any speed gains.

Usually you do not need to adjust the tree unless you have very little memory or very few entities compared to the amount of memory. If you have very little memory, you may need to shrink the tree to reduce the amount of memory it takes. If you have lots of memory, you can increase the depth of the tree to increase search speed.

TREEMAX

TREEMAX sets a limit on the maximum number of nodes or levels in the graphic tree for the current memory configuration.

32 User-Assigned Variables

The user-assigned variables are no default value, and are intended for third-party developers. These variables are used to store numeric and string information with no direct effect on the drawing.

USERI1-5

USERI1-5 are five integer variables with no default value. They are saved with the drawing, and are intended for use by third-party developers.

USERR1-5

USERR1-5 are five real variables with no default value. They are saved with the drawing, and are intended for use by third-party developers.

USERS1-5

USERS1-5 are five string variables with no default value. They are not saved with the drawing, and are intended for use by third-party developers.

33 Macro Variables

The macro variables control the behavior of DIESEL expressions in macros.

MACROTRACE

MACROTRACE controls the display of DIESEL expression evaluations. This is a debugging tool for DIESEL expressions.

> 0 = OFF (the default). MACROTRACE is disabled.
> 1 = ON. An evaluation of all DIESEL strings is displayed at the `Command:` prompt.

MODEMACRO

MODEMACRO controls the display of strings and DIESEL expressions on the status line. You can enter a string or a DIESEL expression.

34 Date and Time Variables

The date and time variables store information on the dates, times, and durations of an editing session. All of the variables are read-only, so they must be set by other commands.

CDATE

CDATE is the current date and time in calendar format. Calendar format is a real number with the following values:

YYYYMMDD.HHMMSSmsec

YYYY = Year
MM = Month
DD = Day
HH = Hour
MM = Minutes
SS = Seconds
msec = milliseconds

DATE

DATE is the current date and time in Julian-date format. Hours, minutes, and seconds are displayed in decimal format.

TDCREATE

TDCREATE stores the drawing-creation date as a Julian number.

TDINDWG

TDINDWG stores the total time that the drawing spends in the drawing editor in numbers of days.

TDUPDATE

TDUPDATE stores the date and time of the last drawing update as a Julian date.

TDUSTIMER

TDUSTIMER stores the elapsed time of the current drawing session in number of days.

35 Error Variables

The error variables give information on on-line program errors and the capability to reset those errors relative to peripheral input/output. For a complete listing of error codes, see Chapter 13 on error messages.

ERRNO

ERRNO stores the error code produced by on-line applications such as AutoLISP and ADS programs.

RE-INIT

RE-INIT reinitializes peripherals and the ACAD.PGP file. Valid entries are any of the following, or a sum of the desired options:

> 1 = Reinitialize the digitizer port.
> 2 = Reinitialize the plotter port.
> 4 = Reinitialize the digitizer.
> 8 = Reinitialize the display.
> 16 = Reload the ACAD.PGP file.

Index

C

G

H

J-K

L

M

AUPREC, 1138
LUNITS, 1138
LUPREC, 1138
UNITMODE, 1138
user-assigned
USERI1-5, 1179
USERR1-5, 1179
USERS1-5, 1179
view/viewport
CVPORT, 1170
MAXACTVP, 1170
VIEWCTR, 1170
VIEWSIZE, 1170
VSMAX, 1171
VSMIN, 1171
XRECTL, 155
xref
VISRETAIN, 1167
XREFCTL, 1168
system-setting variables
ACADPREFIX, 1126-1127
ACADVER, 1127
LOGINNAME, 1127
PLATFORM, 1127
SYSCODEPAG, 1127-1128
TEMPPREFIX, 1128

T

tables, 291
creating, 324-325
in databases, 502-504
current, 297, 311
data
deleting from databases, 474-475
entering, 322
deleting from DBMS, 325
displaying, 305
file-descriptor, troubleshooting, 426
indexes, 325-326
page, 100

rows
adding, 300, 312, 328
deleting, 312, 322-323
editing, 298-299, 313
selecting, 319-322
updating, 323
viewing, 300, 313
symbol, 423
TABLET command, 1017-1021
Tablet mode on/off (Ctrl-T) keyboard
shortcut, 28
tablets
digitizer, 38, 1017
menus, 38-39, 371
TABMODE menu system variable, 1154
TABSURF command, 1021-1024
tag names, 148
Tagged Image File Format raster file,
1030
TARGET dview system variable, 1172
targets, objects, snap selection, 440-442
TCODE error message, 424
TDCREATE date/time system variable,
1180
TDINDWG date/time system variable,
1181
TDUPDATE date/time system variable,
1181
TDUSTIMER date/time system variable, 1181
TEdit dimensioning command,
174-176, 665-668
Template/Output File dialog box, 564
templates, 39
files, 520
for attribute extraction, 150-152
temporary files, corrupted, 410
TEMPPREFIX system-setting variable,
1128
Terminate DBMS Driver dialog box, 509
Test dialog box, 379
TEST.DCL file, 376-378

U

V

W

X-Z